2020

D1262556

U.S.
COIN
Digest

The Complete Guide to Current Market Values

David C. Harper, Editor
Richard Giedroyc, Market Analyst

Copyright ©2019 F+W Media, Inc.

All rights reserved. No portion of this publication may be reproduced or transmitted in any form or by any means, electronic or mechanical, including photocopy, recording, or any information storage and retrieval system, without permission in writing from the publisher, except by a reviewer who may quote brief passages in a critical article or review to be printed in a magazine or newspaper, or electronically transmitted on radio, television, or the Internet.

Published by

Krause Publications, a division of F+W Media, Inc.
5225 Joerns Drive, Suite 2 • Stevens Point, WI 54481
715-445-2214 • 888-457-2873
www.krausebooks.com

To order books or other products call toll-free 1-855-864-2579
or visit us online at www.shopnumismaster.com

ISBN-13: 978-1-4402-4899-3
ISBN-10: 1-4402-4899-0

Designed by Sandi Carpenter
Edited by Tracy L. Schmidt

Printed in China

10 9 8 7 6 5 4 3 2 1

Front cover images left to right:
Large Cent, 1793, KM#12; Standing Liberty Quarter, Type 1, 1917, KM#141; Coronet Head Quarter Eagle, 1846D, KM#72

Back cover images top to bottom:
Lincoln Cent, 1969S, Doubled Die Obverse, KM#201; Mercury Dime, 1942/41D, KM#140; Liberty Cap Dime, 1830, Medium 10 C, KM#48; Buffalo Nickel, 1918/17D, KM#134; Hawaii, 10 Cents (UMI KENETA), 1883, KM#3; Flowing Hair Dollar, 1794, KM#17; Morgan Dollar, 1893S, KM#110; Philippines, 5 Centavos, 1918S, KM#173; Panama-Pacific Exposition, Octagonal $50, 1915S, KM#139; Alabama Centennial Half Dollar, 2X2, 1921, KM#148.1

All images courtesy of Heritage Auctions – coins.ha.com

Contents

Preface

Since 1952, Krause Publications has built its business and reputation by serving the needs of coin collectors. Three questions dominate every collector's thinking.

The first is: "What is it?" We hope the photographs in this price guide will help you identify the coins you own.

The second question is: "What's it worth?" The prices contained in this volume are intended to serve as a retail guide. That means if you want to buy a specific coin in a specific grade, the price listed will be approximately what you would have to pay at the time this book was compiled. The prices listed are neither an offer to buy nor an offer to sell the coins listed. They are simply a guide assembled for your convenience by the authors. Remember that prices fluctuate. What dealers will pay to buy coins from you is a question beyond the scope of this book.

The third question is: "How do I buy a specific coin?" There are several thousand coin dealers across America who are ready, willing and able to serve your needs. To find them, you can consult the phone book in your local area, but beyond that, there is a whole hobby world out there and newspapers and magazines that feature advertisements by dealers who want to fill your needs. For more information on numismatic products and pricing go to www.numismaster.com.

Photo Credits

We wish to thank the following auction houses and individuals for the fabulous color images contained within these pages.

Mike Locke   Jay M. Galst, M.D.   Chester L. Krause

Heritage Numismatic Auctions, Inc.
www.HeritageCoins.com

Stack's
www.stacks.com

Ken Potter
www.koinpro.com

Professional Coin Grading Service
www.pcgs.com

Introduction

The authors have organized this book in a manner that we hope you will find both logical and useful.

Value listings

Values listed in the price guide are average retail prices. These are the approximate prices collectors can expect to pay when purchasing coins from dealers. They are not offers to buy or sell. The pricing section should be considered a guide only; actual selling prices will vary.

The values were compiled by Krause Publications' independent staff of market analysts. They derived the values listed by monitoring auction results, business on electronic dealer trading networks and at major shows, and in consultation with a panel of dealers. For rare coins, when only a few specimens of a particular date and mintmark are known, a confirmed transaction may occur only once every several years. In those instances, the most recent auction result is listed.

Grading

Values are listed for coins in various states of preservation, or grades. Standards used in determining grade for U.S. coins are those set by the American Numismatic Association (www.money.org). See Chapter 3 for more on grading.

Precious metal content

Throughout this book precious metal content is indicated in troy ounces. One troy ounce equals 480 grains, or 31.103 grams. This is followed by ASW or AGW, which stand for Actual Silver (Gold) Weight.

Dates and mintmarks

The dates listed are the individual dates that appear on each coin. The letter that follows the date is the mintmark and indicates where the coin was struck: "C" – Charlotte, N.C. (1838-1861); "CC" – Carson City, Nev. (1870-1893); "D" – Dahlonega, Ga. (1838-1861), and Denver (1906-present); "O" – New Orleans (1838-1909); "P" – Philadelphia (1793-present), coins without mintmarks also were struck at Philadelphia; "S" – San Francisco (1854-present); and "W" – West Point, N.Y. (1984-present).

A slash mark in a date indicates an overdate. This means a new date was engraved on a die over an old date. For example, if the date is listed as "1899/8," an 1898 die had a 9 engraved over the last 8 in the date. Portions of the old numeral are still visible on the coin.

A slash mark in a mintmark listing indicates an overmintmark (example: "1922-P/D"). The same process as above occurred, but this time a new mintmark was engraved over an old.

See Chapter 3, "U.S. Minting Varieties and Errors," for more information on overdates and overmintmarks.

1 Type Identification Guide

United States coins are often given nicknames based on their obverse design. This Type Identification Guide is a start for coin identification. It also shows the changes in the sizes of various denominations over time.

Half Cent

Liberty Cap

Draped Bust   Classic Head   Braided Hair

Large Cent

Liberty Cap   Draped Bust   Classic Head

Coronet   Braided Hair   Flowing Hair

Small Cent

Flying Eagle

Indian Head

Lincoln

Shield

Silver 3 Cents

Coronet

Half Dime

Flowing Hair

Draped Bust

Liberty Cap

Seated Liberty

Nickel

Shield

Liberty

Buffalo

Jefferson

Jefferson
large profile

Jefferson
large facing portrait

Dime

Draped Bust

Liberty Cap

Seated Liberty

Barber

Mercury

Roosevelt

Twenty Cents

Seated Liberty within circle of stars

Quarter

Draped Bust

Liberty Cap

Seated Liberty

Barber

Standing Liberty

Washington

50 State

Half Dollar

Flowing Hair

Draped Bust

Capped Bust

Seated Liberty

Barber

Walking Liberty

Franklin

Kennedy

Dollar

Flowing Hair

Gobrecht

Draped Bust

Seated Liberty

Morgan

Trade

Peace

Eisenhower

Dollar

Susan B. Anthony

Liberty Head - Type 1

Indian Head - Type 2

Sacagawea

Indian Head - Type 3

$2.50 Gold Quarter Eagle

Liberty Cap   Turban Head   Coronet Head   Indian Head

$3.00 Gold

Indian Head with headress

$5.00 Gold Half Eagle

Liberty Cap   Turban Head   Classic Head

Coronet Head   Indian Head

$10.00 Gold Eagle

Liberty Cap   Coronet Head   Indian Head

$20.00 Gold Double Eagle

Coronet Head   Saint-Gaudens

2 How to Grade

Better condition equals better value

Grading is one of the most important factors in buying and selling coins as collectibles. Unfortunately, it's also one of the most controversial. Since the early days of coin collecting in the United States, buying through the mail has been a convenient way for collectors to acquire coins. As a result, there has always been a need in numismatics for a concise way to classify the amount of wear on a coin and its condition in general.

A look back

In September 1888, Dr. George Heath, a physician in Monroe, Mich., published a four-page pamphlet titled *The American Numismatist*. Publication of subsequent issues led to the founding of the American Numismatic Association, and *The Numismatist*, as it's known today, is the association's official journal. Heath's first issues were largely devoted to selling world coins from his collection. There were no formal grades listed with the coins and their prices, but the following statement by Heath indicates that condition was a consideration for early collectors:

"The coins are in above average condition," Heath wrote, "and so confident am I that they will give satisfaction, that I agree to refund the money in any unsatisfactory sales on the return of the coins."

As coin collecting became more popular and *The Numismatist* started accepting paid advertising from others, grading became more formal. The February 1892 issue listed seven "classes" for the condition of coins (from worst to best): mutilated, poor, fair, good, fine, uncirculated, and proof. Through the years, the hobby has struggled with developing a grading system that would be accepted by all and could apply to all coins. The hobby's growth was accompanied by a desire for more grades, or classifications, to more precisely define a coin's condition. The desire for more precision, however, was at odds with the basic concept of grading: to provide a concise method for classifying a coin's condition.

For example, even the conservatively few 1892 classifications included fudge factors.

"To give flexibility to this classification," *The Numismatist* said, "such modification of find, good and fair, as 'extremely,' 'very,' 'almost,' etc., are used to express slight variations from the general condition."

The debate over grading continued for decades in *The Numismatist*. A number of articles and letters prodded the ANA to write grading guidelines and endorse them as the association's official standards. Some submitted specific suggestions for terminology and accompanying standards for each grade. But grading remained a process of "instinct" gained through years of collecting or dealing experience.

A formal grading guide in book form finally appeared in 1958, but it was the work of two individuals rather than the ANA. *A Guide to the Grading of United States Coins* by Martin R. Brown and John W. Dunn was a break-through in the great grading debate. Now collectors had a reference that gave them specific guidelines for specific coins and could be studied and restudied at home.

The first editions of Brown and Dunn carried text only, no illustrations. For the fourth edition, in 1964, publication was assumed by Whitman Publishing Co. of Racine, Wis., and line drawings were added to illustrate the text.

The fourth edition listed six principal categories for circulated coins (from worst to best): good, very good, fine, very fine, extremely fine, and about uncirculated. But again, the desire for more precise categories was evidenced. In the book's introduction, Brown and Dunn wrote, "Dealers will sometimes advertise coins that are graded G-VG, VG-F, F-VF, VF-XF. Or the description may be ABT. G. or VG plus, etc. This means that the coin in question more than meets minimum standards for the lower grade but is not quite good enough for the higher grade."

When the fifth edition appeared, in 1969, the "New B & D Grading System" was introduced. The six principal categories for circulated coins were still intact, but variances within those categories were now designated by up to four letters: "A," "B," "C" or "D." For example, an EF-A coin was "almost about uncirculated." An EF-B was "normal extra fine" within the B & D standards. EF-C had a "normal extra fine" obverse, but the reverse was "obviously not as nice as obverse due to poor strike or excessive wear." EF-D had a "normal extra fine" reverse but a problem obverse.

But that wasn't the end. Brown and Dunn further listed 29 problem points that could appear on a coin – from No. 1 for an "edge bump" to No. 29 for "attempted re-engraving outside of the Mint." The number could be followed by the letter "O" or "R" to designate whether the problem appeared on the obverse or reverse and a Roman numeral corresponding to a clock face to designate where the problem appears on the obverse or reverse. For example, a coin described as "VG-B-9-O-X" would grade "VG-B"; the "9" designated a "single rim nick"; the "O" indicated the nick was on the obverse; and the "X" indicated it appeared at the 10 o'clock position, or upper left, of the obverse.

The authors' goal was noble – to create the perfect grading system. They again, however, fell victim to the age-old grading-system problem: Precision comes at the expense of brevity. Dealer Kurt Krueger wrote in the January 1976 issues of *The Numismatist*, "Under the new B & D system, the numismatist must contend with a minimum of 43,152 different grading combinations! Accuracy is apparent, but simplicity has been lost." As a result, the "New B & D Grading System" never caught on in the marketplace.

The 1970s saw two important grading guides make their debut. The first was *Photo-*

grade by James F. Ruddy. As the title implies, Ruddy uses photographs instead of line drawings to show how coins look in the various circulated grades. Simplicity is also a virtue of Ruddy's book. Only seven circulated grades are listed (about good, good, very good, fine, very fine, extremely fine, and about uncirculated), and the designations stop there.

In 1977 the longtime call for the ANA to issue grading standards was met with the release of *Official A.N.A. Grading Standards for United States Coins*. Like Brown and Dunn, the first edition of the ANA guide used line drawings to illustrate coins in various states of wear. But instead of using adjectival descriptions, the ANA guide adopted a numerical system for designating grades.

The numerical designations were based on a system used by Dr. William H. Sheldon in his book *Early American Cents*, first published in 1949. He used a scale of 1 to 70 to designate the grades of large cents.

"On this scale," Sheldon wrote, "1 means that the coin is identifiable and not mutilated – no more than that. A 70-coin is one in flawless Mint State, exactly as it left the dies, with perfect mint color and without a blemish or nick."

(Sheldon's scale also had its pragmatic side. At the time, a No. 2 large cent was worth about twice a No. 1 coin; a No. 4 was worth about twice a No. 2, and so on up the scale.)

With the first edition of its grading guide, the ANA adopted the 70-point scale for grading all U.S. coins. It designated 10 categories of circulated grades: AG-3, G-4, VG-8, F-12, VF-20, VF-30, EF-40, EF-45, AU-50, and AU-55. The third edition, released in 1987, replaced the line drawings with photographs, and another circulated grade was added: AU-58. A fourth edition was released in 1991.

Grading circulated U.S. coins

Dealers today generally use either the ANA guide or *Photograde* when grading circulated coins for their inventories. (Brown and Dunn is now out of print.) Many local coin shops sell both books. Advertisers in *Numismatic News*, *Coins* magazine, and *Coin Prices* must indicate which standards they are using in grading their coins. If the standards are not listed, they must conform to ANA standards.

Following are some general guidelines, accompanied by photos, for grading circulated U.S. coins. Grading even circulated pieces can be subjective, particularly when attempting to draw the fine line between, for example, AU-55 and AU-58. Two longtime collectors or dealers can disagree in such a case.

But by studying some combination of the following guidelines, the ANA guide, and *Photograde*, and by looking at a lot of coins at shops and shows, collectors can gain enough grading knowledge to buy circulated coins confidently from dealers and other collectors. The more you study, the more knowledge and confidence you will gain. When you decide which series of coins you want to collect, focus on the guidelines for that particular series. Read them, reread them, and then refer back to them again and again.

AU-50

AU-50 (about uncirculated): Just a slight trace of wear, result of brief exposure to circulation or light rubbing from mishandling, may be evident on elevated design areas. These imperfections may appear as scratches or dull spots, along with bag marks or edge nicks. At least half of the original mint luster generally is still evident.

Indian cent

Lincoln cent

Buffalo nickel

Jefferson nickel

AU-50

Mercury dime

Standing Liberty quarter

Washington quarter

Walking Liberty half dollar

Morgan dollar

Barber coins

XF-40

XF-40 (extremely fine): The coin must show only slight evidence of wear on the highest points of the design, particularly in the hair lines of the portrait on the obverse. The same may be said for the eagle's feathers and wreath leaves on the reverse of most U.S. coins. A trace of mint luster may still show in protected areas of the coin's surface.

Indian cent

Lincoln cent

Buffalo nickel

Jefferson nickel

XF-40

Mercury dime

Standing Liberty quarter

Washington quarter

Walking Liberty half dollar

Morgan dollar

Barber coins

VF-20

VF-20 (very fine): The coin will show light wear at the fine points in the design, though they may remain sharp overall. Although the details may be slightly smoothed, all lettering and major features must remain sharp.

Indian cent: All letters in "Liberty" are complete but worn. Headdress shows considerable flatness, with flat spots on the tips of the feathers.

Lincoln cent: Hair, cheek, jaw, and bow-tie details will be worn but clearly separated, and wheat stalks on the reverse will be full with no weak spots.

Buffalo nickel: High spots on hair braid and cheek will be flat but show some detail, and a full horn will remain on the buffalo.

Jefferson nickel: Well over half of the major hair detail will remain, and the pillars on Monticello will remain well defined, with the triangular roof partially visible.

Mercury dime: Hair braid will show some detail, and three-quarters of the detail will remain in the feathers. The two diagonal bands on the fasces will show completely but will be worn smooth at the middle, with the vertical lines sharp.

Standing Liberty quarter: Rounded contour of Liberty's right leg will be flattened, as will the high point of the shield.

Washington quarter: There will be considerable wear on the hair curls, with feathers on the right and left of the eagle's breast showing clearly.

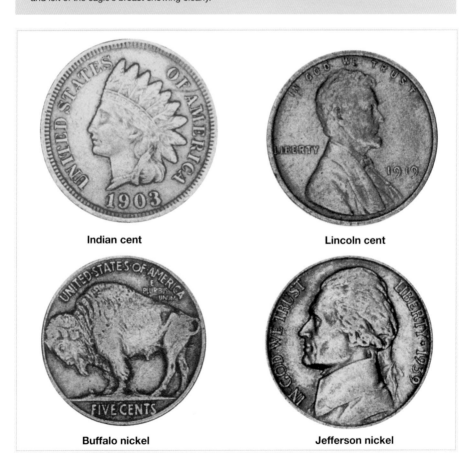

Indian cent

Lincoln cent

Buffalo nickel

Jefferson nickel

VF-20

Walking Liberty half dollar: All lines of the skirt will show but will be worn on the high points. Over half the feathers on the eagle will show.
Morgan dollar: Two-thirds of the hair lines from the forehead to the ear must show. Ear should be well defined. Feathers on the eagle's breast may be worn smooth.
Barber coins: All seven letters of "Liberty" on the headband must stand out sharply. Head wreath will be well outlined from top to bottom.

Mercury dime

Standing Liberty quarter

Washington quarter

Walking Liberty half dollar

Morgan dollar

Barber coins

F-12

F-12 (fine): Coins show evidence of moderate to considerable but generally even wear on all high points, though all elements of the design and lettering remain bold. Where the word "Liberty" appears in a headband, it must be fully visible. On 20th century coins, the rim must be fully raised and sharp.

Indian cent

Lincoln cent

Buffalo nickel

Jefferson nickel

F-12

Mercury dime

Standing Liberty quarter

Washington quarter

Walking Liberty half dollar

Morgan dollar

Barber coins

VG-8

VG-8 (very good): The coin will show considerable wear, with most detail points worn nearly smooth. Where the word "Liberty" appears in a headband, at least three letters must show. On 20th century coins, the rim will start to merge with the lettering.

Indian cent

Lincoln cent

Buffalo nickel

Jefferson nickel

VG-8

Mercury dime

Standing Liberty quarter

Washington quarter

Walking Liberty half dollar

Morgan dollar

Barber coins

G-4

G-4 (good): Only the basic design remains distinguishable in outline form, with all points of detail worn smooth. The word "Liberty" has disappeared, and the rims are almost merging with the lettering.

About good or fair: The coin will be identifiable by date and mint but otherwise badly worn, with only parts of the lettering showing. Such coins are of value only as fillers in a collection until a better example of the date and mintmark can be obtained. The only exceptions would be rare coins.

Indian cent

Lincoln cent

Buffalo nickel

Jefferson nickel

G-4

Mercury dime

Standing Liberty quarter

Washington quarter

Walking Liberty half dollar

Morgan dollar

Barber coins

Grading uncirculated U.S. coins

The subjectivity of grading and the trend toward more classifications becomes more acute when venturing into uncirculated, or mint-state, coins. A minute difference between one or two grade points can mean a difference in value of hundreds or even thousands of dollars. In addition, the standards are more difficult to articulate in writing and illustrate through drawings or photographs. Thus, the possibilities for differences of opinion on one or two grade points increase in uncirculated coins.

Back in Dr. George Heath's day and continuing through the 1960s, a coin was either uncirculated or it wasn't. Little distinction was made between uncirculated coins of varying condition, largely because there was little if any difference in value. When *Numismatic News* introduced its value guide in 1962 (the forerunner of today's Coin Market section in the *News*), it listed only one grade of uncirculated for Morgan dollars.

But as collectible coins increased in value and buyers of uncirculated coins became more picky, distinctions within uncirculated grade started to surface. In 1975 *Numismatic News* still listed only one uncirculated grade in Coin Market, but added this note: "Uncirculated and proof specimens in especially choice condition will also command proportionately higher premiums than these listed."

The first edition of the ANA guide listed two grades of uncirculated, MS-60 and MS-65, in addition to the theoretical but non-existent MS-70 (a flawless coin). MS-60 was described as "typical uncirculated" and MS-65 as "choice uncirculated." *Numismatic News* adopted both designations for Coin Market. In 1981, when the second edition of the ANA grading guide was released, MS-67 and MS-63 were added. In 1985 *Numismatic News* started listing six grades of uncirculated for Morgan dollars: MS-60, MS-63, MS-65, MS-65+, and MS-63 prooflike.

Then in 1986, a new entity appeared that has changed the nature of grading and trading uncirculated coins ever since. A group of dealers led by David Hall of Newport Beach, Calif., formed the Professional Coin Grading Service. For a fee, collectors could submit a coin through an authorized PCGS dealer and receive back a professional opinion of its grade.

Collectors have a variety of grading services to choose from. This set of Arkansas half dollars that appeared in an Early American History Auctions sale used two of the services.

The concept was not new; the ANA had operated an authentication service since 1972 and a grading service since 1979. A collector or dealer could submit a coin directly to the service and receive a certificate giving the service's opinion on authenticity and grade. The grading service was the source of near constant debate among dealers and ANA officials. Dealers charged that ANA graders were too young and inexperienced, and that their grading was inconsistent.

Grading stability was a problem throughout the coin business in the early 1980s, not just with the ANA service. Standards among uncirculated grades would tighten during a bear market and loosen during a bull market. As a result, a coin graded MS-65 in a bull market may have commanded only MS-63 during a bear market.

PCGS created several innovations in the grading business in response to these problems:

1. Coins could be submitted through PCGS-authorized dealers only.

2. Each coin would be graded by at least three members of a panel of "top graders," all prominent dealers in the business. (Since then, however, PCGS does not allow its graders to also deal in coins.)

3. After grading, the coin would be encapsulated in an inert, hard-plastic holder with a serial number and the grade indicated on the holder.

4. PCGS-member dealers pledged to make a market in PCGS-graded coins and honor the grades assigned.

5. In one of the most far-reaching moves, PCGS said it would use all 11 increments of uncirculated on the 70-point numerical scale: MS-60, MS-61, MS-62, MS-63, MS-64, MS-65, MS-66, MS-67, MS-68, MS-69, and MS-70.

Numerous other commercial grading services followed in the steps of PCGS and third-party grading is an accepted part of the hobby.

How should a collector approach the buying and grading of uncirculated coins? Collecting uncirculated coins worth thousands of dollars implies a higher level of numismatic expertise by the buyer. Those buyers without that level of expertise should cut their teeth on more inexpensive coins, just as today's experienced collectors did. Inexperienced collectors can start toward that level by studying the guidelines for mint-state coins in the ANA grading guide and looking at lots of coins at shows and shops.

Study the condition and eye appeal of a coin and compare it to other coins of the same series. Then compare prices. Do the more expensive coins look better? If so, why? Start to make your own judgments concerning relationships between condition and value. Experience remains the best teacher in the field of grading.

Grading U.S. proof coins

Because proof coins are struck by a special process using polished blanks, they receive their own grading designation. A coin does not start out being a proof and then become mint state if it becomes worn. Once a proof coin, always a proof coin.

In the ANA system, proof grades use the same numbers as circulated and uncirculated grades, and the amount of wear on the coin corresponds to those grades. But the number is preceded by the word "proof." For example, Proof-65, Proof-55, Proof-45, and so on. In addition, the ANA says a proof coin with many marks, scratches or other defects should be called an "impaired proof."

3 U.S. Minting Varieties and Errors

Most are common, some are rare

Introduction

The P.D.S. cataloging system used here to list minting varieties was originally compiled by Alan Herbert in 1971. PDS stands for the three main divisions of the. minting process, "planchet," "die" and "striking." Two more divisions cover collectible modifications after the strike, as well as non-collectible alterations, counterfeits and damaged coins.

This listing includes 445 classes, each a distinct part of the minting process or from a specific non-mint change in the coin. Classes from like causes are grouped together. The PDS system applies to coins of the world, but is based on U.S. coinage with added classes for certain foreign minting practices.

Price ranges are based on a U.S. coin in MS-60 grade (uncirculated.) The ranges may be applied in general to foreign coins of similar size or value although collector values are not usually as high as for U.S. coins. Prices are only a guide as the ultimate price is determined by a willing buyer and seller.

To define minting varieties, "A coin which exhibits a variation of any kind from the normal, as a result of any portion of the minting process, whether at the planchet stage, as a result of a change or modification of the die, or during the striking process. It includes those classes considered to be intentional changes, as well as those caused by normal wear and tear on the dies or other minting equipment and classes deemed to be 'errors'."

One of the most unusual error coins – a Roosevelt dime struck on a nail – sold for more than $42,000 through Heritage Auctions in early 2016. A zinc-coated sixpenny nail found its way into the coinage production line during the minting of Roosevelt dimes, and apparently escaped through normal distribution channels.

The three causes are represented as follows:
1. (I) = Intentional Changes
2. (W) = Wear and Tear
3. (E) = Errors
Note: A class may show more than one cause and could be listed as (IWE).

Images Courtesy of Heritage Auctions

Rarity level

The rarity ratings are based on the following scale:

1 - Very Common. Ranges from every coin struck down to 1,000,000.

2 - Common. From 1,000,000 down to 100,000.

3 - Scarce. From 100,000 down to 10,000.

4 - Very Scarce. From 10,000 down to 1,000.

5 - Rare. From 1,000 down to 100.

6 - Very Rare. From 100 down to 10.

7 - Extremely Rare. From 10 down to 1.

Unknown: If there is no confirmed report of a piece fitting a particular class, it is listed as Unknown. Reports of finds by readers would be appreciated in order to update future presentations.

An Unknown does not mean that your piece automatically is very valuable. Even a Rarity 7 piece, extremely rare, even unique, may have a very low collector value because of a lack of demand or interest in that particular class.

Classes, definitions and price ranges are based on material previously offered in Alan Herbert's book, *The Official Price Guide to Minting Varieties and Errors.*

Pricing information has also been provided by John A. Wexler and Ken Potter, with special pricing and technical advice from Del Romines.

Also recommended is the *Cherrypicker's Guide to Rare Die Varieties* by Bill Fivaz and J.T. Stanton. Check your favorite coin shop, numismatic library or book seller for availability of the latest edition.

Quick check index

If you have a coin and are not sure where to look for the possible variety:

If your coin shows doubling, first check V-B-I.

Then try II-A, II-B, II-C, II-I (4 & 5), III-J, III-L, or IV-C.

If part of the coin is missing, check III-B, III-C, or III-D.

If there is a raised line of coin metal, check II-D, II-G.

If there is a raised area of coin metal, check II-E, II-F, or III-F.

If the coin is out of round, and too thin, check III-G.

If coin appears to be the wrong metal, check III-A, III-E, III-F-3 and III-G.

If the die appears to have been damaged, check II-E, II-G. (Damage to the coin itself usually is not a minting variety.)

If the coin shows incomplete or missing design, check II-A, II-E, III-B-3, III-B-5 or III-D.

If only part of the planchet was struck, check III-M.

If something was struck into the coin, check III-J and III-K.

If something has happened to the edge of the coin, check II-D-6, II-E-10, III-I, III-M and III-O.

If your coin shows other than the normal design, check II-A or II-C.

If a layer of the coin metal is missing, or a clad layer is missing, check III-B and III-D.

If you have an unstruck blank, or planchet, check I-G.

If your coin may be a restrike, check IV-C.

If your coin has a counterstamp, countermark, additional engraving or apparent official modifications, check IV-B and V-A-8.

Do not depend on the naked eye to examine your coins. Use a magnifying lens whenever possible, as circulation damage, wear and alterations frequently can be mistaken for legitimate minting varieties.

The planchet varieties

DIVISION I

The first division of the PDS System includes those minting varieties t hat occur in the manufacture of the planchet upon which the coins will ultimately be struck and includes classes resulting from faulty metallurgy, mechanical damage, faulty processing, or equipment or human malfunction prior to the actual coin striking.

●PLANCHET ALLOY MIX (I-A)

This section includes those classes pertaining to mixing and processing the various metals which will be used to make a coin alloy.

I-A-1 Improper Alloy Mix (WE), Rarity Level: 3-4, Values: $5 to $10.

I-A-2 Slag Inclusion Planchet (WE), Rarity Level: 5-6, Values: $25 up.

●DAMAGED AND DEFECTIVE PLANCHETS (I-B)

To be a class in this section the blank, or planchet, must for some reason not meet the normal standards or must have been damaged in processing. The classes cover the areas of defects in the melting, rolling, punching and processing of the planchets up to the point where they are sent to the coin presses to be struck.

I-B-1 Defective Planchet (WE), Rarity Level: 6, Values: $25 up.

I-B-2 Mechanically Damaged Planchet (WE), Rarity Level: –, Values: No Value. (See values for the coin struck on a mechanically damaged planchet.)

I-B-3 Rolled Thin Planchet (WE), Rarity Level: 6 - (Less rare on half cents of 1795, 1797 and restrikes of 1831-52.) Values: $10 up.

I-B-4 Rolled Thick Planchet (WE), Rarity Level: 7 - (Less rare in Colonial copper coins. Notable examples occur on the restrike half cents of 1840-52.) Values: $125 up.

I-B-5 Tapered Planchet (WE), Rarity Level: 7, Values: $25 up.

I-B-6 Partially Unplated Planchet (WE), Rarity Level: 6, Values: $15 up.

I-B-7 Unplated Planchet (WE), Rarity Level: 6-7, Values: $50 up.

I-B-8 Bubbled Plating Planchet (WE), Rarity Level: 1, Values: No Value.

I-B-9 Included Gas Bubble Planchet (WE), Rarity Level: 6-7, Values: $50 up.

I-B-10 Partially Unclad Planchet (WE), Rarity Level: 6, Values: $20 up.

I-B-11 Unclad Planchet (WE), Rarity Level: 6-7, Values: $50 up.

I-B-12 Undersize Planchet (WE), Rarity Level: 7, Values: $250 up.

I-B-13 Oversize Planchet (WE), Rarity Level: 7, Values: $250 up.

I-B-14 Improperly Prepared Proof Planchet (WE), Rarity Level: 7, Values: $100 up.

I-B-15 Improperly Annealed Planchet (WE), Rarity Level: - , Values: No Value.

I-B-16 Faulty Upset Edge Planchet (WE), Rarity Level: 5-6, Values: $10 up.

I-B-17 Rolled-In Metal Planchet (WE), Rarity Level: 6-7, Values: $50 up.

I-B-18 Weld Area Planchet (WE), Rarity Level: Unknown, Values: No Value Established. (See values for the coins struck on weld area planchets.)

I-B-19 Strike Clip Planchet (WE), Rarity Level: 7, Values: $150 up.

I-B-20 Unpunched Center-Hole Planchet (WE), Rarity Level: 5-7, Values: $5 and up.

I-B-21 Incompletely Punched Center-Hole Planchet (WE), Rarity Level: 6-7, Values: $15 up.

I-B-22 Uncentered Center-Hole Planchet (WE), Rarity Level: 6-7, Values: $10 up.

I-B-23 Multiple Punched Center-Hole Planchet (WE), Rarity Level: 7, Values: $35 up.

I-B-24 Unintended Center-Hole Planchet (WE), Rarity Level: Unknown, Values: -.

I-B-25 Wrong Size or Shape Center-Hole Planchet (IWE), Rarity Level: 5-7, Values: $10 up.

●CLIPPED PLANCHETS (I-C)

Clipped blanks, or planchets, occur when the strip of coin metal fails to move forward between successive strokes of the gang punch to clear the previously punched holes, in the same manner as a cookie cutter overlapping a previously cut hole in the dough. The size of the clip is a function of the amount of overlap of the next punch.

The overlapping round punches produce a missing arc with curve matching the outside circumference of the blanking punch. Straight clips occur when the punch overlaps the beginning or end of a strip which has had the end sheared or sawed off. Ragged clips occur in the same manner when the ends of the strip have been left as they were rolled out.

The term "clip" as used here should not be confused with the practice of clipping or shaving small pieces of metal from a bullion coin after it is in circulation.

I-C-1 Disc Clip Planchet (WE), Rarity Level: 3-5, Values: $5 up.

I-C-2 Curved Clip Planchet - (To 5%) (WE), Rarity Level: 5-6, Values: $5 up.

I-C-3 Curved Clip Planchet - (6 to 10%) (WE), Rarity Level: 6, Values: $10 up.

I-C-4 Curved Clip Planchet - (11 to 25%) (WE), Rarity Level: 5-6, Values: $15 up.

I-C-5 Curved Clip Planchet - (26 to 60%) (WE), Rarity Level: 6-7, Values: $25 up.

I-C-6 Double Curved Clip Planchet (WE), Rarity Level: 6, Values: $10 up.

I-C-7 Triple Curved Clip Planchet (WE), Rarity Level: 5-6, Values: $25 up.

I-C-8 Multiple Curved Clip Planchet (WE), Rarity Level: 6-7, Values: $35 up.

I-C-9 Overlapping Curved Clipped Planchet (WE), Rarity Level: 6-7, Values: $50 up.

I-C-10 Incompletely Punched Curved Clip Planchet (WE), Rarity Level: 6, Values: $35 up.

I-C-11 Oval Curved Clip Planchet (WE), Rarity Level: 6-7, Values: $50 up.

I-C-12 Crescent Clip Planchet - (61% or more) (WE), Rarity Level: 7, Values: $200 up.

I-C-13 Straight Clip Planchet (WE), Rarity Level: 6, Values: $30 up.

I-C-14 Incompletely Sheared Straight Clip Planchet (WE), Rarity Level: 6, Values: $50 up.

I-C-15 Ragged Clip Planchet (WE), Rarity Level: 6-7, Values: $35 up.

I-C-16 Outside Corner Clip Planchet (E), Rarity Level: -, Values: No Value.

I-C-17 Inside Corner Clip Planchet (E), Rarity Level: -, Values: No Value.

I-C-18 Irregularly Clipped Planchet (E) Rarity Level: -, Values: Value not established.

I-C-19 Incompletely Punched Scalloped or Multi-Sided Planchet (E), Rarity Level: 7, Values: $25 up.

I-C-2

● **L**AMINATED, SPLIT, OR BROKEN PLANCHET **(I-D)**

For a variety of reasons the coin metal may split into thin layers (delaminate) and either split completely off the coin, or be retained. Common causes are included gas or alloy mix problems. Lamination cracks usually enter the surface of the planchet at a very shallow angle or are at right angles to the edge. The resulting layers differ from slag in that they appear as normal metal.

Lamination cracks and missing metal of any size below a split planchet are too common in the 35 percent silver 1942-1945 nickels to be collectible or have any significant value.

I-D-1 Small Lamination Crack Planchet (W), Rarity Level: 4-5, Values: $1 up.

I-D-2 Large Lamination Crack Planchet (W), Rarity Level: 3-4, Values: $5 up.

I-D-3 Split Planchet (W), Rarity Level: 5-6, Values: $15 up.

I-D-4 Hinged Split Planchet (W), Rarity Level: 6-7, Values: $75 up.

I-D-5 Clad Planchet With a Clad Layer Missing (W), Rarity Level: 5-6, Values: $35 up.

I-D-6 Clad Planchet With Both Clad Layers Missing (W), Rarity Level: 6-7, Values: $75 up.

I-D-7 Separated Clad Layer (W), Rarity Level: 5, Values: $25 up.

I-D-8 Broken Planchet (WE), Rarity Level: 3-4, Values: $5 up.

● **W**RONG STOCK PLANCHET **(I-E)**

The following classes cover those cases where the wrong coin metal stock was run through the blanking press, making blanks of the correct diameter, but of the wrong thickness, alloy or metal or a combination of the wrong thickness and the wrong metal.

I-E-1 Half Cent Stock Planchet (IE), Rarity Level: Unknown, Values: No Value Established.

I-E-2 Cent Stock Planchet (IE), Rarity Level: Unknown, Values: No Value Established.

I-E-3 Two Cent Stock Planchet (E), Rarity Level: Unknown, Values: No Value Established.

I-E-4 Three Cent Silver Stock Planchet (E), Rarity Level: Unknown, Values: No Value Established.

I-E-5 Three Cent Nickel Stock Planchet (E), Rarity Level: Unknown, Values: No Value Established.

I-E-6 Half Dime Stock Planchet (E), Rarity Level: Unknown, Values: No Value Established.

I-E-7 Dime Stock Planchet (E), Rarity Level: 7, Values: $200 up.

I-E-8 Twenty Cent Stock Planchet (E), Rarity Level: Unknown, Values: No Value Established.

I-E-9 Quarter Stock Planchet (E), Rarity Level: Unknown, Values: No Value Established.

I-E-10 Half Dollar Stock Planchet (E), Rarity Level: Unknown, Values: No Value Established.

I-E-11 Dollar Stock Planchet (E), Rarity Level: 7, Values: $300 up.

I-E-12 Token or Medal Stock Planchet (E), Rarity Level: Unknown, Values: No Value Established.

I-E-13 Wrong Thickness Spoiled Planchet (IWE), Rarity Level: Unknown, Values: No Value Established.

I-E-14 Correct Thickness Spoiled Planchet (IWE), Rarity Level: Unknown, Values: No Value Established.

I-E-15 Cut Down Struck Token Planchet (IWE), Rarity Level: Unknown, Values: No Value Established.

I-E-16 Experimental or Pattern Stock Planchet (IE), Rarity Level: Unknown, Values: No Value Established.

I-E-17 Proof Stock Planchet (IE), Rarity Level: Unknown, Values: No Value Established.

I-E-18 Adjusted Specification Stock Planchet (IE), Rarity Level: 7, Values: $25 up.

I-E-19 Trial Strike Stock Planchet (IE), Rarity Level: Unknown, Values: No Value Established.

I-E-20 U.S. Punched Foreign Stock Planchet (E), Rarity Level: 7, Values: $75 up.

I-E-21 Foreign Punched Foreign Stock Planchet (E), Rarity Level: 7, Values: $75 up.

I-E-22 Non-Standard Coin Alloy Planchet (IE), Rarity Level: 7, Values: Unknown.

●EXTRA METAL ON A BLANK, OR PLANCHET (I-F)

True extra metal is only added to the blank during the blanking operation. This occurs as metal is scraped off the sides of the blanks as they are driven down through the thimble, or lower die in the blanking press. The metal is eventually picked up by a blank passing through, welded to it by the heat of friction.

A second form of extra metal has been moved to this section, the sintered coating planchet, the metal deposited on the planchet in the form of dust during the annealing operation.

I-F-1 Extra Metal on a Type 1 Blank (W), Rarity Level: 7, Values: $50 up.

I-F-2 Extra Metal on a Type 2 Planchet (W), Rarity Level: 6-7, Values: $75 up.

I-F-3 Sintered Coating Planchet (W), Rarity Level: 7, Values: $75 up.

●NORMAL OR ABNORMAL PLANCHETS (I-G)

This section consists of the two principal forms – the blank as it comes from the blanking press – and in the form of a planchet after it has passed through the upsetting mill. It also includes a class for purchased planchets and one for planchets produced by the mint.

I-G-1 Type I Blank (IWE), Rarity Level: 3-5, Values: $2 up.

I-G-2 Type II Planchet (IWE), Rarity Level: 3-4, Values: 50 up.

I-G-3 Purchased Planchet (I), Rarity Level: 1, Values: No Value.

I-G-4 Mint Made Planchet (I), Rarity Level: 1, Values: No Value.

I-G-5 Adjustment-Marked Planchet (I), Rarity Level: Unknown, Values: No Value.

I-G-6 Hardness Test-Marked Planchet (I), Rarity Level: -, Values: No Value Established.

Note: There are no classes between I-G-6 and I-G-23

I-G-23 Proof Planchet (IE), Rarity Level: 6-7, Values: $1 up.

●COIN METAL STRIP (I-H)

When the coin metal strip passes through the blanking press it goes directly to a chopper. This cuts the remaining web into small pieces to be sent back to the melting furnace. Pieces of the web or the chopped up web may escape into the hands of collectors.

I-H-1 Punched Coin Metal Strip (IWE), Rarity Level: 4-6, Values: $5 up, depending on size, denomination and number of holes showing.

I-H-2 Chopped Coin Metal Strip (IE), Rarity Level: 3-5, Values: $5 up.

The die varieties

DIVISION II

Die varieties may be unique to a given die, but will repeat for the full life of the die unless a further change occurs. Anything that happens to the die will affect the appearance of the struck coin. This includes all the steps of the die making:

- Cutting a die blank from a tool steel bar.
- Making the design.
- Transferring it to a model.
- Transferring it to the master die or hub.
- The hubbing process of making the die.
- Punching in the mintmark.
- Heat treating of the die.

The completed dies are also subject to damage in numerous forms, plus wear and tear during the striking process and repair work done with abrasives. All of these factors can affect how the struck coin looks.

•ENGRAVING VARIETIES (II-A)

In all cases in this section where a master die, or master hub is affected by the class, the class will affect all the working hubs and all working dies descending from it.

Identification as being on a master die or hub depends on it being traced to two or more of the working hubs descended from the same master tools.

II-A-1 Overdate (IE), Rarity Level: 1-7, Values: $1 up.

II-A-2 Doubled Date (IE), Rarity Level: 1-7, Values: $1 up.

II-A-3 Small Date (IE), Rarity Level: 2-5, Values: $1 up.

II-A-4 Large Date (IE), Rarity Level: 2-5, Values: $1 up.

II-A-5 Small Over Large Date (IE), Rarity Level: 4-6, Values: $15 up.

II-A-6 Large Over Small Date (IE), Rarity Level: 3-5, Values: $10 up.

II-A-7 Blundered Date (E), Rarity Level: 6-7, Values: $50 up.

II-A-8 Corrected Blundered Date (IE), Rarity Level: 3-5, Values: $5 up.

II-A-9 Wrong Font Date Digit (IE), Rarity Level: 5-6, Values: Minimal.

II-A-10 Worn, Broken or Damaged Punch (IWE), Rarity Level: 5-6, Values: $5 up.

II-A-11 Expedient Punch (IWE), Rarity Level: 5-6, Values: $10 up.

II-A-12 Blundered Digit (E), Rarity Level: 4-5, Values: $50 up.

II-A-13 Corrected Blundered Digit (IE), Rarity Level: 3-6, Values: $10 up.

II-A-14 Doubled Digit (IWE), Rarity Level: 2-6, Values: $2 up.

II-A-15 Wrong Style or Font Letter or Digit (IE), Rarity Level: 3-5, Values: Minimal.

II-A-1

II-A-2

II-A-2

II-A-16 One Style or Font Over Another (IE), Rarity Level: 4-6, Values: $10 up.

II-A-17 Letter Over Digit (E), Rarity Level: 6-7, Values: $25 up.

II-A-18 Digit Over Letter (E), Rarity Level: 6-7, Values: $25 up.

II-A-19 Omitted Letter or Digit (IWE), Rarity Level: 4-6, Values: $5 up.

II-A-20 Blundered Letter (E), Rarity Level: 6-7, Values: $50 up.

II-A-21 Corrected Blundered Letter (IE), Rarity Level: 1-3, Values: $10 up.

II-A-22 Doubled Letter (IWE), Rarity Level: 2-6, Values: $2 up.

II-A-23 Blundered Design Element (IE), Rarity Level: 6-7, Values: $50 up.

II-A-24 Corrected Blundered Design Element (IE), Rarity Level: 3-5, Values: $10 up.

II-A-25 Large Over Small Design Element (IE), Rarity Level: 4-6, Values: $2 up.

II-A-26 Omitted Design Element (IWE), Rarity Level: 5-7, Values: $10 up.

II-A-27 Doubled Design Element (IWE), Rarity Level: 2-6, Values: $2 up.

II-A-28 One Design Element Over Another (IE), Rarity Level: 3-6, Values: $5 up.

II-A-29 Reducing Lathe Doubling (WE), Rarity Level: 6-7, Values: $50 up.

II-A-30 Extra Design Element (IE), Rarity Level: 3-5, Values: $10 up.

II-A-31 Modified Design (IWE), Rarity Level: 1-5, Values: No Value up.

II-A-32 Normal Design (I), Rarity Level: 1, Values: No Extra Value.

II-A-33 Design Mistake (IE), Rarity Level: 2-6, Values: $1 up.

II-A-34 Defective Die Design (IWE), Rarity Level: 1, Values: No Value.

II-A-35 Pattern (I), Rarity Level: 6-7, Values: $100 up.

II-A-36 Trial Design (I), Rarity Level: 5-7, Values: $100 up.

II-A-37 Omitted Designer's Initial (IWE), Rarity Level: 3-7, Values: $1 up.

II-A-38 Layout Mark (IE), Rarity Level: 5-7, Values: Minimal.

II-A-39 Abnormal Reeding (IWE), Rarity Level: 2-5, Values: $1 up.

II-A-40 Modified Die or Hub (IWE), Rarity Level: 1-5, Values: No Value up.

II-A-41 Numbered Die (I), Rarity Level: 3-5, Values: $5 up.

II-A-42 Plugged Die (IW), Rarity Level: 5-6, Values: Minimal.

II-A-43 Cancelled Die (IE), Rarity Level: 3-6, Values: No Value up.

II-A-44 Hardness Test Marked Die (IE), Rarity Level: 7, Values: $100 up.

II-A-45 Coin Simulation (IE), Rarity Level: 6-7, Values: $100 up, but may be illegal to own.

II-A-46 Punching Mistake (IE), Rarity Level: 2-6, Values: $1 up.

II-A-47 Small Over Large Design (IE), Rarity Level: 4-6, Values: $5 up.

II-A-48 Doubled Punch (IE), Rarity Level: 5-7, Values: $5 up.

II-A-49 Mint Display Sample (I) Rarity Level: 7, Values not established.

II-A-50 Center Dot, Stud or Circle (IE) Rarity Level: 7, much more common on early cents, Values not established

●**Hub doubling varieties (II-B)**

This section includes eight classes of hub doubling. Each class is from a different cause, described by the title of the class. At the latest count over 2,500 doubled dies have been reported in the U.S. coinage, the most famous being examples of the 1955, 1969-S and 1972 cent dies.

II-B-I Rotated Hub Doubling (WE), Rarity Level: 3-6, Values: $1 up

II-B-II Distorted Hub Doubling (WE), Rarity Level: 3-6, Values: $1 up.

II-B-III Design Hub Doubling (IWE), Rarity Level: 3-6, Values: $1 up to five figure amounts.

II-B-IV Offset Hub Doubling (WE), Rarity Level: 4-6, Values: $15 up.

II-B-V Pivoted Hub Doubling (WE), Rarity Level: 3-6, Values: $10 up.

II-B-VI Distended Hub Doubling (WE), Rarity Level: 2-5, Values: $1 up.

II-B-VII Modified Hub Doubling (IWE), Rarity Level: 2-5, Values: $1 up.

II-B-VIII Tilted Hub Doubling (WE), Rarity Level: 4-6, Values: $5 up.

●**Mintmark varieties (II-C)**

Mintmarks are punched into U.S. coin dies by hand (Up to 1985 for proof coins, to 1990 for cents and nickels and 1991 for other denominations). Variations resulting from mistakes in the punching are listed in this section. Unless exceptionally mispunched, values are usually estimated at 150 percent of numismatic value. Slightly tilted or displaced mintmarks have no value.

II-C-1 Doubled Mintmark (IE), Rarity Level: 2-6, Values: 50 cents up.

II-C-2 Separated Doubled Mintmark (IE), Rarity Level: 5-6, Values: $15 up.

II-C-3 Over Mintmark (IE), Rarity Level: 3-6, Values: $2 up.

II-C-4 Tripled Mintmark (IE), Rarity Level: 3-5, Values: 50 up.

II-C-5 Quadrupled Mintmark (IE), Rarity Level: 4-6, Values: $1 up.

II-C-6 Small Mintmark (IE), Rarity Level: 2-5, Values: No Extra Value up.

II-C-7 Large Mintmark (IE), Rarity Level: 2-5, Values: No Extra Value up.

II-C-8 Large Over Small Mintmark (IE), Rarity Level: 2-5, Values: $2 up.

II-C-9 Small Over Large Mintmark (IE), Rarity Level: 3-6, Values: $5 up.

II-C-10 Broken Mintmark Punch (W), Rarity Level: 5-6, Values: $5 up.

II-C-11 Omitted Mintmark (IWE), Rarity Level: 4-7, Values: $125 up.

II-C-12 Tilted Mintmark (IE), Rarity Level: 5-7, Values: $5 up.

II-C-13 Blundered Mintmark (E), Rarity Level: 4-6, Values: $5 up.

II-C-14 Corrected Horizontal Mintmark (IE), Rarity Level: 4-6, Values: $5 up.

II-C-15 Corrected Upside Down Mintmark (IE), Rarity Level: 4-6, Values: $5 up.

II-C-16 Displaced Mintmark (IE), Rarity Level: 4-6, Values: $5 to $10.

II-C-17 Modified Mintmark (IWE), Rarity Level: 1-4, Values: No Extra Value up.

II-C-18 Normal Mintmark (I), Rarity Level: 1, Values: No Extra Value.

II-C-19 Doubled Mintmark Punch (I), Rarity Level: 6-7, Values: No Extra Value up.

II-C-20 Upside Down Mintmark (E) Rarity Level 6-7, Values: $5 up.

II-C-21 Horizontal Mintmark (E) Rarity Level 6-7, Values: $5 up.

II-C-22 Wrong Mintmark (E) Rarity Level 6-7, Values $15 up. (Example has a D mintmark in the date, but was used at Philadelphia.)

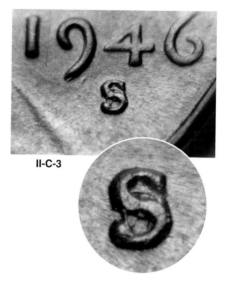

II-C-3

II-C-3

II-C-1

II-C-4

●**DIE, COLLAR AND HUB CRACKS (II-D)**

Cracks in the surface of the die allow coin metal to be forced into the crack during the strike, resulting in raised irregular lines of coin metal above the normal surface of the coin. These are one of the commonest forms of die damage and wear, making them easily collectible.

Collar cracks and hub cracks are added to this section because the causes and effects are similar or closely associated.

Die cracks, collar cracks and hub cracks are the result of wear and tear on the tools, with intentional use assumed for all classes.

II-D-1 Die Crack (W), Rarity Level: 1-3, Values: 10 to $1, $25 up on a proof coin with a rarity level of 6-7.

II-D-2 Multiple Die Cracks (W), Rarity Level: 1-3, Values: 25 cents to $2.

II-D-3 Head-To-Rim Die Crack (Lincoln Cent) (W), Rarity Level: 2-6, Values: 25 to $10 for multiple die cracks.

II-D-4 Split Die (W), Rarity Level: 5-6, Values: $10 up.

II-D-5 Rim-To-Rim Die Crack (W), Rarity Level: 2-5, Values: $1 up.

II-D-6 Collar Crack (W), Rarity Level: 4-6, Values: $10 up.

II-D-7 Hub Crack (W), Rarity Level: 3-5, Values: $1-$2.

●**DIE BREAKS (II-E)**

Breaks in the surface of the die allow coin metal to squeeze into the resulting holes, causing raised irregular areas above the normal surface of the coin. Die chips and small die breaks are nearly as common as the die cracks, but major die breaks, which extend in from the edge of the coin, are quite rare on the larger coins.

If the broken piece of the die is retained, the resulting design will be above or below the level of the rest of the surface.

II-E-1 Die Chip (W), Rarity Level: 1-2, Values: 10 to $1.

II-E-2 Small Die Break (W), Rarity Level: 1-3, Values: 10 to $2.

II-E-3 Large Die Break (W), Rarity Level: 3-5, Values: $1 to $50 and up.

II-E-4 Rim Die Break (W), Rarity Level: 2-3, Values: 25 cents to $5.

II-E-5 Major Die Break (WE), Rarity Level: 3-6, Values: $5 to $100 and up.

II-E-6 Retained Broken Die (W), Rarity Level: 3-5, Values: $1 to $10 and up.

II-E-7 Retained Broken Center of the Die (W), Rarity Level: 6-7, Values: $100 up.

II-E-8 Laminated Die (W), Rarity Level: 3-5, Values: 10 cents to $5.

II-E-9 Chipped Chrome Plating (W), Rarity Level: 4-5, Values: $10 to $25 on proofs.

II-E-10 Collar Break (W), Rarity Level: 4-6, Values: $5 to $25 and up.

II-E-11 Broken Letter or Digit on an Edge Die (W), Rarity Level: 4-6, Values: Minimal.

II-E-12 "Bar" Die Break (W), Rarity Level: 3-5, Values: 25 to $20.

II-E-13 Hub Break (W), Rarity Level: 4-6, Values: 50 to $10 and up.

●**"BIE" VARIETIES (II-F)**

A series of small die breaks or die chips in the letters of "LIBERTY" mostly on the wheat-reverse Lincoln cent are actively collected. The name results from the resemblance to an "I" between the "B" and "E" on many of the dies, but they are found between all of the letters in different cases. Well over 1,500 dies are known and cataloged. Numerous more recent examples are known.

II-F-1 ILI Die Variety (W), Rarity Level: 4-5, Values: 25 cents to $10.

II-F-2 LII Die Variety (W), Rarity Level: 3-5, Values: 50 cents to $15.

II-F-3 IIB Die Variety (W), Rarity Level: 3-5, Values: 50 cents to $15.

II-F-4 BIE Die Variety (W), Rarity Level: 3-5, Values: $1 to $20.

II-F-5 EIR Die Variety (W), Rarity Level: 3-5, Values: 50 to $15.

II-F-6 RIT Die Variety (W), Rarity Level: 4-5, Values: $2 to $25.

II-F-7 TIY Die Variety (W), Rarity Level: 4-5, Values: $5 to $30.

II-F-8 TYI Die Variety (W), Rarity Level: 4-5, Values: $2 to $25.

●**WORN AND DAMAGED DIES, COLLARS AND HUBS (II-G)**

Many dies are continued deliberately in service after they have been damaged, dented, clashed or show design transfer, since none of these classes actually affect anything but the appearance of the coin. The root cause is wear, but intent or mistakes may enter the picture.

II-G-1 Dented Die, Collar or Hub (IWE), Rarity Level: 3-5, Values: 25 to $5.

II-G-2 Damaged Die, Collar or Hub (IWE), Rarity Level: 3-5, Values: 25 to $5.

II-G-3 Worn Die, Collar or Hub (IWE), Rarity Level: 2-3, Values: No Extra Value to Minimal Value.

II-G-4 Pitted or Rusted Die, Collar or Hub (IWE), Rarity Level: 3-4, Values: No Extra Value, marker only.

II-G-5

II-G-5 Heavy Die Clash (IWE), Rarity Level: 4-5, Values: $1 to $10 and up.

II-G-6 Heavy Collar Clash (IWE), Rarity Level: 3-4, Values: $1 to $5 and up.

II-G-7 Heavy Design Transfer (IWE), Rarity Level: 3-4, Values: 10 cents to $1.

●DIE PROGRESSIONS (II-H)

The progression section consists of three classes. These are useful as cataloging tools for many different die varieties, but especially the die cracks and die breaks which may enlarge, lengthen or increase in number.

II-H-1 Progression (W), Rarity Level: 3-5, Values: $1 up.

II-H-2 Die Substitution (IW), Rarity Level: 2-4, Values: No Extra Value to Minimal Value.

II-H-3 Die Repeat (I), Rarity Level: 2-4, Values: No Extra Value to Minimal Value.

●DIE SCRATCHES, POLISHED AND ABRADED DIES (II-I)

This section consists of those classes having to do with the use of an abrasive in some form to intentionally polish proof dies, or repair the circulating die surface. Several classes which previously were referred to as "polished" now are listed as "abraded."

II-I-1 Die Scratch (IW), Rarity Level: 1-2, Values: No Extra Value to 10 cents to 25 cents, as a marker.

II-I-2 Polished (proof) Die (IW), Rarity Level: 1, Values: No Extra Value.

II-I-3 Abraded (Circulation) Die (IW), Rarity Level: 1-2, Values: No Extra Value up to $10.

II-I-4 Inside Abraded Die Doubling (IW), Rarity Level: 1-3, Values: No Extra Value to $1.

II-I-5 Outside Abraded Die Doubling (IW), Rarity Level: 1-3, Values: No Extra Value to $1.

II-I-6 Lathe Marks (IW), Rarity Level: 5-7, Values: No Extra Value, marker only.

Striking varieties

DIVISION III

Once the dies are made and the planchets have been prepared, they are struck by a pair of dies and become a coin. In this division, we list the misstrikes resulting from human or mechanical malfunction in the striking process. These are one-of-a-kind varieties, but there may be many similar coins that fall in a given class. Multiples and combinations of classes must be considered on a case by case basis. The first several sections match the planchet sections indicated in the title.

●STRUCK ON DEFECTIVE ALLOY MIX PLANCHETS (III-A)

This section includes those classes of coins struck on planchets that were made from a defective alloy.

III-A-1 Struck on an Improper Alloy Mix Planchet (IE), Rarity Level: 2-3, Values: 10 cents to $2.

III-A-2 Struck on a Planchet With Slag Inclusions(IE), Rarity Level: 5-6, Values: $10 up.

●STRUCK ON DAMAGED, DEFECTIVE OR ABNORMAL PLANCHET (III-B)

Coins get struck on many strange objects. The more common of course are planchets which have been damaged in some way in the production process. In most of the classes in this section intent is at least presumed, if not specifically listed as a cause.

III-B-1 Struck on a Defective Planchet (IWE), Rarity Level: 4-6, Values: $5 to $10 and up.

III-B-2 Struck on a Mechanically Damaged Planchet (IWE), Rarity Level: 5-6, Values: $10 to $20 and up.

III-B-3 Struck on a Rolled Thin Planchet (IWE), Rarity Level: 5-6, Values: $2 to $5 and up.

III-B-4 Struck on a Rolled Thick Planchet (IWE), Rarity Level: 5-6, Values: $35 to $50 and up.

III-B-5 Struck on a Tapered Planchet (WE), Rarity Level: 4-6, Values: $2 to $5 and up.

III-B-6 Struck on a Partially Unplated Planchet (WE), Rarity Level: 5, Values: $10 up.

III-B-7 Struck on an Unplated Planchet (WE), Rarity Level: 6-7, Values: $100 up.

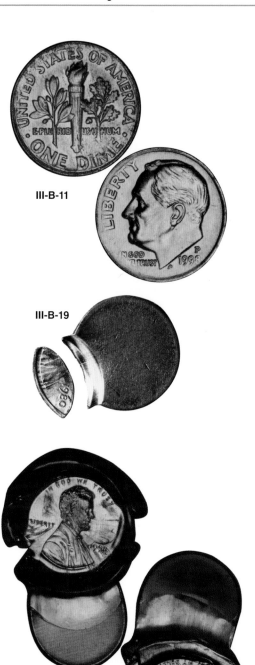

III-B-11

III-B-19

III-B-29

III-B-8 Struck on a Bubbled Plating Planchet (IWE), Rarity Level: 1, Values: No Value.

III-B-9 Struck on an Included Gas Bubble Planchet (WE), Rarity Level: 5-6, Values: $5 up.

III-B-10 Struck on a Partially Unclad Planchet (WE), Rarity Level: 5-6, Values: $5 up.

III-B-11 Struck on an Unclad Planchet (WE), Rarity Level: 4-5, Values: $5 and up.

III-B-12 Struck on an Undersize Planchet (WE), Rarity Level: 4-6, Values: Minimal.

III-B-13 Struck on an Oversize Planchet (WE), Rarity Level: 6-7, Values: Minimal.

III-B-14 Struck on an Improperly Prepared Proof Planchet (IWE), Rarity Level: 3-5, Values: $5 up.

III-B-15 Struck on an Improperly Annealed Planchet (IWE), Rarity Level: 4-5, Values: $5 up.

III-B-16 Struck on a Faulty Upset Edge Planchet (IWE), Rarity Level: 4-5, Values: $1 to $2.

III-B-17 Struck on a Rolled In Metal Planchet (WE), Rarity Level: 4-6, Values: $2 up.

III-B-18 Struck on a Weld Area Planchet (WE), Rarity Level: 6, Values: $25 to $50.

III-B-19 Struck on a Strike Clip Planchet (W), Rarity Level: 6-7, Values: $25 up.

III-B-20 Struck on an Unpunched Center Hole Planchet (WE), Rarity Level: 4-6, Values: $1 and up.

III-B-21 Struck on an Incompletely Punched Center Hole Planchet (WE), Rarity Level: 6-7, Values: $5 up.

III-B-22 Struck on an Uncentered Center Hole Planchet (WE), Rarity Level: 6-7, Values: $10 up.

III-B-23 Struck on a Multiple Punched Center Hole Planchet (WE), Rarity Level: 7, Values: $25 up.

III-B-24 Struck on an Unintended Center Hole Planchet (WE), Rarity Level: 6-7, Values: $25 and up.

III-B-25 Struck on a Wrong Size or Shape Center Hole Planchet (WE), Rarity Level: 5-7, Values: $5 up.

III-B-26 Struck on Scrap Coin Metal (E), Rarity Level: 4-6, Values: $10 up.

III-B-27 Struck on Junk Non Coin Metal (E), Rarity Level: 4-6, Values: $15 up.

III-B-28 Struck on a False Planchet (E), Rarity Level: 3-5, Values: $35 up.

III-B-29 Struck on Bonded Planchets (E), Rarity Level: 6-7, Values: $50 up.

•STRUCK ON A CLIPPED PLANCHET (III-C)

Coins struck on clipped blanks, or planchets, exhibit the same missing areas as they did before striking, modified by the metal flow from the strike which rounds the edges and tends to move metal into the missing areas. Values for blanks will run higher than planchets with similar clips.

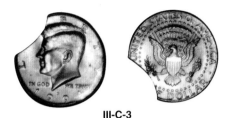

III-C-3

III-C-1 Struck on a Disc Clip Planchet (WE), Rarity Level: 4-5, Values: $1 on regular coins, $20 and up for clad coins.

III-C-2 Struck on a Curved Clip Planchet - to 5% (WE), Rarity Level: 3-5, Values: 50 cents up.

III-C-3 Struck on a Curved Clip Planchet - (6 to 10%) (WE), Rarity Level: 4-5, Values: $1 up.

III-C-4 Struck on a Curved Clip Planchet - (11 to 25%) (WE), Rarity Level: 4-5, Values: $2 up.

III-C-5 Struck on a Curved Clip Planchet - (26 to 60%) (WE), Rarity Level: 4-6, Values: $10 up.

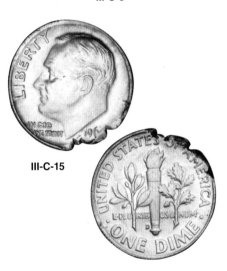

III-C-15

III-C-6 Struck on a Double Curved Clip Planchet (WE), Rarity Level: 3-4, Values: $2 up.

III-C-7 Struck on a Triple Curved Clip Planchet (WE), Rarity Level: 4-5, Values: $5 up.

III-C-8 Struck on a Multiple Curved Clip Planchet (WE), Rarity Level: 4-6, Values: $5 up.

III-C-9 Struck on an Overlapping Curved Clipped Planchet (WE), Rarity Level: 5-6, Values: $15 up.

III-C-10 Struck on an Incomplete Curved Clip Planchet (WE), Rarity Level: 4-5, Values: $10 up.

III-C-11 Struck on an Oval Clip Planchet (WE), Rarity Level: 5-6, Values: $20 up.

III-C-12 Struck on a Crescent Clip Planchet - (61% or more) (WE), Rarity Level: 6-7, Values: $100 up.

III-C-13 Struck on a Straight Clip Planchet (E), Rarity Level: 4-6, Values: $10 up.

III-C-14 Struck on an Incomplete Straight Clip Planchet (WE), Rarity Level: 5-6, Values: $20 up.

III-C-15 Struck on a Ragged Clip Planchet (E), Rarity Level: 4-6, Values: $15 up.

III-C-16 Struck on an Outside Corner Clip Planchet (E), Rarity Level: 7, Values: $100 up.

III-C-17 Struck on an Inside Corner Clip Planchet (E), Rarity Level: Unknown outside mint., Values: -.

III-C-18 Struck on an Irregularly Clipped Planchet (E), Rarity Level: 6-7, Values: $20 up.

III-C-19 Struck on an Incompletely Punched Scalloped or Multi-Sided Planchet (E), Rarity Level: 7, Values: $20 up.

•STRUCK ON A LAMINATED, SPLIT OR BROKEN PLANCHET (III-D)

This section has to do with the splitting, cracking or breaking of a coin parallel to the faces of the coin, or at least very nearly parallel, or breaks at right angles to the faces of the coin.

Lamination cracks and missing metal of any size below a split planchet are too common in the 35-percent silver 1942-1945 nickels to be collectible or have any significant value.

III-D-1 Struck on a Small Lamination Crack Planchet (W), Rarity Level: 3-4, Values: 10 up.

III-D-2 Struck on a Large Lamination Crack Planchet (W), Rarity Level: 3-6, Values: $1 up.

III-D-3 Struck on a Split Planchet (W), Rarity Level: 4-6, Values: $5 up.

III-D-4 Struck on a Hinged Split Planchet (W), Rarity Level: 5-6, Values: $35 up.

III-D-5 Struck on a Planchet With a Clad Layer Missing (W), Rarity Level: 4-5, Values: $15 up.

III-D-6 Struck on a Planchet With Both Clad Layers Missing (W), Rarity Level: 4-5, Values: $25 up.

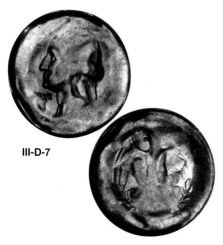

III-D-7

III-E-2

III-D-7 Struck on a Separated Clad Layer or Lamination (W), Rarity Level: 6-7, Values: $75 up.

III-D-8 Struck on a Broken Planchet Before the Strike (W), Rarity Level: 3-5, Values: $10 up.

III-D-9 Broken Coin During or After the Strike (W), Rarity Level: 4-6, Values: $20 up.

III-D-10 Struck Coin Fragment Split or Broken During or After the Strike (W), Rarity Level: 3-5, Values: $5 up.

III-D-11 Reedless Coin Broken During or After the Strike (W), Rarity Level: Unknown, Values: -.

●STRUCK ON WRONG STOCK PLANCHETS (III-E)

These classes cover those cases where the wrong stock was run through the blanking press, making planchets of the correct diameter, but of the wrong thickness, alloy or metal or a combination of incorrect thickness and metal.

III-E-1 Struck on a Half Cent-Stock Planchet (IE), Rarity Level: Unknown, Values: No Value Established.

III-E-2 Struck on a Cent-Stock Planchet (IE), Rarity Level: Unknown, Values: No Value Established.

III-E-3 Struck on a Two-Cent-Stock Planchet (E), Rarity Level: Unknown, Values: -.

III-E-4 Struck on a Three-Cent-Silver Stock Planchet (E), Rarity Level: Unknown, Values: -.

III-E-5 Struck on a Three-Cent-Nickel Stock Planchet (E), Rarity Level: Unknown, Values: -.

III-E-6 Struck on a Half Dime-Stock Planchet (E), Rarity Level: Unknown, Values: -.

III-E-7 Struck on a Dime-Stock Planchet (E), Rarity Level: 5-6, Values: $20 up.

III-E-8 Struck on a Twenty-Cent-Stock Planchet (E), Rarity Level: Unknown, Values: -.

III-E-9 Struck on a Quarter-Stock Planchet (E), Rarity Level: 6, Values: $50 up.

III-E-10 Struck on a Half Dollar-Stock Planchet (E), Rarity Level: 6-7, Values: $100 up.

III-E-11 Struck on a Dollar-Stock Planchet (E), Rarity Level: 6-7, Values: $300 up.

III-E-12 Struck on a Token/Medal-Stock Planchet (E), Rarity Level: 7, Values: No Value Established.

III-E-13 Struck on a Wrong Thickness Spoiled Planchet (IWE), Rarity Level: 7, Values: $50 up.

III-E-14 Struck on a Correct Thickness Spoiled Planchet (IWE), Rarity Level: Unknown, Values: No Value Established.

III-E-15 Struck on a Cut Down Struck Token (IWE), Rarity Level: 6-7, Values: $50 up.

III-E-16 Struck on an Experimental or Pattern-Stock Planchet (IE), Rarity Level: 7, Values: $50 up.

III-E-17 Struck on a Proof-Stock Planchet (IE), Rarity Level: 7, Values: $100 up.

III-E-18 Struck on an Adjusted Specification-Stock Planchet (IE), Rarity Level: 3-7, Values: No Value to $5 and up.

III-E-19 Struck on a Trial Strike-Stock Planchet (IE), Rarity Level: Unknown, Values: No Value Established.

III-E-20 U.S. Coin Struck on a Foreign-Stock Planchet. (E), Rarity Level: 5, Values: $35 up.

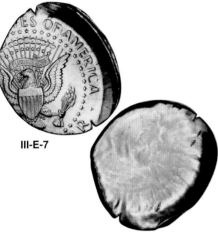

III-E-7

III-G-18

III-E-21 Foreign Coin Struck on a Foreign-Stock Planchet (E), Rarity Level: 5-6, Values: $25 up.

III-E-22 Struck on a Non-Standard Coin Alloy (IE), Rarity Level: 4-7, Values: $20 up.

●Extra metal (III-F)

The term "extra metal" for the purpose of this section includes both extra metal added to the blank during the blanking operation and metal powder added to the planchet during the annealing operation.

III-F-1 Struck on a Type 1 Blank With Extra Metal (W), Rarity Level: Unknown, Values: -.

III-F-2 Struck on a Type 2 Planchet With Extra Metal (W), Rarity Level: 4-5, Values: $10 up.

III-F-3 Struck on a Sintered Coating Planchet (W), Rarity Level: 6-7, Values: $35 up.

●Struck on normal or abnormal blanks, or planchets (III-G)

This section includes coins struck on either a blank, as it comes from the blanking press, or as a planchet that has passed through the upsetting mill. Added to this section are those planchets which are normal until they are struck by the wrong dies. These differ from the wrong stock planchets because the wrong stock planchets are already a variety before they are struck.

III-G-1 Struck on a Type 1 Blank (IWE), Rarity Level: 4-6, Values: $10 up.

III-G-2 Struck on a Type 2 Planchet (I), Rarity Level: 1, Values: No Extra Value.

III-G-3 Struck on a Purchased Planchet (I), Rarity Level: 1, Values: No Extra Value.

III-G-4 Struck on a Mint-Made Planchet (I), Rarity Level: 1, Values: No Extra Value.

III-G-5 Struck on an Adjustment-Marked Planchet (I), Rarity Level: 4-7, Values: Minimal, and may reduce value of coin in some cases.

III-G-6 Struck on a Hardness Test-Marked Planchet (I), Rarity Level: 6-7, Values: $10 up.

III-G-7 Wrong Planchet or Metal on a Half Cent Planchet (IE), Rarity Level: 5-7, Values: $100 up.

III-G-8 Wrong Planchet or Metal on a Cent Planchet (IE), Rarity Level: 3-6, Values: $25 up.

III-G-9 Wrong Planchet or Metal on a Nickel Planchet (E), Rarity Level: 4-6, Values: $35 up

III-G-10 Wrong Planchet or Metal on a Dime Planchet (E), Rarity Level: 4-6, Values: $50 up.

III-G-11 Wrong Planchet or Metal on a Quarter Planchet (E), Rarity Level: 4-6. Values: $100 up.

III-G-12 Wrong Planchet or Metal on a Half Dollar Planchet (E), Rarity Level: 6-7, Values: $500 up.

III-G-13 Wrong Planchet or Metal on a Dollar Planchet (E), Rarity Level: 7, Values: $500 up.

III-G-14 Wrong Planchet or Metal on a Gold Planchet (E), Rarity Level: 7, Values: $1000 up.

III-G-15 Struck on a Wrong Series Planchet (IE), Rarity Level: 6-7, Values: $1500 up.

III-G-16 U.S. Coin Struck on a Foreign Planchet (E), Rarity Level: 5-7, Values: $35 up.

III-G-17 Foreign Coin Struck on a U.S. Planchet (E), Rarity Level: 6-7, Values: $50 up.

III-G-18 Foreign Coin Struck on a Wrong Foreign Planchet (E), Rarity Level: 6-7, Values: $50 up.

III-G-19 Struck on a Medal Planchet (E), Rarity Level: 6-7, Values: $100 up.

III-G-20 Medal Struck on a Coin Planchet (IE), Rarity Level: 3-5, Values: $10 up.

III-G-21 Struck on an Official Sample Planchet (IE), Rarity Level: Unknown, Values: No Value Established.

III-G-22 Struck Intentionally on a Wrong Planchet (I), Rarity Level: 6-7, Values: Mainly struck as Presentation Pieces, full numismatic value.

III-G-23 Non-Proof Struck on a Proof Planchet (IE), Rarity Level: 6-7, Values: $500 up.

●STRUCK ON COIN METAL STRIP (III-H)

Pieces of the coin metal strip do manage at times to escape into the coin press.

III-H-1 (See I-H-1 Punched Coin Metal Strip), Rarity Level: Impossible, Values: -.

III-H-2 Struck on Chopped Coin Metal Strip (E), Rarity Level: 6-7, Values: $25 up.

●DIE ADJUSTMENT STRIKES (III-I)

As the dies are set up and adjusted in the coin press, variations in the strike occur until the dies are properly set. Test strikes are normally scrapped, but on occasion reach circulation.

III-I-1 Die Adjustment Strike (IE), Rarity Level: 5-6, Values: $35 up.

III-I-2 Edge Strike (E), Rarity Level: 5-6, Values: $10 to $20 and up.

III-I-3 Weak Strike (W), Rarity Level: 1, Values: No Extra Value.

III-I-4 Strong Strike (IWE), Rarity Level: 1, Values: No value except for the premium that might be paid for a well struck coin.

III-I-5 Jam Strike (IE), Rarity Level: 7, Values: $50 up.

III-I-6 Trial Piece Strike (I), Rarity Level: 6-7, Values: $100 up.

III-I-7 Edge-Die Adjustment Strike (I), Rarity Level: 5-7, Values: $5 up.

III-I-8 Uniface Strike (I), Rarity Level 7, Values: $50 up.

III-I-3

●INDENTED, BROCKAGE AND COUNTER-BROCKAGE STRIKES (III-J)

Indented and uniface strikes involve an extra unstruck planchet between one of the dies and the planchet being struck. Brockage strikes involve a struck coin between one of the dies and the planchet and a counter-brockage requires a brockage coin between one of the dies and the planchet.

A cap, or capped die strike results when a coin sticks to the die and is squeezed around it in the shape of a bottle cap.

III-J-1 Indented Strike (W), Rarity Level: 3-6, Values: $5 up.

III-J-2 Uniface Strike (W), Rarity Level: 3-5, Values: $15 up.

III-J-3 Indented Strike By a Smaller Planchet (WE), Rarity Level: 5-7, Values: $100 up.

III-J-4 Indented Second Strike (W), Rarity Level: 3-5, Values: $10 up, about the same as a regular double strike of comparable size.

III-J-5 Partial Brockage Strike (W), Rarity Level: 3-6, Values: $15 up.

III-J-6 Full Brockage Strike (W), Rarity Level: 3-6, Values: $5 up.

III-J-7 Brockage Strike of a Smaller Coin (WE), Rarity Level: 6-7, Values: $200 up.

III-J-8 Brockage Strike of a Struck Coin Fragment (WE), Rarity Level: 4-6, Values: $5 up.

III-J-9 Brockage Second Strike (WE), Rarity Level: 3-5, Values: $5 up.

III-J-10 Partial Counter-Brockage Strike (WE), Rarity Level: 3-5, Values: $10 up.

III-J-11 Full Counter-Brockage Strike (WE), Rarity Level: 5-7, Values: $100 up.

III-J-12 Counter-Brockage Second Strike (WE), Rarity Level: 4-6, Values: $10 up.

III-J-13 Full Brockage-Counter-Brockage Strike (WE), Rarity Level: 6-7, Values: $150 up.

III-J-14 Multiple Brockage or Counter-Brockage Strike (WE), Rarity Level: 5-7, Values: $100 up.

III-J-15 Capped Die Strike (WE), Rarity Level: 6-7, Values: $500 up.

III-J-16 Reversed Capped Die Strike (WE), Rarity Level: 7, Values: $1,000 up.

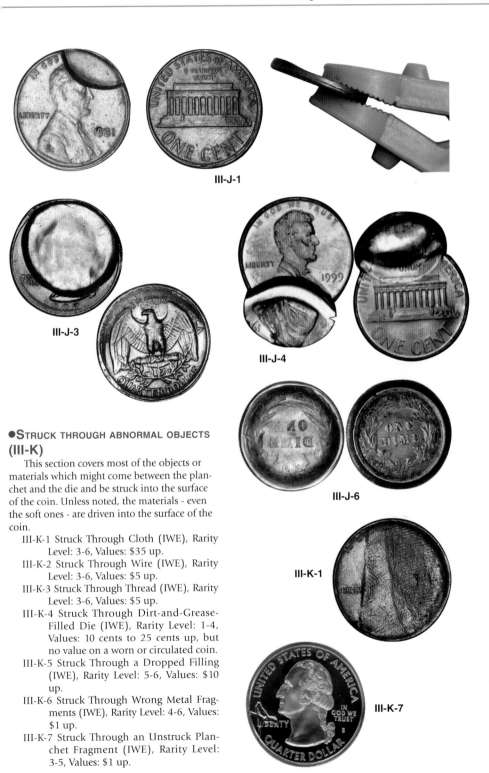

III-J-1

III-J-3

III-J-4

III-J-6

III-K-1

III-K-7

●**STRUCK THROUGH ABNORMAL OBJECTS (III-K)**

This section covers most of the objects or materials which might come between the planchet and the die and be struck into the surface of the coin. Unless noted, the materials - even the soft ones - are driven into the surface of the coin.

III-K-1 Struck Through Cloth (IWE), Rarity Level: 3-6, Values: $35 up.

III-K-2 Struck Through Wire (IWE), Rarity Level: 3-6, Values: $5 up.

III-K-3 Struck Through Thread (IWE), Rarity Level: 3-6, Values: $5 up.

III-K-4 Struck Through Dirt-and-Grease-Filled Die (IWE), Rarity Level: 1-4, Values: 10 cents to 25 cents up, but no value on a worn or circulated coin.

III-K-5 Struck Through a Dropped Filling (IWE), Rarity Level: 5-6, Values: $10 up.

III-K-6 Struck Through Wrong Metal Fragments (IWE), Rarity Level: 4-6, Values: $1 up.

III-K-7 Struck Through an Unstruck Planchet Fragment (IWE), Rarity Level: 3-5, Values: $1 up.

III-K-7

III-K-8

III-K-8

III-K-8

III-K-8 Struck Through a Rim Burr (IWE), Rarity Level: 3-5, Values: $1 to $2 and up.

III-K-9 Struck Through plit-Off Reeding (IWE), Rarity Level: 5-6, Values: $25 up.

III-K-10 Struck Through a Feed Finger (IWE), Rarity Level: 5-7, Values: $25 to $50 and up.

III-K-11 Struck Through Miscellaneous Objects (IWE), Rarity Level: 4-6, Values: $1 up.

III-K-12 Struck Through Progression (IWE), Rarity Level: 4-6, Values: $1 up.

Note: Some 1987 through 1994 quarters are found without mintmarks, classed as III-K-4, a Filled Die. Values depend on market conditions. Filled dies have value ONLY on current, uncirculated grade coins.

•DOUBLE STRIKES (III-L)

Only coins which receive two or more strikes by the die pair fall in this section and are identified by the fact that both sides of the coin are affected. Unless some object interferes, an equal area of both sides of the coin will be equally doubled.

The exception is the second strike with a loose die, which will double only one side of a coin, but is a rare form usually occurring only on proofs. A similar effect is flat field doubling from die chatter.

III-L-1 Close Centered Double Strike (WE), Rarity Level: 4-6, Values: $15 up.

III-L-2 Rotated Second Strike Over a Centered First Strike (WE), Rarity Level: 4-6, Values: $15 up.

III-L-3 Off-Center Second Strike Over a Centered First Strike (WE), Rarity Level: 4-6, Values: $15 up.

III-L-4 Off-Center Second Strike Over an Off-Center First Strike (WE), Rarity Level: 4-6, Values: $10 up.

III-L-5 Off-Center Second Strike Over a Broadstrike (WE), Rarity Level: 5-6, Values: $20 up.

III-L-6 Centered Second Strike Over an Off-Center First Strike (WE), Rarity Level: 5-6, Values: $50 up.

III-L-7 Obverse Struck Over Reverse (WE), Rarity Level: 5-6, Values: $25 up.

III-L-8 Nonoverlapping Double Strike (WE), Rarity Level: 5-6 Values: $20 up.

III-L-9 Struck Over a Different Denomination or Series (WE), Rarity Level: 6, Values: $300 and up.

III-L-10 Chain Strike (WE), Rarity Level: 6, Values: $300 up for the pair of coins that were struck together.

III-L-11 Second-Strike Doubling From a Loose Die (W), Rarity Level: 6-7, Values: $200 up.

III-L-12 Second-Strike Doubling From a Loose Screw Press Die (W), Rarity Level: 5-6, Values: $100 up.

III-L-13 Second Strike on an Edge Strike (WE), Rarity Level: 5-6, Values: $20 up.

III-L-14 Folded Planchet Strike (WE), Rarity Level: 5-7, Values: $100 up.

III-L-15 Triple Strike (WE), Rarity Level: 6-7, Values: $100 up.

III-L-16 Multiple Strike (WE), Rarity Level: 6-7, Values: $200 up.

III-L-17 U.S. Coin Struck Over a Struck Foreign Coin (WE), Rarity Level: 6-7, Values: $300 up.

III-L-18 Foreign Coin Struck Over a Struck U.S. Coin (WE), Rarity Level: 6-7, Values: $400 up.

III-L-19 Foreign Coin Struck Over a Struck Foreign Coin (WE), Rarity Level: 7, Values: $500 up.

III-L-20 Double Strike on Scrap or Junk (E), Rarity Level: 6, Values: $50 up.

III-L-21 Struck on a Struck Token or Medal (E), Rarity Level: 5-6, Values: $100 up.

III-L-22 Double-Struck Edge Motto or Design (E), Rarity Level: 6-7, Values: $200 up.

III-L-23 One Edge Motto or Design Struck Over Another (E), Rarity Level: 7, Values: $300 up.

III-L-24 Flat Field Doubling (W), Rarity Level: 2-3, Values: $1 to $5.

III-L-25 Territorial Struck over Struck U.S. Coin: (I) Rarity Level: 6-7, Values: $200 up.

III-L-26 Pattern Struck over Struck U.S. Coin: (I) Rarity Level: 6-7, Values: $200 up.

III-L-27 Pattern Struck over Struck Pattern:(I) Rarity Level 6-7, Values: $200 up.

III-L-28 Pattern Struck Over Foreign Coin:(I) Rarity Level 6-7, Values - $200 up.

●COLLAR STRIKING VARIETIES (III-M)

The collar is often referred to as the "Third Die," and is involved in a number of forms of misstrikes. The collar normally rises around the planchet, preventing it from squeezing sideways between the dies and at the same time forming the reeding on reeded coins.

If the collar is out of position or tilted, a partial collar strike results; if completely missing, it causes a broadstrike; if the planchet is not entirely between the dies, an off-center strike.

III-M-1 Flanged Partial Collar Strike (WE), Rarity Level: 5-6, Values: $20 up.

III-M-2 Reversed Flanged Partial Collar Strike (WE), Rarity Level: 6-7, Values: $35 up.

III-M-3 Tilted Partial Collar Strike (WE), Rarity Level: 5-6, Values: $20 up.

III-M-4 Centered Broadstrike (WE), Rarity Level: 5-6, Values: $5 up.

III-L-3

III-L-3

III-L-4

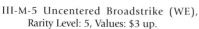

III-M-5   **III-M-8**

III-M-5 Uncentered Broadstrike (WE), Rarity Level: 5, Values: $3 up.
III-M-6 Reversed Broadstrike (WE), Rarity Level: 6, Values: $10 up.
III-M-7 Struck Off-Center 10-30% (W), Rarity Level: 3-6, Values: $3 up.
III-M-8 Struck Off-Center 31-70% (W), Rarity Level: 4-6, Values: $5 up.
III-M-9 Struck Off-Center 71% or More (W), Rarity Level: 3-5, Values: $2 up.
III-M-10 Rotated Multi-sided Planchet Strike (W), Rarity Level: 5-6, Values: $10 up.
III-M-11 Wire Edge Strike (IWE), Rarity Level: 1-2, Values: No Extra Value.
III-M-12 Struck With the Collar Too High (WE), Rarity Level: 6-7, Values: $20 up.
III-M-13 Off-Center Slide Strike (W), Rarity Level:3-6 $4 up.

●MISALIGNED AND ROTATED (DIE) STRIKE VARIETIES (III-N)
One (rarely both) of the dies may be Offset Misaligned, off to one side, or may be tilted (Vertically Misaligned). One die may either have been installed so that it is turned in relation to the other die, or may turn in the holder, or the shank may break allowing the die face to rotate in relation to the opposing die.
Vertical misaligned dies are rarely found, and like rotated dies, find only limited collector interest. Ninety and 180 degree rotations are the most popular. Rotations of 14 degrees or less have no value. The 1989-D Congress dollar is found with a nearly 180 degree rotated reverse, currently retailing for around $2,000. Only about 30 have been reported to date.
III-N-1 Offset Die Misalignment Strike (WE), Rarity Level: 3-5, Values: $2 up.
III-N-2 Vertical Die Misalignment Strike (WE), Rarity Level: 4-6, Values: $1 up.
III-N-3 Rotated Die Strike - 15 to 45 Degrees (IWE), Rarity Level: 4-6, Values: $2 up.
III-N-4 Rotated Die Strike - 46 to 135 Degrees (IWE), Rarity Level: 5-6, Values: $10 up.

III-N-5 Rotated Die Strike - 136 to 180 Degrees (IWE), Rarity Level: 5-6, Values: $25 up.

●LETTERED AND DESIGN EDGE STRIKE VARIETIES (III-O)
Early U.S. coins and a number of foreign coins have either lettered edges, or designs on the edge of the coin. Malfunctions of the application of the motto or design to the edge fall in this section.
III-O-1 Overlapping Edge Motto or Design (WE), Rarity Level: 3-4, Values: $5 to $10 and up.
III-O-2 Wrong Edge Motto or Design (WE), Rarity Level: 5-6-7, Values: $50 up.
III-O-3 Missing Edge Motto, Design or Security Edge (IWE), Rarity Level: 5-6-7, Values: $50 up.
III-O-4 Jammed Edge Die Strike (W), Rarity Level: 6, Values: $10 up.
III-O-5 Misplaced Segment of an Edge Die (E), Rarity Level: 4-7, Values: $25 up.
III-O-6 Reeded Edge Struck Over a Lettered Edge (IE), Rarity Level: 3-6, Values: No Extra Value up.

●DEFECTIVE STRIKES AND MISMATCHED DIES (III-P)
The final section of the Striking Division covers coins which are not properly struck for reasons other than those in previous classes, such as coins struck with mismatched (muled) dies. The mismatched die varieties must be taken on a case by case basis, while the otherclasses presently have little collector demand or premium.
III-P-1 Defective Strike (WE), Rarity Level: 1, Values: No Extra Value.
III-P-2 Mismatched Die Strike (E), Rarity Level: 4-7, Values: $25 up.
III-P-3 Single-Strike Proof (WE), Rarity Level: 4-5, Values: Minimal.
III-P-4 Single Die-Proof Strike (IE), Rarity Level: 5-6, Values: $100 up.
III-P-5 Reversed Die Strike (I), Rarity Level: 4-5, Values: No Extra Value to Minimal.

Official Mint modifications

DIVISION IV

Several mint produced varieties occur after the coin has been struck, resulting in the addition of the fourth division to my PDS System. Since most of these coins are either unique or are special varieties, each one must be taken on a case by case basis. All classes listed here are by definition intentional.

I have not listed values as the coins falling in these classes which are sold through regular numismatic channels, are cataloged with the regular issues or are covered in specialized catalogs in their particular area.

●MATTE PROOFS (IV-A)

Matte proofs as a section include several of the forms of proof coins which have the striking characteristics of a mirror proof but have been treated AFTER striking to give them a grainy, non-reflective surface.

IV-A-1 Matte Proof (I), Rarity Level: 3-5, Values: Normal Numismatic Value.

IV-A-2 Matte Proof on One Side (I), Rarity Level: 7, Values: Normal Numismatic Value.

IV-A-3 Sandblast Proof (I), Rarity Level: 4-6, Values: Normal Numismatic Value.

●ADDITIONAL ENGRAVING (IV-B)

This section includes any added markings which are placed on the struck coin and struck coins which later were cut into pieces for various purposes. The warning is repeated: Anything done to a coin after the strike is extremely difficult to authenticate and is much easier to fake than a die struck coin.

IV-B-1 Counterstamp and Countermark (I), Rarity Level: 3-6, Values: Normal Numismatic Value.

IV-B-2 Perforated and Cut Coins (I), Rarity Level: 4-6, Values: Normal Numismatic Value.

●RESTRIKES (IV-C)

Restrikes cover a complicated mixture of official use of dies from a variety of sources. Whether or not some were officially sanctioned is always a problem for the collector.

IV-C-1 Restrike on the Same Denomination Planchet (I), Rarity Level: 4-6, Values: Normal Numismatic Value.

IV-C-2 Restrike on a Different Denomination or Series Planchet (I), Rarity Level: 4-6, Values: Normal Numismatic Value.

IV-C-3 Restrike on a Foreign Coin (I), Rarity Level: 6-7, Values: Normal Numismatic Value.

IV-C-4 Restrike on a Token or Medal (I), Rarity Level: 5-6, Values: Normal Numismatic Value.

IV-C-5 Restruck With the Original Dies (I), Rarity Level: 4-6, Values: Normal Numismatic Value.

IV-C-6 Restruck With Mismatched Dies (I), Rarity Level: 4-6, Values: Normal Numismatic Value.

IV-C-7 Copy Strike With New Dies (I), Rarity Level: 3-5, Values: Normal Numismatic Value.

IV-C-8 Fantasy Strike (I), Rarity Level: 4-6, Values: Normal Numismatic Value.

After strike modifications

DIVISION V

This division includes both modifications that have value to collectors – and those that don't. I needed a couple of divisions to cover other things that happen to coins to aid in cataloging them. This avoids the false conclusion that an unlisted coin is quite rare, when the exact opposite is more likely to be the case.

●COLLECTIBLE MODIFICATIONS AFTER STRIKE (V-A)

This section includes those classes having to do with deliberate modifications of the coin done with a specific purpose or intent which makes them of some value to collectors. Quite often these pieces were made specifically to sell to collectors, or at least to the public under the guise of being collectible.

V-A-1 Screw Thaler, Rarity Level: 5-6, Values: Normal Numismatic Value.

V-A-2 Love Token, Rarity Level: 3-6, Values: $10 up.

V-A-3 Satirical or Primitive Engraving, Rarity Level: 6-7, Values: $5 up.

V-A-4 Elongated Coin, Rarity Level: 2-7, Values: 50 cents to $1 and up.

V-A-5 Coin Jewelry, Rarity Level: 2-5, Values: $1 up.

V-A-6 Novelty Coin, Rarity Level: 1-3, Values: No Value up to $5 to $10.

V-A-7 Toning, Rarity Level: 3-6, Values: No value up, depending on coloration. Easily faked.

V-A-8 Mint Modification, Rarity Level: 4-7, Values: $5 up. Easily faked.

V-A-9 Mint Packaging Mistake, Rarity Level: 5-7, Values: Nominal $1. Very easily faked.

●ALTERATIONS AND DAMAGE AFTER THE STRIKE(V-B)

This section includes those changes in a coin which have no collector value. In most cases their effect on the coin is to reduce or entirely eliminate any collector value - and in the case of counterfeits they are actually illegal to even own.

V-B-1 Machine Doubling Damage: NOTE: Machine doubling damage is defined as: "Damage to a coin after the strike, due to die bounce or chatter or die displacement, showing on the struck coin as scrapes on the sides of the design elements, with portions of the coin metal in the relief elements either displaced sideways or downward, depending on the direction of movement of the loose die." Machine doubling damage, or MDD, is by far the most common form of doubling found on almost any coin in the world. Rarity Level: 0, Values: Reduces the coin's value.

V-B-2 Accidental or Deliberate Damage, Rarity Level: 0, Values: Reduces the coin's value.

V-B-3 Test Cut or Mark, Rarity Level: 0, Values: Reduces value of coin to face or bullion value.

V-B-4 Alteration, Rarity Level: 0, Values: Reduces value to face or bullion value.

V-B-5 Whizzing, Rarity Level: 0, Values: Reduces value sharply and may reduce it to face or bullion value.

V-B-6 Counterfeit, Copy, Facsimile, Forgery or Fake, Rarity Level: 0, Values: No Value and may be illegal to own.

V-B-7 Planchet Deterioration. Very common on copper-plated zinc cents. Rarity level: 0, Values: No Value.

4 American Coin History

U.S. Mint founded in 1792

At peak production, the U.S. Mint strikes nearly 30 billion coins a year. Who would have thought it possible at its founding? In July 1792, a site for the new U.S. Mint not yet having been secured, 1,500 silver half dismes were struck on a small screw press in the cellar of a Philadelphia building owned by sawmaker John Harper. Though some have since categorized these early emissions of the fledgling U.S. Mint as patterns, it is clear that first President George Washington – who is said to have deposited the silver from which the coins were struck – considered this small batch of half dismes to be the first official U.S. coins.

The law establishing the Mint dates to April 2, 1792. From that early legislative birth has flowed the coins that have underpinned the workings of U.S. commerce for over two centuries. It must be remembered that the Mint was born in chaos. It was a time shortly after the Revolutionary War and as hard as it was to win independence from Great Britain, setting up American government finances on a sound basis was to prove almost as daunting.

First United States Mint, Philadelphia Pa.   1854

At first a cumbersome system was proposed by Robert Morris, a Revolutionary War financier and first superintendent of finance. Refinements tendered by Thomas Jefferson and Alexander Hamilton then firmly placed the nation on an easily understood decimal system of coinage. They were working with a hodgepodge system that grew up in the Colonial period.

Despite a dire need for coinage in the Colonies, Great Britain considered it a royal right and granted franchises sparingly. Much of the Colonial economy, therefore, revolved around barter, with food staples, crops, and goods serving as currency. Indian wampum or bead money also was used, first in the fur trade and later as a form of money for Colonial use.

Copper pieces were produced around 1616 for Sommer Islands (now Bermuda), but coinage within the American Colonies apparently didn't begin until 1652, when John Hull struck silver threepence, sixpence and shillings under authority of the General Court of Massachusetts. This coinage continued, with design changes (willow, oak, and pine trees), through 1682. Most of the coins were dated 1652, apparently to avoid legal problems with England.

In 1658 Cecil Calvert, second Lord Baltimore, commissioned coins to be struck in England for use in Maryland. Other authorized and unauthorized coinages – including those of Mark Newby, John Holt, William Wood, and Dr. Samuel Higley – all became part of the landscape of circulating coins. In the 1780s there were influxes of counterfeit British halfpence and various state coinages.

The Articles of Confederation had granted individual states the right to produce copper coins. Many states found this to be appealing, and merchants in the mid-1780s traded copper coins of Vermont, Connecticut, Massachusetts, New Jersey, and New York. Not all were legal issues; various entrepreneurs used this as an invitation to strike imitation state coppers and British halfpence. Mutilated and worn foreign coins also circulated in abundance. Included among these were coins of Portugal, Great Britain, and France, with the large majority of the silver arriving from Spain.

The accounting system used by the states was derived from the British system of pounds, shillings, and pence. Each state was allowed to set its own rates at which foreign gold and silver coins would trade in relation to the British pound.

In 1782 Robert Morris, newly named superintendent of finance, was appointed to head a committee to determine the values and weights of the gold and silver coins in circulation. Asked simply to draw up a table of values, Morris took the opportunity to propose the establishment of a federal mint. In his Jan. 15, 1782, report (largely prepared by his assistant, Gouverneur Morris), Morris noted that the exchange rates between the states were complicated.

He observed that a farmer in New Hampshire would be hard-pressed if asked to determine the value of a bushel of wheat in South Carolina. Morris recorded that an amount of wheat worth four shillings in his home state of New Hampshire would be worth 21 shillings and eightpence under the accounting system used in South Carolina.

Morris claimed these difficulties plagued not only farmers, but that "they are perplexing to most Men and troublesome to all." Morris further pressed for the adoption of an American coin to solve the problems of the need for small change and debased foreign coinages in circulation.

In essence, what he was advocating was a monometallic system based on silver.

He said that gold and silver had fluctuated throughout history. Because these fluctuations resulted in the more valuable metal leaving the country, any nation that adopted a bimetallic coinage was doomed to have its gold or silver coins disappear from circulation.

Gouverneur Morris calculated the rate at which the Spanish dollar traded to the British pound in the various states. Leaving out South Carolina, because it threw off his calculations, Gouverneur Morris arrived at a common denominator of 1,440. Robert Morris, therefore, recommended a unit of value of 1/1,440, equivalent to a quarter grain of silver. He suggested the striking of a silver 100-unit coin, or cent; a silver 500-unit coin, or quint; a silver 1,000-unit coin, or mark; and two copper coins, one of eight units and the other of five units.

On Feb. 21, 1782, the Grand Committee of Congress approved the proposal and directed Morris to press forward and report with a plan to establish a mint. Morris had already done so. Apparently feeling confident that Congress would like his coinage ideas, Morris (as shown by his diary) began efforts at the physical establishment prior to his January 1782 report. He had already engaged Benjamin Dudley to acquire necessary equipment for the mint and hoped to have sample coins available to submit with his original report to Congress.

It wasn't until April 23, 1783, that Morris was able to send his Nova Constellatio patterns to Congress and suggest that he was ready to report on establishing a mint. Apparently nothing came of Morris' efforts. Several committees looked into the matter, but nothing was accomplished. Dudley was eventually discharged as Morris' hopes dimmed.

Thomas Jefferson was the next to offer a major plan. Jefferson liked the idea of a decimal system of coinage, but disliked Morris' basic unit of value. As chairman of the Currency Committee, Jefferson reviewed Morris' plan and formulated his own ideas.

To test public reaction, Jefferson gave his "Notes on Coinage" to The Providence Gazette, and Country Journal, which published his plan in its July 24, 1784, issue. Jefferson disagreed with Morris' suggestion for a 1/1,440 unit of value and instead proposed a decimal coinage based on the dollar, with the lowest unit of account being the mil, or 1/1,000.

"The most easy ratio of multiplication and division is that by ten," Jefferson wrote. "Every one knows the facility of Decimal Arithmetic."

Jefferson argued that although Morris' unit would have eliminated the unwanted fraction that occurred when merchants converted British farthings to dollars, this was of little significance. After all, the original idea of establishing a mint was to get rid of foreign currencies.

Morris' unit, Jefferson said, was too cumbersome for use in normal business transactions. According to Jefferson, under Morris' plan a horse valued at 80 Spanish dollars would require a notation of six figures and would be shown as 115,200 units.

Jefferson' coinage plan suggested the striking of a dollar, or unit; half dollar, or five-tenths; a double tenth, or fifth of a dollar, equivalent to a pistareen; a tenth, equivalent to a Spanish bit; and a one-fifth copper coin, relating to the British farthing. He also wanted a gold coin of $10, corresponding to the British double guinea; and a copper one-hundredth coin, relating to the British halfpence.

In reference to his coinage denominations, Jefferson said, it was important that the coins "coincide in value with some of the known coins so nearly, that the people may by quick reference in the mind, estimate their value." The Spanish dollar was the most commonly used coin in trade, so it was natural basis for the new U.S. silver dollar. In the Spanish system, the coin was called an eight reales, or piece of eight.

More than a year, however, passed without any further action on his plan or that proposed by Morris. In a letter to William Grayson, a member of the Continental Congress, Washington expressed concern for the establishment of a national coinage system, terming it "indispensably necessary." Washington also complained of the coinage in circulation: "A man must travel with a pair of scales in his pocket, or run the risk of receiving gold at one-fourth less than it counts."

On May 13, 1785, the 13-member Grand Committee, to whom Jefferson's plan had been submitted, filed its report, generally favoring Jefferson's coinage system. The committee did, however, make slight alterations, including the elimination of the gold $10 coin, the addition of a gold $5 coin, and the dropping of Jefferson's double tenth, which it replaced with a quarter dollar. The committee also added a coin equal to 1/200 of a dollar (half cent). On July 6, 1785, Congress unanimously approved the Grand Committee's plan. It failed, however, to set a standard weight for the silver dollar or to order plans drawn up for a mint.

Several proposals were offered for a contract coinage. On April 21, 1787, the board accepted a proposal by James Jarvis to strike 300 tons of copper coin at the federal standard. Jarvis, however, delivered slightly less than 9,000 pounds of his contract. The contract was voided the following year for his failure to meet scheduled delivery times, but helped to delay further action on a mint. Concerted action on a coinage system and a mint would wait until the formation of the new government.

Alexander Hamilton, named in September 1789 to head the new Treasury, offered three different methods by which the new nation could achieve economic stability, including the funding of the national debt, establishment of the Bank of North America and the founding of the U.S. Mint. On Jan. 21, 1791, Hamilton submitted to Congress a "Report on the Establishment of a Mint."

Hamilton agreed with Jefferson that the dollar seemed to be best suited to serve as the basic unit, but believed it necessary to establish a proper weight and fineness for the new coin. To do so, Hamilton had several Spanish coins assayed to determine the fine weight of the Spanish dollar. He also watched the rate at which Spanish dollars traded for fine gold (24 3/4 grains per dollar) on the world market.

From his assays and observations he determined that the Spanish dollar contained 371 grains of silver. He then multiplied 24 3/4 by 15 (the gold value of silver times his suggested bimetallic ratio) and arrived at 371 1/4 as the proper fine silver weight for the new silver dollar.

The Spanish dollar actually contained 376 grains of pure silver when new, 4 3/4 grains more than Hamilton's proposed silver dollar.

Hamilton also wanted a bimetallic ratio of 15-to-1. Hamilton said his ratio was closer to Great Britain's, which would be important for trade, and Holland's, which would be important for repaying loans from that country.

His report suggested the striking of a gold $10; gold dollar; silver dollar; silver tenth, or disme; and copper one-hundredth and half-hundredth. Hamilton felt the last of these, the half cent, was necessary because it would enable merchants to lower their prices, which would help the poor.

Congress passed the act establishing the U.S. Mint April 2, 1792. It reinstated several coin denominations left out by Hamilton and dropped his gold dollar. In gold, the act authorized at $10 coin, or "eagle"; a $5 coin, or "half eagle"; and a $2.50 coin, or "quarter eagle." In silver were to be a dollar, half dollar, quarter dollar, disme, and half disme, and in copper a cent and half cent.

Though it established a sound system of U.S. coinage, the act failed to address the problem of foreign coins in circulation. It was amended in February 1793 to cancel their legal-tender status within three years of the mint's opening.

Coinage totals at the first mint in Philadelphia were understandably low. Skilled coiners, assayers and others who could handle the mint's daily operations were in short supply in the United States. Also in want were adequate equipment and supplies of metal for coinage. Much of the former had to be built or imported. Much of the latter was also imported or salvaged from various domestic sources, including previously struck tokens and coins, and scrap metal.

Coinage began in earnest in 1793 with the striking of half cents and cents at the new mint located at Seventh Street between Market and Arch streets in Philadelphia. Silver coinage followed in 1794, with half dimes, half dollars, and dollars. Gold coinage did not begin until 1795 with the minting of the first $5 and $10 coins. Silver dimes and quarters and gold $2.50 coins did not appear until 1796.

Under the bimetallic system of coinage by which gold and silver served as equal representations of the unit of value, much of the success and failure of the nation's coinage to enter and remain in circulation revolved around the supply and valuation of precious metals. From the Mint's beginning, slight miscalculations in the proper weight for the silver dollar and a proper bimetallic ratio led gold and silver to disappear from circulation. The U.S. silver dollar traded at par with Spanish and Mexican dollars, but because the U.S. coin was lighter, it was doomed to be exported.

A depositor at the first mint could make a profit at the mint's expense by sending the coins to the West Indies. There they could be traded at par for the heavier Spanish or Mexican eight reales, which were then shipped back to the United States for recoinage. As a result, few early silver dollars entered domestic circulation; most failed to escape the melting pots.

Gold fared no better. Calculations of the bimetallic ratio by which silver traded for gold on the world market were also askew at first and were always subject to fluctuations. Gold coins either disappeared quickly after minting or never entered circulation, languishing in bank vaults. These problems led President Jefferson to halt coinage of the gold $10 and the silver dollar in 1804.

The gold $10 reappeared in 1838 at a new, lower weight standard. The silver dollar, not coined for circulation since 1803, returned in 1836 with a limited mintage. Full-scale coinage waited until 1840.

Nor was the coinage of copper an easy matter for the first mint. Severe shortages of the metal led the mint to explore various avenues of obtaining sufficient supplies for striking cents and half cents.

Witness, for example, the half-cent issues of 1795 and 1797 struck over privately issued tokens of the New York firm of Talbot, Allum & Lee because of a shortage of copper for the federal issue. Rising copper prices and continued shortages forced the mint to lower the cent's weight from 208 grains to 168 grains in 1795.

In 1798, because of the coinage shortage, the legal-tender status of foreign coins was restored. Several more extensions were given during the 1800s, ending with the withdrawal of legal-tender status for Spanish coins in 1857.

A new law made the mint lower the standard weight of all gold coins in 1834. This reflected market conditions and in effect recognized a higher gold price when bought with silver coins. For example, $5 in silver coins bought a new, lighter $5 gold piece, meaning the buyer got less gold. This led to the melting of great numbers of the older, heavier gold coins as speculators grabbed a 4.7 percent profit.

By the 1850s discovery of gold in California made silver more expensive in terms of gold. All silver quickly disappeared from circulation. Congress reacted in 1853 by lowering the weight of the silver half dime, dime, quarter, and half dollar, hoping to keep silver in circulation. A new gold coin of $20 value, the "double eagle," was introduced to absorb a great amount of the gold from Western mines.

Not long after, silver was discovered in Nevada. By the mid-1870s the various mines that made up what was known as the Comstock Lode (named after its colorful early proprietor, Henry P. Comstock) had hit the mother lode. Large supplies of silver from the Comstock, combined with European demonetization, caused a severe drop in its value. Silver coins were made heavier as a result in 1873.

Also, it was believed that the introduction of a heavier, 420-grain silver dollar in 1873, known as the Trade dollar, would create a market for much of the Comstock silver, bolster its price, and at the same time wrest control from Great Britain of lucrative trade with the Orient. It didn't. Large numbers of Trade dollars eventually flooded back into the United States. They were demonetized in 1887.

Morgan dollars were introduced in 1878 as a panacea to the severe economic problems following the Civil War. Those who proudly carried the banner of free silver contended that by taking the rich output of the Comstock mines and turning it into silver dollars, a cheaper, more plentiful form of money would become available. This was supposed to give the economy a boost.

The Free Silver Movement reached its peak in 1896 when William Jennings Bryan attempted to gain the White House on a plank largely based on restoration of the free and unlimited coinage of the standard 412.5-grain silver dollar. He failed. Silver failed. In 1900 the United States officially adopted a gold standard.

Silver continued to be a primary coinage metal until 1964, when rising prices led the Mint to remove it from the dime and quarter. Mintage of the silver dollar had ended in 1935. The half dollar continued to be coined through 1970 with a 40 percent silver composition. It, too, was then made of copper-nickel clad metal.

Gold coinage ended in 1933 and exists today only in commemorative issues and American Eagle bullion coins with fictive face values. A clad composition of copper and nickel is now the primary coinage metal. Even the cent is no longer all copper; a copper-coated zinc composition has been used since 1982.

Precious-metal supplies were also linked to the opening of additional mints, which served the parent facility in Philadelphia. The impact of gold discoveries in the 1820s in the southern Appalachian Mountains was directly tied to the construction of branch mints in Dahlonega, Ga., and Charlotte, N.C., in 1838. These new mints struck only gold coins. New Orleans also became the site of a branch mint in the same year as Dahlonega and Charlotte. It took in some of the outflow of gold from Southern mines, but also struck silver coins.

Discovery of gold in California in the late 1840s created a gold rush, and from it sprang a great western migration. Private issues of gold coinage, often of debased quality, were prevalent, and the cost of shipping the metal eastward for coinage at Philadelphia was high. A call for an official branch mint was soon heard and heeded in 1852 with the authorization of the San Francisco Mint, which began taking deposits in 1854.

The discovery of silver in the Comstock Lode led to yet another mint. Located only a short distance via Virginia & Truckee Railroad from the fabulous Comstock Lode, the Carson City mint began receiving bullion in early 1870.

Denver, also located in a mineral-rich region, became the site of an assay office in 1863 when the government purchased the Clark, Gruber & Co. private mint. It became a U.S. branch mint in 1906. Now four mints exist. They are in Denver, Philadelphia, San Francisco and West Point, N.Y. The latter strikes current precious metal coinage for collectors and investors.

5 How Are Coins Made?

Mints are really factories

Copper, nickel, silver, and gold are pretty much the basic coin metals for the United States. When mixed with tin, copper becomes bronze, and this alloy was used in cents. Current cents have a pure zinc core. There have been patterns made of aluminum, but these never were issued for use in circulation. Platinum joined gold and silver as a precious metal used in U.S. coinage starting in 1997.

There are three basic parts of the minting process: (1) the making of the planchet, which is divided into the selection and processing of the metal and the preparation of the planchets, (2) the making of the dies, and (3) the use of the dies to strike the planchets. To help you remember these three parts, think of "P," "D," and "S" for planchet, die, and striking.

Making the 'blanks'

The piece of metal that becomes a coin is known as a "blank." This is a usually round, flat piece that has been punched or cut from a sheet or strip of coin metal.

Before a blank can become a coin it has to be processed, cleaned, softened, and given what is known as an "upset edge" – a raised ridge or rim around both sides. The blank then becomes a "planchet" and is ready to be struck into a coin by the dies. First they go through what looks like a monstrous cement mixer. A huge cylinder revolves slowly as the planchets are fed in at one end and spiral their way through. This is an annealing oven, which heats the planchets to soften them. When they come out the end, they fall into a bath where they are cleaned with a diluted acid or soap solution. As the final step, they go through the upsetting mill, the machine that puts the raised rim on the blank and turns it into a planchet, ready to be struck. In a different department the process of making the dies used to strike the coins has already begun.

Preparing the dies

For those who haven't studied metallurgy, the concept of hard metal flowing about is pretty hard to swallow, but this is actually what happens. It is basically the same process as the one used in an auto plant to turn a flat sheet of steel into a fender with multiple curves and sharp bends. The cold metal is moved about by the pressure applied.

To make the metal move into the desired design, there has to be a die. Actually, there have to be two dies, because one of the laws of physics is that for every action there has to be an equal and opposite reaction. You cannot hold a piece of metal in midair and strike one side of it. Instead you make two dies, fix one, and drive the other one against it – with a piece of metal in between to accept the design from each die.

A die is a piece of hard metal, like steel, with a design on its face that helps to form a mirror image on the struck coin. Early dies were made by hand. Engravers used hand tools, laboriously cutting each letter, each digit, and each owl or eagle or whatever design was being used into the face of the die. Notice that this is "into" the surface of the die. Each part of the die design is a hole or cavity of varying shape and depth.

This is because we want a mirror image on the coin, but we want it raised, or in "relief." To make a relief image on a coin, the image on the die has to be recessed into the face of the die, or "incuse." Of course, if we want an incuse image on the coin, such as the gold $2.50 and $5 coins of 1908-1929, the design on the die face would have to be in relief.

To fully understand this, take a coin from your pocket and a piece of aluminum foil. Press the foil down over the coin design and rub it with an eraser. When you take the foil off and look at the side that was in contact with the coin, you have a perfect copy of a die. Everywhere there is a relief design on the coin there is an incuse design on your foil "die."

From sketchbook to coin

The design process begins with an artist's sketch. This is translated into a three-dimensional relief design that is hand-carved from plaster or, in recent years, from a form of plastic.

The plaster or plastic design is then transformed into a "galvano," which is an exact copy of the design that has been plated with a thin layer of copper. This is used as a template or pattern in a reducing lathe, which cuts the design into a die blank.

This die becomes the master die, from which all of the following steps descend. The process can be reversed so that the designs will be cut in relief, forming a tool called a "hub," which is simply a piece of steel with the design in relief, exactly the same as the relief design on the intended coin.

To make working dies, pieces of special steel are prepared, with one end shaped with a slight cone. The die blank is softened by heating it. Then the hub is forced into the face of the die, forming the incuse, mirror-image design in the face of the die.

The process usually has to be repeated because the die metal will harden from the

A galvano of the 1976 half dollar goes on the reducing lathe.

pressure. The die is removed, softened, and returned to the hubbing press for a second impression from the hub. As you can imagine, it takes several hundred tons per square inch to force the hub into the die. Logically, this process is called "hubbing" a die.

The advantage of hubbing a die is that thousands of working dies can be made from a single hub, each one for all practical purposes as identical as the proverbial peas in a pod. This enables, for example, U.S. mints to strike billions of one-cent coins each year, each with the identical design.

Die making has come a long way from the early days. Philadelphia used to make all dies and then shipped them to the branch mints. Now Denver has its own die shop and creates dies of its own.

Striking the coin

Yesterday's die might strike only a few hundred coins. Today it is not unusual for a die to strike well over a million coins.

The coin press used to strike modern coins is a complicated piece of equipment that consists basically of a feed system to place the planchets in position for the stroke of the hammer die to form a coin. This process takes only a fraction of a second, so the press has to operate precisely to spew out the hundreds of coins that are struck every minute.

The end of the early hammered coinage came with the introduction of the collar, which often is called the "third" die. The collar is nothing more than a steel plate with a hole in it. This hole is the exact diameter of the intended coin and often is lined with carbide to prolong its life. It surrounds the lower, or fixed, die. Its sole purpose is to contain the coin metal to keep it from spreading too far sideways under the force of the strike.

If the intended coin has serrations, or "reeds," on the edge, then the collar has the matching design. The strike forces the coin metal against the serrations in the collar, forming the reeded edge at the same time that the two dies form the front and back, or obverse and reverse, of the coin.

Lettered-edge coins are produced usually by running the planchets through an edge-lettering die, or by using a segmented collar that is forced against the edge of the planchet during the strike by hydraulic pressure.

Several hundred tons were required to drive a hub into a die. Not as much but still significant amounts of force are needed to strike coins. A cent requires about 30 tons per square inch. A silver dollar took 150 tons. Other denominations fall between.

Modern coin presses apply pressure in a variety of ways. A ram, carrying the moving or "hammer" die, is forced against the planchet. Most commonly this is with the mechanical advantage of a "knuckle" or connected pieces to which pressure is applied from the side.

A binful of blanks are ready for the coin press.

When the joint straightens – like straightening your finger – the ram at the end of the piece is driven into the planchet. Once the strike is complete, at the final impact of the die pair, the coin has been produced. It is officially a coin now, and it's complete and ready to be spent.

Making proof coins

Proof coins started out as special presentation pieces. They were and still are struck on specially prepared planchets with specially prepared dies. Today the definition of a proof coin also requires that it be struck two or more times.

Currently all proof versions of circulating U.S. coins are struck at the San Francisco Mint, but some of the proof commemorative coins have been struck at the other mints. West Point currently strikes proof American Eagles of silver, gold, and platinum, and they carry a "W" mintmark.

After the proof blanks are punched from the strip, they go through the annealing oven, but on a conveyor belt rather than being tumbled in the revolving drum. After cleaning and upsetting they go into a huge vibrating machine where they are mixed with steel pellets that look like tiny footballs. The movement of the steel pellets against the planchets burnishes, or smooths, the surface so any scratches and gouges the planchets pick up during processing are smoothed over.

Proof dies get an extra polishing before the hubbing process. They are made at Philadelphia and shipped to the branch mints. When the proof dies arrive at San Francisco, they are worked on by a team of specialists who use diamond dust and other polishing agents to turn the fields of the proof dies into mirrorlike surfaces. The incuse design is sandblasted to make the surface rough, producing what is known as a "frosted" design. Because collectors like the frosted proofs, the design is periodically swabbed with acid to keep the surface rough and increase the number of frosted proofs from each die. This process has been around about a quarter century, so frosted examples of earlier proofs are considerably scarcer.

The presses that strike proof coins usually are hand-operated rather than automatic. Some of the newer presses use equipment such as vacuum suction devices to pick up the planchets, place them in the coining chamber, and then remove the struck coins. This avoids handling the pieces any more than necessary.

On a hand-operated press, the operator takes a freshly washed and dried planchet and, using tongs, places it in the collar. The ram with the die descends two or more times before the finished coin is removed from the collar and carefully stored in a box for transport to storage or the packaging line. After each strike the operator wipes the dies to make sure that lint or other particles don't stick to the dies and damage the coins as they are struck.

Proof dies are used for only a short time. Maximum die life is usually less than 10,000 coins, varying with the size of the coin and the alloy being struck.

CIRCULATION COINAGE

HALF CENT

Liberty Cap Half Cent
Head facing left.
KM# 10 • 6.74 g., Copper, 22 mm. •
Designer: Henry Voigt

Date	Mintage	G4	VG8	F12	VF20	XF40	MS60
1793	35,334	3,400	6,000	10,500	13,500	17,000	55,000

Head facing right.
KM# 14 • Copper, 6.74 g. (1794-95) and 5.44 g.
(1795-97), 23.5 mm. • **Designer:** Robert Scot
(1794) and John Smith Gardner (1795) **Note:** The
"lettered edge" varieties have TWO HUNDRED FOR
A DOLLAR inscribed around the edge. The "pole"
varieties have a pole upon which the cap is hanging,
resting on Liberty's shoulder. The "punctuated date"
varieties have a comma after the 1 in the date. The
1797 "1 above 1" variety has a second 1 above the
1 in the date.

Date	Mintage	G4	VG8	F12	VF20	XF40	MS60
1794 Normal Relief Head	81,600	600	910	1,000	1,500	4,625	34,000
1794 High Relief Head	Inc. above	600	910	1,000	1,500	4,625	34,000
1795 lettered edge, pole	25,600	560	750	1,350	1,700	3,600	18,000
1795 plain edge, no pole	109,000	600	850	1,075	1,700	4,000	14,000
1795 lettered edge, punctuated date	Inc. above	560	770	1,185	1,825	5,500	17,250
1795 plain edge, punctuated date	Inc. above	525	770	1,125	1,700	4,750	17,000
1796 pole	5,090	17,000	20,000	28,500	45,000	65,000	150,000
1796 no pole	1,390	25,000	34,000	90,000	120,000	165,000	300,000
1797 plain edge	119,215	500	675	1,250	1,725	3,100	15,000
1797 lettered edge	Inc. above	1,100	1,900	3,650	13,500	43,000	50,000
1797 1 above 1	Inc. above	575	1,095	1,528	1,975	4,100	14,500
1797 gripped edge	Inc. above	15,500	38,500	48,000	60,000	72,000	—

Draped Bust Half Cent
Draped bust right, date at angle
below. Value within thin wreath.
KM# 33 • 5.44 g., Copper, 23.5 mm. •
Obv. Legend: LIBERTY **Rev. Legend:** UNITED
STATES OF AMERICA **Designer:** Robert Scot **Note:**
The wreath on the reverse was redesigned slightly
in 1802, resulting in "reverse of 1800" and "reverse
of 1802" varieties. The "stems" varieties have stems
extending from the wreath above and on both
sides of the fraction on the reverse. On the 1804
"crosslet 4" variety, a serif appears at the far right
of the crossbar on the 4 in the date. The "spiked
chin" variety appears to have a spike extending from
Liberty's chin, the result of a damaged die. Varieties
of the 1805 strikes are distinguished by the size of
the 5 in the date. Varieties of the 1806 strikes are
distinguished by the size of the 6 in the date.

Stemless   Stems

Date	Mintage	G4	VG8	F12	VF20	XF40	MS60
1800	211,530	80.00	115	200	300	475	1,800
1802/0 rev. 1800	14,366	24,000	18,000	32,000	40,500	70,000	—
1802/0 rev. 1802	Inc. above	650	1,650	5,000	6,950	18,500	—
1803	97,900	50.00	100	165	360	775	2,800
1804 plain 4, stemless wreath	1,055,312	95.00	120	155	200	600	1,400
1804 plain 4, stems	Inc. above	70.00	100	155	285	880	3,400
1804 crosslet 4, stemless	Inc. above	70.00	100	155	200	600	1,400
1804 crosslet 4, stems	Inc. above	70.00	100	155	200	600	1,400
1804 spiked chin	Inc. above	70.00	100	155	200	400	2,300
1805 small 5, stemless	814,464	70.00	100	155	200	600	1,400
1805 small 5, stems	Inc. above	700	1,300	3,000	6,000	11,000	—
1805 large 5, stems	Inc. above	70.00	100	155	200	550	1,400

Date	Mintage	G4	VG8	F12	VF20	XF40	MS60
1806 small 6, stems	356,000	155	300	500	900	2,500	9,000
1806 small 6, stemless	Inc. above	70.00	100	155	200	550	1,400
1806 large 6, stems	Inc. above	70.00	100	155	200	600	1,400
1807	476,000	70.00	100	155	200	600	2,400
1808/7	400,000	135	215	500	1,150	2,900	85,000
1808	Inc. above	70.00	100	155	235	550	2,400

Classic Head Half Cent
Classic head left, flanked by stars, date below. Value within wreath.
KM# 41 • 5.44 g., Copper, 23.5 mm. •
Rev. Legend: UNITED STATES OF AMERICA
Designer: John Reich **Note:** Restrikes listed were produced privately in the mid-1800s. The 1831 restrikes have two varieties with different sized berries in the wreath on the reverse. The 1828 strikes have either 12 or 13 stars on the obverse.

Date	Mintage	G4	VG8	F12	VF20	XF40	MS60
1809/6	1,154,572	65.00	80.00	125	150	300	800
1809	Inc. above	65.00	80.00	92.00	94.00	155	550
1809 circle in 0	Inc. above	65.00	80.00	135	350	460	4,000
1810	215,000	65.00	80.00	135	180	600	2,000
1811 Close Date	63,140	250	500	1,390	1,600	4,000	30,000
1811 Wide Date Inc. Above	—	250	500	1,495	1,600	4,000	30,000
1811 restrike, reverse of 1802, uncirculated	—	250	500	1,200	—	—	—
1825	63,000	55.00	90.00	100	110	210	700
1826	234,000	55.00	90.00	100	110	120	420
1828 13 stars	606,000	55.00	90.00	100	110	115	260
1828 12 stars	Inc. above	55.00	90.00	100	150	275	800
1829	487,000	55.00	90.00	100	110	205	350
1831 original	2,200	—	—	—	—	50,000	—
1831 1st restrike, lg. berries, reverse of 1836	—	—	—	—	—	—	—
1831 2nd restrike, sm. berries, reverse of 1840, proof	—	—	—	—	—	—	—
1832	154,000	55.00	90.00	100	110	115	300
1833	120,000	55.00	90.00	100	110	115	265
1834	141,000	55.00	90.00	100	110	115	265
1835	398,000	55.00	90.00	100	110	115	265
1836 original, proof	—	—	—	—	—	—	—
1836 restrike, reverse of 1840, proof	—	—	—	—	—	—	—

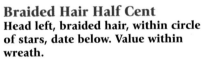

Braided Hair Half Cent
Head left, braided hair, within circle of stars, date below. Value within wreath.
KM# 70 • 5.44 g., Copper, 23 mm. • **Rev. Legend:** UNITED STATES OF AMERICA **Designer:** Christian Gobrecht **Note:** 1840-1849 and 1852 strikes, both originals and restrikes, are known in proof only; mintages are unknown. The small-date varieties of 1849, both originals and restrikes are known in proof only. The restrikes were produced clandestinely by Philadelphia Mint personnel in the mid-1800s.

Date	Mintage	G4	VG8	F12	VF20	XF40	MS60	PF60Brn
1840 original	—	—	—	—	—	—	—	3,250
1840 1st restrike	—	—	—	—	—	—	—	3,250
1840 2nd restrike	—	—	—	—	—	—	—	5,500
1841 original	—	—	—	—	—	—	—	3,250
1841 1st restrike	—	—	—	—	—	—	—	3,250
1841 2nd restrike	—	—	—	—	—	—	—	6,000
1842 original	—	—	—	—	—	—	—	3,250
1842 1st restrike	—	—	—	—	—	—	—	3,250
1842 2nd restrike	—	—	—	—	—	—	—	6,000
1843 original	—	—	—	—	—	—	—	3,250
1843 1st restrike	—	—	—	—	—	—	—	3,250
1843 2nd restrike	—	—	—	—	—	—	—	6,500
1844 original	—	—	—	—	—	—	—	3,250
1844 1st restrike	—	—	—	—	—	—	—	3,250
1844 2nd restrike	—	—	—	—	—	—	—	6,000
1845 original	—	—	—	—	—	—	—	6,000
1845 1st restrike	—	—	—	—	—	—	—	3,250
1845 2nd restrike	—	—	—	—	—	—	—	6,000

Date	Mintage	G4	VG8	F12	VF20	XF40	MS60	PF60Brn
1846 original	—	—	—	—	—	—	—	3,250
1846 1st restrike	—	—	—	—	—	—	—	3,250
1846 2nd restrike	—	—	—	—	—	—	—	6,000
1847 original	—	—	—	—	—	—	—	3,250
1847 1st restrike	—	—	—	—	—	—	—	3,250
1847 2nd restrike	—	—	—	—	—	—	—	6,000
1848 original	—	—	—	—	—	—	—	6,000
1848 1st restrike	—	—	—	—	—	—	—	3,250
1848 2nd restrike	—	—	—	—	—	—	—	6,000
1849 original, small date	—	—	—	—	—	—	—	3,250
1849 1st restrike small date	—	—	—	—	—	2,500	3,100	3,250
1849 large date	39,864	56.00	75.00	83.00	110	150	325	—
1850	39,812	115	160	195	210	270	500	—
1851	147,672	56.00	75.00	83.00	85.00	90.00	175	—
1852 original	—	12,000	45,000	20,000	25,000	30,000	—	90,000
1852 1st restrike	—	—	—	—	—	—	900	5,000
1852 2nd restrike	—	—	—	—	—	—	900	7,000
1853	129,694	56.00	75.00	83.00	85.00	90.00	175	—
1854	55,358	56.00	75.00	83.00	85.00	90.00	175	—
1855	56,500	56.00	75.00	83.00	85.00	90.00	175	3,250
1856	40,430	56.00	75.00	83.00	85.00	90.00	180	3,250
1857	35,180	56.00	75.00	83.00	85.00	100	300	3,250

CENT

Flowing Hair Cent
Chain.
KM# 11 • 13.48 g., Copper, 26-27 mm. •
Designer: Henry Voigt

Date	Mintage	G4	VG8	F12	VF20	XF40	MS60
1793 AMERI	36,103	9,575	14,000	22,000	38,000	75,000	170,000
1793 AMERICA	Inc. above	5,600	9,950	16,000	29,000	66,000	150,000
1793 periods after "LIBERTY	Inc. above	6,550	10,000	18,500	28,000	66,000	145,000

Wreath.
KM# 12 • 13.48 g., Copper, 26-28 mm. •
Designer: Henry Voigt

Date	Mintage	G4	VG8	F12	VF20	XF40	MS60
1793 vine and bars edge	63,353	3,000	4,000	6,600	9,000	18,000	50,000
1793 lettered edge	Inc. above	3,000	4,750	7,200	12,000	22,000	78,000
1793 strawberry leaf; 4 known	—	135,000	220,000	600,000	—	—	—

Liberty Cap Cent
KM# 13 • Copper, 13.48 g., 29 mm. •
Designer: Joseph Wright **Note:** The heavier pieces
were struck on a thicker planchet. The Liberty design
on the obverse was revised slightly in 1794, but the
1793 design was used on some 1794 strikes. A 1795
"lettered edge" variety has ONE HUNDRED FOR A
DOLLAR and a leaf inscribed on the edge.

Date	Mintage	G4	VG8	F12	VF20	XF40	MS60
1793 cap	11,056	6,000	9,500	13,000	35,000	60,000	265,000
1794 NO FRACTION BAR	Inc. above	500	800	1,350	2,750	8,000	33,000
1794 head '93	918,521	1,075	1,560	2,100	5,000	12,000	115,000
1794 head '94	Inc. above	400	600	800	1,950	3,750	14,750
1794 head '95	Inc. above	400	600	800	1,950	3,750	10,000
1794 starred rev.	Inc. above	23,000	35,000	65,000	220,000	360,000	—
1795 Lettered Edge	Inc. above	325	475	1,250	1,950	3,200	11,000
1795 plain edge	501,500	325	475	1,250	1,950	3,250	7,000
1795 reeded edge	Inc. above	160,000	540,000	1,000,000	—	—	—

Date	Mintage	G4	VG8	F12	VF20	XF40	MS60
1795 Jefferson head plain edge	Inc. above	16,000	19,000	30,000	45,000	120,000	—
1795 Jefferson head lettered edge	Inc. above	70,000	75,000	140,000	220,000	—	—

KM# 13a • 10.89 g., Copper, 29 mm. •
Designer: John Smith Gardner

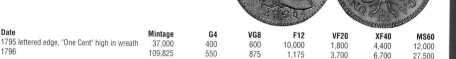

Date	Mintage	G4	VG8	F12	VF20	XF40	MS60
1795 lettered edge, "One Cent" high in wreath	37,000	400	600	10,000	1,800	4,400	12,000
1796	109,825	550	875	1,175	3,700	6,700	27,500

Draped Bust Cent
Draped bust right, date at angle below. Value within wreath.

KM# 22 • 10.98 g., Copper, 29 mm. •
Obv. Legend: LIBERTY **Rev. Legend:** UNITED
STATES OF AMERICA **Designer:** Robert Scot
Note: The 1801 "3 errors" variety has the fraction
on the reverse reading "1/000," has only one stem
extending from the wreath above and on both
sides of the fraction on the reverse, and UNITED in
UNITED STATES OF AMERICA appears as "Iinited".

Stemless   Stems

Date	Mintage	G4	VG8	F12	VF20	XF40	MS60
1796 reverse of 1794	363,375	500	700	1,600	2,650	7,500	35,000
1796 reverse of 1795	Inc. above	475	650	1,200	4,500	9,500	23,000
1796 reverse of 1797	Inc. above	350	500	925	1,875	4,500	9,500
1796 Liberty error	Inc. above	1,150	1,550	2,200	4,700	12,000	—
1797 reverse of 1795 plain edge	897,510	225	1,500	2,100	2,800	4,500	27,000
1797 reverse of 1795 gripped edge	Inc. above	425	1,500	2,100	2,750	5,800	27,000
1797 stems	Inc. above	225	350	650	1,325	2,200	4,100
1797 stemless	Inc. above	225	1,300	1,750	2,600	6,000	27,750
1797 reverse of 1795	—	—	—	—	—	—	8,500
1798 reverse of 1795	—	—	—	—	—	—	6,000
1798 reverse of 1796	Inc. above	2,500	5,000	8,000	12,000	17,500	23,000
1798 1st hair style	Inc. above	250	375	550	900	1,700	12,500
1798 2nd hair style	Inc. above	235	300	450	600	2,100	9,000
1798/7	1,841,745	475	700	1,000	1,050	1,400	13,000
1799	42,540	4,200	9,500	14,500	31,000	120,000	720,000
1799/98	Inc. above	8,800	12,000	22,000	43,000	165,000	—
1800	2,822,175	175	355	475	950	1,700	10,000
1800/798	Inc. above	175	355	500	900	3,000	—
1800/79	Inc. above	175	355	500	825	2,000	18,000
1801	1,362,837	175	355	500	825	1,750	12,750
1801 3 errors	Inc. above	300	650	1,200	2,750	6,000	—
1801 1/000	Inc. above	200	355	525	875	4,000	14,250
1801 100/000	Inc. above	200	355	525	900	5,525	38,000
1802	3,435,100	75.00	120	225	460	1,125	6,000
1802 stemless	Inc. above	125	200	225	550	1,350	4,200
1802 1/000	Inc. above	200	275	475	650	1,700	6,800
1803 small date, small fraction	2,471,353	150	240	350	525	1,100	5,600
1803 small date, large fraction	Inc. above	150	240	350	525	1,100	4,400
1803 large date, small fraction	Inc. above	9,000	14,000	22,500	38,000	120,000	—
1803 large date, large fraction	Inc. above	350	500	875	1,950	3,600	40,000
1803 1/100 over 1/1000	—	200	355	500	925	1,750	17,000
1803 Stemless wreath	—	200	355	425	775	1,600	12,000
1804	96,500	2,300	3,500	4,500	8,350	13,000	225,000
1804 Restrike of 1860	—	—	—	475	500	550	900
1805	941,116	150	200	300	500	1,100	4,200
1806	348,000	150	250	400	625	1,725	6,800
1807 small fraction	727,221	170	250	380	1,200	9,000	55,000
1807 large fraction	Inc. above	150	200	350	700	1,325	12,000
1807/6 large 7/6	Inc. above	200	350	500	725	1,050	12,000
1807/6 small 7/6	Inc. above	2,400	5,000	8,500	30,000	65,000	—
1807 Comet Variety	Inc. above	250	350	600	1,200	2,300	17,500

CENT

Classic Head Cent
Classic head left, flanked by stars, date below. Value within wreath.
KM# 39 • 10.89 g., Copper, 29 mm. •
Rev. Legend: UNITED STATES OF AMERICA
Designer: John Reich

Date	Mintage	G4	VG8	F12	VF20	XF40	MS60
1808	1,109,000	175	250	525	975	2,000	9,750
1809	222,867	300	600	875	1,325	3,300	12,500
1810/09	1,458,500	175	250	525	990	1,950	10,000
1810	Inc. above	175	250	525	925	1,600	10,500
1811/10	218,025	350	500	775	1,625	6,000	22,000
1811	Inc. above	250	400	600	1,150	2,400	10,000
1812 small date	1,075,500	175	250	525	845	1,890	8,500
1812 large date	—	175	250	525	845	1,690	8,500
1813	418,000	175	250	525	845	1,690	8,500
1814 Plain 4	357,830	175	250	525	845	1,690	8,500
1814 Crosslet 4	Inc. above	175	250	525	845	1,690	8,500

Coronet Cent
Coronet head left, within circle of stars, date below. Value within wreath.
KM# 45 • 10.89 g., Copper, 28-29 mm. •
Rev. Legend: UNITED STATES OF AMERICA
Designer: Robert Scot

Date	Mintage	G4	VG8	F12	VF20	XF40	MS60
1816	2,820,982	38.00	42.00	100	150	280	600
1817 13 obverse stars	3,948,400	30.00	35.00	100	125	200	690
1817 15 obverse stars	Inc. above	40.00	50.00	150	225	660	2,600
1818	3,167,000	28.00	34.00	90.00	130	180	425
1819 Large date, 9/8	2,671,000	—	—	—	—	—	—
1819	—	30.00	32.00	90.00	130	300	825
1819/8	—	30.00	32.00	90.00	130	300	825
1819 Large date	Inc. above	26.00	33.00	90.00	130	185	650
1819 Small date	Inc. above	30.00	36.00	90.00	130	205	550
1820 Large date, 20/19	4,407,550	35.00	41.00	90.00	130	425	1,325
1820 Large date	—	31.00	38.00	90.00	130	180	375
1820 Small date	—	30.00	38.00	90.00	130	225	600
1821	389,000	44.00	65.00	190	385	1,225	8,500
1822	2,072,339	32.00	39.00	49.50	110	185	1,100
1823 Included in 1824 mintage	—	175	275	550	875	2,600	21,000
1823/22 Included in 1824 mintage	—	175	300	485	900	2,200	19,000
1823 Restrike	—	500	600	650	750	800	1,700
1824	1,262,000	70.00	150	200	310	575	2,700
1824/22	Inc. above	150	175	225	450	875	6,000
1825	1,461,100	37.50	39.50	65.00	110	340	1,950
1826	1,517,425	60.00	80.00	105	175	275	800
1826/25	Inc. above	175	200	300	450	1,000	9,000
1827	2,357,732	21.00	25.00	36.00	80.00	150	925
1828 Large date	2,260,624	30.00	50.00	65.00	80.00	130	1,150
1828 Small date	—	27.00	36.00	50.00	110	250	2,600
1829 Large letters	1,414,500	45.00	55.00	85.00	175	350	1,100
1829 Medium letters	Inc. above	65.00	85.00	130	175	500	5,000
1830 Large letters	1,711,500	20.00	25.00	30.00	60.00	120	875
1830 Medium letters	Inc. above	50.00	100	250	650	1,600	7,500
1831 Large letters	3,359,260	25.00	45.00	60.00	80.00	135	550
1831 Medium letters	—	50.00	100	250	650	235	650
1832 Large letters	2,362,000	25.00	45.00	60.00	80.00	135	640
1832 Medium letters	—	50.00	80.00	95.00	200	225	750
1833	2,739,000	25.00	45.00	60.00	80.00	135	500
1834 Large 8, stars and letters	1,855,100	40.00	50.00	80.00	120	180	950
1834 Large 8 & stars, medium letters	Inc. above	600	875	1,350	2,000	4,500	8,800
1834 Large 8, small stars, medium letters	Inc. above	25.00	50.00	80.00	150	225	950
1834 Small 8 & stars	Inc. above	25.00	50.00	80.00	150	225	950
1835 Large 8 & stars	3,878,400	25.00	65.00	150	175	400	1,200
1835 Head '36	—	25.00	65.00	125	150	325	900

Date	Mintage	G4	VG8	F12	VF20	XF40	MS60
1835 Small 8 & stars	—	25.00	65.00	125	150	325	900
1836	2,111,000	25.00	45.00	60.00	80.00	135	600
1837 Plain hair cords, medium letters	5,558,300	25.00	45.00	60.00	80.00	135	290
1837 Plain hair cords, small letters	Inc. above	25.00	45.00	60.00	80.00	135	290
1837 Head '38	Inc. above	25.00	45.00	60.00	80.00	135	290
1838	6,370,200	25.00	45.00	60.00	80.00	135	290
1839 Head '38, beaded hair cords	3,128,661	45.00	65.00	80.00	120	185	500
1839/36 Plain hair cords	Inc. above	450	880	1,250	2,150	5,500	—
1839 Silly head	Inc. above	25.00	45.00	60.00	80.00	135	675
1839 Booby head	Inc. above	25.00	45.00	60.00	80.00	135	700

Braided Hair Cent
Head left, braided hair, within circle of stars, date below. Value within wreath.
KM# 67 • 10.89 g., Copper, 27.5 mm. • **Rev. Legend:** UNITED STATES OF AMERICA **Designer:** Christian Gobrecht **Note:** 1840 and 1842 strikes are known with both small and large dates, with little difference in value. A slightly larger Liberty head and larger reverse lettering were used beginning in 1843.

Date	Mintage	G4	VG8	F12	VF20	XF40	MS60
1839 Petite Head	3,128,661	25.00	45.00	60.00	80.00	135	900
1840 Large date	2,462,700	25.00	45.00	60.00	80.00	135	575
1840 Small date	Inc. above	25.00	45.00	60.00	80.00	135	575
1840 Small date over large 18	Inc. above	30.00	40.00	60.00	100	150	1,000
1841	1,597,367	25.00	65.00	95.00	160	200	800
1842 Small date	2,383,390	28.00	31.00	37.00	55.00	95.00	600
1842 Large date	Inc. above	28.00	31.00	37.00	55.00	95.00	600
1843 Petite Head, small date	2,425,342	29.00	31.00	42.00	55.00	95.00	600
1843 Petite Head, (rev '44)	Inc. above	29.00	31.00	42.00	55.00	95.00	600
1843 Mature Head	—	29.00	31.00	42.00	55.00	95.00	725
1844	2,398,752	29.00	31.00	42.00	55.00	95.00	600
1844/81	Inc. above	125	200	250	300	500	1,650
1845	3,894,804	18.00	30.00	50.00	68.00	75.00	190
1846 Small date	4,120,800	18.00	30.00	50.00	68.00	75.00	190
1846 MD	Inc. above	18.00	30.00	50.00	68.00	75.00	190
1846 TD	Inc. above	36.00	75.00	100	150	260	1,650
1847	6,183,669	18.00	40.00	45.00	68.00	100	300
1847/7	Inc. above	100	150	200	225	375	1,400
1848	6,415,799	18.00	30.00	50.00	68.00	75.00	190
1849	4,178,500	18.00	30.00	25.00	68.00	75.00	190
1850	4,426,844	18.00	30.00	50.00	68.00	75.00	190
1851	9,889,707	18.00	30.00	50.00	68.00	75.00	190
1851/81	Inc. above	85.00	105	150	175	225	600
1852	5,063,094	18.00	30.00	50.00	68.00	75.00	190
1853	6,641,131	18.00	30.00	50.00	68.00	75.00	190
1854	4,236,156	18.00	30.00	50.00	68.00	75.00	190
1855 Slanted 5's	1,574,829	18.00	30.00	50.00	68.00	75.00	190
1855 Upright 5's	Inc. above	18.00	30.00	50.00	68.00	75.00	190
1855 Slanted 5's Knob on Ear	Inc. above	65.00	75.00	105	150	195	400
1856 Slanted 5	2,690,463	18.00	30.00	50.00	68.00	75.00	190
1856 Upright 5	Inc. above	18.00	32.00	40.00	48.00	65.00	190
1857 Large date	333,456	100	180	210	260	285	450
1857 Small date	Inc. above	100	160	200	275	350	525

Flying Eagle Cent
Flying eagle above date. Value within wreath.
KM# 85 • 4.67 g., Copper-Nickel, 19 mm. •
Obv. Legend: UNITED STATES OF AMERICA **Designer:** James B. Longacre **Note:** On the large-letter variety of 1858, the "A" and "M" in AMERICA are connected at their bases; on the small-letter variety, the two letters are separated.

Large letters – AM touch at bottom

Small letters – Space between AM

Date	Mintage	G4	VG8	F12	VF20	XF40	AU50	MS60	MS65	Prf65
1856	Est. 2500	6,100	6,550	8,800	10,500	12,000	14,000	15,000	62,500	27,000
1857	17,450,000	21.00	32.00	36.00	65.00	160	240	450	4,000	25,500
1858/7	Inc. below	55.00	75.00	150	325	650	1,100	2,900	70,000	—

Date	Mintage	G4	VG8	F12	VF20	XF40	AU50	MS60	MS65	Prf65
1858 large letters	24,600,000	21.00	32.00	36.00	45.00	140	180	450	3,250	17,500
1858 small letters	Inc. above	21.00	32.00	36.00	45.00	140	180	475	3,300	26,000

Indian Head Cent
Indian head with headdress left above date. Value within wreath.

KM# 87 • 4.67 g., Copper-Nickel, 19 mm. •
Obv. Legend: UNITED STATES OF AMERICA
Designer: James B. Longacre

Date	Mintage	G4	VG8	F12	VF20	XF40	AU50	MS60	MS65	Prf65
1859	36,400,000	12.00	15.00	20.00	40.00	130	215	340	2,390	4,175

Indian head with headdress left above date. Value within wreath, shield above.

KM# 90 • 4.67 g., Copper-Nickel, 19 mm. •
Obv. Legend: UNITED STATES OF AMERICA
Designer: James B. Longacre

Date	Mintage	G4	VG8	F12	VF20	XF40	AU50	MS60	MS65	Prf65
1860 Rounded Bust	20,566,000	10.00	15.00	22.00	40.00	60.00	90.00	220	1,500	2,200
1860	1,000	—	—	—	—	—	—	—	—	—
1860 Pointed Bust	Inc. above	15.00	20.00	30.00	50.00	75.00	190	285	3,200	—
1861	10,100,000	23.00	26.00	40.00	55.00	120	135	185	1,200	1,900
1862	28,075,000	9.00	10.00	11.00	22.00	45.00	60.00	125	900	2,600
1863	49,840,000	8.00	9.00	10.00	22.00	45.00	60.00	100	850	1,900
1864	13,740,000	20.00	23.00	60.00	65.00	155	195	260	1,200	2,665

Indian head with headdress left above date. Value within wreath, shield above.

KM# 90a • 3.11 g., Bronze, 19 mm. •
Obv. Legend: UNITED STATES OF AMERICA
Designer: James B. Longacre **Note:** The 1864 "L" variety has the designer's initial in Liberty's hair to the right of her neck.

1864 "L"

Date	Mintage	G4	VG8	F12	VF20	XF40	AU50	MS60	MS65	Prf65
1864	39,233,714	12.00	17.00	25.00	44.00	60.00	70.00	100	700	1,100
1864 L pointed bust	Inc. above	45.00	65.00	150	215	270	350	450	1,750	60,000
1865 plain 5	35,429,286	11.00	12.00	17.00	23.00	50.00	60.00	75.00	775	400
1865 fancy 5	Inc. above	11.00	12.00	17.00	21.00	33.00	50.00	75.00	775	—
1866	9,826,500	45.00	52.00	125	175	225	260	310	1,250	1,350
1867	9,821,000	40.00	55.00	110	135	225	250	240	1,325	425
1867/1867	Inc. above	90.00	114	200	300	750	830	1,350	—	—
1868	10,266,500	45.00	60.00	75.00	125	180	265	310	1,300	700
1869/9	6,420,000	125	245	435	600	875	950	1,000	2,300	—
1869	Inc. above	110	175	275	325	550	600	700	2,450	725
1870 Bold N	5,275,000	55.00	125	275	350	525	640	720	1,600	725
1870 Shallow N*	Inc. above	70.00	130	230	475	525	560	—	—	—
1871 Bold N	3,929,500	130	185	300	320	525	575	685	2,200	1,450
1871 Shallow N*	Included above	115	125	235	500	600	650	—	—	—
1872 Bold N	4,042,000	115	165	290	415	575	720	875	3,000	1,100
1872 Shallow N*	Included above	120	190	340	400	460	550	—	—	—
1873 closed 3	11,676,500	20.00	40.00	60.00	85.00	160	210	300	1,500	1,000
1873 open 3	Inc. above	20.00	60.00	80.00	100	210	275	290	1,325	—
1873 Double Liberty die 1	Inc. above	300	675	800	1,175	2,300	3,650	6,600	36,000	—
1873 Double Liberty die 2	Inc. above	—	75.00	250	400	500	900	4,200	—	—
1874	14,187,500	18.00	30.00	50.00	59.00	115	145	200	995	480
1875	13,528,000	35.00	55.00	75.00	90.00	165	282	350	780	1,450
1876	7,944,000	25.00	35.00	60.00	100	250	300	360	1,200	480
1877	852,500	550	800	1,000	1,250	1,720	2,950	3,300	13,000	5,900
1878	5,799,850	23.00	30.00	60.00	125	275	325	950	1,500	585
1879	16,231,200	6.00	8.00	14.00	28.00	100	120	180	585	585
1880	38,964,955	3.00	4.00	5.00	9.00	25.00	40.00	65.00	575	585
1881	39,211,575	3.00	4.00	5.00	7.00	20.00	25.00	50.00	500	585
1882	38,581,100	3.00	3.25	4.00	8.00	20.00	33.00	55.00	570	585
1883	45,589,109	2.75	3.00	3.50	6.00	19.00	25.00	55.00	570	500

Date	Mintage	G4	VG8	F12	VF20	XF40	AU50	MS60	MS65	Prf65
1884	23,261,742	3.50	4.00	10.00	15.00	60.00	85.00	120	425	1,000
1885	11,765,384	7.00	8.00	10.00	25.00	90.00	140	185	725	1,170
1886 Type 1 obverse	17,654,290	4.00	6.00	15.00	45.00	145	155	190	1,150	800
1886 Type 2 obverse	Inc. above	6.00	8.00	22.00	75.00	180	210	240	2,050	7,500
1887	45,226,483	1.50	1.60	2.50	4.00	13.00	21.00	45.00	600	800
1888	37,494,414	2.50	3.00	4.00	6.00	17.00	20.00	75.00	750	585
1888/7	Included above	1,525	8,700	4,100	6,200	9,300	10,575	—	—	—
1889	48,869,361	1.70	2.10	2.25	5.00	9.00	21.00	33.00	625	845
1890	57,182,854	1.50	1.75	2.00	4.00	8.00	20.00	40.00	850	585
1891	47,072,350	1.75	2.25	2.50	4.00	10.00	18.00	40.00	800	585
1892	37,649,832	1.50	2.75	3.50	4.00	16.00	55.00	80.00	560	660
1893	46,642,195	1.50	2.25	2.50	4.00	8.00	18.00	38.00	900	585
1894	16,752,132	4.50	5.00	11.00	16.00	38.00	48.00	65.00	590	650
1894/94	Inc. above	45.00	55.00	85.00	170	400	900	1,150	4,500	585
1895	38,343,636	1.75	2.00	2.50	3.00	9.00	18.00	38.00	170	585
1896	39,057,293	1.75	2.00	2.50	3.00	10.00	21.00	40.00	295	585
1897	50,466,330	1.35	1.75	1.85	3.00	8.00	19.00	38.00	375	750
1898	49,823,079	1.35	1.80	2.00	3.00	8.00	19.00	38.00	300	585
1899	53,600,031	1.35	1.80	2.00	3.00	8.00	19.00	38.00	485	800
1900	66,833,764	1.35	1.80	2.00	3.00	8.00	19.00	38.00	550	585
1901	79,611,143	1.35	1.80	2.00	3.00	8.00	19.00	38.00	250	690
1902	87,376,722	1.35	1.80	2.00	3.00	8.00	19.00	38.00	250	550
1903	85,094,493	1.35	1.80	2.00	3.00	8.00	19.00	38.00	250	585
1904	61,328,015	1.35	1.80	2.00	3.00	8.00	19.00	38.00	450	585
1905	80,719,163	1.35	1.80	2.00	3.00	8.00	19.00	38.00	500	585
1906	96,022,255	1.35	1.80	2.00	3.00	8.00	19.00	38.00	250	585
1907	108,138,618	1.35	1.80	2.00	3.00	8.00	19.00	38.00	250	585
1908	32,327,987	1.35	1.80	2.00	3.00	8.00	19.00	38.00	250	585
1908S	1,115,000	90.00	100	115	140	180	250	280	1,250	—
1909	14,370,645	10.00	12.00	13.00	14.00	18.00	26.00	43.00	550	585
1909S	309,000	290	460	550	640	790	850	1,360	3,500	—

Lincoln Cent
Wheat Ears.

KM# 132 • 3.11 g., Bronze, 19 mm. •
Designer: Victor D. Brenner **Note:** The 1909 "VDB"
varieties have the designer's initials inscribed at the
6 o'clock position on the reverse. The initials were
removed until 1918, when they were restored on
the obverse • MS60 and MS63 prices are for brown
coins and MS65 prices are for coins that are at least
90% original red.

1922 Plain

Date	Mintage	G4	VG8	F12	VF20	XF40	AU50	MS60	MS65	Prf65
1909 VDB	27,995,000	9.00	10.00	11.00	12.00	14.00	15.00	20.00	105	27,000
1909 VDB Doubled Die Obverse	Inc. above	—	—	45.00	60.00	80.00	90.00	110	1,300	—
1909S VDB	484,000	580	625	720	750	865	910	1,400	4,150	—
1909	72,702,618	2.00	2.50	3.25	4.00	5.00	12.00	15.00	140	900
1909S	1,825,000	65.00	70.00	88.00	118	132	210	300	675	—
1909S/S S over horizontal S	Inc. above	100	115	125	170	230	260	300	1,150	—
1910	146,801,218	0.30	0.40	0.50	0.60	4.00	8.00	16.00	180	1,400
1910S	6,045,000	11.00	15.00	16.00	20.00	43.00	65.00	90.00	550	—
1911	101,177,787	0.35	0.45	1.25	1.75	6.00	9.00	16.00	360	1,075
1911D	12,672,000	5.00	6.00	8.00	22.00	46.00	97.00	115	850	—
1911S	4,026,000	32.00	40.00	45.00	50.00	100	120	160	1,050	—
1912	68,153,060	1.00	1.25	2.50	6.00	14.00	23.00	30.00	475	1,200
1912D	10,411,000	6.00	8.00	10.00	26.00	63.00	145	165	1,600	—
1912S	4,431,000	18.00	20.00	25.00	43.00	68.00	95.00	155	950	—
1913	76,532,352	0.65	0.75	1.25	3.00	16.00	25.00	30.00	180	1,075
1913D	15,804,000	3.00	3.50	4.50	10.50	38.00	95.00	120	1,225	—
1913S	6,101,000	9.00	13.00	17.00	25.00	50.00	125	170	1,300	—
1914	75,238,432	0.35	0.60	2.00	8.00	17.00	35.00	50.00	475	1,465
1914D	1,193,000	175	185	210	450	725	1,775	1,925	16,000	—
1914S	4,137,000	19.00	21.00	25.00	32.00	78.00	190	275	5,000	—
1915	29,092,120	1.50	3.00	4.50	16.00	52.00	65.00	75.00	450	1,800
1915D	22,050,000	1.35	2.50	3.50	7.00	22.00	4.00	65.00	1,000	—
1915S	4,833,000	15.00	18.00	23.00	29.00	60.00	122	175	4,600	—
1916	131,833,677	0.30	0.35	0.65	2.00	7.00	12.00	17.00	300	4,000
1916D	35,956,000	0.65	2.00	3.00	6.00	16.00	33.00	80.00	1,300	—
1916S	22,510,000	1.35	2.75	4.00	9.00	25.00	42.00	95.00	1,000	—
1917	196,429,785	0.25	0.30	0.35	1.50	4.00	12.00	14.00	325	—

Date	Mintage	G4	VG8	F12	VF20	XF40	AU50	MS60	MS65	Prf65
1917 Doubled Die Obverse	Inc. above	125	195	300	390	1,000	1,500	2,500	13,000	—
1917D	55,120,000	0.85	1.00	2.50	6.00	35.00	40.00	65.00	800	—
1917S	32,620,000	0.40	0.65	1.00	2.00	10.00	25.00	65.00	6,900	—
1918	288,104,634	0.25	0.30	0.35	0.55	4.00	8.00	11.00	315	—
1918D	47,830,000	0.75	1.25	2.50	5.00	18.00	31.00	70.00	1,000	—
1918S	34,680,000	0.25	0.75	1.00	3.25	10.00	30.00	60.00	10,000	—
1919	392,021,000	0.25	0.30	0.35	0.40	1.00	5.00	7.00	100	—
1919D	57,154,000	0.65	0.90	1.50	4.00	12.00	24.00	55.00	1,475	—
1919S	139,760,000	0.20	0.35	1.25	2.00	5.00	44.00	75.00	1,150	—
1920	310,165,000	0.15	0.20	0.45	1.00	2.50	7.00	13.00	150	—
1920D	49,280,000	1.00	1.25	2.50	7.00	16.00	32.00	65.00	1,450	—
1920S	46,220,000	0.45	0.50	1.25	2.25	11.00	31.00	95.00	1,550	—
1921	39,157,000	0.40	0.50	0.75	2.50	9.50	20.00	37.00	360	—
1921S	15,274,000	1.20	2.25	3.25	6.00	60.00	100	170	11,200	—
1922D	7,160,000	16.00	20.00	21.00	23.00	65.00	100	160	1,300	—
1922D Weak Rev	Inc. above	22.00	23.00	24.00	25.50	34.00	65.00	95.00	355	—
1922D Weak D	Inc. above	20.00	30.00	40.00	50.00	105	150	225	1,500	—
1922 No D Die 2 Strong Rev	Inc. above	425	475	625	650	1,275	2,600	8,000	130,000	—
1922 No D Die 3 Weak Rev	Inc. above	140	210	320	375	550	725	1,330	—	—
1923	74,723,000	0.30	0.40	0.50	1.00	5.00	10.00	12.00	160	—
1923S	8,700,000	4.75	6.00	7.25	10.50	60.00	90.00	185	16,000	—
1924	75,178,000	0.20	0.35	0.45	1.00	4.50	9.00	16.00	450	—
1924D	2,520,000	29.00	33.00	38.00	42.00	120	160	260	11,250	—
1924S	11,696,000	1.25	1.50	2.75	5.35	65.00	90.00	130	16,500	—
1925	139,949,000	0.25	0.35	0.45	0.70	3.00	6.50	8.00	125	—
1925D	22,580,000	0.75	1.50	2.60	5.00	14.00	26.00	55.00	800	—
1925S	26,380,000	0.50	1.00	1.50	2.75	10.00	25.00	75.00	16,100	—
1926	157,088,000	0.25	0.35	0.45	0.60	1.65	5.00	6.00	65.00	—
1926D	28,020,000	1.00	1.70	2.75	5.25	13.00	28.00	75.00	600	—
1926S	4,550,000	8.00	9.00	11.00	16.50	60.00	100	120	2,090	—
1927	144,440,000	0.20	0.25	0.35	0.60	1.60	5.25	7.50	135	—
1927D	27,170,000	1.00	1.50	1.75	3.00	7.50	25.00	50.00	575	—
1927S	14,276,000	1.40	1.85	2.25	5.25	13.00	36.00	55.00	2,275	—
1928	134,116,000	0.20	0.25	0.35	0.60	1.45	4.00	7.50	125	—
1928D	31,170,000	0.75	1.00	1.50	3.50	7.00	17.00	32.00	815	—
1928S Small S	17,266,000	0.75	1.40	2.25	3.50	8.00	27.00	60.00	2,500	—
1928S Large S	Inc. above	1.65	2.85	4.25	7.50	15.00	45.00	110	1,000	—
1929	185,262,000	0.20	0.25	0.35	0.55	2.75	4.50	5.50	115	—
1929D	41,730,000	0.30	0.70	1.00	2.25	6.00	12.00	21.00	485	—
1929S	50,148,000	0.35	0.75	1.50	2.80	7.00	13.00	17.00	200	—
1930	157,415,000	0.20	0.25	0.35	0.60	1.25	2.75	4.00	35.00	—
1930D	40,100,000	0.25	0.35	0.60	0.90	2.00	5.50	9.00	140	—
1930S	24,286,000	0.25	0.55	0.75	2.00	4.00	6.50	9.50	95.00	—
1931	19,396,000	0.65	0.75	1.10	2.00	4.00	9.50	17.00	120	—
1931D	4,480,000	4.25	5.00	6.00	7.00	12.50	33.50	45.00	900	—
1931S	866,000	59.00	65.00	70.00	75.00	82.00	85.00	145	690	—
1932	9,062,000	1.60	1.95	2.85	3.50	7.50	11.00	15.00	100	—
1932D	10,500,000	1.50	1.90	2.00	2.50	4.15	9.00	16.00	140	—
1933	14,360,000	1.50	1.80	2.65	2.85	6.50	10.00	14.00	77.00	—
1933D	6,200,000	3.50	4.25	5.25	6.50	12.00	17.00	21.00	150	—
1934	219,080,000	0.15	0.25	0.30	0.45	1.25	4.00	9.00	25.00	—
1934D	28,446,000	0.35	0.50	0.80	1.25	5.50	9.00	20.00	30.00	—
1935	245,338,000	0.15	0.20	0.25	0.40	0.90	1.50	5.00	20.00	—
1935D	47,000,000	0.20	0.30	0.40	0.55	0.95	2.50	5.50	20.00	—
1935S	38,702,000	0.25	0.35	0.60	1.75	3.00	5.00	11.00	44.00	—
1936 (Proof in Satin Finish)	309,637,569	0.15	0.20	0.30	0.40	0.85	1.40	1.90	10.00	2,250
1936 Brilliant Proof	Inc. above	—	—	—	—	—	—	—	—	2,300
1936 DDO	Inc. above	—	—	25.00	50.00	80.00	125	175	1,000	—
1936D	40,620,000	0.20	0.30	0.40	0.55	0.90	1.50	4.00	15.00	—
1936S	29,130,000	0.20	0.30	0.45	0.60	1.50	2.25	5.00	18.00	—
1937	309,179,320	0.15	0.20	0.30	0.40	0.50	0.75	1.75	13.50	275
1937D	50,430,000	0.20	0.30	0.40	0.60	0.80	1.20	2.65	15.00	—
1937S	34,500,000	0.20	0.30	0.40	0.55	0.90	1.25	2.75	16.50	—
1938	156,696,734	0.15	0.20	0.30	0.40	0.50	1.20	2.25	18.00	175
1938D	20,010,000	0.20	0.30	0.45	0.60	1.00	1.50	3.50	20.00	—
1938S	15,180,000	0.30	0.40	0.50	0.70	1.00	1.75	3.00	15.00	—
1939	316,479,520	0.15	0.20	0.30	0.40	0.45	0.75	1.00	16.00	165
1939D	15,160,000	0.35	0.45	0.50	0.60	0.95	1.75	3.00	18.00	—
1939S	52,070,000	0.30	0.40	0.50	0.60	0.80	1.20	2.50	16.00	—
1940	586,825,872	0.10	0.20	0.30	0.35	0.45	0.75	1.00	12.00	130
1940D	81,390,000	0.20	0.30	0.40	0.55	0.75	1.10	2.00	11.00	—
1940S	112,940,000	0.20	0.30	0.40	0.55	0.70	1.25	2.50	12.50	—
1941	887,039,100	0.10	0.20	0.30	0.35	0.45	0.60	1.25	10.00	170
1941 Doubled Die Obv	Inc. above	35.00	50.00	70.00	80.00	95.00	135	200	1,000	—
1941D	128,700,000	0.20	0.30	0.40	0.55	0.90	1.35	2.20	12.50	—
1941S	92,360,000	0.20	0.30	0.40	0.55	0.95	1.75	2.50	15.00	—
1942	657,828,600	0.10	0.20	0.30	0.35	0.40	0.55	0.85	11.00	145

Date	Mintage	G4	VG8	F12	VF20	XF40	AU50	MS60	MS65	Prf65
1942D	206,698,000	0.20	0.25	0.30	0.35	0.45	0.60	1.00	12.00	—
1942S	85,590,000	0.25	0.35	0.45	0.85	1.25	2.50	5.00	18.00	—
1943 Copper planchet error	—	—	—	35,000	42,000	45,000	80,000	155,000	—	—
1943S Copper planchet error	—	—	—	125,000	150,000	185,000	275,000	—	—	—

KM# 132a • 2.70 g., Zinc Coated Steel, 19 mm. •
Designer: Victor D. Brenner

Date	Mintage	G4	VG8	F12	VF20	XF40	AU50	MS60	MS65	Prf65
1943	684,628,670	0.20	0.30	0.35	0.45	0.60	0.85	1.25	18.00	—
1943D	217,660,000	0.35	0.40	0.45	0.50	0.70	1.00	1.50	—	—
1943D/D RPM	Inc. above	30.00	38.00	50.00	65.00	90.00	125	200	—	—
1943S	191,550,000	0.40	0.45	0.50	0.65	0.90	1.40	4.00	28.00	—

1955 Double die

KM# A132 • 3.11 g., Brass, 19 mm. •
Designer: Victor D. Brenner **Note:** KM#132 design
and composition resumed • MS60 prices are for
brown coins and MS65 prices are for coins that are
at least 90% original red.

Date	Mintage	XF40	MS65	Prf65
1944	1,435,400,000	0.30	8.00	—
1944D	430,578,000	0.40	14.00	—
1944D/S Type 1	Inc. above	115	3,300	—
1944D/S Type 2	Inc. above	115	2,500	—
1944S	282,760,000	0.35	8.00	—
1945	1,040,515,000	0.40	13.50	—
1945D	226,268,000	0.40	8.00	—
1945S	181,770,000	0.40	7.50	—
1946	991,655,000	0.25	13.50	—
1946D	315,690,000	0.30	10.00	—
1946S	198,100,000	0.30	13.50	—
1946S/D	—	70.00	650	—
1947	190,555,000	0.45	18.50	—
1947D	194,750,000	0.35	7.50	—
1947S	99,000,000	0.35	8.00	—
1948	317,570,000	0.35	18.50	—
1948D	172,637,000	0.40	12.00	—
1948S	81,735,000	0.40	12.00	—
1949	217,775,000	0.40	18.00	—
1949D	153,132,000	0.40	15.00	—
1949S	64,290,000	0.50	10.00	—
1950	272,686,386	0.35	16.50	85.00
1950D	334,950,000	0.35	12.50	—
1950S	118,505,000	0.30	9.00	—
1951	295,633,500	0.40	16.50	80.00
1951D	625,355,000	0.30	8.50	—
1951S	136,010,000	0.40	9.00	—
1952	186,856,980	0.40	16.00	50.00
1952D	746,130,000	0.30	8.50	—
1952S	137,800,004	0.60	12.00	—
1953	256,883,800	0.25	18.00	40.00
1953D	700,515,000	0.25	8.50	—
1953S	181,835,000	0.40	8.00	—
1954	71,873,350	0.25	20.00	19.00
1954D	251,552,500	0.25	8.50	—
1954S	96,190,000	0.25	10.00	—
1955	330,958,000	0.25	9.00	20.00
1955 Doubled Die	Inc. above	1,450	28,000	—

Note: The 1955 "doubled die" has distinct doubling of the date
and lettering on the obverse.

1955D	563,257,500	0.20	8.00	—
1955S	44,610,000	0.35	7.50	—
1956	421,414,384	0.20	12.00	5.00

Date	Mintage	XF40	MS65	Prf65
1956D	1,098,201,100	0.20	7.00	—
1957	283,787,952	0.20	7.50	4.00
1957D	1,051,342,000	0.20	6.00	—
1958	253,400,652	0.20	9.00	6.50
1958D	800,953,300	0.20	7.00	—

Lincoln Memorial.

Small date   Large date

Small date   Large date

KM# 201 • 3.11 g., Brass, 19 mm. • **Rev. Designer:**
Frank Gasparro **Note:** MS60 prices are for brown
coins and MS65 prices are for coins that are at least
90% original red. The dates were modified in 1960,
1970 and 1982, resulting in large-date and small-
date varieties for those years. The 1972 "doubled
die" shows doubling of IN GOD WE TRUST. The
1979-S and 1981-S Type II proofs have a clearer
mint mark than the Type I proofs of those years.
Some 1982 cents have the predominantly copper
composition; others have the predominantly zinc
composition. They can be distinguished by weight.

Date	Mintage	XF40	MS65	Prf65
1959	610,864,291	—	15.00	6.50
1959D	1,279,760,000	—	7.50	—
1960 small date, low 9	588,096,602	1.85	12.00	16.00
1960 large date, high 9	Inc. above	—	8.00	7.50
1960 small over large date	Inc. above	—	—	600
1960D small date, low 9	1,580,884,000	—	10.00	—
1960D large date, high 9	Inc. above	—	8.00	—
1960D/D small over large date	Inc. above	—	300	—

CENT

Date	Mintage	XF40	MS65	Prf65
1961	756,373,244	—	8.50	9.00
1961D	1,753,266,700	—	18.00	—
1962	609,263,019	—	8.00	8.00
1962D	1,793,148,400	—	14.00	—
1963	757,185,645	—	10.00	6.00
1963D	1,774,020,400	—	12.00	—
1964	2,652,525,762	—	8.50	6.00
1964D	3,799,071,500	—	10.00	—
1965	1,497,224,900	—	10.00	—
1965 SMS	Inc. above	—	7.50	—
1966	2,188,147,783	—	10.00	—
1966 SMS	Inc. above	—	8.00	—
1967	3,048,667,100	—	12.00	—
1967 SMS	Inc. above	—	8.00	—
1968	1,707,880,970	—	12.00	—
1968D	2,886,269,600	—	12.50	—
1968S	261,311,510	—	10.00	4.50
1969	1,136,910,000	—	7.00	—
1969D	4,002,832,200	—	10.00	—
1969S	547,309,631	—	15.00	5.50
1969S Doubled Die Obverse	Inc. above	10,000	—	100,000
1970	1,898,315,000	—	8.00	—
1970D	2,891,438,900	—	6.00	—
1970S small date, level 7	Inc. above	30.00	65.00	60.00
1970S large date, low 7	Inc. above	—	15.00	5.00
1970S Doubled Die Obverse	Inc. above	—	20,000	15,000
1971	1,919,490,000	—	20.00	—
1971D	2,911,045,600	—	6.50	—
1971S	528,354,192	—	7.50	5.50
1971S Doubled Die Obverse	—	—	—	400
1972	2,933,255,000	—	6.00	—
1972 Doubled Die Obverse	Inc. above	240	585	—
1972D	2,665,071,400	—	12.00	—
1972S	380,200,104	—	26.50	5.50
1973	3,728,245,000	—	8.00	—
1973D	3,549,576,588	—	11.00	—
1973S	319,937,634	—	10.00	5.50
1974	4,232,140,523	—	12.00	—
1974D	4,235,098,000	—	9.00	—
1974S	412,039,228	—	12.00	5.00
1975	5,451,476,142	—	8.00	—
1975D	4,505,245,300	—	13.50	—
1975S	2,845,450	—	—	5.00
1976	4,674,292,426	—	14.00	—
1976D	4,221,592,455	—	16.00	—
1976S	4,149,730	—	—	6.00
1977	4,469,930,000	—	16.00	—
1977D	4,149,062,300	—	16.00	—
1977S	3,251,152	—	—	5.00
1978	5,558,605,000	—	16.00	—
1978D	4,280,233,400	—	14.00	—
1978S	3,127,781	—	—	5.00
1979	6,018,515,000	—	12.00	—
1979D	4,139,357,254	—	8.00	—
1979S type I, proof	3,677,175	—	—	5.00
1979S type II, proof	—	—	—	10.00
1980	7,414,705,000	—	6.50	—
1980D	5,140,098,660	—	12.00	—
1980S	3,554,806	—	—	5.00
1981	7,491,750,000	—	8.50	—
1981D	5,373,235,677	—	9.00	—
1981S type I, proof	4,063,083	—	—	5.00
1981S type II, proof	—	—	—	42.00
1982 large date	10,712,525,000	—	7.00	—
1982 small date	Inc. above	—	9.00	—
1982D large date	6,012,979,368	—	7.50	—
1982S	3,857,479	—	—	5.00

KM# 201a • 2.50 g., Copper Plated Zinc, 19 mm.
• **Note:** MS60 prices are for brown coins and MS65 prices are for coins that are at least 90% original red.

Date	Mintage	XF40	MS65	Prf65
1982 large date	—	—	6.00	—
1982 small date	—	—	9.00	—
1982D large date	—	—	8.00	—
1982D small date	—	—	6.00	—

KM# 201b • Copper Plated Zinc, 19 mm. •
Note: MS60 prices are for brown coins and MS65 prices are for coins that are at least 90% original red.

Date	Mintage	XF40	MS65	Prf65
1983	7,752,355,000	—	7.00	—
1983 Doubled Die	Inc. above	135	290	—
1983D	6,467,199,428	—	5.50	—
1983S	3,279,126	—	—	3.50
1984	8,151,079,000	—	7.50	—
1984 Doubled Die	Inc. above	90.00	250	—
1984D	5,569,238,906	—	6.50	—
1984S	3,065,110	—	—	3.50
1985	5,648,489,887	—	4.50	—
1985D	5,287,399,926	—	4.50	—
1985S	3,362,821	—	—	3.50
1986	4,491,395,493	—	5.00	—
1986D	4,442,866,698	—	8.00	—
1986S	3,010,497	—	—	3.50
1987	4,682,466,931	—	7.50	—
1987D	4,879,389,514	—	5.50	—
1987S	4,227,728	—	—	3.50
1988	6,092,810,000	—	10.00	—
1988D	5,253,740,443	—	6.00	—
1988S	3,262,948	—	—	3.50
1989	7,261,535,000	—	6.50	—
1989D	5,345,467,111	—	6.50	—
1989S	3,220,194	—	—	5.00
1990	6,851,765,000	—	5.00	—
1990D	4,922,894,533	—	5.50	—
1990S	3,299,559	—	—	3.50
1990 no S, Proof only	Inc. above	—	—	4,650
1991	5,165,940,000	—	6.50	—
1991D	4,158,442,076	—	5.50	—
1991S	2,867,787	—	—	3.50
1992	4,648,905,000	—	5.50	—
1992D	4,448,673,300	—	5.50	—
1992D Close AM, Proof Reverse Die	Inc. above	—	—	—
1992S	4,176,560	—	—	3.50
1993	5,684,705,000	—	5.00	—
1993D	6,426,650,571	—	4.50	—
1993S	3,394,792	—	—	3.50
1994	6,500,850,000	—	6.00	—
1994D	7,131,765,000	—	4.50	—
1994S	3,269,923	—	—	3.50
1995	6,411,440,000	—	5.00	—
1995 Doubled Die Obverse	Inc. above	20.00	60.00	—
1995D	7,128,560,000	—	4.50	—
1995S	2,707,481	—	—	3.50
1996	6,612,465,000	—	4.50	—
1996D	6,510,795,000	—	4.50	—
1996S	2,915,212	—	—	3.50
1997	4,622,800,000	—	3.00	—
1997D	4,576,555,000	—	3.50	—
1997S	2,796,678	—	—	4.00
1998	5,032,155,000	—	3.00	—

Date	Mintage	XF40	MS65	Prf65
1998 Wide AM, reverse from proof die	Inc. above	—	110	—
1998D	5,255,353,500	—	3.00	—
1998S	2,957,286	—	—	4.00
1999	5,237,600,000	—	3.00	—
1999 Wide AM, reverse from proof die	Inc. above	—	450	—
1999D	6,360,065,000	—	3.00	—
1999S	3,362,462	—	—	3.50
2000 Wide AM, reverse from proof die	Inc. above	—	45.00	—
2000	5,503,200,000	—	3.00	—
2000D	8,774,220,000	—	3.00	—
2000S	4,063,361	—	—	3.50
2001	4,959,600,000	—	3.00	—
2001D	5,374,990,000	—	3.00	—
2001S	3,099,096	—	—	3.50
2002	3,260,800,000	—	3.00	—
2002D	4,028,055,000	—	3.00	—
2002S	3,157,739	—	—	3.50
2003	3,300,000,000	—	3.50	—
2003D	3,548,000,000	—	3.50	—
2003S	3,116,590	—	—	3.50
2004	3,379,600,000	—	3.50	—
2004D	3,456,400,000	—	3.50	—
2004S	2,992,069	—	—	3.50
2005	3,935,600,000	—	2.50	—
2005 Satin Finish	1,160,000	—	4.00	—
2005D	3,764,450,000	—	2.50	—
2005D Satin Finish	1,160,000	—	4.00	—
2005S	3,273,000	—	—	3.50
2006	4,290,000,000	—	2.00	—
2006 Satin Finish	847,361	—	4.00	—
2006D	3,944,000,000	—	2.50	—
2006D Satin Finish	847,361	—	4.00	—
2006S	2,923,105	—	—	3.50
2007	3,762,400,000	—	2.00	—
2007 Satin Finish	895,628	—	4.00	—
2007D	3,638,800,000	—	2.00	—
2007D Satin Finish	895,628	—	4.00	—
2007S	2,577,166	—	—	3.50
2008	2,558,800,000	—	2.25	—
2008 Satin Finish	745,464	—	4.00	—
2008D	2,849,600,000	—	2.25	—
2008D Satin Finish	745,464	—	4.00	—
2008S	2,169,561	—	—	4.50

Lincoln Bicentennial
Bust right. Log cabin.

KM# 441 • 2.50 g., Copper Plated Zinc, 19 mm. • **Subject:** Early Childhood in Kentucky **Rev. Designer:** Richard Masters and James Licaretz

Date	Mintage	XF40	MS65	Prf65
2009	284,400,000	—	1.50	—
2009D	350,400,000	—	1.50	—

KM# 441a • 3.31 g., Brass, 19 mm. • **Subject:** Early childhood in Kentucky **Rev. Designer:** Richard Masters and James Licaretz

Date	Mintage	XF40	MS65	Prf65
2009 Satin finish	784,614	—	4.00	—
2009D Satin finish	784,614	—	4.00	—
2009S	2,995,615	—	—	4.00

Lincoln seated on log.

KM# 442 • 2.50 g., Copper Plated Zinc, 19 mm. • **Subject:** Formative years in Indiana **Rev. Designer:** Charles Vickers

Date	Mintage	XF40	MS65	Prf65
2009	376,000,000	—	1.50	—
2009D	363,600,000	—	1.50	—

KM# 442a • 3.11 g., Brass, 19 mm. • **Subject:** Formative years in Indiana **Rev. Designer:** Charles Vickers

Date	Mintage	XF40	MS65	Prf65
2009 Satin finish	784,614	—	4.00	—
2009D Satin finish	784,614	—	4.00	—
2009S	2,995,615	—	—	4.00

Lincoln standing before Illinois Statehouse.

KM# 443 • 2.50 g., Copper Plated Zinc, 19 mm. • **Subject:** Professional life in Illinois **Rev. Designer:** Joel Iskowitz and Don Everhart

Date	Mintage	XF40	MS65	Prf65
2009	316,000,000	—	1.50	—
2009D	336,000,000	—	1.50	—

KM# 443a • 3.11 g., Brass, 19 mm. • **Subject:** Professional life in Illinois **Rev. Designer:** Joel Iskowitz and Don Everhart

Date	Mintage	XF40	MS65	Prf65
2009 Satin finish	784,614	—	4.00	—
2009D Satin finish	784,614	—	4.00	—
2009S	2,995,615	—	—	4.00

Capitol Building.

KM# 444 • 2.50 g., Copper Plated Zinc, 19 mm. • **Subject:** Presidency in Washington, DC **Rev. Designer:** Susan Gamble and Joseph Menna

Date	Mintage	XF40	MS65	Prf65
2009	129,600,000	—	1.50	—
2009D	198,000,000	—	1.50	—

KM# 444a • 3.11 g., Brass, 19 mm. • **Subject:** Presidency in Washington, DC **Rev. Designer:** Susan Ganmble and Joseph Menna

Date	Mintage	XF40	MS65	Prf65
2009 Satin finish	784,614	—	4.00	—
2009D Satin finish	784,614	—	4.00	—
2009S	2,995,615	—	—	4.00

CENT

Lincoln - Shield Reverse
Lincoln bust right. Shield.

KM# 468 • 2.50 g., Copper Plated Zinc, 19 mm. •
Obv. Designer: Victor D. Brenner **Rev. Designer:**
Lyndall Bass and Joseph Menna

Date	Mintage	XF40	MS65	Prf65
2010	1,963,630,000	—	1.50	—
2010 Satin finish	583,912	—	—	—
2010D	2,047,200,000	—	1.50	—
2010D Satin finish	583,912	—	—	—
2010S	1,689,364	—	—	4.00
2011	2,006,800,000	—	1.50	—
2011D	2147483647	—	1.50	—
2011S	1,673,010	—	—	4.00
2012	3,132,000,000	—	1.50	—
2012D	2,883,200,000	—	1.50	—
2012S	1,237,415	—	—	4.00
2013	3,750,400,000	—	1.50	—
2013D	3,319,600,000	—	1.50	—
2013S	1,237,926	—	—	4.00
2014	3,990,800,000	—	1.50	—
2014D	4,155,600,000	—	1.50	—
2014S	—	—	—	4.00
2015	4,691,512,561	—	—	—
2015D	4,674,212,561	—	—	—
2015S	710,183	—	—	—
2016	4,698,000,000	—	1.50	—
2016D	4,420,400,000	—	1.50	—
2016S	—	—	—	4.00
2017	—	—	1.50	—
2017D	—	—	1.50	—
2017S Enhanced Unc.	225,000	—	10.00	—
2017S	—	—	—	4.00
2018	—	—	1.50	—
2018D	—	—	1.50	—
2018S Proof	—	—	—	4.00
2018S Reverse Proof	—	—	—	6.00

2 CENTS

Shield in front of crossed arrows, banner above, date below. Value within wheat wreath.

KM# 94 • 6.22 g., Copper-Tin-Zinc, 23 mm. • **Rev. Legend:** UNITED STATES OF AMERICA **Designer:** James B. Longacre **Note:** The motto IN GOD WE TRUST was modified in 1864, resulting in small-motto and large-motto varieties for that year.

Small motto   Large motto

Date	Mintage	G4	VG8	F12	VF20	XF40	AU50	MS60	MS65	Prf65
1864 small motto	19,847,500	225	350	425	470	800	900	1,500	3,375	85,000
1864 large motto	Inc. above	16.50	18.50	20.00	27.50	45.00	72.00	88.00	390	8,000
1865 fancy 5	13,640,000	13.00	15.00	22.00	27.00	40.00	65.00	90.00	650	2,800
1865 plain 5	Inc. above	10.00	12.00	14.00	19.00	35.00	50.00	60.00	650	2,800
1866	3,177,000	14.00	16.00	19.00	30.00	55.00	70.00	80.00	750	1,300
1867	2,938,750	15.00	18.00	30.00	40.00	55.00	80.00	150	800	2,800
1867 double die obverse	Inc. above	110	150	275	370	640	1,100	1,700	8,500	—
1868	2,803,750	15.00	19.00	32.00	60.00	75.00	120	170	1,200	2,800
1869	1,546,000	17.00	35.00	45.00	60.00	90.00	150	190	1,100	2,250
1869 repunched 18	Inc. above	25.00	35.00	65.00	125	275	450	—	—	—
1869/8 die crack	Inc. above	100	130	250	325	500	750	—	—	—
1870	861,250	35.00	45.00	70.00	95.00	115	230	285	2,250	2,800
1871	721,250	42.00	57.00	75.00	95.00	130	175	250	1,695	3,000
1872	65,000	450	500	585	775	1,250	1,565	2,700	9,100	2,800
1873 closed 3 proof only	Est. 600	1,075	1,250	1,350	1,450	1,550	1,700	2,300	4,500	5,325
1873 open 3 proof only	Est. 500	1,125	1,300	1,475	1,600	1,775	1,950	—	—	5,000

SILVER 3 CENTS

Silver 3 Cents - Type 1
Shield within star, no outlines in star. Roman numeral in designed C, within circle of stars.

KM# 75 • 0.80 g., 0.750 Silver 0.0193 oz. ASW, 14 mm. • **Obv. Legend:** UNITED STATES OF AMERICA **Designer:** James B. Longacre

Date	Mintage	G4	VG8	F12	VF20	XF40	AU50	MS60	MS65	Prf65
1851	5,447,400	33.00	49.00	65.00	73.00	105	200	210	760	—
1851O	720,000	40.00	53.00	56.00	110	180	265	525	3,000	—
1852	18,663,500	33.00	49.00	52.00	65.00	75.00	170	210	590	—
1853	11,400,000	33.00	49.00	52.00	65.00	75.00	170	210	590	—

CENT

Silver 3 Cents - Type 2

Shield within star, three outlines in star. Roman numeral in designed C, within circle of stars.

KM# 80 • 0.75 g., 0.900 Silver 0.0217 oz. ASW, 14 mm. • **Obv. Legend:** UNITED STATES OF AMERICA **Designer:** James B. Longacre

Date	Mintage	G4	VG8	F12	VF20	XF40	AU50	MS60	MS65	Prf65
1854	671,000	43.00	55.00	65.00	75.00	100	160	260	3,775	30,000
1855	139,000	43.00	55.00	70.00	150	250	425	700	7,800	16,000
1856	1,458,000	43.00	55.00	65.00	75.00	100	185	235	2,300	10,000
1857	1,042,000	43.00	55.00	65.00	75.00	100	200	370	3,000	9,000
1858	1,604,000	43.00	55.00	65.00	75.00	100	160	280	1,620	5,000

Silver 3 Cents - Type 3

Shield within star, two outlines in star. Roman numeral in designed C, within circle of stars.

KM# 88 • 0.75 g., 0.900 Silver 0.0217 oz. ASW, 14 mm. • **Obv. Legend:** UNITED STATES OF AMERICA **Designer:** James B. Longacre

Date	Mintage	G4	VG8	F12	VF20	XF40	AU50	MS60	MS65	Prf65
1859	365,000	43.00	55.00	65.00	75.00	100	150	185	825	1,700
1860	287,000	43.00	55.00	65.00	75.00	80.00	150	185	1,125	5,000
1861	498,000	43.00	55.00	65.00	75.00	80.00	180	220	750	1,700
1862	343,550	43.00	55.00	65.00	75.00	80.00	150	185	875	1,450
1862/1	Inc. above	43.00	55.00	65.00	75.00	80.00	165	260	950	—
1863	21,460	460	525	600	750	775	825	1,050	3,960	1,700
1863/62 proof only; Rare	Inc. above	—	—	—	—	—	—	—	—	5,440
1864	12,470	460	525	600	750	775	825	1,050	2,900	1,700
1865	8,500	460	525	600	750	775	825	1,750	3,900	1,700
1866	22,725	450	500	550	600	700	800	900	3,500	1,700
1867	4,625	460	525	600	750	800	1,200	1,700	15,000	1,500
1868	4,100	650	750	925	1,350	1,800	2,400	4,000	25,000	1,700
1869	5,100	460	525	600	750	800	1,000	1,500	7,300	1,645
1869/68 proof only; Rare	Inc. above	—	—	—	—	—	—	—	—	8,500
1870	4,000	460	525	600	750	775	950	1,425	4,500	1,600
1871	4,360	460	525	600	750	775	825	1,000	1,600	1,565
1872	1,950	600	750	950	1,400	1,800	2,300	2,800	12,000	1,500
1873 proof only	600	—	—	—	—	775	900	—	—	2,700

NICKEL 3 CENTS

Coronet head left, date below. Roman numeral value within wreath.

KM# 95 • 1.94 g., Copper-Nickel, 17.9 mm. • **Obv. Legend:** UNITED STATES OF AMERICA **Designer:** James B. Longacre

Date	Mintage	G4	VG8	F12	VF20	XF40	AU50	MS60	MS65	Prf65
1865	11,382,000	11.00	14.00	17.00	26.00	33.00	65.00	90.00	475	3,350
1866	4,801,000	16.50	18.00	20.00	25.00	33.00	65.00	90.00	475	860
1867	3,915,000	16.50	18.00	20.00	25.00	33.00	65.00	90.00	475	775
1868	3,252,000	16.50	18.00	20.00	25.00	33.00	65.00	90.00	475	825
1869	1,604,000	12.00	19.50	20.00	25.00	33.00	65.00	90.00	600	500
1870	1,335,000	14.00	18.00	20.00	25.00	33.00	65.00	90.00	475	2,550
1871	604,000	17.50	22.50	20.00	25.00	33.00	65.00	90.00	850	600
1872	862,000	13.00	15.00	18.00	33.50	43.50	68.00	160	995	580
1873 Closed 3	1,173,000	10.00	15.00	25.00	35.00	70.00	75.00	145	950	720
1873 Open 3	Inc. above	18.00	20.00	25.00	35.00	75.00	100	180	1,500	—
1874	790,000	17.50	19.00	25.00	33.00	41.00	66.00	160	790	675
1875	228,000	19.00	25.00	29.00	40.00	70.00	82.00	175	950	870
1876	162,000	20.50	22.00	30.00	50.00	49.50	97.00	240	1,350	540
1877 proof	Est. 900	1,000	1,025	1,075	1,125	1,275	1,350	—	—	5,000
1878 proof	2,350	615	750	775	800	—	—	—	—	—
1879	41,200	70.00	80.00	96.00	140	190	225	320	925	475
1880	24,955	100	115	130	200	250	300	350	935	675
1881	1,080,575	9.00	12.00	15.00	25.00	40.00	60.00	100	585	600
1882	25,300	130	150	180	240	275	325	425	1,700	500
1883	10,609	325	375	425	500	600	1,300	—	—	515
1884	5,642	700	900	1,050	1,350	1,900	4,000	5,500	18,000	675
1885	4,790	800	1,100	1,425	2,200	3,000	3,900	3,600	12,000	500
1886 proof	4,290	320	330	345	385	385	420	—	—	625

NICKEL 3 CENTS

Date	Mintage	G4	VG8	F12	VF20	XF40	AU50	MS60	MS65	Prf65
1887/6 proof	7,961	350	390	415	450	460	515	—	—	600
1887	Inc. above	305	355	395	440	455	500	540	1,200	500
1888	41,083	54.00	63.00	70.00	80.00	150	225	325	650	600
1889	21,561	90.00	115	145	225	250	300	375	660	460

HALF DIME

Flowing Hair Half Dime
KM# 15 • 1.35 g., 0.892 Silver 0.0387 oz. ASW, 16.5 mm. • Designer: Robert Scot

Date	Mintage	G4	VG8	F12	VF20	XF40	MS60
1794	86,416	1,500	1,700	26,500	3,850	8,000	18,000
1795	Inc. above	1,500	1,500	2,700	2,800	7,350	10,000

Draped Bust Half Dime
Draped bust right. Small eagle.
KM# 23 • 1.35 g., 0.892 Silver 0.0387 oz. ASW, 16.5 mm. • Designer: Robert Scot

Date	Mintage	G4	VG8	F12	VF20	XF40	MS60
1796	10,230	1,400	1,750	3,000	4,100	9,500	20,000
1796 LIKERTY	Inc. above	1,400	1,800	3,050	4,100	9,600	20,500
Note: In 1796 the word LIBERTY was spelled LIKERTY on a die.							
1796/5	Inc. above	2,300	2,850	4,200	5,200	7,900	25,000
1797 13 stars	44,527	2,300	3,000	5,000	5,800	12,250	43,000
1797 15 stars	Inc. above	1,500	18,750	3,000	4,600	6,000	15,000
1797 16 stars	Inc. above	1,700	2,300	3,300	4,200	7,000	15,500

Draped bust right, flanked by stars, date at angle below. Heraldic eagle.
KM# 34 • 1.35 g., 0.892 Silver 0.0387 oz. ASW, 16.5 mm. • Obv. Legend: LIBERTY Rev. Legend: UNITED STATES OF AMERICA Designer: Robert Scot

Date	Mintage	G4	VG8	F12	VF20	XF40	MS60
1800	24,000	1,300	1,400	2,000	2,600	4,500	13,000
1800 LIBEKTY	Inc. above	1,400	1,600	2,500	3,000	5,000	15,000
1801	33,910	1,300	1,400	2,000	3,600	5,500	18,500
1802	3,060	60,000	75,000	95,000	120,000	200,000	—
1803 Large 8	37,850	1,250	1,450	2,000	3,900	6,750	13,000
1803 Small 8	Inc. above	2,000	2,750	3,800	5,600	9,500	62,500
1805	15,600	1,400	1,500	2,400	3,700	9,500	—

Liberty Cap Half Dime
Classic head left, flanked by stars, date below. Eagle with arrows in talons, banner above.
KM# 47 • 1.35 g., 0.892 Silver 0.0387 oz. ASW, 15.5 mm. • Rev. Legend: UNITED STATES OF AMERICA Designer: William Kneass

Date	Mintage	G4	VG8	F12	VF20	XF40	AU50	MS60	MS65
1829	1,230,000	40.00	55.00	70.00	90.00	135	270	375	1,980
1830	1,240,000	40.00	55.00	70.00	90.00	135	270	375	1,980
1831	1,242,700	40.00	55.00	70.00	90.00	135	270	375	1,980
1832	965,000	40.00	55.00	70.00	90.00	135	270	375	1,980
1833	1,370,000	40.00	55.00	70.00	90.00	135	270	375	1,980
1834	1,480,000	40.00	55.00	70.00	90.00	135	270	375	1,980
1835 large date and 5C.	2,760,000	40.00	55.00	70.00	90.00	135	270	375	1,980
1835 large date, small 5C.	Inc. above	40.00	55.00	70.00	90.00	135	270	375	1,980
1835 small date, large 5C.	Inc. above	40.00	55.00	70.00	90.00	135	270	375	1,980
1835 small date and 5C.	Inc. above	40.00	55.00	70.00	90.00	135	270	375	1,980
1836 large 5C.	1,900,000	40.00	55.00	70.00	90.00	135	270	375	1,980
1836 small 5C.	Inc. above	40.00	55.00	70.00	90.00	135	270	375	1,980
1837 large 5C.	2,276,000	40.00	55.00	70.00	160	225	350	425	5,600
1837 small 5C.	Inc. above	175	200	250	300	425	875	2,200	9,100

Seated Liberty Half Dime

Seated Liberty, no stars around border, date below. Value within wreath.

KM# 60 • 1.34 g., 0.900 Silver 0.0388 oz. ASW, 15.5 mm. • **Rev. Legend:** UNITED STATES OF AMERICA **Designer:** Christian Gobrecht **Note:** A design modification in 1837 resulted in small-date and large-date varieties for that year.

Date	Mintage	G4	VG8	F12	VF20	XF40	AU50	MS60	MS65
1837 small date	Inc. above	45.00	60.00	95.00	155	215	460	625	2,625
1837 large date	Inc. above	45.00	60.00	95.00	155	215	460	525	2,600
1838O	70,000	110	165	310	610	1,700	2,550	4,200	23,500

Seated Liberty, stars around top 1/2 of border, date below. Value within wreath.

KM# 62.1 • 1.34 g., 0.900 Silver 0.0388 oz. ASW, 15.5 mm. • **Rev. Legend:** UNITED STATES OF AMERICA **Designer:** Christian Gobrecht **Note:** The two varieties of 1838 are distinguished by the size of the stars on the obverse. The 1839-O with reverse of 1838-O was struck from rusted reverse dies. The result is a bumpy surface on this variety's reverse.

Date	Mintage	G4	VG8	F12	VF20	XF40	AU50	MS60	MS65
1838 large stars	2,255,000	17.00	22.00	26.00	42.00	95.00	190	250	1,250
1838 small stars	Inc. above	17.00	31.00	42.00	90.00	175	350	675	3,200
1839	1,069,150	17.00	32.00	35.00	43.00	88.00	200	275	1,700
1839O	1,034,039	18.00	35.00	43.00	53.00	135	325	875	7,800
1839O reverse 1838O	Inc. above	450	650	1,100	1,600	2,600	—	—	—
1840	1,344,085	17.00	30.00	35.00	42.00	85.00	195	250	1,625
1840O	935,000	23.00	29.00	33.00	80.00	135	550	1,625	14,000

Seated Liberty, stars around top 1/2 of border, date below.

KM# 62.2 • 1.34 g., 0.900 Silver 0.0388 oz. ASW, 15.5 mm. • **Rev. Legend:** UNITED STATES OF AMERICA **Designer:** Christian Gobrecht **Note:** In 1840 drapery was added to Liberty's left elbow. Varieties for the 1848 Philadelphia strikes are distinguished by the size of the numerals in the date.

Date	Mintage	G4	VG8	F12	VF20	XF40	AU50	MS60	MS65
1840	Inc. above	26.00	38.00	65.00	135	225	325	500	2,500
1840O	Inc. above	32.00	55.00	105	250	775	1,275	11,500	—
1841	1,150,000	17.00	30.00	35.00	40.00	53.00	75.00	155	1,025
1841O	815,000	75.00	95.00	110	150	240	440	1,100	6,600
1842	815,000	17.00	30.00	35.00	40.00	63.00	140	165	1,100
1842O	350,000	75.00	115	210	325	500	950	1,400	12,750
1843	1,165,000	17.00	30.00	35.00	40.00	63.00	140	210	1,300
1844	430,000	22.00	36.00	30.00	65.00	90.00	185	300	1,300
1844O	220,000	150	200	325	575	1,100	1,650	6,300	22,000
1845	1,564,000	17.00	30.00	35.00	40.00	48.00	97.00	205	1,050
1845/1845	Inc. above	23.00	40.00	50.00	60.00	75.00	175	200	1,175
1846	27,000	750	1,150	1,750	2,400	3,800	6,000	17,000	—
1847	1,274,000	17.00	30.00	35.00	40.00	63.00	110	195	1,200
1848 medium date	668,000	17.00	30.00	35.00	40.00	53.00	75.00	350	3,100
1848 large date	Inc. above	27.00	32.00	43.00	66.00	175	340	510	3,100
1848O	600,000	19.00	23.00	32.00	75.00	195	425	560	2,375
1849/8	1,309,000	45.00	65.00	95.00	140	200	360	750	1,825
1849/6	Inc. above	45.00	65.00	95.00	140	200	360	775	2,650
1849	Inc. above	17.00	30.00	35.00	40.00	63.00	110	260	1,850
1849O	140,000	50.00	75.00	170	225	525	875	1,775	7,900
1850	955,000	17.00	30.00	35.00	40.00	63.00	110	240	770
1850O	690,000	25.00	30.00	38.00	63.00	110	275	700	4,500
1851	781,000	17.00	30.00	35.00	40.00	63.00	110	240	880
1851O	860,000	24.00	26.00	30.00	42.00	105	185	410	3,400
1852	1,000,500	17.00	30.00	35.00	40.00	63.00	140	165	1,000
1852O	260,000	31.00	42.00	64.00	135	240	425	900	7,800
1853	135,000	60.00	80.00	110	200	310	550	700	1,880
1853O	160,000	300	400	775	1,200	2,500	3,400	10,600	30,000

Seated Liberty, stars around top 1/2 of border, arrows at date. Value within wreath.

KM# 76 • 1.24 g., 0.900 Silver 0.0359 oz. ASW
Rev. Legend: UNITED STATES OF AMERICA
Designer: Christian Gobrecht

Date	Mintage	G4	VG8	F12	VF20	XF40	AU50	MS60	MS65	Prf65
1853	13,210,020	17.00	30.00	35.00	40.00	50.00	95.00	200	950	100,000
1853O	2,200,000	17.00	30.00	47.00	60.00	70.00	115	270	3,500	—
1854	5,740,000	17.00	30.00	35.00	40.00	63.00	95.00	200	1,170	8,800
1854O	1,560,000	17.00	30.00	35.00	40.00	76.00	165	300	3,200	—
1855	1,750,000	17.00	30.00	35.00	40.00	53.00	100	200	1,400	8,800
1855O	600,000	17.00	30.00	35.00	64.00	135	200	575	4,000	—

Seated Liberty, stars around top 1/2 of border, date below. Value within wreath.

KM# A62.2 • 1.24 g., 0.900 Silver 0.0359 oz.
ASW **Rev. Legend:** UNITED STATES OF AMERICA
Designer: Christian Gobrecht **Note:** On the 1858/
inverted date variety, the date was engraved into the
die upside down and then re-engraved right side up.
Another 1858 variety has the date doubled.

Date	Mintage	G4	VG8	F12	VF20	XF40	AU50	MS60	MS65	Prf65
1856	4,880,000	17.00	30.00	35.00	40.00	63.00	140	165	680	8,225
1856O	1,100,000	17.00	30.00	35.00	53.00	110	200	460	1,800	—
1857	7,280,000	17.00	30.00	35.00	37.00	40.00	80.00	165	580	4,600
1857O	1,380,000	15.00	17.00	30.00	45.00	50.00	140	315	1,100	—
1858	3,500,000	17.00	30.00	35.00	37.00	68.00	80.00	165	680	3,750
1858 inverted date	Inc. above	75.00	140	185	285	400	440	875	3,200	—
1858 double date	Inc. above	60.00	75.00	135	225	375	700	1,250	—	—
1858O	1,660,000	17.00	30.00	35.00	48.00	75.00	145	285	1,300	—
1859	340,000	17.00	30.00	35.00	54.00	84.00	145	230	800	2,950
1859O	560,000	17.00	28.00	55.00	85.00	125	225	400	1,500	—

Seated Liberty, date below. Value within wreath.

KM# 91 • 1.24 g., 0.900 Silver 0.0359 oz. ASW **Obv.
Legend:** UNITED STATES OF AMERICA **Designer:**
Christian Gobrecht

Date	Mintage	G4	VG8	F12	VF20	XF40	AU50	MS60	MS65	Prf65
1860	799,000	17.00	30.00	35.00	40.00	63.00	90.00	175	575	890
1860O	1,060,000	17.00	30.00	35.00	45.00	60.00	125	195	830	—
1861	3,361,000	17.00	30.00	35.00	40.00	63.00	75.00	175	575	890
1861/0	Inc. above	30.00	43.00	67.00	130	285	375	500	1,725	—
1862	1,492,550	17.00	30.00	35.00	40.00	63.00	75.00	185	575	890
1863	18,460	195	270	325	375	500	600	750	1,480	890
1863S	100,000	30.00	50.00	100	125	275	380	700	4,500	—
1864	48,470	315	425	810	900	1,150	1,300	1,450	2,500	890
1864S	90,000	110	145	175	230	500	675	925	3,375	—
1865	13,500	300	425	650	700	950	1,000	1,125	2,200	890
1865S	120,000	55.00	75.00	110	175	325	600	1,100	6,700	—
1866	10,725	280	360	580	700	825	850	900	2,500	890
1866S	120,000	30.00	42.00	44.00	72.00	180	325	450	4,000	—
1867	8,625	450	490	725	825	900	1,075	1,200	2,800	890
1867S	120,000	45.00	65.00	95.00	130	215	285	600	2,900	—
1868	89,200	50.00	65.00	105	180	280	425	650	1,500	890
1868S	280,000	17.00	24.00	32.00	40.00	63.00	155	285	1,800	—
1869	208,600	17.00	24.00	31.00	40.00	62.00	135	225	1,025	890
1869S	230,000	17.00	24.00	31.00	38.00	52.00	135	375	3,400	—
1870	536,600	17.00	24.00	28.00	31.00	63.00	75.00	175	850	890
1870S unique	—	—	—	—	—	—	—	—	—	—
Note: 1870S, Superior Galleries, July 1986, brilliant uncirculated, $253,000.										
1871	1,873,960	17.00	24.00	28.00	31.00	63.00	75.00	175	625	890
1871S	161,000	24.00	35.00	45.00	70.00	85.00	190	270	1,160	—
1872	2,947,950	17.00	24.00	28.00	31.00	63.00	75.00	175	625	890
1872S mint mark in wreath	837,000	17.00	24.00	28.00	31.00	63.00	75.00	180	635	—
1872S mint mark below wreath	Inc. above	17.00	24.00	28.00	31.00	63.00	75.00	180	595	—
1873	712,600	17.00	24.00	28.00	31.00	63.00	75.00	175	625	890
1873S	324,000	17.00	24.00	28.00	31.00	63.00	75.00	175	600	—

HALF DIME

5 CENTS

Shield Nickel

Draped garland above shield, date below. Value within center of rays between stars.

KM# 96 • 5.00 g., Copper-Nickel, 20.5 mm. • **Obv. Legend:** IN GOD WE TRUST **Rev. Legend:** UNITED STATES OF AMERICA **Designer:** James B. Longacre

Date	Mintage	G4	VG8	F12	VF20	XF40	AU50	MS60	MS65	Prf65
1866	14,742,500	29.00	38.00	65.00	75.00	150	250	335	1,500	2,850
1867	2,019,000	30.00	36.00	56.00	105	220	255	380	3,000	32,000

Draped garland above shield, date below. Value within circle of stars.

KM# 97 • 5.00 g., Copper-Nickel **Obv. Legend:** IN GOD WE TRUST **Rev. Legend:** UNITED STATES OF AMERICA

Date	Mintage	G4	VG8	F12	VF20	XF40	AU50	MS60	MS65	Prf65
1867	28,890,500	19.00	22.00	30.00	45.00	60.00	120	150	600	925
1868 Rev'67	28,817,000	25.00	28.00	30.00	35.00	62.00	115	175	650	1,000
1868 Rev'68	Inc. above	22.00	34.00	36.00	45.00	77.00	144	188	—	—
Note: Star points to center of A in STATES.										
1869	16,395,000	21.00	28.00	30.00	45.00	70.00	120	150	660	700
1870	4,806,000	27.00	35.00	60.00	75.00	100	160	230	1,300	800
1871	561,000	75.00	95.00	140	210	310	340	525	2,150	900
1872	6,036,000	60.00	70.00	85.00	100	125	180	240	1,500	675
1873 Open 3	4,550,000	40.00	50.00	65.00	80.00	115	135	230	1,525	—
1873 Closed 3	Inc. above	50.00	60.00	70.00	135	195	235	375	1,900	600
1874	3,538,000	31.00	45.00	74.00	94.00	130	165	245	1,125	700
1875	2,097,000	58.00	62.00	100	140	175	230	290	1,375	1,000
1876	2,530,000	45.00	54.00	125	150	200	215	255	1,500	800
1877 proof	Est. 900	—	—	—	1,800	2,000	2,100	—	—	5,200
1878 proof	2,350	—	—	1,100	—	—	—	—	—	1,200
1879	29,100	390	600	750	900	1,200	—	1,725	2,800	625
1879/8	Inc. above	—	—	—	—	—	—	—	—	750
1880	19,995	1,900	—	—	—	—	8,000	10,000	—	680
1881	72,375	260	500	530	550	750	800	980	2,800	675
1882	11,476,600	28.00	30.00	32.00	40.00	60.00	120	160	525	490
Note: Many exist with excess metal at numeral 2 & 3 these should not be confused with the following overdate.										
1883	1,456,919	25.00	35.00	38.00	40.00	65.00	115	160	675	500
Note: Many exist with excess metal at numeral 2 & 3 these should not be confused with the following overdate.										
1883/2	Inc. above	220	300	535	670	880	1,100	1,750	5,000	—

Liberty Nickel

Liberty head left, within circle of stars, date below. Roman numeral value within wreath, without CENTS below.

KM# 111 • 5.00 g., Copper-Nickel, 21.2 mm. • **Rev. Legend:** UNITED STATES OF AMERICA **Designer:** Charles E. Barber

Date	Mintage	G4	VG8	F12	VF20	XF40	AU50	MS60	MS65	Prf65
1883	5,479,519	8.00	9.00	10.00	12.00	14.00	20.00	26.00	255	525

Liberty head left, within circle of stars, date below. Roman numeral value within wreath, CENTS below.

KM# 112 • 5.00 g., Copper-Nickel, 21.2 mm. • **Rev. Legend:** UNITED STATES OF AMERICA

Date	Mintage	G4	VG8	F12	VF20	XF40	AU50	MS60	MS65	Prf65
1883	16,032,983	20.00	28.00	35.00	59.00	85.00	120	170	510	500
1884	11,273,942	23.00	35.00	50.00	65.00	80.00	140	200	1,150	550
1885	1,476,490	500	600	925	990	1,350	1,550	1,700	5,400	1,400
1886	3,330,290	210	360	425	490	700	775	900	4,200	620
1887	15,263,652	16.00	25.00	35.00	50.00	75.00	120	145	750	525
1888	10,720,483	30.00	48.00	60.00	125	185	250	290	1,200	525

Date	Mintage	G4	VG8	F12	VF20	XF40	AU50	MS60	MS65	Prf65
1889	15,881,361	12.00	21.00	24.00	65.00	75.00	140	165	700	525
1890	16,259,272	11.00	22.00	35.00	50.00	60.00	125	150	875	525
1891	16,834,350	5.00	15.00	22.00	40.00	55.00	125	160	750	525
1892	11,699,642	5.00	8.00	27.00	50.00	75.00	125	140	850	525
1893	13,370,195	7.00	12.00	27.00	50.00	75.00	125	140	1,275	525
1894	5,413,132	18.00	30.00	100	170	250	300	335	1,150	525
1895	9,979,884	7.00	11.00	29.00	55.00	70.00	115	135	1,200	525
1896	8,842,920	12.00	25.00	40.00	65.00	100	150	200	1,125	525
1897	20,428,735	2.00	4.00	8.00	29.00	50.00	70.00	110	850	525
1898	12,532,087	2.00	4.00	15.00	17.00	60.00	110	135	625	525
1899	26,029,031	2.00	4.00	8.00	12.00	30.00	75.00	110	625	525
1900	27,255,995	2.00	4.00	8.00	12.00	30.00	75.00	110	450	525
1901	26,480,213	2.00	4.00	8.00	12.00	30.00	75.00	110	450	525
1902	31,480,579	2.00	4.00	8.00	12.00	30.00	75.00	110	450	525
1903	28,006,725	2.00	4.00	8.00	12.00	30.00	75.00	110	450	525
1904	21,404,984	2.00	4.00	8.00	12.00	30.00	75.00	110	450	525
1905	29,827,276	2.00	4.00	5.00	12.00	30.00	75.00	110	450	525
1906	38,613,725	2.00	4.00	8.00	12.00	30.00	75.00	110	750	525
1907	39,214,800	2.00	4.00	8.00	12.00	30.00	75.00	110	525	525
1908	22,686,177	2.00	4.00	8.00	12.00	30.00	75.00	110	850	525
1909	11,590,526	4.00	6.00	7.00	12.00	30.00	75.00	110	625	525
1910	30,169,353	2.00	4.00	8.00	12.00	30.00	75.00	110	450	525
1911	39,559,372	2.00	4.00	8.00	12.00	30.00	75.00	110	360	525
1912	26,236,714	2.00	4.00	8.00	12.00	30.00	75.00	110	450	525
1912D	8,474,000	4.00	5.00	11.00	38.00	105	200	260	1,425	—
1912S	238,000	135	175	250	575	955	1,225	1,350	—	—
1913 5 known	—	—	—	—	—	—	—	—	—	—

Note: 1913, Heritage Sale, January 2010, Proof-64 (Olsen), $3,737,500. Private treaty, 2007, (Eliasburg) Proof-66 $5 million.

Buffalo Nickel
American Bison standing on a mound.

KM# 133 • 5.00 g., Copper-Nickel, 21.2 mm. •
Designer: James Earle Fraser

Date	Mintage	G4	VG8	F12	VF20	XF40	AU50	MS60	MS65	Prf65
1913	30,993,520	10.00	12.00	14.00	16.00	20.00	26.00	48.00	140	3,150
1913D	5,337,000	15.00	18.00	29.00	31.00	36.00	63.00	67.00	325	—
1913S	2,105,000	44.00	46.00	50.00	60.00	75.00	92.00	160	685	—

American Bison standing on a line.

KM# 134 • 5.00 g., Copper-Nickel, 21.2 mm. • **Designer:** James Earle Fraser **Note:** In 1913 the reverse design was modified so the ground under the buffalo was represented as a line rather than a mound. On the 1937D 3-legged variety, the buffalo's right front leg is missing, the result of a damaged die.

1937D 3-legged   1918/17D   1937D 3-legged

Date	Mintage	G4	VG8	F12	VF20	XF40	AU50	MS60	MS65	Prf65
1913	29,858,700	10.00	11.00	12.00	15.00	20.00	25.00	50.00	300	2,500
1913D	4,156,000	150	180	200	220	245	280	315	1,000	—
1913S	1,209,000	200	265	300	390	550	675	850	2,500	—
1914	20,665,738	14.00	16.00	19.00	23.00	30.00	40.00	50.00	455	2,250
1914/3	Inc. above	110	250	400	460	550	760	1,800	30,000	—
1914D	3,912,000	90.00	120	150	190	300	400	430	1,500	—
1914/3D	Inc. above	90.00	200	300	400	590	800	3,200	—	—
1914S	3,470,000	25.00	37.00	61.00	75.00	90.00	185	210	1,800	—
1914/3S	Inc. above	210	400	650	900	1,300	2,000	4,100	—	—
1915	20,987,270	5.00	6.00	9.00	12.00	16.00	42.00	48.00	315	2,100
1915D	7,569,500	18.00	30.00	40.00	50.00	105	154	200	1,170	—
1915S	1,505,000	50.00	60.00	130	150	375	525	615	3,400	—
1916	63,498,066	4.50	6.00	8.00	10.00	14.00	25.00	60.00	260	3,250
1916 2 Feathers	Inc. above	40.00	—	65.00	—	—	—	—	200	—
1916/16	Inc. above	3,400	4,400	8,500	15,000	16,000	27,000	55,000	—	—
1916D	13,333,000	18.00	33.00	43.00	52.00	80.00	105	190	1,500	—
1916S	11,860,000	12.00	24.00	35.00	39.00	100	150	200	2,250	—
1917	51,424,029	5.00	6.00	9.00	12.00	20.00	35.00	61.00	600	—
1917 2 Feathers	Inc. above	30.00	—	40.00	—	—	—	—	145	—
1917D	9,910,800	20.00	50.00	70.00	85.00	135	255	360	2,100	—

Date	Mintage	G4	VG8	F12	VF20	XF40	AU50	MS60	MS65	Prf65
1917S	4,193,000	22.00	90.00	111	160	200	270	700	4,340	—
1917S 2 Feathers	Inc. above	40.00	60.00	85.00	—	—	—	—	255	—
1918	32,086,314	5.00	6.00	9.00	12.00	33.00	48.00	150	1,070	—
1918/17D	8,362,314	875	1,295	2,700	4,250	8,000	10,500	32,000	250,000	—
1918D	Inc. above	21.00	40.00	105	135	290	425	550	3,400	—
1918 2 Feathers	Inc. above	40.00	—	85.00	—	—	—	—	275	—
1918S	4,882,000	13.00	56.00	90.00	120	185	370	680	12,000	—
1919	60,868,000	2.00	3.25	8.00	12.00	16.00	27.00	51.00	500	—
1919D	8,006,000	14.50	32.00	115	145	275	365	670	6,650	—
1919S	7,521,000	7.00	32.00	90.00	140	230	375	610	10,500	—
1920	63,093,000	1.25	1.75	5.00	9.00	13.50	26.00	54.00	600	—
1920D	9,418,000	8.50	17.50	37.00	140	275	340	560	4,400	—
1920S	9,689,000	24.00	45.00	65.00	100	250	350	580	14,000	—
1921	10,663,000	3.25	5.50	18.00	27.00	50.00	100	145	925	—
1921S	1,557,000	110	190	210	500	900	1,000	2,400	8,000	—
1923	35,715,000	1.75	2.75	6.00	9.00	13.00	45.00	54.00	615	—
1923S	6,142,000	17.00	25.00	66.00	120	335	490	600	5,300	—
1924	21,620,000	1.25	1.75	5.00	10.00	22.00	44.00	69.00	850	—
1924D	5,258,000	19.00	30.00	66.00	85.00	220	300	380	5,600	—
1924S	1,437,000	31.50	90.00	280	310	875	1,550	2,325	17,000	—
1925	35,565,100	2.00	4.00	5.00	13.00	24.00	28.00	39.00	400	—
1925D	4,450,000	11.00	22.00	44.00	112	200	280	410	3,400	—
1925S	6,256,000	5.00	10.00	18.00	110	245	310	550	18,800	—
1926	44,693,000	1.50	2.50	4.00	6.00	14.00	20.00	29.00	195	—
1926D	5,638,000	10.50	21.00	35.00	85.00	210	290	335	3,660	—
1926S	970,000	24.00	52.00	175	350	825	2,650	4,100	90,000	—
1927	37,981,000	1.00	1.50	3.00	5.00	13.00	21.00	36.00	275	—
1927D	5,730,000	3.50	5.00	9.00	50.00	120	160	180	3,600	—
1927S	3,430,000	1.75	3.00	16.00	47.00	112	240	810	11,000	—
1928	23,411,000	2.00	2.25	2.50	7.00	11.00	25.00	40.00	300	—
1928D	6,436,000	2.00	3.00	5.00	23.00	38.00	51.00	80.00	525	—
1928S	6,936,000	2.00	3.00	5.00	14.00	38.00	100	245	2,160	—
1929	36,446,000	1.00	1.50	2.00	7.00	13.00	21.00	33.00	400	—
1929D	8,370,000	1.00	1.50	3.00	18.00	41.00	60.00	125	875	—
1929S	7,754,000	1.00	1.50	1.90	7.00	16.00	31.00	45.00	370	—
1930	22,849,000	2.00	2.25	2.50	7.00	16.00	21.00	30.00	250	—
1930S	5,435,000	2.00	2.25	2.50	9.00	16.00	38.00	70.00	375	—
1931S	1,200,000	15.00	18.00	21.00	28.00	40.00	50.00	63.00	350	—
1934	20,213,003	1.75	2.00	2.50	4.00	9.50	28.00	50.00	255	—
1934D	7,480,000	1.75	3.00	7.00	13.00	19.00	50.00	80.00	600	—
1935	58,264,000	1.00	1.25	1.60	2.00	3.00	12.00	28.00	135	—
1935 Double Die Rev.	Inc. above	80.00	95.00	125	185	480	900	3,200	22,000	—
1935D	12,092,000	2.00	2.50	3.00	11.00	24.00	50.00	70.00	275	—
1935S	10,300,000	1.00	1.50	1.60	2.00	4.00	21.00	50.00	230	—
1936	119,001,420	1.00	1.50	1.60	2.00	4.00	10.00	28.00	83.00	2,155
1936 Brilliant	Inc. above	—	—	—	—	—	—	—	—	2,300
1936D	24,814,000	1.00	1.50	1.60	2.00	4.00	25.00	32.00	100	—
1936D 3-1/2 leg	Inc. above	400	600	925	1,100	2,465	3,375	12,000	—	—
1936D/S	Inc. above	—	—	10.00	16.00	25.00	—	—	—	—
1936S	14,930,000	1.00	1.50	1.60	2.00	4.00	12.00	35.00	107	—
1937	79,485,769	1.00	1.50	1.60	2.00	4.00	10.00	21.00	60.00	1,540
1937D	17,826,000	1.00	1.50	1.60	2.00	4.00	10.00	31.00	63.00	—
1937D 3-legged	Inc. above	330	355	400	500	750	900	2,000	30,000	—
1937S	5,635,000	1.00	1.50	1.60	2.00	4.00	11.00	28.00	60.00	—
1938D	7,020,000	2.00	2.35	3.00	4.25	4.50	9.25	16.00	60.00	—
1938D/D	Inc. above	—	—	6.00	8.00	12.00	22.00	40.00	80.00	—
1938D/S	Inc. above	9.00	12.00	14.00	18.00	22.00	33.00	50.00	140	—

Jefferson Nickel
Monticello, mintmark to right side.
KM# 192 • 5.00 g., Copper-Nickel, 21.2 mm. •
Designer: Felix Schlag **Note:** Some 1939 strikes
have doubling of the word MONTICELLO on the
reverse.

Date	Mintage	VG8	F12	VF20	XF40	MS60	MS65	65FS	Prf65
1938	19,515,365	0.50	0.75	1.00	2.25	7.50	18.00	125	140
1938D	5,376,000	1.00	1.25	1.50	2.00	4.00	25.00	95.00	—
1938S	4,105,000	1.75	2.00	2.50	3.00	5.25	12.00	165	—
1939 T I, wavy steps, Rev. of 1939	120,627,535	—	—	—	—	3.00	30.00	300	125
1939 T II, even steps, Rev. of 1940	Inc. above	—	0.20	0.25	0.30	4.00	45.00	50.00	130
1939 doubled MONTICELLO T II	Inc. above	40.00	60.00	90.00	165	375	1,100	2,000	—
1939D T IT II, wavy steps, Rev. of 1939	3,514,000	—	—	10.00	17.50	75.00	160	275	—
1939D T IIT II, even steps, Rev. of 1940	Inc. above	4.00	5.00	8.00	14.00	35.00	75.00	400	—
1939S T IT I, wavy steps, Rev. of 1939	6,630,000	0.45	0.60	1.50	4.00	17.00	45.00	250	—

5 CENTS

Date	Mintage	VG8	F12	VF20	XF40	MS60	MS65	65FS	Prf65
1939S T IIT II, even steps, Rev. of 1940	Inc. above	—	—	—	5.00	24.00	250	275	—
1940	176,499,158	—	—	—	0.25	1.00	12.00	60.00	125
1940D	43,540,000	—	0.20	0.30	0.40	1.50	2.75	25.00	—
1940S	39,690,000	0.25	0.40	0.50	1.25	4.50	20.00	55.00	—
1941	203,283,720	—	—	—	0.20	0.75	20.00	55.00	90.00
1941D	53,432,000	—	0.20	0.30	0.50	2.25	7.50	25.00	—
1941S	43,445,000	0.25	0.40	0.50	1.35	5.00	14.00	60.00	—
1942	49,818,600	—	—	—	0.40	5.00	22.00	75.00	68.00
1942D	13,938,000	1.00	1.75	3.00	5.00	38.00	65.00	85.00	—
1942D D over horizontal D	Inc. above	35.00	60.00	100	165	1,400	—	25,000	—

Note: Fully Struck Full Step nickels command higher prices. Bright, Fully Struck coins command even higher prices. 1938 thru 1989 - 5 Full Steps. 1990 to date - 6 Full Steps. Without bag marks or nicks on steps.

Monticello, mint mark above.

KM# 192a • 0.350 Copper-Silver-Manganese, 21.2 mm. • **Designer:** Felix Schlag **Note:** War-time composition nickels have the mint mark above MONTICELLO on the reverse.

1943/2P

Date	Mintage	VG8	F12	VF20	XF40	MS60	MS65	65FS	Prf65
1942P	57,900,600	1.87	1.93	2.13	2.00	9.00	20.00	75.00	150
1942S	32,900,000	1.87	1.93	2.13	2.45	8.00	19.00	170	—
1943P	271,165,000	1.87	1.93	2.13	2.00	5.00	20.00	40.00	—
1943P DDO	Inc. above	—	—	32.00	54.00	125	575	1,100	—
1943/2P	Inc. above	35.00	50.00	75.00	110	300	775	1,000	—
1943D	15,294,000	2.12	2.18	2.38	2.05	4.00	18.00	40.00	—
1943S	104,060,000	1.87	1.93	2.13	2.15	6.75	18.50	48.00	—
1944P	119,150,000	1.87	1.93	2.13	2.15	10.00	28.00	75.00	—
1944D	32,309,000	1.92	1.98	2.18	2.25	10.00	22.50	65.00	—
1944S	21,640,000	1.92	1.98	2.18	2.15	8.50	20.00	185	—
1945P	119,408,100	1.87	1.93	2.13	2.15	6.00	28.00	120	—
1945D	37,158,000	1.97	2.03	2.28	2.30	5.50	20.00	40.00	—
1945S	58,939,000	1.87	1.93	2.13	2.15	5.00	18.00	250	—

Note: Fully Struck Full Step nickels command higher prices. Bright, Fully Struck coins command even higher prices. 1938 thru 1989 - 5 Full Steps. 1990 to date - 6 Full Steps. Without bag marks or nicks on steps.

Pre-war design resumed.

KM# A192 • 5.00 g., Copper-Nickel, 21.2 mm. • **Edge:** Plain **Designer:** Felix Schlag

Date	Mintage	XF40	MS65	Prf65
1946	161,116,000	0.25	35.00	—
1946D	45,292,200	0.35	22.00	—
1946D/D	Inc. above	—	1,750	—
1946S	13,560,000	0.40	15.00	—
1947	95,000,000	0.25	18.00	—
1947D	37,822,000	0.30	18.00	—
1947S	24,720,000	0.25	20.00	—
1948	89,348,000	0.25	25.00	—
1948D	44,734,000	0.35	19.00	—
1948S	11,300,000	0.50	15.00	—
1949	60,652,000	0.30	40.00	—
1949D	36,498,000	0.40	18.00	—
1949D/S	Inc. above	65.00	550	—
1949S	9,716,000	0.90	25.00	—
1950	9,847,386	0.75	25.00	75.00
1950D	2,630,030	10.00	28.00	—
1951	28,609,500	0.50	35.00	70.00
1951D	20,460,000	0.50	22.00	—
1951S	7,776,000	1.10	28.00	—
1952	64,069,980	0.25	35.00	42.00
1952D	30,638,000	0.45	30.00	—

Date	Mintage	XF40	MS65	Prf65
1952S	20,572,000	0.25	30.00	—
1953	46,772,800	0.25	26.00	45.00
1953D	59,878,600	0.25	25.00	—
1953S	19,210,900	0.25	35.00	—
1954	47,917,350	—	37.50	20.00
1954D	117,136,560	—	40.00	—
1954S	29,384,000	0.20	35.00	—
1954S/D	Inc. above	20.00	165	—
1955	8,266,200	0.45	25.00	17.00
1955D	74,464,100	—	25.00	—
1955D/S	Inc. above	25.00	300	—
1956	35,885,384	—	16.00	3.00
1956D	67,222,940	—	26.00	—
1957	39,655,952	—	35.00	2.50
1957D	136,828,900	—	22.00	—
1958	17,963,652	0.20	36.00	8.00
1958D	168,249,120	—	13.00	—

Note: Fully Struck Full Step nickels command higher prices. Bright, Fully Struck coins command even higher prices. 1938 thru 1989 - 5 Full Steps. 1990 to date - 6 Full Steps. Without bag marks or nicks on steps.

	Mintage	XF40	MS65	Prf65
1959	28,397,291	—	22.00	1.40
1959D	160,738,240	—	22.00	—
1960	57,107,602	—	30.00	1.25
1960D	192,582,180	—	25.00	—
1961	76,668,244	—	40.00	1.00
1961D	229,342,760	—	35.00	—
1962	100,602,019	—	24.00	1.00
1962D	280,195,720	—	110	—
1963	178,851,645	—	4.00	1.00
1963D	276,829,460	—	100	—
1964	1,028,622,762	—	5.00	1.00
1964D	1,787,297,160	—	12.00	—
1965	136,131,380	—	12.00	—

5 CENTS

Date	Mintage	XF40	MS65	Prf65
1965SMS	2,360,000	—	12.00	—
1966	156,208,283	—	10.00	—
1966SMS	2,261,583	—	15.00	—
1967	107,325,800	—	8.00	—
1967SMS	1,863,344	—	12.00	—
1968 none minted	—	—	—	—
1968D	91,227,880	—	6.00	—
1968S	103,437,510	—	5.00	0.75
1969 none minted	—	—	—	—
1969D	202,807,500	—	5.00	—
1969S	123,099,631	—	7.50	0.75
1970 none minted	—	—	—	—
1970D	515,485,380	—	12.00	—
1970S	241,464,814	—	30.00	0.75
1971	106,884,000	—	9.00	—
1971D	316,144,800	—	4.50	—
1971S	3,220,733	—	—	1.00
1972	202,036,000	—	4.00	—
1972D	351,694,600	—	3.00	—
1972S	3,260,996	—	—	1.00
1973	384,396,000	—	5.00	—
1973D	261,405,000	—	4.00	—
1973S	2,760,339	—	—	0.75
1974	601,752,000	—	12.00	—
1974D	277,373,000	—	5.00	—
1974S	2,612,568	—	—	0.75
1975	181,772,000	—	6.00	—
1975D	401,875,300	—	6.00	—
1975S	2,845,450	—	—	0.75
1976	367,124,000	—	8.00	—
1976D	563,964,147	—	6.00	—
1976S	4,149,730	—	—	0.75
1977	585,376,000	—	8.50	—
1977D	297,313,460	—	6.50	—
1977S	3,251,152	—	—	0.75
1978	391,308,000	—	7.00	—
1978D	313,092,780	—	5.00	—
1978S	3,127,781	—	—	0.75
1979	463,188,000	—	8.50	—
1979D	325,867,672	—	5.50	—
1979S type I, proof	3,677,175	—	—	0.75
1979S type II, proof	—	—	—	2.00
1980P	593,004,000	—	6.50	—
1980D	502,323,448	—	5.50	—
1980S	3,554,806	—	—	0.75
1981P	657,504,000	—	5.00	—
1981D	364,801,843	—	6.00	—
1981S type I, proof	4,063,083	—	—	2.00
1981S type II, proof	—	—	—	2.50
1982P	292,355,000	—	15.00	—
1982D	373,726,544	—	14.00	—
1982S	3,857,479	—	—	1.50
1983P	561,615,000	—	9.00	—
1983D	536,726,276	—	6.00	—
1983S	3,279,126	—	—	1.50
1984P	746,769,000	—	5.00	—
1984D	517,675,146	—	4.75	—
1984S	3,065,110	—	—	1.50
1985P	647,114,962	—	4.75	—
1985D	459,747,446	—	4.75	—
1985S	3,362,821	—	—	1.50
1986P	536,883,483	—	5.00	—
1986D	361,819,140	—	4.75	—
1986S	3,010,497	—	—	3.00
1987P	371,499,481	—	5.00	—
1987D	410,590,604	—	4.50	—
1987S	4,227,728	—	—	1.25
1988P	771,360,000	—	4.50	—
1988D	663,771,652	—	5.00	—
1988S	3,262,948	—	—	1.75
1989P	898,812,000	—	4.50	—
1989D	570,842,474	—	6.00	—
1989S	3,220,194	—	—	1.50
1990P	661,636,000	—	4.50	—
1990D	663,938,503	—	5.50	—
1990S	3,299,559	—	—	1.50
1991P	614,104,000	—	4.50	—

Date	Mintage	XF40	MS65	Prf65
1991D	436,496,678	—	4.50	—
1991S	2,867,787	—	—	1.50
1992P	399,552,000	—	5.00	—
1992D	450,565,113	—	4.00	—
1992S	4,176,560	—	—	1.00
1993P	412,076,000	—	4.00	—
1993D	406,084,135	—	4.00	—
1993S	3,394,792	—	—	1.00
1994P	722,160,000	—	4.00	—
1994P Special	167,703	—	—	—
Uncirculated matte finish				
1994D	715,762,110	—	4.00	—
1994S	3,269,923	—	—	1.00
1995P	774,156,000	—	4.00	—
1995D	888,112,000	—	4.50	—
1995S	2,707,481	—	—	1.50
1996P	829,332,000	—	4.00	—
1996D	817,736,000	—	4.00	—
1996S	2,915,212	—	—	1.50
1997P	470,972,000	—	4.75	—
1997P Special	25,000	—	—	—
Uncirculated matte finish				
1997D	466,640,000	—	4.50	—
1997S	1,975,000	—	—	1.50
1998P	688,272,000	—	3.75	—
1998D	635,360,000	—	3.75	—
1998S	2,957,286	—	—	1.25
1999P	1,212,000,000	—	3.75	—
1999D	1,066,720,000	—	3.75	—
1999S	3,362,462	—	—	1.25
2000P	846,240,000	—	3.75	—
2000D	1,509,520,000	—	3.75	—
2000S	4,063,361	—	—	1.00
2001P	675,704,000	—	3.75	—
2001D	627,680,000	—	3.75	—
2001S	3,099,096	—	—	1.00
2002P	539,280,000	—	3.75	—
2002D	691,200,000	—	3.75	—
2002S	3,157,739	—	—	1.00
2003P	441,840,000	—	3.75	—
2003D	383,040,000	—	3.75	—
2003S	3,116,590	—	—	1.00

Jefferson - Westward Expansion - Lewis & Clark Bicentennial

Jefferson era peace medal design: two clasped hands, pipe and hatchet.

KM# 360 • 5.00 g., Copper-Nickel, 21.2 mm.
• **Obv. Designer:** Felix Schlag **Rev. Designer:** Norman E. Nemeth

Date	Mintage	MS65	Prf65
2004P	361,440,000	1.50	—
2004D	372,000,000	1.50	—
2004S	2,992,069	—	5.00

Lewis and Clark's Keelboat.

KM# 361 • 5.00 g., Copper-Nickel, 21.2 mm. •
Obv. Designer: Felix Schlag **Rev. Designer:** Al Maletsky

Date	Mintage	MS65	Prf65
2004P	366,720,000	1.50	—
2004D	344,880,000	1.50	—
2004S	2,965,422	—	5.00

5 CENTS

Thomas Jefferson large profile right. American Bison right.

KM# 368 • 5.00 g., Copper-Nickel, 21.2 mm. • **Obv. Designer:** Joe Fitzgerald and Don Everhart II **Rev. Designer:** Jamie Franki and Norman E. Nemeth

Date	Mintage	MS65	Prf65
2005P	448,320,000	1.50	—
2005P Satin Finish	1,160,000	4.00	—
2005D	487,680,000	1.50	—
2005D Satin Finish	1,160,000	4.00	—
2005S	3,344,679	—	6.50

Jefferson, large profile. Pacific coastline.

KM# 369 • 5.00 g., Copper-Nickel, 21.2 mm. • **Subject:** Ocean in View!, oh the joy! **Obv. Designer:** Joe Fitzgerald and Don Everhart **Rev. Designer:** Joe Fitzgerald and Donna Weaver

Date	Mintage	MS65	Prf65
2005P	394,080,000	1.25	—
2005P Satin Finish	1,160,000	4.00	—
2005D	411,120,000	1.25	—
2005D Satin Finish	1,160,000	4.00	—
2005S	3,344,679	—	5.50

Jefferson large facing portrait - Enhanced Monticello Reverse

Jefferson head facing. Monticello, enhanced design.

KM# 381 • 5.00 g., Copper-Nickel, 21.2 mm. • **Subject:** Jefferson facing head **Obv. Designer:** Jamie N. Franki and Donna Weaver **Rev. Designer:** Felix Schlag and John Mercanti

Date	Mintage	MS65	Prf65	Date	Mintage	MS65	Prf65
2006P	693,120,000	2.50	—	2011D	540,240,000	1.50	—
2006P Satin finish	847,361	4.00	—	2011S	1,673,010	—	4.00
2006D	809,280,000	2.50	—	2012P	464,640,000	1.50	—
2006D Satin finish	847,361	4.00	—	2012D	558,960,000	1.50	—
2006S	3,054,436	—	5.00	2012S	1,237,415	—	4.00
2007P	571,680,000	2.50	—	2013P	607,440,000	1.50	—
2007P Satin finish	895,628	4.00	—	2013D	615,600,000	1.50	—
2007D	626,160,000	2.50	—	2013S	1,237,926	—	3.00
2007D Satin finish	895,628	4.00	—	2014P	—	1.50	—
2007S	2,577,166	—	4.00	2014D	—	1.50	—
2008P	279,840,000	2.50	—	2014S	—	—	3.00
2008P Satin finish	745,464	4.00	—	2015P	753,092,561	2.50	—
2008D	345,600,000	2.50	—	2015D	846,932,561	2.50	—
2008D Satin finish	745,464	4.00	—	2015S	710,183	—	3.00
2008S	2,169,561	—	4.00	2016P	786,960,000	2.50	—
2009P	39,840,000	3.50	—	2016D	759,600,000	2.50	—
2009P Satin finish	784,614	4.00	—	2016S	—	—	3.00
2009D	46,800,000	1.75	—	2017P	—	2.50	—
2009D Satin finish	784,614	4.00	—	2017D	—	2.50	—
2009S	2,179,867	—	3.00	2017S Enhanced Unc.	225,000	12.00	—
2010P	260,640,000	1.50	—	2017S	—	—	3.00
2010P Satin finish	—	4.00	—	2018P	—	2.50	—
2010D	229,920,000	1.50	—	2018D	—	2.50	—
2010D Satin finish	—	4.00	—	2018S	—	—	3.00
2010S	1,689,216	—	3.00	2018S	—	—	5.00
2011P	450,000,000	1.50	—				

5 CENTS

DIME

Draped Bust Dime

Draped bust right. Small eagle.

KM# 24 • 2.70 g., 0.892 Silver 0.0774 oz. ASW, 19 mm. • **Designer:** Robert Scot

Date	Mintage	G4	VG8	F12	VF20	XF40	MS60
1796	22,135	2,400	3,400	4,500	7,500	8,500	22,000
1797 13 stars	25,261	2,650	3,700	6,500	8,000	16,000	65,000
1797 16 stars	Inc. above	2,650	3,700	4,900	6,750	12,000	38,000

Draped bust right. Heraldic eagle.

KM# 31 • 2.70 g., 0.892 Silver 0.0774 oz. ASW,
19 mm. • **Obv. Legend:** LIBERTY **Rev. Legend:**
UNITED STATES OF AMERICA **Designer:** Robert
Scot **Note:** The 1805 strikes have either 4 or 5
berries on the olive branch held by the eagle.

Date	Mintage	G4	VG8	F12	VF20	XF40	MS60
1798 large 8	27,550	715	900	1,300	2,000	3,300	11,000
1798 small 8	Inc. above	1,325	1,850	3,000	6,000	11,000	50,000
1798/97 13 stars	Inc. above	2,200	4,000	6,000	7,700	11,000	41,000
1798/97 16 stars	Inc. above	825	1,100	1,450	2,200	3,300	6,700

Note: The 1798 overdates have either 13 or 16 stars under the clouds on the reverse; Varieties of the regular 1798 strikes are distinguished by the size of the 8 in the date.

Date	Mintage	G4	VG8	F12	VF20	XF40	MS60
1800	21,760	975	1,225	1,600	2,200	3,600	22,000
1801	34,640	1,000	1,550	1,950	3,250	5,200	43,000
1802	10,975	1,475	2,250	2,425	3,300	5,700	30,000
1803	33,040	1,150	1,600	1,825	2,200	4,500	66,000
1804 13 stars	8,265	3,300	5,500	8,800	14,000	27,000	—
1804 14 stars	Inc. above	4,650	6,300	12,000	23,500	45,000	—
1805 5 berries	Inc. above	625	925	1,450	2,100	2,700	6,500
1805 4 berries	120,780	600	925	1,075	1,650	2,600	5,500
1807	165,000	560	775	1,050	1,425	2,600	5,500

Liberty Cap Dime

Draped bust left, flanked by stars, date below. Eagle with arrows in talons, banner above, value below.

KM# 42 • 2.70 g., 0.892 Silver 0.0774 oz. ASW, 18.8
mm. • **Rev. Legend:** UNITED STATES OF AMERICA
Designer: John Reich **Note:** The 1820 varieties are
distinguished by the size of the 0 in the date. The
1823 overdates have either large E's or small E's in
UNITED STATES OF AMERICA on the reverse.

Date	Mintage	G4	VG8	F12	VF20	XF40	AU50	MS60	MS65
1809	51,065	660	880	1,350	2,400	3,300	4,400	5,500	25,000
1811/9	65,180	200	350	880	1,250	1,650	2,200	3,300	29,000
1814 small date	421,500	100	150	225	350	660	1,025	1,675	22,000
1814 large date	Inc. above	75.00	120	185	270	540	700	1,250	10,500
1814 large date with period	Inc. above	46.00	60.00	85.00	195	500	775	2,000	—
1814 STATESOF	Inc. above	325	550	650	825	1,450	1,800	3,000	24,500
1820 large O	942,587	85.00	125	185	300	600	725	1,300	13,000
1820 small O	Inc. above	50.00	80.00	105	225	525	980	1,650	15,000
1820 STATESOF	Inc. above	225	300	475	650	1,200	2,000	4,000	17,500
1821 large date	1,186,512	80.00	130	185	270	580	825	1,450	16,500
1821 small date	Inc. above	80.00	130	185	270	600	925	2,450	12,000
1822	100,000	2,100	3,000	3,600	6,600	8,800	12,000	18,500	70,000
1823/22 large E's	440,000	50.00	80.00	102	185	450	560	2,300	19,000
1823/22 small E's	Inc. above	125	200	290	450	750	1,000	1,450	18,000
1824/22	—	125	200	250	560	900	1,225	1,650	18,000
1825	510,000	125	200	240	270	600	800	1,425	16,500
1827	1,215,000	125	200	210	270	520	750	1,475	14,000
1827/7	Inc. above	250	—	—	750	1,100	1,500	—	—
1828 large date	125,000	125	200	250	500	925	1,600	3,500	—

Draped bust left, flanked by stars, date below. Eagle with arrows in talons, banner above, value below.

KM# 48 • Silver, 18.5 mm. • **Rev. Legend:** UNITED
STATES OF AMERICA **Designer:** John Reich **Note:**
The three varieties of 1829 strikes and two varieties
of 1830 strikes are distinguished by the size of
"10C." on the reverse. On the 1833 "high 3" variety,
the last 3 in the date is higher thatn the first 3. The
two varieties of the 1834 strikes are distinguished by
the size of the 4 in the date.

Date	Mintage	G4	VG8	F12	VF20	XF40	AU50	MS60	MS65
1828 small date	Inc. above	60.00	80.00	125	200	400	725	1,250	14,000
1829 very large 10C.	770,000	60.00	70.00	100	195	455	700	1,325	—
1829 large 10C.	Inc. above	65.00	85.00	100	160	400	725	1,375	9,400
1829 medium 10C.	Inc. above	37.50	42.00	54.00	85.00	255	525	900	8,500
1829 small 10C.	Inc. above	37.50	42.00	56.00	90.00	270	460	920	8,700

DIME

Date	Mintage	G4	VG8	F12	VF20	XF40	AU50	MS60	MS65
1829 curl base 2	Inc. above	5,800	9,500	16,500	30,000	—	—	—	—
1830 large 10C.	510,000	37.50	46.00	56.00	95.00	255	440	900	8,500
1830 small 10C.	Inc. above	65.00	75.00	100	160	350	500	1,450	13,500
1830/29	Inc. above	50.00	60.00	90.00	150	350	600	1,350	22,000
1831	771,350	30.00	40.00	70.00	95.00	210	350	875	8,250
1832	522,500	30.00	40.00	70.00	95.00	210	350	875	8,250
1833	485,000	30.00	40.00	70.00	95.00	210	350	875	8,250
1833 last 3 high	Inc. above	30.00	40.00	70.00	95.00	210	350	875	8,250
1834 small 4	635,000	30.00	40.00	70.00	95.00	210	350	875	8,250
1834 large 4	Inc. above	30.00	40.00	70.00	95.00	210	350	875	8,250
1835	1,410,000	30.00	40.00	70.00	95.00	210	350	875	8,250
1836	1,190,000	30.00	40.00	70.00	95.00	210	350	875	11,000
1837	1,042,000	30.00	40.00	70.00	95.00	210	350	875	13,500

Seated Liberty Dime
Seated Liberty, date below.
Value within wreath.

KM# 61 • 2.67 g., 0.900 Silver 0.0773 oz. ASW, 17.9 mm. • **Rev. Legend:** UNITED STATES OF AMERICA **Designer:** Christian Gobrecht

Date	Mintage	G4	VG8	F12	VF20	XF40	AU50	MS60	MS65
1837 flat top	Inc. above	45.00	60.00	105	250	550	700	925	6,300
1837 curly top	Inc. above	45.00	65.00	110	285	550	700	925	8,000
1838O	406,034	125	200	250	425	800	950	3,600	24,000

Seated Liberty, stars around top 1/2 of border, date below. Value within wreath.

KM# 63.1 • 2.67 g., 0.900 Silver 0.0773 oz. ASW, 17.9 mm. • **Obv. Designer:** Christian Gobrecht **Rev. Legend:** UNITED STATES OF AMERICA **Note:** The 1839-O with reverse of 1838-O variety was struck from rusted dies, it has a bumpy reverse surface.

No drapery at elbow

Date	Mintage	G4	VG8	F12	VF20	XF40	AU50	MS60	MS65
1838 small stars	1,992,500	30.00	45.00	60.00	85.00	180	320	600	4,000
1838 large stars	Inc. above	22.00	30.00	40.00	60.00	150	315	450	2,500
1838 partial drapery	Inc. above	25.00	40.00	75.00	140	215	325	505	—
1839	1,053,115	14.00	28.00	35.00	55.00	145	310	400	2,500
1839O	1,323,000	30.00	50.00	70.00	135	240	400	725	7,500
1839O reverse 1838O	Inc. above	155	200	325	500	1,000	—	—	—
1840	1,358,580	14.00	17.00	25.00	40.00	120	300	350	3,000
1840O	1,175,000	60.00	85.00	125	200	500	1,125	7,000	40,000

KM# 63.2 • 2.67 g., 0.900 Silver 0.0773 oz. ASW, 17.9 mm. • **Rev. Legend:** UNITED STATES OF AMERICA **Designer:** Christian Gobrecht **Note:** Drapery added to Liberty's left elbow

Drapery at elbow

Date	Mintage	G4	VG8	F12	VF20	XF40	AU50	MS60	MS65
1840	Inc. above	90.00	125	175	300	750	1,225	2,700	27,000
1841	1,622,500	24.00	26.00	28.00	34.00	55.00	155	425	4,000
1841O	2,007,500	28.00	40.00	50.00	100	175	350	800	8,500
1841O large O	Inc. above	500	800	1,100	2,325	—	—	—	—
1842	1,887,500	20.00	25.00	28.00	32.00	48.00	145	350	3,500
1842O	2,020,000	30.00	50.00	70.00	200	425	860	3,500	15,000
1843	1,370,000	18.00	25.00	28.00	34.00	50.00	145	475	4,500
1843/1843	Inc. above	18.00	30.00	35.00	50.00	75.00	200	300	—
1843O	150,000	175	350	495	1,000	2,650	10,000	65,000	—
1844	72,500	185	300	385	625	1,000	1,900	4,000	24,500
1845	1,755,000	24.00	26.00	28.00	36.00	50.00	175	425	1,985
1845/1845	Inc. above	24.00	27.00	29.00	55.00	90.00	185	—	—
1845O	230,000	100	155	240	500	900	2,685	11,000	—
1846	31,300	200	375	600	1,075	2,200	7,000	18,000	—

Date	Mintage	G4	VG8	F12	VF20	XF40	AU50	MS60	MS65
1847	245,000	24.00	35.00	38.00	60.00	200	425	1,400	8,300
1848	451,500	26.00	29.00	33.00	55.00	95.00	165	700	4,500
1849	839,000	25.00	27.00	30.00	40.00	70.00	175	350	2,000
1849O	300,000	30.00	35.00	70.00	135	350	900	2,100	8,000
1850	1,931,500	15.00	17.00	20.00	65.00	80.00	175	295	4,000
1850O	510,000	30.00	45.00	75.00	125	300	800	1,725	7,800
1851	1,026,500	25.00	27.00	29.00	40.00	75.00	215	400	4,000
1851O	400,000	30.00	34.00	47.00	125	300	875	2,200	16,000
1852	1,535,500	18.00	21.00	26.00	33.00	55.00	145	275	2,350
1852O	430,000	32.00	50.00	100	200	350	550	2,100	—
1853	95,000	140	200	325	500	650	775	950	2,500

Seated Liberty, stars around top 1/2 of border, arrows at date. Value within wreath.

KM# 77 • 2.49 g., 0.900 Silver 0.072 oz. ASW
Rev. Legend: UNITED STATES OF AMERICA
Designer: Christian Gobrecht

Date	Mintage	G4	VG8	F12	VF20	XF40	AU50	MS60	MS65	Prf65
1853	12,078,010	18.00	22.00	28.00	35.00	55.00	140	350	1,500	—
1853O	1,100,000	23.00	45.00	100	125	285	650	2,400	—	—
1854	4,470,000	22.00	23.00	24.00	30.00	60.00	145	325	1,500	18,000
1854O	1,770,000	23.00	27.00	30.00	40.00	80.00	200	425	5,000	—
1855	2,075,000	21.00	22.00	24.00	35.00	55.00	145	325	2,375	22,750

Seated Liberty, stars around top 1/2 of border, date below. Value within wreath.

KM# A6.3.2 • 2.49 g., 0.900 Silver 0.072 oz. ASW
Rev. Legend: UNITED STATES OF AMERICA
Designer: Christian Gobrecht

Date	Mintage	G4	VG8	F12	VF20	XF40	AU50	MS60	MS65	Prf65
1856 small date	5,780,000	22.00	23.00	24.00	35.00	58.00	140	275	2,000	9,750
1856 large date	Inc. above	45.00	60.00	100	135	200	300	625	7,700	—
1856O	1,180,000	24.00	50.00	60.00	100	160	350	750	5,500	—
1856S	70,000	250	400	600	1,100	1,500	2,150	7,000	—	—
1857	5,580,000	22.00	23.00	24.00	35.00	48.00	145	275	1,650	5,500
1857O	1,540,000	23.00	25.00	30.00	32.00	57.00	165	375	2,200	—
1858	1,540,000	22.00	23.00	24.00	30.00	52.00	145	275	1,650	3,800
1858O	290,000	23.00	27.00	39.00	75.00	175	350	800	8,000	—
1858S	60,000	150	225	350	750	1,200	1,800	7,000	25,500	—
1859	430,000	23.00	26.00	27.00	36.00	57.00	165	275	2,000	2,500
1859O	480,000	25.00	28.00	33.00	38.00	80.00	225	330	—	—
1859S	60,000	200	300	500	950	2,650	6,000	16,000	85,000	—
1860S	140,000	75.00	100	165	325	600	900	2,000	42,300	—

UNITED STATES OF AMERICA replaced stars. Value within wreath.

KM# 92 • 2.49 g., 0.900 Silver 0.072 oz. ASW
Obv. Legend: UNITED STATES OF AMERICA
Obv. Designer: Christian Gobrecht **Note:** The 1873 "closed-3" and "open-3" varieties are distinguished by the amount of space between the upper left and lower left serifs of the 3 in the date.

Date	Mintage	G4	VG8	F12	VF20	XF40	AU50	MS60	MS65	Prf65
1860	607,000	23.00	25.00	26.00	35.00	40.00	85.00	200	1,050	1,500
1860O	40,000	550	750	1,400	2,000	4,250	8,000	16,500	—	—
1861	1,884,000	22.00	23.00	24.00	27.00	35.00	80.00	175	1,050	1,450
1861S	172,500	160	275	450	650	850	1,150	6,000	—	—
1862	847,550	24.00	25.00	27.00	30.00	45.00	80.00	180	1,000	1,500
1862S	180,750	160	250	325	600	950	2,300	3,800	35,000	—
1863	14,460	600	850	900	950	1,075	1,200	1,300	—	1,200
1863S	157,500	125	175	300	450	800	1,100	3,200	32,000	—
1864	11,470	275	450	600	800	900	1,025	1,200	—	1,550
1864S	230,000	125	150	250	350	700	900	1,200	—	—
1865	10,500	400	600	750	850	950	1,050	1,200	—	1,800
1865S	175,000	125	200	350	650	1,700	2,600	6,600	—	—
1866	8,725	660	775	875	975	1,125	1,325	1,600	—	1,550
1866S	135,000	125	200	275	425	900	1,400	3,200	—	—
1867	6,625	550	725	825	930	990	1,275	1,400	—	1,200
1867S	140,000	125	180	250	375	650	1,375	2,000	9,500	—
1868	464,000	25.00	27.00	34.00	45.00	70.00	145	275	2,950	1,250
1868S	260,000	75.00	100	150	250	500	600	900	5,000	—

DIME

Date	Mintage	G4	VG8	F12	VF20	XF40	AU50	MS60	MS65	Prf65
1869	256,600	28.00	31.00	43.00	85.00	155	200	375	2,900	1,100
1869S	450,000	25.00	27.00	30.00	38.00	250	325	500	3,600	—
1870	471,000	22.00	23.00	24.00	27.00	50.00	100	250	2,300	1,300
1870S	50,000	300	350	600	750	900	1,025	1,375	7,000	—
1871	907,710	18.00	20.00	30.00	36.00	45.00	130	260	—	1,100
1871CC	20,100	2,450	4,000	5,250	8,000	10,750	23,000	40,000	—	—
1871S	320,000	29.00	75.00	125	200	350	725	1,400	12,000	—
1872	2,396,450	20.00	22.00	23.00	26.00	40.00	75.00	160	—	1,100
1872CC	35,480	900	1,200	2,375	3,375	11,000	17,500	73,000	—	—
1872S	190,000	26.00	75.00	125	175	325	500	1,700	—	—
1873 closed 3	1,568,600	18.00	21.00	45.00	60.00	80.00	125	250	1,300	1,100
1873 open 3	Inc. above	26.00	34.00	60.00	80.00	150	275	775	12,000	—
1873CC	12,400	—	—	—	—	—	—	—	—	—

Note: 1873-CC, Heritage Sale, April 1999, MS-64, $632,500.

Seated Liberty, arrows at date.
Value within wreath.

KM# 105 • 2.50 g., 0.900 Silver 0.0723 oz. ASW
Obv. Legend: UNITED STATES OF AMERICA
Designer: Christian Gobrecht

Date	Mintage	G4	VG8	F12	VF20	XF40	AU50	MS60	MS65	Prf65
1873	2,378,500	24.00	27.00	32.00	63.00	175	300	450	4,500	3,500
1873CC	18,791	2,900	3,150	3,500	7,500	13,000	38,500	63,000	—	—
1873S	455,000	16.00	19.00	30.00	60.00	160	470	800	7,500	—
1874	2,940,700	16.00	19.00	25.00	40.00	130	275	350	3,450	4,100
1874CC	10,817	6,000	8,500	12,000	17,000	28,000	50,000	70,000	—	—
1874S	240,000	26.00	40.00	64.00	100	210	420	800	—	—

Seated Liberty, date below.
Value within wreath.

KM# A92 • 2.50 g., 0.900 Silver 0.0723 oz. ASW
Obv. Legend: UNITED STATES OF AMERICA
Designer: Christian Gobrecht **Note:** On the 1876-CC doubled-obverse variety, doubling appears in the words OF AMERICA in the legend.

Date	Mintage	G4	VG8	F12	VF20	XF40	AU50	MS60	MS65	Prf65
1875	10,350,700	13.00	21.00	22.00	25.00	35.00	75.00	175	600	1,100
1875CC mint mark in wreath	4,645,000	33.00	36.00	38.00	60.00	83.00	190	360	2,600	—
1875CC mint mark under wreath	Inc. above	24.00	26.00	28.00	46.00	68.00	185	360	3,600	—
1875S mint mark in wreath	9,070,000	22.00	23.00	24.00	27.00	40.00	85.00	225	1,850	—
1875S mint mark under wreath	Inc. above	22.00	23.00	24.00	27.00	40.00	80.00	175	900	—
1876 Type 1 rev	11,461,150	12.00	13.00	14.00	26.00	28.00	75.00	175	750	1,100
1876 Type 2 rev	Inc. above	25.00	30.00	35.00	45.00	65.00	145	205	—	—
1876CC Type 1 rev	8,270,000	33.00	36.00	38.00	56.00	80.00	175	300	—	—
1876CC Type 2 rev	Inc. above	40.00	44.00	55.00	75.00	140	155	275	—	—
1876CC doubled die obverse	Inc. above	35.00	40.00	55.00	100	185	340	600	—	—
1876S Type 1 rev	10,420,000	21.00	22.00	24.00	27.00	35.00	85.00	175	1,400	—
1876S Type 2 rev	Inc. above	28.00	30.00	32.00	41.00	50.00	100	190	—	—
1877 Type 1 rev	7,310,510	20.00	22.00	23.00	26.00	35.00	80.00	170	725	1,000
1877 Type 2 rev	Inc. above	26.00	32.00	40.00	50.00	60.00	110	170	—	—
1877CC Type 1 rev	7,700,000	30.00	36.00	38.00	53.00	130	185	300	1,995	—
1877CC Type 2 rev	Inc. above	38.00	40.00	50.00	72.00	90.00	125	210	—	—
1877S Type 1 rev	2,340,000	—	—	—	—	—	—	—	—	—
1877S Type 2 rev	Inc. above	20.00	22.00	23.00	27.00	40.00	80.00	175	—	—
1878 Type 1 rev	1,678,800	22.00	30.00	40.00	55.00	85.00	150	—	—	—
1878 Type 2 rev	Inc. above	21.00	22.00	23.00	26.00	40.00	80.00	175	1,000	1,100
1878CC Type 1 rev	200,000	145	170	225	350	600	800	—	—	—
1878CC Type 2 rev	Inc. above	225	250	325	400	500	850	1,300	4,000	—
1879	15,100	225	250	290	300	400	485	575	1,000	1,100
1880	37,335	160	210	275	310	400	450	550	1,200	1,100
1881	24,975	175	230	270	325	400	475	550	1,575	1,100
1882	3,911,100	20.00	22.00	23.00	26.00	35.00	80.00	170	650	1,100
1883	7,675,712	20.00	22.00	23.00	26.00	35.00	80.00	170	550	1,100
1884	3,366,380	20.00	22.00	23.00	26.00	35.00	80.00	170	615	1,100
1884S	564,969	26.00	28.00	35.00	55.00	105	270	600	4,800	—
1885	2,533,427	20.00	22.00	23.00	26.00	35.00	80.00	165	625	1,100
1885S	43,690	575	890	1,000	1,225	2,200	4,000	5,500	—	—
1886	6,377,570	10.00	12.00	14.00	26.00	35.00	80.00	165	595	1,100
1886S	206,524	29.00	45.00	55.00	80.00	110	175	475	—	—
1887	11,283,939	10.00	12.00	13.00	17.00	35.00	80.00	165	625	1,100
1887S	4,454,450	13.00	14.00	23.00	26.00	30.00	80.00	165	550	—
1888	5,496,487	20.00	22.00	23.00	26.00	35.00	80.00	165	550	1,100

Date	Mintage	G4	VG8	F12	VF20	XF40	AU50	MS60	MS65	Prf65
1888S	1,720,000	20.00	22.00	23.00	26.00	35.00	95.00	325	3,350	—
1889	7,380,711	20.00	22.00	23.00	26.00	35.00	80.00	165	550	1,100
1889S	972,678	23.00	25.00	28.00	46.00	75.00	155	325	4,500	—
1890	9,911,541	21.00	22.00	23.00	26.00	40.00	80.00	175	715	1,100
1890S	1,423,076	22.00	23.00	28.00	45.00	75.00	140	225	1,400	—
1891	15,310,600	13.00	13.00	14.00	25.00	40.00	80.00	175	560	1,100
1891O	4,540,000	20.00	23.00	30.00	32.00	40.00	80.00	175	1,050	1,100
1891O /horizontal O	Inc. above	65.00	95.00	125	175	225	400	—	—	—
1891S	3,196,116	14.00	23.00	24.00	27.00	40.00	80.00	175	825	—
1891S/S	Inc. above	25.00	30.00	40.00	85.00	135	250	—	—	—

Barber Dime
Laureate head right, date at angle below. Value within wreath.
KM# **113** • 2.50 g., 0.900 Silver 0.0723 oz. ASW, 17.9 mm. • **Obv. Legend:** UNITED STATES OF AMERICA **Designer:** Charles E. Barber

Date	Mintage	G4	VG8	F12	VF20	XF40	AU50	MS60	MS65	Prf65
1892	12,121,245	10.00	11.00	19.00	24.00	30.00	65.00	105	450	1,000
1892O	3,841,700	8.00	17.00	35.00	56.00	70.00	85.00	135	1,225	—
1892S	990,710	60.00	92.00	185	215	235	270	340	2,800	—
1893/2	3,340,792	130	160	195	235	330	550	1,300	5,200	—
1893	Inc. above	8.00	12.00	17.00	28.00	40.00	66.00	130	775	1,000
1893O	1,760,000	25.00	37.00	110	140	165	200	265	1,950	—
1893S	2,491,401	10.50	16.00	42.00	50.00	85.00	130	315	1,800	—
1894	1,330,972	17.00	38.00	125	140	190	225	265	1,125	1,200
1894O	720,000	65.00	100	200	325	370	675	1,850	11,025	—
1894S	24	—	—	—	—	—	—	—	—	1,700,000

Note: 1894S, Eliasberg Sale, May 1996, Prf-64, $451,000.

Date	Mintage	G4	VG8	F12	VF20	XF40	AU50	MS60	MS65	Prf65
1895	690,880	145	185	370	495	570	650	840	1,900	1,000
1895O	440,000	440	550	825	1,300	2,175	2,585	5,850	33,000	—
1895S	1,120,000	42.00	54.00	125	180	205	270	450	3,150	—
1896	2,000,762	9.25	23.00	56.00	75.00	91.00	100	145	1,025	1,000
1896O	610,000	70.00	160	300	320	450	675	1,100	7,800	—
1896S	575,056	72.00	190	240	285	335	440	675	2,900	—
1897	10,869,264	3.00	4.00	7.00	16.00	35.00	74.00	120	425	1,000
1897O	666,000	75.00	120	280	360	440	550	1,000	2,950	—
1897S	1,342,844	18.00	30.00	75.00	135	180	250	470	2,800	—
1898	16,320,735	4.00	5.00	8.00	15.00	20.00	72.00	120	425	1,000
1898O	2,130,000	12.00	30.00	100	150	195	290	450	3,000	—
1898S	1,702,507	8.00	18.00	34.00	50.00	100	140	450	2,050	—
1899	19,580,846	3.75	4.50	7.00	11.00	20.00	72.00	120	425	1,000
1899O	2,650,000	8.00	18.00	70.00	100	145	200	350	3,700	—
1899S	1,867,493	7.00	16.00	38.00	40.00	48.00	95.00	320	2,100	—
1900	17,600,912	2.75	3.05	3.50	10.00	20.00	72.00	120	500	1,100
1900O	2,010,000	14.00	34.00	120	155	245	295	550	3,300	—
1900S	5,168,270	2.75	3.05	14.00	24.00	33.00	70.00	175	1,350	—
1901	18,860,478	2.75	3.05	3.50	10.00	20.00	72.00	120	475	1,000
1901O	5,620,000	4.00	6.00	14.00	26.00	85.00	185	560	1,800	—
1901S	593,022	350	440	490	535	600	1,000	1,420	3,320	—
1902	21,380,777	4.00	6.00	7.00	9.00	20.00	72.00	120	575	1,000
1902O	4,500,000	4.00	6.00	14.00	35.00	65.00	175	400	3,300	—
1902S	2,070,000	11.00	25.00	56.00	85.00	135	185	380	3,125	—
1903	19,500,755	2.75	3.05	3.50	7.50	20.00	72.00	140	800	1,000
1903O	8,180,000	3.75	4.50	16.00	23.00	51.00	95.00	205	2,875	—
1903S	613,300	85.00	120	315	400	510	850	925	2,400	—
1904	14,601,027	2.75	3.05	3.50	7.50	20.00	72.00	120	750	1,000
1904S	800,000	45.00	60.00	145	205	280	450	800	3,600	—
1905	14,552,350	2.75	3.05	3.50	10.00	20.00	72.00	120	550	1,000
1905O	3,400,000	4.00	8.00	36.00	54.00	100	135	275	1,120	—
1905O micro O	Inc. above	50.00	70.00	110	300	700	1,050	2,325	8,800	—
1905S	6,855,199	3.00	5.00	9.00	22.00	43.00	100	190	900	—
1906	19,958,406	2.75	3.05	3.55	7.50	20.00	72.00	120	475	1,000
1906D	4,060,000	2.75	3.05	3.55	18.00	20.00	70.00	145	900	—
1906O	2,610,000	6.00	15.00	50.00	74.00	95.00	125	200	975	—
1906S	3,136,640	2.75	4.05	15.00	23.00	48.00	135	250	800	—
1907	22,220,575	2.75	3.05	3.55	7.50	20.00	72.00	120	420	1,000
1907D	4,080,000	2.75	3.05	14.00	20.00	43.00	105	240	1,500	—
1907O	5,058,000	2.75	6.75	42.00	55.00	65.00	95.00	195	1,025	—
1907S	3,178,470	2.75	3.05	18.00	29.00	65.00	175	340	1,750	—
1908	10,600,545	2.75	3.05	3.55	7.50	20.00	72.00	120	500	1,000
1908D	7,490,000	2.75	3.05	3.55	16.00	34.00	65.00	125	620	—
1908O	1,789,000	4.25	14.00	47.00	65.00	90.00	135	260	800	—
1908S	3,220,000	4.00	5.25	12.00	24.00	48.00	155	285	1,100	—
1909	10,240,650	2.75	3.05	3.55	7.50	20.00	72.00	120	450	1,000

DIME

Date	Mintage	G4	VG8	F12	VF20	XF40	AU50	MS60	MS65	Prf65
1909D	954,000	7.00	19.00	60.00	95.00	135	200	440	1,800	—
1909O	2,287,000	2.75	7.75	11.75	24.00	60.00	170	275	1,425	—
1909S	1,000,000	11.00	22.00	83.00	125	190	280	490	2,100	—
1910	11,520,551	2.75	3.05	3.55	7.50	20.00	72.00	120	450	1,000
1910D	3,490,000	2.75	2.75	11.00	20.00	48.00	100	195	1,275	—
1910S	1,240,000	6.00	13.00	52.00	75.00	105	200	370	1,700	—
1911	18,870,543	2.75	8.05	8.55	9.50	20.00	72.00	120	450	1,000
1911D	11,209,000	2.75	3.05	3.55	9.50	20.00	72.00	120	450	—
1911S	3,520,000	3.50	5.00	8.00	25.00	40.00	105	200	800	—
1912	19,350,700	2.75	3.05	3.55	7.50	20.00	72.00	120	470	1,000
1912D	11,760,000	2.75	3.05	3.55	7.50	20.00	72.00	120	450	—
1912S	3,420,000	2.75	3.05	3.55	13.00	35.00	85.00	165	975	—
1913	19,760,622	2.75	3.05	3.55	7.50	20.00	72.00	120	450	975
1913S	510,000	35.00	65.00	125	185	220	300	600	2,625	—
1914	17,360,655	2.75	3.05	3.55	7.00	20.00	72.00	120	415	1,000
1914D	11,908,000	2.75	5.75	8.75	11.75	20.00	72.00	120	465	—
1914S	2,100,000	2.75	5.25	6.75	21.00	45.00	80.00	130	1,000	—
1915	5,620,450	2.75	3.05	3.55	7.00	20.00	72.00	120	450	1,000
1915S	960,000	7.00	11.00	35.00	50.00	75.00	125	205	1,300	—
1916	18,490,000	2.75	3.05	3.55	8.35	20.00	72.00	120	465	—
1916S	5,820,000	2.75	3.05	3.55	8.35	20.00	72.00	120	450	—

Mercury Dime

KM# 140 • 2.50 g., 0.900 Silver 0.0723 oz. ASW, 17.8 mm. • **Designer:** Adolph A. Weinman
Note: All specimens listed as -65FSB are for fully struck MS-65 coins with fully split and rounded horizontal bands on the fasces.

Mint mark

Full split bands

Date	Mintage	G4	VG8	F12	VF20	XF40	AU50	MS60	MS63	MS65	65FSB
1916	22,180,080	2.50	3.50	6.00	7.50	10.50	22.50	40.00	58.00	105	165
1916D	264,000	825	1,275	2,300	3,300	5,300	8,250	11,250	17,750	24,000	48,500
1916S	10,450,000	3.00	3.50	6.50	7.85	12.00	19.00	21.00	89.00	200	800
1917	55,230,000	—	3.50	6.50	7.00	8.50	9.50	10.50	55.00	170	375
1917D	9,402,000	—	3.50	6.50	12.00	19.00	46.00	77.00	255	925	5,650
1917S	27,330,000	—	3.50	6.50	7.00	18.00	30.00	85.00	165	400	1,265
1918	26,680,000	—	3.50	6.50	7.00	10.00	28.00	37.00	140	355	1,325
1918D	22,674,800	—	3.50	6.50	7.00	11.00	26.00	38.00	250	680	27,500
1918S	19,300,000	—	3.50	6.50	7.00	9.00	20.00	32.00	230	700	7,450
1919	35,740,000	—	3.50	6.50	7.00	8.50	9.00	20.00	170	325	685
1919D	9,939,000	—	3.50	6.50	11.00	24.00	38.00	195	525	1,200	38,500
1919S	8,850,000	—	3.50	6.50	10.00	45.00	85.00	260	575	1,400	14,350
1920	59,030,000	—	3.50	6.50	7.00	8.50	9.50	13.00	105	240	540
1920D	19,171,000	—	3.50	6.50	7.00	8.00	20.00	37.00	305	600	4,750
1920S	13,820,000	—	3.50	6.50	9.00	9.00	17.00	34.00	370	11,225	8,250
1921	1,230,000	28.00	40.00	115	290	430	700	1,140	2,025	2,900	4,350
1921D	1,080,000	40.00	150	200	375	600	975	1,400	2,200	3,645	5,200
1923	50,130,000	—	3.50	6.50	7.00	8.50	9.50	11.00	60.00	350	340
1923S	6,440,000	—	3.50	6.50	19.00	70.00	63.00	200	410	1,200	7,450
1924	24,010,000	—	3.50	6.50	7.00	8.50	11.00	22.00	95.00	181	500
1924D	6,810,000	—	3.50	6.50	8.00	20.00	60.00	85.00	425	900	1,365
1924S	7,120,000	—	3.50	6.50	25.00	50.00	92.00	270	525	1,495	16,750
1925	25,610,000	—	3.50	6.50	7.00	8.50	9.50	14.00	75.00	275	990
1925D	5,117,000	—	3.00	4.50	11.00	42.00	110	157	660	1,520	3,500
1925S	5,850,000	—	3.00	18.00	30.00	80.00	105	200	550	1,050	4,650
1926	32,160,000	—	3.50	6.50	7.00	8.50	9.50	10.50	50.00	205	525
1926D	6,828,000	—	3.50	6.50	18.00	32.00	44.00	160	280	500	2,500
1926S	1,520,000	7.50	10.00	45.00	70.00	240	400	1,150	1,700	3,300	6,750
1927	28,080,000	—	3.50	6.50	7.00	8.50	9.50	10.50	51.00	145	350
1927D	4,812,000	—	3.50	6.50	8.50	24.00	77.00	102	350	1,015	8,500
1927S	4,770,000	—	3.50	6.50	18.00	35.00	50.00	265	600	1,200	7,600
1928	19,480,000	—	3.50	6.50	7.00	8.50	9.50	14.00	55.00	135	345
1928D	4,161,000	—	3.50	6.50	11.50	24.00	52.00	87.00	385	750	2,750
1928S Large S	7,400,000	—	3.50	6.50	7.00	7.00	16.50	31.00	340	600	6,500

DIME

Date	Mintage	G4	VG8	F12	VF20	XF40	AU50	MS60	MS63	MS65	65FSB
1928S Small S	Inc. above	—	3.50	6.50	7.00	9.50	17.00	41.00	360	440	2,000
1929	25,970,000	—	3.50	6.50	7.00	8.50	9.50	10.00	35.00	72.00	175
1929D	5,034,000	—	3.50	6.50	7.00	10.50	13.50	17.00	32.00	73.00	225
1929S	4,730,000	—	3.50	6.50	7.00	9.50	11.50	16.00	40.00	125	560
1929S Doubled Die Obv	Inc. above	—	8.00	11.00	16.00	25.00	40.00	60.00	150	335	1,150
1930	6,770,000	—	3.50	6.50	7.00	9.50	11.50	11.00	45.00	115	575
1930S	1,843,000	—	3.50	6.50	7.00	8.50	15.00	36.00	140	195	685
1931	3,150,000	—	3.50	6.50	7.00	8.50	10.00	17.50	73.00	150	800
1931D	1,260,000	4.75	6.75	8.00	13.00	18.00	42.50	45.00	135	500	375
1931 Doubled Die Obv & Rev	Inc. above	—	—	20.00	27.50	50.00	70.00	90.00	225	485	650
1931S	1,800,000	—	3.50	6.50	8.00	9.00	20.00	36.00	140	280	2,500
1931S Doubled Die Obv	Inc. above	—	7.50	10.00	13.00	25.00	35.00	60.00	220	425	3,850
1934	24,080,000	—	3.00	3.30	3.80	4.10	5.60	10.00	36.00	53.00	130
1934D	6,772,000	—	3.00	3.30	3.80	7.50	14.00	18.00	56.00	80.00	320
1935	58,830,000	—	3.00	3.30	3.80	4.10	5.60	6.00	19.00	32.00	68.00
1935D	10,477,000	—	3.00	3.30	3.80	6.50	7.00	14.00	45.00	85.00	500
1935S	15,840,000	—	3.00	3.30	3.80	4.10	5.60	14.00	30.00	37.00	360
1936	87,504,130	—	3.00	3.30	3.80	4.10	5.60	6.00	17.00	28.00	84.00
1936 Doubled Die Obv	Inc. above	—	—	—	8.00	15.00	25.00	35.00	105	165	—
1936D	16,132,000	—	3.00	3.30	3.80	4.10	8.50	17.00	38.00	55.00	290
1936S	9,210,000	—	3.00	3.30	3.80	4.10	5.60	9.00	32.00	36.00	88.00
1937	56,865,756	—	3.00	3.30	3.80	4.10	5.60	6.00	12.00	25.00	52.00
1937 Doubled Die Obv	Inc. above	—	—	—	—	6.00	9.00	12.00	50.00	105	175
1937D	14,146,000	—	3.00	3.30	3.80	4.10	5.60	7.00	28.00	40.00	105
1937S	9,740,000	—	3.00	3.30	3.80	4.10	5.60	9.00	26.00	33.00	190
1937S Doubled Die Obv	Inc. above	—	—	—	—	5.00	8.00	12.00	55.00	135	275
1938	22,198,728	—	3.00	3.30	3.80	4.10	5.60	6.00	15.00	28.00	80.00
1938D	5,537,000	—	3.00	3.30	3.80	4.10	5.60	6.00	21.00	32.00	62.00
1938S	8,090,000	—	3.00	3.30	3.80	4.10	5.60	9.00	29.00	40.00	160
1939	67,749,321	—	3.00	3.30	3.80	4.10	5.60	6.00	10.00	28.00	170
1939 Doubled Die Obv	Inc. above	—	—	—	—	4.00	6.00	8.00	30.00	45.00	450
1939D	24,394,000	—	3.00	3.30	3.80	4.10	5.60	6.00	10.00	28.00	49.00
1939S	10,540,000	—	3.00	7.30	7.80	8.10	9.60	8.00	30.00	37.00	765
1940	65,361,827	—	3.00	3.30	3.80	4.10	5.60	6.00	11.00	30.00	48.00
1940D	21,198,000	—	3.00	3.30	3.80	4.10	5.60	6.00	13.00	32.00	48.00
1940S	21,560,000	—	3.00	3.30	3.80	4.10	5.60	6.00	12.00	32.00	95.00
1941	175,106,557	—	3.00	3.30	3.80	4.10	5.60	6.00	10.00	30.00	46.00
1941 Doubled Die Obv	Inc. above	—	—	—	—	10.00	16.00	30.00	105	175	295
1941D	45,634,000	—	3.00	3.30	3.80	4.10	5.60	6.00	15.00	24.00	46.00
1941D Doubled Die Obv	Inc. above	—	—	—	—	9.00	14.00	20.00	72.00	135	250
1941S Small S	43,090,000	—	3.00	3.30	3.80	4.10	5.60	6.00	11.00	30.00	46.00
1941S Large S	Inc. above	—	4.00	5.00	8.00	15.00	25.00	60.00	160	265	425
1941S Doubled Die Rev	Inc. above	—	4.00	4.50	5.00	5.50	6.00	7.50	30.00	70.00	85.00
1942	205,432,329	—	3.00	3.30	3.80	4.10	5.60	6.00	11.00	24.00	46.00
1942/41	Inc. above	290	325	365	420	485	800	2,400	4,100	12,000	35,000
1942D	60,740,000	—	3.00	3.30	3.80	4.10	5.60	6.00	16.00	27.00	46.00
1942/41D	Inc. above	275	310	315	350	370	490	790	5,050	12,000	26,500
1942S	49,300,000	—	3.00	3.30	3.80	4.10	5.60	6.00	21.00	26.00	145
1943	191,710,000	—	3.00	3.30	3.80	4.10	5.60	6.00	11.00	28.00	50.00
1943D	71,949,000	—	3.00	3.30	3.80	4.10	5.60	6.00	17.00	28.00	47.00
1943S	60,400,000	—	3.00	3.30	3.80	4.10	5.60	6.00	16.00	27.00	66.00
1944	231,410,000	—	3.00	3.30	3.80	4.10	5.60	6.00	10.00	25.00	75.00
1944D	62,224,000	—	3.00	3.30	3.80	4.10	5.60	6.00	17.00	25.00	46.00
1944S	49,490,000	—	3.00	3.30	3.80	4.10	5.60	6.00	19.00	30.00	50.00
1945	159,130,000	—	3.00	3.30	3.80	4.10	5.60	6.00	10.00	26.00	97.50
1945D	40,245,000	—	3.00	3.30	3.80	4.10	5.60	6.00	13.00	26.00	46.50
1945S	41,920,000	—	3.00	3.30	3.80	4.10	5.60	6.00	15.00	26.00	105
1945S micro S	Inc. above	3.25	4.00	6.00	9.00	13.00	20.00	30.00	38.00	110	685

DIME

Roosevelt Dime

KM# 195 • 2.50 g., 0.900 Silver 0.0723 oz. ASW, 17.9 mm. • **Designer:** John R. Sinnock

Mint mark 1946-64

Date	Mintage	G4	VG8	F12	VF20	XF40	AU50	MS60	MS65	Prf65
1946	225,250,000	—	—	—	—	3.00	3.30	3.80	5.00	—
1946D	61,043,500	—	—	—	—	3.00	3.30	3.80	5.00	—
1946S	27,900,000	—	—	—	—	3.00	3.30	3.80	5.00	—
1947	121,520,000	—	—	—	—	3.00	3.30	3.80	12.00	—
1947D	46,835,000	—	—	—	—	3.00	3.30	4.00	16.00	—
1947S	34,840,000	—	—	—	—	3.00	3.30	3.50	12.00	—

Date	Mintage	G4	VG8	F12	VF20	XF40	AU50	MS60	MS65	Prf65
1948	74,950,000	—	—	—	—	3.00	3.30	3.25	10.00	—
1948D	52,841,000	—	—	—	—	3.00	3.30	5.00	14.00	—
1948S	35,520,000	—	—	—	—	3.00	3.30	4.50	15.00	—
1949	30,940,000	—	—	3.00	3.30	5.00	8.50	12.00	25.00	—
1949D	26,034,000	—	—	3.00	3.30	5.00	5.50	7.00	20.00	—
1949S	13,510,000	—	—	3.00	3.30	8.00	15.00	35.00	60.00	—
1950	50,181,500	—	—	—	3.30	3.60	5.30	6.00	12.00	60.00
1950D	46,803,000	—	—	—	—	—	1.63	3.25	10.00	—
1950S	20,440,000	—	—	3.00	3.30	5.00	9.00	23.00	35.00	—
1951	102,937,602	—	—	—	—	—	3.00	3.30	13.00	60.00
1951D	56,529,000	—	—	—	—	—	1.73	2.80	12.00	—
1951S	31,630,000	—	—	—	3.00	3.30	5.00	10.00	18.00	—
1952	99,122,073	—	—	—	—	—	3.00	3.30	20.00	45.00
1952D	122,100,000	—	—	—	—	—	3.00	3.30	10.00	—
1952S	44,419,500	—	—	—	3.00	3.30	5.00	5.50	16.00	—
1953	53,618,920	—	—	—	—	—	3.00	3.30	12.00	40.00
1953D	136,433,000	—	—	—	—	—	3.00	3.30	11.00	—
1953S	39,180,000	—	—	—	—	—	3.70	3.00	12.50	—
1954	114,243,503	—	—	—	—	—	3.00	3.30	10.00	24.00
1954D	106,397,000	—	—	—	—	—	3.00	3.30	15.00	—
1954S	22,860,000	—	—	—	—	—	3.00	3.30	10.00	—
1955	12,828,381	—	—	—	3.00	3.30	3.80	4.10	8.50	20.00
1955D	13,959,000	—	—	—	3.00	3.30	3.80	4.10	8.50	—
1955S	18,510,000	—	—	—	3.00	3.30	3.80	4.10	8.00	—
1956	109,309,384	—	—	—	—	—	3.00	3.30	9.50	12.00
1956D	108,015,100	—	—	—	—	—	3.00	3.30	9.00	—
1957	161,407,952	—	—	—	—	—	3.00	3.30	8.50	10.00
1957D	113,354,330	—	—	—	—	—	3.00	3.30	7.50	—
1958	32,785,652	—	—	—	—	—	3.00	3.30	11.00	10.00
1958D	136,564,600	—	—	—	—	—	3.00	3.30	10.00	—
1959	86,929,291	—	—	—	—	—	3.00	3.30	8.00	10.00
1959D	164,919,790	—	—	—	—	—	3.00	3.30	8.50	—
1960	72,081,602	—	—	—	—	—	3.00	3.30	8.50	10.00
1960D	200,160,400	—	—	—	—	—	3.00	3.30	7.50	—
1961	96,758,244	—	—	—	—	—	3.00	3.30	8.00	10.00
1961D	209,146,550	—	—	—	—	—	3.00	3.30	6.50	—
1962	75,668,019	—	—	—	—	—	3.00	3.30	6.50	10.00
1962D	334,948,380	—	—	—	—	—	3.00	3.30	7.00	—
1963	126,725,645	—	—	—	—	—	3.00	3.30	7.50	10.00
1963D	421,476,530	—	—	—	—	—	3.00	3.30	7.00	—
1964	933,310,762	—	—	—	—	—	3.00	3.30	7.50	10.00
1964D	1,357,517,180	—	—	—	—	—	3.00	3.30	7.00	—

KM# 195a • 2.27 g., Copper-Nickel Clad Copper, 17.91 mm. • **Designer:** John R. Sinnock **Note:** The 1979-S and 1981-S Type II proofs have clearer mint marks than the Type I proofs of those years. On the 1982 no-mint-mark variety, the mint mark was inadvertently left off.

Mint mark 1968- present   1982 No mint mark

Date	Mintage	MS65	Prf65
1965	1,652,140,570	6.00	—
1965SMS	—	2.00	—
1966	1,382,734,540	6.50	—
1966SMS	—	2.25	—
1967	2,244,007,320	7.00	—
1967SMS	—	3.50	—
1968	424,470,000	6.50	—
1968D	480,748,280	6.50	—
1968S	3,041,506	—	4.00
1968 no S error	—	—	7,500
1969	145,790,000	7.00	—
1969D	563,323,870	6.00	—
1969S	2,934,631	—	4.00
1970	345,570,000	5.50	—
1970D	754,942,100	5.00	—
1970S	2,632,810	—	4.00
1970S No S	—	—	1,300
1971	162,690,000	10.00	—
1971D	377,914,240	8.00	—

Date	Mintage	MS65	Prf65
1971S	3,220,733	—	4.00
1972	431,540,000	7.50	—
1972D	330,290,000	8.50	—
1972S	3,260,996	—	4.00
1973	315,670,000	6.00	—
1973D	455,032,426	5.50	—
1973S	2,760,339	—	4.00
1974	470,248,000	5.50	—
1974D	571,083,000	4.50	—
1974S	2,612,568	—	4.00
1975	585,673,900	4.50	—
1975D	313,705,300	4.50	—
1975S	2,845,450	—	4.00
1976	568,760,000	4.50	—
1976D	695,222,774	4.50	—
1976S	4,149,730	—	4.00
1977	796,930,000	4.50	—
1977D	376,607,228	8.00	—
1977S	3,251,152	—	4.00
1978	663,980,000	5.00	—
1978D	282,847,540	4.50	—
1978S	3,127,781	—	4.00
1979	315,440,000	5.50	—
1979D	390,921,184	5.00	—
1979S type I	3,677,175	—	5.00
1979S type II	—	—	2.00
1980P	735,170,000	6.00	—
1980D	719,354,321	5.00	—
1980S	3,554,806	—	4.00
1981P	676,650,000	4.00	—
1981D	712,284,143	4.00	—
1981S type I	—	—	4.00
1981S type II	—	—	6.50

DIME

Date	Mintage	MS65	Prf65
1982P	519,475,000	8.50	—
1982 no mint mark	Inc. above	200	—
1982D	542,713,584	3.20	—
1982S	3,857,479	—	4.00
1983P	647,025,000	6.00	—
1983D	730,129,224	4.00	—
1983S	3,279,126	—	4.00
1984P	856,669,000	4.00	—
1984D	704,803,976	3.50	—
1984S	3,065,110	—	4.00
1985P	705,200,962	5.00	—
1985D	587,979,970	3.50	—
1985S	3,362,821	—	4.00
1986P	682,649,693	3.50	—
1986D	473,326,970	3.50	—
1986S	3,010,497	—	4.00
1987P	762,709,481	4.50	—
1987D	653,203,402	4.50	—
1987S	4,227,728	—	4.00
1988P	1,030,550,000	5.50	—
1988D	962,385,488	5.50	—
1988S	3,262,948	—	3.00
1989P	1,298,400,000	4.00	—
1989D	896,535,597	5.00	—
1989S	3,220,194	—	4.00
1990P	1,034,340,000	4.50	—
1990D	839,995,824	5.50	—
1990S	3,299,559	—	4.00
1991P	927,220,000	5.00	—
1991D	601,241,114	5.00	—
1991S	2,867,787	—	3.00
1992P	593,500,000	4.50	—
1992D	616,273,932	4.50	—
1992S	2,858,981	—	4.00
1993P	766,180,000	3.50	—
1993D	750,110,166	4.50	—
1993S	2,633,439	—	7.00
1994P	1,189,000,000	4.00	—
1994D	1,303,268,110	5.50	—
1994S	2,484,594	—	5.00
1995P	1,125,500,000	4.00	—
1995D	1,274,890,000	4.50	—
1995S	2,010,384	—	20.00
1996P	1,421,163,000	3.00	—
1996D	1,400,300,000	5.00	—
1996W	1,457,949	24.00	—
1996S	2,085,191	—	3.50
1997P	991,640,000	4.00	—
1997D	979,810,000	3.00	—
1997S	1,975,000	—	14.00
1998P	1,163,000,000	2.75	—
1998D	1,172,250,000	2.75	—
1998S	2,078,494	—	4.00
1999P	2,164,000,000	2.75	—
1999D	1,397,750,000	2.75	—
1999S	2,557,897	—	4.00
2000P	1,842,500,000	2.75	—
2000D	1,818,700,000	2.75	—
2000S	3,097,440	—	1.00
2001P	1,369,590,000	2.75	—
2001D	1,412,800,000	2.75	—
2001S	2,249,496	—	3.75
2002P	1,187,500,000	2.75	—
2002D	1,379,500,000	3.00	—
2002S	2,268,913	—	2.50
2003P	1,085,500,000	3.00	—
2003D	986,500,000	3.00	—
2003S	2,076,165	—	2.60
2004P	1,328,000,000	3.00	—
2004D	1,159,500,000	3.00	—
2004S	1,804,396	—	4.75
2005P	1,412,000,000	2.75	—
2005P Satin Finish	—	4.00	—
2005D	1,423,500,000	2.75	—
2005D Satin Finish	—	4.00	—
2005S	2,275,000	—	2.60
2006P	1,381,000,000	2.50	—
2006P Satin Finish	—	4.00	—
2006D	1,447,000,000	2.50	—
2006D Satin Finish	—	4.00	—
2006S	2,000,428	—	2.50
2007P	1,047,500,000	2.00	—
2007P Satin Finish	—	3.00	—
2007D	1,042,000,000	2.00	—
2007D Satin Finish	—	3.00	—
2007S	1,702,116	—	2.50
2008P	391,000,000	1.25	—
2008 Satin Finish	—	2.50	—
2008D	624,500,000	1.25	—
2008D Satin Finish	—	2.50	—
2008S	1,405,674	—	2.50
2009P	96,500,000	1.25	—
2009P Satin Finish	—	1.00	—
2009D	49,500,000	1.25	—
2009D Satin Finish	—	1.00	—
2009S	1,482,502	—	2.50
2010P	557,000,000	4.00	—
2010P Satin Finish	—	2.00	—
2010D	562,000,000	4.00	—
2010D Satin Finish	—	2.00	—
2010S	1,103,815	—	2.50
2011P	748,000,000	4.00	—
2011D	754,000,000	4.00	—
2011S	1,098,835	—	2.50
2012P	808,000,000	4.00	—
2012D	868,000,000	4.00	—
2012S	841,972	—	2.50
2013P	1,086,500,000	4.00	—
2013D	1,025,500,000	4.00	—
2013S	821,031	—	2.50
2014P	1,125,845,813	2.00	—
2014D	1,177,345,813	2.00	—
2014S	764,641	—	2.50
2015P	1,543,712,561	2.00	—
2015D	1,497,722,561	2.00	—
2015S	462,393	—	2.50
2016P	1,517,000,000	2.00	—
2016D	1,437,000,000	2.00	—
2016S	—	—	2.50
2017P	—	2.00	—
2017D	—	2.00	—
2017S Enhanced Unc.	225,000	12.00	—
2017S	—	—	2.50

KM# 195b • 2.50 g., 0.900 Silver 0.0723 oz. ASW, 17.9 mm. • **Designer:** John R. Sinnock

Date	Mintage	Prf65
1992S	1,317,579	5.00
1993S	761,353	7.00
1994S	785,329	7.00
1995S	838,953	8.00
1996S	830,021	7.00
1997S	821,678	14.00
1998S	878,792	7.00
1999S	804,565	7.00
1999S	1,317,579	7.00
1999S	761,353	7.00
1999S	785,329	7.00
1999S	838,953	7.00
2000S	965,921	5.50
2001S	849,600	5.00
2002S	888,826	5.00
2003S	1,090,425	4.75
2004S	1,175,934	5.00
2005S	1,069,679	5.00
2006S	1,054,008	4.50
2007S	875,050	6.00
2008S	763,887	6.50
2009S	697,365	6.75
2010S	585,401	6.75
2011S	574,175	6.75
2012S	395,443	6.75
2013S	821,031	6.75
2014S	467,074	6.75

DIME

Date	Mintage	Prf65	Date	Mintage	Prf65
2015P	74,430	10.00	2016S	—	6.75
Note: Available only in March of Dimes silver set.			2017S	—	6.75
2015W	74,430	10.00	2018S Reverse	—	9.00
Note: Available only in March of Dimes silver set.			Proof		
2015S	247,790	6.75	2018S	—	6.75

20 CENTS

Seated Liberty within circle of stars, date below. Eagle with arrows in talons, value below.

KM# 109 • 5.00 g., 0.900 Silver 0.1447 oz. ASW, 22 mm. • Rev. Legend: UNITED STATES OF AMERICA Designer: William Barber

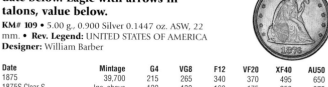

Date	Mintage	G4	VG8	F12	VF20	XF40	AU50	MS60	MS65	Prf65
1875	39,700	215	265	340	370	495	650	875	4,400	7,700
1875S Clear S	Inc. above	120	130	160	175	250	375	650	2,700	—
1875S	1,155,000	85.00	100	130	145	250	375	650	2,500	—
Note: 1875-S exists as a branch mint proof										
1875S over horizontal S	Inc. above	105	140	160	200	235	375	550	4,500	—
Note: Also known as filled S										
1875S as	Inc. above	—	150	170	190	230	280	365	1,250	—
1875CC	133,290	280	300	400	450	715	1,075	2,200	9,300	—
1876	15,900	210	260	330	450	525	625	1,000	5,200	7,000
1876CC	10,000	—	—	—	—	—	160,000	220,000	585,000	—
1877 proof only	510	—	—	—	—	4,100	4,600	—	—	7,700
1878 proof only	600	—	—	—	—	2,400	2,700	—	—	8,000

QUARTER

Draped Bust Quarter
Draped bust right. Small eagle.

KM# 25 • 6.74 g., 0.892 Silver 0.1933 oz. ASW, 27.5 mm. • Designer: Robert Scot

Date	Mintage	G4	VG8	F12	VF20	XF40	AU50	MS60	MS65
1796	6,146	10,750	16,000	22,000	30,000	49,750	60,000	70,000	375,000

Draped bust right, flanked by stars, date at angle below. Heraldic eagle.

KM# 36 • 6.74 g., 0.892 Silver 0.1933 oz. ASW, 27.5 mm. • Obv. Legend: LIBERTY Rev. Legend: UNITED STATES OF AMERICA Designer: Robert Scot

Date	Mintage	G4	VG8	F12	VF20	XF40	AU50	MS60	MS65
1804	6,738	4,000	6,500	8,500	14,000	30,000	48,000	95,000	360,000
1805	121,394	375	600	1,250	1,650	3,500	5,000	11,000	84,000
1806/5	206,124	375	650	1,365	1,550	4,100	6,000	14,000	100,000
1806	Inc. above	375	600	1,040	1,650	3,500	5,000	11,000	84,000
1807	220,643	375	600	935	1,650	3,500	5,000	11,000	84,000

DIME

Liberty Cap Quarter

Draped bust left, flanked by stars, date below. Eagle with arrows in talons, banner above, value below.

KM# 44 • 6.74 g., 0.892 Silver 0.1933 oz. ASW, 27 mm. • **Rev. Legend:** UNITED STATES OF AMERICA **Designer:** John Reich **Note:** Varieties of the 1819 strikes are distinguished by the size of the 9 in the date. Varieties of the 1820 strikes are distinguished by the size of the 0 in the date. One 1822 variety and one 1828 variety have "25" engraved over "50" in the denomination. The 1827 restrikes were produced privately using dies sold as scrap by the U.S. Mint.

Date	Mintage	G4	VG8	F12	VF20	XF40	AU50	MS60	MS65
1815	89,235	130	360	500	700	950	1,500	4,000	24,000
1818/15	361,174	110	200	375	650	1,600	1,700	4,000	24,000
1818	Inc. above	110	150	255	300	1,500	1,700	4,000	24,000
1819 small 9	144,000	110	150	255	300	1,500	1,700	4,000	30,000
1819 large 9	Inc. above	110	150	255	300	1,500	1,700	4,000	45,000
1820 small 0	127,444	110	150	255	300	1,500	1,700	6,000	30,000
1820 large 0	Inc. above	110	150	255	300	1,500	1,700	4,000	40,000
1821	216,851	110	150	255	300	1,500	1,700	3,600	24,000
1822	64,080	255	425	600	950	1,100	2,250	5,700	—
1822 25/50C.	Inc. above	6,000	11,500	18,000	26,000	35,000	45,000	55,000	—
1823/22	17,800	50,000	60,000	80,000	100,000	125,000	175,000	275,000	—
1824/2	—	800	1,225	2,250	2,650	4,750	8,500	23,000	—
1825/22	168,000	525	700	1,050	1,450	4,500	7,200	15,000	—
1825/23	Inc. above	160	220	350	500	1,500	1,700	3,500	28,000
1825/24	Inc. above	150	220	300	530	1,500	1,700	3,400	30,000
1827 original curl base 2	4,000	—	—	—	100,000	—	—	140,000	550,000
1827 restrike, square base 2	Inc. above	—	—	—	—	—	—	—	85,000
1828	102,000	140	200	325	700	1,500	1,800	4,000	25,000
1828 25/50C.	Inc. above	1,000	1,700	2,250	3,600	7,500	11,500	17,000	—

Draped bust left, flanked by stars, date below. Eagle with arrows in talons, value below.

KM# 55 • 0.892 Silver, 24.3 mm. • **Rev. Legend:** UNITED STATES OF AMERICA **Designer:** William Kneass **Note:** Varieties of the 1831 strikes are distinguished by the size of the lettering on the reverse.

Date	Mintage	G4	VG8	F12	VF20	XF40	AU50	MS60	MS65
1831 small letter rev.	398,000	80.00	115	130	160	300	475	1,750	19,000
1831 large letter rev.	Inc. above	80.00	115	130	160	300	475	1,750	28,000
1832	320,000	80.00	115	130	160	300	475	1,750	19,000
1833	156,000	80.00	115	130	160	300	475	1,750	19,000
1834	286,000	80.00	115	130	160	300	475	1,750	19,000
1834 No period after C	Inc. above	160	220	260	310	600	900	1,850	28,500
1834 0 over 0	Inc. above	—	—	—	—	—	—	—	—
1835	1,952,000	80.00	115	130	160	250	475	1,750	25,000
1836	472,000	80.00	115	130	160	250	475	1,750	45,500
1837	252,400	80.00	115	130	160	250	475	1,750	19,000
1838	832,000	80.00	115	130	160	250	475	1,750	23,000

Seated Liberty Quarter

Seated Liberty, stars around top 1/2 of border, date below. Eagle with arrows in talons, value below.

KM# 64.1 • 6.68 g., 0.900 Silver 0.1933 oz. ASW, 24.3 mm. • **Rev. Legend:** UNITED STATES OF AMERICA **Designer:** Christian Gobrecht

Date	Mintage	G4	VG8	F12	VF20	XF40	AU50	MS60	MS65
1838	Inc. above	30.00	35.00	48.00	160	400	700	1,410	33,000
1839	491,146	28.00	35.00	45.00	160	350	650	1,410	36,000
18400	425,200	35.00	45.00	60.00	165	350	900	2,000	28,500

Drapery added to Liberty's left elbow, stars around top 1/2 of border. Eagle with arrows in talons, value below.

KM# 64.2 • 6.68 g., 0.900 Silver 0.1933 oz. ASW, 24.3 mm. • **Rev. Legend:** UNITED STATES OF AMERICA **Designer:** Christian Gobrecht

Date	Mintage	G4	VG8	F12	VF20	XF40	AU50	MS60	MS65
1840	188,127	31.00	35.00	60.00	150	310	560	1,575	17,000
18400	Inc. above	40.00	48.00	100	175	300	475	1,275	17,000
1841	120,000	56.00	85.00	120	230	385	710	1,125	6,500
18410	452,000	40.00	45.00	55.00	170	265	375	900	9,000
1842 small date	88,000	—	—	—	—	—	—	—	—
1842 large date	Inc. above	60.00	78.00	130	230	350	660	1,625	11,000
18420 small date	769,000	575	1,000	1,400	2,500	6,650	11,000	27,000	—
18420 large date	Inc. above	40.00	45.00	60.00	125	275	500	1,300	—
1843	645,600	30.00	35.00	45.00	75.00	100	210	590	4,100
18430	968,000	40.00	70.00	140	330	1,100	1,350	2,000	17,000
1844	421,200	38.00	40.00	45.00	55.00	80.00	250	660	11,250
18440	740,000	40.00	45.00	60.00	80.00	200	425	1,200	10,200
1845	922,000	30.00	35.00	40.00	60.00	105	185	600	4,950
1846	510,000	46.00	57.00	67.00	88.00	250	375	700	5,000
1847	734,000	20.00	30.00	35.00	45.00	60.00	185	500	5,000
18470	368,000	125	175	325	700	920	1,350	7,500	—
1848	146,000	30.00	60.00	100	140	300	500	1,050	9,800
1849	340,000	20.00	25.00	30.00	80.00	125	270	900	8,600
18490	—	1,100	1,400	2,300	3,000	6,700	8,000	17,000	—
1850	190,800	32.00	46.00	105	160	275	600	1,300	10,750
18500	412,000	40.00	105	175	210	475	800	1,400	12,500
1851	160,000	60.00	90.00	150	300	450	900	1,100	6,000
18510	88,000	400	650	800	1,000	2,300	3,000	6,000	—
1852	177,060	65.00	100	150	250	450	660	1,025	4,600
18520	96,000	200	275	700	1,350	1,900	6,000	10,000	—
1853 recut date	44,200	1,500	2,000	2,700	3,400	4,000	4,950	6,500	10,600

Seated Liberty, arrows at date. Rays around eagle.

KM# 78 • 6.22 g., 0.900 Silver 0.180 oz. ASW, 24.3 mm. • **Rev. Legend:** UNITED STATES OF AMERICA **Designer:** Christian Gobrecht

Date	Mintage	G4	VG8	F12	VF20	XF40	AU50	MS60	MS65	Prf65
1853	15,210,020	20.00	26.00	38.00	45.00	95.00	295	900	10,000	85,000
1853/4	Inc. above	60.00	100	150	300	450	700	1,500	33,000	—
18530	1,332,000	40.00	60.00	100	150	475	1,000	4,000	22,000	—

Seated Liberty, arrows at date. Eagle with arrows in talons, value below.

KM# 81 • 6.22 g., 0.900 Silver 0.180 oz. ASW, 24.3 mm. • **Rev. Legend:** UNITED STATES OF AMERICA **Designer:** Christian Gobrecht

Date	Mintage	G4	VG8	F12	VF20	XF40	AU50	MS60	MS65	Prf65
1854	12,380,000	30.00	33.00	40.00	42.00	82.00	135	625	5,100	24,000
18540	1,484,000	37.00	45.00	50.00	55.00	125	300	900	15,000	—
18540 huge O	Inc. above	650	1,390	1,625	1,900	4,500	13,500	—	—	—
1855	2,857,000	30.00	35.00	40.00	45.00	85.00	150	600	9,000	23,500
18550	176,000	110	165	300	500	775	1,750	2,600	—	—
1855S	396,400	100	150	250	400	800	1,100	2,000	23,000	—

QUARTER

Seated Liberty, date below. Eagle with arrows in talons, value below.

KM# A64.2 • 6.22 g., 0.900 Silver 0.180 oz. ASW, 24.3 mm. • **Rev. Legend:** UNITED STATES OF AMERICA **Designer:** Christian Gobrecht

Date	Mintage	G4	VG8	F12	VF20	XF40	AU50	MS60	MS65	Prf65
1856	7,264,000	21.00	35.00	40.00	45.00	70.00	105	375	2,530	11,000
1856O	968,000	37.00	45.00	80.00	130	270	475	850	12,000	—
1856S	286,000	230	280	490	675	1,600	2,250	7,500	38,000	—
1856S/S	Inc. above	500	800	1,100	1,850	8,000	11,000	33,000	—	—
1857	9,644,000	20.00	25.00	30.00	50.00	75.00	100	325	2,530	10,000
1857O	1,180,000	27.00	35.00	95.00	120	150	350	1,100	—	—
1857S	82,000	180	290	380	650	975	1,600	3,600	—	—
1858	7,368,000	20.00	25.00	32.00	50.00	75.00	135	350	2,530	5,000
1858O	520,000	37.00	45.00	75.00	125	275	725	3,500	22,000	—
1858S	121,000	250	375	575	840	2,400	4,400	25,000	—	—
1859	1,344,000	30.00	35.00	40.00	50.00	80.00	200	400	3,800	4,500
1859O	260,000	60.00	80.00	110	160	300	1,000	2,450	22,000	—
1859S	80,000	450	600	950	1,400	4,000	12,000	48,000	—	—
1860	805,400	20.00	25.00	40.00	80.00	110	185	480	4,600	3,500
1860O	388,000	37.00	45.00	50.00	100	225	350	850	12,000	—
1860S	56,000	1,000	1,375	2,900	4,860	9,000	14,250	55,000	—	—
1861	4,854,600	21.00	35.00	40.00	45.00	63.00	180	325	2,475	4,500
1861S	96,000	600	800	1,250	1,500	2,100	11,000	33,000	—	—
1862	932,550	27.00	35.00	40.00	48.00	85.00	180	400	2,900	3,500
1862S	67,000	200	300	500	600	1,250	2,400	4,600		—
1863	192,060	40.00	48.00	60.00	125	285	425	625	3,750	3,500
1864	94,070	150	225	300	400	500	800	1,300	6,000	3,500
1864S	20,000	800	1,000	1,300	1,625	4,000	5,700	11,000	—	—
1865	59,300	70.00	80.00	180	350	500	700	1,275	13,000	4,150
1865S	41,000	200	300	375	650	1,000	1,150	3,500	17,500	—
1866 unique	—	—	—	—	—	—	—	—	—	—

Seated Liberty, date below. In God We Trust above eagle.

KM# 98 • 6.22 g., 0.900 Silver 0.180 oz. ASW, 24.3 mm. • **Rev. Legend:** UNITED STATES OF AMERICA **Designer:** Christian Gobrecht **Note:** The 1873 closed-3 and open-3 varieties are distinguished by the amount of space between the upper left and lower left serifs in the 3.

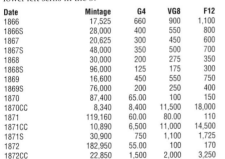

Date	Mintage	G4	VG8	F12	VF20	XF40	AU50	MS60	MS65	Prf65
1866	17,525	660	900	1,100	1,250	1,400	1,550	2,075	8,000	1,900
1866S	28,000	400	550	800	1,200	1,500	2,100	4,500	—	—
1867	20,625	300	450	600	880	1,350	1,700	2,500	—	1,750
1867S	48,000	350	500	700	1,100	2,100	7,800	10,000	—	—
1868	30,000	200	275	350	450	700	950	1,600	7,800	1,890
1868S	96,000	125	175	300	675	800	1,300	—	15,000	—
1869	16,600	450	550	750	850	1,025	1,300	1,775	9,000	2,300
1869S	76,000	200	250	400	600	1,100	1,500	400	7,000	—
1870	87,400	65.00	100	150	250	400	600	900	5,200	2,100
1870CC	8,340	8,400	11,500	18,000	23,500	37,000	85,000	220,000	—	—
1871	119,160	60.00	80.00	110	160	300	400	675	6,500	2,300
1871CC	10,890	6,500	11,000	14,500	19,000	33,000	65,000	125,000	—	—
1871S	30,900	750	1,100	1,725	2,800	4,000	5,000	6,250	19,000	—
1872	182,950	55.00	100	170	275	425	650	1,350	6,500	2,300
1872CC	22,850	1,500	2,000	3,250	6,500	12,000	18,000	55,000	—	—
1872S	83,000	1,800	2,100	3,000	3,700	4,600	6,000	8,500	35,000	—
1873 closed 3	212,600	350	550	850	1,200	3,300	4,400	22,000	—	2,000
1873 open 3	Inc. above	100	125	175	265	345	580	1,100	5,600	—
1873CC 6 known	4,000	—	—	—	—	70,000	80,000	150,000	—	—

Note: 1873CC, Heritage, April 1999, MS-62, $106,375.

Seated Liberty, arrows at date. In God We Trust above eagle.

KM# 106 • 6.25 g., 0.900 Silver 0.1808 oz. ASW, 24.3 mm. • Rev. Legend: UNITED STATES OF AMERICA Designer: Christian Gobrecht

Date	Mintage	G4	VG8	F12	VF20	XF40	AU50	MS60	MS65	Prf65
1873	1,271,700	29.00	35.00	40.00	65.00	190	400	800	3,200	5,500
1873CC	12,462	4,600	8,500	11,500	17,000	24,000	45,000	85,000	165,000	—
1873S	156,000	88.00	117	165	220	350	475	1,600	14,500	—
1874	471,900	21.00	35.00	45.00	75.00	200	400	800	3,300	5,500
1874S	392,000	33.00	38.00	52.00	100	250	425	800	3,500	—

Seated Liberty, date below. In God We Trust above eagle.

KM# A98 • 6.25 g., 0.900 Silver 0.1808 oz. ASW, 24.3 mm. • Rev. Legend: UNITED STATES OF AMERICA Designer: Christian Gobrecht Note: The 1876-CC fine-reeding variety has a more finely reeded edge.

Date	Mintage	G4	VG8	F12	VF20	XF40	AU50	MS60	MS65	Prf65
1875	4,293,500	30.00	33.00	35.00	46.00	73.00	165	275	1,500	1,900
1875CC	140,000	200	300	700	840	1,150	1,600	3,500	22,000	—
1875S	680,000	34.00	44.00	65.00	125	150	235	600	3,000	—
1876	17,817,150	24.00	26.00	30.00	47.00	52.00	80.00	110	1,750	1,900
1876CC Ty1 rev. sm wide CC	4,944,000	55.00	75.00	120	160	250	350	500	3,950	—
1876CC Ty1 rev. sm close CC	Inc. above	50.00	70.00	115	140	180	300	500	3,950	—
1876CC Ty1 rev. tall CC	Inc. above	50.00	70.00	115	140	200	300	500	3,950	—
1876CC Ty2 rev. sm CC	Inc. above	50.00	70.00	115	140	200	300	500	3,950	—
1876CC Ty2 rev tall CC	Inc. above	55.00	75.00	120	160	250	350	500	3,950	—
1876S	8,596,000	20.00	23.00	32.00	40.00	52.00	110	275	1,700	—
1877	10,911,710	22.00	29.00	35.00	42.00	52.00	110	275	1,300	1,600
1877CC	4,192,000	47.00	70.00	100	125	200	285	500	2,050	—
1877S	8,996,000	20.00	33.00	35.00	42.00	52.00	110	275	1,500	—
1877S over horizontal S	Inc. above	41.00	62.00	90.00	200	300	500	825	3,400	—
1878	2,260,800	30.00	33.00	35.00	42.00	52.00	110	275	1,950	1,600
1878CC	996,000	65.00	75.00	85.00	125	250	375	825	—	—
1878S	140,000	200	300	500	750	1,000	1,350	2,400	—	—
1879	14,700	150	210	275	400	450	550	650	1,900	1,500
1880	14,955	150	210	275	400	450	550	650	2,100	1,600
1881	12,975	150	210	275	400	450	550	650	1,900	1,600
1882	16,300	150	210	275	400	450	550	650	1,900	1,600
1883	15,439	150	210	275	400	450	550	650	2,300	1,600
1884	8,875	225	300	350	400	500	550	650	2,000	1,600
1885	14,530	150	210	275	400	450	550	675	2,200	1,600
1886	5,886	300	350	450	525	700	850	1,000	2,300	1,600
1887	10,710	200	250	325	400	550	625	850	2,300	1,600
1888	10,833	200	250	325	400	550	575	650	2,250	1,600
1888S	1,216,000	32.00	36.00	39.00	50.00	70.00	200	350	3,000	—
1889	12,711	175	210	275	325	400	475	700	1,800	1,600
1890	80,590	125	150	175	250	275	350	500	1,900	1,600
1891	3,920,600	20.00	30.00	35.00	42.00	70.00	110	275	1,300	1,600
1891O	68,000	350	500	880	1,300	2,200	3,500	6,500	25,000	—
1891S	2,216,000	25.00	28.00	32.00	43.00	68.00	160	275	1,675	—

Barber Quarter

Laureate head right, flanked by stars, date below. Heraldic eagle.

KM# 114 • 6.25 g., 0.900 Silver 0.1808 oz. ASW, 24.3 mm. • Obv. Legend: IN GOD WE TRUST Rev. Legend: UNITED STATES OF AMERICA Designer: Charles E. Barber

Date	Mintage	G4	VG8	F12	VF20	XF40	AU50	MS60	MS65	Prf65
1892	8,237,245	9.00	10.00	22.00	39.00	63.00	110	220	800	1,300
1892 Type 2 Rev	Inc. above	10.00	12.00	25.00	44.00	70.00	130	250	1,125	1,500
1892O	2,640,000	13.00	19.00	38.00	55.00	88.00	135	300	1,425	—
1892O Type 2 Rev	Inc. above	15.00	23.50	44.00	61.00	98.00	155	340	1,600	—
1892S	964,079	60.00	85.00	105	145	200	330	550	4,000	—
1892S Type 2 Rev	Inc. above	28.00	53.00	82.00	125	175	275	525	3,600	—

Date	Mintage	G4	VG8	F12	VF20	XF40	AU50	MS60	MS65	Prf65
1893	5,484,838	9.00	11.00	25.00	45.00	55.00	110	220	1,250	1,300
1893O	3,396,000	9.00	13.00	27.00	52.00	100	150	325	1,300	—
1893O MM far right	Inc. above	11.50	15.50	30.00	58.00	118	170	245	1,760	—
1893S	1,454,535	16.00	33.00	59.00	110	165	330	385	—	—
1893S MM far right	Inc. above	20.00	38.00	65.00	125	190	320	435	3,875	—
1894	3,432,972	10.00	11.00	27.00	32.00	77.00	125	220	960	1,300
1894O	2,852,000	10.00	16.00	38.00	72.00	120	185	275	1,500	—
1894O MM far right	Inc. above	12.00	18.00	42.00	81.00	138	190	270	1,450	—
1894S	2,648,821	10.00	16.00	38.00	72.00	120	185	275	—	—
1894S MM far right	Inc. above	10.00	13.00	34.50	71.00	115	190	295	1,775	—
1895	4,440,880	10.00	11.00	25.00	33.00	65.00	115	220	1,300	1,300
1895O	2,816,000	10.00	17.00	38.00	66.00	120	230	325	—	—
1895O MM far right	Inc. above	9.00	16.00	36.00	60.00	110	175	300	1,600	—
1895S	1,764,681	16.00	31.00	66.00	110	160	245	355	—	—
1895S MM far right	Inc. above	15.00	27.00	62.00	100	120	210	315	3,000	—
1896	3,874,762	10.00	11.00	20.00	35.00	72.00	115	220	800	1,050
1896O	1,484,000	54.00	95.00	175	425	550	880	1,050	7,000	—
1896S	188,039	700	1,600	2,000	3,550	4,800	6,250	10,000	45,000	—
1897	8,140,731	10.00	11.00	18.00	27.00	60.00	90.00	245	800	1,450
1897O	1,414,800	38.00	95.00	175	340	375	615	800	2,475	—
1897S	542,229	125	275	600	720	895	1,415	1,800	6,450	—
1898	11,100,735	10.00	11.00	19.00	30.00	63.00	90.00	245	800	1,450
1898O	1,868,000	13.00	25.00	66.00	130	250	440	880	6,100	—
1898S	1,020,592	10.00	16.00	44.00	60.00	140	330	980	5,800	—
1899	12,624,846	10.00	11.00	19.00	45.00	63.00	90.00	245	800	1,450
1899O	2,644,000	11.00	19.00	33.00	60.00	120	250	440	2,100	—
1899S	708,000	26.00	55.00	93.00	105	130	330	1,100	4,300	—
1900	10,016,912	11.00	12.00	20.00	31.00	63.00	115	230	1,150	1,450
1900O	3,416,000	13.00	25.00	60.00	105	150	375	725	3,000	—
1900S	1,858,585	10.00	12.00	31.00	44.00	65.00	200	650	2,475	—
1901	8,892,813	25.00	30.00	40.00	53.00	60.00	115	275	875	1,450
1901O	1,612,000	55.00	75.00	185	400	750	1,200	1,725	6,600	—
1901S	72,664	3,100	7,800	15,000	16,750	25,500	28,000	37,500	70,000	—
1902	12,197,744	8.00	9.00	16.00	27.00	40.00	90.00	245	800	1,450
1902O	4,748,000	10.00	13.00	80.00	100	120	220	500	2,900	—
1902S	1,524,612	17.00	22.00	44.00	77.00	140	275	500	2,750	—
1903	9,670,064	8.00	9.00	17.00	29.00	100	90.00	245	1,600	1,450
1903O	3,500,000	10.00	11.00	33.00	55.00	105	210	440	3,300	—
1903S	1,036,000	13.00	21.00	52.00	77.00	125	230	570	2,200	—
1904	9,588,813	8.00	11.00	17.00	30.00	58.00	110	220	1,300	1,450
1904O	2,456,000	20.00	37.00	55.00	140	190	365	875	4,000	—
1905	4,968,250	27.00	31.00	42.00	55.00	60.00	115	220	850	1,450
1905O	1,230,000	47.00	65.00	110	210	260	300	550	4,000	—
1905S	1,884,000	29.00	37.00	80.00	90.00	95.00	180	500	3,300	—
1906	3,656,435	8.00	9.00	16.00	27.00	55.00	90.00	245	900	1,450
1906D	3,280,000	8.00	16.00	20.00	35.00	57.00	125	220	1,500	—
1906O	2,056,000	10.00	14.00	33.00	51.00	95.00	165	240	1,250	—
1907	7,192,575	8.00	9.00	14.00	27.00	53.00	90.00	245	800	1,450
1907D	2,484,000	8.00	9.00	22.00	42.00	65.00	200	330	2,200	—
1907O	4,560,000	10.00	11.00	16.00	33.00	55.00	115	220	1,300	—
1907S	1,360,000	10.00	15.00	38.00	60.00	170	280	500	2,800	—
1908	4,232,545	8.00	9.00	16.00	27.00	55.00	90.00	245	800	1,450
1908D	5,788,000	8.00	9.00	14.00	30.00	55.00	90.00	245	800	—
1908O	6,244,000	8.00	9.00	14.00	30.00	55.00	90.00	220	900	—
1908S	784,000	28.00	60.00	130	140	330	500	900	2,875	—
1909	9,268,650	8.00	9.00	14.00	30.00	55.00	90.00	245	800	1,450
1909D	5,114,000	8.00	9.00	14.00	30.00	55.00	90.00	245	800	—
1909O	712,000	100	165	540	900	2,000	3,100	4,000	7,250	—
1909S	1,348,000	10.00	11.00	30.00	46.00	77.00	200	330	1,550	—
1910	2,244,551	8.00	9.00	14.00	30.00	55.00	90.00	245	800	1,450
1910D	1,500,000	8.00	18.00	38.00	75.00	135	250	450	1,600	—
1911	3,720,543	8.00	9.00	14.00	30.00	55.00	90.00	220	800	1,450
1911D	933,600	27.00	37.00	140	275	400	500	800	3,200	—
1911S	988,000	10.00	13.00	46.00	82.00	210	300	490	1,350	—
1912	4,400,700	8.00	9.00	14.00	27.00	46.00	90.00	245	800	1,450
1912S	708,000	22.00	28.00	65.00	90.00	110	260	490	1,500	—
1913	484,613	26.00	41.00	100	160	330	440	940	2,100	1,450
1913D	1,450,800	12.00	15.00	38.00	53.00	85.00	170	350	920	—
1913S	40,000	1,225	2,400	4,500	7,000	9,550	12,000	14,250	31,000	—
1914	6,244,610	8.00	9.00	14.00	27.00	46.00	90.00	245	800	1,450
1914D	3,046,000	8.00	9.00	14.00	27.00	46.00	90.00	245	800	—
1914S	264,000	125	145	400	525	990	1,100	1,550	4,800	—
1915	3,480,450	8.00	9.00	14.00	27.00	46.00	90.00	245	800	1,450
1915D	3,694,000	8.00	9.00	14.00	27.00	46.00	90.00	245	800	—
1915S	704,000	22.00	37.00	55.00	82.00	88.00	175	250	990	—
1916	1,788,000	8.00	9.00	14.00	27.00	46.00	90.00	245	800	—
1916D	6,540,800	8.00	9.00	14.00	27.00	46.00	90.00	245	800	—
1916D/D	Inc. above	12.00	16.00	21.00	32.00	59.00	148	280	—	—

QUARTER

Standing Liberty Quarter
Right breast exposed; Type 1.

KM# 141 • 6.25 g., 0.900 Silver 0.1808 oz. ASW, 24.3 mm. • **Designer:** Hermon A. MacNeil

Right breast exposed

Date	Mintage	G4	VG8	F12	VF20	XF40	AU50	MS60	MS65	MS65FH
1916	52,000	3,000	4,100	5,800	6,800	8,750	10,000	13,000	26,000	36,500
1917	8,792,000	18.00	38.00	80.00	90.00	110	165	205	330	850
1917D	1,509,200	19.00	55.00	80.00	100	150	190	300	825	1,650
1917S	1,952,000	22.00	62.00	95.00	130	170	340	400	925	3,200

Right breast covered; Type 2. Three stars below eagle.

KM# 145 • 6.25 g., 0.900 Silver 0.1808 oz. ASW, 24.3 mm. • **Designer:** Hermon A. MacNeil

Right breast covered | Right breast covered | Mint mark

Date	Mintage	G4	VG8	F12	VF20	XF40	AU50	MS60	MS65	MS65FH
1917	13,880,000	16.00	35.00	46.00	55.00	88.00	155	210	610	900
1917D	6,224,400	32.00	35.00	125	170	200	245	300	1,400	3,350
1917S	5,522,000	29.00	36.00	80.00	120	215	250	300	930	3,650
1918	14,240,000	12.00	18.00	24.00	25.00	35.00	70.00	110	440	1,750
1918D	7,380,000	18.00	32.00	62.00	95.00	120	225	285	1,350	4,850
1918S	11,072,000	13.00	15.00	35.00	55.00	70.00	95.00	220	1,200	10,500
1918/17S	Inc. above	1,400	1,925	3,300	4,800	6,500	10,000	16,250	85,000	320,000
1919	11,324,000	26.00	40.00	53.00	60.00	81.00	140	170	530	1,275
1919D	1,944,000	60.00	80.00	250	345	600	685	900	4,000	37,500
1919S	1,836,000	55.00	80.00	245	475	525	650	1,400	8,000	31,500
1920	27,860,000	11.00	13.00	20.00	26.00	47.00	70.00	170	540	1,850
1920D	3,586,400	125	135	150	205	245	300	525	1,900	6,850
1920S	6,380,000	13.00	18.00	23.00	30.00	50.00	115	315	2,000	24,000
1921	1,916,000	130	150	390	435	550	800	1,450	2,300	5,500
1923	9,716,000	14.00	21.00	41.00	55.00	90.00	112	225	505	3,850
1923S	1,360,000	320	420	540	600	1,140	1,475	2,300	3,900	7,500
1924	10,920,000	11.00	13.00	20.00	32.00	55.00	75.00	160	432	1,550
1924D	3,112,000	40.00	50.00	88.00	193	235	280	310	470	4,350
1924S	2,860,000	20.00	25.00	37.00	50.00	145	190	260	2,140	5,650
1925	12,280,000	8.00	10.00	14.00	20.00	42.50	60.00	125	525	950
1926	11,316,000	8.00	10.00	14.00	20.00	42.50	60.00	125	425	1,650
1926D	1,716,000	8.00	15.00	21.00	40.00	80.00	115	150	395	25,000
1926S	2,700,000	8.00	10.00	10.00	40.00	80.00	210	500	2,750	26,000
1927	11,912,000	8.00	10.00	14.00	20.00	42.50	60.00	125	525	1,150
1927D	976,400	15.00	18.00	32.00	50.00	110	185	220	525	2,450
1927S	396,000	35.00	50.00	65.00	135	550	1,680	4,500	11,500	185,000
1928	6,336,000	8.00	10.00	14.00	20.00	42.50	60.00	125	525	1,850
1928D	1,627,600	8.00	10.00	14.00	20.00	42.50	60.00	125	525	4,950
1928S Large S	2,644,000	8.00	10.00	14.00	20.00	42.50	60.00	125	525	—
1928S Small S	Inc. above	8.00	10.00	14.00	20.00	42.50	60.00	125	525	900
1929	11,140,000	8.00	10.00	14.00	20.00	42.50	60.00	125	525	795
1929D	1,358,000	8.00	10.00	14.00	20.00	42.50	60.00	125	525	5,850
1929S	1,764,000	8.00	10.00	14.00	20.00	42.50	60.00	125	525	795
1930	5,632,000	8.00	10.00	14.00	20.00	42.50	60.00	125	525	795
1930S	1,556,000	8.00	10.00	14.00	20.00	42.50	60.00	125	525	845

Washington Quarter

KM# 164 • 6.25 g., 0.900 Silver 0.1808 oz. ASW, 24.3 mm. • **Designer:** John Flanagan

Mint mark 1932-64

Date	Mintage	G4	VG8	F12	VF20	XF40	AU50	MS60	MS65	Prf65
1932	5,404,000	9.00	10.00	10.00	12.00	14.00	17.00	27.00	230	—
1932D	436,800	60.00	75.00	85.00	100	135	250	1,025	7,600	—
1932S	408,000	45.00	50.00	60.00	63.00	100	162	300	2,300	—
1934 Medium Motto	31,912,052	5.00	6.00	7.00	8.00	8.50	9.00	20.00	90.00	—
1934 Heavy Motto	Inc. Above	6.00	7.00	9.00	12.50	15.00	25.00	45.00	225	—
1934 Light Motto	Inc. Above	6.00	7.00	10.00	13.00	17.00	25.00	45.00	290	—
1934 Doubled Die Obverse	Inc. Above	60.00	80.00	140	180	200	295	800	3,000	—
1934D Medium Motto	3,527,200	5.00	6.00	10.00	17.00	25.00	45.00	200	480	—
1934D Heavy Motto	Inc. Above	5.00	7.50	12.50	20.00	30.00	80.00	240	450	—
1935	32,484,000	5.00	6.00	7.00	8.00	11.00	14.00	19.00	70.00	—
1935D	5,780,000	5.00	6.00	9.00	14.00	35.00	65.00	260	420	—
1935S	5,660,000	5.00	6.00	7.00	8.00	13.00	30.00	82.00	260	—
1936	41,303,837	5.00	6.00	7.00	8.00	12.00	17.00	22.00	85.00	1,070
1936D	5,374,000	5.00	8.00	9.00	25.00	60.00	165	530	900	—
1936S	3,828,000	5.00	6.00	7.00	15.00	20.00	35.00	92.00	247	—
1937	19,701,542	5.00	6.00	7.00	12.00	14.00	17.00	31.00	80.00	360
1937 Double Die Obverse	Inc. Above	95.00	140	250	350	600	800	1,650	8,000	—
1937D	7,189,600	5.00	6.00	7.00	9.00	21.00	32.00	60.00	135	—
1937S	1,652,000	5.00	6.00	8.00	19.00	38.00	62.00	195	325	—
1938	9,480,045	5.00	6.00	7.00	8.00	24.00	40.00	100	200	165
1938S	2,832,000	5.00	6.00	7.00	11.00	20.00	40.00	85.00	120	—
1939	33,548,795	5.00	6.00	7.00	12.00	14.00	15.00	22.00	65.00	250
1939D	7,092,000	5.00	6.00	7.00	12.00	15.00	24.00	41.00	100	—
1939S	2,628,000	5.00	6.00	7.00	10.00	30.00	40.00	105	240	—
1940	35,715,246	5.00	6.00	7.00	8.00	9.00	12.00	21.00	45.00	160
1940D	2,797,600	5.00	6.00	8.00	11.00	30.00	45.00	110	260	—
1940S	8,244,000	5.00	6.00	7.00	8.00	9.00	15.00	25.00	36.00	—
1941	79,047,287	—	—	—	—	—	8.00	9.00	30.00	175
1941 Double Die Obv.	Inc. Above	—	—	—	20.00	30.00	50.00	65.00	120	—
1941D	16,714,800	—	—	—	—	—	12.00	28.00	58.00	—
1941S	16,080,000	—	—	—	—	—	10.00	25.00	55.00	—
1941 Lg S	Inc. Above	—	4.00	8.00	10.00	15.00	40.00	85.00	300	—
1942	102,117,123	—	—	—	—	—	8.00	8.50	25.00	135
1942D	17,487,200	—	—	—	—	—	9.00	16.00	33.00	—
1942D Double Die Obv.	Inc. Above	—	—	—	—	—	700	1,800	9,000	—
1942D Double Die Rev.	Inc. Above	—	18.00	35.00	50.00	65.00	120	300	1,550	—
1942S	19,384,000	—	—	—	—	—	19.00	63.00	110	—
1943	99,700,000	—	—	—	—	—	8.00	8.50	35.00	—
1943 Double Die Obv.	Inc. Above	—	—	—	—	—	4,200	6,000	13,750	—
1943D	16,095,600	—	—	—	—	—	14.00	25.00	44.00	—
1943S	21,700,000	—	—	—	—	—	11.00	23.00	45.00	—
1943S Double Die Obv.	Inc. Above	—	145	—	—	—	300	525	1,600	—
1943 Trumpet tail S	Inc. Above	6.00	12.00	18.00	30.00	45.00	80.00	140	500	—
1944	104,956,000	—	—	—	—	—	8.00	8.50	25.00	—
1944D	14,600,800	—	—	—	—	—	9.00	16.00	34.00	—
1944S	12,560,000	—	—	—	—	—	9.00	13.00	27.00	—
1945	74,372,000	—	—	—	—	—	8.00	8.50	30.00	—
1945D	12,341,600	—	—	—	—	—	11.00	16.00	33.00	—
1945S	17,004,001	—	—	—	—	—	8.00	9.00	28.00	—
1946	53,436,000	—	—	—	—	—	8.00	8.50	34.00	—
1946D	9,072,800	—	—	—	—	—	8.00	9.00	35.00	—
1946S	4,204,000	—	—	—	—	—	8.00	8.50	26.00	—
1947	22,556,000	—	—	—	—	—	8.00	9.00	28.00	—
1947D	15,338,400	—	—	—	—	—	8.00	9.00	32.00	—
1947S	5,532,000	—	—	—	—	—	8.00	9.00	20.00	—
1948	35,196,000	—	—	—	—	—	8.00	8.50	20.00	—
1948D	16,766,800	—	—	—	—	—	8.00	11.00	45.00	—
1948S	15,960,000	—	—	—	—	—	8.00	9.00	30.00	—
1949	9,312,000	—	—	—	—	—	13.00	31.00	65.00	—
1949D	10,068,400	—	—	—	—	—	15.00	23.00	33.00	—
1950	24,971,512	—	—	—	—	—	8.00	8.50	26.00	65.00
1950D	21,075,600	—	—	—	—	—	8.00	8.50	26.00	—
1950D/S	Inc. Above	18.00	21.00	30.00	49.00	120	185	215	3,300	—
1950S	10,284,004	—	—	—	—	—	8.00	8.50	26.00	—

QUARTER

Date	Mintage	G4	VG8	F12	VF20	XF40	AU50	MS60	MS65	Prf65
1950S/D	Inc. Above	18.00	21.00	30.00	49.00	155	260	325	680	—
1950S/S	Inc. Above	6.00	7.00	8.00	10.00	—	18.00	35.00	135	—
1951	43,505,602	—	—	—	—	—	8.00	8.50	26.00	60.00
1951D	35,354,800	—	—	—	—	—	8.00	8.50	26.00	—
1951S	9,048,000	—	—	—	—	—	8.00	8.50	26.00	—
1952	38,862,073	—	—	—	—	—	8.00	8.50	26.00	46.00
1952D	49,795,200	—	—	—	—	—	8.00	8.50	26.00	—
1952S	13,707,800	—	—	—	—	—	8.00	8.50	26.00	—
1953	18,664,920	—	—	—	—	—	8.00	8.50	26.00	44.00
1953D	56,112,400	—	—	—	—	—	8.00	8.50	26.00	—
1953S	14,016,000	—	—	—	—	—	8.00	8.50	26.00	—
1954	54,645,503	—	—	—	—	—	8.00	8.50	26.00	18.00
1954D	42,305,500	—	—	—	—	—	8.00	8.50	26.00	—
1954S	11,834,722	—	—	—	—	—	8.00	8.50	26.00	—
1955	18,558,381	—	—	—	—	—	8.00	8.50	26.00	22.00
1955D	3,182,400	—	—	—	—	—	8.00	8.50	26.00	—
1956	44,813,384	—	—	—	—	—	8.00	8.50	26.00	15.00
1956 Double Bar 5	Inc. Above	—	5.60	5.70	5.80	6.50	9.00	20.00	125	—
1956 Type B rev, proof rev die	Inc. Above	—	—	8.00	12.00	18.00	25.00	35.00	275	—
1956D	32,334,500	—	—	—	—	—	8.00	8.50	26.00	—
1957	47,779,952	—	—	—	—	—	8.00	8.50	26.00	15.00
1957 Type B rev, proof rev die	Inc. Above	—	—	—	5.60	10.00	20.00	40.00	125	—
1957D	77,924,160	—	—	—	—	—	8.00	8.50	26.00	—
1958	7,235,652	—	—	—	—	—	8.00	8.50	26.00	15.00
1958 Type B rev, proof rev die	Inc. Above	—	—	—	5.60	10.00	16.00	24.00	90.00	—
1958D	78,124,900	—	—	—	—	—	8.00	8.50	26.00	—
1959	25,533,291	—	—	—	—	—	8.00	8.50	26.00	15.00
1959 Type B rev, proof rev die	Inc. Above	—	—	—	5.80	8.00	12.00	18.00	65.00	—
1959D	62,054,232	—	—	—	—	—	8.00	8.50	26.00	—
1960	30,855,602	—	—	—	—	—	8.00	8.50	26.00	15.00
1960 Type B rev, proof rev die	Inc. Above	—	—	—	5.10	10.00	16.00	24.00	90.00	—
1960D	63,000,324	—	—	—	—	—	8.00	8.50	26.00	—
1961	40,064,244	—	—	—	—	—	8.00	8.50	26.00	15.00
1961 Type B rev, proof rev die	Inc. Above	—	—	—	5.80	10.00	14.00	20.00	200	—
1961D	83,656,928	—	—	—	—	—	8.00	8.50	26.00	—
1962	39,374,019	—	—	—	—	—	8.00	8.50	26.00	15.00
1962 Type B rev, proof rev die	Inc. Above	—	—	—	8.00	12.00	15.00	30.00	175	—
1962D	127,554,756	—	—	—	—	—	8.00	8.50	26.00	—
1963	77,391,645	—	—	—	—	—	8.00	8.50	26.00	15.00
1963 Type B rev, proof rev die	Inc. Above	—	—	—	5.80	5.90	8.00	15.00	50.00	—
1963D	135,288,184	—	—	—	—	—	8.00	8.50	26.00	—
1964	564,341,347	—	—	—	—	—	8.00	8.50	26.00	15.00
1964 Type B rev, proof rev die	Inc. Above	—	—	—	5.80	9.00	10.00	18.00	75.00	—
1964 SMS	Inc. Above	—	—	—	—	—	250	750	1,400	—
1964D	704,135,528	—	—	—	—	—	8.00	8.50	26.00	—
1964D Type C rev, clad rev die	Inc. Above	—	—	—	40.00	55.00	75.00	125	450	—

KM# 164a • 5.67 g., Copper-Nickel Clad Copper, 24.3 mm. • **Designer:** John Flanagan

Date	Mintage	MS65	Prf65
1965	1,819,717,540	10.00	—
1965 SMS	2,360,000	9.00	—
1966	821,101,500	7.50	—
1966 SMS	2,261,583	9.00	—
1967	1,524,031,848	10.00	—
1967 SMS	1,863,344	9.00	—
1968	220,731,500	10.00	—
1968D	101,534,000	7.00	—
1968S	3,041,506	—	2.00

Date	Mintage	MS65	Prf65
1969	176,212,000	14.00	—
1969D	114,372,000	8.00	—
1969S	2,934,631	—	2.25
1970	136,420,000	12.00	—
1970D	417,341,364	6.00	—
1970S	2,632,810	—	2.00
1971	109,284,000	12.00	—
1971D	258,634,428	6.00	—
1971S	3,220,733	—	2.00
1972	215,048,000	7.50	—
1972D	311,067,732	6.00	—
1972S	3,260,996	—	2.00
1973	346,924,000	8.00	—
1973D	232,977,400	7.00	—
1973S	2,760,339	—	1.75
1974	801,456,000	6.00	—
1974D	353,160,300	8.00	—
1974S	2,612,568	—	2.10
1975 none minted	—	—	—
1975D none minted	—	—	—
1975S none minted	—	—	—

QUARTER

Colonial drummer, torch at top left within ring of stars.

KM# 204 • 5.67 g., Copper-Nickel Clad Copper, 24.3 mm. • **Rev. Designer:** Jack L. Ahr

Date	Mintage	MS60	MS65	Prf65
1976	809,784,016	0.50	7.00	—
1976D	860,118,839	0.50	8.00	—
1976S	4,149,730	—	—	3.25

Bicentennial design, drummer boy.

KM# 204a • 5.75 g., Silver Clad, 24.3 mm. • **Rev. Designer:** Jack L. Ahr

Date	Mintage	MS60	MS65	Prf65
1976S	4,908,319	1.85	6.00	—
1976S	3,998,621	1.85	6.00	4.50

Eagle, regular design resumed.

KM# A164a • 5.67 g., Copper-Nickel Clad Copper, 24.3 mm. • **Edge:** Reeded **Note:** KM#164 design and composition resumed. The 1979-S and 1981 Type II proofs have clearer mint marks than the Type I proofs for those years.

Date	Mintage	MS65	Prf65
1977	468,556,000	7.50	—
1977D	256,524,978	8.00	—
1977S	3,251,152	—	2.75
1978	521,452,000	6.00	—
1978D	287,373,152	7.00	—
1978S	3,127,781	—	2.75
1979	515,708,000	8.00	—
1979D	489,789,780	7.00	—
1979S T-I	3,677,175	—	2.50
1979S T-II	Inc. above	—	4.00
1980P	635,832,000	8.00	—
1980D	518,327,487	8.50	—
1980S	3,554,806	—	2.75
1981P	601,716,000	7.50	—
1981D	575,722,833	6.50	—

Date	Mintage	MS65	Prf65
1981S T-I	4,063,083	—	2.75
1981S T-II	Inc. above	—	7.50
1982P	500,931,000	28.00	—
1982D	480,042,788	15.00	—
1982S	3,857,479	—	4.00
1983P	673,535,000	50.00	—
1983D	617,806,446	30.00	—
1983S	3,279,126	—	3.00
1984P	676,545,000	14.50	—
1984D	546,483,064	12.50	—
1984S	3,065,110	—	3.00
1985P	775,818,962	12.50	—
1985D	519,962,888	10.00	—
1985S	3,362,821	—	3.00
1986P	551,199,333	11.00	—
1986D	504,298,660	15.00	—
1986S	3,010,497	—	3.00
1987P	582,499,481	10.50	—
1987D	655,594,696	8.50	—
1987S	4,227,728	—	3.00
1988P	562,052,000	10.00	—
1988D	596,810,688	7.50	—
1988S	3,262,948	—	3.00
1989P	512,868,000	16.00	—
1989D	896,535,597	7.50	—
1989S	3,220,194	—	3.00
1990P	613,792,000	12.00	—
1990D	927,638,181	6.00	—
1990S	3,299,559	—	4.50
1991P	570,968,000	10.00	—
1991D	630,966,693	12.00	—
1991S	2,867,787	—	3.00
1992P	384,764,000	20.00	—
1992D	389,777,107	12.00	—
1992S	2,858,981	—	3.00
1993P	639,276,000	7.50	—
1993D	645,476,128	8.50	—
1993S	2,633,439	—	3.00
1994P	825,600,000	8.00	—
1994D	880,034,110	8.00	—
1994S	2,484,594	—	3.00
1995P	1,004,336,000	7.50	—
1995D	1,103,216,000	6.50	—
1995S	2,117,496	—	6.00
1996P	925,040,000	7.50	—
1996D	906,868,000	11.00	—
1996S	1,750,244	—	4.00
1997P	595,740,000	22.50	—
1997D	599,680,000	17.00	—
1997S	2,055,000	—	9.00
1998P	896,268,000	14.00	—
1998D	821,000,000	18.00	—
1998S	2,086,507	—	9.00

KM# A164b • 6.25 g., 0.900 Silver 0.1808 oz. ASW, 24.3 mm. •

Date	Mintage	MS65	Prf65
1992S	1,317,579	—	6.80
1993S	761,353	6.80	—
1994S	785,329	8.00	—
1995S	838,953	—	8.00
1996S	775,021	—	—
1997S	741,678	—	8.00
1998S	878,792	—	6.80

QUARTER

50 State Quarters

Delaware

KM# 293 • 5.67 g., Copper-Nickel Clad Copper, 24.3 mm.

Date	Mintage	MS63	MS65	Prf65
1999P	373,400,000	1.00	5.00	—
1999D	401,424,000	1.00	7.00	—
1999S	3,713,359	—	—	3.50

KM# 293a • 6.25 g., 0.900 Silver 0.1808 oz. ASW, 24.3 mm.

Date	Mintage	MS63	MS65	Prf65
1999S	804,565	—	—	20.00

Pennsylvania

KM# 294 • 5.67 g., Copper-Nickel Clad Copper, 24.3 mm.

Date	Mintage	MS63	MS65	Prf65
1999P	349,000,000	1.00	5.00	—
1999D	358,332,000	1.00	4.00	—
1999S	3,713,359	—	—	3.50

KM# 294a • 6.25 g., 0.900 Silver 0.1808 oz. ASW, 24.3 mm.

Date	Mintage	MS63	MS65	Prf65
1999S	804,565	—	—	20.00

New Jersey

KM# 295 • 5.67 g., Copper-Nickel Clad Copper, 24.3 mm.

Date	Mintage	MS63	MS65	Prf65
1999P	363,200,000	1.00	5.00	—
1999D	299,028,000	1.00	4.00	—
1999S	3,713,359	—	—	3.50

KM# 295a • 6.25 g., 0.900 Silver 0.1808 oz. ASW, 24.3 mm.

Date	Mintage	MS63	MS65	Prf65
1999S	804,565	—	—	20.00

Georgia

KM# 296 • 5.67 g., Copper-Nickel Clad Copper, 24.3 mm.

Date	Mintage	MS63	MS65	Prf65
1999P	451,188,000	1.00	4.50	—
1999D	488,744,000	1.00	4.50	—
1999S	3,713,359	—	—	3.50

KM# 296a • 6.25 g., 0.900 Silver 0.1808 oz. ASW, 24.3 mm.

Date	Mintage	MS63	MS65	Prf65
1999S	804,565	—	—	20.00

Connecticut

KM# 297 • 5.67 g., Copper-Nickel Clad Copper, 24.3 mm.

Date	Mintage	MS63	MS65	Prf65
1999P	688,744,000	0.80	6.00	—
1999D	657,480,000	0.80	5.00	—
1999S	3,713,359	—	—	3.50

KM# 297a • 6.25 g., 0.900 Silver 0.1808 oz. ASW, 24.3 mm.

Date	Mintage	MS63	MS65	Prf65
1999S	804,565	—	—	20.00

Massachusetts

KM# 305 • 5.67 g., Copper-Nickel Clad Copper, 24.3 mm.

Date	Mintage	MS63	MS65	Prf65
2000P	629,800,000	0.80	7.00	—
2000D	535,184,000	0.80	8.00	—
2000S	4,078,747	—	—	3.00

KM# 305a • 6.25 g., 0.900 Silver 0.1808 oz. ASW, 24.3 mm.

Date	Mintage	MS63	MS65	Prf65
2000S	965,921	—	—	9.00

QUARTER

Maryland

KM# 306 • 5.67 g., Copper-Nickel Clad Copper, 24.3 mm.

Date	Mintage	MS63	MS65	Prf65
2000P	678,200,000	0.80	6.00	—
2000D	556,526,000	0.80	6.00	—
2000S	4,078,747	—	—	3.00

KM# 306a • 6.25 g., 0.900 Silver 0.1808 oz. ASW, 24.3 mm.

Date	Mintage	MS63	MS65	Prf65
2000S	965,921	—	—	9.00

South Carolina

KM# 307 • 5.67 g., Copper-Nickel Clad Copper, 24.3 mm.

Date	Mintage	MS63	MS65	Prf65
2000P	742,756,000	0.80	6.00	—
2000D	566,208,000	0.80	9.00	—
2000S	4,078,747	—	—	3.00

KM# 307a • 6.25 g., 0.900 Silver 0.1808 oz. ASW, 24.3 mm.

Date	Mintage	MS63	MS65	Prf65
2000S	965,921	—	—	9.00

New Hampshire

KM# 308 • 5.67 g., Copper-Nickel Clad Copper, 24.3 mm.

Date	Mintage	MS63	MS65	Prf65
2000P	673,040,000	0.80	8.00	—
2000D	495,976,000	0.80	9.00	—
2000S	4,078,747	—	—	3.00

KM# 308a • 6.25 g., 0.900 Silver 0.1808 oz. ASW, 24.3 mm.

Date	Mintage	MS63	MS65	Prf65
2000S	965,921	—	—	9.00

Virginia

KM# 309 • 5.67 g., Copper-Nickel Clad Copper, 24.3 mm.

Date	Mintage	MS63	MS65	Prf65
2000P	943,000,000	0.80	6.50	—
2000D	651,616,000	0.80	6.50	—
2000S	4,078,747	—	—	3.00

KM# 309a • 6.25 g., 0.900 Silver 0.1808 oz. ASW, 24.3 mm.

Date	Mintage	MS63	MS65	Prf65
2000S	965,921	—	—	9.50

New York

KM# 318 • 5.67 g., Copper-Nickel Clad Copper, 24.3 mm.

Date	Mintage	MS63	MS65	Prf65
2001P	655,400,000	0.80	5.50	—
2001D	619,640,000	0.80	5.50	—
2001S	3,094,140	—	—	4.00

KM# 318a • 6.25 g., 0.900 Silver 0.1808 oz. ASW, 24.3 mm.

Date	Mintage	MS63	MS65	Prf65
2001S	889,697	—	—	9.50

North Carolina

KM# 319 • 5.67 g., Copper-Nickel Clad Copper, 24.3 mm.

Date	Mintage	MS63	MS65	Prf65
2001P	627,600,000	1.00	5.50	—
2001D	427,876,000	1.00	6.50	—
2001S	3,094,140	—	—	4.00

KM# 319a • 6.25 g., 0.900 Silver 0.1808 oz. ASW, 24.3 mm.

Date	Mintage	MS63	MS65	Prf65
2001S	889,697	—	—	9.50

QUARTER

Rhode Island

KM# 320 • 5.67 g., Copper-Nickel Clad Copper, 24.3 mm.

Date	Mintage	MS63	MS65	Prf65
2001P	423,000,000	0.80	5.50	—
2001D	447,100,000	0.80	6.00	—
2001S	3,094,140	—	—	4.00

KM# 320a • 6.25 g., 0.900 Silver 0.1808 oz. ASW, 24.3 mm.

Date	Mintage	MS63	MS65	Prf65
2001S	889,697	—	—	9.50

Vermont

KM# 321 • 5.67 g., Copper-Nickel Clad Copper, 24.3 mm.

Date	Mintage	MS63	MS65	Prf65
2001P	423,400,000	0.80	6.50	—
2001D	459,404,000	0.80	6.50	—
2001S	3,094,140	—	—	4.00

KM# 321a • 6.25 g., 0.900 Silver 0.1808 oz. ASW, 24.3 mm.

Date	Mintage	MS63	MS65	Prf65
2001S	889,697	—	—	9.50

Kentucky

KM# 322 • 5.67 g., Copper-Nickel Clad Copper, 24.3 mm.

Date	Mintage	MS63	MS65	Prf65
2001P	353,000,000	1.00	6.50	—
2001D	370,564,000	1.00	7.00	—
2001S	3,094,140	—	—	4.00

KM# 322a • 6.25 g., 0.900 Silver 0.1808 oz. ASW, 24.3 mm.

Date	Mintage	MS63	MS65	Prf65
2001S	889,697	—	—	9.50

Tennessee

KM# 331 • 5.67 g., Copper-Nickel Clad Copper, 24.3 mm.

Date	Mintage	MS63	MS65	Prf65
2002P	361,600,000	1.40	6.50	—
2002D	286,468,000	1.40	7.00	—
2002S	3,084,245	—	—	2.30

KM# 331a • 6.25 g., 0.900 Silver 0.1808 oz. ASW, 24.3 mm.

Date	Mintage	MS63	MS65	Prf65
2002S	892,229	—	—	8.50

Ohio

KM# 332 • 5.67 g., Copper-Nickel Clad Copper, 24.3 mm.

Date	Mintage	MS63	MS65	Prf65
2002P	217,200,000	0.80	5.50	—
2002D	414,832,000	0.80	5.50	—
2002S	3,084,245	—	—	2.30

KM# 332a • 6.25 g., 0.900 Silver 0.1808 oz. ASW, 24.3 mm.

Date	Mintage	MS63	MS65	Prf65
2002S	892,229	—	—	8.50

Louisiana

KM# 333 • 5.67 g., Copper-Nickel Clad Copper, 24.3 mm.

Date	Mintage	MS63	MS65	Prf65
2002P	362,000,000	0.80	5.50	—
2002D	402,204,000	0.80	6.00	—
2002S	3,084,245	—	—	2.30

KM# 333a • 6.25 g., 0.900 Silver 0.1808 oz. ASW, 24.3 mm.

Date	Mintage	MS63	MS65	Prf65
2002S	892,229	—	—	8.50

QUARTER

Indiana

KM# 334 • 5.67 g., Copper-Nickel Clad Copper, 24.3 mm.

Date	Mintage	MS63	MS65	Prf65
2002P	362,600,000	0.80	5.00	—
2002D	327,200,000	0.80	5.00	—
2002S	3,084,245	—	—	2.30

KM# 334a • 6.25 g., 0.900 Silver 0.1808 oz. ASW, 24.3 mm.

Date	Mintage	MS63	MS65	Prf65
2002S	892,229	—	—	8.50

Mississippi

KM# 335 • 5.67 g., Copper-Nickel Clad Copper, 24.3 mm.

Date	Mintage	MS63	MS65	Prf65
2002P	290,000,000	0.80	5.00	—
2002D	289,600,000	0.80	5.00	—
2002S	3,084,245	—	—	2.30

KM# 335a • 6.25 g., 0.900 Silver 0.1808 oz. ASW, 24.3 mm.

Date	Mintage	MS63	MS65	Prf65
2002S	892,229	—	—	8.50

Illinois

KM# 343 • 5.67 g., Copper-Nickel Clad Copper, 24.3 mm.

Date	Mintage	MS63	MS65	Prf65
2003P	225,800,000	1.10	5.00	—
2003D	237,400,000	1.10	5.00	—
2003S	3,408,516	—	—	2.30

KM# 343a • 6.25 g., 0.900 Silver 0.1808 oz. ASW, 24.3 mm.

Date	Mintage	MS63	MS65	Prf65
2003S	1,257,555	—	—	8.50

Alabama

KM# 344 • 5.67 g., Copper-Nickel Clad Copper, 24.3 mm.

Date	Mintage	MS63	MS65	Prf65
2003P	225,000,000	0.65	5.00	—
2003D	232,400,000	0.65	5.00	—
2003S	3,408,516	—	—	2.30

KM# 344a • 6.25 g., 0.900 Silver 0.1808 oz. ASW, 24.3 mm.

Date	Mintage	MS63	MS65	Prf65
2003S	1,257,555	—	—	8.50

Maine

KM# 345 • 5.67 g., Copper-Nickel Clad Copper, 24.3 mm.

Date	Mintage	MS63	MS65	Prf65
2003P	217,400,000	0.65	5.00	—
2003D	213,400,000	0.65	5.00	—
2003S	3,408,516	—	—	2.30

KM# 345a • 6.25 g., 0.900 Silver 0.1808 oz. ASW, 24.3 mm.

Date	Mintage	MS63	MS65	Prf65
2003S	1,257,555	—	—	8.50

Missouri

KM# 346 • 5.67 g., Copper-Nickel Clad Copper, 24.3 mm.

Date	Mintage	MS63	MS65	Prf65
2003P	225,000,000	0.65	5.00	—
2003D	228,200,000	0.65	5.00	—
2003S	3,408,516	—	—	2.30

KM# 346a • 6.25 g., 0.900 Silver 0.1808 oz. ASW, 24.3 mm.

Date	Mintage	MS63	MS65	Prf65
2003S	1,257,555	—	—	8.50

QUARTER

Arkansas

KM# 347 • 5.67 g., Copper-Nickel Clad Copper, 24.3 mm.

Date	Mintage	MS63	MS65	Prf65
2003P	228,000,000	0.65	5.00	—
2003D	229,800,000	0.65	5.00	—
2003S	3,408,516	—	—	2.30

KM# 347a • 6.25 g., 0.900 Silver 0.1808 oz. ASW, 24.3 mm.

Date	Mintage	MS63	MS65	Prf65
2003S	1,257,555	—	—	8.50

Michigan

KM# 355 • 5.67 g., Copper-Nickel Clad Copper, 24.3 mm.

Date	Mintage	MS63	MS65	Prf65
2004P	233,800,000	0.65	5.00	—
2004D	225,800,000	0.65	5.00	—
2004S	2,740,684	—	—	2.30

KM# 355a • 6.25 g., 0.900 Silver 0.1808 oz. ASW, 24.3 mm.

Date	Mintage	MS63	MS65	Prf65
2004S	1,781,810	—	—	8.50

Florida

KM# 356 • 5.67 g., Copper-Nickel Clad Copper, 24.3 mm.

Date	Mintage	MS63	MS65	Prf65
2004P	240,200,000	0.65	5.00	—
2004D	241,600,000	0.65	5.00	—
2004S	2,740,684	—	—	2.30

KM# 356a • 6.25 g., 0.900 Silver 0.1808 oz. ASW, 24.3 mm.

Date	Mintage	MS63	MS65	Prf65
2004S	1,781,810	—	—	8.50

Texas

KM# 357 • 5.67 g., Copper-Nickel Clad Copper, 24.3 mm.

Date	Mintage	MS63	MS65	Prf65
2004P	278,800,000	0.65	5.00	—
2004D	263,000,000	0.65	5.00	—
2004S	2,740,684	—	—	2.30

KM# 357a • 6.25 g., 0.900 Silver 0.1808 oz. ASW, 24.3 mm.

Date	Mintage	MS63	MS65	Prf65
2004S	1,781,810	—	—	8.50

Iowa

KM# 358 • 5.67 g., Copper-Nickel Clad Copper, 24.3 mm.

Date	Mintage	MS63	MS65	Prf65
2004P	213,800,000	0.65	5.00	—
2004D	251,800,000	0.65	5.00	—
2004S	2,740,684	—	—	2.30

KM# 358a • 6.25 g., 0.900 Silver 0.1808 oz. ASW, 24.3 mm.

Date	Mintage	MS63	MS65	Prf65
2004S	1,781,810	—	—	8.50

Wisconsin

KM# 359 • 5.67 g., Copper-Nickel Clad Copper, 24.3 mm.

Date	Mintage	MS63	MS65	Prf65
2004P	226,400,000	0.65	5.00	—
2004D	226,800,000	0.65	5.00	—
2004D Extra Leaf Low	Est. 9000	135	190	—
2004D Extra Leaf High	Est. 3000	175	285	—
2004S	2,740,684	—	—	2.30

KM# 359a • 6.25 g., 0.900 Silver 0.1808 oz. ASW, 24.3 mm.

Date	Mintage	MS63	MS65	Prf65
2004S	1,781,810	—	—	8.50

California

KM# 370 • 5.67 g., Copper-Nickel Clad Copper, 24.3 mm.

Date	Mintage	MS63	MS65	Prf65
2005P	257,200,000	0.65	5.00	—
2005P Satin Finish	1,160,000	1.50	4.50	—
2005D	263,200,000	0.65	5.00	—
2005D Satin Finish	1,160,000	1.50	4.50	—
2005S	3,262,960	—	—	2.30

KM# 370a • 6.25 g., 0.900 Silver 0.1808 oz. ASW, 24.3 mm.

Date	Mintage	MS63	MS65	Prf65
2005S	1,679,600	—	—	8.50

Minnesota

KM# 371 • 5.67 g., Copper-Nickel Clad Copper, 24.3 mm.

Date	Mintage	MS63	MS65	Prf65
2005P	226,400,000	0.65	5.00	—
2005P Satin Finish	1,160,000	1.50	4.50	—
2005D	226,800,000	0.65	5.00	—
2005D Satin Finish	1,160,000	1.50	4.50	—
2005S	3,262,960	—	—	2.30

KM# 371a • 6.25 g., 0.900 Silver 0.1808 oz. ASW, 24.3 mm.

Date	Mintage	MS63	MS65	Prf65
2005S	1,679,600	—	—	8.50

Oregon

KM# 372 • 5.67 g., Copper-Nickel Clad Copper, 24.3 mm.

Date	Mintage	MS63	MS65	Prf65
2005P	316,200,000	0.65	5.00	—
2005P Satin Finish	1,160,000	1.50	4.50	—
2005D	404,000,000	0.65	5.00	—
2005D Satin Finish	1,160,000	1.50	4.50	—
2005S	3,262,960	—	—	2.30

KM# 372a • 6.25 g., 0.900 Silver 0.1808 oz. ASW, 24.3 mm.

Date	Mintage	MS63	MS65	Prf65
2005S	1,679,600	—	—	8.50

Kansas

KM# 373 • 5.67 g., Copper-Nickel Clad Copper, 24.3 mm.

Date	Mintage	MS63	MS65	Prf65
2005P	263,400,000	0.65	5.00	—
2005P Satin Finish	1,160,000	1.50	4.50	—
2005D	300,000,000	0.65	5.00	—
2005D Satin Finish	1,160,000	1.50	4.50	—
2005S	3,262,960	—	—	2.30

KM# 373a • 6.25 g., 0.900 Silver 0.1808 oz. ASW, 24.3 mm.

Date	Mintage	MS63	MS65	Prf65
2005S	1,679,600	—	—	8.50

West Virginia

KM# 374 • 5.67 g., Copper-Nickel Clad Copper, 24.3 mm.

Date	Mintage	MS63	MS65	Prf65
2005P	365,400,000	0.65	5.00	—
2005P Satin Finish	1,160,000	1.50	4.50	—
2005D	356,200,000	0.65	5.00	—
2005D Satin Finish	1,160,000	1.50	4.50	—
2005S	3,262,960	—	—	2.30

KM# 374a • 6.25 g., 0.900 Silver 0.1808 oz. ASW, 24.3 mm.

Date	Mintage	MS63	MS65	Prf65
2005S	1,679,600	—	—	8.50

Nevada

KM# 382 • 5.67 g., Copper-Nickel Clad Copper, 24.3 mm.

Date	Mintage	MS63	MS65	Prf65
2006P	277,000,000	0.65	5.00	—
2006P Satin Finish	847,361	1.50	4.50	—
2006D	312,800,000	0.65	5.00	—
2006D Satin Finish	847,361	1.50	4.50	—
2006S	2,862,078	—	—	2.30

KM# 382a • 6.25 g., 0.900 Silver 0.1808 oz. ASW, 24.3 mm.

Date	Mintage	MS63	MS65	Prf65
2006S	1,571,839	—	—	8.50

QUARTER

Nebraska

KM# 383 • 5.67 g., Copper-Nickel Clad Copper, 24.3 mm.

Date	Mintage	MS63	MS65	Prf65
2006P	318,000,000	0.65	5.00	—
2006P Satin Finish	847,361	1.50	4.50	—
2006D	273,000,000	0.65	5.00	—
2006D Satin Finish	847,361	1.50	4.50	—
2006S	2,862,078	—	—	2.30

KM# 383a • 6.25 g., 0.900 Silver 0.1808 oz. ASW, 24.3 mm.

Date	Mintage	MS63	MS65	Prf65
2006S	1,571,839	—	—	8.50

Colorado

KM# 384 • 5.67 g., Copper-Nickel Clad Copper, 24.3 mm.

Date	Mintage	MS63	MS65	Prf65
2006P	274,800,000	0.65	5.00	—
2006P Satin Finish	847,361	1.50	4.50	—
2006D	294,200,000	0.65	5.00	—
2006D Satin Finish	847,361	1.50	4.50	—
2006S	2,862,078	—	—	2.30

KM# 384a • 6.25 g., 0.900 Silver 0.1808 oz. ASW, 24.3 mm.

Date	Mintage	MS63	MS65	Prf65
2006S	1,571,839	—	—	8.50

North Dakota

KM# 385 • 5.67 g., Copper-Nickel Clad Copper, 24.3 mm.

Date	Mintage	MS63	MS65	Prf65
2006P	305,800,000	0.65	5.00	—
2006P Satin Finish	847,361	1.50	4.50	—
2006D	359,000,000	0.65	5.00	—
2006D Satin Finish	847,361	1.50	4.50	—
2006S	2,862,078	—	—	2.30

KM# 385a • 6.25 g., 0.900 Silver 0.1808 oz. ASW, 24.3 mm.

Date	Mintage	MS63	MS65	Prf65
2006S	1,571,839	—	—	8.50

South Dakota

KM# 386 • 5.67 g., Copper-Nickel Clad Copper, 24.3 mm.

Date	Mintage	MS63	MS65	Prf65
2006P	245,000,000	0.65	5.00	—
2006P Satin Finish	847,361	1.50	4.50	—
2006D	265,800,000	0.65	5.00	—
2006D Satin Finish	847,361	1.50	4.50	—
2006S	2,862,078	—	—	2.30

KM# 386a • 6.25 g., 0.900 Silver 0.1808 oz. ASW, 24.3 mm.

Date	Mintage	MS63	MS65	Prf65
2006S	1,571,839	—	—	8.50

Montana

KM# 396 • 5.67 g., Copper-Nickel Clad Copper, 24.3 mm.

Date	Mintage	MS63	MS65	Prf65
2007P	257,000,000	0.65	5.00	—
2007P Satin Finish	895,628	1.50	4.50	—
2007D	256,240,000	0.65	5.00	—
2007D Satin Finish	895,628	1.50	4.50	—
2007S	2,374,778	—	—	2.30

KM# 396a • 6.25 g., 0.900 Silver 0.1808 oz. ASW, 24.3 mm.

Date	Mintage	MS63	MS65	Prf65
2007S	1,299,878	—	—	8.50

Washington

KM# 397 • 5.67 g., Copper-Nickel Clad Copper, 24.3 mm.

Date	Mintage	MS63	MS65	Prf65
2007P	265,200,000	0.65	5.00	—
2007P Satin Finish	895,628	1.50	4.50	—
2007D	280,000,000	0.65	5.00	—
2007D Satin Finish	895,628	1.50	4.50	—
2007S	2,374,778	—	—	2.30

KM# 397a • 6.25 g., 0.900 Silver 0.1808 oz. ASW, 24.3 mm.

Date	Mintage	MS63	MS65	Prf65
2007S	1,299,878	—	—	8.50

QUARTER

Idaho

KM# 398 • 5.67 g., Copper-Nickel Clad Copper, 24.3 mm.

Date	Mintage	MS63	MS65	Prf65
2007P	294,600,000	0.65	5.00	—
2007P Satin finish	895,628	1.50	4.50	—
2007D	286,800,000	0.65	5.00	—
2007D Satin finish	895,628	1.50	4.50	—
2007S	2,374,778	—	—	2.30

KM# 398a • 6.25 g., 0.900 Silver 0.1808 oz. ASW, 24.3 mm.

Date	Mintage	MS63	MS65	Prf65
2007S	1,299,878	—	—	8.50

Wyoming

KM# 399 • 5.67 g., Copper-Nickel Clad Copper, 24.3 mm.

Date	Mintage	MS63	MS65	Prf65
2007P	243,600,000	0.65	5.00	—
2007P Satin finish	895,628	1.50	4.50	—
2007D	320,800,000	0.65	5.00	—
2007 Satin finish	895,628	1.50	4.50	—
2007S	2,374,778	—	—	2.30

KM# 399a • 6.25 g., 0.900 Silver 0.1808 oz. ASW, 24.3 mm.

Date	Mintage	MS63	MS65	Prf65
2007S	1,299,878	—	—	8.50

Utah

KM# 400 • 5.67 g., Copper-Nickel Clad Copper, 24.3 mm.

Date	Mintage	MS63	MS65	Prf65
2007P	255,000,000	0.65	5.00	—
2007P Satin finish	895,628	1.50	4.50	—
2007D	253,200,000	0.65	5.00	—
2007D Satin finish	895,628	1.50	4.50	—
2007S	2,374,778	—	—	2.30

KM# 400a • 6.25 g., 0.900 Silver 0.1808 oz. ASW

Date	Mintage	MS63	MS65	Prf65
2007S	1,299,878	—	—	8.50

Oklahoma

KM# 421 • 5.67 g., Copper-Nickel Clad Copper, 24.3 mm.

Date	Mintage	MS63	MS65	Prf65
2008P	222,000,000	0.65	5.00	—
2008P Satin finish	745,464	1.50	4.50	—
2008D	194,600,000	0.65	5.00	—
2008D Satin finish	745,464	1.50	4.50	—
2008S	2,100,000	—	—	2.30

KM# 421a • 6.25 g., 0.900 Silver 0.1808 oz. ASW, 24.3 mm.

Date	Mintage	MS63	MS65	Prf65
2008S	1,200,000	—	—	8.50

New Mexico

KM# 422 • 5.67 g., Copper-Nickel Clad Copper, 24.3 mm.

Date	Mintage	MS63	MS65	Prf65
2008P	244,200,000	0.65	5.00	—
2008P Satin finish	745,464	1.50	4.50	—
2008D	244,400,000	0.65	5.00	—
2008D Satin finish	745,464	1.50	4.50	—
2008S	2,100,000	—	—	2.30

KM# 422a • 6.25 g., 0.900 Silver 0.1808 oz. ASW, 24.3 mm.

Date	Mintage	MS63	MS65	Prf65
2008S	1,200,000	—	—	8.50

Arizona

KM# 423 • 5.67 g., Copper-Nickel Clad Copper, 24.3 mm.

Date	Mintage	MS63	MS65	Prf65
2008P	244,600,000	0.65	5.00	—
2008P Satin finish	745,464	1.50	4.50	—
2008D	265,000,000	0.65	5.00	—
2008D Satin finish	745,464	1.50	4.50	—
2008S	2,100,000	—	—	2.30

KM# 423a • 6.25 g., 0.900 Silver 0.1808 oz. ASW, 24.3 mm.

Date	Mintage	MS63	MS65	Prf65
2008S	1,200,000	—	—	8.50

QUARTER

Alaska

KM# 424 • 5.67 g., Copper-Nickel Clad Copper, 24.3 mm.

Date	Mintage	MS63	MS65	Prf65
2008P	251,800,000	0.65	5.00	—
2008P Satin finish	745,464	1.50	4.50	—
2008D	254,000,000	0.65	5.00	—
2008D Satin finish	745,464	1.50	4.50	—
2008S	2,100,000	—	—	2.30

KM# 424a • 6.25 g., 0.900 Silver 0.1808 oz. ASW, 24.3 mm.

Date	Mintage	MS63	MS65	Prf65
2008S	1,200,000	—	—	8.50

Hawaii

KM# 425 • 5.67 g., Copper-Nickel Clad Copper, 24.3 mm.

Date	Mintage	MS63	MS65	Prf65
2008P	254,000,000	0.65	5.00	—
2008P Satin finish	745,464	1.50	4.50	—
2008D	263,600,000	0.65	5.00	—
2008D Satin finish	745,464	1.50	4.50	—
2008S	2,100,000	—	—	2.30

KM# 425a • 6.25 g., 0.900 Silver 0.1808 oz. ASW, 24.3 mm.

Date	Mintage	MS63	MS65	Prf65
2008S	1,200,000	—	—	8.50

DC and Territories

District of Columbia

KM# 445 • 5.67 g., Copper-Nickel Clad Copper, 24.3 mm.

Date	Mintage	MS63	MS65	Prf65
2009P	83,600,000	0.75	5.00	—
2009D	88,800,000	0.75	5.00	—
2009S	2,113,478	—	—	3.75

KM# 445a • 6.25 g., 0.900 Silver 0.1808 oz. ASW, 24.3 mm.

Date	Mintage	MS63	MS65	Prf65
2009S	996,548	—	—	7.75

Puerto Rico

KM# 446 • 5.67 g., Copper-Nickel Clad Copper, 24.3 mm.

Date	Mintage	MS63	MS65	Prf65
2009P	53,200,000	0.75	5.00	—
2009D	86,000,000	0.75	5.00	—
2009S	2,113,478	—	—	3.75

KM# 446a • 6.25 g., 0.900 Silver 0.1808 oz. ASW, 24.3 mm.

Date	Mintage	MS63	MS65	Prf65
2009S	996,548	—	—	7.75

Guam

KM# 447 • 5.67 g., Copper-Nickel Clad Copper, 24.3 mm.

Date	Mintage	MS63	MS65	Prf65
2009P	45,000,000	0.75	5.00	—
2009D	42,600,000	0.75	5.00	—
2009S	2,113,478	—	—	3.75

KM# 447a • 6.25 g., 0.900 Silver 0.1808 oz. ASW, 24.3 mm.

Date	Mintage	MS63	MS65	Prf65
2009S	996,548	—	—	7.75

American Samoa

KM# 448 • 5.67 g., Copper-Nickel Clad Copper, 24.3 mm.

Date	Mintage	MS63	MS65	Prf65
2009P	42,600,000	0.75	5.00	—
2009D	39,600,000	0.75	5.00	—
2009S	2,113,478	—	—	3.75

KM# 448a • 6.25 g., 0.900 Silver 0.1808 oz. ASW, 24.3 mm.

Date	Mintage	MS63	MS65	Prf65
2009S	996,548	—	—	7.75

US Virgin Islands

KM# 449 • 5.67 g., Copper-Nickel Clad Copper, 24.3 mm.

Date	Mintage	MS63	MS65	Prf65
2009P	41,000,000	0.75	5.00	—
2009D	41,000,000	0.75	5.00	—
2009S	2,113,478	—	—	3.75

KM# 449a • 6.25 g., 0.900 Silver 0.1808 oz. ASW, 24.3 mm.

Date	Mintage	MS63	MS65	Prf65
2009S	996,548	—	—	7.75

Northern Mariana Islands

KM# 466 • 5.67 g., Copper-Nickel Clad Copper

Date	Mintage	MS63	MS65	Prf65
2009P	35,200,000	0.75	5.00	—
2009D	37,600,000	0.75	5.00	—
2009S	2,113,478	—	—	3.75

KM# 466a • 6.25 g., 0.900 Silver 0.1808 oz. ASW

Date	Mintage	MS63	MS65	Prf65
2009S	996,548	—	—	7.75

America the Beautiful

Hot Springs, Ark.

KM# 469 • 5.67 g., Copper-Nickel Clad Copper, 24.3 mm.

Date	Mintage	MS63	MS65	Prf65
2010P	35,600,000	0.75	5.00	—
2010D	34,000,000	0.75	5.00	—
2010S	1,401,903	—	—	3.75

KM# 469a • 6.25 g., 0.900 Silver 0.1808 oz. ASW

Date	Mintage	MS63	MS65	Prf65
2010S	859,435	—	—	7.75

Yellowstone National Park

KM# 470 • 5.67 g., Copper-Nickel Clad Copper, 24.3 mm.

Date	Mintage	MS63	MS65	Prf65
2010P	33,600,000	0.75	5.00	—
2010D	34,800,000	0.75	5.00	—
2010S	1,402,756	—	—	3.75

KM# 470a • 6.25 g., 0.900 Silver 0.1808 oz. ASW

Date	Mintage	MS63	MS65	Prf65
2010	859,435	—	—	7.75

Yosemite National Park

KM# 471 • 5.67 g., Copper-Nickel Clad Copper, 24.3 mm.

Date	Mintage	MS63	MS65	Prf65
2010P	35,200,000	0.75	5.00	—
2010D	34,800,000	0.75	5.00	—
2010S	1,400,215	—	—	3.75

KM# 471a • 6.25 g., 0.900 Silver 0.1808 oz. ASW

Date	Mintage	MS63	MS65	Prf65
2010	859,435	—	—	7.75

Grand Canyon National Park

KM# 472 • 5.67 g., Copper-Nickel Clad Copper, 24.3 mm.

Date	Mintage	MS63	MS65	Prf65
2010P	34,800,000	0.75	5.00	—
2010D	35,400,000	0.75	5.00	—
2010S	1,399,970	—	—	3.75

KM# 472a • 6.25 g., 0.900 Silver 0.1808 oz. ASW

Date	Mintage	MS63	MS65	Prf65
2010	859,435	—	—	7.75

QUARTER

Mount Hood National Park

KM# 473 • 5.67 g., Copper-Nickel Clad Copper, 24.3 mm.

Date	Mintage	MS63	MS65	Prf65
2010P	34,400,000	0.75	5.00	—
2010D	34,400,000	0.75	5.00	—
2010S	1,397,101	—	—	3.75

KM# 473a • 6.25 g., 0.900 Silver 0.1808 oz. ASW

Date	Mintage	MS63	MS65	Prf65
2010S	859,435	—	—	7.75

Gettysburg National Military Park

KM# 494 • 5.67 g., Copper-Nickel Clad Copper, 24 mm.

Date	Mintage	MS63	MS65	Prf65
2011P	30,800,000	0.75	5.00	—
2011D	30,400,000	0.75	5.00	—
2011S	1,271,553	—	—	3.75

KM# 494a • 6.25 g., 0.900 Silver 0.1808 oz. ASW

Date	Mintage	MS63	MS65	Prf65
2011S	722,076	—	—	7.75

Glacier National Park

KM# 495 • 5.67 g., Copper-Nickel Clad Copper, 24 mm.

Date	Mintage	MS63	MS65	Prf65
2011P	30,400,000	0.75	5.00	—
2011D	31,200,000	0.75	5.00	—
2011S	1,268,452	—	—	3.75

KM# 495a • 6.25 g., 0.900 Silver 0.1808 oz. ASW

Date	Mintage	MS63	MS65	Prf65
2011S	722,076	—	—	7.75

Olympic National Park

KM# 496 • 5.67 g., Copper-Nickel Clad Copper, 24 mm.

Date	Mintage	MS63	MS65	Prf65
2011P	30,400,000	0.75	5.00	—
2011D	30,600,000	0.75	5.00	—
2011S	1,267,361	—	—	3.75

KM# 496a • 6.25 g., 0.900 Silver 0.1808 oz. ASW

Date	Mintage	MS63	MS65	Prf65
2011S	722,076	—	—	7.75

Vicksburg National Military Park

KM# 497 • 5.67 g., Copper-Nickel Clad Copper, 24 mm.

Date	Mintage	MS63	MS65	Prf65
2011P	30,800,000	0.75	5.00	—
2011D	33,400,000	0.75	5.00	—
2011S	1,267,691	—	—	3.75

KM# 497a • 6.25 g., 0.900 Silver 0.1808 oz. ASW

Date	Mintage	MS63	MS65	Prf65
2011S	722,076	—	—	7.75

Chickasaw National Recreation Area

KM# 498 • 5.67 g., Copper-Nickel Clad Copper, 24 mm.

Date	Mintage	MS63	MS65	Prf65
2011P	73,800,000	0.75	5.00	—
2011D	69,400,000	0.75	5.00	—
2011S	1,266,010	—	—	3.75

KM# 498a • 6.25 g., 0.900 Silver 0.1808 oz. ASW

Date	Mintage	MS63	MS65	Prf65
2011S	722,076	—	—	7.75

El Yunque National Forest

KM# 519 • 5.67 g., Copper-Nickel Clad Copper, 24.3 mm.

Date	Mintage	MS63	MS65	Prf65
2012P	25,800,000	0.75	5.00	—
2012D	25,800,000	0.75	5.00	—
2012S	1,010,361	—	7.50	—
2012S	1,679,240	—	—	3.75

KM# 519a • 6.25 g., 0.900 Silver 0.1808 oz. ASW, 24.3 mm.

Date	Mintage	MS63	MS65	Prf65
2012S	557,891	—	—	7.75

Chaco Culture National Historic Park

KM# 520 • 5.71 g., Copper-Nickel Clad Copper, 24.3 mm.

Date	Mintage	MS63	MS65	Prf65
2012P	22,000,000	0.75	8.00	—
2012D	22,000,000	0.75	8.00	—
2012S	960,049	—	10.00	—
2012S	1,389,020	—	—	4.00

KM# 520a • 6.25 g., 0.900 Silver 0.1808 oz. ASW, 24.3 mm.

Date	Mintage	MS63	MS65	Prf65
2012S	557,891	—	—	7.75

Acadia National Park

KM# 521 • 5.67 g., Copper-Nickel Clad Copper, 24.3 mm.

Date	Mintage	MS63	MS65	Prf65
2012P	24,800,000	0.75	5.00	—
2012D	21,606,000	0.75	5.00	—
2012S	960,409	—	7.50	—
2012S	1,409,120	—	—	3.75

KM# 521a • 6.25 g., 0.900 Silver 0.1808 oz. ASW, 24.3 mm.

Date	Mintage	MS63	MS65	Prf65
2012S	557,891	—	—	7.75

Hawai'i Volcanoes National Park

KM# 522 • 5.67 g., Copper-Nickel Clad Copper, 24.3 mm.

Date	Mintage	MS63	MS65	Prf65
2012P	46,200,000	0.75	5.00	—
2012D	78,600,000	0.75	5.00	—
2012S	961,272	—	7.50	—
2012S	1,407,520	—	—	3.75

KM# 522a • 6.25 g., 0.900 Silver 0.1808 oz. ASW, 24.3 mm.

Date	Mintage	MS63	MS65	Prf65
2012S	557,891	—	—	7.75

Denali National Park

KM# 523 • 5.67 g., Copper-Nickel Clad Copper, 24.3 mm.

Date	Mintage	MS63	MS65	Prf65
2012P	135,400,000	0.75	5.00	—
2012D	166,600,000	0.75	5.00	—
2012S	957,856	—	7.50	—
2012S	1,401,920	—	—	3.75

KM# 523a • 6.25 g., 0.900 Silver 0.1808 oz. ASW, 24.3 mm.

Date	Mintage	MS63	MS65	Prf65
2012S	557,891	—	—	7.75

White Mountain National Forest

KM# 542 • 5.67 g., Copper-Nickel Clad Copper, 24.3 mm.

Date	Mintage	MS63	MS65	Prf65
2013P	68,800,000	0.75	5.00	—
2013D	107,600,000	0.75	5.00	—
2013S	950,080	—	7.50	—
2013S	990,144	—	—	3.75

KM# 542a • 6.25 g., 0.900 Silver 0.1808 oz. ASW, 24.3 mm.

Date	Mintage	MS63	MS65	Prf65
2013S	579,409	—	—	7.75

QUARTER

Perry's Victory and International Peace Memorial

KM# 543 • 5.67 g., Copper-Nickel Clad Copper, 24.3 mm.

Date	Mintage	MS63	MS65	Prf65
2013P	107,800,000	0.75	5.00	—
2013D	131,600,000	0.75	5.00	—
2013S	913,563	—	7.50	—
2013S	947,992	—	—	3.75

KM# 543a • 6.25 g., 0.900 Silver 0.1808 oz. ASW, 24.3 mm.

Date	Mintage	MS63	MS65	Prf65
2013S	579,409	—	—	7.75

Great Basin National Park

KM# 544 • 5.67 g., Copper-Nickel Clad Copper, 24.3 mm.

Date	Mintage	MS63	MS65	Prf65
2013P	122,400,000	0.75	5.00	—
2013D	141,400,000	0.75	5.00	—
2013S	911,525	—	7.50	—
2013S	945,867	—	—	3.75

KM# 544a • 6.25 g., 0.900 Silver 0.1808 oz. ASW, 24.3 mm.

Date	Mintage	MS63	MS65	Prf65
2013S	579,409	—	—	7.75

Fort McHenry National Monument and Historic Shrine

KM# 545 • 5.67 g., Copper-Nickel Clad Copper, 24.3 mm.

Date	Mintage	MS63	MS65	Prf65
2013P	120,000,000	0.75	5.00	—
2013D	151,400,000	0.75	5.00	—
2013S	911,451	—	7.50	—
2013S	946,514	—	—	3.75

KM# 545a • 6.25 g., 0.900 Silver 0.1808 oz. ASW, 24.3 mm.

Date	Mintage	MS63	MS65	Prf65
2013S	579,409	—	—	7.75

Mount Rushmore National Memorial

KM# 546 • 5.67 g., Copper-Nickel Clad Copper, 24.3 mm.

Date	Mintage	MS63	MS65	Prf65
2013P	231,800,000	0.75	5.00	—
2013D	272,400,000	0.75	5.00	—
2013S	920,695	—	7.50	—
2013S	959,244	—	—	3.75

KM# 546a • 6.25 g., 0.900 Silver 0.1808 oz. ASW, 24.3 mm.

Date	Mintage	MS63	MS65	Prf65
2013S	579,409	—	—	7.75

Great Smoky Mountains National Park

KM# 566 • 5.67 g., Copper-Nickel Clad Copper, 24.3 mm.

Date	Mintage	MS63	MS65	Prf65
2014P	73,593,253	0.75	5.00	—
2014D	99,793,253	0.75	5.00	—
2014S	1,360,780	—	7.50	—
2014S	882,444	—	—	3.75

KM# 566a • 6.25 g., 0.900 Silver 0.1808 oz. ASW, 24.3 mm.

Date	Mintage	MS63	MS65	Prf65
2014S	586,325	—	—	7.75

Shenandoah National Park

KM# 567 • 5.67 g., Copper-Nickel Clad Copper, 24.3 mm.

Date	Mintage	MS63	MS65	Prf65
2014P	113,191,404	0.75	5.00	—
2014D	198,191,404	0.75	5.00	—
2014S	1,266,720	—	7.50	—
2014S	846,579	—	—	3.75

KM# 567a • 6.25 g., 0.900 Silver 0.1808 oz. ASW, 24.3 mm.

Date	Mintage	MS63	MS65	Prf65
2014S	586,325	—	—	7.75

Arches National Park

KM# 568 • 5.67 g., Copper-Nickel Clad Copper,
24.3 mm.

Date	Mintage	MS63	MS65	Prf65
2014P	214,589,782	0.75	5.00	—
2014D	251,789,782	0.75	5.00	—
2014S	1,235,720	—	7.50	—
2014S	844,957	—	—	3.75

KM# 568a • 6.25 g., 0.900 Silver 0.1808 oz. ASW,
24.3 mm.

Date	Mintage	MS63	MS65	Prf65
2014S	586,325	—	—	7.75

Great Sand Dunes National Park

KM# 569 • 5.67 g., Copper-Nickel Clad Copper,
24.3 mm.

Date	Mintage	MS63	MS65	Prf65
2014P	159,988,214	0.75	5.00	—
2014D	172,188,214	0.75	5.00	—
2014S	1,176,760	—	7.50	—
2014S	843,389	—	—	3.75

KM# 569a • 6.25 g., 0.900 Silver 0.1808 oz. ASW,
24.3 mm.

Date	Mintage	MS63	MS65	Prf65
2014S	586,325	—	—	7.75

Everglades National Park

KM# 570 • 5.67 g., Copper-Nickel Clad Copper,
24.3 mm.

Date	Mintage	MS63	MS65	Prf65
2014P	157,989,610	0.75	5.00	—
2014D	142,788,410	0.75	5.00	—
2014S	1,180,900	—	7.50	—
2014S	856,549	—	—	3.75

KM# 570a • 6.25 g., 0.900 Silver 0.1808 oz. ASW,
24.3 mm.

Date	Mintage	MS63	MS65	Prf65
2014S	586,325	—	—	7.75

Homestead National Monument of America

KM# 597 • 5.67 g., Copper-Nickel Clad Copper,
24.3 mm.

Date	Mintage	MS63	MS65	Prf65
2015P	214,400,000	0.75	5.00	—
2015D	248,600,000	0.75	5.00	—
2015S	—	—	—	3.75

KM# 597a • 6.25 g., 0.900 Silver 0.1808 oz. ASW,
24.3 mm.

Date	Mintage	MS63	MS65	Prf65
2015S	—	—	—	7.75

Kisatchie National Forest

KM# 598 • 5.67 g., Copper-Nickel Clad Copper,
24.3 mm.

Date	Mintage	MS63	MS65	Prf65
2015P	397,200,000	0.75	5.00	—
2015D	379,600,000	0.75	5.00	—
2015S	—	—	—	3.75

Blue Ridge Parkway

KM# 599 • 5.67 g., Copper-Nickel Clad Copper,
24.3 mm.

Date	Mintage	MS63	MS65	Prf65
2015P	325,616,000	0.75	5.00	—
2015D	505,200,000	0.75	5.00	—
2015S	—	—	—	3.75

KM# 599a • 6.25 g., 0.900 Silver 0.1808 oz. ASW,
24.3 mm.

Date	Mintage	MS63	MS65	Prf65
2015S	—	—	—	7.75

QUARTER

Bombay Hook
National Wildlife Refuge

KM# 600 • 5.67 g., Copper-Nickel Clad Copper, 24.3 mm.

Date	Mintage	MS63	MS65	Prf65
2015P	275,000,000	0.75	5.00	—
2015D	206,400,000	0.75	5.00	—
2015S	—	—	—	3.75

KM# 600a • 6.25 g., 0.900 Silver 0.1808 oz. ASW, 24.3 mm.

Date	Mintage	MS63	MS65	Prf65
2015S	—	—	—	7.75

Saratoga National Historical Park

KM# 601 • 5.67 g., Copper-Nickel Clad Copper, 24.3 mm.

Date	Mintage	MS63	MS65	Prf65
2015P	223,000,000	0.75	5.00	—
2015D	215,800,000	0.75	5.00	—
2015S	—	—	—	3.75

KM# 601a • 6.25 g., 0.900 Silver 0.1808 oz. ASW, 24.3 mm.

Date	Mintage	MS63	MS65	Prf65
2015S	—	—	—	7.75

Shawnee National Forest

KM# 635 • 5.67 g., Copper-Nickel Clad Copper, 24.3 mm.

Date	Mintage	MS63	MS65	Prf65
2016P	—	0.75	5.00	—
2016D	—	0.75	5.00	—
2016S Proof	—	—	—	3.75

KM# 635a • 6.25 g., 0.900 Silver 0.1808 oz. ASW, 24.3 mm.

Date	Mintage	MS63	MS65	Prf65
2016S Proof	—	—	—	7.75

Cumberland Gap
National Historical Park

KM# 636 • 5.67 g., Copper-Nickel Clad Copper, 24.3 mm.

Date	Mintage	MS63	MS65	Prf65
2016P	—	0.75	5.00	—
2016D	—	0.75	5.00	—
2016S Proof	—	—	—	3.75

KM# 636a • 6.25 g., 0.900 Silver 0.1808 oz. ASW, 24.3 mm.

Date	Mintage	MS63	MS65	Prf65
2016S Proof	—	—	—	7.75

Harper's Ferry
National Historical Park

KM# 637 • 5.67 g., Copper-Nickel Clad Copper, 24.3 mm.

Date	Mintage	MS63	MS65	Prf65
2016P	—	0.75	5.00	—
2016D	—	0.75	5.00	—
2016S Proof	—	—	—	3.75

KM# 637a • 6.25 g., 0.900 Silver 0.1808 oz. ASW, 24.3 mm.

Date	Mintage	MS63	MS65	Prf65
2016S Proof	—	—	—	7.75

Theodore Roosevelt
National Park

KM# 638 • 5.67 g., Copper-Nickel Clad Copper, 24.3 mm.

Date	Mintage	MS63	MS65	Prf65
2016P	—	0.75	5.00	—
2016D	—	0.75	5.00	—
2016S Proof	—	—	—	3.75

KM# 638a • 6.25 g., 0.900 Silver 0.1808 oz. ASW, 24.3 mm.

Date	Mintage	MS63	MS65	Prf65
2016S Proof	—	—	—	7.75

QUARTER

Fort Moultrie (Fort Sumter) National Monument

KM# 639 • 5.67 g., Copper-Nickel Clad Copper, 24.3 mm.

Date	Mintage	MS63	MS65	Prf65
2016P	—	0.75	5.00	—
2016D	—	0.75	5.00	—
2016S Proof	—	—	—	3.75

KM# 639a • 6.25 g., 0.900 Silver 0.1808 oz. ASW, 24.3 mm.

Date	Mintage	MS63	MS65	Prf65
2016S Proof	—	—	—	7.75

Effigy Mounds National Monument

KM# 653 • 5.67 g., Copper-Nickel Clad Copper, 24.3 mm.

Date	Mintage	MS63	MS65	Prf65
2017P	—	0.75	5.00	—
2017D	—	0.75	5.00	—
2017S Enhanced Unc.	225,000	—	15.00	—
2017S Proof	—	—	—	3.75

KM# 653a • 6.25 g., 0.900 Silver 0.1808 oz. ASW, 24.3 mm.

Date	Mintage	MS63	MS65	Prf65
2017S Proof	—	—	—	7.75

Frederick Douglass National Historic Site

KM# 654 • 5.67 g., Copper-Nickel Clad Copper, 24.3 mm.

Date	Mintage	MS63	MS65	Prf65
2017P	—	0.75	5.00	—
2017D	—	0.75	5.00	—
2017S Enhanced Unc.	225,000	—	15.00	—
2017S Proof	—	—	—	3.75

KM# 654a • 6.25 g., 0.900 Silver 0.1808 oz. ASW, 24.3 mm.

Date	Mintage	MS63	MS65	Prf65
2017S Proof	—	—	—	7.75

Ozark National Scenic Riverways

KM# 655 • 5.67 g., Copper-Nickel Clad Copper, 24.3 mm.

Date	Mintage	MS63	MS65	Prf65
2017P	—	0.75	5.00	—
2017D	—	0.75	5.00	—
2017S Enhanced Unc.	225,000	—	15.00	—
2017S Proof	—	—	—	3.75

KM# 655a • 6.25 g., 0.900 Silver 0.1808 oz. ASW, 24.3 mm.

Date	Mintage	MS63	MS65	Prf65
2017S Proof	—	—	—	7.75

Ellis Island (Statue of Liberty National Monument)

KM# 656 • 5.67 g., Copper-Nickel Clad Copper, 24.3 mm.

Date	Mintage	MS63	MS65	Prf65
2017P	—	0.75	5.00	—
2017D	—	0.75	5.00	—
2017S Enhanced Unc.	225,000	—	15.00	—
2017S Proof	—	—	—	3.75

KM# 656a • 6.25 g., 0.900 Silver 0.1808 oz. ASW, 24.3 mm.

Date	Mintage	MS63	MS65	Prf65
2017S Proof	—	—	—	7.75

George Rogers Clark National Historical Park

KM# 657 • 5.67 g., Copper-Nickel Clad Copper, 24.3 mm.

Date	Mintage	MS63	MS65	Prf65
2017P	—	0.75	5.00	—
2017D	—	0.75	5.00	—
2017S Enhanced Unc.	225,000	—	15.00	—
2017S Proof	—	—	—	3.75

KM# 657a • 6.25 g., 0.900 Silver 0.1808 oz. ASW, 24.3 mm.

Date	Mintage	MS63	MS65	Prf65
2017S Proof	—	—	—	7.75

QUARTER

Pictured Rocks National Lakeshore

KM# 669 • 5.67 g., Copper-Nickel Clad Copper, 24.3 mm.

Date	Mintage	MS63	MS65	Prf65
2018P	—	0.75	5.00	—
2018D	—	0.75	5.00	—
2018S Proof	—	—	—	3.75

KM# 669a • 6.25 g., 0.900 Silver 0.1808 oz. ASW, 24.3 mm.

Date	Mintage	MS63	MS65	Prf65
2018S Proof	—	—	—	7.75
2018S Reverse Proof	—	—	—	9.00

Apostle Islands National Lakeshore

KM# 670 • 5.67 g., Copper-Nickel Clad Copper, 24.3 mm.

Date	Mintage	MS63	MS65	Prf65
2018P	—	0.75	5.00	—
2018D	—	0.75	5.00	—
2018S Proof	—	—	—	3.75

KM# 670a • 6.25 g., 0.900 Silver 0.1808 oz. ASW, 24.3 mm.

Date	Mintage	MS63	MS65	Prf65
2018S Proof	—	—	—	7.75
2018S Reverse Proof	—	—	—	9.00

Voyageurs National Park

KM# 671 • 5.67 g., Copper-Nickel Clad Copper, 24.3 mm.

Date	Mintage	MS63	MS65	Prf65
2018P	—	0.75	5.00	—
2018D	—	0.75	5.00	—
2018S Proof	—	—	—	3.75

KM# 671a • 6.25 g., 0.900 Silver 0.1808 oz. ASW, 24.3 mm.

Date	Mintage	MS63	MS65	Prf65
2018S Proof	—	—	—	7.75
2018S Reverse Proof	—	—	—	9.00

Cumberland Island National Seashore

KM# 672 • 5.67 g., Copper-Nickel Clad Copper, 24.3 mm.

Date	Mintage	MS63	MS65	Prf65
2018P	—	0.75	5.00	—
2018D	—	0.75	5.00	—
2018S Proof	—	—	—	3.75

KM# 672a • 6.25 g., 0.900 Silver 0.1808 oz. ASW, 24.3 mm.

Date	Mintage	MS63	MS65	Prf65
2018S Proof	—	—	—	7.75
2018S Reverse Proof	—	—	—	9.00

Block Island National Wildlife Refuge

KM# 673 • 5.67 g., Copper-Nickel Clad Copper, 24.3 mm.

Date	Mintage	MS63	MS65	Prf65
2018P	—	0.75	5.00	—
2018D	—	0.75	5.00	—
2018S Proof	—	—	—	3.75

KM# 673a • 6.25 g., 0.900 Silver 0.1808 oz. ASW, 24.3 mm.

Date	Mintage	MS63	MS65	Prf65
2018S Proof	—	—	—	7.75
2018S Reverse Proof	—	—	—	9.00

QUARTER

Flowing Hair Half Dollar

KM# 16 • 13.48 g., 0.892 Silver 0.3866 oz. ASW, 32.5 mm. • **Designer:** Robert Scot **Note:** The 1795 "recut date" variety had the date cut into the dies twice, so both sets of numbers are visible on the coin. The 1795 "3 leaves" variety has three leaves under each of the eagle's wings on the reverse.

Date	Mintage	G4	VG8	F12	VF20	XF40	MS60
1794	23,464	4,600	6,900	8,500	24,000	40,000	230,000
1795	299,680	1,600	1,800	2,040	2,950	8,950	32,000
1795 recut date	Inc. above	1,070	1,375	3,500	4,000	12,000	—
1795 3 leaves	Inc. above	2,400	3,000	4,500	6,600	18,000	54,000

Draped Bust Half Dollar
Draped bust right. Small eagle.

KM# 26 • 13.48 g., 0.892 Silver 0.3866 oz. ASW, 32.5 mm. • **Designer:** Robert Scot

Date	Mintage	G4	VG8	F12	VF20	XF40	MS60
1796 15 obverse stars	3,918	33,000	40,000	50,000	75,000	112,000	260,000
1796 16 obverse stars	Inc. above	34,000	41,000	50,000	75,000	112,000	260,000
1797	Inc. above	40,000	45,000	53,000	70,000	108,000	255,000

Draped bust right, flanked by stars, date at angle below. Heraldic eagle.

KM# 35 • 13.48 g., 0.892 Silver 0.3866 oz. ASW, 32.5 mm. • **Obv. Legend:** LIBERTY **Rev. Legend:** UNITED STATES OF AMERICA **Designer:** Robert Scot **Note:** The two varieties of the 1803 strikes are distinguished by the size of the 3 in the date. The several varieties of the 1806 strikes are distinguished by the style of 6 in the date, size of the stars on the obverse, and whether the stem of the olive branch held by the reverse eagle extends through the claw.

Date	Mintage	G4	VG8	F12	VF20	XF40	MS60
1801	30,289	1,200	1,750	2,500	2,875	5,000	63,000
1802	29,890	1,200	1,750	2,400	2,500	5,800	55,000
1803 small 3	188,234	500	600	625	1,000	1,800	26,500
1803 large 3	Inc. above	300	400	500	750	1,625	22,000
1805	211,722	220	400	460	700	1,925	22,000
1805/4	Inc. above	375	650	1,000	1,575	3,200	30,000
1806 knobbed 6, large stars	839,576	220	250	350	630	1,725	—
1806 knobbed 6, small stars	Inc. above	250	325	500	700	2,000	11,500

HALF DOLLAR

Date	Mintage	G4	VG8	F12	VF20	XF40	MS60
1806 knobbed 6, stem not through claw	Inc. above	70,000	90,000	100,000	112,000	116,000	—
1806 pointed-top 6, stem not through claw	Inc. above	250	300	400	640	1,725	10,000
1806 pointed-top 6, stem through claw	Inc. above	250	300	400	700	1,725	9,000
1806/5	Inc. above	300	375	600	850	2,200	14,000
1806 /inverted 6	Inc. above	375	500	925	1,425	3,500	27,250
1807	301,076	220	300	400	680	1,000	9,000

Capped Bust Half Dollar
Draped bust left, flanked by stars, date at angle below. 50 C. below eagle.

KM# 37 • 13.48 g., 0.892 Silver 0.3866 oz. ASW, 32.5 mm. • **Rev. Legend:** UNITED STATES OF AMERICA **Designer:** John Reich **Note:** There are three varieties of the 1807 strikes. Two are distinguished by the size of the stars on the obverse. The third was struck from a reverse die that had a 5 cut over a 2 in the "50C" denomination. Two varieties of the 1811 are distinguished by the size of the 8 in the date. A third has a period between the 8 and second 1 in the date. One variety of the 1817 has a period between the 1 and 7 in the date. Two varieties of the 1820 are distinguished by the size of the date. On the 1823 varieties, the "broken 3" appears to be almost separated in the middle of the 3 in the date; the "patched 3" has the error repaired; the "ugly 3" has portions of its detail missing. The 1827 "curled-2" and "square-2" varieties are distinguished by the numeral's base -- either curled or square. Among the 1828 varieties, "knobbed 2" and "no knob" refers to whether the upper left serif of the digit is rounded. The 1830 varieties are distinguished by the size of the 0 in the date. The four 1834 varieties are distinguished by the sizes of the stars, date and letters in the inscriptions. The 1836 "50/00" variety was struck from a reverse die that has "50" recut over "00" in the denomination.

Date	Mintage	G4	VG8	F12	VF20	XF40	AU50	MS60	MS65
1807 small stars	750,500	220	330	660	1,050	2,000	5,000	16,000	70,000
1807 large stars	Inc. above	200	250	450	750	1,250	2,700	11,000	150,000
1807 50/20 C.	Inc. above	175	200	300	475	750	1,650	7,000	65,000
1807 bearded goddess	—	700	1,100	2,500	4,000	7,000	12,000	—	—
1808	1,368,600	70.00	95.00	140	240	325	1,300	3,200	19,000
1808/7	Inc. above	95.00	150	200	275	875	1,500	5,000	23,000
1809 IIIIIII edge	Inc. above	90.00	125	175	300	700	1,200	5,000	40,000
1809 Normal edge	1,405,810	95.00	130	180	260	600	780	2,350	22,000
1809 XXXX edge	Inc. above	175	225	275	380	1,000	1,600	9,000	—
1810	1,276,276	85.00	105	130	220	390	500	2,200	22,000
1811 small 8	1,203,644	85.00	105	130	200	375	725	2,200	16,000
1811 large 8	Inc. above	85.00	105	130	200	390	950	1,850	23,000
1811 dated 18.11	Inc. above	125	150	250	400	625	1,100	6,500	35,000
1812	1,628,059	85.00	105	130	185	350	680	1,975	12,500
1812/1 small 8	Inc. above	125	150	200	300	600	1,150	3,300	21,000
1812/1 large 8	Inc. above	1,700	2,600	4,500	7,250	10,000	21,000	—	—
1812 Single leaf below wing	Inc. above	350	600	850	1,600	3,300	5,500	—	—
1813	1,241,903	85.00	95.00	110	185	500	1,000	2,600	22,000
1813 50/UNI reverse	1,241,903	150	175	250	425	850	1,300	2,700	42,500
1814	1,039,075	70.00	100	110	200	480	625	1,700	11,500
1814/3	Inc. above	175	225	300	450	825	1,950	4,400	30,000
1814 E/A in States	Inc. above	175	250	400	500	1,175	2,600	7,500	—
1814 Single leaf below wing	Inc. above	175	250	400	600	2,000	3,500	7,000	—
1815/2	47,150	1,400	2,000	3,300	3,600	5,400	9,000	17,500	115,000
1817	1,215,567	85.00	130	180	260	400	900	2,900	17,000
1817/3	Inc. above	200	275	500	700	1,275	2,850	8,500	37,000
1817/4	—	85,000	115,000	135,000	175,000	275,000	350,000	—	—
1817 dated 181.7	Inc. above	85.00	105	135	175	625	1,250	3,700	28,000
1817 Single leaf below wing	Inc. above	85.00	105	135	200	625	1,900	2,700	—
1818	1,960,322	60.00	75.00	95.00	160	300	650	1,700	13,500
1818/7 Large 8	Inc. above	80.00	90.00	165	200	550	1,400	3,400	25,000
1818/7 Small 8	Inc. above	95.00	105	155	250	525	1,300	2,750	22,000
1819	2,208,000	65.00	80.00	95.00	145	350	475	1,900	2,000
1819/8 small 9	Inc. above	70.00	80.00	115	200	475	725	2,200	22,000
1819/8 large 9	Inc. above	70.00	80.00	95.00	135	400	600	4,000	26,500
1820 Curl Base 2, small date	751,122	100	175	225	300	725	1,000	3,400	40,000
1820 Square Base 2 with knob, large date	Inc. above	100	175	200	250	500	1,000	3,800	22,000
1820 Square Base 2 without knob, large date	Inc. above	85.00	120	175	200	650	900	3,300	33,000

Date	Mintage	G4	VG8	F12	VF20	XF40	AU50	MS60	MS65
1820 E's without Serifs	Inc. above	600	850	1,350	3,300	7,500	11,000	25,000	—
1820/19 Square Base 2	Inc. above	85.00	125	150	250	800	1,200	2,400	37,000
1820/19 Curled Base 2	Inc. above	85.00	125	150	250	750	1,000	3,300	41,000
1821	1,305,797	70.00	77.00	125	160	250	375	1,700	16,000
1822	1,559,573	80.00	100	120	175	330	400	1,300	14,000
1822/1	Inc. above	75.00	90.00	120	175	600	1,175	2,350	21,000
1823	1,694,200	75.00	105	120	150	210	340	1,200	11,000
1823 broken 3	Inc. above	150	175	250	400	800	1,350	6,000	50,000
1823 patched 3	Inc. above	125	150	200	340	800	1,575	4,500	23,000
1823 ugly 3	Inc. above	125	150	200	340	700	2,200	6,000	33,000
1824	3,504,954	65.00	80.00	105	150	175	275	1,075	12,000
1824/21	Inc. above	90.00	125	150	175	350	625	2,100	21,500
1824/4	Inc. above	65.00	70.00	125	160	325	670	2,200	10,000
1824 1824/various dates	Inc. above	80.00	95.00	125	155	350	1,100	3,300	16,000
1825	2,943,166	65.00	78.00	80.00	90.00	170	275	1,100	11,000
1826	4,004,180	45.00	62.00	70.00	80.00	120	210	1,100	9,600
1827 curled 2	5,493,400	65.00	75.00	85.00	95.00	360	450	1,300	20,000
1827 square 2	Inc. above	45.00	58.00	82.00	95.00	120	210	1,100	10,750
1827/6	Inc. above	100	125	150	200	450	1,100	1,900	13,500
1828 curled-base 2, no knob	3,075,200	45.00	58.00	82.00	95.00	120	210	1,300	9,600
1828 curled-base 2, knobbed 2	Inc. above	64.00	75.00	100	160	250	600	2,000	12,750
1828 small 8s, square-base 2, large letters	Inc. above	45.00	58.00	82.00	95.00	120	440	1,275	9,000
1828 small 8s, square-base 2, small letters	Inc. above	125	150	175	250	400	800	2,200	25,500
1828 large 8s, square-base 2	Inc. above	45.00	58.00	70.00	95.00	120	210	1,275	12,500
1829	3,712,156	45.00	58.00	70.00	95.00	120	475	1,275	9,000
1829 Large letters	Inc. above	45.00	58.00	70.00	95.00	120	210	1,275	13,000
1829/7	Inc. above	68.00	80.00	125	160	300	790	1,400	21,000
1830 Small O rev	4,764,800	45.00	58.00	67.00	95.00	120	210	1,275	9,000
1830 Large O	Inc. above	45.00	58.00	67.00	95.00	120	210	1,275	9,000
1830 Large letter rev	Inc. above	800	1,100	1,600	3,300	5,500	8,800	14,000	—
1831	5,873,660	45.00	58.00	82.00	95.00	120	235	1,275	6,500
1832 small letters	4,797,000	45.00	58.00	82.00	95.00	120	235	1,275	9,000
1832 large letters	Inc. above	45.00	58.00	82.00	95.00	120	235	1,275	9,000
1833	5,206,000	45.00	58.00	62.00	65.00	120	235	1,275	9,000
1834 small date, large stars, small letters	6,412,004	45.00	58.00	82.00	95.00	120	235	1,275	9,000
1834 small date, small stars, small letters	Inc. above	45.00	58.00	82.00	95.00	120	235	1,275	9,000
1834 large date, small letters	Inc. above	45.00	58.00	82.00	95.00	120	235	1,275	9,000
1834 large date, large letters	Inc. above	45.00	58.00	82.00	95.00	120	235	1,275	9,000
1835	5,352,006	45.00	69.00	82.00	95.00	120	235	1,275	9,000
1836	6,545,000	45.00	75.00	82.00	95.00	120	235	1,275	9,000
1836	Inc. above	45.00	58.00	82.00	95.00	120	235	2,300	—
1836 50/00	Inc. above	125	150	200	300	450	800	2,600	30,000

Bust Half Dollar
Draped bust left, flanked by stars, date at angle below. "50 Cents" below eagle.
KM# 58 • 13.48 g., 0.892 Silver 0.3866 oz. ASW, 30 mm. • **Rev. Legend:** UNITED STATES OF AMERICA
Edge: Reeded. **Designer:** Christian Gobrecht

Date	Mintage	G4	VG8	F12	VF20	XF40	AU50	MS60	MS65
1836	1,200	880	1,100	1,600	1,950	4,000	4,700	8,800	68,000

HALF DOLLAR

Draped bust left, flanked by stars, date at angle below. "50 Cents" below eagle.

KM# 58a • 13.36 g., 0.900 Silver 0.3866 oz. ASW, 30 mm. • **Rev. Legend:** UNITED STATES OF AMERICA
Edge: Reeded. **Designer:** Christian Gobrecht

Date	Mintage	G4	VG8	F12	VF20	XF40	AU50	MS60	MS65
1837	3,629,820	60.00	70.00	77.00	100	175	345	1,500	16,500

Draped bust left, flanked by stars, date below. "HALF DOL." below eagle.

KM# 65 • 13.36 g., 0.900 Silver 0.3866 oz. ASW, 30 mm. • **Rev. Legend:** UNITED STATES OF AMERICA
Designer: Christian Gobrecht

Date	Mintage	G4	VG8	F12	VF20	XF40	AU50	MS60	MS65
1838	3,546,000	60.00	70.00	77.00	100	175	345	1,500	16,500
1838O proof only	Est. 20	—	—	—	—	275,000	300,000	375,000	
1839	1,392,976	60.00	74.00	130	175	235	450	1,300	27,000
1839O	116,000	400	600	900	1,175	1,780	2,400	6,700	60,000

Seated Liberty Half Dollar
Seated Liberty, date below. "HALF DOL." below eagle.

KM# 68 • 13.36 g., 0.900 Silver 0.3866 oz. ASW, 30.6 mm. • **Rev. Legend:** UNITED STATES OF AMERICA
Designer: Christian Gobrecht

Date	Mintage	G4	VG8	F12	VF20	XF40	AU50	MS60	MS65
1839 no drapery from elbow	Inc. above	40.00	120	325	550	1,150	1,950	6,300	125,000
1839 drapery	Inc. above	46.00	65.00	70.00	105	240	450	1,300	14,500
1840 small letters	1,435,008	30.00	40.00	50.00	55.00	120	235	650	7,000
1840 reverse 1838	Inc. above	150	210	360	500	1,000	1,600	3,800	—
1840O	855,100	40.00	50.00	80.00	175	320	425	1,500	—
1841	310,000	38.00	45.00	70.00	140	300	600	1,200	8,500
1841O	401,000	35.00	50.00	95.00	130	225	650	1,100	9,000
1842 small date	2,012,764	35.00	50.00	65.00	80.00	135	375	1,250	14,000
1842 medium date	Inc. above	35.00	50.00	60.00	100	160	375	950	7,500
1842O small date	957,000	600	850	1,200	1,800	3,000	6,000	13,000	—
1842O medium date	Inc. above	45.00	50.00	60.00	70.00	250	500	1,600	18,000
1843	3,844,000	40.00	45.00	55.00	80.00	150	210	750	6,500
1843O	2,268,000	50.00	55.00	60.00	70.00	195	375	1,300	22,000
1844	1,766,000	40.00	45.00	55.00	90.00	130	250	600	8,500
1844O	2,005,000	45.00	55.00	70.00	125	160	450	1,300	12,000
1844/18440	Inc. above	375	600	800	1,200	2,300	4,850	7,000	—
1845	589,000	35.00	60.00	70.00	110	180	350	800	—
1845O	2,094,000	35.00	50.00	55.00	80.00	125	250	425	7,000

Date	Mintage	G4	VG8	F12	VF20	XF40	AU50	MS60	MS65
1845O no drapery	Inc. above	75.00	100	125	150	400	770	1,125	—
1846 medium date	2,210,000	35.00	50.00	60.00	70.00	150	400	825	7,200
1846 tall date	Inc. above	45.00	50.00	80.00	110	350	500	600	15,000
1846 /horizontal 6	Inc. above	225	300	525	925	1,600	2,500	4,400	16,000
1846O medium date	2,304,000	50.00	60.00	95.00	170	235	400	1,400	18,000
1846O tall date	Inc. above	250	350	500	950	1,600	2,200	8,700	—
1847/1846	1,156,000	1,150	1,750	2,500	3,500	8,500	11,000	22,000	—
1847	Inc. above	30.00	50.00	60.00	80.00	180	215	550	6,400
1847O	2,584,000	45.00	60.00	65.00	90.00	200	250	950	12,000
1848	580,000	40.00	53.00	100	160	275	600	1,100	13,000
1848O	3,180,000	35.00	45.00	55.00	100	200	400	1,100	23,000
1849	1,252,000	35.00	60.00	65.00	125	150	300	900	11,000
1849O	2,310,000	45.00	550	60.00	175	400	780	1,500	16,000
1850	227,000	225	400	450	525	850	1,200	2,000	26,000
1850O	2,456,000	50.00	55.00	65.00	80.00	175	350	700	13,000
1851	200,750	650	700	800	900	1,200	2,300	3,400	10,750
1851O	402,000	35.00	85.00	125	150	300	800	1,200	9,500
1852	77,130	275	400	475	700	700	1,200	1,825	10,000
1852O	144,000	275	425	610	750	1,000	1,700	3,300	33,000
1853O mintage unrecorded	—	135,000	180,000	220,000	300,000	400,000	—	—	—

Seated Liberty, arrows at date. Rays around eagle.

KM# 79 • 12.44 g., 0.900 Silver 0.360 oz. ASW **Rev. Legend:** UNITED STATES OF AMERICA **Designer:** Christian Gobrecht

Date	Mintage	G4	VG8	F12	VF20	XF40	AU50	MS60	MS65	Prf65
1853	3,532,708	30.00	65.00	80.00	115	200	400	1,350	20,000	150,000
1853O	1,328,000	45.00	65.00	80.00	115	225	475	2,300	35,000	—

Seated Liberty, arrows at date. "HALF DOL." below eagle.

KM# 82 • 12.44 g., 0.900 Silver 0.360 oz. ASW **Rev. Legend:** UNITED STATES OF AMERICA **Designer:** Christian Gobrecht

Date	Mintage	G4	VG8	F12	VF20	XF40	AU50	MS60	MS65	Prf65
1854	2,982,000	36.50	42.00	55.00	75.00	110	315	500	8,000	25,000
1854O	5,240,000	36.50	42.00	60.00	70.00	130	185	500	6,750	—
1855	759,500	38.50	42.00	55.00	70.00	150	350	750	12,000	30,000
1855/4	Inc. above	65.00	90.00	190	360	500	1,025	1,850	11,000	55,000
1855O	3,688,000	39.50	42.00	60.00	70.00	130	300	500	8,600	—
1855S	129,950	400	1,000	1,200	1,600	2,950	5,825	32,000	—	—

Seated Liberty, date below. "HALF DOL." below eagle.

KM# A68 • 12.44 g., 0.900 Silver 0.360 oz. ASW **Rev. Legend:** UNITED STATES OF AMERICA **Designer:** Christian Gobrecht

Date	Mintage	G4	VG8	F12	VF20	XF40	AU50	MS60	MS65	Prf65
1856	938,000	35.00	50.00	55.00	70.00	180	300	500	4,600	18,000
1856O	2,658,000	40.00	50.00	60.00	80.00	145	265	375	6,200	—
1856S	211,000	75.00	125	200	375	1,000	1,750	4,500	—	—
1857	1,988,000	35.00	45.00	55.00	70.00	100	200	375	4,400	18,500
1857O	818,000	40.00	45.00	55.00	70.00	100	200	1,300	10,000	—
1857S	158,000	100	150	200	350	1,200	1,800	3,000	15,000	—
1858	4,226,000	35.00	45.00	550	70.00	90.00	150	375	4,200	6,000
1858O	7,294,000	40.00	50.00	55.00	70.00	100	150	375	6,300	—
1858S	476,000	45.00	65.00	100	225	300	500	1,500	13,000	—
1859	748,000	45.00	60.00	65.00	80.00	160	310	420	4,200	5,000
1859O	2,834,000	45.00	65.00	70.00	95.00	155	310	625	7,600	—
1859S	566,000	35.00	45.00	55.00	150	225	500	1,200	6,300	—
1860	303,700	40.00	45.00	60.00	70.00	125	250	550	4,200	5,000
1860O	1,290,000	35.00	50.00	55.00	125	200	425	650	4,400	—
1860S	472,000	45.00	80.00	105	135	250	450	1,275	—	—
1861	2,888,400	45.00	50.00	65.00	80.00	120	250	450	4,000	5,000
1861O	2,532,633	60.00	80.00	100	150	240	835	1,425	5,400	—
1861O CSA Obv, cracked die	Inc. above	300	450	650	1,200	3,700	4,400	13,000	—	—
1861S	939,500	45.00	55.00	80.00	100	300	650	1,000	17,500	—
1862	253,550	60.00	85.00	120	200	350	600	850	6,000	5,000
1862S	1,352,000	45.00	65.00	70.00	75.00	220	325	1,000	22,000	—
1863	503,660	35.00	60.00	80.00	125	185	350	650	7,000	5,000
1863S	916,000	35.00	60.00	80.00	175	360	600	1,200	11,250	—
1864	379,570	35.00	55.00	100	250	360	650	1,100	6,000	5,000
1864S	658,000	70.00	95.00	175	275	415	725	1,600	13,000	—
1865	511,900	70.00	95.00	135	180	450	700	1,300	4,500	5,000
1865S	675,000	75.00	105	150	200	400	725	1,825	55,000	—
1866 proof, unique	—	—	—	—	—	—	—	—	—	—
1866S	60,000	375	528	840	1,100	1,800	2,300	8,000	63,000	—

Seated Liberty, date below. "IN GOD WE TRUST above eagle."

KM# 99 • 12.44 g., 0.900 Silver 0.360 oz. ASW **Rev. Legend:** UNITED STATES OF AMERICA **Designer:** Christian Gobrecht

Date	Mintage	G4	VG8	F12	VF20	XF40	AU50	MS60	MS65	Prf65
1866	745,625	45.00	60.00	65.00	90.00	160	215	600	4,850	3,000
1866S	994,000	55.00	60.00	85.00	144	216	300	700	11,000	—
1867	449,925	60.00	70.00	105	155	240	350	700	4,300	3,000
1867S	1,196,000	47.00	55.00	80.00	115	200	336	1,200	11,000	—
1868	418,200	55.00	60.00	80.00	155	275	400	675	7,000	3,000
1868S	1,160,000	54.00	58.00	80.00	135	230	375	900	11,000	—
1869	795,900	50.00	60.00	70.00	90.00	125	230	650	9,000	3,000
1869S	656,000	55.00	60.00	70.00	115	175	375	850	6,500	—
1870	634,900	40.00	60.00	70.00	90.00	160	275	675	7,750	3,300
1870CC	54,617	1,100	2,400	4,750	5,500	1,000	27,500	70,000	—	—
1870S	1,004,000	60.00	75.00	100	150	400	550	2,000	30,000	—
1871	1,204,560	35.00	55.00	70.00	80.00	140	220	550	4,000	3,300
1871CC	153,950	475	725	1,275	1,500	3,000	5,400	27,000	—	—
1871S	2,178,000	40.00	50.00	60.00	80.00	160	325	800	7,000	—

Date	Mintage	G4	VG8	F12	VF20	XF40	AU50	MS60	MS65	Prf65
1872	881,550	40.00	45.00	55.00	70.00	150	300	650	6,000	2,150
1872CC	272,000	300	475	700	1,250	1,750	3,900	20,000	—	—
1872S	580,000	40.00	50.00	80.00	200	300	550	1,000	12,750	—
1873 closed 3	801,800	40.00	450	60.00	100	190	260	600	6,000	2,150
1873 open 3	Inc. above	2,750	4,000	4,500	5,000	7,000	12,500	45,000	—	—
1873CC	122,500	400	600	990	1,800	2,095	5,000	10,000	80,000	—
1873S no arrows	5,000	—	—	—	—	—	—	—	—	—

Note: 1873S no arrows, no specimens known to survive.

Seated Liberty, arrows at date. "IN GOD WE TRUST" above eagle.

KM# 107 • 12.50 g., 0.900 Silver 0.3617 oz. ASW **Rev. Legend:** UNITED STATES OF AMERICA **Designer:** Christian Gobrecht

Date	Mintage	G4	VG8	F12	VF20	XF40	AU50	MS60	MS65	Prf65
1873	1,815,700	35.00	45.00	60.00	70.00	175	380	725	13,000	8,000
1873CC	214,560	200	400	650	950	2,000	2,750	7,500	43,000	—
1873S	233,000	40.00	100	150	175	400	600	1,950	28,000	—
1874	2,360,300	35.00	45.00	60.00	70.00	200	350	725	1,300	8,000
1874CC	59,000	1,100	1,350	1,825	2,650	4,900	7,700	14,000	93,000	—
1874S	394,000	75.00	150	180	200	300	575	1,350	19,500	—

Seated Liberty, date below. "IN GOD WE TRUST" above eagle.

KM# A99 • 12.50 g., 0.900 Silver 0.3617 oz. ASW **Rev. Legend:** UNITED STATES OF AMERICA **Designer:** Christian Gobrecht

Date	Mintage	G4	VG8	F12	VF20	XF40	AU50	MS60	MS65	Prf65
1875	6,027,500	35.00	45.00	55.00	70.00	95.00	200	350	2,800	2,500
1875CC	1,008,000	60.00	100	175	250	400	800	1,300	7,000	—
1875S	3,200,000	35.00	40.00	60.00	70.00	125	200	330	2,600	—
1876	8,419,150	45.00	60.00	65.00	70.00	100	175	380	2,850	2,500
1876CC	1,956,000	80.00	90.00	115	175	340	600	950	4,825	—
1876S	4,528,000	36.50	55.00	65.00	70.00	100	200	540	3,000	—
1877	8,304,510	36.50	50.00	60.00	70.00	100	200	335	2,650	2,500
1877CC	1,420,000	85.00	105	125	175	300	400	1,000	5,800	—
1877S	5,356,000	36.50	42.00	55.00	70.00	100	200	330	2,700	—
1878	1,378,400	38.50	75.00	100	105	190	210	330	4,200	2,500
1878CC	62,000	850	1,200	2,000	2,400	3,200	4,500	10,000	57,500	—
1878S	12,000	24,000	34,000	35,500	37,000	54,500	65,000	85,000	210,000	—
1879	5,900	255	280	380	625	800	900	1,380	2,700	2,500
1880	9,755	255	280	380	460	660	760	1,100	3,000	2,500
1881	10,975	390	500	540	600	690	760	880	3,500	2,500
1882	5,500	255	280	380	460	660	760	880	4,000	2,500
1883	9,039	255	280	380	460	660	760	925	2,600	2,600
1884	5,275	265	330	385	475	660	770	1,465	3,800	2,500
1885	6,130	275	330	400	475	660	770	1,000	3,600	2,500
1886	5,886	300	375	400	425	660	770	880	3,450	2,500
1887	5,710	375	425	475	525	660	930	1,080	3,300	2,500
1888	12,833	250	300	375	600	660	810	980	3,500	2,500
1889	12,711	200	250	400	475	660	875	1,000	3,600	2,500
1890	12,590	200	250	400	475	620	770	880	3,400	2,500
1891	200,600	60.00	85.00	125	150	200	336	600	3,325	2,500

Barber Half Dollar

Laureate head right, flanked by stars, date below. Heraldic eagle.
KM# 116 • 12.50 g., 0.900 Silver 0.3617 oz. ASW, 30.6 mm. • **Obv. Legend:** IN GOD WE TRUST **Rev. Legend:** UNITED STATES OF AMERICA **Designer:** Charles E. Barber

Date	Mintage	G4	VG8	F12	VF20	XF40	AU50	MS60	MS65	Prf65
1892	935,245	30.00	35.00	70.00	145	225	410	530	2,500	1,990
1892O	390,000	285	375	525	580	600	775	900	2,600	—
1892O micro O	Inc. above	3,200	6,500	9,000	11,000	15,000	18,000	30,000	84,500	—
1892S	1,029,028	275	320	465	625	725	950	1,050	5,500	—
1893	1,826,792	20.00	40.00	70.00	204	225	360	750	2,700	1,990
1893O	1,389,000	35.00	57.00	170	350	400	500	900	8,800	—
1893S	740,000	140	185	500	660	975	1,825	2,000	17,500	—
1894	1,148,972	26.00	54.00	145	175	325	440	530	1,925	1,990
1894O	2,138,000	23.00	29.00	82.00	210	270	450	530	5,000	—
1894S	4,048,690	22.00	29.00	65.00	125	260	475	575	6,000	—
1895	1,835,218	22.00	29.00	165	195	260	400	530	2,500	1,990
1895O	1,766,000	32.00	57.00	115	205	350	410	720	5,000	—
1895S	1,108,086	31.00	45.00	195	250	425	475	545	4,800	—
1896	950,762	40.00	48.00	150	200	260	320	475	3,500	1,990
1896O	924,000	45.00	60.00	350	600	2,250	2,700	5,500	20,500	—
1896S	1,140,948	110	185	210	450	900	1,170	2,200	5,000	—
1897	2,480,731	21.00	29.00	30.00	145	225	310	530	2,500	1,990
1897O	632,000	145	190	575	710	935	1,200	1,725	7,700	—
1897S	933,900	120	200	375	600	1,975	2,200	2,600	6,600	—
1898	2,956,735	20.00	23.00	55.00	125	225	425	530	2,500	1,990
1898O	874,000	29.00	84.00	300	420	600	800	1,400	6,500	—
1898S	2,358,550	23.00	40.00	80.00	145	375	575	1,420	5,000	—
1899	5,538,846	19.00	23.00	60.00	85.00	225	280	312	1,720	1,990
1899O	1,724,000	21.00	32.00	68.00	145	400	500	660	4,800	—
1899S	1,686,411	19.00	35.00	135	185	205	370	720	5,700	—
1900	4,762,912	16.00	20.00	55.00	145	225	340	620	2,400	1,990
1900O	2,744,000	25.00	38.00	105	250	275	350	1,100	9,500	—
1900S	2,560,322	15.00	20.00	55.00	125	180	275	550	7,600	—
1901	4,268,813	15.00	20.00	55.00	125	225	300	600	2,400	1,990
1901O	1,124,000	15.00	29.00	147	330	1,100	1,350	1,925	12,500	—
1901S	847,044	30.00	44.00	200	525	900	1,600	3,750	12,000	—
1902	4,922,777	15.00	20.00	55.00	125	235	340	600	2,350	1,990
1902O	2,526,000	16.00	20.00	60.00	125	230	300	900	7,500	—
1902S	1,460,670	16.00	20.00	105	155	375	490	1,100	4,000	—
1903	2,278,755	16.00	20.00	55.00	125	225	340	550	5,800	1,990
1903O	2,100,000	16.00	20.00	55.00	125	300	415	770	3,800	—
1903S	1,920,772	16.00	20.00	80.00	125	375	440	900	3,100	—
1904	2,992,670	16.00	20.00	55.00	145	225	400	630	3,200	1,990
1904O	1,117,600	16.00	20.00	165	175	600	925	1,525	10,400	—
1904S	553,038	50.00	140	390	820	3,000	7,000	13,250	36,000	—
1905	662,727	16.00	32.00	120	170	225	475	700	4,700	1,990
1905O	505,000	26.00	40.00	170	220	350	420	860	4,000	—
1905S	2,494,000	16.00	20.00	75.00	125	235	390	660	6,600	—
1906	2,638,675	16.00	20.00	55.00	125	225	340	530	1,720	1,990
1906D	4,028,000	16.00	20.00	55.00	125	225	340	530	2,450	—
1906O	2,446,000	16.00	20.00	55.00	125	225	350	850	5,100	—
1906S	1,740,154	16.00	40.00	80.00	145	225	330	800	2,500	—
1907	2,598,575	16.00	20.00	55.00	145	225	400	530	1,720	1,990
1907D	3,856,000	16.00	20.00	55.00	145	225	450	530	1,720	—
1907O	3,946,000	16.00	20.00	55.00	145	225	340	530	1,720	—
1907S	1,250,000	16.00	40.00	90.00	145	425	810	2,500	9,300	—
1908	1,354,545	16.00	20.00	55.00	145	225	340	530	1,720	1,990
1908D	3,280,000	16.00	20.00	55.00	145	225	340	530	2,350	—
1908O	5,360,000	16.00	20.00	55.00	145	225	340	530	2,875	—
1908S	1,644,828	16.00	20.00	55.00	145	400	625	990	3,600	—
1909	2,368,650	16.00	20.00	55.00	145	225	340	530	1,845	1,990
1909O	925,400	16.00	20.00	80.00	145	480	625	990	4,800	—
1909S	1,764,000	16.00	20.00	55.00	145	275	440	660	3,300	—
1910	418,551	16.00	35.00	75.00	185	315	355	535	3,500	1,990

Date	Mintage	G4	VG8	F12	VF20	XF40	AU50	MS60	MS65	Prf65
1910S	1,948,000	16.00	20.00	75.00	145	220	410	720	2,800	—
1911	1,406,543	16.00	20.00	55.00	145	225	340	530	1,720	1,990
1911D	695,080	16.00	20.00	55.00	145	225	340	530	1,720	—
1911S	1,272,000	16.00	20.00	55.00	145	390	440	700	3,500	—
1912	1,550,700	16.00	20.00	55.00	145	225	340	530	1,720	1,990
1912D	2,300,800	16.00	20.00	55.00	145	225	400	530	1,720	—
1912S	1,370,000	16.00	20.00	55.00	145	225	360	550	3,100	—
1913	188,627	65.00	100	185	385	770	1,250	1,600	3,900	1,990
1913D	534,000	16.00	20.00	55.00	145	175	340	530	3,000	—
1913S	604,000	16.00	20.00	85.00	155	325	450	660	3,750	—
1914	124,610	150	170	360	500	880	1,100	1,425	5,800	1,990
1914S	992,000	16.00	20.00	55.00	145	240	400	585	3,300	—
1915	138,450	75.00	125	300	425	600	975	1,320	5,500	1,990
1915D	1,170,400	16.00	20.00	55.00	145	225	340	530	1,800	—
1915S	1,604,000	16.00	20.00	55.00	145	225	340	530	1,720	—

Walking Liberty Half Dollar

Liberty walking left wearing U.S. flag gown, sunrise at left. Eagle advancing left.

KM# 142 • 12.50 g., 0.900 Silver 0.3617 oz. ASW, 30.6 mm. • **Designer:** Adolph A. Weinman **Note:** The mint mark appears on the obverse below the word "Trust" on 1916 and some 1917 issues. Starting with some 1917 issues and continuing through the remainder of the series, the mint mark was changed to the reverse, at about the 8 o'clock position near the rim.

Obverse mint mark	Reverse mint mark
1916-1917	1917-1947

Date	Mintage	G4	VG8	F12	VF20	XF40	AU50	MS60	MS65	Prf65
1916	608,000	44.00	75.00	130	180	240	310	450	2,300	—
1916D	1,014,400	44.00	75.00	130	180	170	265	680	2,600	—
1916S	508,000	80.00	150	220	350	495	900	1,600	6,100	—
1917	12,292,000	14.00	15.00	21.00	23.00	35.00	85.00	150	1,065	—
1917D obv. mint mark	765,400	21.00	30.00	68.00	130	265	400	725	7,395	—
1917S obv. mint mark	952,000	23.00	37.00	170	300	800	1,275	3,000	26,000	—
1917D rev. mint mark	1,940,000	15.00	16.00	38.00	110	280	475	1,125	16,000	—
1917S rev. mint mark	5,554,000	14.00	15.00	16.00	27.00	67.00	275	700	13,750	—
1918	6,634,000	15.00	16.00	17.00	60.00	100	370	600	5,000	—
1918D	3,853,040	15.00	22.00	38.00	93.00	190	425	1,350	27,500	—
1918S	10,282,000	14.00	15.00	31.00	55.00	85.00	225	600	18,000	—
1919	962,000	21.00	27.00	65.00	240	595	1,000	2,200	8,000	—
1919D	1,165,000	22.00	65.00	210	370	895	2,000	5,000	210,000	—
1919S	1,552,000	16.00	24.00	60.00	350	975	1,600	3,650	25,500	—
1920	6,372,000	15.00	16.00	18.00	35.00	60.00	200	425	3,400	—
1920D	1,551,000	15.00	17.00	55.00	200	400	800	3,100	16,750	—
1920S	4,624,000	14.00	16.00	20.00	85.00	200	700	1,100	16,500	—
1921	246,000	130	175	280	625	1,820	3,000	5,750	22,000	—
1921D	208,000	210	340	625	1,250	2,625	5,050	8,500	46,000	—
1921S	548,000	90.00	115	220	680	3,700	6,800	20,000	110,000	—
1923S	2,178,000	16.00	21.00	41.00	180	560	1,450	2,600	16,250	—
1927S	2,392,000	13.00	14.00	16.00	44.00	222	600	1,600	8,500	—
1928S Large S	1,940,000	19.50	22.00	28.00	90.00	290	675	1,700	7,000	—
1928S Small S	Inc. above	13.00	14.00	15.00	80.00	170	675	1,200	11,000	—
1929D	1,001,200	12.00	14.00	16.00	35.00	80.00	220	450	2,675	—
1929S	1,902,000	12.00	13.00	15.00	25.00	145	220	500	2,800	—
1933S	1,786,000	15.00	16.00	19.00	32.00	70.00	260	700	3,125	—
1934	6,964,000	9.00	10.00	12.00	17.00	18.00	29.00	80.00	300	—
1934D	2,361,400	9.00	10.00	12.00	17.00	18.00	18.00	105	155	—
1934S	3,652,000	9.00	10.00	12.00	17.00	42.00	105	345	2,700	—
1935	9,162,000	9.00	10.00	12.00	17.00	18.00	29.00	60.00	230	—
1935D	3,003,800	9.00	10.00	12.00	17.00	18.00	75.00	155	1,500	—
1935S	3,854,000	9.00	10.00	12.00	17.00	42.00	130	265	2,000	—
1936	12,617,901	9.00	10.00	12.00	17.00	18.00	29.00	42.00	200	3,100
1936D	4,252,400	9.00	10.00	12.00	17.00	18.00	42.00	95.00	415	—
1936S	3,884,000	9.00	10.00	12.00	17.00	18.00	75.00	165	575	—
1937	9,527,728	9.00	10.00	12.00	17.00	18.00	29.00	64.00	160	975
1937D	1,676,000	9.00	10.00	12.00	17.00	18.00	18.00	120	205	—
1937S	2,090,000	9.00	10.00	12.00	17.00	18.00	75.00	180	500	—
1938	4,118,152	9.00	10.00	12.00	17.00	18.00	50.00	100	245	785

HALF DOLLAR

Date	Mintage	G4	VG8	F12	VF20	XF40	AU50	MS60	MS65	Prf65
1938D	491,600	65.00	75.00	90.00	105	170	220	485	1,250	—
1939	6,820,808	9.00	10.00	12.00	17.00	18.00	40.00	57.00	200	600
1939D	4,267,800	9.00	10.00	12.00	17.00	18.00	29.00	57.00	140	—
1939S	2,552,000	9.00	10.00	12.00	17.00	18.00	100	175	225	—
1940	9,167,279	9.00	10.00	12.00	17.00	18.00	29.00	50.00	158	575
1940S	4,550,000	9.00	10.00	12.00	17.00	18.00	50.00	65.00	285	—
1941	24,207,412	9.00	10.00	12.00	17.00	18.00	29.00	45.00	90.00	500
1941D	11,248,400	9.00	10.00	12.00	17.00	18.00	29.00	52.00	110	—
1941S Small S	8,098,000	9.00	10.00	12.00	17.00	18.00	43.00	85.00	610	—
1941S Large S	Inc. above	9.00	10.00	12.00	17.00	18.00	29.00	80.00	525	—
1942	47,839,120	9.00	10.00	12.00	17.00	18.00	29.00	47.00	100	600
1942D	10,973,800	9.00	10.00	12.00	17.00	18.00	29.00	52.00	180	—
1942S	12,708,000	9.00	10.00	12.00	17.00	18.00	29.00	52.00	300	—
1943	53,190,000	9.00	10.00	12.00	17.00	18.00	29.00	45.00	83.00	—
1943D	11,346,000	9.00	10.00	12.00	17.00	18.00	29.00	55.00	160	—
1943D Double Die Obverse	Inc. above	9.00	10.00	12.00	17.00	18.00	50.00	78.00	500	—
1943S	13,450,000	9.00	10.00	12.00	17.00	18.00	29.00	65.00	230	—
1944	28,206,000	9.00	10.00	12.00	17.00	18.00	29.00	52.00	130	—
1944D	9,769,000	9.00	10.00	12.00	17.00	18.00	29.00	62.00	110	—
1944S	8,904,000	9.00	10.00	12.00	17.00	18.00	30.00	67.00	250	—
1945	31,502,000	9.00	10.00	12.00	17.00	18.00	29.00	57.00	120	—
1945D	9,966,800	9.00	10.00	12.00	17.00	18.00	29.00	62.00	90.00	—
1945S	10,156,000	9.00	10.00	12.00	17.00	18.00	52.00	67.00	120	—
1946	12,118,000	9.00	10.00	12.00	17.00	18.00	29.00	57.00	90.00	—
1946 Double Die Reverse	Inc. above	—	—	80.00	90.00	100	155	400	1,800	—
1946D	2,151,000	9.00	10.00	12.00	17.00	18.00	65.00	70.00	120	—
1946S	3,724,000	9.00	10.00	12.00	17.00	18.00	65.00	80.00	95.00	—
1947	4,094,000	9.00	10.00	12.00	17.00	18.00	29.00	58.00	130	—
1947D	3,900,600	9.00	10.00	12.00	17.00	18.00	58.00	68.00	100	—

Franklin Half Dollar
Franklin bust right. Liberty Bell, small eagle at right.

KM# 199 • 12.50 g., 0.900 Silver 0.3617 oz. ASW, 30.6 mm. • **Designer:** John R. Sinnock **Note:** The type I reverse is distinguished by the eagle having four full feathers on the wing closest the bell, whereas the type II reverse eagle has three full feathers.

Mint mark

Date	Mintage	G4	VG8	F12	VF20	XF40	AU50	MS60	MS65	65FBL	65CAM
1948	3,006,814	—	—	—	—	—	12.00	18.00	66.00	190	—
1948D	4,028,600	—	—	—	—	—	12.00	18.00	90.00	260	—
1949	5,614,000	—	—	—	—	—	15.00	33.00	100	250	—
1949D	4,120,600	—	—	—	—	—	24.00	48.00	250	1,750	—
1949S	3,744,000	—	—	—	—	—	27.00	65.00	125	700	—
1950	7,793,509	—	—	—	—	—	14.00	23.00	250	285	2,000
1950D	8,031,600	—	—	—	—	—	16.00	24.00	200	900	—
1951	16,859,602	—	—	—	—	—	12.00	18.00	85.00	340	1,500
1951D	9,475,200	—	—	—	—	—	22.00	33.00	125	540	—
1951S	13,696,000	—	—	—	—	—	12.00	20.00	125	750	—
1952	21,274,073	—	—	—	—	—	10.00	15.00	64.00	210	775
1952D	25,395,600	—	—	—	—	—	8.50	9.00	95.00	450	—
1952S	5,526,000	—	—	—	—	—	44.00	55.00	130	1,500	—
1953	2,796,920	—	—	—	—	—	20.00	26.00	63.00	1,000	475
1953D	20,900,400	—	—	—	—	—	10.00	19.00	88.00	400	—
1953S	4,148,000	—	—	—	—	—	22.00	32.00	100	160	—
1954	13,421,503	—	—	—	—	—	10.00	16.00	75.00	225	175
1954D	25,445,580	—	—	—	—	—	10.00	15.50	90.00	235	—
1954S	4,993,400	—	—	—	—	—	14.00	15.00	75.00	440	—
1955	2,876,381	—	—	—	—	—	14.00	20.00	95.00	140	120
1955 Bugs Bunny	Inc. above	—	—	9.00	12.00	14.00	18.50	25.00	95.00	750	—
1956 Type 1 rev.	4,701,384	—	—	—	—	—	10.00	15.00	60.00	125	300
1956 Type 2 rev.	Inc. above	—	—	—	—	—	—	—	—	—	40.00
1957 Type 1 rev.	6,361,952	—	—	—	—	—	10.00	15.00	60.00	95.00	—
1957 Type 2 rev.	Inc. above	—	—	—	—	—	—	—	—	—	55.00
1957D	19,966,850	—	—	—	—	—	10.00	14.00	30.00	100	—
1958 Type 1 rev.	4,917,652	—	—	—	—	—	10.00	13.00	75.00	110	—

Date	Mintage	G4	VG8	F12	VF20	XF40	AU50	MS60	MS65	65FBL	65CAM
1958 Type 2 rev.	Inc. above	—	—	—	—	—	15.00	20.00	—	—	60.00
1958D	23,962,412	—	—	—	—	—	10.00	13.00	60.00	80.00	—
1959 Type 1 rev.	7,349,291	—	—	—	—	—	10.00	15.00	75.00	250	—
1959 Type 2 rev.	Inc. above	—	—	—	—	—	16.00	25.00	90.00	—	75.00
1959D	13,053,750	—	—	—	—	—	10.00	16.00	85.00	215	—
1960 Type 1 rev.	7,715,602	—	—	—	—	—	10.00	16.00	75.00	340	—
1960 Type 2 rev.	Inc. above	—	—	—	—	—	—	—	—	—	45.00
1960D	18,215,812	—	—	—	—	—	10.00	16.00	120	1,350	—
1961 Type 1 rev.	11,318,244	—	—	—	—	—	10.00	14.00	175	1,300	—
1961 Type 2 rev.	Inc. above	—	—	—	—	—	—	—	—	—	40.00
1961 Double die rev.	Inc. above	—	—	—	—	—	—	—	—	—	3,500
1961D	20,276,442	—	—	—	—	—	10.00	12.00	150	875	—
1962 Type 1 rev.	12,932,019	—	—	—	—	—	10.00	14.00	175	1,850	—
1962 Type 2 rev.	Inc. above	—	—	—	—	—	—	—	—	—	35.00
1962D	35,473,281	—	—	—	—	—	10.00	13.00	200	800	—
1963 Type 1 rev.	25,239,645	—	—	—	—	—	10.00	13.00	60.00	1,200	—
1963 Type 2 rev.	Inc. above	—	—	—	—	—	—	—	—	—	35.00
1963D	67,069,292	—	—	—	—	—	10.00	12.00	75.00	165	—

Kennedy Half Dollar

KM# 202 • 12.50 g., 0.900 Silver 0.3617 oz. ASW, 30.6 mm. • **Obv. Designer:** Gilroy Roberts **Rev. Designer:** Frank Gasparro **Edge:** Reeded

Mint mark 1964

Date	Mintage	XF40	MS60	MS65	Prf65
1964	277,254,766	8.00	13.00	35.00	45.00
1964 Accented Hair	Inc. above	—	—	—	125
1964D	156,205,446	8.00	13.00	25.00	—

KM# 202a • 11.50 g., 0.400 Silver 0.1479 oz. ASW, 30.6 mm. • **Obv. Designer:** Gilroy Roberts **Rev. Designer:** Frank Gasparro **Edge:** Reeded

Mint mark 1968 - present

Date	Mintage	MS60	MS65	Prf65
1965	65,879,366	6.10	14.50	—
1965 SMS	2,360,000	—	15.00	—

Date	Mintage	MS60	MS65	Prf65
1966	108,984,932	6.10	22.50	—
1966 SMS	2,261,583	—	17.00	—
1967	295,046,978	6.10	18.50	—
1967 SMS	1,863,344	—	18.00	—
1968D	246,951,930	6.10	16.50	—
1968S	3,041,506	—	—	8.56
1969D	129,881,800	6.10	20.00	—
1969S	2,934,631	—	—	8.56
1970D	2,150,000	8.50	100	—
1970S	2,632,810	—	—	12.00

KM# 202b • 11.34 g., Copper-Nickel Clad Copper, 30.6 mm. • **Obv. Designer:** Gilroy Roberts **Rev. Designer:** Frank Gasparro

Date	Mintage	XF40	MS60	MS65	Prf65
1971	155,640,000	—	1.00	17.50	—
1971D	302,097,424	—	1.00	12.00	—
1971S	3,244,183	—	—	—	5.00
1972	153,180,000	—	1.00	15.50	—
1972D	141,890,000	—	1.00	14.50	—
1972S	3,267,667	—	—	—	5.00
1973	64,964,000	—	1.00	20.00	—
1973D	83,171,400	—	1.00	12.00	—
1973S	2,769,624	—	—	—	5.00
1974	201,596,000	—	1.00	25.00	—
1974D	79,066,300	—	1.00	17.00	—
1974D DDO	Inc. above	24.00	32.00	165	—
1974S	2,617,350	—	—	—	5.00
1975 none minted					
1975D none minted					
1975S none minted					

Independence Hall.

KM# 205 • 11.20 g., Copper-Nickel, 30.6 mm. • **Obv. Designer:** Gilroy Roberts **Rev. Designer:** Seth Huntington

Date	Mintage	MS60	MS65	Prf65
1976	234,308,000	1.00	16.50	—
1976D	287,565,248	1.00	14.00	—
1976S	7,059,099	—	—	5.00

Bicentennial design, Independence Hall.

KM# 205a • 11.50 g., 0.400 Silver 0.1479 oz. ASW, 30.6 mm. • **Rev. Designer:** Seth Huntington

Date	Mintage	MS60	MS65	Prf65
1976S	4,908,319	—	15.00	8.70
1976S	3,998,621	—	—	8.70

Regular design resumed.

KM# A202b • 11.34 g., Copper-Nickel Clad Copper, 30.61 mm. • **Edge:** Reeded **Note:** KM#202b design and composition resumed. The 1979-S and 1981-S Type II proofs have clearer mint marks than the Type I proofs of those years.

Date	Mintage	MS65	Prf65
1977	43,598,000	12.50	—
1977D	31,449,106	16.50	—
1977S	3,251,152	—	4.50
1978	14,350,000	12.00	—
1978D	13,765,799	15.00	—
1978S	3,127,788	—	5.00
1979	68,312,000	13.50	—
1979D	15,815,422	13.50	—
1979S Type I	3,677,175	—	5.00
1979S Type II	Inc. above	—	18.00
1980P	44,134,000	12.50	—
1980D	33,456,449	17.50	—
1980S	3,547,030	—	5.00
1981P	29,544,000	9.00	—
1981D	27,839,533	12.00	—
1981S Type I	4,063,083	—	5.00
1981S Type II	Inc. above	—	18.50
1982P	10,819,000	18.50	—
1982P no initials FG	Inc. above	110	—
1982D	13,140,102	20.00	—
1982S	38,957,479	—	5.00
1983P	34,139,000	22.50	—
1983D	32,472,244	12.50	—
1983S	3,279,126	—	5.00
1984P	26,029,000	12.00	—
1984D	26,262,158	18.00	—
1984S	3,065,110	—	6.00
1985P	18,706,962	16.50	—
1985D	19,814,034	12.50	—
1985S	3,962,138	—	5.00
1986P	13,107,633	17.50	—
1986D	15,336,145	14.00	—
1986S	2,411,180	—	6.00
1987P	2,890,758	16.50	—
1987D	2,890,758	12.50	—
1987S	4,407,728	—	5.00
1988P	13,626,000	16.50	—
1988D	12,000,096	10.00	—
1988S	3,262,948	—	5.00
1989P	24,542,000	13.00	—
1989D	23,000,216	13.00	—
1989S	3,220,194	—	5.00
1990P	22,780,000	17.50	—

Date	Mintage	MS65	Prf65
1990D	20,096,242	20.00	—
1990S	3,299,559	—	5.00
1991P	14,874,000	12.50	—
1991D	15,054,678	16.00	—
1991S	2,867,787	—	5.00
1992P	17,628,000	10.00	—
1992D	17,000,106	10.00	—
1992S	2,858,981	—	5.00
1993P	15,510,000	12.00	—
1993D	15,000,006	10.00	—
1993S	2,633,439	—	5.00
1994P	23,718,000	12.00	—
1994D	23,828,110	8.50	—
1994S	2,484,594	—	5.00
1995P	26,496,000	10.00	—
1995D	26,288,000	8.00	—
1995S	2,010,384	—	12.00
1996P	24,442,000	10.00	—
1996D	24,744,000	10.00	—
1996S	2,085,191	—	9.00
1997P	20,882,000	14.00	—
1997D	19,876,000	13.50	—
1997S	1,975,000	—	10.00
1998P	15,646,000	12.50	—
1998D	15,064,000	12.50	—
1998S	2,078,494	—	7.00
1999P	8,900,000	11.00	—
1999D	10,682,000	10.00	—
1999S	2,557,897	—	8.00
2000P	22,600,000	12.00	—
2000D	19,466,000	12.00	—
2000S	3,082,944	—	5.00
2001P	21,200,000	10.00	—
2001D	19,504,000	9.00	—
2001S	2,235,000	—	5.00
2002P	3,100,000	10.00	—
2002D	2,500,000	10.50	—
2002S	2,268,913	—	5.00
2003P	2,500,000	6.00	—
2003D	2,500,000	6.00	—
2003S	2,076,165	—	5.00
2004P	2,900,000	4.50	—
2004D	2,900,000	4.50	—
2004S	1,789,488	—	6.00
2005P	3,800,000	6.00	—
2005P Satin finish	1,160,000	8.00	—
2005D	3,500,000	5.00	—
2005D Satin finish	1,160,000	10.00	—
2005S	2,275,000	—	5.00
2006P	2,400,000	4.50	—
2006P Satin finish	847,361	12.00	—
2006D	2,000,000	4.50	—
2006D Satin finish	847,361	14.00	—
2006S	1,934,965	—	6.00
2007P	2,400,000	4.50	—
2007P Satin finish	—	8.00	—
2007D	2,400,000	4.50	—
2007D Satin finish	—	8.00	—
2007S	1,702,116	—	6.00
2008P	1,700,000	4.50	—
2008P Satin finish	—	8.50	—
2008D	1,700,000	4.50	—
2008D Satin finish	—	8.50	—
2008S	1,405,674	—	9.00
2009P	1,900,000	4.50	—
2009P Satin finish	—	8.50	—
2009D	1,900,000	4.50	—
2009D Satin finish	—	8.50	—
2009S	1,482,502	—	6.00
2010P	1,800,000	4.50	—
2010P Satin finish	—	8.50	—
2010D	1,700,000	4.50	—
2010D Satin finish	—	8.50	—
2010S	1,103,815	—	13.00
2011P	1,750,000	4.50	—
2011D	1,700,000	4.50	—
2011S	1,098,835	—	9.00

HALF DOLLAR

Date	Mintage	MS65	Prf65
2012P	1,800,000	4.50	—
2012D	1,700,000	4.50	—
2012S	841,972	—	9.00
2013P	5,000,000	4.50	—
2013D	4,600,000	4.50	—
2013S	821,031	—	9.00
2014D	2,445,813	4.50	—
2014P	2,845,813	4.50	—
2014S	761,641	—	9.00

KM# A202c • 12.50 g., 0.900 Silver 0.3617 oz. ASW, 30.6 mm. • **Designer:** Gilroy Roberts

Date	Mintage	Prf65
1992S	1,317,579	13.20
1993S	761,353	15.20
1994S	785,329	13.20
1995S	838,953	46.00
1996S	830,021	15.20
1997S	821,678	35.00
1998S Matte Finish	62,350	—
1998S	878,792	13.20
1999S	804,565	15.20
2000S	965,921	13.20
2001S	849,600	13.20
2002S	888,816	13.20
2003S	1,040,425	13.20
2004S	1,175,935	13.20
2005S	1,069,679	14.20
2006S	988,140	14.20
2007S	1,384,797	15.70
2008S	620,684	14.20
2009S	697,365	13.20
2010S	585,401	14.20
2011S	574,175	14.20
2012S	395,443	175
2013S	451,342	14.20
2014S	467,074	12.00

Restored 1964 portrait.

KM# A202b.1 • 11.34 g., Copper-Nickel Clad Copper, 30.61 mm. • **Subject:** 50th anniversary of Kennedy half dollar **Edge:** Reeded

Date	Mintage	MS65	Prf65
2014P	197,608	6.00	—
Note: In anniversary sets only.			
2014D	197,608	6.00	—

Date	Mintage	MS65	Prf65
Note: In anniversary sets only.			
2015P	2,512,561	4.50	—
2015D	2,512,561	4.50	—
2015S	462,393	—	9.00
2016P	2,100,000	4.50	—
2016D	2,100,000	4.50	—
2016S	—	—	9.00
2017P	—	4.50	—
2017D	—	4.50	—
2017S Enhanced Unc.	225,000	15.00	—
2017S	—	—	9.00
2018P	—	4.50	—
2018D	—	4.50	—
2018S Proof	—	—	9.00

KM# A202c.1 • 12.50 g., 0.900 Silver 0.3617 oz. ASW, 30.61 mm. • **Subject:** 50th anniversary of Kennedy half dollar **Note:** In anniversary sets only.

Date	Mintage	Prf65
2014D	221,134	—

KM# A202c.2 • 12.50 g., 0.900 Silver 0.3617 oz. ASW, 30.61 mm. • **Subject:** 50th anniversary of Kennedy half dollar **Note:** In anniversary sets only.

Date	Mintage	Prf65
2014S Enhanced Unc.	221,134	—

KM# A202c.3 • 12.50 g., 0.900 Silver 0.3617 oz. ASW, 30.61 mm. • **Subject:** 50th anniversary of Kennedy half dollar

Date	Mintage	Prf65
2014P	221,134	30.00
Note: In anniversary sets only.		
2015S	247,790	9.00
2016S	—	9.00
2017S	—	9.00
2018S Reverse Proof	—	15.00
2018S	—	9.00

KM# A202c.4 • 12.50 g., 0.900 Silver 0.3617 oz. ASW, 30.61 mm. • **Subject:** 50th anniversary of Kennedy half dollar **Note:** In anniversary sets only.

Date	Mintage	Prf65
2014W	221,134	30.00
Note: Reverse Proof		

Kennedy head left, dual dates below. Presidential seal.

KM# 587 • 23.33 g., 0.9999 Gold 0.750 oz. AGW, 30.61 mm. • **Subject:** John F. Kennedy Half Dollar, 50th Anniversary **Obv. Designer:** Gilroy Roberts **Rev. Designer:** Frank Gasparro

Date	Mintage	Prf65
1964-2014W	73,772	1,100

DOLLAR

Flowing Hair Dollar

KM# 17 • 26.96 g., 0.892 Silver 0.7732 oz. ASW, 39-40 mm. • **Designer:** Robert Scot **Note:** The two 1795 varieties have either two or three leaves under each of the eagle's wings on the reverse.

Date	Mintage	G4	VG8	F12	VF20	XF40	MS60	MS63
1794	1,758	57,500	100,000	125,000	155,000	300,000	1,000,000	1,500,000
1795 2 leaves	203,033	2,000	2,600	3,700	5,600	10,750	63,000	135,000
1795 3 leaves	Inc. above	2,000	2,200	4,125	6,000	11,500	63,000	135,000
1795 Silver plug	Inc. above	4,200	6,000	15,500	21,000	28,500	115,000	235,000

Draped Bust Dollar
Small eagle.

KM# 18 • 26.96 g., 0.892 Silver 0.7732 oz. ASW, 39-40 mm. • **Designer:** Robert Scot

Date	Mintage	G4	VG8	F12	VF20	XF40	MS60	MS63
1795 Off-center bust	Inc. above	1,600	2,100	3,300	4,750	9,000	41,000	125,000
1795 Centered bust	—	1,700	2,000	3,300	4,750	9,000	41,000	115,000
1796 small date, small letters	72,920	1,600	1,900	3,300	5,300	9,000	54,000	175,000
1796 small date, large letters	Inc. above	1,600	2,000	3,300	5,300	9,000	95,000	—
1796 large date, small letters	Inc. above	1,600	1,900	3,300	5,300	9,000	95,000	165,000
1797 9 stars left, 7 stars right, small letters	7,776	1,600	2,500	4,200	6,000	14,750	65,000	—
1797 9 stars left, 7 stars right, large letters	Inc. above	1,600	1,900	3,500	4,500	9,000	70,000	210,000
1797 10 stars left, 6 stars right	Inc. above	1,600	2,250	3,300	5,600	10,500	65,000	112,000
1798 13 stars	327,536	1,600	2,100	3,300	4,500	12,500	113,000	—
1798 15 stars	Inc. above	2,050	2,750	4,700	9,180	16,150	95,000	—

Draped bust right, flanked by stars, date below. Heraldic eagle.

KM# 32 • 26.96 g., 0.892 Silver 0.7732 oz. ASW, 39-40 mm. • **Obv. Legend:** LIBERTY **Rev. Legend:** UNITED STATES OF AMERICA **Designer:** Robert Scot **Note:** The 1798 "knob 9" variety has a serif on the lower left of the 9 in the date. The 1798 varieties are distinguished by the number of arrows held by the eagle on the reverse and the number of berries on the olive branch. On the 1798 "high-8" variety, the 8 in the date is higher than the other numerals. The 1799 varieties are distinguished by the number and positioning of the stars on the obverse and by the size of the berries in the olive branch on the reverse. On the 1700 "irregular date" variety, the first 9 in the date is smaller than the other numerals. Some varieties of the 1800 strikes had letters in the legend cut twice into the dies; as between the numerals in the date are wider than other varieties and the 8 is lower than the other numerals. The 1800 "small berries" variety refers to the size of the berries in the olive branch on the reverse. The 1800 "12 arrows" and "10 arrows" varieties refer to the number of arrows held by the eagle. The 1800 "Americai" variety appears to have the faint outline of an "I" after "America" in the reverse legend. The "close" and "wide" varieties of the 1802 refer to the amount of space between the numerals in the date. The 1800 large-3 and small-3 varieties are distinguished by the size of the 3 in the date.

Date	Mintage	G4	VG8	F12	VF20	XF40	MS60	MS63
1798 knob 9, 4 stripes	423,515	1,000	1,650	2,600	3,175	4,000	23,000	57,000
1798 knob 9, 10 arrows	Inc. above	1,000	1,650	2,600	3,175	4,000	23,000	57,000
1798 knob 9, 5 stripes	Inc. above	—	—	—	—	—	—	124,500
1798 pointed 9, 4 berries	Inc. above	1,000	1,650	2,600	3,175	4,000	23,000	57,000
1798 5 berries, 12 arrows	Inc. above	1,000	1,650	2,600	3,175	4,000	23,000	57,000
1798 high 8	Inc. above	1,000	1,650	2,600	3,175	4,000	23,000	57,000
1798 13 arrows	Inc. above	1,000	1,650	2,600	3,175	4,000	23,000	57,000
1799/98 13-star reverse	Inc. above	1,000	1,650	2,600	3,175	4,000	20,000	54,000
1799/98 15-star reverse	Inc. above	1,000	1,650	2,600	3,175	4,000	20,000	54,000
1799 irregular date, 13-star reverse	Inc. above	1,000	1,650	2,600	3,175	4,000	23,000	200,000
1799 irregular date, 15-star reverse	Inc. above	1,000	1,650	2,600	3,175	4,000	23,000	200,000
1799 perfect date, 7- and 6-star obverse, no berries	Inc. above	1,020	1,650	2,600	3,175	4,000	23,000	200,000
1799 perfect date, 7- and 6-star obverse, small berries	Inc. above	1,020	1,650	2,600	3,175	4,000	23,000	200,000
1799 perfect date, 7- and 6-star obverse, medium large berries	Inc. above	1,020	1,650	2,600	3,175	4,000	23,000	200,000
1799 perfect date, 7- and 6-star obverse, extra large berries	Inc. above	1,000	1,650	2,600	3,175	4,000	23,000	200,000
1799 8 stars left, 5 stars right on obverse	Inc. above	1,000	1,650	2,600	3,175	4,000	23,000	200,000
1800 R" in "Liberty" double cut	220,920	1,000	1,650	2,600	3,175	4,000	23,000	107,000
1800 first 'T' in "States" double cut	Inc. above	1,000	1,650	2,600	3,175	4,000	23,000	107,000
1800 both letters double cut	Inc. above	1,000	1,650	2,600	3,175	4,000	23,000	107,000
1800 T' in "United" double cut	Inc. above	1,000	1,650	2,600	3,175	4,000	23,000	107,000
1800 very wide date, low 8	Inc. above	1,000	1,150	1,550	2,500	5,800	23,000	—
1800 small berries	Inc. above	1,000	1,150	1,475	2,500	5,800	23,000	107,000
1800 dot date	Inc. above	1,000	1,150	1,475	2,500	5,800	23,000	107,000
1800 12 arrows	Inc. above	1,000	1,150	1,475	2,500	5,800	23,000	—
1800 10 arrows	Inc. above	1,000	1,150	1,475	2,500	5,800	23,000	—
1800 Americai	Inc. above	1,000	1,150	1,475	2,500	5,800	23,000	107,000
1801	54,454	900	1,175	1,690	3,000	5,800	28,000	68,000
1801 proof restrike	—	—	—	—	—	—	—	—
1802/1 close	Inc. above	930	1,200	2,300	2,600	4,600	25,500	—
1802/1 wide	Inc. above	930	1,200	2,300	2,600	4,600	25,500	—
1802 close, perfect date	Inc. above	975	1,100	1,675	2,500	3,500	23,000	60,000
1802 wide, perfect date	Inc. above	930	1,100	1,675	2,500	3,500	23,000	55,000
1802 proof restrike, mintage unrecorded	—	—	—	—	—	—	—	—
1803 large 3	85,634	1,000	1,100	1,700	2,400	4,200	28,000	112,000
1803 small 3	Inc. above	1,000	1,100	1,700	3,000	4,200	24,000	54,000
1803 proof restrike, mintage unrecorded	—	—	—	—	—	—	—	—
1804 15 known	—	—	—	—	—	—	—	—

Note: 1804, Childs Sale, Aug. 1999, Prf-68, $4,140,000.

DOLLAR

Gobrecht Dollar
C Gobrecht F. in base. Eagle flying left amid stars.
KM# 59.1 • 26.73 g., 0.900 Silver 0.7734 oz. ASW, 38.1 mm. • **Obv. Designer:** Christian Gobrecht **Rev. Legend:** UNITED STATES OF AMERICA **Edge:** Plain.

Date	Mintage	G4	VG8	F12	VF20	XF40	AU50	MS60	MS63	MS65	Prf65
1836	1,000	—	—	—	11,500	14,850	18,000	—	—	—	75,000

C. Gobrecht F. in base. Eagle flying in plain field.
KM# 59.2 • 26.73 g., 0.900 Silver 0.7734 oz. ASW, 38.1 mm. • **Obv. Designer:** Christian Gobrecht. **Edge:** Plain.

Date	Mintage	G4	VG8	F12	VF20	XF40	AU50	MS60	MS63	MS65	Prf65
1836 Restrike	—	—	—	—	—	—	17,500	—	—	—	68,000

C. Gobrecht F. in base.
KM# 59a.1 • 26.73 g., 0.900 Silver 0.7734 oz. ASW, 38.1 mm. • **Obv. Legend:** Eagle flying left amid stars. **Edge:** Plain.

Date	Mintage	G4	VG8	F12	VF20	XF40	AU50	MS60	MS63	MS65	Prf65
1836	600	—	—	—	—	—	—	—	—	—	—

C. Gobrecht F. in base. Eagle flying left amid stars.
KM# 59a.2 • 26.73 g., 0.900 Silver 0.7734 oz. ASW, 38.1 mm. • **Edge:** Reeded.

Date	Mintage	G4	VG8	F12	VF20	XF40	AU50	MS60	MS63	MS65	Prf65
1836 Restrike	—	—	—	—	—	—	—	—	—	—	—

Designer's name omitted in base. Eagle in plain field.

KM# 59a.3 • 26.73 g., 0.900 Silver 0.7734 oz. ASW, 38.1 mm. • **Edge:** Reeded.

Date	Mintage	G4	VG8	F12	VF20	XF40	AU50	MS60	MS63	MS65	Prf65
1839	300	—	—	—	—	—	27,500	—	—	—	95,000

KM# 59a.4 • 26.73 g., 0.900 Silver 0.7734 oz. ASW, 38.1 mm. •

Date	Mintage	G4	VG8	F12	VF20	XF40	AU50	MS60	MS63	MS65	Prf65
1839 Restrike	—	—	—	—	—	—	26,500	—	—	—	90,000

Note: All other combinations are restrikes of the late 1850's.

Seated Liberty Dollar
Seated Liberty, date below. No motto above eagle.

KM# 71 • 26.73 g., 0.900 Silver 0.7734 oz. ASW, 38.1 mm. • **Rev. Legend:** UNITED STATES OF AMERICA
Designer: Christian Gobrecht

Date	Mintage	G4	VG8	F12	VF20	XF40	AU50	MS60	MS63	MS65	Prf65
1840	61,005	450	465	475	490	500	800	6,000	14,000	—	76,000
1841	173,000	385	420	420	435	600	900	2,200	7,500	28,000	220,000
1842	184,618	385	400	500	600	800	825	2,200	3,400	—	76,000
1843	165,100	410	420	465	520	575	875	2,000	6,000	—	125,000
1844	20,000	300	350	420	500	900	1,400	4,850	12,000	—	72,000
1845	24,500	540	600	700	800	900	1,100	6,000	31,000	—	55,000
1846	110,600	265	495	525	565	700	860	1,800	5,000	65,000	95,000
1846O	59,000	280	370	420	500	700	2,000	5,800	17,000	—	—
1847	140,750	395	425	470	490	520	1,122	2,650	4,200	57,000	60,000
1848	15,000	350	450	550	650	1,650	2,150	6,600	12,000	—	62,000
1849	62,600	300	350	400	500	840	900	2,300	5,650	85,000	66,000
1850	7,500	500	600	750	1,000	1,800	3,000	7,700	14,000	—	42,000
1850O	40,000	575	665	825	1,500	2,000	3,450	9,500	22,000	—	—
1851	1,300	5,000	9,500	9,800	10,000	17,000	23,000	33,000	50,000	120,000	80,000
1851 Restrike	—	—	—	—	—	—	—	—	—	—	75,000
1852	1,100	2,200	2,700	3,600	5,100	16,000	25,000	30,000	60,000	120,000	80,000
1852 Restrike	—	—	—	—	—	—	—	—	—	—	53,000
1853	46,110	350	450	550	650	1,000	1,200	3,200	5,000	72,000	82,000
1853 Restrike	—	—	—	—	—	—	—	—	—	—	—
1854	33,140	1,200	1,600	2,200	3,000	4,000	5,800	9,200	18,000	85,000	65,000
1855	26,000	1,000	1,250	1,750	2,600	3,800	5,000	8,750	30,000	—	45,000
1856	63,500	450	600	800	1,300	1,700	2,900	4,300	10,000	—	26,000
1857	94,000	450	600	800	1,300	1,800	3,000	4,400	5,800	72,000	24,000
1858 proof only	Est. 800	—	—	3,200	3,800	5,850	6,800	—	—	—	32,000
Note: Later restrike.											
1859	256,500	300	350	450	520	1,250	1,540	2,500	5,200	72,000	10,000
1859O	360,000	300	420	450	460	550	730	1,650	4,340	42,000	—
1859S	20,000	600	750	900	1,325	1,725	3,400	8,800	18,000	—	—
1860	218,930	340	380	430	535	995	1,600	2,100	5,600	45,000	10,000
1860O	515,000	200	240	350	420	490	940	1,825	2,800	48,000	—

Date	Mintage	G4	VG8	F12	VF20	XF40	AU50	MS60	MS63	MS65	Prf65
1861	78,500	425	550	800	1,100	2,200	2,600	3,900	6,600	51,000	10,000
1862	12,090	425	550	800	1,500	2,600	3,200	6,000	9,100	55,000	10,000
1863	27,660	400	850	1,200	1,700	2,600	2,750	3,600	5,400	46,000	10,000
1864	31,170	350	450	725	900	1,300	2,525	3,750	8,800	48,000	10,000
1865	47,000	400	550	650	850	1,625	1,950	4,400	8,000	75,000	10,000
1866 2 known without motto	—	—	—	—	—	—	—	—	—	—	—

Seated Liberty, date below. "IN GOD WE TRUST" above eagle.

KM# 100 • 26.73 g., 0.900 Silver 0.7734 oz. ASW, 38.1 mm. • **Rev. Legend:** UNITED STATES OF AMERICA
Designer: Christian Gobrecht **Note:** In 1866 the motto was added to the reverse above the eagle.

Date	Mintage	G4	VG8	F12	VF20	XF40	AU50	MS60	MS63	MS65	Prf65
1866	49,625	400	475	500	700	880	1,550	2,400	4,500	80,000	9,500
1867	47,525	290	300	360	575	975	1,225	2,100	4,500	50,000	9,500
1868	162,700	280	300	400	575	880	1,175	2,100	6,300	75,000	9,500
1869	424,300	290	300	360	500	600	1,175	2,100	4,600	75,000	9,500
1870	416,000	265	425	500	600	912	1,200	1,800	4,000	45,000	9,500
1870CC	12,462	700	1,000	1,225	1,700	3,950	5,500	24,000	36,750	—	—
1870S 12-15 known	—150,000	200,000	275,000	400,000	500,000	850,000	1,500,000		—	—	—
Note: 1870S, Eliasberg Sale, April 1997, EF-45 to AU-50, $264,000.											
1871	1,074,760	300	360	460	520	630	700	1,700	3,300	52,000	9,500
1871CC	1,376	2,200	3,000	4,500	6,000	11,000	20,000	55,000	147,000	225,000	—
1872	1,106,450	340	435	450	575	630	650	1,800	3,200	50,000	9,500
1872CC	3,150	1,600	2,000	2,400	3,100	5,400	8,000	21,000	75,000	100,000	—
1872S	9,000	750	1,000	1,220	1,375	1,610	2,800	7,000	26,000	—	—
1873	293,600	425	475	500	550	700	900	1,600	3,150	8,000	9,500
1873CC	2,300	7,000	9,500	13,000	18,000	23,000	40,000	110,000	—	—	—
1873S none known	700	—	—	—	—	—	—	—	—	—	—

Trade Dollar
Seated Liberty, "IN GOD WE TRUST" in base above date. TRADE DOLLAR below eagle.

KM# 108 • 27.22 g., 0.900 Silver 0.7876 oz. ASW, 38.1 mm. • **Rev. Legend:** UNITED STATES OF AMERICA.
Designer: William Barber

Date	Mintage	G4	VG8	F12	VF20	XF40	AU50	MS60	MS65	Prf65
1873	397,500	110	125	130	145	225	280	525	9,500	7,000
1873CC	124,500	250	300	450	600	1,250	2,500	7,100	95,000	—
1873S	703,000	110	125	130	150	225	350	1,200	24,000	—
1874	987,800	110	125	130	145	560	1,000	2,100	13,000	5,900
1874CC	1,373,200	200	250	300	400	825	1,400	2,500	30,000	—
1874S	2,549,000	110	125	130	135	465	880	1,400	14,500	—
1875	218,900	320	400	500	700	975	1,150	2,125	13,000	10,500
1875CC	1,573,700	250	280	425	400	877	1,000	2,000	32,000	—
1875S	4,487,000	110	120	125	135	225	300	880	7,900	—
1875S/CC	Inc. above	175	225	325	450	775	1,200	4,500	48,000	—

Date	Mintage	G4	VG8	F12	VF20	XF40	AU50	MS60	MS65	Prf65
1876	456,150	325	425	550	700	1,125	300	925	7,900	5,900
1876CC	509,000	370	500	600	800	950	1,100	6,600	—	—
1876CC DDR	Inc. above	—	—	375	650	1,250	2,000	8,500	—	—
1876S	5,227,000	100	120	125	130	225	300	1,125	11,000	—
1877	3,039,710	167	190	225	262	385	500	825	7,900	5,900
1877CC	534,000	370	500	600	825	1,200	1,900	4,000	60,000	—
1877S	9,519,000	110	120	125	155	265	350	900	7,900	—
1878 proof only	900	700	800	900	1,000	1,100	1,200	—	—	5,900
1878CC	97,000	550	800	1,200	1,700	3,400	6,500	15,000	130,000	—
1878S	4,162,000	110	120	125	130	275	365	1,000	7,900	—
1879 proof only	1,541	600	700	800	900	1,000	1,500	—	—	5,900
1880 proof only	1,987	600	700	800	900	1,000	1,500	—	—	5,900
1881 proof only	960	600	700	800	900	1,000	1,500	—	—	5,900
1882 proof only	1,097	600	700	800	900	1,000	1,500	—	—	5,900
1883 proof only	979	600	700	800	900	1,000	1,500	—	—	5,900
1884 proof only	10	—	—	—	—	—	—	—	—	750,000

Note: 1884, Eliasberg Sale, April 1997, Prf-66, $396,000.

Date	Mintage	G4	VG8	F12	VF20	XF40	AU50	MS60	MS65	Prf65
1885 proof only	5	—	—	—	—	—	—	—	—	—

Note: 1885, Eli asberg Sale, April 1997, Prf-65, $907,500.

Morgan Dollar

Laureate head left, date below flanked by stars. Eagle within 1/2 wreath.

KM# 110 • 26.73 g., 0.900 Silver 0.7734 oz. ASW, 38.1 mm. • **Obv. Legend:** E • PLURIBUS • UNUM **Rev. Legend:** UNITED STATES OF AMERICA **Designer:** George T. Morgan **Note:** 65DMPL values are for coins grading MS-65 deep-mirror prooflike. The 1878 "8 tail feathers" and "7 tail feathers" varieties are distinguished by the number of feathers in the eagle's tail. On the "reverse of 1878" varieties, the top of the top feather in the arro ws held by the eagle is straight across and the eagle's breast is concave. On the "reverse of 1879 varieties," the top feather in the arrows held by the eagle is slanted and the eagle's breast is convex. The 1890-CC "tail-bar" variety has a bar extending from the arrow feathers to the wreath on the reverse, the result of a die gouge. The Pittman Act of 1918 authorized the melting of 270 Million pieces of various dates. They were not individually recorded.

7 Tail feathers   7/8 Tail feathers   8 Tail feathers

Date	Mintage	VG8	F12	VF20	XF40	AU50	MS60	MS63	MS64	MS65	65DMPL	Prf65
1878 8 tail feathers	750,000	80.00	85.00	90.00	95.00	125	200	295	450	1,125	20,000	9,000
1878 7 over 8 tail feathers	9,759,550	47.00	50.00	55.00	60.00	80.00	220	267	502	1,400	14,500	—
1878 7 tail feathers, reverse of 1878	—	47.00	48.00	50.00	55.00	65.00	85.00	140	490	825	9,250	11,000
1878 7 tail feathers, reverse of 1879	—	47.00	48.00	50.00	55.00	65.00	130	165	500	1,520	21,250	135,000
1878CC	2,212,000	125	128	135	150	220	385	465	485	1,757	9,100	—
1878S	9,744,000	35.00	40.00	42.00	46.00	50.00	65.00	97.00	115	302	8,500	—
1879	14,807,100	26.00	27.00	29.00	38.00	44.00	60.00	100	146	302	10,000	6,800
1879CC	756,000	145	200	325	1,550	2,700	5,200	7,200	9,850	22,000	34,000	—
1879CC capped CC	—	200	215	420	950	1,670	4,250	6,250	7,825	39,500	54,000	—
1879O	2,887,000	53.00	56.00	57.00	58.00	65.00	100	315	606	2,450	20,000	—
1879S reverse of 1878	9,110,000	65.00	68.00	72.00	80.00	90.00	275	750	1,627	5,000	16,000	—
1879S reverse of 1879	—	26.00	27.00	29.00	38.00	44.00	70.00	73.00	80.00	145	1,200	—
1880	12,601,335	26.00	27.00	29.00	38.00	48.00	52.00	95.00	130	782	4,800	6,800
1880CC reverse of 1878	591,000	178	185	205	220	295	575	660	900	1,160	15,000	—
1880CC 80/79 reverse of 1878	—	200	240	280	345	420	650	782	1,175	4,100	—	—
1880CC 8/7 reverse of 1878	—	180	210	245	300	370	610	760	1,310	2,900	—	—
1880CC reverse of 1879	—	150	200	260	290	350	490	627	900	1,160	7,000	—

DOLLAR

Date	Mintage	VG8	F12	VF20	XF40	AU50	MS60	MS63	MS64	MS65	65DMPL	Prf65
1880CC 8/7 high 7 reverse of 1879	—	185	215	255	300	365	535	789	—	1,900	—	—
1880CC 8/7 low 7 reverse of 1879	—	185	215	255	300	355	535	789	—	1,900	10,500	—
1880O	5,305,000	26.00	27.00	29.00	38.00	54.00	110	365	1,375	14,000	62,500	—
1880S	8,900,000	26.00	27.00	29.00	38.00	44.00	55.00	67.00	80.00	145	1,250	—
1880S 8/7 crossbar	—	67.00	68.00	75.00	77.00	110	120	360	435	550	—	—
1881	9,163,975	26.00	27.00	29.00	39.00	49.00	70.00	80.00	155	587	12,250	5,200
1881CC	296,000	400	433	360	476	400	460	587	632	725	3,200	—
1881O	5,708,000	25.00	34.00	36.00	36.00	40.00	70.00	86.00	185	900	10,250	—
1881S	12,760,000	26.00	27.00	35.00	36.00	50.00	55.00	70.00	88.00	151	900	—
1882	11,101,100	26.00	27.00	29.00	36.00	42.00	50.00	80.00	132	325	6,000	5,000
1882CC	1,133,000	113	116	118	120	145	225	250	265	450	1,900	—
1882O	6,090,000	51.00	52.00	53.00	53.00	59.00	65.00	85.00	140	590	3,450	—
1882O/S	—	65.00	70.00	90.00	91.00	127	197	525	1,670	51,000	55,000	—
1882S	9,250,000	26.00	27.00	35.00	36.00	49.00	53.00	67.00	80.00	140	2,750	—
1883	12,291,039	26.00	45.00	46.00	46.00	48.00	67.00	91.00	97.00	185	1,475	5,200
1883CC	1,204,000	105	107	110	115	155	225	243	270	400	1,200	—
1883O	8,725,000	26.00	27.00	29.00	38.00	43.00	55.00	65.00	67.00	151	1,150	—
1883S	6,250,000	26.00	43.00	46.00	65.00	165	1,025	2,400	6,450	39,500	—	—
1884	14,070,875	51.00	51.00	53.00	58.00	54.00	65.00	80.00	100	250	3,950	4,800
1884CC	1,136,000	137	27.00	155	158	160	175	243	262	365	1,500	—
1884O	9,730,000	26.00	27.00	29.00	38.00	38.00	45.00	68.00	72.00	120	900	—
1884S	3,200,000	26.00	45.00	46.00	80.00	223	11,400	47,000	130,000	225,000	215,000	—
1885	17,787,767	26.00	27.00	29.00	35.00	40.00	50.00	70.00	87.00	160	1,050	4,850
1885CC	—	550	575	625	628	640	645	750	800	1,000	2,600	—
1885O	9,185,000	26.00	27.00	29.00	38.00	43.00	55.00	60.00	77.00	130	1,065	—
1885S	1,497,000	21.05	60.00	70.00	110	275	310	600	1,500	40,000	—	—
1886	19,963,886	26.00	27.00	29.00	38.00	43.00	50.00	64.00	74.00	130	1,000	5,200
1886O	10,710,000	34.00	35.00	40.00	57.00	70.00	900	2,950	6,600	145,000	—	—
1886S	750,000	65.00	67.00	80.00	100	150	380	460	680	1,625	26,000	—
1887	20,290,710	26.00	27.00	29.00	38.00	43.00	55.00	60.00	80.00	130	1,125	5,600
1887/6	—	58.00	59.00	60.00	61.00	160	335	500	600	1,625	23,000	—
1887O	11,550,000	26.00	27.00	45.00	57.00	68.00	98.00	165	355	1,525	17,000	—
1887/6O	—	48.00	59.00	55.00	70.00	225	525	2,000	3,400	33,750	—	—
1887S	1,771,000	26.00	45.00	46.00	47.00	57.00	145	280	570	1,520	25,300	—
1888	19,183,833	26.00	45.00	48.00	48.00	59.00	60.00	75.00	90.00	165	2,250	5,200
1888O	12,150,000	26.00	45.00	46.00	47.00	60.00	75.00	100	120	485	4,000	—
1888O Hot Lips	—	80.00	145	300	700	3,100	—	—	—	—	—	—
1888S	657,000	105	130	140	—	175	345	445	800	2,600	—	—
1889	21,726,811	26.00	27.00	45.00	55.00	68.00	80.00	82.00	90.00	225	3,400	5,200
1889CC	350,000	665	850	1,300	4,000	6,400	26,750	47,000	95,000	278,000	—	—
1889O	11,875,000	17.05	45.00	48.00	50.00	54.00	240	3,655	1,250	4,750	26,500	—
1889S	700,000	53.00	65.00	80.00	85.00	100	300	370	725	1,450	29,500	—
1890	16,802,590	26.00	25.05	45.00	57.00	65.00	70.00	85.00	160	1,000	15,000	5,200
1890CC	2,309,041	95.00	97.00	105	120	195	500	975	1,190	2,750	11,500	—
1890CC tail bar	—	125	145	245	390	700	1,450	3,300	4,700	—	—	—
1890O	10,701,000	26.00	27.00	45.00	56.00	61.00	70.00	135	260	1,375	9,750	—
1890S	8,230,373	26.00	27.00	45.00	56.00	61.00	75.00	115	250	975	9,000	—
1891	8,694,206	26.00	27.00	56.00	56.00	58.00	80.00	185	500	3,400	24,500	4,800
1891CC	1,618,000	120	124	132	170	320	480	750	1,000	3,250	28,000	—
1891CC Spitting Eagle	—	105	115	135	185	260	605	850	1,375	5,500	—	—
1891O	7,954,529	26.00	27.00	45.00	58.00	64.00	210	385	600	4,500	32,000	—
1891S	5,296,000	26.00	27.00	45.00	55.00	61.00	100	150	280	1,125	18,000	—
1892	1,037,245	26.00	48.00	49.00	52.00	100	290	430	975	2,800	18,000	4,500
1892CC	1,352,000	190	210	260	390	655	1,325	2,500	3,350	6,275	32,500	—
1892O	2,744,000	17.05	25.05	45.00	56.00	78.00	295	450	750	3,700	45,000	—
1892S	1,200,000	45.00	50.00	130	255	1,325	39,000	90,000	180,000	200,000	175,000	—
1893	378,792	165	170	190	210	365	925	1,390	2,400	10,000	—	5,200
1893CC	677,000	370	420	575	1,600	2,175	5,000	7,200	14,600	77,000	85,500	—
1893O	300,000	210	230	340	570	775	3,325	6,800	16,000	165,000	210,000	—
1893S	100,000	3,300	3,825	4,800	7,100	20,500	160,000	300,000	350,000	700,000	650,000	—
1894	110,972	680	900	925	1,025	1,100	3,500	5,600	10,600	35,000	80,000	6,400
1894O	1,723,000	43.00	48.00	50.00	155	1,325	4,600	10,500	56,000	58,000	—	—
1894S	1,260,000	68.00	60.00	95.00	130	500	900	1,400	2,300	5,350	—	—
1895 proof only	12,880	30,000	32,000	34,000	34,750	34,750	38,000	43,500	54,000	60,000	69,000	—	81,600
1895O	450,000	192	250	258	455	925	15,000	55,000	86,000	185,000	—	—
1895S	400,000	400	525	700	1,000	1,325	4,000	5,640	7,300	20,000	32,500	—
1896	9,967,762	26.00	27.00	29.00	38.00	43.00	55.00	68.00	70.00	190	1,100	4,800
1896O	4,900,000	43.00	46.00	47.00	47.80	160	990	5,900	36,000	150,000	140,000	—
1896S	5,000,000	43.00	45.00	55.00	165	825	2,400	3,850	5,600	11,750	85,000	—
1897	2,822,731	26.00	27.00	29.00	38.00	43.00	55.00	75.00	70.00	215	2,700	4,900
1897O	4,004,000	26.00	27.00	40.00	49.00	95.00	1,000	4,650	14,000	70,000	60,000	—
1897S	5,825,000	26.00	27.00	48.00	49.00	55.00	90.00	145	225	465	2,300	—
1898	5,884,735	26.00	27.00	29.00	38.00	43.00	55.00	68.00	70.00	185	950	5,200
1898O	4,440,000	26.00	27.00	29.00	38.00	43.00	55.00	68.00	80.00	160	1,100	—
1898S	4,102,000	45.00	46.00	47.00	50.00	95.00	270	410	690	1,450	13,000	—

Date	Mintage	VG8	F12	VF20	XF40	AU50	MS60	MS63	MS64	MS65	65DMPL	Prf65
1899	330,846	85.00	110	120	130	145	185	210	312	600	2,500	5,200
1899O	12,290,000	26.00	27.00	45.00	54.00	59.00	65.00	78.00	85.00	160	1,300	—
1899S	2,562,000	26.00	27.00	47.00	52.00	185	375	600	1,000	1,790	17,500	—
1900	8,880,938	26.00	27.00	29.00	38.00	43.00	55.00	68.00	70.00	155	30,000	5,200
1900O	12,590,000	26.00	27.00	45.00	—	60.00	66.00	80.00	85.00	170	5,000	—
1900O/CC	—	70.00	75.00	105	120	180	375	840	1,260	1,950	15,000	—
1900S	3,540,000	26.00	48.00	50.00	57.00	85.00	290	390	575	1,450	25,000	—
1901	6,962,813	47.00	48.00	55.00	85.00	215	3,100	12,100	54,000	450,000	—	4,800
1901 doubled die reverse	—	275	450	900	2,000	3,850	—	—	—	—	—	—
1901O	13,320,000	50.00	53.00	53.00	54.00	59.00	71.00	82.00	85.00	160	9,000	—
1901S	2,284,000	45.00	50.00	51.00	60.00	195	465	900	1,150	2,100	23,000	—
1902	7,994,777	42.00	46.00	47.00	50.00	56.00	90.00	170	220	375	17,500	5,800
1902O	8,636,000	43.00	44.00	47.00	—	59.00	65.00	80.00	85.00	190	14,000	—
1902S	1,530,000	102	105	140	160	250	425	745	810	1,900	12,000	—
1903	4,652,755	50.00	51.00	53.00	54.00	55.00	70.00	115	140	230	23,000	4,950
1903O	4,450,000	330	350	375	385	420	425	420	432	600	6,800	—
1903S	1,241,000	80.00	105	195	300	1,450	5,500	7,700	8,000	10,400	32,500	—
1903S Micro S	—	155	245	500	1,250	—	—	—	—	—	—	—
1904	2,788,650	43.00	44.00	45.00	47.00	60.00	135	255	515	1,870	65,000	5,000
1904O	3,720,000	43.00	44.00	45.00	46.00	50.00	60.00	75.00	80.00	180	1,125	—
1904S	2,304,000	26.00	27.00	80.00	110	570	2,550	4,650	5,600	7,800	20,000	—
1921	44,690,000	26.00	27.00	29.00	35.00	38.00	40.00	50.00	80.00	125	11,250	10,000
1921D	20,345,000	26.00	27.00	29.00	35.00	38.00	42.00	90.00	135	325	—	—
1921S	21,695,000	26.00	27.00	29.00	35.00	38.00	42.00	90.00	145	690	—	—

Peace Dollar
Liberty Head left. Eagle facing right perched on rock.
KM# 150 • 26.73 g., 0.900 Silver 0.7734 oz. ASW, 38.1 mm. • **Designer:** Anthony DeFrancisci

Date	Mintage	G4	VG8	F12	VF20	XF40	AU50	MS60	MS63	MS64	MS65
1921	1,006,473	65.00	85.00	90.00	100	140	150	285	400	800	1,800
1921 rev ray over first L in DOLLAR Vam 3	—	—	—	—	—	200	250	475	—	—	—
1922	51,737,000	19.00	20.00	21.00	23.00	25.00	25.00	36.00	52.00	69.00	125
1922D	15,063,000	19.00	20.00	21.00	23.00	25.00	25.00	66.00	85.00	130	590
1922S	17,475,000	19.00	—	21.00	23.00	25.00	25.00	64.00	100	250	1,375
1923	30,800,000	19.00	20.00	21.00	23.00	25.00	25.00	36.00	39.00	55.00	120
1923D	6,811,000	19.00	20.00	21.00	23.00	33.00	34.00	76.00	165	340	965
1923S	19,020,000	19.00	20.00	21.00	23.00	25.00	25.00	62.00	90.00	315	2,200
1924	11,811,000	19.00	20.00	21.00	23.00	25.00	25.00	36.00	40.00	55.00	130
1924S	1,728,000	19.00	20.00	21.00	37.00	40.00	45.00	225	455	1,075	6,000
1925	10,198,000	19.00	20.00	21.00	23.00	25.00	25.00	36.00	40.00	60.00	115
1925S	1,610,000	19.00	20.00	21.00	29.00	37.00	48.00	105	260	690	21,200
1926	1,939,000	19.00	20.00	21.00	29.00	37.00	45.00	65.00	110	140	400
1926D	2,348,700	19.00	20.00	21.00	23.00	37.00	60.00	100	260	350	875
1926S	6,980,000	19.00	20.00	21.00	23.00	35.00	45.00	70.00	105	230	720
1927	848,000	19.00	31.00	32.00	34.00	45.00	55.00	98.00	170	575	1,450
1927D	1,268,900	19.00	30.00	30.00	37.00	46.00	100	165	420	1,075	3,250
1927S	866,000	19.00	32.00	32.00	42.00	56.00	81.00	230	525	1,375	7,400
1928	360,649	185	240	245	250	255	265	400	615	1,290	4,600
1928S	1,632,000	19.00	34.00	38.00	40.00	49.00	70.00	215	450	950	17,000
1934	954,057	19.00	31.00	43.00	46.00	50.00	55.00	125	190	300	525
1934D Large D	1,569,500	19.00	37.00	40.00	44.00	52.00	55.00	130	300	435	1,180
1934D Small D	—	19.00	35.00	38.00	40.00	52.00	55.00	130	410	575	1,575
1934S	1,011,000	—	34.00	40.00	60.00	150	500	2,300	4,000	6,450	9,375
1935	1,576,000	19.00	33.00	36.00	39.00	48.00	65.00	95.00	140	220	490
1935S 3 Rays	1,964,000	19.00	41.00	42.00	45.00	50.00	95.00	285	495	570	1,200
1935S 4 Rays	—	19.00	41.00	42.00	50.00	54.00	100	275	465	570	1,100

DOLLAR

Eisenhower Dollar

KM# 203 • 22.80 g., Copper-Nickel Clad Copper, 38 mm. • **Designer:** Frank Gasparro

Date	Mintage	MS63	MS65	Prf65
1971	47,799,000	5.00	185	—
1971D	68,587,424	4.00	40.00	—
1972 Low Relief	75,890,000	18.00	80.00	—
1972 High Relief	Inc. above	100	1,500	—
1972 Modified High Relief	Inc. above	25.00	125	—
1972D	92,548,511	8.00	27.00	—
1973	2,000,056	12.00	65.00	—
1973D	2,000,000	12.00	45.00	—
1973S	2,769,624	—	—	12.00
1974	27,366,000	9.00	45.00	—
1974D	35,466,000	7.50	22.00	—
1974S	2,617,350	—	—	11.00

KM# 203a • 24.59 g., 0.400 Silver 0.3162 oz. ASW, 38.1 mm. • **Designer:** Frank Gasparro

Date	Mintage	MS63	MS65	Prf65
1971S	6,868,530	7.50	22.00	11.00
1971S	4,265,234	—	—	—
1971S Peg Leg "R" Variety	Inc. above	—	—	17.00
1971S Partial Peg Leg "R" Variety	Inc. above	—	—	18.00
1972S	2,193,056	7.50	18.50	—
1972S	1,811,631	—	—	9.00
1973S	1,833,140	7.50	20.00	—
1973S	1,005,617	—	—	45.00
1974S	1,720,000	7.50	18.50	—
1974S	1,306,579	—	—	11.00

Moon behind Liberty Bell.

Type I	Type II
Squared "T"	Slant-top "T"

KM# 206 • 22.68 g., Copper-Nickel Clad Copper, 38.1 mm. • **Rev. Designer:** Dennis R. Williams **Note:** In 1976 the lettering on the reverse was changed to thinner letters, resulting in the Type II variety for that year. The Type I variety was minted 1975 and dated 1976.

Date	Mintage	MS63	MS65	Prf65
1976 type I	117,337,000	12.00	125	—
1976 type II	Inc. above	7.50	24.00	—
1976D type I	103,228,274	10.00	50.00	—
1976D type II	Inc. above	7.00	22.00	—
1976S type I	2,909,369	—	—	10.00
1976S type II	4,149,730	—	—	9.00

Bicentennial design, moon behind Liberty Bell.

KM# 206a • 24.59 g., 0.400 Silver 0.3162 oz. ASW **Rev. Designer:** Dennis R. Williams

Date	Mintage	MS63	MS65	Prf65
1976S	4,908,319	7.50	18.00	14.00
1976S	3,998,621	—	—	—

Regular design resumed.

KM# A203 • Copper-Nickel Clad Copper, 38.1 mm. • **Designer:** Frank Gasparro

Date	Mintage	MS63	MS65	Prf65
1977	12,596,000	5.50	20.00	—
1977D	32,983,006	8.00	25.00	—
1977S	3,251,152	—	—	9.00
1978	25,702,000	6.50	35.00	—
1978D	33,012,890	6.50	30.00	—
1978S	3,127,788	—	—	9.00

Susan B. Anthony Dollar

Susan B. Anthony bust right. Eagle landing on moon, symbolic of Apollo manned moon landing.

KM# 207 • 8.10 g., Copper-Nickel Clad Copper, 26.5 mm. • **Edge:** Reeded **Designer:** Frank Gasparro **Note:** The 1979-S and 1981-S Type II coins have a clearer mint mark than the Type I varieties for those years.

Date	Mintage	MS63	PF65
1979P Near date	360,222,000	30.00	—
1979P	Inc. above	2.50	—
1979D	288,015,744	2.50	—
1979S Proof, Type I	3,677,175	—	6.00
1979S Proof, Type II	Inc. above	—	85.00
1979S	109,576,000	2.50	—
1980P	27,610,000	2.50	—
1980D	41,628,708	2.50	—
1980S	20,422,000	5.00	—
1980S Proof	3,547,030	—	5.00
1981P	3,000,000	5.00	—
1981D	3,250,000	5.00	—
1981S	3,492,000	5.00	—
1981S Proof, Type I	4,063,083	—	7.00
1981S Proof, Type II	Inc. above	—	225
1999P	29,592,000	3.00	—
1999P Proof	Est. 750000	—	22.00
1999D	11,776,000	3.00	—

Sacagawea Dollar
Sacagawea bust right, with baby on back. Eagle in flight left.

KM# 310 • 8.07 g., Copper-Zinc-Manganese-Nickel Clad Copper, 26.5 mm. • **Obv. Designer:** Glenda Goodacre **Rev. Designer:** Thomas D. Rodgers

Date	Mintage	MS63	PF65
2000P	767,140,000	2.00	—
2000P Goodacre Presentation	5,000	—	—
2000D	518,916,000	2.00	—
2000D from Millennium Set	5,500	10.00	—
2000S	4,048,000	—	5.00
2001P	62,468,000	2.25	—
2001D	70,909,500	2.25	—
2001S	3,084,000	—	16.00
2002P	3,865,610	3.00	—
2002D	3,732,000	2.75	—
2002S	3,157,739	—	10.00
2003P	3,090,000	4.50	—
2003D	3,090,000	4.75	—
2003S	3,116,590	—	8.00
2004P	2,660,000	3.50	—
2004D	2,660,000	4.00	—
2004S	2,992,069	—	7.50
2005P	2,520,000	3.00	—
2005P Satin Finish	1,160,000	5.00	—
2005D	2,520,000	3.00	—
2005D Satin Finish	1,160,000	5.00	—
2005S	3,273,000	—	6.00
2006P	4,900,000	3.25	—
2006P Satin Finish	847,361	4.50	—
2006D	2,800,000	3.50	—
2006D Satin Finish	847,361	4.00	—
2006S	3,054,436	—	9.00
2007P	3,640,000	2.25	—
2007P Satin Finish	895,628	4.00	—
2007D	3,920,000	2.25	—
2007D Satin Finish	895,628	4.00	—
2007S	2,577,166	—	6.50
2008P	1,820,000	2.00	—
2008P Satin Finish	745,464	4.00	—
2008D	1,820,000	3.50	—
2008D Satin Finish	745,464	4.00	—
2008S	2,169,561	—	16.00

Native American Dollar - Planting crops reverse
Sacagawea bust right with baby on back. Native American female planting corn, beans and squash.

KM# 467 • 8.07 g., Copper-Zinc-Manganese-Nickel Clad Copper, 26.5 mm. • **Obv. Designer:** Glenda Goodacre **Rev. Designer:** Norm Nemeth **Edge Lettering:** E PLURIBUS UNUM, date, mint mark **Note:** Date and mint mark on edge

Date	Mintage	MS63	PF65
2009P	37,380,000	2.00	—
2009P Satin finish	784,614	4.00	—
2009D	33,880,000	2.00	—
2009D Satin finish	784,614	4.00	—
2009S	2,179,867	—	6.00

Native American Dollar - Hiawatha belt reverse
Sacagawea bust right with baby on back. Hiawatha belt and bundle of five arrows.

KM# 474 • 8.07 g., Copper-Zinc-Manganese-Nickel Clad Copper, 26.5 mm. • **Obv. Designer:** Glenda Goodacre **Rev. Designer:** Thomas Cleveland and Charles L. Vickers **Edge Lettering:** E PLURIBUS UNUM, date, mint mark **Note:** Date and mint mark on edge

Date	Mintage	MS63	PF65
2010P	32,060,000	2.00	—
2010P Satin Finish	583,897	4.00	—
2010D	48,720,000	2.00	—
2010D Satin Finish	583,897	4.00	—
2010S	1,689,364	—	12.50

Native American Dollar - Peace pipe reverse
Sacagawea bust right with baby on back. Hands passing peace pipe.

KM# 503 • 8.07 g., Copper-Zinc-Manganese-Nickel Clad Copper, 26.5 mm. • **Obv. Designer:** Glenna Goodacre **Rev. Designer:** Richard Masters and Joseph Menna **Edge Lettering:** E PLURIBUS UNUM, date, mint mark **Note:** Date and mint mark on edge

Date	Mintage	MS63	PF65
2011P	29,400,000	2.00	—
2011D	48,160,000	2.00	—
2011S	1,453,276	—	8.00

DOLLAR

Native American Dollar - Horse reverse
Sacagawea bust right with baby on back. Horse and Native American profile facing left.

KM# 528 • 8.07 g., Copper-Zinc-Manganese-Nickel Clad Copper, 26.5 mm. • **Obv. Designer:** Glenda Goodacre **Rev. Designer:** Thomas Cleveland and Phebe Hemphill **Edge Lettering:** E PLURIBUS UNUM, date, mint mark **Note:** Date and mint mark on edge

Date	Mintage	MS63	PF65
2012P	2,800,000	2.00	—
2012D	3,080,000	2.00	—
2012S	1,189,445	—	12.50

Native American Dollar - Delaware Treaty of 1778
Turtle, turkey and wolf.

KM# 551 • 8.07 g., Copper-Zinc-Manganese-Nickel Clad Copper, 26.5 mm. • **Edge:** E PLURIBUS UNUM, date, mint mark **Note:** Date and mint mark on edge.

Date	Mintage	MS63	PF65
2013P	1,820,000	2.00	—
2013D	1,820,000	2.00	—
2013S	1,192,690	—	12.50

Native American Dollar - Native Hospitality

KM# 575 • 8.07 g., Copper-Zinc-Manganese-Nickel Clad Copper, 26.5 mm. •

Date	Mintage	MS63	PF65
2014P	3,080,000	2.00	—
2014D	2,800,000	2.00	—
2014S	—	—	12.50

KM# 575.1 • 8.07 g., Copper-Zinc-Manganese-Nickel Clad Copper, 26.5 mm. • **Note:** In 2014 American $1 Coin & Currency Sets only.

Date	Mintage	MS63	PF65
2014D Enhanced Unc.	50,000	5.00	—

Native American Dollar - Mohawk Ironworkers

KM# 603 • 8.07 g., Copper-Zinc-Manganese-Nickel Clad Copper, 26.5 mm. •

Date	Mintage	MS63	PF65
2015P	2,467,651	2.00	—
2015D	3,042,741	2.00	—
2015S	661,165	—	12.50

KM# 603.1 • 8.07 g., Copper-Zinc-Manganese-Nickel Clad Copper, 26.5 mm. • **Note:** In 2015 American $1 Coin & Currency Sets only.

Date	Mintage	MS63	PF65
2015W Enhanced Unc.	87,239	5.00	—

Native American Dollar - Code Talkers

KM# 618 • 8.07 g., Copper-Zinc-Manganese-Nickel Clad Copper, 26.5 mm. •

Date	Mintage	MS63	PF65
2016P	2,800,000	2.00	—
2016D	2,100,000	2.00	—
2016S	—	—	12.50

Native American Dollar - Sequoyah

KM# 640 • 8.07 g., Copper-Zinc-Manganese-Nickel Clad Copper, 26.5 mm. •

Date	Mintage	MS63	PF65
2017P	—	2.00	—
2017D	—	2.00	—
2017S Proof	—	—	12.50

Native American Dollar - Jim Thorpe

KM# 680 • 8.07 g., Copper-Zinc-Manganese-Nickel Clad Copper, 26.5 mm. •

Date	Mintage	MS63	PF65
2018P	—	2.00	—
2018D	—	2.00	—
2018S Proof	—	—	—

Presidents

George Washington

KM# 401 • 8.07 g., Copper-Zinc-Manganese-Nickel Clad Copper, 26.5 mm. **Note:** Date and mint mark incuse on edge.

Date	Mintage	MS63	MS65	Prf65
2007P	176,680,000	2.00	3.00	—
2007P Satin Finish	895,628	2.00	4.00	—
-2007 Plain edge error	Inc. above	175	275	—
2007D	163,680,000	2.00	3.00	—
2007D Satin Finish	895,628	2.00	4.00	—
2007S	3,883,103	—	—	3.00

John Adams

KM# 402 • 8.07 g., Copper-Zinc-Manganese-Nickel Clad Copper, 26.5 mm. **Note:** Date and mint mark incuse on edge.

Date	Mintage	MS63	MS65	Prf65
2007P	112,420,000	2.00	3.00	—
2007P Double edge lettering	Inc. above	45.00	65.00	—
2007D Plain edge error	Inc. above	60.00	70.00	—
2007P Satin Finish	895,628	2.00	4.00	—
2007D	112,140,000	2.00	3.00	—
2007D Satin Finish	895,628	2.00	4.00	—
2007S	3,877,409	—	—	3.00

Thomas Jefferson

KM# 403 • 8.07 g., Copper-Zinc-Manganese-Nickel Clad Copper, 26.5 mm. **Note:** Date and mint mark incuse on edge.

Date	Mintage	MS63	MS65	Prf65
2007P	100,800,000	2.00	3.00	—
2007P Satin Finish	895,628	2.00	4.00	—
2007D	102,810,000	2.00	3.00	—
2007D Satin Finish	895,628	2.00	4.00	—
2007S	3,877,573	—	—	3.00

James Madison

KM# 404 • 8.07 g., Copper-Zinc-Manganese-Nickel Clad Copper, 26.5 mm. **Note:** Date and mint mark incuse on edge.

Date	Mintage	MS63	MS65	Prf65
2007P	84,560,000	2.00	3.00	—
2007P Satin Finish	895,628	2.00	4.00	—
2007D	87,780,000	2.00	3.00	—
2007D Satin Finish	895,628	2.00	4.00	—
2007S	3,876,829	—	—	3.00

James Monroe

KM# 426 • 8.07 g., Copper-Zinc-Manganese-Nickel Clad Copper, 26.5 mm.

Date	Mintage	MS63	MS65	Prf65
2008P	64,260,000	2.00	3.00	—
2008P Satin Finish	745,464	2.00	4.00	—
2008D	60,230,000	2.00	3.00	—
2008D Satin Finish	745,464	2.00	4.00	—
2008S	3,000,000	—	—	4.00

John Quincy Adams

KM# 427 • 8.07 g., Copper-Zinc-Manganese-Nickel Clad Copper, 26.5 mm. **Note:** Date and mint mark incuse on edge.

Date	Mintage	MS63	MS65	Prf65
2008P	57,540,000	2.00	3.00	—
2008P Satin Finish	745,464	2.00	4.00	—
2008D	57,720,000	2.00	3.00	—
2008D Satin Finish	745,464	2.00	4.00	—
2008S	3,000,000	—	—	4.00

DOLLAR

KM# 428 • 8.07 g., Copper-Zinc-Manganese-Nickel Clad Copper, 26.5 mm. **Note:** Date and mint mark incuse on edge.

Date	Mintage	MS63	MS65	Prf65
2008P	61,180,000	2.00	3.00	—
2008P Satin Finish	745,464	2.00	4.00	—
2008D	61,070,000	2.00	3.00	—
2008D Satin Finish	745,464	2.00	4.00	—
2008S	3,000,000	—	—	4.00

Martin van Buren

KM# 429 • 8.07 g., Copper-Zinc-Manganese-Nickel Clad Copper, 26.5 mm. **Note:** Date and mint mark incuse on edge.

Date	Mintage	MS63	MS65	Prf65
2008P	51,520,000	2.00	3.00	—
2008P Satin Finish	745,464	2.00	4.00	—
2008D	50,960,000	2.00	3.00	—
2008D Satin Finish	745,464	2.00	4.00	—
2008S	3,000,000	—	—	4.00

William Henry Harrison

KM# 450 • 8.07 g., Copper-Zinc-Manganese-Nickel Clad Copper, 26.5 mm. **Note:** Date and mint mark on edge

Date	Mintage	MS63	MS65	Prf65
2009P	43,260,000	2.00	3.00	—
2009P Satin Finish	784,614	2.00	4.00	—
2009D	55,160,000	2.00	3.00	—
2009P Satin Finish	784,614	2.00	4.00	—
2009S	2,224,827	—	—	3.00

John Tyler

KM# 451 • 8.07 g., Copper-Zinc-Manganese-Nickel Clad Copper, 26.5 mm. **Note:** Date and mint mark on edge.

Date	Mintage	MS63	MS65	Prf65
2009P	43,540,000	2.00	3.00	—
2009P Satin Finish	784,614	2.00	4.00	—
2009D	43,540,000	2.00	3.00	—
2009D Satin Finish	784,614	2.00	4.00	—
2009S	2,224,827	—	—	3.00

James K. Polk

KM# 452 • 8.07 g., Copper-Zinc-Manganese-Nickel Clad Copper, 26.5 mm. **Note:** Date and mint mark on edge

Date	Mintage	MS63	MS65	Prf65
2009P	46,620,000	2.00	3.00	—
2009P Satin Finish	784,614	2.00	4.00	—
2009D	41,720,000	2.00	3.00	—
2009D Satin Finish	784,614	2.00	4.00	—
2009S	2,224,827	—	—	3.00

Zachary Taylor

KM# 453 • 8.07 g., Copper-Zinc-Manganese-Nickel Clad Copper, 26.5 mm. **Note:** Date and mint mark on edge.

Date	Mintage	MS63	MS65	Prf65
2009P	41,580,000	2.00	3.00	—
2009P Satin Finish	784,614	2.00	4.00	—
2009D	36,680,000	2.00	3.00	—
2009D Satin Finish	784,614	2.00	4.00	—
2009S	2,224,827	—	—	3.00

Millard Filmore

KM# 475 • 8.07 g., Copper-Zinc-Manganese-Nickel Clad Copper, 26.5 mm. **Note:** Date and mint mark on edge.

Date	Mintage	MS63	MS65	Prf65
2010P	37,520,000	2.00	3.00	—
2010P Satin Finish	583,897	2.00	4.00	—
2010D	36,960,000	2.00	3.00	—
2010D Satin Finish	583,897	2.00	4.00	—
2010S	2,224,827	—	—	4.00

DOLLAR

Franklin Pierce

KM# 476 • 8.07 g., Copper-Zinc-Manganese-Nickel Clad Copper, 26.5 mm. **Note:** Date and mint mark on edge.

Date	Mintage	MS63	MS65	Prf65
2010P	38,220,000	2.00	3.00	—
2010P Satin Finish	583,897	2.00	4.00	—
2010D	38,360,000	2.00	3.00	—
2010D Satin Finish	583,897	2.00	4.00	—
2010S	2,224,827	—	—	4.00

James Buchanan

KM# 477 • 8.07 g., Copper-Zinc-Manganese-Nickel Clad Copper, 26.5 mm. **Note:** Date and mint mark on edge.

Date	Mintage	MS63	MS65	Prf65
2010P	36,820,000	2.00	3.00	—
2010P Satin Finish	583,897	2.00	4.00	—
2010D	36,540,000	2.00	3.00	—
2010D Satin Finish	583,897	2.00	4.00	—
2010S	2,224,827	—	—	4.00

Abraham Lincoln

KM# 478 • 8.07 g., Copper-Zinc-Manganese-Nickel Clad Copper, 26.5 mm. **Note:** Date and mint mark on edge.

Date	Mintage	MS63	MS65	Prf65
2010P	49,000,000	2.00	3.00	—
2010P Satin Finish	583,897	2.00	4.00	—
2010D	48,020,000	2.00	3.00	—
2010D Satin Finish	583,897	2.00	4.00	—
2010S	2,224,827	—	—	4.00

Andrew Johnson

KM# 499 • 8.07 g., Copper-Zinc-Manganese-Nickel Clad Copper, 26.5 mm. **Note:** Date and mint mark on edge.

Date	Mintage	MS63	MS65	Prf65
2011P	35,560,000	2.00	3.00	—
2011D	37,100,000	2.00	3.00	—
2011S	1,706,916	—	—	4.00

Ulysses S. Grant

KM# 500 • 8.07 g., Copper-Zinc-Manganese-Nickel Clad Copper, 26.5 mm. **Note:** Date and mint mark on edge.

Date	Mintage	MS63	MS65	Prf65
2011P	38,080,000	2.00	3.00	—
2011D	37,940,000	2.00	3.00	—
2011S	1,706,916	—	—	4.00

Rutherford B. Hayes

KM# 501 • 8.07 g., Copper-Zinc-Manganese-Nickel Clad Copper, 26.5 mm. **Note:** Date and mint mark on edge.

Date	Mintage	MS63	MS65	Prf65
2011P	37,660,000	2.00	3.00	—
2011D	36,820,000	2.00	3.00	—
2011S	1,706,916	—	—	4.00

James Garfield

KM# 502 • 8.07 g., Copper-Zinc-Manganese-Nickel Clad Copper, 26.5 mm. **Note:** Date and mint mark on edge.

DOLLAR

Date	Mintage	MS63	MS65	Prf65
2011P	37,100,000	2.00	3.00	—
2011D	37,100,000	2.00	3.00	—
2011S	1,706,916	—	—	4.00

Chester A. Arthur

KM# 524 • 8.07 g., Copper-Zinc-Manganese-Nickel Clad Copper, 26.5 mm. **Note:** Date and mintmark on edge.

Date	Mintage	MS63	MS65	Prf65
2012P	6,020,000	2.00	3.00	—
2012D	4,060,000	2.00	3.00	—
2012S	—	—	—	5.00

Grover Cleveland, first term

KM# 525 • 8.07 g., Copper-Zinc-Manganese-Nickel Clad Copper, 26.5 mm. **Note:** Date and mint mark on edge

Date	Mintage	MS63	MS65	Prf65
2012P	5,460,000	2.00	3.00	—
2012D	4,060,000	2.00	3.00	—
2012S	1,438,710	—	—	5.00

Benjamin Harrison

KM# 526 • 8.07 g., Copper-Zinc-Manganese-Nickel Clad Copper, 26.5 mm. **Note:** Date at mint mark on edge

Date	Mintage	MS63	MS65	Prf65
2012P	5,640,001	2.00	3.00	—
2012D	4,200,000	2.00	3.00	—
2012S	1,438,710	—	—	5.00

Grover Cleveland, second term

KM# 527 • 8.07 g., Copper-Zinc-Manganese-Nickel Clad Copper, 26.5 mm. **Note:** Date and mint mark on edge

Date	Mintage	MS63	MS65	Prf65
2012P	10,680,000	2.00	3.00	—
2012D	3,920,000	2.00	3.00	—
2012S	1,438,710	—	—	5.00

William McKinley

KM# 547 • 8.07 g., Copper-Zinc-Manganese-Nickel Clad Copper, 26.5 mm. **Note:** Date and mint mark on edge.

Date	Mintage	MS63	MS65	Prf65
2013P	4,760,000	2.00	3.00	—
2013D	3,365,100	2.00	3.00	—
2013S	1,449,415	—	—	5.00

Theodore Roosevelt

KM# 548 • 8.07 g., Copper-Zinc-Manganese-Nickel Clad Copper, 26.5 mm. **Note:** Date and mint mark on edge.

Date	Mintage	MS63	MS65	Prf65
2013P	5,310,700	2.00	3.00	—
2013D	3,920,000	2.00	3.00	—
2013S	1,449,415	—	—	5.00

William Howard Taft

KM# 549 • 8.07 g., Copper-Zinc-Manganese-Nickel Clad Copper, 26.5 mm. **Note:** Date and mint mark on edge.

Date	Mintage	MS63	MS65	Prf65
2013P	4,760,000	2.00	3.00	—
2013D	3,360,000	2.00	3.00	—
2013S	1,449,415	—	—	5.00

Woodrow Wilson

KM# 550 • 8.07 g., Copper-Zinc-Manganese-Nickel Clad Copper, 26.5 mm. **Note:** Date and mint mark on edge.

Date	Mintage	MS63	MS65	Prf65
2013P	4,620,000	2.00	3.00	—
2013D	3,360,000	2.00	3.00	—
2013S	1,449,415	—	—	5.00

Warren G. Harding

KM# 571 • 8.07 g., Copper-Zinc-Manganese-Nickel Clad Copper, 26.5 mm. **Note:** Date and mint mark on edge.

Date	Mintage	MS63	MS65	Prf65
2014P	6,160,000	2.00	3.00	—
2014D	3,780,000	2.00	3.00	—
2014S	—	—	—	5.00

Calvin Coolidge

KM# 572 • 8.07 g., Copper-Zinc-Manganese-Nickel Clad Copper, 26.5 mm. **Note:** Date and mint mark on edge.

Date	Mintage	MS63	MS65	Prf65
2014P	4,480,000	2.00	5.00	—
2014D	3,780,000	2.00	5.00	—
2014S	—	—	—	5.00

Herbert Hoover

KM# 573 • 8.07 g., Copper-Zinc-Manganese-Nickel Clad Copper, 26.5 mm. **Note:** Date and mint mark on edge.

Date	Mintage	MS63	MS65	Prf65
2014P	4,944,886	2.00	3.00	—
2014D	4,208,459	2.00	3.00	—
2014S	1,373,569	—	—	5.00

Franklin D. Roosevelt

KM# 574 • 8.07 g., Copper-Zinc-Manganese-Nickel Clad Copper, 26.5 mm. **Note:** Date and mint mark on edge.

Date	Mintage	MS63	MS65	Prf65
2014P	4,760,000	2.00	3.00	—
2014D	3,920,000	2.00	3.00	—
2014S	—	—	—	5.00

Harry S. Truman

KM# 606 • 8.07 g., Copper-Zinc-Manganese-Nickel Clad Copper, 26.5 mm. **Note:** Date and mint mark on edge.

Date	Mintage	MS63	MS65	Prf65
2015P	4,900,000	2.00	3.00	—
2015D	3,500,000	2.00	3.00	—
2015S	836,777	—	—	5.00
2015P Reverse Proof	17,000	—	—	—

Note: In 2015 Truman Coin and Chronicles Sets only, including 1oz. silver Presidential medal and U.S. postage stamp

DOLLAR

DOLLAR

Dwight D. Eisenhower

KM# 607 • 8.07 g., Copper-Zinc-Manganese-Nickel Clad Copper, 26.5 mm. **Note:** Date and mint mark on edge.

Date	Mintage	MS63	MS65	Prf65
2015P	4,900,000	2.00	3.00	—
2015D	3,645,998	2.00	3.00	—
2015S	836,777	—	—	5.00
2015P Reverse Proof	17,000	—	—	—

Note: In 2015 Eisenhower Coin and Chronicles Sets only, including 1oz. silver Presidential medal and U.S. postage stamp

John F. Kennedy

KM# 608 • 8.07 g., Copper-Zinc-Manganese-Nickel Clad Copper, 26.5 mm. **Note:** Date and mint mark on edge.

Date	Mintage	MS63	MS65	Prf65
2015P	6,160,000	2.00	3.00	—
2015D	5,180,000	2.00	3.00	—
2015S	836,777	—	—	5.00
2015P Reverse Proof	50,000	—	—	—

Note: In 2015 Kennedy Coin and Chronicles Sets only, including 1oz. silver Presidential medal and U.S. postage stamp

Lyndon B. Johnson

KM# 609 • 8.07 g., Copper-Zinc-Manganese-Nickel Clad Copper, 26.5 mm. **Note:** Date and mint mark on edge.

Date	Mintage	MS63	MS65	Prf65
2015P	7,840,000	2.00	3.00	—
2015D	4,200,000	2.00	3.00	—
2015S	836,777	—	—	5.00
2015P Reverse Proof	25,000	—	—	—

Note: In 2015 Johnson Coin and Chronicles Sets only, including 1oz. silver Presidential medal and U.S. postage stamp

Richard M. Nixon

KM# 619 • 8.07 g., Copper-Zinc-Manganese-Nickel Clad Copper, 26.5 mm. **Note:** Date and mint mark on edge.

Date	Mintage	MS63	MS65	Prf65
2016P	5,460,000	2.00	3.00	—
2016D	4,340,000	2.00	3.00	—
2016S	—	—	—	5.00

Gerald Ford

KM# 620 • 8.07 g., Copper-Zinc-Manganese-Nickel Clad Copper, 26.5 mm. **Note:** Date and mint mark on edge.

Date	Mintage	MS63	MS65	Prf65
2016P	5,460,000	2.00	3.00	—
2016D	5,040,000	2.00	3.00	—
2016S	—	—	—	5.00

Ronald Reagan

KM# 621 • 8.07 g., Copper-Zinc-Manganese-Nickel Clad Copper, 26.5 mm. **Note:** Date and mint mark on edge.

Date	Mintage	MS63	MS65	Prf65
2016P	7,140,000	2.00	3.00	—
2016D	5,880,000	2.00	3.00	—
2016S	—	—	—	5.00
2016S Reverse Proof				
2017S Enhanced Unc.	225,000	—	15.00	—

Note: In 2016 Reagan Coin and Chronicles Sets only, including 1oz. silver Presidential medal and U.S. postage stamp

GOLD

$1

Liberty Head - Type 1
Liberty head left within circle of stars. Value, date within 3/4 wreath.

KM# 73 1.67 g., 0.900 Gold 0.0484 oz. AGW, 13 mm. • **Rev. Legend:** UNITED STATES OF AMERICA **Designer:** James B. Longacre **Note:** On the "closed wreath" varieties of 1849, the wreath on the reverse extends closer to the numeral 1.

Date	Mintage	F12	VF20	XF40	AU50	MS60
1849 open wreath	688,567	177	227	257	310	700
1849 small head, no L	—	—	—	—	—	—
1849 closed wreath	Inc. above	130	200	240	285	450
1849C closed wreath	11,634	800	1,000	1,400	2,000	8,300
1849C open wreath	Inc. above	100,000	150,000	200,000	300,000	500,000
1849D open wreath	21,588	900	1,250	2,000	2,350	4,400
1849O open wreath	215,000	160	270	300	345	940
1850	481,953	190	227	277	310	325
1850C	6,966	800	1,150	1,725	2,875	6,800
1850D	8,382	900	1,200	1,950	2,875	9,800
1850O	14,000	250	500	750	875	2,600
1851	3,317,671	177	227	257	310	325
1851C	41,267	750	1,000	1,400	1,675	2,800
1851D	9,882	850	1,150	1,900	2,200	4,600
1851O	290,000	177	227	257	310	675
1852	2,045,351	—	75.00	130	185	220
1852C	9,434	750	1,000	1,350	2,200	4,000
1852D	6,360	850	1,150	1,725	2,200	7,000
1852O	140,000	177	227	257	310	985
1853	4,076,051	177	227	257	310	325
1853C	11,515	750	1,000	1,525	1,775	4,300
1853D	6,583	850	1,150	1,725	2,400	7,500
1853O	290,000	177	227	257	310	550
1854	736,709	177	227	257	310	325
1854D	2,935	1,200	1,800	3,500	6,000	9,800
1854S	14,632	225	350	475	1,050	2,450

Indian Head - Type 2
Indian head with headdress left. Value, date within wreath.

KM# 83 1.67 g., 0.900 Gold 0.0484 oz. AGW, 15 mm. • **Obv. Legend:** UNITED STATES OF AMERICA **Designer:** James B. Longacre

Date	Mintage	F12	VF20	XF40	AU50	MS60
1854	902,736	80.00	180	300	520	1,025
1855	758,269	80.00	180	300	520	1,025
1855C	9,803	1,200	2,000	2,750	5,500	14,000
1855D	1,811	4,500	7,500	20,000	25,000	40,000
1855O	55,000	950	1,100	1,275	1,800	6,750
1856S	24,600	460	700	1,400	2,200	6,750

Indian Head - Type 3
Indian head with headdress left. Value, date within wreath.

KM# 86 • 1.67 g., 0.900 Gold 0.0484 oz. AGW, 15 mm. • **Obv. Legend:** UNITED STATES OF AMERICA **Designer:** James B. Longacre **Note:** The 1856 varieties are distinguished by whether the 5 in the date is slanted or upright. The 1873 varieties are distinguished by the amount of space between the upper left and lower left serifs in the 3.

Date	Mintage	F12	VF20	XF40	AU50	MS60	Prf65
1856 upright 5	1,762,936	203	243	258	303	450	—
1856 slanted 5	Inc. above	203	243	310	335	310	60,000
1856D	1,460	2,900	5,000	8,000	9,200	24,000	—
1857	774,789	203	243	258	303	310	30,000
1857C	13,280	650	800	1,500	2,800	8,000	—
1857D	3,533	800	1,300	1,800	3,350	9,000	—

DOLLAR GOLD

Date	Mintage	F12	VF20	XF40	AU50	MS60	Prf65
1857S	10,000	200	425	650	1,000	4,000	—
1858	117,995	203	243	258	303	307	23,000
1858D	3,477	900	1,050	1,900	2,675	6,300	—
1858S	10,000	310	480	750	1,050	4,200	—
1859	168,244	203	243	258	303	325	16,000
1859C	5,235	1,200	1,800	2,800	3,600	6,000	—
1859D	4,952	950	1,200	1,800	2,800	8,000	—
1859S	15,000	200	275	475	1,000	3,700	—
1860	36,668	161	211	221	246	310	13,000
1860D	1,566	2,000	2,800	5,000	9,000	16,000	—
1860S	13,000	325	375	525	680	2,250	—
1861	527,499	161	211	221	246	420	13,000
1861D mintage unrecorded	—	12,000	18,000	30,000	60,000	70,000	—
1862	1,361,390	203	243	258	303	350	17,000
1863	6,250	450	700	1,200	2,200	4,700	17,000
1864	5,950	400	550	650	750	1,100	17,000
1865	3,725	500	600	800	900	1,200	15,000
1866	7,130	300	350	500	600	900	12,000
1867	5,250	300	350	500	650	1,000	13,000
1868	10,525	300	350	500	600	950	13,000
1869	5,925	300	350	500	600	900	12,000
1870	6,335	300	350	500	600	775	11,500
1870S	3,000	450	600	850	1,200	2,000	—
1871	3,930	250	300	375	450	700	14,000
1872	3,530	225	275	325	400	800	14,000
1873 closed 3	125,125	325	400	625	725	1,250	27,000
1873 open 3	Inc. above	182	232	242	267	475	—
1874	198,820	182	232	275	300	325	18,000
1875	420	2,500	3,000	4,300	5,000	9,000	26,000
1876	3,245	300	325	400	500	900	12,500
1877	3,920	300	325	400	550	725	14,000
1878	3,020	300	325	400	500	700	12,000
1879	3,030	250	275	325	375	500	11,000
1880	1,636	250	275	325	375	500	10,000
1881	7,707	182	232	242	267	450	10,595
1882	5,125	182	232	242	267	450	8,500
1883	11,007	182	232	242	267	450	8,500
1884	6,236	182	232	242	267	450	8,500
1885	12,261	182	232	242	267	450	8,500
1886	6,016	182	232	242	267	450	8,500
1887	8,543	182	232	242	267	450	8,500
1888	16,580	182	232	242	267	450	8,500
1889	30,729	182	232	242	267	325	8,500

$2.50 (QUARTER EAGLE)

Liberty Cap
Liberty cap on head, right, flanked by stars.
Heraldic eagle.

KM# 27 • 4.37 g., 0.916 Gold 0.1287 oz. AGW, 20 mm. • **Obv. Legend:**
LIBERTY **Rev. Legend:** UNITED STATES OF AMERICA **Designer:** Robert
Scot **Note:** The 1796 "no stars" variety does not have stars on the obverse.
The 1804 varieties are distinguished by the number of stars on the obverse.

Date	Mintage	F12	VF20	XF40	MS60
1796 no stars	963	45,000	70,000	90,000	240,000
1796 stars	432	50,000	60,000	76,000	160,000
1797	427	11,500	17,500	30,000	175,000
1798 close date	1,094	4,000	6,000	13,000	58,000
1798 wide date	Inc. above	3,500	8,100	13,000	110,000
1802/1	3,035	3,500	5,500	12,000	28,000
1804 13-star reverse	3,327	45,000	80,000	130,000	—
1804 14-star reverse	Inc. above	6,000	8,000	12,000	28,000
1805	1,781	3,500	5,500	12,000	28,000
1806/4	1,616	3,500	5,100	12,000	28,000
1806/5	Inc. above	3,500	7,500	14,400	73,000
1807	6,812	3,500	5,500	12,000	28,000

Turban Head
Turban on head left flanked by stars.
Banner above eagle.

KM# 40 • 4.37 g., 0.916 Gold 0.1287 oz. AGW, 20 mm. •
Rev. Legend: UNITED STATES OF AMERICA **Designer:** John Reich

Date	Mintage	F12	VF20	XF40	MS60
1808	2,710	18,000	31,000	60,000	155,000

Turban on head left within circle of stars. Banner above eagle.

KM# 46 • 4.37 g., 0.916 Gold 0.1287 oz. AGW, 18.5 mm. • **Rev. Legend:** UNITED STATES OF AMERICA **Designer:** John Reich

Date	Mintage	F12	VF20	XF40	MS60
1821	6,448	6,000	8,000	14,250	28,000
1824/21	2,600	6,000	8,000	11,250	30,000
1825	4,434	6,000	8,000	11,250	25,500
1826/25	760	8,000	10,500	14,000	55,000
1827	2,800	6,000	8,000	11,250	28,000

Turban on head left within circle of stars. Banner above eagle.

KM# 49 • 4.37 g., 0.916 Gold 0.1287 oz. AGW, 18.2 mm. • **Rev. Legend:** UNITED STATES OF AMERICA **Designer:** John Reich

Coronet Head
Coronet head left within circle of stars. No motto above eagle.

KM# 72 • 4.18 g., 0.900 Gold 0.121 oz. AGW, 18 mm. • **Rev. Legend:** UNITED STATES OF AMERICA **Designer:** Christian Gobrecht

Date	Mintage	F12	VF20	XF40	AU50	MS60	Prf65
1840	18,859	650	850	1,000	2,200	6,000	—
1840C	12,822	1,000	1,200	3,000	3,200	8,000	—
1840D	3,532	1,800	2,400	7,000	8,200	31,000	—
1840O	33,580	350	500	1,000	1,700	8,000	—
1841	—	—	42,000	95,000	105,000	—	—
1841C	10,281	950	1,200	1,900	4,000	13,500	—
1841D	4,164	1,350	1,800	4,300	8,000	24,000	—
1842	2,823	900	1,100	3,000	5,500	16,500	125,000
1842C	6,729	1,250	1,650	3,000	5,000	18,500	—
1842D	4,643	1,500	2,000	5,000	6,500	30,000	—
1842O	19,800	265	425	1,000	1,450	7,700	—
1843	100,546	180	240	350	1,450	2,000	125,000
1843C small date, Crosslet 4	26,064	1,500	1,950	4,400	6,300	19,000	—
1843C large date, Plain 4	Inc. above	850	1,200	1,600	2,625	6,000	—
1843D small date, Crosslet 4	36,209	900	1,500	2,000	3,100	5,000	—
1843O small date, Crosslet 4	288,002	195	250	300	500	1,400	—
1843O large date, Plain 4	76,000	255	300	450	1,625	4,000	—
1844	6,784	300	375	770	2,100	6,700	150,000
1844C	11,622	1,000	1,450	2,450	3,750	14,000	—
1844D	17,332	1,050	1,350	2,000	3,750	5,300	—
1845	91,051	275	300	400	2,700	1,100	150,000
1845D	19,460	1,100	1,350	1,800	2,350	8,000	—
1845O	4,000	650	900	2,200	5,850	20,000	—
1846	21,598	270	310	400	700	4,000	150,000
1846C	4,808	800	1,400	2,500	4,700	13,500	—
1846D	19,303	780	1,485	2,000	3,000	8,000	—
1846O	66,000	300	350	490	925	3,900	—
1847	29,814	300	350	525	770	3,375	—
1847C	23,226	900	1,200	1,650	2,550	5,950	—
1847D	15,784	900	1,350	1,900	2,400	6,500	—
1847O	124,000	275	310	350	850	3,250	—
1848	7,497	400	500	900	2,600	4,900	150,000
1848 CAL.	1,389	—	28,000	34,000	46,000	68,000	—

Date	Mintage	F12	VF20	XF40	MS60
1829	3,403	5,200	6,250	8,600	19,000
1830	4,540	5,200	6,250	8,600	19,000
1831	4,520	5,200	6,250	8,600	19,000
1832	4,400	5,200	6,250	8,600	19,000
1833	4,160	5,200	6,250	8,600	19,000
1834	4,000	—	—	50,000	175,000

Classic Head
Classic head left within circle of stars. No motto above eagle.

KM# 56 • 4.18 g., 0.899 Gold 0.1208 oz. AGW, 18.2 mm. • **Rev. Legend:** UNITED STATES OF AMERICA **Designer:** William Kneass

Date	Mintage	F12	VF20	XF40	MS60
1834	112,234	280	480	775	3,000
1835	131,402	280	480	775	3,000
1836	547,986	280	480	775	3,000
1837	45,080	450	700	975	3,800
1838	47,030	350	700	900	3,000
1838C	7,880	2,500	4,000	7,000	23,000
1839	27,021	600	850	1,500	9,000
1839C	18,140	1,700	3,250	5,000	23,000
1839/8	Inc. above	—	—	—	—
1839D	13,674	2,000	3,500	5,800	26,000
1839O	17,781	850	1,500	3,000	12,000

1848 "Cal." reverse

$2.50 GOLD

Date	Mintage	F12	VF20	XF40	AU50	MS60	Prf65
1848 C	16,788	950	1,200	2,450	2,875	9,000	—
1848D	13,771	1,250	1,800	2,500	3,500	7,300	—
1849	23,294	400	500	700	900	2,700	—
1849C	10,220	—	1,600	2,600	4,500	13,000	—
1849D	10,945	1,500	2,000	2,700	3,500	12,000	—
1850	252,923	220	315	325	375	825	—
1850C	9,148	800	1,200	2,200	3,300	11,000	—
1850D	12,148	850	1,350	2,400	3,500	11,800	—
1850O	84,000	240	275	400	900	3,400	—
1851	1,372,748	240	275	295	315	485	—
1851C	14,923	800	1,200	1,800	3,000	6,750	—
1851D	11,264	900	1,350	2,000	3,200	9,000	—
1851O	148,000	270	300	415	600	4,000	—
1852	1,159,681	240	275	295	315	400	—
1852C	9,772	975	1,200	1,800	3,500	8,000	—
1852D	4,078	900	1,350	3,000	5,600	14,000	—
1852O	140,000	270	300	350	1,200	1,880	—
1853	1,404,668	240	275	295	315	420	—
1853D	3,178	900	1,600	2,900	4,100	13,500	—
1854	596,258	240	275	295	315	400	—
1854C	7,295	900	1,200	2,500	3,900	9,000	—
1854D	1,760	1,700	2,700	5,800	9,000	23,000	—
1854O	153,000	250	300	350	425	1,250	—
1854S	246	—	225,000	300,000	400,000	—	—
1855	235,480	240	275	295	315	425	—
1855C	3,677	1,450	2,500	4,000	6,000	17,000	—
1855D	1,123	2,100	2,800	6,000	12,000	43,000	—
1856	384,240	240	275	295	315	350	120,000
1856C	7,913	985	1,225	2,100	3,300	10,000	—
1856D	874	6,500	8,500	15,000	26,000	71,000	—
1856O	21,100	300	400	850	1,500	6,400	—
1856S	71,120	240	275	500	1,300	3,800	—
1857	214,130	240	275	295	315	320	120,000
1857D	2,364	1,025	1,350	2,300	3,200	11,000	—
1857O	34,000	240	275	295	315	3,500	—
1857S	69,200	240	275	295	315	4,900	—
1858	47,377	240	275	375	400	1,200	75,000
1858C	9,056	1,000	1,400	2,450	3,300	6,000	—
1859	39,444	240	275	320	350	1,300	80,000
1859D	2,244	1,150	1,550	2,500	3,300	14,000	—
1859S	15,200	275	350	900	2,000	4,000	—
1860	22,675	240	275	295	400	1,000	35,000
1860C	7,469	1,050	1,400	2,100	2,800	14,000	—
1860S	35,600	300	350	525	900	3,200	—
1861	1,283,878	240	275	295	370	600	35,000
1861S	24,000	325	400	725	3,000	6,000	—
1862	98,543	275	325	500	1,500	4,100	45,000
1862/1	Inc. above	650	850	1,650	3,000	8,800	—
1862S	8,000	1,100	1,675	2,175	3,900	14,000	—
1863	30	—	—	—	—	—	95,000
1863S	10,800	550	650	2,100	4,500	16,000	—
1864	2,874	3,100	4,500	9,000	18,000	70,000	50,000
1865	1,545	2,950	3,750	8,500	17,000	—	50,000
1865S	23,376	600	725	1,300	2,000	4,000	—
1866	3,110	650	975	2,600	4,700	13,000	40,000
1866S	38,960	400	450	700	1,150	5,100	—
1867	3,250	180	300	650	1,300	5,200	30,000
1867S	28,000	180	300	500	1,200	3,400	—
1868	3,625	375	450	500	625	2,300	40,000
1868S	34,000	240	300	350	825	3,000	—
1869	4,345	340	375	520	770	2,800	36,000
1869S	29,500	345	430	600	900	2,950	—
1870	4,555	245	300	400	750	3,650	40,000
1870S	16,000	245	300	400	770	3,600	—
1871	5,350	290	450	600	850	2,000	36,000
1871S	22,000	240	260	260	475	1,850	—
1872	3,030	350	425	800	1,050	4,000	30,000
1872S	18,000	325	375	475	700	3,800	—
1873 closed 3	178,025	240	260	260	340	500	36,000
1873 open 3	Inc. above	240	260	260	280	425	—
1873S	27,000	240	260	260	600	1,600	—
1874	3,940	240	260	260	675	2,000	40,000
1875	420	3,000	4,000	6,000	10,000	25,000	80,000
1875S	11,600	240	260	260	625	3,200	—
1876	4,221	300	500	870	950	2,800	30,000
1876S	5,000	300	450	700	1,000	2,600	—
1877	1,652	300	360	725	940	2,750	36,000

Date	Mintage	F12	VF20	XF40	AU50	MS60	Prf65
1877S	35,400	240	260	260	280	575	—
1878	286,260	240	260	260	280	300	36,000
1878S	178,000	240	260	260	280	300	—
1879	88,990	240	260	260	280	400	28,000
1879S	43,500	240	260	260	475	1,800	—
1880	2,996	240	260	260	600	1,100	30,000
1881	691	950	1,500	2,500	4,500	10,000	25,000
1882	4,067	240	260	260	425	1,075	23,000
1883	2,002	400	725	1,350	2,500	4,700	22,000
1884	2,023	240	350	500	625	1,700	24,000
1885	887	400	600	1,600	2,600	5,000	24,000
1886	4,088	280	340	475	550	1,250	24,000
1887	6,282	280	340	475	550	800	26,000
1888	16,098	240	260	260	280	300	25,000
1889	17,648	240	260	260	280	300	24,000
1890	8,813	240	260	260	280	300	17,000
1891	11,040	240	260	260	280	300	17,000
1891 Double die reverse	Inc. above	—	—	—	—	—	—
1892	2,545	240	260	260	280	800	17,000
1893	30,106	240	260	260	280	400	17,000
1894	4,122	240	260	260	280	600	16,000
1895	6,199	240	260	260	280	475	15,000
1896	19,202	240	260	260	280	300	15,000
1897	29,904	240	260	260	280	300	15,000
1898	24,165	240	260	260	280	300	15,000
1899	27,350	240	260	260	280	300	15,000
1900	67,205	240	260	260	280	300	15,000
1901	91,322	240	260	260	280	300	15,000
1902	133,733	240	260	260	280	300	15,000
1903	201,257	240	260	260	280	300	15,000
1904	160,960	240	260	260	280	300	15,000
1905	217,944	240	260	260	280	300	15,000
1906	176,490	240	260	260	280	300	15,000
1907	336,448	240	260	260	280	300	15,000

Indian Head

KM# 128 • 4.18 g., 0.900 Gold 0.121 oz. AGW, 18 mm. • **Designer:** Bela Lyon Pratt

Date	Mintage	VF20	XF40	AU50	MS60	MS63	MS65	Prf65
1908	565,057	—	260	260	350	600	2,450	23,750
1909	441,899	—	260	260	350	600	4,689	37,000
1910	492,682	—	260	260	350	600	2,700	26,500
1911	704,191	—	260	260	350	600	3,300	26,000
1911D D strong D	55,680	2,600	2,950	3,775	7,200	14,000	46,000	—
1911D 1D weak D	Inc. above	—	1,800	2,600	4,500	—	—	—
1912	616,197	—	260	260	350	1,025	13,500	26,000
1913	722,165	—	260	260	350	675	3,425	24,000
1914	240,117	—	260	330	465	2,400	16,000	26,000
1914D	448,000	—	260	260	395	1,000	12,000	—
1915	606,100	—	260	260	350	500	3,300	31,500
1925D	578,000	—	260	260	350	500	1,325	—
1926	446,000	—	260	260	350	500	1,325	—
1927	388,000	—	260	260	350	500	1,325	—
1928	416,000	—	260	260	350	500	1,325	—
1929	532,000	—	260	260	350	500	1,325	—

$3 GOLD

$3

Indian head with headdress, left. Value, date within wreath.

KM# 84 • 5.02 g., 0.900 Gold 0.1451 oz. AGW, 20.5 mm. • **Obv. Legend:** UNITED STATES OF AMERICA **Designer:** James B. Longacre **Note:** The 1873 "closed-3" and "open-3" varieties are distinguished by the amount of space between the upper left and lower left serifs of the 3 in the date.

Date	Mintage	VF20	XF40	AU50	MS60	MS65	Prf65
1854	138,618	775	1,000	1,000	1,700	13,000	—
1854D	1,120	13,000	22,000	37,000	70,000	—	—
1854O	24,000	1,525	3,000	4,500	38,000	—	—
1855	50,555	775	925	1,050	1,700	33,000	150,000
1855S	6,600	1,400	3,125	6,300	32,000	—	—

Date	Mintage	VF20	XF40	AU50	MS60	MS65	Prf65
1856	26,010	775	925	1,000	2,300	34,500	120,000
1856S	34,500	900	1,325	2,400	10,750	—	—
1857	20,891	775	1,000	1,150	2,850	33,000	120,000
1857S	14,000	950	2,000	3,900	19,000	—	—
1858	2,133	1,100	2,000	3,300	10,000	—	93,000
1859	15,638	925	1,100	1,200	2,900	20,500	53,000
1860	7,155	925	1,250	1,750	3,300	30,000	53,000
1860S	7,000	1,150	2,450	7,000	23,000	—	—
1861	6,072	1,300	2,450	3,400	6,450	26,000	53,000
1862	5,785	1,300	3,600	4,100	6,450	34,000	53,000
1863	5,039	1,300	2,450	3,600	7,000	28,000	53,000
1864	2,680	1,450	3,000	5,000	7,700	36,000	53,000
1865	1,165	2,400	4,000	7,700	13,000	48,000	55,000
1866	4,030	1,100	1,350	1,800	4,500	32,000	53,000
1867	2,650	1,100	1,350	2,300	4,400	33,000	53,000
1868	4,875	1,100	1,350	1,800	3,700	28,000	53,000
1869	2,525	1,100	1,350	2,000	3,700	40,000	53,000
1870	3,535	1,100	1,600	1,800	3,800	43,000	53,000
1870S unique	—	—	1,000,000	—	—	—	—
Note: H. W. Bass Collection. AU50, cleaned. Est. value, $1,250,000.							
1871	1,330	1,100	1,600	2,000	4,000	32,000	52,000
1872	2,030	1,100	1,450	2,300	4,500	33,000	53,000
1873 closed 3, mintage unknown	—	4,800	8,800	12,500	25,000	—	—
1873 open 3, proof only	25	—	—	—	—	—	135,000
1874	41,820	800	1,000	1,100	1,700	12,500	55,000
1875 proof only	20	—	—	—	—	—	235,000
1876	45	—	—	22,000	—	—	72,000
1877	1,488	4,000	6,600	8,750	23,000	—	55,000
1878	82,324	775	1,000	1,100	1,700	8,000	55,000
1879	3,030	925	1,200	1,800	2,750	12,000	40,000
1880	1,036	1,300	1,800	3,150	4,400	16,000	35,000
1881	554	2,500	4,000	7,000	13,000	55,000	32,500
1882	1,576	1,200	1,600	2,100	3,400	22,000	30,000
1883	989	1,500	2,200	2,700	3,600	22,000	30,000
1884	1,106	1,600	2,400	3,100	4,400	22,000	30,000
1885	910	1,600	2,400	3,100	5,050	25,000	27,500
1886	1,142	1,300	2,000	2,600	4,200	38,000	26,000
1887	6,160	900	1,300	1,800	2,500	14,000	26,500
1888	5,291	900	1,300	1,600	2,500	10,500	32,000
1889	2,429	900	1,300	1,900	2,800	10,500	26,500

$5 (HALF EAGLE)

Liberty Cap

Liberty Cap on head, right, flanked by stars. Small eagle.
KM# 19 • 8.75 g., 0.916 Gold 0.2577 oz. AGW

Date	Mintage	F12	VF20	XF40	MS60
1795	8,707	16,000	22,000	26,000	68,000
1796/95	6,196	22,000	28,000	40,000	165,000
1797 15 obverse stars	Inc. above	25,000	35,000	60,000	230,000
1797 16 obverse stars	Inc. above	25,000	35,000	60,000	210,000
1798	—	75,000	130,000	230,000	—

Liberty cap on head, right, flanked by stars. Large Heraldic eagle.
KM# 28 • 8.75 g., 0.916 Gold 0.2577 oz. AGW, 25 mm. • **Obv. Legend:** LIBERTY **Rev. Legend:** UNITED STATES OF AMERICA **Designer:** Robert Scot

Date	Mintage	F12	VF20	XF40	MS60
1795	Inc. above	8,000	17,000	26,000	80,000
1797/95	3,609	8,000	13,000	19,500	130,000
1797 15 star obv.; Unique	—	—	—	—	—
Note: Smithsonian collection					
1797 16 star obv.; Unique	—	—	—	—	—
Note: Smithsonian collection					

$3 GOLD

Date	Mintage	F12	VF20	XF40	MS60
1798 small 8	24,867	4,200	5,000	8,500	34,000
1798 large 8, 13-star reverse	Inc. above	3,600	4,300	11,200	22,000
1798 large 8, 14-star reverse	Inc. above	3,500	4,300	8,500	—
1799 small reverse stars	7,451	3,300	3,900	7,000	20,000
1799 large reverse stars	Inc. above	3,950	4,750	9,000	24,500
1800	37,628	3,200	3,800	6,800	17,000
1802/1	53,176	3,200	3,800	6,800	17,000
1803/2	33,506	3,200	3,800	6,800	17,000
1804 small 8	30,475	3,850	3,200	3,800	17,000
1804 small 8 over large 8	Inc. above	3,200	3,800	6,800	17,000
1805	33,183	3,200	3,800	6,800	17,000
1806 pointed 6	64,093	3,200	3,800	6,800	17,000
1806 round 6	Inc. above	3,200	3,800	7,400	17,000
1807	32,488	3,200	3,800	6,800	17,000

Turban Head
Capped draped bust, left, flanked by stars. Heraldic eagle.
KM# 38 • 8.75 g., 0.916 Gold 0.2577 oz. AGW, 25 mm. • **Rev. Legend:** UNITED STATES OF AMERICA **Designer:** John Reich

Date	Mintage	F12	VF20	XF40	MS60
1807	51,605	2,600	3,300	5,500	11,000
1808	55,578	2,600	3,300	5,500	11,000
1808/7	Inc. above	2,600	3,200	5,500	11,000
1809/8	33,875	2,600	3,200	5,500	11,000
1810 small date, small 5	100,287	9,000	19,000	30,000	85,000
1810 small date, large 5	Inc. above	2,600	3,250	5,500	10,200
1810 large date, small 5	Inc. above	17,250	55,000	75,000	150,000
1810 large date, large 5	Inc. above	2,600	3,300	5,500	11,000
1811 small 5	99,581	2,600	3,300	5,500	11,000
1811 tall 5	Inc. above	2,600	3,200	6,500	12,500
1812	58,087	2,600	3,300	5,500	11,000

Capped head, left, within circle of stars. Heraldic eagle.
KM# 43 • 8.75 g., 0.916 Gold 0.2577 oz. AGW, 25 mm. • **Rev. Legend:** UNITED STATES OF AMERICA **Designer:** John Reich

Date	Mintage	F12	VF20	XF40	MS60
1813	95,428	3,000	4,200	6,500	10,000
1814/13	15,454	4,200	5,400	7,000	20,000
1815	635	28,000	40,000	165,000	195,000
Note: 1815, private sale, Jan. 1994, MS-61, $150,000					
1818	48,588	4,200	5,500	12,000	17,000
1818 5D over 50 Inc. Above	—	4,500	55,000	85,000	21,000
1819	51,723	25,000	35,000	50,000	110,000
1819 5D over 50 Inc. Above	—	27,000	37,000	56,000	110,000
1820 curved-base 2, small letters	263,806	—	—	—	—
1820 curved-base 2, large letters	Inc. above	—	—	—	22,000
1820 square-base 2	Inc. above	4,200	5,400	10,000	17,000
1821	34,641	27,000	45,000	60,000	185,000
1822 3 known	—	—	—	6,000,000	—
1823	14,485	4,200	5,400	11,000	23,000
1824	17,340	5,600	9,000	26,000	34,000
1825/21	29,060	6,800	11,250	27,000	73,000
1825/24	Inc. above	—	—	—	—
1826	18,069	5,000	9,500	20,000	68,000
1827	24,913	5,000	9,500	20,000	68,000
1828/7	28,029	11,000	27,000	58,000	105,000
Note: 1828/7, Bowers & Merena, June 1989, XF, $20,900.					
1828	Inc. above	10,000	20,000	37,000	105,000
1829 large planchet	57,442	—	—	—	300,000
Note: 1829 large planchet, Superior, July 1985, MS-65, $104,500.					
1829 small planchet	Inc. above	—	—	—	300,000
Note: 1829 small planchet, private sale, 1992 (XF-45), $89,000.					
1830 small "5D".	126,351	12,000	26,000	40,000	54,000
1830 large "5D".	Inc. above	12,000	26,500	40,000	55,000

$5 GOLD

Date	Mintage	F12	VF20	XF40	MS60
1831	140,594	12,000	26,500	40,000	75,000
1832 curved-base 2, 12 stars	157,487	75,000	100,000	125,000	—
1832 square-base 2, 13 stars	Inc. above	13,000	26,500	40,000	65,000
1833 large date	Inc. above	13,000	26,500	40,000	55,000
1833 small date	193,630	13,000	26,500	40,000	52,000
1834 plain 4	50,141	13,000	26,500	40,000	54,500
1834 crosslet 4	Inc. above	13,000	26,500	40,000	62,000

Classic Head

Classic head, left, within circle of stars. No motto above eagle.

KM# 57 • 8.36 g., 0.899 Gold 0.2416 oz. AGW, 22.5 mm. • **Rev. Legend:** UNITED STATES OF AMERICA **Designer:** William Kneass

Date	Mintage	VF20	XF40	MS60	MS65	PF65
1834 plain 4	658,028	650	800	3,800	65,000	—
1834 crosslet 4	Inc. above	1,750	3,000	21,000	—	—
1835	371,534	480	695	3,800	—	—
1836	553,147	480	650	3,800	68,000	—
1837	207,121	500	935	5,200	100,000	—
1838	286,588	500	800	3,800	95,000	—
1838C	17,179	3,900	10,000	67,000	—	—
1838D	20,583	4,600	6,800	26,000	—	—

Coronet Head

Coronet head, left, within circle of stars. No motto above eagle.

KM# 69 • 8.36 g., 0.900 Gold 0.2419 oz. AGW, 21.6 mm. • **Rev. Legend:** UNITED STATES OF AMERICA **Designer:** Christian Gobrecht **Note:** Varieties for 1843 are distinguished by the size of the numerals in the date. One 1848 variety has "Cal." incsribed on the reverse, indicating it was made from California gold. The 1873 "closed-3" and "open-3" varieties are distinguished by the amount of space between the upper left and lower left serifs in the 3 in the date.

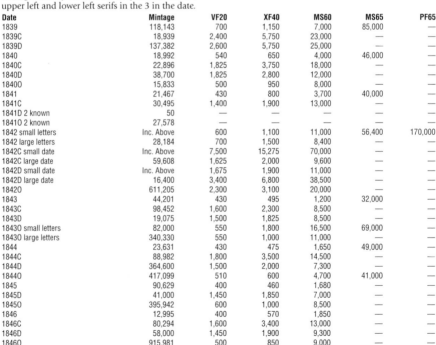

Date	Mintage	VF20	XF40	MS60	MS65	PF65
1839	118,143	700	1,150	7,000	85,000	—
1839C	18,939	2,400	5,750	23,000	—	—
1839D	137,382	2,600	5,750	25,000	—	—
1840	18,992	540	650	4,000	46,000	—
1840C	22,896	1,825	3,750	18,000	—	—
1840D	38,700	1,825	2,800	12,000	—	—
1840O	15,833	500	950	8,000	—	—
1841	21,467	430	800	3,700	40,000	—
1841C	30,495	1,400	1,900	13,000	—	—
1841D 2 known	50	—	—	—	—	—
1841O 2 known	27,578	—	—	—	—	—
1842 small letters	Inc. Above	600	1,100	11,000	56,400	170,000
1842 large letters	28,184	700	1,500	8,400	—	—
1842C small date	Inc. Above	7,500	15,275	70,000	—	—
1842C large date	59,608	1,625	2,000	9,600	—	—
1842D small date	Inc. Above	1,675	1,900	11,000	—	—
1842D large date	16,400	3,400	6,800	38,500	—	—
1842O	611,205	2,300	3,100	20,000	—	—
1843	44,201	430	495	1,200	32,000	—
1843C	98,452	1,600	2,300	8,500	—	—
1843D	19,075	1,500	1,825	8,500	—	—
1843O small letters	82,000	550	1,800	16,500	69,000	—
1843O large letters	340,330	550	1,000	11,000	—	—
1844	23,631	430	475	1,650	49,000	—
1844C	88,982	1,800	3,500	14,500	—	—
1844D	364,600	1,500	2,000	7,300	—	—
1844O	417,099	510	600	4,700	41,000	—
1845	90,629	400	460	1,680	—	—
1845D	41,000	1,450	1,850	7,000	—	—
1845O	395,942	600	1,000	8,500	—	—
1846	12,995	400	570	1,850	—	—
1846C	80,294	1,600	3,400	13,000	—	—
1846D	58,000	1,450	1,900	9,300	—	—
1846O	915,981	500	850	9,000	—	—
1847	84,151	400	460	1,500	—	—

$5 GOLD

Date	Mintage	VF20	XF40	MS60	MS65	PF65
1847C	64,405	1,400	2,000	8,000	75,000	—
1847D	12,000	1,450	2,425	7,000	—	—
1847O	260,775	2,500	7,400	20,000	—	—
1848	64,472	400	550	2,000	—	—
1848C	47,465	1,725	1,850	14,000	—	—
1848D	133,070	1,400	2,570	11,000	—	—
1849	64,823	400	460	2,500	24,000	—
1849C	39,036	1,500	1,825	8,100	—	—
1849D	64,491	1,600	2,350	13,000	—	—
1850	63,591	400	500	2,200	54,000	—
1850C	43,984	1,650	1,900	8,800	—	—
1850D	377,505	1,450	1,850	20,000	—	—
1851	49,176	400	460	1,900	40,000	—
1851C	62,710	1,400	1,750	10,500	—	—
1851D	41,000	1,400	1,700	9,000	—	—
1851O	573,901	750	1,525	10,000	—	—
1852	72,574	400	460	1,500	—	—
1852C	91,584	1,725	2,375	6,000	—	—
1852D	305,770	1,550	1,900	7,000	—	—
1853	65,571	400	460	1,200	60,000	—
1853C	89,678	1,900	2,350	500	—	—
1853D	160,675	1,500	2,400	5,800	—	—
1854	39,283	400	460	1,750	—	—
1854C	56,413	1,400	2,100	10,500	—	—
1854D	46,000	1,600	2,100	7,100	69,000	—
1854O	268	430	650	6,300	—	—
1854S	117,098	—	—	—	—	—

Note: 1854S, Bowers & Merena, Oct. 1982, AU-55, $170,000.

Date	Mintage	VF20	XF40	MS60	MS65	PF65
1855	39,788	400	460	1,650	—	—
1855C	22,432	1,500	2,000	10,000	63,000	—
1855D	11,100	1,450	2,300	12,000	—	—
1855O	61,000	1,325	2,400	17,000	—	—
1855S	197,990	650	900	10,000	—	—
1856	28,457	400	460	1,775	—	—
1856C	19,786	1,500	1,900	12,000	—	—
1856D	10,000	1,550	2,000	7,500	—	—
1856O	105,100	800	1,500	11,000	—	—
1856S	98,188	500	650	6,000	—	—
1857	31,360	400	460	1,600	—	150,000
1857C	17,046	1,400	1,750	6,600	—	—
1857D	13,000	1,800	2,000	9,500	—	—
1857O	87,000	800	1,500	12,000	—	—
1857S	15,136	430	550	8,000	—	—
1858	38,856	500	600	2,800	34,000	120,000
1858C	15,362	1,600	2,500	7,500	—	—
1858D	18,600	1,650	2,000	9,000	—	—
1858S	16,814	1,400	2,800	25,000	—	—
1859	31,847	430	500	5,300	—	93,000
1859C	10,366	1,400	1,850	8,000	90,000	—
1859D	13,220	1,650	2,000	7,500	—	—
1859S	19,825	1,450	3,000	21,000	—	—
1860	14,813	500	960	3,250	—	95,000
1860C	14,635	1,750	2,400	9,500	—	—
1860D	21,200	1,650	2,400	11,500	—	—
1860S	688,150	1,750	3,000	25,000	—	—
1861	6,879	450	510	1,600	34,000	95,000
1861C	1,597	5,100	9,100	25,000	—	—
1861D	18,000	22,000	37,000	79,000	—	—
1862	9,500	2,000	4,900	28,000	—	100,000
1862S	2,472	3,500	8,100	38,000	—	—
1861S	4,465	2,500	5,500	—	—	—
1863	17,000	3,000	7,500	45,000	—	95,000
1863S	4,220	2,800	4,000	35,000	—	—
1864	3,888	1,500	3,500	18,000	—	95,000
1864S	1,295	16,000	37,000	80,000	200,000	—
1865	27,612	5,000	10,000	32,000	—	95,000
1865S	9,000	2,000	4,300	12,500	—	—
1866S	9,000	1,800	4,200	—	—	—

Coronet head, left, within circle of stars. IN GOD WE TRUST above eagle.

KM# 101 • 8.36 g., 0.900 Gold 0.2419 oz. AGW, 21.6 mm. • **Rev. Legend:** UNITED STATES OF AMERICA **Designer:** Christian Gobrecht

$5 GOLD

$5 GOLD

Date	Mintage	VF20	XF40	AU50	MS60	MS63	MS65	Prf65
1866	6,730	900	1,800	2,800	11,000	35,000	—	60,000
1866S	34,920	1,100	2,400	6,500	18,500	—	—	—
1867	6,920	800	1,700	2,250	9,000	—	—	50,000
1867S	29,000	925	1,850	6,000	25,000	30,000	—	—
1868	5,725	500	750	2,200	10,000	—	—	50,000
1868S	52,000	475	1,350	2,700	15,000	—	—	—
1869	1,785	1,100	2,725	5,100	12,000	25,000	—	50,000
1869S	31,000	575	2,000	2,500	19,250	—	—	—
1870	4,035	780	1,500	2,500	13,000	—	—	75,000
1870CC	7,675	14,000	27,200	39,400	90,000	—	—	—
1870S	17,000	1,250	2,000	4,300	21,000	—	—	—
1871	3,230	700	1,100	4,300	7,500	—	—	70,000
1871CC	20,770	4,500	9,000	16,200	46,000	—	—	—
1871S	25,000	450	900	3,000	12,000	30,000	—	—
1872	1,690	925	1,900	3,900	10,600	19,000	—	70,000
1872CC	16,980	3,300	8,225	12,000	—	—	—	—
1872S	36,400	770	960	1,650	11,000	—	—	—
1873 closed 3	49,305	345	345	345	850	4,300	20,000	65,000
1873 open 3	63,200	345	345	345	700	3,150	14,500	—
1873CC	7,416	6,000	12,000	21,000	65,000	—	—	—
1873S	31,000	525	825	1,600	16,000	—	—	—
1874	3,508	750	1,225	1,850	9,000	19,000	—	65,000
1874CC	21,198	2,000	3,800	9,100	30,000	—	—	—
1874S	16,000	800	1,525	2,500	—	—	—	—
1875	220	70,000	75,000	122,000	—	—	—	175,000
1875CC	11,828	3,000	5,500	6,950	36,000	90,000	—	—
1875S	9,000	1,900	2,250	3,500	—	—	—	—
1876	1,477	1,500	3,500	4,500	12,000	20,000	37,000	55,000
1876CC	6,887	5,000	6,500	11,000	34,000	—	—	—
1876S	4,000	2,800	6,350	9,000	—	—	—	—
1877	1,152	1,750	3,000	5,000	9,500	—	—	65,000
1877CC	8,680	2,700	4,400	10,000	40,000	—	—	—
1877S	26,700	470	600	1,900	7,500	17,000	—	—
1878	131,740	360	360	360	500	1,700	8,200	55,000
1878CC	9,054	3,500	8,000	13,750	60,000	—	—	—
1878S	144,700	360	360	360	700	3,800	17,000	—
1879	301,950	360	360	360	360	1,300	8,000	55,000
1879CC	17,281	1,875	2,450	5,000	23,000	—	—	—
1879S	426,200	360	360	360	500	1,450	22,000	—
1880	3,166,436	360	360	360	360	550	1,700	43,000
1880CC	51,017	850	1,050	5,000	10,500	37,000	—	—
1880S	1,348,900	360	360	360	360	550	8,000	—
1881	5,708,802	360	360	360	360	450	1,500	36,000
1881/80	Inc. above	585	600	625	1,000	2,750	—	—
1881CC	13,886	1,400	2,800	5,200	18,500	40,000	—	—
1881S	969,000	360	360	360	360	525	3,300	—
1882	2,514,568	360	360	360	360	410	3,400	36,000
1882CC	82,817	850	1,350	1,750	10,500	34,250	—	—
1882S	969,000	360	360	360	360	525	1,500	—
1883	233,461	360	360	360	475	1,200	12,500	36,000
1883CC	12,958	1,650	2,750	5,750	17,000	43,000	—	—
1883S	83,200	360	360	360	625	1,500	—	—
1884	191,078	360	360	360	360	1,325	—	36,000
1884CC	16,402	900	1,350	3,900	19,000	—	—	—
1884S	177,000	360	360	360	360	975	12,500	—
1885	601,506	360	360	360	360	565	5,000	34,000
1885S	1,211,500	360	360	360	360	525	1,750	—
1886	388,432	360	360	360	360	650	5,250	34,000
1886S	3,268,000	360	360	360	360	410	1,500	—
1887	87	—	—	26,000	—	—	—	9,300
1887S	1,912,000	360	360	360	360	560	4,000	—
1888	18,296	360	360	360	630	1,500	12,000	36,000
1888S	293,900	360	360	360	1,050	3,700	—	—
1889	7,565	450	475	600	1,225	4,250	—	36,000
1890	4,328	550	650	925	2,750	6,000	—	36,000
1890CC	53,800	650	750	1,300	1,850	6,000	43,000	—
1891	61,413	360	360	360	600	1,300	—	32,000
1891CC	208,000	750	800	975	1,800	4,000	31,000	—
1892	753,572	360	360	360	360	520	1,500	32,000
1892CC	82,968	650	725	900	2,000	6,725	38,000	—
1892O	10,000	1,700	2,000	2,475	5,200	—	—	—
1892S	298,400	360	360	360	360	1,850	—	—
1893	1,528,197	360	360	360	360	410	1,950	36,000
1893CC	60,000	800	1,200	1,500	2,400	7,600	29,000	—
1893O	110,000	360	360	360	1,025	4,750	—	—
1893S	224,000	360	360	360	360	650	7,300	—
1894	957,955	360	360	360	360	525	3,200	32,000

Date	Mintage	VF20	XF40	AU50	MS60	MS63	MS65	Prf65
1894O	16,600	450	550	725	1,550	8,800	—	—
1894S	55,900	360	360	360	3,550	10,000	—	—
1895	1,345,936	360	360	360	360	410	1,500	29,000
1895S	112,000	360	360	360	1,900	4,100	16,500	—
1896	59,063	360	360	360	360	675	6,800	25,000
1896S	155,400	360	360	360	1,000	4,450	20,000	—
1897	867,883	360	360	360	360	485	1,820	27,500
1897S	354,000	360	360	360	775	3,850	—	—
1898	633,495	360	360	360	360	650	3,300	25,000
1898S	1,397,400	360	360	360	360	1,175	6,700	—
1899	1,710,729	380	400	405	440	460	2,100	25,000
1899S	1,545,000	360	360	360	360	720	7,250	—
1900	1,405,730	360	360	360	360	485	2,000	25,000
1900S	329,000	360	360	360	500	420	11,000	—
1901	616,040	360	360	360	360	485	1,675	25,000
1901S	3,648,000	360	360	360	360	485	2,000	—
1902	172,562	360	360	360	360	650	1,500	25,000
1902S	939,000	360	360	360	360	485	2,000	—
1903	227,024	360	360	360	360	925	1,690	25,000
1903S	1,855,000	360	360	360	360	485	1,900	—
1904	392,136	360	360	360	360	520	2,000	25,000
1904S	97,000	360	360	360	825	3,000	9,200	—
1905	302,308	360	360	360	360	485	2,600	27,500
1905S	880,700	360	360	360	625	1,225	6,000	—
1906	348,820	360	360	360	360	485	2,000	25,000
1906D	320,000	360	360	360	360	515	2,000	—
1906S	598,000	360	360	360	360	725	4,450	—
1907	626,192	360	360	360	360	485	2,000	25,000
1907D	888,000	360	360	360	360	485	2,000	—
1908	421,874	360	360	360	360	485	2,000	—

Indian Head

KM# 129 • 8.36 g., 0.900 Gold 0.2419 oz. AGW, 21.6 mm. • **Designer:** Bela Lyon Pratt

Date	Mintage	VF20	XF40	AU50	MS60	MS63	MS65	Prf65
1908	578,012	360	380	400	440	600	8,700	40,000
1908D	148,000	360	380	400	520	860	27,000	—
1908S	82,000	360	380	900	2,200	7,400	20,000	—
1909	627,138	360	380	400	440	860	8,700	43,000
1909D	3,423,560	360	380	400	440	860	8,700	—
1909O	34,200	4,200	5,600	13,000	34,200	76,000	455,000	—
1909S	297,200	390	400	475	1,900	8,500	55,000	—
1910	604,250	350	380	400	440	1,060	8,700	43,000
1910D	193,600	350	380	400	525	2,025	28,500	—
1910S	770,200	350	380	400	1,100	9,300	65,000	—
1911	915,139	350	380	400	440	1,095	8,700	43,000
1911D	72,500	600	800	1,500	7,500	34,000	185,000	—
1911S	1,416,000	350	380	525	700	3,100	50,000	—
1912	790,144	350	380	400	440	925	8,700	43,000
1912S	392,000	400	410	525	1,600	14,000	165,000	—
1913	916,099	350	380	400	440	995	8,700	43,000
1913S	408,000	400	440	450	1,700	13,500	130,000	—
1914	247,125	350	380	400	500	16,000	13,500	43,000
1914D	247,000	350	380	400	500	2,500	20,000	—
1914S	263,000	390	415	435	1,600	6,500	105,000	—
1915	588,075	350	380	400	440	860	8,700	46,000
1915S	164,000	350	380	400	2,125	10,200	120,000	—
1916S	240,000	385	395	435	990	4,225	40,000	—
1929	662,000	—	15,000	17,000	28,250	48,500	110,000	—

$5 GOLD

$10 (EAGLE)

Liberty Cap
Small eagle.
KM# 21 • 17.50 g., 0.916 Gold 0.5154 oz. AGW, 33 mm. • **Designer:** Robert Scot

Date	Mintage	F12	VF20	XF40	MS60
1795 13 leaves	5,583	24,000	30,000	45,000	95,000
1795 9 leaves	Inc. above	45,000	75,000	90,000	225,000
1796	4,146	25,000	30,000	45,000	100,000
1797 small eagle	3,615	40,000	50,000	75,000	230,000

Liberty cap on head, right, flanked by stars. Heraldic eagle.
KM# 30 • 17.50 g., 0.916 Gold 0.5154 oz. AGW, 33 mm. • **Obv. Legend:** LIBERTY **Rev. Legend:** UNITED STATES OF AMERICA **Designer:** Robert Scot

Date	Mintage	F12	VF20	XF40	MS60
1797 large eagle	10,940	8,500	15,000	19,000	47,600
1798/97 9 stars left, 4 right	900	11,000	15,000	32,000	125,000
1798/97 7 stars left, 6 right	842	40,000	55,000	90,000	435,000
1799 large star obv	37,449	8,000	10,000	15,000	26,000
1799 small star obv	Inc. above	8,500	11,000	15,000	32,000
1800	5,999	8,000	10,000	15,000	26,000
1801	44,344	8,000	10,000	15,000	26,000
1803 extra star	15,017	8,000	10,000	15,000	26,000
1803 large stars rev	Inc. above	7,500	9,000	14,000	28,000
1804 crosslet 4	3,757	16,000	22,000	30,000	70,000
1804 plain 4	—	—	—	—	—

Coronet Head
Old-style head, left, within circle of stars. No motto above eagle.
KM# 66.1 • 16.72 g., 0.900 Gold 0.4837 oz. AGW, 27 mm. • **Rev. Legend:** UNITED STATES OF AMERICA **Designer:** Christian Gobrecht

Date	Mintage	VF20	XF40	MS60	MS65	PF65
1838	7,200	3,600	8,500	65,000	—	1,500,000
1839/8 Type of 1838	25,801	1,750	4,600	26,000	—	1,500,000
1839 large letters	Inc. above	1,200	4,000	26,000	—	—

New-style head, left, within circle of stars. No motto above eagle.
KM# 66.2 • 16.72 g., 0.900 Gold 0.4837 oz. AGW, 27 mm. • **Rev. Legend:** UNITED STATES OF AMERICA **Designer:** Christian Gobrecht

Date	Mintage	VF20	XF40	MS60	MS65	PF65
1839 small letters	12,447	3,400	9,700	38,000	—	—
1840	47,338	850	1,100	8,175	—	—
1841	63,131	925	1,000	11,000	—	—

Date	Mintage	VF20	XF40	MS60	MS65	PF65
1841O	2,500	7,100	11,250	—	—	—
1842 small date	81,507	850	1,100	13,000	—	—
1842 large date	Inc. above	850	1,100	16,000	89,000	—
1842O	27,400	1,300	1,600	52,000	—	—
1843	75,462	850	1,100	15,250	—	—
1843O	175,162	850	1,100	10,600	—	—
1844	6,361	2,100	4,200	23,000	—	—
1844O	118,700	850	1,100	14,000	—	—
1845	26,153	850	1,100	15,000	—	—
1845O	47,500	850	1,100	15,000	—	—
1845O repunched	Inc. above	975	1,400	—	—	—
1846	20,095	1,025	1,400	19,000	—	—
1846O	81,780	1,200	2,100	13,500	—	—
1846/5	Inc. above	1,200	2,000	—	—	—
1847	862,258	850	1,100	3,750	—	—
1847O	571,500	850	1,100	5,400	—	—
1848	145,484	850	1,100	6,100	—	—
1848O	38,850	1,325	3,400	14,000	86,000	—
1849	653,618	850	1,100	3,300	—	—
1849O	23,900	1,750	2,500	23,000	—	—
1850 large date	291,451	850	1,100	4,600	—	—
1850 small date	Inc. above	850	1,100	6,750	—	—
1850O	57,500	1,150	1,900	20,000	227,000	—
1851	176,328	850	1,100	4,000	—	—
1851O	263,000	850	1,100	8,000	—	—
1852	263,106	850	1,100	1,880	—	—
1852O	18,000	1,500	2,500	82,000	—	—
1853	201,253	850	1,100	3,450	—	—
1853/2	Inc. above	850	1,100	14,500	—	—
1853O	51,000	1,050	1,500	14,000	—	—
1854	54,250	850	1,100	5,500	—	—
1854O small date	52,500	850	1,100	11,000	—	—
1854O large date	Inc. above	850	1,100	9,250	—	—
1854S	123,826	1,050	1,300	11,000	—	—
1855	121,701	850	1,100	4,000	—	—
1855O	18,000	1,050	3,600	26,000	—	—
1855S	9,000	850	1,100	—	—	—
1856	60,490	1,300	2,500	3,350	—	—
1856O	14,500	850	1,100	27,000	—	—
1856S	68,000	850	1,100	11,250	—	—
1857	16,606	1,430	1,490	12,750	—	—
1857O	5,500	2,000	3,300	—	—	—
1857S	26,000	1,800	1,950	11,000	—	—
1858	2,521	5,000	7,000	24,300	—	—
1858O	20,000	1,350	1,550	11,000	—	—
1858S	11,800	850	1,100	—	—	—
1859	16,093	1,400	1,600	10,000	—	165,000
1859O	2,300	6,000	12,000	—	—	—
1859S	7,000	4,500	6,000	—	—	—
1860	15,105	1,260	1,300	7,500	—	165,000
1860O	11,100	1,900	2,100	16,000	—	—
1860S	5,000	5,000	11,000	—	—	—
1861	113,233	3,600	8,500	5,300	83,750	165,000
1861S	15,500	—	9,600	—	—	—
1862	10,995	1,020	2,000	17,000	—	165,000
1862S	12,500	6,000	7,000	—	—	—
1863	1,248	13,000	32,000	68,000	—	165,000
1863S	10,000	6,000	10,000	105,000	—	—
1864	3,580	8,000	10,000	55,000	—	165,000
1864S	2,500	—	60,000	—	—	—
1865	4,005	3,400	5,150	37,000	—	165,000
1865S	16,700	8,000	11,000	—	—	—
1865S over inverted 186	Inc. above	5,125	6,175	—	—	—
1866S without motto	8,500	11,000	15,000	—	—	—

New-style head, left, within circle of stars. "IN GOD WE TRUST" above eagle.

KM# **102** • 16.72 g., 0.900 Gold 0.4837 oz. AGW, 27 mm. • **Rev. Legend:** UNITED STATES OF AMERICA **Designer:** Christian Gobrecht

$10 GOLD

$10 GOLD

Date	Mintage	VF20	XF40	AU50	MS60	MS63	MS65	Prf65
1866	3,780	1,800	3,100	7,000	34,000	—	—	75,000
1866S	11,500	3,300	5,800	7,500	22,000	—	—	—
1867	3,140	800	1,400	1,750	37,000	—	—	64,000
1867S	9,000	4,000	7,000	8,000	—	—	—	—
1868	10,655	800	1,000	1,550	14,000	—	—	58,000
1868S	13,500	1,700	2,200	3,500	20,000	—	—	—
1869	1,855	1,550	3,900	5,025	32,250	—	—	58,000
1869S	6,430	2,075	3,500	6,100	23,500	—	—	—
1870	4,025	1,075	1,725	3,000	26,500	—	—	64,000
1870CC	5,908	34,000	53,000	80,000	—	—	—	—
1870S	8,000	1,600	4,500	4,850	31,200	—	—	—
1871	1,820	1,300	2,675	4,800	40,000	—	—	64,000
1871CC	8,085	4,400	13,000	20,000	53,000	135,000	—	—
1871S	16,500	1,400	1,875	3,400	22,000	—	—	—
1872	1,650	2,100	3,900	7,550	13,750	27,000	—	64,000
1872CC	4,600	8,000	11,500	26,250	45,000	65,000	—	—
1872S	17,300	900	1,575	2,400	23,500	—	—	—
1873 closed 3	825	8,500	18,500	32,000	70,000	—	—	85,000
1873CC	4,543	11,000	24,000	47,000	—	—	—	—
1873S	12,000	1,250	2,795	4,000	26,000	—	—	—
1874	53,160	680	690	760	1,425	11,000	48,000	64,000
1874CC	16,767	3,000	4,700	11,750	63,000	155,000	—	—
1874S	10,000	1,250	1,950	5,000	—	—	—	—
1875	120	55,000	80,000	150,000	—	—	—	150,000

Note: 1875, Akers, Aug. 1990, Proof, $115,000.

Date	Mintage	VF20	XF40	AU50	MS60	MS63	MS65	Prf65
1875CC	7,715	4,500	9,000	14,000	86,000	155,000	—	—
1876	732	4,800	8,000	23,500	68,000	—	—	85,000
1876CC	4,696	4,800	12,000	18,500	—	—	—	—
1876S	5,000	2,000	4,000	6,700	32,000	—	—	—
1877	817	4,300	6,700	9,500	55,000	—	—	55,000
1877CC	3,332	7,500	10,250	21,000	42,000	—	—	—
1877S	17,000	850	1,350	1,850	27,000	—	—	—
1878	73,800	680	680	690	800	4,800	25,000	55,000
1878CC	3,244	6,700	18,200	37,000	—	—	—	—
1878S	26,100	825	925	1,000	12,000	25,500	—	—
1879	384,770	660	660	660	675	2,800	13,750	49,000
1879/78	Inc. above	800	840	950	1,000	2,500	—	—
1879CC	1,762	18,500	18,800	41,125	—	—	—	—
1879O	1,500	9,500	16,000	21,500	72,500	—	—	—
1879S	224,000	660	660	660	1,095	6,250	—	—
1880	1,644,876	660	660	660	675	1,325	—	60,000
1880CC	11,190	1,850	2,550	4,300	38,000	—	—	—
1880O	9,200	900	2,000	4,000	20,000	—	—	—
1880S	506,250	660	660	660	675	1,400	—	—
1881	3,877,260	660	660	660	675	925	15,750	55,000
1881CC	24,015	1,300	1,800	2,725	7,100	32,000	—	—
1881O	8,350	800	1,000	3,200	16,000	—	—	—
1881S	970,000	660	660	660	675	1,300	—	—
1882	2,324,480	660	660	660	675	740	—	55,000
1882CC	6,764	1,750	2,750	4,600	30,000	63,000	—	—
1882O	10,820	1,400	1,700	2,600	9,600	34,000	—	—
1882S	132,000	660	660	660	675	1,800	31,000	—
1883	208,740	660	660	660	675	1,125	—	55,000
1883CC	12,000	1,500	2,000	3,750	32,000	—	—	—
1883O	800	—	25,000	60,000	—	—	—	—
1883S	38,000	660	660	660	675	9,000	—	—
1884	76,905	660	660	660	675	3,450	—	60,000
1884CC	9,925	1,475	2,700	5,000	14,000	44,000	—	—
1884S	124,250	660	660	660	675	4,000	—	—
1885	253,527	660	660	660	675	1,620	30,000	48,000
1885S	228,000	660	660	660	675	1,000	—	—
1886	236,160	660	660	660	675	1,875	—	53,000
1886S	826,000	660	660	660	675	850	—	—
1887	53,680	660	660	660	675	5,300	—	88,000
1887S	817,000	660	660	660	675	1,350	—	—
1888	132,996	660	660	660	675	3,450	—	45,000
1888O	21,335	660	660	660	1,100	7,000	—	—
1888S	648,700	660	660	660	675	925	—	—
1889	4,485	750	900	1,175	3,375	8,500	—	50,000
1889S	425,400	660	660	660	675	1,075	—	—
1890	58,043	660	660	660	675	3,400	16,500	43,000
1890CC	17,500	1,125	1,350	1,675	3,800	16,000	—	—
1891	91,868	660	660	660	675	2,000	—	40,000
1891CC	103,732	1,000	1,200	1,400	3,000	7,500	43,000	—
1892	797,552	660	660	660	675	740	6,600	37,000
1892CC	40,000	1,125	1,550	1,700	4,400	31,500	—	—
1892O	28,688	660	660	660	1,225	7,500	—	—
1892S	115,500	660	660	660	675	2,100	—	—

Date	Mintage	VF20	XF40	AU50	MS60	MS63	MS65	Prf65
1893	1,840,895	660	660	660	675	740	7,500	37,000
1893CC	14,000	1,125	1,375	3,000	20,000	—	—	—
1893O	17,000	660	660	660	675	4,800	—	—
1893S	141,350	660	660	660	675	1,600	—	—
1894	2,470,778	660	660	660	675	740	12,750	37,000
1894O	107,500	660	660	660	675	4,350	—	—
1894S	25,000	660	660	660	3,600	—	—	—
1895	567,826	660	660	660	675	740	9,850	37,000
1895O	98,000	660	660	660	1,100	7,000	—	—
1895S	49,000	660	660	660	675	8,500	—	—
1896	76,348	660	660	660	675	1,200	—	37,000
1896S	123,750	660	660	660	675	7,100	—	—
1897	1,000,159	660	660	660	675	740	3,600	37,000
1897O	42,500	660	660	660	675	6,600	23,000	—
1897S	234,750	660	660	660	675	5,250	—	—
1898	812,197	660	660	660	675	740	6,300	37,000
1898S	473,600	660	660	660	675	1,525	—	—
1899	1,262,305	660	660	660	675	740	2,320	37,000
1899O	37,047	660	660	660	675	7,850	32,000	—
1899S	841,000	660	660	660	675	1,550	16,000	—
1900	293,960	660	660	660	675	740	3,500	34,000
1900S	81,000	660	660	660	675	4,600	19,000	—
1901	1,718,825	660	660	660	675	740	2,260	34,000
1901O	72,041	660	660	660	1,050	3,400	—	—
1901S	2,812,750	660	660	660	675	740	2,500	—
1902	82,513	660	660	660	675	1,300	10,500	34,000
1902S	469,500	660	660	660	675	740	2,260	—
1903	125,926	660	660	660	675	740	8,100	34,000
1903O	112,771	660	660	660	675	2,300	20,500	—
1903S	538,000	660	660	660	675	740	2,260	—
1904	162,038	660	660	660	675	1,500	6,150	37,000
1904O	108,950	660	660	660	675	2,800	20,000	—
1905	201,078	660	660	660	675	980	5,875	34,000
1905S	369,250	660	660	660	675	4,400	—	—
1906	165,497	660	660	660	675	1,025	6,500	34,000
1906D	981,000	660	660	660	675	740	6,000	—
1906O	86,895	660	660	660	1,125	4,350	23,000	—
1906S	457,000	660	660	660	675	2,300	15,750	—
1907	1,203,973	660	660	660	675	750	2,260	37,000
1907D	1,030,000	660	660	660	675	1,550	12,000	—
1907S	210,500	660	660	660	675	3,550	—	—

Indian Head
No motto to left of eagle.
KM# 125 • 16.72 g., 0.900 Gold 0.4837 oz. AGW, 27 mm. • **Designer:** Augustus Saint-Gaudens **Note:** 1907 varieties are distinguished by whether the edge is rolled or wired, and whether the legend E PLURIBUS UNUM has periods between each word.

Date	Mintage	VF20	XF40	AU50	MS60	MS63	MS65	Prf65
1907 wire edge, periods before and after legend	500	11,000	16,500	19,000	38,000	39,000	70,000	—
1907 same, without stars on edge, unique	—	—	—	—	—	—	—	—
1907 rolled edge, periods	42	24,500	38,000	48,000	73,000	115,000	275,000	—
1907 without periods	239,406	—	665	670	1,120	1,950	5,500	—
1908 without motto	33,500	—	665	670	1,310	4,600	15,000	—
1908D without motto	210,000	—	665	670	1,300	5,700	41,000	—

"IN GOD WE TRUST" left of eagle.
KM# 130 • 16.72 g., 0.900 Gold 0.4837 oz. AGW, 27 mm. • **Designer:** Augustus Saint-Gaudens

Date	Mintage	VF20	XF40	AU50	MS60	MS63	MS65	Prf65
1908	341,486	—	665	670	810	1,400	4,050	55,000
1908D	836,500	—	665	760	1,225	3,500	24,000	—
1908S	59,850	900	975	1,250	3,600	12,600	23,000	—
1909	184,863	—	665	670	750	1,500	20,500	72,500
1909D	121,540	—	665	670	1,200	4,000	28,000	—

$10 GOLD

Date	Mintage	VF20	XF40	AU50	MS60	MS63	MS65	Prf65
1909S	292,350	—	665	880	1,800	5,500	16,950	—
1910	318,704	—	665	670	720	895	5,700	68,000
1910D	2,356,640	—	665	670	720	990	5,950	—
1910S	811,000	—	665	670	900	4,875	41,000	—
1911	505,595	—	665	670	720	890	5,000	55,000
1911D	30,100	1,600	2,000	2,550	8,500	27,000	220,000	—
1911S	51,000	950	1,100	1,200	2,900	10,000	25,000	—
1912	405,083	—	665	670	720	875	8,000	55,000
1912S	300,000	—	665	670	1,425	4,850	31,500	—
1913	442,071	—	665	670	720	1,000	5,200	55,000
1913S	66,000	840	950	1,170	5,500	17,750	—	—
1914	151,050	—	665	670	720	1,425	7,400	60,000
1914D	343,500	—	665	670	800	1,375	11,000	—
1914S	208,000	850	975	1,125	1,800	4,300	30,500	—
1915	351,075	—	665	670	720	1,320	6,000	55,000
1915S	59,000	1,050	1,225	1,600	5,500	19,700	60,000	—
1916S	138,500	—	665	670	1,750	5,300	22,250	—
1920S	126,500	16,500	23,000	30,000	55,000	90,000	200,000	—
1926	1,014,000	—	665	670	720	825	2,325	—
1930S	96,000	14,000	19,750	24,000	36,500	44,000	88,000	—
1932	4,463,000	—	665	670	720	820	2,300	—
1933	312,500	130,000	140,000	145,000	165,000	225,000	600,000	—

$20 (DOUBLE EAGLE)

Liberty Head

Coronet head, left, within circle of stars. "TWENTY D." below eagle, no motto above eagle.

KM# 74.1 • 33.44 g., 0.900 Gold 0.9675 oz. AGW, 34 mm. • **Rev. Legend:** UNITED STATES OF AMERICA **Designer:** James B. Longacre

Date	Mintage	VF20	XF40	AU50	MS60	MS63	MS65	Prf65
1849 unique, in Smithsonian collection	1	—	—	—	—	—	—	—
1850	1,170,261	2,100	3,100	6,895	15,000	53,000	195,000	—
1850O	141,000	5,000	7,000	13,250	63,000	—	—	—
1851	2,087,155	1,825	1,900	2,200	5,250	21,250	—	—
1851O	315,000	2,500	4,000	6,000	28,000	—	—	—
1852	2,053,026	1,800	1,825	2,200	5,400	20,000	—	—
1852O	190,000	2,150	4,000	6,000	34,500	—	—	—
1853	1,261,326	1,800	1,900	2,000	5,300	30,000	165,000	—
1853/2	Inc. above	2,000	3,000	4,800	27,000	—	—	—
1853O	71,000	2,700	6,600	11,500	35,000	—	—	—
1854 SD	757,899	1,800	2,000	9,000	25,850	—	—	—
1854 LD	Inc. above	3,000	4,100	11,000	36,000	61,000	—	—
1854O	3,250	92,000	176,000	290,000	—	—	—	—
1854S	141,468	2,750	3,700	12,000	29,000	47,500	86,000	—
1855	364,666	1,800	1,825	2,400	11,000	60,000	60,000	—
1855O	8,000	14,500	36,000	45,000	120,000	—	—	—
1855S	879,675	1,800	1,825	2,200	7,000	22,000	—	—
1856	329,878	1,800	2,100	3,300	7,900	36,000	—	—
1856O	2,250	175,000	220,000	335,000	—	—	—	—
1856S	1,189,750	1,800	1,900	2,200	6,000	16,000	37,000	—
1857	439,375	1,800	1,900	2,425	10,000	37,500	—	—
1857O	30,000	4,600	9,200	13,200	82,000	250,000	—	—
1857S	970,500	1,800	1,825	2,200	4,300	7,000	10,500	—
1858	211,714	1,800	1,825	3,000	9,250	35,000	—	—
1858O	35,250	4,600	8,300	19,000	53,000	180,000	—	—
1858S	846,710	1,800	1,900	2,400	8,800	40,000	—	—
1859	43,597	3,000	6,000	12,000	30,000	—	—	—
1859O	9,100	15,000	28,000	52,000	130,000	—	—	—
1859S	636,445	1,800	1,900	2,350	13,250	58,000	—	—
1860	577,670	1,800	1,825	2,150	5,400	18,000	72,000	—
1860O	6,600	12,000	34,000	50,000	—	—	—	—
1860S	544,950	1,800	2,200	2,800	6,500	35,000	—	—
1861	2,976,453	1,800	1,825	2,250	5,000	18,500	55,000	225,000
1861O	17,741	15,000	36,000	55,000	160,000	—	—	—
1861S	768,000	1,800	2,300	2,600	15,000	40,000	—	—

$10 GOLD

Coronet head, left, within circle of stars. Paquet design, "TWENTY D." below eagle.

KM# 93 • 33.44 g., 0.900 Gold 0.9675 oz. AGW
Rev. Legend: UNITED STATES OF AMERICA **Note:** In 1861 the reverse was redesigned by Anthony C. Paquet, but it was withdrawn soon after its release. The letters in the inscriptions on the Paquet-reverse variety are taller than on the regular reverse.

$20 GOLD

Date	Mintage	VF20	XF40	AU50	MS60	MS63	MS65	Prf65
1861 2 Known	—	—	—	—	—	—	—	—
Note: 1861 Paquet reverse, Bowers & Merena, Nov. 1988, MS-67, $660,000.								
1861S	—	22,000	56,000	90,000	—	—	—	—
Note: Included in mintage of 1861S, KM#74.1								

Longacre design resumed.

KM# A74.1 • 33.44 g., 0.900 Gold 0.9675 oz. AGW

Date	Mintage	VF20	XF40	AU50	MS60	MS63	MS65	Prf65
1862	92,133	4,800	11,000	18,000	40,000	—	—	400,000
1862S	854,173	2,000	2,400	2,700	16,000	46,000	—	—
1863	142,790	3,600	7,500	12,000	31,500	90,000	—	400,000
1863S	966,570	2,100	2,200	4,500	11,000	34,000	—	—
1864	204,285	3,000	5,000	8,250	24,000	76,000	240,000	400,000
1864S	793,660	1,800	2,190	2,700	9,500	42,000	—	—
1865	351,200	2,000	2,400	3,100	7,000	20,000	70,000	400,000
1865S	1,042,500	1,700	1,775	2,300	6,750	13,750	30,000	—
1866S	Inc. below	10,000	20,000	35,000	150,000	—	—	—

Coronet head, left, within circle of stars. TWENTY D. below eagle. "IN GOD WE TRUST" above eagle.

KM# 74.2 • 33.44 g., 0.900 Gold 0.9675 oz. AGW, 34 mm. • **Rev. Legend:** UNITED STATES OF AMERICA **Designer:** James B. Longacre

Date	Mintage	VF20	XF40	AU50	MS60	MS63	MS65	Prf65
1866	698,775	1,330	2,200	3,700	12,500	55,000	—	290,000
1866S	842,250	1,750	2,300	4,100	22,000	—	—	—
1867	251,065	1,330	1,700	2,100	5,000	28,000	—	290,000
1867S	920,750	1,330	1,475	1,985	11,000	—	—	—
1868	98,600	1,700	2,100	3,700	18,500	60,000	—	290,000
1868S	837,500	1,330	1,700	2,000	9,500	—	—	—
1869	175,155	1,600	1,700	2,100	11,000	33,000	245,000	290,000
1869S	686,750	1,330	1,750	2,100	5,300	38,000	—	—
1870	155,185	1,330	1,800	3,600	15,000	48,000	—	325,000
1870CC	3,789	175,000	240,000	345,000	—	—	—	—
1870S	982,000	1,330	1,525	1,590	5,100	56,000	—	—
1871	80,150	1,600	1,650	3,275	6,800	40,000	—	—
1871CC	17,387	12,500	36,000	52,000	120,000	225,000	—	—
1871S	928,000	1,330	1,625	1,700	4,400	19,500	—	—
1872	251,880	1,330	1,625	2,000	3,400	24,000	—	—
1872CC	26,900	5,000	9,500	15,000	62,000	—	—	—
1872S	780,000	1,330	1,625	1,625	3,000	25,000	—	—
1873 closed 3	Est. 208925	1,330	1,625	1,700	3,800	—	—	325,000
1873 open 3	Est. 1500900	1,330	1,390	1,410	1,575	7,100	190,000	—

$20 GOLD

Date	Mintage	VF20	XF40	AU50	MS60	MS63	MS65	Prf65
1873CC	22,410	4,000	8,100	16,250	45,000	125,000	—	—
1873S closed 3	1,040,600	1,330	1,400	1,400	2,300	18,500	—	—
1873S open 3	Inc. above	1,330	1,500	1,500	5,600	6,700	—	—
1874	366,800	1,330	1,625	1,625	2,100	17,250	—	325,000
1874CC	115,085	3,000	3,475	5,000	24,000	—	—	—
1874S	1,214,000	1,450	1,475	1,475	1,950	24,000	—	—
1875	295,740	1,450	1,475	1,475	1,950	6,200	—	—
1875CC	111,151	2,400	3,350	4,000	11,000	30,000	—	—
1875S	1,230,000	1,330	1,625	1,625	1,650	10,000	—	—
1876	583,905	1,330	1,625	1,625	1,650	12,000	—	325,000
1876CC	138,441	2,600	3,400	3,900	10,300	28,000	—	—
1876S	1,597,000	1,330	1,390	1,410	1,500	6,500	185,000	—

Coronet head, left, within circle of stars.   "TWENTY DOLLARS" below eagle.

KM# 74.3 • 33.44 g., 0.900 Gold 0.9675 oz. AGW **Rev. Legend:** UNITED STATES OF AMERICA

Date	Mintage	VF20	XF40	AU50	MS60	MS63	MS65	Prf65
1877	397,670	1,290	1,290	1,290	1,900	12,000	—	125,000
1877CC	42,565	3,000	3,400	6,000	27,000	—	—	—
1877S	1,735,000	1,290	1,290	1,290	1,575	13,700	42,500	—
1878	543,645	1,290	1,290	1,290	1,500	9,100	—	125,000
1878CC	13,180	5,500	8,000	12,250	42,500	—	—	—
1878S	1,739,000	1,290	1,290	1,290	1,500	14,250	—	—
1879	207,630	1,290	1,290	1,290	2,000	14,000	53,000	125,000
1879CC	10,708	6,100	11,000	19,000	58,000	—	—	—
1879O	2,325	26,500	40,000	54,000	125,000	—	—	—
1879S	1,223,800	1,290	1,290	1,290	2,000	34,000	—	—
1880	51,456	1,310	1,450	2,050	10,000	35,000	—	125,000
1880S	836,000	1,290	1,290	1,290	3,200	20,000	49,500	—
1881	2,260	17,500	25,000	40,000	110,000	—	—	145,000
1881S	727,000	1,290	1,290	1,290	1,750	21,000	—	—
1882	630	30,000	50,000	85,000	125,000	—	—	210,000
1882CC	39,140	2,600	3,000	4,500	13,250	83,000	—	—
1882S	1,125,000	1,290	1,290	1,290	1,590	12,750	—	—
1883 proof only	92	—	—	—	—	—	—	225,000
1883CC	59,962	2,600	2,700	4,800	10,000	36,500	—	—
1883S	1,189,000	1,290	1,290	1,290	1,480	5,000	—	—
1884 proof only	71	—	—	—	—	—	—	245,000
1884CC	81,139	2,500	2,700	3,500	9,500	43,000	—	—
1884S	916,000	1,290	1,290	1,290	1,475	3,500	37,500	—
1885	828	20,000	30,000	45,000	70,000	115,000	—	90,000
1885CC	9,450	6,000	12,000	16,000	38,000	115,000	—	—
1885S	683,500	1,290	1,290	1,290	1,725	3,000	—	—
1886	1,106	38,000	70,000	88,000	125,000	145,000	—	87,000
1887	121	—	—	—	—	—	—	165,000
1887S	283,000	1,290	1,290	1,290	1,500	13,000	37,500	—
1888	226,266	1,290	1,290	1,290	1,800	10,000	28,000	85,000
1888S	859,600	1,290	1,290	1,290	1,600	3,600	39,000	—
1889	44,111	1,290	1,290	1,450	2,000	13,000	—	85,000
1889CC	30,945	3,000	3,600	5,000	11,500	40,000	—	—
1889S	774,700	1,290	1,290	1,290	1,600	2,800	20,000	—
1890	75,995	1,290	1,290	1,290	1,295	7,200	—	85,000
1890CC	91,209	2,600	3,100	4,500	9,000	38,500	—	—
1890S	802,750	1,290	1,290	1,290	1,310	3,400	23,000	—
1891	1,442	14,000	21,000	36,000	75,000	136,000	—	87,000
1891CC	5,000	7,800	12,000	23,000	41,000	80,000	—	—
1891S	1,288,125	1,290	1,290	1,290	1,295	2,225	—	—
1892	4,523	4,500	6,800	9,000	22,000	35,000	55,000	84,000
1892CC	27,265	2,700	3,000	4,100	11,950	52,000	—	—
1892S	930,150	1,290	1,290	1,290	1,295	2,300	19,000	—
1893	344,339	1,290	1,290	1,290	1,295	2,450	—	160,000
1893CC	18,402	2,700	3,600	6,000	13,000	47,000	—	—
1893S	996,175	1,290	1,290	1,290	1,295	2,900	—	—
1894	1,368,990	1,290	1,290	1,290	1,295	1,750	23,000	84,000

Date	Mintage	VF20	XF40	AU50	MS60	MS63	MS65	Prf65
1894S	1,048,550	1,290	1,290	1,290	1,295	2,400	19,000	—
1895	1,114,656	1,290	1,290	1,290	1,295	1,800	18,000	84,000
1895S	1,143,500	1,290	1,290	1,290	1,295	1,900	11,000	—
1896	792,663	1,290	1,290	1,290	1,295	1,675	17,500	84,000
1896S	1,403,925	1,290	1,290	1,290	1,295	1,800	25,000	—
1897	1,383,261	1,290	1,290	1,290	1,295	1,750	19,000	84,000
1897S	1,470,250	1,290	1,290	1,290	1,295	1,750	16,000	—
1898	170,470	1,290	1,290	1,290	1,295	2,600	—	84,000
1898S	2,575,175	1,290	1,290	1,290	1,295	1,800	8,000	—
1899	1,669,384	1,290	1,290	1,290	1,295	1,675	9,000	84,000
1899S	2,010,300	1,290	1,290	1,290	1,295	2,150	19,000	—
1900	1,874,584	1,290	1,290	1,290	1,295	1,430	4,600	84,000
1900S	2,459,500	1,290	1,290	1,290	1,295	1,900	17,500	—
1901	111,526	1,290	1,290	1,290	1,295	1,800	4,100	84,000
1901S	1,596,000	1,290	1,290	1,290	1,295	3,000	17,000	—
1902	31,254	1,290	1,290	1,290	1,295	9,000	—	84,000
1902S	1,753,625	1,290	1,290	1,290	1,295	2,900	29,000	—
1903	287,428	1,290	1,290	1,290	1,295	1,400	2,900	84,000
1903S	954,000	1,290	1,290	1,290	1,295	1,800	12,000	—
1904	6,256,797	1,290	1,290	1,290	1,295	1,495	2,700	84,000
1904S	5,134,175	1,290	1,290	1,290	1,295	1,400	2,600	—
1905	59,011	1,290	1,290	1,600	2,250	13,000	85,000	84,000
1905S	1,813,000	1,290	1,290	1,290	1,295	2,500	18,000	—
1906	69,690	1,290	1,290	1,600	2,100	6,700	32,000	84,000
1906D	620,250	1,290	1,290	1,290	1,295	3,400	16,000	—
1906S	2,065,750	1,290	1,290	1,290	1,150	1,950	22,000	—
1907	1,451,864	1,290	1,290	1,290	1,310	1,400	7,000	84,000
1907D	842,250	1,290	1,290	1,290	1,425	3,125	6,000	—
1907S	2,165,800	1,290	1,290	1,290	1,400	2,025	21,000	—

Saint-Gaudens High Relief
Roman numerals in date. No motto below eagle.
KM# 126 • 33.44 g., 0.900 Gold 0.9675 oz. AGW, 34 mm. • **Edge:** Plain. **Designer:** Augustus Saint-Gaudens

Date	Mintage	VF20	XF40	AU50	MS60	MS63	MS65	Prf65
MCMVII (1907) high relief, unique, AU-55, 150,000								
MCMVII (1907) high relief, wire rim	11,250	7,000	8,500	9,800	13,500	24,950	42,500	—
MCMVII (1907) high relief, flat rim	Inc. above	7,000	8,500	9,800	13,500	24,950	38,750	—

Saint-Gaudens
Arabic numerals in date. No motto below eagle.
KM# 127 • 33.44 g., 0.900 Gold 0.9675 oz. AGW, 34 mm. • **Edge:** Lettered; large letters. **Designer:** Augustus Saint-Gaudens

Date	Mintage	VF20	XF40	AU50	MS60	MS63	MS65	Prf65
1907 large letters on edge, unique	—	—	—	—	—	—	—	—
1907 small letters on edge	361,667	1,290	1,290	1,290	1,290	1,900	3,250	—
1908	4,271,551	1,290	1,290	1,290	1,290	1,365	1,725	—
1908D	663,750	1,290	1,290	1,290	1,290	1,365	5,650	—

Saint-Gaudens
"IN GOD WE TRUST" below eagle.
KM# 131 • 33.44 g., 0.900 Gold 0.9675 oz. AGW, 34 mm. • **Designer:** Augustus Saint-Gaudens

Date	Mintage	VF20	XF40	AU50	MS60	MS63	MS65	Prf65
1908	156,359	1,290	1,290	1,290	1,400	1,800	20,000	75,000
1908 Roman finish; Prf64 Rare	—	—						
Note: Rare								
1908D	349,500	1,290	1,290	1,290	1,360	1,875	4,250	—
1908S	22,000	2,800	3,300	4,400	9,800	20,000	45,000	
1909/8	161,282	1,400	1,600	1,650	2,000	3,950	38,000	—
1909	Inc. Above	1,290	1,290	1,290	1,290	2,300	34,000	75,000
1909D	52,500	1,290	1,290	1,290	2,800	5,000	26,750	—
1909S	2,774,925	1,290	1,290	1,290	1,290	1,395	4,100	—
1910	482,167	1,290	1,290	1,290	1,290	1,365	6,400	80,000
1910D	429,000	1,290	1,290	1,290	1,290	1,365	2,625	—
1910S	2,128,250	1,290	1,290	1,290	1,290	1,410	5,100	—
1911	197,350	1,290	1,290	1,290	1,290	2,165	17,800	74,000
1911D	846,500	1,290	1,290	1,290	1,290	1,365	2,500	—
1911S	775,750	1,290	1,290	1,290	1,290	1,365	3,950	—
1912	149,824	1,290	1,290	1,290	1,290	2,225	24,000	74,000
1913	168,838	1,290	1,290	1,290	1,290	2,300	60,000	79,000
1913D	393,500	1,290	1,290	1,290	1,290	1,890	4,550	—
1913S	34,000	1,290	1,290	1,800	2,200	4,400	29,000	—
1914	95,320	1,290	1,290	1,290	1,290	2,750	16,250	79,000
1914D	453,000	1,290	1,290	1,290	1,290	1,365	2,750	—
1914S	1,498,000	1,290	1,290	1,290	1,290	1,365	2,050	—
1915	152,050	1,290	1,290	1,290	1,290	2,050	16,000	90,000
1915S	567,500	1,290	1,290	1,290	1,290	1,365	1,975	—
1916S	796,000	1,290	1,290	1,290	1,290	1,600	2,975	—
1920	228,250	1,290	1,290	1,290	1,290	1,700	85,000	—
1920S	558,000	11,000	15,500	24,000	75,000	75,000	250,000	—
1921	528,500	—	65,000	79,500	90,000	225,000	585,000	—
1922	1,375,500	1,290	1,290	1,290	1,290	1,365	3,150	—
1922S	2,658,000	1,290	1,290	2,000	2,300	4,000	38,000	—
1923	566,000	1,320	1,320	1,320	1,325	1,450	3,600	—
1923D	1,702,250	1,290	1,290	1,290	1,290	1,365	1,807	—
1924	4,323,500	1,290	1,290	1,290	1,290	1,365	1,775	—
1924D	3,049,500	1,320	1,320	1,320	5,000	6,800	73,000	—
1924S	2,927,500	1,320	1,320	1,750	9,000	9,000	140,000	—
1925	2,831,750	1,290	1,290	1,290	1,290	1,365	1,775	—
1925D	2,938,500	1,600	1,900	2,500	8,500	9,500	85,000	—
1925S	3,776,500	1,900	2,300	3,300	16,000	16,000	150,000	—
1926	816,750	1,290	1,290	1,290	1,290	1,425	1,775	—
1926D	481,000	8,000	9,000	10,000	19,000	19,000	170,000	—
1926S	2,041,500	1,650	1,760	1,900	5,625	5,625	22,500	—
1927	2,946,750	1,290	1,290	1,290	1,290	1,365	1,600	—
1927D	180,000	240,000	300,000	500,000	1,000,000	1,000,000	1,600,000	—
1927S	3,107,000	7,500	10,000	13,000	35,000	35,000	110,000	—
1928	8,816,000	1,290	1,290	1,290	1,290	1,365	1,600	—
1929	1,779,750	9,000	11,000	13,000	17,000	30,000	75,000	—
1930S	74,000	33,000	37,000	42,000	60,000	84,000	165,000	—
1931	2,938,250	13,000	16,000	20,000	30,000	50,000	105,000	—
1931D	106,500	13,000	16,000	26,000	36,000	60,000	125,000	—
1932	1,101,750	13,000	16,000	20,000	25,000	70,000	102,000	—
1933	445,500	—	—	—	—	—	9,000,000	—

Note: Sotheby/Stack's Sale, July 2002. Thirteen known, only one currently available.
1907 extremely high relief, unique —
1907 extremely high relief, lettered edge —
Note: 1907 extremely high relief, lettered edge, Prf-68, private sale, 1990, $1,500,000.

COMMEMORATIVE COINAGE 1892-1954

All commemorative half dollars of 1892-1954 have the following specifications: diameter — 30.6 millimeters; weight — 12.500 grams; composition — 0.900 silver, 0.3617 ounces actual silver weight. Values for PDS sets contain one example each from the Philadelphia, Denver and San Francisco mints. Type coin prices are the most inexpensive single coin available from the date and mint mark combinations listed.

QUARTER

Columbian Exposition
KM# 115 • 6.25 g., 0.900 Silver 0.1808 oz. ASW, 24.3 mm. • **Obv.** Queen Isabella bust left **Rev:** Female kneeling with distaff and spindle

Date	Mintage	AU50	MS60	MS63	MS64	MS65
1893	24,214	290	350	465	785	1,325

HALF DOLLAR

Columbian Exposition
KM# 117 • 12.50 g., 0.900 Silver 0.3617 oz. ASW, 30.6 mm. • **Obv.** Christopher Columbus bust right **Rev:** Santa Maria sailing left, two globes below **Obv. Designer:** Charles E. Barber **Rev. Designer:** George T. Morgan

Date	Mintage	AU50	MS60	MS63	MS64	MS65
1892	950,000	24.00	45.00	85.00	125	375
1893	1,550,405	24.00	25.00	75.00	145	330

Panama-Pacific Exposition
KM# 135 • 12.50 g., 0.900 Silver 0.3617 oz. ASW, 30.6 mm. • **Obv.** Columbia standing, sunset in background **Rev:** Eagle standing on shield **Designer:** Charles E. Barber

Date	Mintage	AU50	MS60	MS63	MS64	MS65
1915 S	27,134	360	475	725	790	1,300

Illinois Centennial-Lincoln
KM# 143 • 12.50 g., 0.900 Silver 0.3617 oz. ASW, 30.6 mm. • **Obv.** Abraham Lincon bust right **Rev:** Eagle standing left **Obv. Designer:** George T. Morgan **Rev. Designer:** John R. Sinnock

Date	Mintage	AU50	MS60	MS63	MS64	MS65
1918	100,058	155	170	180	210	295

Maine Centennial
KM# 146 • 12.50 g., 0.900 Silver 0.3617 oz. ASW, 30.6 mm. • **Obv.** Arms of the State of Maine **Rev:** Legend within wreath **Designer:** Anthony de Francisci

Date	Mintage	AU50	MS60	MS63	MS64	MS65
1920	50,028	100	160	165	170	370

Pilgrim Tercentenary
KM# 147.1 • 12.50 g., 0.900 Silver 0.3617 oz. ASW, 30.6 mm. • **Obv.** William Bradford half-length left **Rev:** Mayflower sailing left **Designer:** Cyrus E. Dallin

Date	Mintage	AU50	MS60	MS63	MS64	MS65
1920	152,112	88.00	105	110	120	180

COMMEMORATIVE COINAGE 1892-1954

Pilgrim Tercentenary

KM# 147.2 • 12.50 g., 0.900 Silver 0.3617 oz. ASW, 30.6 mm. • **Obv.** William Bradford half-length left, 1921 added at left **Rev:** Mayflower sailing left **Designer:** Cyrus E. Dallin

Date	Mintage	AU50	MS60	MS63	MS64	MS65
1921	20,053	155	160	175	240	275

2x2

Alabama Centennial

KM# 148.1 • 12.50 g., 0.900 Silver 0.3617 oz. ASW, 30.6 mm. • **Obv.** William W. Bibb and T.E. Kilby conjoint busts left. "2x2" at right above stars **Rev:** Ealge left on shield **Designer:** Laura G. Fraser **Note:** Fake 2x2" counterstamps exist.

Date	Mintage	AU50	MS60	MS63	MS64	MS65
1921	6,006	300	320	465	475	1,235

Alabama Centennial

KM# 148.2 • 12.50 g., 0.900 Silver 0.3617 oz. ASW, 30.6 mm. • **Obv.** William W. Bibb and T.E. Kilby conjoint busts left **Rev:** Eagle standing left on shield **Obv. Designer:** Laura G. Fraser

Date	Mintage	AU50	MS60	MS63	MS64	MS65
1921	59,038	135	210	360	375	1,050

Missouri Centennial

KM# 149.1 • 12.50 g., 0.900 Silver 0.3617 oz. ASW, 30.6 mm. • **Obv.** Frontiersman in coonskin cap left **Rev:** Frontiersman and Native American standing left **Designer:** Robert Aitken

Date	Mintage	AU50	MS60	MS63	MS64	MS65
1921	15,428	375	475	550	800	1,390

2x4

Missouri Centennial

KM# 149.2 • 12.50 g., 0.900 Silver 0.3617 oz. ASW, 30.6 mm. • **Obv.** Frontiersman in coonskin cap left, 2(star)4 in field at left **Rev:** Frontiersman and Native American standing left **Designer:** Robert Aitken **Note:** Fake "2(star)4" counterstamps exist.

Date	Mintage	AU50	MS60	MS63	MS64	MS65
1921	5,000	600	675	985	1,000	1,360

Grant Memorial

KM# 151.1 • 12.50 g., 0.900 Silver 0.3617 oz. ASW, 30.6 mm. • **Obv.** Grant bust right **Rev:** Birthplace in Point Pleasant, Ohio **Designer:** Laura G. Fraser

Date	Mintage	AU50	MS60	MS63	MS64	MS65
1922	67,405	110	125	160	235	600

Grant Memorial

KM# 151.2 • 12.50 g., 0.900 Silver 0.3617 oz. ASW,
30.6 mm. • **Obv.** Grant bust left, star above the
word GRANT **Rev:** Birthplace in Point Pleasant,
Ohio **Designer:** Laura G. Fraser **Note:** Fake "star"
counterstamps exist.

Date	Mintage	AU50	MS60	MS63	MS64	MS65
1922	4,256	840	1,080	1,495	2,300	4,350

California Diamond Jubilee

KM# 155 • 12.50 g., 0.900 Silver 0.3617 oz. ASW,
30.6 mm. • **Obv.** Fourty-Niner kneeling panning
for gold **Rev:** Grizzly bear walking left **Designer:** Jo
Mora

Date	Mintage	AU50	MS60	MS63	MS64	MS65
1925 S	86,594	200	205	215	350	450

Monroe Doctrine Centennial

KM# 153 • 12.50 g., 0.900 Silver 0.3617 oz. ASW, 30.6
mm. • **Obv.** James Monroe and John Quincy Adams
conjoint busts left **Rev:** Western Hemisphere portraied
by two female figures **Designer:** Chester Beach

Date	Mintage	AU50	MS60	MS63	MS64	MS65
1923 S	274,077	55.00	80.00	130	185	675

Lexington-Concord Sesquicentennial

KM# 156 • 12.50 g., 0.900 Silver 0.3617 oz. ASW,
30.6 mm. • **Obv.** Concord's Minute Man statue
Rev: Old Belfry at Lexington **Designer:** Chester
Beach

Date	Mintage	AU50	MS60	MS63	MS64	MS65
1925	162,013	55.00	95.00	105	135	300

Huguenot-Walloon Tercentenary

KM# 154 • 12.50 g., 0.900 Silver 0.3617 oz. ASW,
30.6 mm. • **Obv.** Huguenot leader Gaspard de
Coligny and William I of Orange conjoint busts
right **Rev:** Nieuw Nederland sailing left **Designer:**
George T. Morgan

Date	Mintage	AU50	MS60	MS63	MS64	MS65
1924	142,080	135	140	175	205	235

Stone Mountain Memorial

KM# 157 • 12.50 g., 0.900 Silver 0.3617 oz. ASW,
30.6 mm. • **Obv.** Generals Robert E. Lee and
Thomas "Stonewall" Jackson mounted left. **Rev:**
Eagle on rock at right **Designer:** Gutzon Borglum

Date	Mintage	AU50	MS60	MS63	MS64	MS65
1925	1,314,709	50.00	70.00	80.00	95.00	180

Fort Vancouver Centennial

KM# 158 • 12.50 g., 0.900 Silver 0.3617 oz. ASW, 30.6 mm. • **Obv.** John McLoughlin bust left **Rev:** Frontiersmen standing with musket, Ft. Vancouver in background **Designer:** Laura G. Fraser

Date	Mintage	AU50	MS60	MS63	MS64	MS65
1925	14,994	325	380	425	440	650

Oregon Trail Memorial

KM# 159 • 12.50 g., 0.900 Silver 0.3617 oz. ASW, 30.6 mm. • **Obv.** Native American standing in full headdress and holding bow, US Map in background **Rev:** Conestoga wagon pulled by oxen left towards sunset **Designer:** James E. and Laura G. Fraser

Date	Mintage	AU50	MS60	MS63	MS64	MS65
1926	47,955	145	170	190	215	255
1926 S	83,055	145	170	190	215	265
1928	6,028	155	180	200	220	260
1933 D	5,008	315	335	360	380	435
1934 D	7,006	200	205	215	225	305
1936	10,006	170	200	215	250	260
1936 S	5,006	175	200	215	225	250
1937 D	12,008	160	180	185	200	225
1938	6,006	170	180	185	200	245
1938 D	6,005	185	220	225	260	325
1938 S	6,006	185	220	225	260	325
1939	3,004	390	400	410	420	425
1939 D	3,004	425	445	490	490	560
1939 S	3,005	460	490	500	600	600

U.S. Sesquicentennial

KM# 160 • 12.50 g., 0.900 Silver 0.3617 oz. ASW, 30.6 mm. • **Obv.** George Washington and Calvin Coolidge conjoint busts right **Rev:** Liberty Bell **Designer:** John R. Sinnock

Date	Mintage	AU50	MS60	MS63	MS64	MS65
1926	141,120	60.00	95.00	125	210	1,275

Vermont Sesquicentennial

KM# 162 • 12.50 g., 0.900 Silver 0.3617 oz. ASW, 30.6 mm. • **Obv.** Ira Allen bust right **Rev:** Catamount advancing left **Obv. Designer:** Charles Keck

Date	Mintage	AU50	MS60	MS63	MS64	MS65
1927	28,142	225	255	265	295	400

Hawaiian Sesquicentennial

KM# 163 • 12.50 g., 0.900 Silver 0.3617 oz. ASW, 30.6 mm. • **Obv.** Captain James Cook bust left **Rev:** Native Hawaiian standing over view of Diamond Head **Designer:** Juliette May Fraser and Chester Beach **Note:** Counterfeits exist.

Date	Mintage	AU50	MS60	MS63	MS64	MS65
1928	10,008	1,700	2,100	2,100	2,475	3,400

Daniel Boone Bicentennial

KM# 165.1 • 12.50 g., 0.900 Silver 0.3617 oz. ASW, 30.6 mm. • **Obv.** Daniel Boone bust left **Rev:** Daniel Boone and Native American standing **Designer:** Augustus Lukeman

Date	Mintage	AU50	MS60	MS63	MS64	MS65
1934	10,007	90.00	112	120	132	165
1935	10,010	145	160	185	200	250
1935 D	5,005	90.00	100	112	160	170
1935 S	5,005	180	190	195	210	230

Daniel Boone Bicentennial

KM# 165.2 • 12.50 g., 0.900 Silver 0.3617 oz.
ASW, 30.6 mm. • **Obv.** Daniel Boone bust left
Rev: Daniel Boone and Native American standing,
"1934" added above the word "PIONEER. **Designer:**
Augustus Lukeman

Date	Mintage	AU50	MS60	MS63	MS64	MS65
1935	10,008	160	170	185	200	220
1935 D	2,003	180	190	195	200	245
1935 S	2,004	180	190	195	210	230
1936	12,012	145	150	160	170	175
1936 D	5,005	145	150	160	170	195
1936 S	5,006	145	150	160	170	195
1937	9,810	150	160	180	205	220
1937 D	2,506	210	215	270	285	285
1937 S	2,506	225	235	270	310	350
1938	2,100	290	310	345	380	450
1938 D	2,100	290	310	345	370	415
1938 S	2,100	290	300	335	340	400

Maryland Tercentenary

KM# 166 • 12.50 g., 0.900 Silver 0.3617 oz. ASW,
30.6 mm. • **Obv.** Lord Baltimore, Cecil Calvert
bust right **Rev:** Maryland state arms **Designer:** Hans
Schuler

Date	Mintage	AU50	MS60	MS63	MS64	MS65
1934	25,015	155	160	170	190	210

Texas Centennial

KM# 167 • 12.50 g., 0.900 Silver 0.3617 oz. ASW,
30.6 mm. • **Obv.** Eagle standing left, large star in
background **Rev:** Winged Victory kneeling beside
Alamo Mission, small busts of Sam Houston and
Stephen Austin at sides **Designer:** Pompeo Coppini

Date	Mintage	AU50	MS60	MS63	MS64	MS65
1934	61,463	130	140	155	165	175
1935	9,994	130	140	155	165	200
1935 D	10,007	130	140	155	165	200
1935 S	10,008	130	140	155	165	200
1936	8,911	130	140	155	165	200
1936 D	9,039	130	140	155	165	200
1936 S	9,055	130	140	155	165	200
1937	6,571	130	140	155	165	215
1937 D	6,605	130	140	155	175	200
1937 S	6,637	130	140	155	165	200
1938	3,780	260	270	275	295	435
1938 D	3,775	260	270	275	285	500
1938 S	3,814	260	270	275	285	400

Arkansas Centennial

KM# 168 • 12.50 g., 0.900 Silver 0.3617 oz. ASW,
30.6 mm. • **Obv.** Liberty and Indian Chief's
conjoint heads left **Rev:** Eagle with outstretched
wings and flag of Arkansas in background **Designer:**
Edward E. Burr

Date	Mintage	AU50	MS60	MS63	MS64	MS65
1935 D	5,505	100	105	110	120	180
1935 S	5,506	100	105	110	120	180
1935	13,012	100	105	110	120	180
1936	9,660	100	105	110	120	175
1936 D	9,660	100	105	110	120	170
1936 S	9,662	100	105	110	120	185
1937	5,505	100	105	110	120	180
1937 D	5,505	100	105	110	120	180
1937 S	5,506	100	105	110	120	400
1938	3,156	135	140	180	225	370
1938 D	3,156	135	140	170	225	275
1938 S	3,156	135	140	170	195	340
1939	2,104	220	240	250	280	650
1939 D	2,104	220	240	250	320	575
1939 S	2,105	220	240	250	320	650

Connecticut Tercentenary

KM# 169 • 12.50 g., 0.900 Silver 0.3617 oz. ASW,
30.6 mm. • **Obv.** Eagle standing left **Rev:** Charter
oak tree **Designer:** Henry Kreiss

Date	Mintage	AU50	MS60	MS63	MS64	MS65
1935	25,018	205	210	220	275	340

COMMEMORATIVE COINAGE 1892-1954

Hudson, N.Y., Sesquicentennial

KM# 170 • 12.50 g., 0.900 Silver 0.3617 oz. ASW, 30.6 mm. • **Obv.** Hudson's ship, the Half Moon sailing right **Rev:** Seal of the City of Hudson **Designer:** Chester Beach

Date	Mintage	AU50	MS60	MS63	MS64	MS65
1935	10,008	600	700	770	800	950

Albany, N.Y., Charter Anniversary

KM# 173 • 12.50 g., 0.900 Silver 0.3617 oz. ASW, 30.6 mm. • **Obv.** Beaver gnawing on maple branch **Rev:** Standing figures of Thomas Dongan, Peter Schuyuler and Robert Livingston **Designer:** Gertrude K. Lathrop

Date	Mintage	AU50	MS60	MS63	MS64	MS65
1936	17,671	210	220	235	240	300

San Diego-Pacific International Exposition

KM# 171 • 12.50 g., 0.900 Silver 0.3617 oz. ASW, 30.6 mm. • **Obv.** Seated female with bear at her side **Rev:** State of California exposition building **Designer:** Robert Aitken

Date	Mintage	AU50	MS60	MS63	MS64	MS65
1935 S	70,132	80.00	90.00	120	130	165
1936 D	30,092	80.00	90.00	120	130	175

San Francisco-Oakland Bay Bridge

KM# 174 • 12.50 g., 0.900 Silver 0.3617 oz. ASW, 30.6 mm. • **Obv.** Grizzly bear facing **Rev:** Oakland Bay Bridge **Designer:** Jacques Schnier

Date	Mintage	AU50	MS60	MS63	MS64	MS65
1936	71,424	140	150	160	175	200

Old Spanish Trail

KM# 172 • 12.50 g., 0.900 Silver 0.3617 oz. ASW, 30.6 mm. • **Obv.** Long-horn cow's head facing **Rev:** The 1535 route of Cabeza de Vaca's expedition and a yucca tree **Designer:** L.W. Hoffecker **Note:** Counterfeits exist.

Date	Mintage	AU50	MS60	MS63	MS64	MS65
1935	10,008	760	830	880	1,000	1,050

Bridgeport, Conn., Centennial

KM# 175 • 12.50 g., 0.900 Silver 0.3617 oz. ASW, 30.6 mm. • **Obv.** P.T. Barnum bust left **Rev:** Eagle standing right **Designer:** Henry Kreiss

Date	Mintage	AU50	MS60	MS63	MS64	MS65
1936	25,015	130	135	145	150	170

Cincinnati Music Center

KM# 176 • 12.50 g., 0.900 Silver 0.3617 oz. ASW, 30.6 mm. • **Obv.** Stephen Foster bust right **Rev:** Kneeling female with lyre **Designer:** Constance Ortmayer

Date	Mintage	AU50	MS60	MS63	MS64	MS65
1936	5,005	280	300	350	390	425
1936 D	5,005	280	300	350	390	425
1936 S	5,006	280	300	350	375	425

Delaware Tercentenary

KM# 179 • 12.50 g., 0.900 Silver 0.3617 oz. ASW, 30.6 mm. • **Obv.** Old Swedes Church in Wilmington **Rev:** Kalmar Nyckel sailing left **Designer:** Carl L. Schmitz

Date	Mintage	AU50	MS60	MS63	MS64	MS65
1936	20,993	180	200	215	245	260

Elgin, Ill., Centennial

KM# 180 • 12.50 g., 0.900 Silver 0.3617 oz. ASW, 30.6 mm. • **Obv.** Pioneer head left **Rev:** Statue group **Designer:** Trygve Rovelstad

Date	Mintage	AU50	MS60	MS63	MS64	MS65
1936	20,015	160	160	170	175	180

Cleveland-Great Lakes Exposition

KM# 177 • 12.50 g., 0.900 Silver 0.3617 oz. ASW, 30.6 mm. • **Obv.** Moses Cleveland bust left **Rev:** Dividers and map of the Great Lakes **Designer:** Brenda Putnam

Date	Mintage	AU50	MS60	MS63	MS64	MS65
1936	50,030	110	120	130	145	180

Columbia, S.C., Sesquicentennial

KM# 178 • 12.50 g., 0.900 Silver 0.3617 oz. ASW, 30.6 mm. • **Obv.** Figure of Justice between capitols of 1786 and 1936 **Rev:** Palmetto tree **Designer:** A. Wolfe Davidson

Date	Mintage	AU50	MS60	MS63	MS64	MS65
1936	9,007	180	190	200	225	250
1936 D	8,009	180	190	200	215	270
1936 S	8,007	180	190	200	215	300

Battle of Gettysburg 75th Anniversary

KM# 181 • 12.50 g., 0.900 Silver 0.3617 oz. ASW, 30.6 mm. • **Obv.** Union and Confederate veteran conjoint busts right **Rev:** Double bladed fasces seperating two shields **Designer:** Frank Vittor

Date	Mintage	AU50	MS60	MS63	MS64	MS65
1936	26,928	425	485	500	510	700

Long Island Tercentenary

KM# 182 • 12.50 g., 0.900 Silver 0.3617 oz. ASW, 30.6 mm. • **Obv.** Dutch settler and Native American conjoint head right **Rev:** Dutch sailing vessel **Designer:** Howard K. Weinman

Date	Mintage	AU50	MS60	MS63	MS64	MS65
1936	81,826	75.00	85.00	95.00	105	190

Rhode Island Tercentenary

KM# 185 • 12.50 g., 0.900 Silver 0.3617 oz. ASW, 30.6 mm. • **Obv.** Roger Williams in canoe hailing Native American **Rev:** Shield with anchor **Designer:** Arthur G. Carey and John H. Benson

Date	Mintage	AU50	MS60	MS63	MS64	MS65
1936	20,013	110	125	130	140	170
1936 D	15,010	110	125	130	140	170
1936 S	15,011	110	125	130	160	225

Lynchburg, Va., Sesquicentennial

KM# 183 • 12.50 g., 0.900 Silver 0.3617 oz. ASW, 30.6 mm. • **Obv.** Sen. Carter Glass bust left **Rev:** Liberty standing, old Lynchburg courthouse at right **Designer:** Charles Keck

Date	Mintage	AU50	MS60	MS63	MS64	MS65
1936	20,013	225	235	250	265	300

Roanoke Island, N.C.

KM# 186 • 12.50 g., 0.900 Silver 0.3617 oz. ASW, 30.6 mm. • **Obv.** Sir Walter Raleigh bust left **Rev:** Ellinor Dare holding baby Virginia, two small ships flanking **Designer:** William M. Simpson

Date	Mintage	AU50	MS60	MS63	MS64	MS65
1937	29,030	180	185	195	200	225

Norfolk, Va., Bicentennial

KM# 184 • 12.50 g., 0.900 Silver 0.3617 oz. ASW, 30.6 mm. • **Obv.** Seal of the City of Norfolk **Rev:** Royal Mace of Norfolk **Designer:** William M. and Marjorie E. Simpson

Date	Mintage	AU50	MS60	MS63	MS64	MS65
1936	16,936	300	305	315	320	475

Arkansas Centennial

KM# 187 • 12.50 g., 0.900 Silver 0.3617 oz. ASW, 30.6 mm. • **Obv.** Eagle with wings outstreatched, Arkansas flag in backgorund **Rev:** Sen. Joseph T. Robinson bust right **Obv. Designer:** Henry Kreiss **Rev. Designer:** Edward E. Burr

Date	Mintage	AU50	MS60	MS63	MS64	MS65
1936	25,265	70.00	80.00	130	145	210

New Rochelle, N.Y.

KM# 191 • 12.50 g., 0.900 Silver 0.3617 oz. ASW, 30.6 mm. • **Obv.** John Pell and a calf **Rev:** Fleur-de-lis from the seal of the city **Designer:** Gertrude K. Lathrop

Date	Mintage	AU50	MS60	MS63	MS64	MS65
1938	15,266	300	310	325	340	365

Wisconsin Territorial Centennial

KM# 188 • 12.50 g., 0.900 Silver 0.3617 oz. ASW, 30.6 mm. • **Obv.** Badger from the Territorial seal **Rev:** Pick axe and mound of lead ore **Designer:** David Parsons

Date	Mintage	AU50	MS60	MS63	MS64	MS65
1936	25,015	105	120	150	142	170

Iowa Statehood Centennial

KM# 197 • 12.50 g., 0.900 Silver 0.3617 oz. ASW, 30.6 mm. • **Obv.** First Capitol building at Iowa City **Rev:** Iowa state seal **Designer:** Adam Pietz

Date	Mintage	AU50	MS60	MS63	MS64	MS65
1946	100,057	65.00	70.00	80.00	90.00	115

York County, Maine, Tercentenary

KM# 189 • 12.50 g., 0.900 Silver 0.3617 oz. ASW, 30.6 mm. • **Obv.** Stockade **Rev:** York County seal **Designer:** Walter H. Rich

Date	Mintage	AU50	MS60	MS63	MS64	MS65
1936	25,015	160	170	180	195	205

Booker T. Washington

KM# 198 • 12.50 g., 0.900 Silver 0.3617 oz. ASW, 30.6 mm. • **Obv.** Booker T. Washington bust right **Rev:** Cabin and NYU's Hall of Fame **Designer:** Isaac S. Hathaway **Note:** Actual mintages are higher, but unsold issues were melted to produce Washington Carver issues.

Date	Mintage	AU50	MS60	MS63	MS64	MS65
1946	1,000,546	20.00	28.00	32.00	45.00	65.00
1946 D	200,113	20.00	28.00	32.00	45.00	65.00
1946 S	500,729	20.00	28.00	32.00	45.00	65.00
1947	100,017	20.00	28.00	60.00	75.00	85.00
1947 D	100,017	20.00	28.00	60.00	75.00	85.00
1947 S	100,017	20.00	28.00	60.00	75.00	85.00
1948	8,005	20.00	28.00	60.00	75.00	85.00
1948 D	8,005	20.00	28.00	60.00	75.00	85.00
1948 S	8,005	20.00	28.00	60.00	75.00	110
1949	6,004	20.00	35.00	45.00	70.00	100
1949 D	6,004	20.00	50.00	60.00	70.00	150
1949 S	6,004	20.00	50.00	60.00	70.00	140
1950	6,004	20.00	40.00	60.00	70.00	100
1950 D	6,004	20.00	28.00	60.00	65.00	105
1950 S	512,091	20.00	28.00	45.00	55.00	95.00

Battle of Antietam 75th Anniversary

KM# 190 • 12.50 g., 0.900 Silver 0.3617 oz. ASW, 30.6 mm. • **Obv.** Generals Robert E. Lee and George McClellan conjoint busts left **Rev:** Burnside Bridge **Designer:** William M. Simpson

Date	Mintage	AU50	MS60	MS63	MS64	MS65
1937	18,028	530	550	570	590	700

COMMEMORATIVE COINAGE 1892-1954

COMMEMORATIVE COINAGE 1892-1954

Date	Mintage	AU50	MS60	MS63	MS64	MS65
1951	51,082	20.00	28.00	40.00	55.00	75.00
1951 D	7,004	20.00	40.00	60.00	75.00	90.00
1951 S	7,004	20.00	25.00	30.00	45.00	70.00

Booker T. Washington and George Washington Carver

KM# 200 • 12.50 g., 0.900 Silver 0.3617 oz. ASW, 30.6 mm. • **Obv.** Booker T. Washington and George Washington Carver conjoint busts right **Rev:** Map of the United States **Designer:** Isaac S. Hathaway

Date	Mintage	AU50	MS60	MS63	MS64	MS65
1951	110,018	20.00	28.00	33.00	45.00	75.00
1951 D	10,004	20.00	30.00	40.00	50.00	90.00
1951 S	10,004	20.00	28.00	55.00	60.00	70.00
1952	2,006,292	20.00	28.00	30.00	35.00	132
1952 D	8,006	20.00	35.00	45.00	85.00	160
1952 S	8,006	20.00	28.00	40.00	65.00	80.00
1953	8,003	20.00	28.00	40.00	55.00	110
1953 D	8,003	20.00	28.00	40.00	55.00	70.00
1953 S	108,020	20.00	28.00	40.00	50.00	75.00
1954	12,006	20.00	28.00	40.00	55.00	104
1954 D	12,006	20.00	28.00	40.00	55.00	100
1954 S	122,024	20.00	28.00	40.00	45.00	75.00

DOLLAR

Lafayette

KM# 118 • 26.73 g., 0.900 Silver 0.7734 oz. ASW, 38.1 mm. • **Obv.** George Washington and Marquis de Lafayette conjoint busts right **Rev:** Lafayette on horseback left **Designer:** Charles E. Barber

Date	Mintage	AU50	MS60	MS63	MS64	MS65
1900	36,026	264	700	1,140	1,680	4,000

Louisiana Purchase Exposition - Jefferson bust

KM# 119 • 1.67 g., 0.900 Gold 0.0484 oz. AGW, 15 mm. • **Obv.** Jefferson bust left **Rev:** Legend and laurel branch **Designer:** Charles E. Barber

Date	Mintage	AU50	MS60	MS63	MS64	MS65
1903	17,500	350	410	504	820	935

Louisiana Purchase Exposition - McKinley bust

KM# 120 • 1.67 g., 0.900 Gold 0.0484 oz. AGW, 15 mm. • **Obv.** William McKinley bust left **Rev:** Legend and laurel branch **Obv. Designer:** Charles E. Barber

Date	Mintage	AU50	MS60	MS63	MS64	MS65
1903	17,500	200	228	456	576	780

Lewis and Clark Exposition

KM# 121 • 1.67 g., 0.900 Gold 0.0484 oz. AGW, 15 mm. • **Obv.** Lewis bust left **Rev:** Clark bust left **Obv. Designer:** Charles E. Barber

Date	Mintage	AU50	MS60	MS63	MS64	MS65
1904	10,025	670	740	960	1,324	3,407
1905	10,041	575	780	1,212	1,440	3,600

Panama-Pacific Exposition

KM# 136 • 1.67 g., 0.900 Gold 0.0484 oz. AGW, 15 mm. • **Obv.** Canal laborer bust left **Rev:** Value within two dolphins **Obv. Designer:** Charles Keck

Date	Mintage	AU50	MS60	MS63	MS64	MS65
1915 S	15,000	270	324	528	576	960

McKinley Memorial

KM# 144 • 1.67 g., 0.900 Gold 0.0484 oz. AGW, 15 mm. • **Obv.** William McKinley head left **Rev:** Memorial building at Niles, Ohio **Obv. Designer:** Charles E. Barber **Rev. Designer:** George T. Morgan

Date	Mintage	AU50	MS60	MS63	MS64	MS65
1916	9,977	390	300	338	475	900
1917	10,000	475	500	600	700	1,050

Grant Memorial

KM# 152.1 • 1.67 g., 0.900 Gold 0.0484 oz.
AGW, 15 mm. • **Obv.** U.S. Grant bust right **Rev:**
Birthplace **Obv. Designer:** Laura G. Fraser **Note:**
Without an incuse "star" above the word GRANT on
the obverse.

Date	Mintage	AU50	MS60	MS63	MS64	MS65
1922	5,000	1,000	1,025	1,125	1,250	1,550

Star

Grant Memorial

KM# 152.2 • 1.67 g., 0.900 Gold 0.0484 oz.
AGW, 15 mm. • **Obv.** U.S. Grant bust right **Rev:**
Birthplace **Obv. Designer:** Laura G. Fraser **Note:**
Variety with an incuse "star" above the word GRANT
on the obverse.

Date	Mintage	AU50	MS60	MS63	MS64	MS65
1922	5,016	1,025	1,100	1,365	1,525	1,685

$2.50 (QUARTER EAGLE)

Panama-Pacific Exposition

KM# 137 • 4.18 g., 0.900 Gold 0.121 oz. AGW, 18
mm. • **Obv.** Columbia holding cadueus while
seated on a hippocamp **Rev:** Eagle standing left
Obv. Designer: Charles E. Barber **Rev. Designer:**
George T. Morgan

Date	Mintage	AU50	MS60	MS63	MS64	MS65
1915 S	6,749	1,525	1,900	2,880	3,120	4,080

U.S. Sesquicentennial

KM# 161 • 4.18 g., 0.900 Gold 0.121 oz. AGW, 18
mm. • **Obv.** Liberty standing holding torch and
scroll **Rev:** Independence Hall **Obv. Designer:** John
R. Sinnock

Date	Mintage	AU50	MS60	MS63	MS64	MS65
1926	46,019	260	350	550	—	1,200

$50

Panama-Pacific Exposition Round

KM# 138 • 83.59 g., 0.900 Gold 2.4187 oz. AGW,
44 mm. • **Obv.** Minerva bust helmeted left **Rev:**
Owl perched on California pin branch **Obv.**
Designer: Robert Aitken **Shape:** Round

Date	Mintage	AU50	MS60	MS63	MS64	MS65
1915 S	483	50,000	65,500	85,000	113,000	175,000

Panama-Pacific Exposition Octagonal

KM# 139 • 83.59 g., 0.900 Gold 2.4187 oz. AGW,
44 mm. • **Obv.** Minerva bust helmeted left **Rev:**
Owl perched on California pine branch **Obv.**
Designer: Robert Aitken **Shape:** Octagon

Date	Mintage	AU50	MS60	MS63	MS64	MS65
1915 S	645	50,000	65,500	80,000	92,000	170,000

COMMEMORATIVE COINAGE 1892-1954

MODERN COMMEMORATIVE COINAGE 1982-PRESENT

All commemorative silver dollar coins of 1982-present have the following specifications: diameter — 38.1 millimeters; weight — 26.730 grams; composition — 0.900 silver, 0.7736 ounces actual silver weight. All commemorative $5 coins of 1982-present have the following specificiations: diameter — 21.6 millimeters; weight — 8.359 grams; composition: 0.900 gold, 0.242 ounces actual gold weight.

Note: In 1982, after a hiatus of nearly 30 years, coinage of commemorative half dollars resumed. Those designated with a 'W' were struck at the West Point Mint. Some issues were struck in copper-nickel. Those struck in silver have the same size, weight and composition as the prior commemorative half-dollar series.

DIME

2016 Centennial Gold Coins

KM# 641 • 3.11 g., 0.9999 Gold 0.100 oz. AGW, 16.5 mm. • Obv. Mercury Note: As KM#140

Date	Mintage	MS65	Prf65
2016W	—	280	—

QUARTER

2016 Centennial Gold Coins

KM# 642 • 7.78 g., 0.9999 Gold 0.250 oz. AGW, 22 mm. • Obv. Standing Liberty Note: As KM#141

Date	Mintage	MS65	Prf65
2016W	—	500	—

HALF DOLLAR

George Washington, 250th Birth Anniversary

KM# 208 • 12.50 g., 0.900 Silver 0.3617 oz. ASW, 30.6 mm. • Obv. George Washington on horseback facing Rev: Mount Vernon Obv. Designer: Elizabeth Jones Rev. Designer: Matthew Peloso

Date	Mintage	MS65	Prf65
1982D	2,210,458	10.00	—
1982S	4,894,044	—	11.00

Congress Bicentennial

KM# 224 • 11.34 g., Copper-Nickel Clad Copper Obv. Statue of Freedom head Rev: Capitol building Obv. Designer: Patricia L. Verani Rev. Designer: William Woodward and Edgar Z. Steever

Date	Mintage	MS65	Prf65
1989D	163,753	7.00	—
1989S	762,198	—	6.00

Statue of Liberty Centennial

KM# 212 • 11.34 g., Copper-Nickel Clad Copper Obv. Statue of Liberty and sunrise Rev: Immigrant family looking toward mainland Obv. Designer: Edgar Z. Steever Rev. Designer: Sherl Joseph Winter

Date	Mintage	MS65	Prf65
1986D	928,008	5.00	—
1986S	6,925,627	—	5.40

Mount Rushmore 50th Anniversary

KM# 228 • 11.34 g., Copper-Nickel Clad Copper Rev: Mount Rushmore portraits Obv. Designer: Marcel Jovine Rev. Designer: T. James Ferrell Edge: Bison standing left

Date	Mintage	MS65	Prf65
1991D	172,754	13.00	—
1991S	753,257	—	10.00

1992 Olympics

KM# 233 • 11.34 g., Copper-Nickel Clad Copper
Obv. Torch and laurel Rev: Female gymnast and
large flag Obv. Designer: William Cousins Rev.
Designer: Steven M. Bieda

Date	Mintage	MS65	Prf65
1992P	161,607	7.00	—
1992S	519,645	—	7.00

World War II 50th Anniversary

KM# 243 • 11.34 g., Copper-Nickel Clad Copper
Obv. Three portraits, plane above, large V in
backgound Rev: Pacific island battle scene Obv.
Designer: George Klauba and T. James Ferrell Rev.
Designer: William J. Leftwich and T. James Ferrell

Date	Mintage	MS65	Prf65
ND-1993P	317,396	—	14.00
ND-1993P	197,072	13.00	—

Columbus Voyage - 500th Anniversary

KM# 237 • 11.34 g., Copper-Nickel Clad Copper
Obv. Columbus standing on shore Rev: Nina, Pinta
and Santa Maria sailing right Obv. Designer: T.
James Ferrell Rev. Designer: Thomas D. Rogers, Sr.

Date	Mintage	MS65	Prf65
1992D	135,702	12.00	—
1992S	390,154	—	11.00

1994 World Cup Soccer

KM# 246 • 11.34 g., Copper-Nickel Clad Copper
Obv. Soccer player with ball Rev: World Cup 94
logo Obv. Designer: Richard T. LaRoche Rev.
Designer: Dean McMullen

Date	Mintage	MS65	Prf65
1994D	168,208	9.00	—
1994P	609,354	—	9.00

James Madison - Bill of Rights

KM# 240 • 12.50 g., 0.900 Silver 0.3617 oz.
ASW Obv. James Madison writing, Montpelier
in background Rev: Statue of Liberty torch Obv.
Designer: T. James Ferrell Rev. Designer: Dean
McMullen

Date	Mintage	MS65	Prf65
1993W	193,346	18.00	—
1993S	586,315	—	15.00

Civil War Battlefield Preservation

KM# 254 • 11.34 g., Copper-Nickel Clad Copper
Obv. Drummer and fenceline Rev: Canon
overlooking battlefield Obv. Designer: Don Troiani
Rev. Designer: T. James Ferrell

Date	Mintage	MS65	Prf65
1995S	119,510	33.00	—
1995S	330,099	—	33.00

MODERN COMMEMORATIVE COINAGE 1982-PRESENT

MODERN COMMEMORATIVE COINAGE 1982-PRESENT

1996 Atlanta Olympics - Basketball

KM# 257 • 11.34 g., Copper-Nickel Clad Copper
Obv. Three players, one jumping for a shot Rev:
Hemisphere and Atlanta Olympics logo Obv.
Designer: Clint Hansen and Al Maletsky Rev.
Designer: T. James Ferrell

Date	Mintage	MS65	Prf65
1995S	171,001	20.00	—
1995S	169,655	—	20.50

1996 Atlanta Olympics - Baseball

KM# 262 • 11.34 g., Copper-Nickel Clad Copper
Obv. Baseball batter at plate, catcher and umpire
Rev: Hemisphere and Atlanta Olympics logo Obv.
Designer: Edgar Z. Steever Rev. Designer: T. James
Ferrell

Date	Mintage	MS65	Prf65
1995S	164,605	20.00	—
1995S	118,087	—	23.00

1996 Atlanta Olympics - Swimming

KM# 267 • 11.34 g., Copper-Nickel Clad Copper
Obv. Swimmer right in butterfly stroke Rev:
Atlanta Olympics logo Obv. Designer: William J.
Krawczewicz and Edgar Z. Steever Rev. Designer:
Malcolm Farley and Thomas D. Rogers, Sr.

Date	Mintage	MS65	Prf65
1996S	49,533	90.00	—
1996S	114,315	—	75.00

1996 Atlanta Olympics - Soccer

KM# 271 • 11.34 g., Copper-Nickel Clad Copper
Obv. Two female soccer players Rev: Atlanta
Olympics logo

Date	Mintage	MS65	Prf65
1996S	52,836	90.00	—
1996S	122,412	—	23.00

U. S. Capitol Visitor Center

KM# 323 • 11.34 g., Copper-Nickel Clad Copper Obv.
Capitol silhouette, 1800 structure in detail Rev: Legend
within circle of stars Obv. Designer: Dean McMullen
Rev. Designer: Alex Shagin and Marcel Jovine

Date	Mintage	MS65	Prf65
2001P	99,157	18.50	—
2001P	77,962	—	21.00

First Flight Centennial

KM# 348 • 11.34 g., Copper-Nickel Clad Copper
Obv. Wright Monument at Kitty Hawk Rev: Wright
Flyer in flight Obv. Designer: John Mercanti Rev.
Designer: Donna Weaver

Date	Mintage	MS65	Prf65
2003P	57,726	17.00	—
2003P	111,569	—	20.00

American Bald Eagle

KM# 438 • 11.34 g., Copper-Nickel Clad Copper,
30.6 mm. • Obv. Two eaglets in nest with egg
Rev: Eagle Challenger facing right, American Flag
in background Obv. Designer: Susan Gamble and
Joseph Menna Rev. Designer: Donna Weaver and
Charles Vickers

Date	Mintage	MS65	Prf65
2008S	120,180	16.00	—
2008S	222,577	—	18.00

U.S. Army

KM# 506 • 11.34 g., Copper-Nickel Clad Copper, 30.6 mm. • **Obv.** Army contributions during peacetime, surveying, building a flood wall and space exploration **Rev:** Continental soldier with musket **Obv. Designer:** Donna Weaver and Charles L. Vickers **Rev. Designer:** Thomas Cleveland and Joseph Menna **Edge:** Reeded

Date	Mintage	MS65	Prf65
2011D	39,461	55.00	—
2011S	68,349	—	54.00

Five-Star Generals - Henry "Hap" Arnold and Omar N. Bradley

KM# 554 • Silver, 30.6 mm. • **Obv.** Two portraits facing **Rev:** Shield

Date	Mintage	MS65	Prf65
2013P	38,097	22.00	—
2013S	47,337	—	35.00

Baseball Hall of Fame

KM# 576 • 11.34 g., Copper-Nickel Clad Copper, 30.6 mm. • **Obv.** Glove **Rev:** Baseball

Date	Mintage	MS65	Prf65
2014S	—	—	24.00
2014D	—	27.00	—

Kennedy Half Dollar

KM# 587 • 23.33 g., 0.9999 Gold 0.750 oz. AGW, 30.61 mm. • **Subject:** John F. Kennedy Half Dollar, 50th Anniversary **Obv. Designer:** Gilroy Roberts **Rev. Designer:** Frank Gasparro

Date	Mintage	Prf65
1964-2014W	73,772	1,100

U.S. Marshals Service, 225th Anniversary

KM# 602 • 11.34 g., Copper-Nickel Clad Copper, 30.61 mm. • **Obv.** Old West and modern Marshals **Rev:** Lady Justice with scale and star, copy of Constitution, books, handcuffs, jug

Date	Mintage	MS65	Prf65
2015S	76,549	19.50	18.95
2015D	30,231	19.50	—

2016 Centennial Gold Coins

KM# 643 • 15.55 g., 0.9999 Gold 0.500 oz. AGW, 27 mm. • **Obv.** Walking Liberty **Note:** As KM#142

Date	Mintage	MS65	Prf65
2016W	—	—	—

National Park Service

KM# 644 • 11.34 g., Copper-Nickel Clad Copper, 30.61 mm. • **Obv.** Hiker and child with frog **Rev:** National Park Service Logo

Date	Mintage	MS65	Prf65
2016D	—	19.50	—
2016S	—	19.50	22.00

Boys Town - 100th Anniversary

KM# 659 • 11.34 g., Copper-Nickel Clad Copper, 30.61 mm. • **Obv.** Older and younger brothers holding hands in 1917 advancing towards Father Flanagan's Boys Town **Rev:** Boys Town neighborhood of homes with young adults

Date	Mintage	MS65	Prf65
2017D	Est. 300000	19.50	—
2017S Proof	Inc. Ab.	—	—

Breast Cancer Awareness

KM# 679 • 11.34 g., Copper-Nickel Clad Copper, 30.61 mm. • **Obv.** Two women battling cancer, with breast cancer awareness ribbon in background and butterfly above **Rev:** Tiger Swallowtail butterfly

Date	Mintage	MS65	Prf65
2018D	Est. 750000	32.00	—
2018S Proof	Inc. Ab.	—	35.00

DOLLAR

1984 Los Angeles Olympics - Discus

KM# 209 • 26.73 g., 0.900 Silver 0.7734 oz. ASW, 38.1 mm. • **Obv.** Trippled discus thrower and

five star logo **Rev:** Eagle bust left **Obv. Designer:** Elizabeth Jones

Date	Mintage	MS65	Prf65
1983P	294,543	19.50	—
1983D	174,014	—	—
1983S	174,014	19.50	—
1983S	1,577,025	—	21.50

1984 Los Angeles Olympics - Stadium Statues

KM# 210 • 26.73 g., 0.900 Silver 0.7734 oz. ASW, 38.1 mm. • **Obv.** Statues at exterior of Los Angeles Memorial Coliseum **Rev:** Eagle standing on rock **Obv. Designer:** Robert Graham

Date	Mintage	MS65	Prf65
1984P	217,954	21.50	—
1984D	116,675	—	—
1984S	116,675	19.50	—
1984S	1,801,210	—	21.50

Statue of Liberty Centennial

KM# 214 • 26.73 g., 0.900 Silver 0.7734 oz. ASW, 38.1 mm. • **Obv.** Statue of Liberty and Ellis Island great hall **Rev:** Statue of Liberty torch **Obv. Designer:** John Mercanti **Rev. Designer:** John Mercanti and Matthew Peloso

Date	Mintage	MS65	Prf65
1986P	723,635	23.00	—
1986S	6,414,638	—	21.00

MODERN COMMEMORATIVE COINAGE 1982-PRESENT

Congress Bicentennial

KM# 225 • 26.73 g., 0.900 Silver 0.7734 oz.
ASW, 38.1 mm. • **Obv.** Statue of Freedom in
clouds and sunburst **Rev:** Mace from the House of
Represenatives **Designer:** William Woodward and
Chester Y. Martin

Date	Mintage	MS65	Prf65
1989D	135,203	23.50	—
1989S	762,198	—	25.00

Constitution Bicentennial

KM# 220 • 26.73 g., 0.900 Silver 0.7734 oz. ASW,
38.1 mm. • **Obv.** Feather pen and document **Rev:**
Group of people **Obv. Designer:** Patricia L. Verani

Date	Mintage	MS65	Prf65
1987P	451,629	25.50	—
1987S	2,747,116	—	19.50

Eisenhower Centennial

KM# 227 • 26.73 g., 0.900 Silver 0.7734 oz. ASW,
38.1 mm. • **Obv.** Two Eisenhower profiles, as
general, left, as President, right **Rev:** Eisenhower
home at Gettysburg **Obv. Designer:** Marcel Jovine and John Mercanti
Rev. Designer: Marcel Jovine and John Mercanti

Date	Mintage	MS65	Prf65
1990W	241,669	29.00	—
1990P	1,144,461	—	25.00

1988 Olympics

KM# 222 • 26.73 g., 0.900 Silver 0.7734 oz. ASW,
38.1 mm. • **Obv.** Olympic torch and Statue of
Liberty torch within laurel wreath **Rev:** Olympic
rings within olive wreath **Obv. Designer:** Patricia
L. Verani **Rev. Designer:** Sherl Joseph Winter

Date	Mintage	MS65	Prf65
1988D	191,368	23.50	—
1988S	1,359,366	—	23.00

MODERN COMMEMORATIVE COINAGE 1982-PRESENT

Mount Rushmore 50th Anniversary

KM# 229 • 26.73 g., 0.900 Silver 0.7734 oz. ASW, 38.1 mm. • **Obv.** Mount Rushmore portraits, wreath below **Rev:** Great seal in rays, United States map in background **Obv. Designer:** Marika Somogyi and Chester Martin **Rev. Designer:** Frank Gasparro

Date	Mintage	MS65	Prf65
1991P	133,139	21.50	—
1991S	738,419	—	21.50

USO 50th Anniversary

KM# 232 • 26.73 g., 0.900 Silver 0.7734 oz. ASW, 38.1 mm. • **Obv.** USO banner **Rev:** Eagle perched right atop globe **Obv. Designer:** Robert Lamb **Rev. Designer:** John Mercanti

Date	Mintage	MS65	Prf65
1991D	124,958	29.50	—
1991S	321,275	—	25.00

Korean War - 38th Anniversary

KM# 231 • 26.73 g., 0.900 Silver 0.7734 oz. ASW, 38.1 mm. • **Obv.** Soldier advancing right up a hill; planes above, ships below **Rev:** Map of Korean peninsula, eagle's head at right **Obv. Designer:** John Mercanti **Rev. Designer:** T. James Ferrell

Date	Mintage	MS65	Prf65
1991D	213,049	29.50	—
1991P	618,488	—	21.50

1992 Olympics - Baseball

KM# 234 • 26.73 g., 0.900 Silver 0.7734 oz. ASW, 38.1 mm. • **Obv.** Baseball pitcher, Nolan Ryan as depicted on card **Rev:** Shield flanked by stylized wreath, olympic rings above **Obv. Designer:** John R. Deecken and Chester Y. Martin **Rev. Designer:** Marcel Jovine

Date	Mintage	MS65	Prf65
1992D	187,552	27.00	—
1992S	504,505	—	26.00

White House Bicentennial

KM# 236 • 26.73 g., 0.900 Silver 0.7734 oz. ASW, 38.1 mm. • **Obv.** White House's north portico **Rev:** John Hoban bust left, main entrance doorway **Obv. Designer:** Edgar Z. Steever **Rev. Designer:** Chester Y. Martin

Date	Mintage	MS65	Prf65
1992D	123,803	27.50	—
1992W	375,851	—	25.00

James Madison - Bill of Rights

KM# 241 • 26.73 g., 0.900 Silver 0.7734 oz. ASW, 38.1 mm. • **Obv.** James Madison bust right, at left **Rev:** Montpelier home **Obv. Designer:** William Krawczewicz and Thomas D. Rogers, Sr. **Rev. Designer:** Dean McMullen and Thomas D. Rogers, Sr.

Date	Mintage	MS65	Prf65
1993D	98,383	34.00	—
1993S	534,001	—	25.50

Columbus Discovery - 500th Anniversary

KM# 238 • 26.73 g., 0.900 Silver 0.7734 oz. ASW, 38.1 mm. • **Obv.** Columbus standing with banner, three ships in background **Rev:** Half view of Santa Maria on left, Space Shuttle Discovery on right **Obv. Designer:** John Mercanti **Rev. Designer:** Thomas D. Rogers, Sr.

Date	Mintage	MS65	Prf65
1992D	106,949	34.00	—
1992P	385,241	—	27.00

World War II 50th Anniversary

KM# 244 • 26.73 g., 0.900 Silver 0.7734 oz. ASW, 38.1 mm. • **Obv.** Soldier on Normandy beach **Rev:** Insignia of the Supreme Headquarters of the AEF above Eisenhower quote **Designer:** Thomas D. Rogers, Sr.

Date	Mintage	MS65	Prf65
1993D	94,708	42.00	—
1993W	342,041	—	42.00

MODERN COMMEMORATIVE COINAGE 1982-PRESENT

1994 World Cup Soccer

KM# 247 • 26.73 g., 0.900 Silver 0.7734 oz. ASW, 38.1 mm. • Obv. Two players with ball Rev: World Cup 94 logo Obv. Designer: Dean McMullen and T. James Ferrell Rev. Designer: Dean McMullen

Date	Mintage	MS65	Prf65
1994D	81,698	32.00	—
1994S	576,978	—	30.00

Vietnam Veterans Memorial

KM# 250 • 26.73 g., 0.900 Silver 0.7734 oz. ASW, 38.1 mm. • Obv. Outstretched hand touching names on the Wall, Washington Monument in background Rev: Service Medals Obv. Designer: John Mercanti Rev. Designer: Thomas D. Rogers, Sr.

Date	Mintage	MS65	Prf65
1994W	57,317	50.00	—
1994P	226,262	—	50.00

Thomas Jefferson 250th Birth Anniversary

KM# 249 • 26.73 g., 0.900 Silver 0.7734 oz. ASW, 38.1 mm. • Obv. Jefferson's head left Rev: Monticello home Designer: T. James Ferrell

Date	Mintage	MS65	Prf65
1993P	266,927	25.00	—
1993S	332,891	—	25.00

National Prisoner of War Museum

KM# 251 • 26.73 g., 0.900 Silver 0.7734 oz. ASW, 38.1 mm. • Obv. Eagle in flight left within circle of barbed wire Rev: National Prisoner of War Museum Obv. Designer: Thomas Nielson and Alfred Maletsky Rev. Designer: Edgar Z. Steever

Date	Mintage	MS65	Prf65
1994W	54,790	50.00	—
1994P	220,100	—	50.00

Women in Military Service Memorial

KM# 252 • 26.73 g., 0.900 Silver 0.7734 oz. ASW, 38.1 mm. • **Obv.** Five uniformed women left **Rev:** Memorial at Arlington National Cemetery **Obv. Designer:** T. James Ferrell **Rev. Designer:** Thomas D. Rogers, Sr.

Date	Mintage	MS65	Prf65
1994W	53,054	25.50	—
1994P	213,201	—	31.50

Civil War

KM# 255 • 26.73 g., 0.900 Silver 0.7734 oz. ASW, 38.1 mm. • **Obv.** Soldier giving water to wounded soldier **Rev:** Chamberlain quote and battlefield monument **Obv. Designer:** Don Troiani and Edgar Z. Steever **Rev. Designer:** John Mercanti

Date	Mintage	MS65	Prf65
1995P	45,866	60.00	—
1995S	437,114	—	48.00

U.S. Capitol Bicentennial

KM# 253 • 26.73 g., 0.900 Silver 0.7734 oz. ASW, 38.1 mm. • **Obv.** Capitol dome, Statue fo Freedom surrounded by stars **Rev:** Eagle on shield, flags flanking **Obv. Designer:** William C. Cousins **Rev. Designer:** John Mercanti

Date	Mintage	MS65	Prf65
1994D	68,352	33.00	—
1994S	279,416	—	36.00

1996 Atlanta Paralympics - Blind runner

KM# 259 • 26.73 g., 0.900 Silver 0.7734 oz. ASW, 38.1 mm. • **Obv.** Blind runner **Rev:** Two clasped hands, Atlanta Olympic logo above **Obv. Designer:** Jim C. Sharpe and Thomas D. Rogers, Sr. **Rev. Designer:** William J. Krawczewicz and T. James Ferrell

Date	Mintage	MS65	Prf65
1995D	28,649	50.00	—
1995P	138,337	—	35.00

1996 Atlanta Olympics - Gymnastics

KM# 260 • 26.73 g., 0.900 Silver 0.7734 oz. ASW, 38.1 mm. • **Obv.** Two gymnasts, female on floor exercise and male on rings **Rev:** Two clasped hands, Atlanta Olympic logo above **Obv. Designer:** James C. Sharpe and Thomas D. Rogers, Sr. **Rev. Designer:** William J. Krawczewicz and T. James Ferrell

Date	Mintage	MS65	Prf65
1995D	42,497	35.00	—
1995P	182,676	—	28.00

1996 Atlanta Olympics - Track and field

KM# 264 • 26.73 g., 0.900 Silver 0.7734 oz. ASW, 38.1 mm. • **Obv.** Two runners on a track, one crossing finish line **Rev:** Two clasped hands, Atlanta Olympic logo above **Obv. Designer:** John Mercanti **Rev. Designer:** William J. Krawczewicz and T. James Ferrell

Date	Mintage	MS65	Prf65
1995D	24,796	55.00	—
1995P	136,935	—	30.00

1996 Atlanta Olympics - Cycling

KM# 263 • 26.73 g., 0.900 Silver 0.7734 oz. ASW, 38.1 mm. • **Obv.** Three cyclists approaching **Rev:** Two clasped hands, Atlanta Olympic logo above **Obv. Designer:** John Mercanti **Rev. Designer:** William J. Krawczewicz and T. James Ferrell

Date	Mintage	MS65	Prf65
1995D	19,662	100	—
1995P	118,795	—	35.00

Special Olympics World Games

KM# 266 • 26.73 g., 0.900 Silver 0.7734 oz. ASW, 38.1 mm. • **Obv.** Eunice Schriver head left; founder of the Special Olympics **Rev:** Special Olympics Logo on an award medal, rose, quote from Schriver **Obv. Designer:** Jamie Wyeth and T. James Ferrell **Rev. Designer:** Thomas D. Rogers, Sr.

Date	Mintage	MS65	Prf65
1995W	89,301	33.00	—
1995P	351,764	—	33.00

1996 Atlanta Paralympics - Wheelchair racer

KM# 268 • 26.73 g., 0.900 Silver 0.7734 oz. ASW, 38.1 mm. • **Obv.** Wheelchair racer approaching with uplifted arms **Rev:** Atlanta Olympics logo **Obv. Designer:** James C. Sharpe and Alfred F. Maletsky **Rev. Designer:** Thomas D. Rogers, Sr.

Date	Mintage	MS65	Prf65
1996D	14,497	165	—
1996P	84,280	—	50.00

1996 Atlanta Olympics - High Jump

KM# A272 • 26.73 g., 0.900 Silver 0.7734 oz. ASW **Obv.** High jumper **Obv. Designer:** T. James Ferrell **Rev. Designer:** Thomas D. Rogers, Sr.

Date	Mintage	MS65	Prf65
1996D	15,697	160	—
1996P	124,502	—	40.00

1996 Atlanta Olympics - Tennis

KM# 269 • 26.73 g., 0.900 Silver 0.7734 oz. ASW, 38.1 mm. • **Obv.** Female tennis player **Rev:** Atlanta Olympics logo **Obv. Designer:** James C. Sharpe and T. James Ferrell **Rev. Designer:** Thomas D. Rogers, Sr.

Date	Mintage	MS65	Prf65
1996D	15,983	140	—
1996P	92,016	—	60.00

1996 Atlanta Olympics - Rowing

KM# 272 • 26.73 g., 0.900 Silver 0.7734 oz. ASW, 38.1 mm. • **Obv.** Four man crew rowing left **Rev:** Atlanta Olympic logo **Obv. Designer:** Bart Forbes and T. James Ferrell **Rev. Designer:** Thomas D. Rogers, Sr.

Date	Mintage	MS65	Prf65
1996D	16,258	140	—
1996P	151,890	—	50.00

National Community Service

KM# 275 • 26.73 g., 0.900 Silver 0.7734 oz. ASW,
38.1 mm. • **Obv.** Female standing with lamp and
shield **Rev:** Legend within wreath **Obv. Designer:**
Thomas D. Rogers, Sr. **Rev. Designer:** William C.
Cousins

Date	Mintage	MS65	Prf65
1996S	101,543	—	34.00
1996S	23,500	106	—

U.S. Botanic Gardens 175th Anniversary

KM# 278 • 26.73 g., 0.900 Silver 0.7734 oz. ASW,
38.1 mm. • **Obv.** National Botanic Gardens
Conservatory building **Rev:** Rose **Obv. Designer:**
Edgar Z. Steever **Rev. Designer:** William C. Cousins

Date	Mintage	MS65	Prf65
1997P	57,272	26.00	—
1997P	264,528	—	40.00

Smithsonian Institution 150th Anniversary

KM# 276 • 26.73 g., 0.900 Silver 0.7734 oz. ASW,
38.1 mm. • **Obv.** Original Smithsonian building,
the "Castle" designed by James Renwick **Rev:**
Female seated with torch and scroll on globe **Obv.
Designer:** Thomas D. Rogers, Sr. **Rev. Designer:**
John Mercanti

Date	Mintage	MS65	Prf65
1996D	31,230	60.00	—
1996P	129,152	—	36.00

Jackie Robinson

KM# 279 • 26.73 g., 0.900 Silver 0.7734 oz. ASW,
38.1 mm. • **Obv.** Jackie Robinson sliding into
base **Rev:** Anniversary logo **Obv. Designer:** Alfred
Maletsky **Rev. Designer:** T. James Ferrell

Date	Mintage	MS65	Prf65
1997S	30,007	75.00	—
1997S	110,495	—	60.00

National Law Enforcement Officers Memorial

KM# 281 • 26.73 g., 0.900 Silver 0.7734 oz. ASW, 38.1 mm. • **Obv.** Male and female officer admiring name on monument **Rev:** Rose on a plain shield **Designer:** Alfred F. Maletsky

Date	Mintage	MS65	Prf65
1997P	28,575	110	—
1997P	110,428	—	60.00

Black Revolutionary War Patriots

KM# 288 • 26.73 g., 0.900 Silver 0.7734 oz. ASW, 38.1 mm. • **Obv.** Crispus Attucks bust right **Rev:** Family standing **Obv. Designer:** John Mercanti **Rev. Designer:** Edward Dwight and Thomas D. Rogers, Sr.

Date	Mintage	MS65	Prf65
1998S	37,210	80.00	—
1998S	75,070	—	52.00

Robert F. Kennedy

KM# 287 • 26.73 g., 0.900 Silver 0.7734 oz. ASW, 38.1 mm. • **Obv.** Kennedy bust facing **Rev:** Eagle on shield, Senate Seal **Obv. Designer:** Thomas D. Rogers, Sr. **Rev. Designer:** James M. Peed and Thomas D. Rogers, Sr.

Date	Mintage	MS65	Prf65
1998S	106,422	34.00	—
1998S	99,020	—	58.00

Dolley Madison

KM# 298 • 26.73 g., 0.900 Silver 0.7734 oz. ASW, 38.1 mm. • **Obv.** Madison bust right, at left **Rev:** Montpelier home **Obv. Designer:** Tiffany & Co. and T. James Ferrell **Rev. Designer:** Tiffany & Co. and Thomas D. Rogers, Sr.

Date	Mintage	MS65	Prf65
1999P	22,948	30.00	—
1999P	158,247	—	30.00

MODERN COMMEMORATIVE COINAGE 1982-PRESENT

Yellowstone

KM# 299 • 26.73 g., 0.900 Silver 0.7734 oz. ASW, 38.1 mm. • **Obv.** Old Faithful gyser erupting **Rev:** Bison and vista as on National Parks shield **Obv. Designer:** Edgar Z. Steever **Rev. Designer:** William C. Cousins

Date	Mintage	MS65	Prf65
1999P	82,563	43.00	—
1999P	187,595	—	43.00

Leif Ericson

KM# 313 • 26.73 g., 0.900 Silver 0.7734 oz. ASW **Obv.** Ericson bust helmeted right **Rev:** Viking ship sailing left **Obv. Designer:** John Mercanti **Rev. Designer:** T. James Ferrell

Date	Mintage	MS65	Prf65
2000P	28,150	67.00	—
2000P	58,612	—	50.00
2000 Iceland	15,947	—	20.00

Library of Congress Bicentennial

KM# 311 • 26.73 g., 0.900 Silver 0.7734 oz. ASW **Obv.** Open and closed book, torch in background **Rev:** Skylight dome above the main reading room **Obv. Designer:** Thomas D. Rogers, Sr. **Rev. Designer:** John Mercanti

Date	Mintage	MS65	Prf65
2000P	52,771	25.00	—
2000P	196,900	—	25.00

Capitol Visitor Center

KM# 324 • 26.73 g., 0.900 Silver 0.7734 oz. ASW **Obv.** Original and current Capital facades **Rev:** Eagle with shield and ribbon **Obv. Designer:** Marika Somogyi **Rev. Designer:** John Mercanti

Date	Mintage	MS65	Prf65
2001P	66,636	36.00	—
2001P	143,793	—	40.00

Native American - Bison

KM# 325 • 26.73 g., 0.900 Silver 0.7734 oz. ASW
Obv. Native American bust right **Rev:** Bison
standing left **Designer:** James E. Fraser

Date	Mintage	MS65	Prf65
2001D	197,131	—	133
2001P	272,869	150	—

2002 Winter Olympics - Salt Lake City

KM# 336 • 26.73 g., 0.900 Silver 0.7734 oz. ASW,
38.1 mm. • **Obv.** Salt Lake City Olympic logo **Rev:**
Stylized skyline with mountains in background
Obv. Designer: John Mercanti **Rev. Designer:**
Donna Weaver

Date	Mintage	MS65	Prf65
2002P	35,388	40.00	—
2002P	142,873	—	36.00

U.S. Military Academy at West Point -Bicentennial

KM# 338 • 26.73 g., 0.900 Silver 0.7734 oz. ASW,
38.1 mm. • **Obv.** Cadet Review flagbearers,
Academy buildings in background **Rev:** Academy
emblems - Corinthian helmet and sword **Obv.**
Designer: T. James Ferrell **Rev. Designer:** John
Mercanti

Date	Mintage	MS65	Prf65
2002W	103,201	25.00	—
2002W	288,293	—	37.50

First Flight Centennial

KM# 349 • 26.75 g., 0.900 Silver 0.774 oz. ASW,
38.1 mm. • **Obv.** Orville and Wilbur Wright busts
left **Rev:** Wright Flyer over dunes **Obv. Designer:**
T. James Ferrell **Rev. Designer:** Norman E. Nemeth
Edge: Reeded

Date	Mintage	MS65	Prf65
2003P	53,761	42.00	—
2003P	193,086	—	40.00

Thomas A. Edison - Electric Light 125th Anniversary

KM# 362 • 23.73 g., 0.900 Silver 0.6866 oz. ASW
Obv. Edison half-length figure facing holding light
bulb **Rev:** Light bulb and rays **Obv. Designer:**
Donna Weaver **Rev. Designer:** John Mercanti

Date	Mintage	MS65	Prf65
2004P	68,031	28.00	—
2004P	213,409	—	28.00

John Marshall, 250th Birth Anniversary

KM# 375 • 26.73 g., 0.900 Silver 0.7734 oz. ASW,
38.1 mm. • **Obv.** Marshall bust left **Rev:** Marshall
era Supreme Court Chamber **Obv. Designer:** John
Mercanti **Rev. Designer:** Donna Weaver

Date	Mintage	MS65	Prf65
2005P	48,953	35.00	—
2005P	141,993	—	30.00

Lewis and Clark Corps of Discovery Bicentennial

KM# 363 • 26.73 g., 0.900 Silver 0.7734 oz. ASW
Obv. Lewis and Clark standing **Rev:** Jefferson
era clasped hands peace medal **Designer:** Donna
Weaver

Date	Mintage	MS65	Prf65
2004P	90,323	28.00	—
2004P	288,492	—	28.00

U.S. Marine Corps, 230th Anniversary

KM# 376 • 26.73 g., 0.900 Silver 0.7734 oz. ASW,
38.1 mm. • **Obv.** Flag Raising at Mt. Suribachi
on Iwo Jima **Rev:** Marine Corps emblem **Obv.
Designer:** Norman E. Nemeth **Rev. Designer:**
Charles Vickers

Date	Mintage	MS65	Prf65
2005P	130,000	46.00	—
2005P	370,000	—	43.00

Benjamin Franklin, 300th Birth Anniversary

KM# 387 • 26.73 g., 0.900 Silver 0.7734 oz. ASW, 38.1 mm. • **Obv.** Youthful Franklin flying kite **Rev:** Revolutionary era "JOIN, or DIE" snake cartoon illustration **Obv. Designer:** Norman E. Nemeth **Rev. Designer:** Charles Vickers

Date	Mintage	MS65	Prf65
2006P	58,000	25.00	—
2006P	142,000	—	26.00

San Francisco Mint Museum

KM# 394 • 26.73 g., 0.900 Silver 0.7734 oz. ASW, 38.1 mm. • **Obv.** 3/4 view of building **Rev:** Reverse of 1880s Morgan silver dollar **Obv. Designer:** Sherl J. Winter **Rev. Designer:** George T. Morgan

Date	Mintage	MS65	Prf65
2006S	65,609	37.00	—
2006S	255,700	—	37.00

Benjamin Franklin, 300th Birth Anniversary

KM# 388 • 26.73 g., 0.900 Silver 0.7734 oz. ASW, 38.1 mm. • **Obv.** Bust 3/4 right, signature in oval below **Rev:** Continental Dollar of 1776 in center **Obv. Designer:** Don Everhart II **Rev. Designer:** Donna Weaver

Date	Mintage	MS65	Prf65
2006P	58,000	30.00	—
2006P	142,000	—	30.00

Jamestown - 400th Anniversary

KM# 405 • 26.73 g., 0.900 Silver 0.7734 oz. ASW, 38.1 mm. • **Obv.** Two settlers and Native American **Rev:** Three ships **Obv. Designer:** Donna Weaver and Don Everhart II **Rev. Designer:** Susan Gamble and Charles Vickers

Date	Mintage	MS65	Prf65
2007P	79,801	30.00	—
2007P	258,802	—	30.00

Central High School Desegregation

KM# 418 • 26.73 g., 0.900 Silver 0.7734 oz. ASW, 38.1 mm. • Obv. Children's feet walking left with adult feet in military boots Rev: Little Rock's Central High School Obv. Designer: Richard Masters and Charles Vickers Rev. Designer: Don Everhart II

Date	Mintage	MS65	Prf65
2007P	66,093	28.00	—
2007P	124,618	—	25.00

Lincoln Bicentennial

KM# 454 • 26.73 g., 0.900 Silver 0.7734 oz. ASW, 38.1 mm. • Obv. 3/4 portrait facing right Rev: Part of Gettysburg Address within wreath Obv. Designer: Justin Kunz and Don Everhart II Rev. Designer: Phebe Hemphill

Date	Mintage	MS65	Prf65
2009P	125,000	33.00	—
2009P	375,000	—	36.00

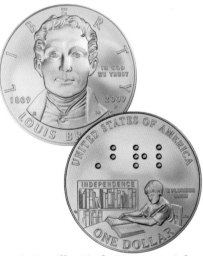

American Bald Eagle

KM# 439 • 26.73 g., 0.900 Silver 0.7734 oz. ASW, 38.1 mm. • Obv. Eagle with flight, mountain in background at right Rev: Great Seal of the United States Obv. Designer: Joel Iskowitz and Don Everhart II Rev. Designer: James Licaretz

Date	Mintage	MS65	Prf65
2008P	110,073	28.00	—
2008P	243,558	—	25.00

Louis Braille Birth Bicentennial

KM# 455 • 26.73 g., 0.900 Silver 0.7734 oz. ASW, 38.1 mm. • Obv. Louis Braille bust facing Rev: School child reading book in Braille, BRL in Braille code above Obv. Designer: Joel Iskowitz and Phebe Hemphill Rev. Designer: Susan Gamble and Joseph Menna

Date	Mintage	MS65	Prf65
2009P	82,639	27.00	—
2009P	135,235	—	25.00

MODERN COMMEMORATIVE COINAGE 1982-PRESENT

American Veterans Disabled for Life

KM# 479 • 0.900 Silver **Obv.** Soldier's feet, crutches **Rev:** Legend within wreath **Obv. Designer:** Don Everhart II **Rev. Designer:** Thomas Cleveland and Joseph Menna

Date	Mintage	MS65	Prf65
2010W	77,859	33.00	—
2010W	189,881	—	32.00

Medal of Honor

KM# 504 • 26.73 g., 0.900 Silver 0.7734 oz. ASW, 38.1 mm. • **Obv.** Medal of Honor designs for Army, Navy and Air Force awards **Rev:** Army infantry soldier carrying another to safety **Obv. Designer:** James Licaretz **Rev. Designer:** Richard Masters and Phebe Hemphill **Edge:** Reeded

Date	Mintage	MS65	Prf65
2011S	44,769	43.00	—
2011S	112,850	—	43.00

Boy Scouts of America, 100th Anniversary

KM# 480 • 0.900 Silver **Obv.** Cub Scout, Boy Scout and Venturer saluting **Rev:** Boy Scouts of America logo **Obv. Designer:** Donna Weaver **Rev. Designer:** Jim Licaretz

Date	Mintage	MS65	Prf65
2010P	105,020	28.00	—
2010P	244,963	—	30.00

U.S. Army

KM# 507 • 26.73 g., 0.900 Silver 0.7734 oz. ASW, 38.1 mm. • **Obv.** Male and female soldier heads looking outward **Rev:** Seven core values of the Army, Eagle from the great seal **Obv. Designer:** Richard Masters and Michael Gaudioso **Rev. Designer:** Susan Gamble and Don Everhart, II **Edge:** Reeded

Date	Mintage	MS65	Prf65
2011S	43,512	43.00	—
2011S	119,829	—	42.00

National Infantry Museum and Soldier Center

KM# 529 • 26.73 g., 0.900 Silver 0.7734 oz. ASW, 38.1 mm. • **Obv.** Infantry soldier advancing left **Rev:** Crossed rifles insignia **Obv. Designer:** Joel Iskowitz and Michael Gaudioso **Rev. Designer:** Ronald D. Sanders and Norman E. Nemeth

Date	Mintage	MS65	Prf65
2012	—	39.00	—
2012	—	—	46.00

Star-Spangled Banner

KM# 530 • 26.73 g., 0.900 Silver 0.7734 oz. ASW, 38.1 mm. • **Obv.** Liberty waving 15 star and stripe flag, Ft. McHenry in background **Rev:** Modern American Flag **Obv. Designer:** Joel Iskowitz and Phebe Hemphill **Rev. Designer:** William C Burgard III and Don Everhart

Date	Mintage	MS65	Prf65
2012	—	42.00	—
2012	—	—	42.00

Five-Star Generals - George C. Marshall and Dwight D. Eisenhower

KM# 553 • 26.73 g., 0.900 Silver 0.7734 oz. ASW, 38.1 mm. • **Obv.** Two busts facing, strips from flag in background **Rev:** Lamp from U.S. Army Command and General Staff College

Date	Mintage	MS65	Prf65
2013W	34,639	55.00	—
2013S	69,290	—	60.00

Girl Scouts of the USA, 100th Anniversary

KM# 552 • 26.73 g., 0.900 Silver 0.7734 oz. ASW, 38.1 mm. • **Obv.** Three busts right **Rev:** Trefoil logo

Date	Mintage	MS65	Prf65
2013W	37,461	37.00	—
2013W	86,353	—	43.00

Baseball Hall of Fame

KM# 577 • 26.73 g., 0.900 Silver 0.7734 oz. ASW **Obv.** Baseball glove **Rev:** Baseball

Date	Mintage	MS65	Prf65
2014P	131,924	55.00	—
2014P	268,076	—	63.00

Civil Rights Act of 1964

KM# 579 • 26.73 g., 0.900 Silver 0.7734 oz. ASW
Obv. Three Civil Rights marchers **Rev:** Torch

Date	Mintage	MS65	Prf65
2014P	—	50.00	—
2014P	—	—	66.00

Mark Twain

KM# 622 • 26.73 g., 0.900 Silver 0.7734 oz. ASW,
38.1 mm. • **Obv.** Twain with pipe, image in smoke
Rev: Book characters

Date	Mintage	MS65	Prf65
2016P	—	35.00	—
2016P	—	—	38.00

National Park Service

KM# 645 • 26.73 g., 0.900 Silver 0.7734 oz. ASW,
38.61 mm. • **Obv.** Yellowstone National Park's Old
Faithful geyers and Bison **Rev:** Latina Folk lorico
dancer and National Park Service Logo

Date	Mintage	MS65	Prf65
2016P	—	40.00	—
2016P Proof	—	—	37.00

March of Dimes - 60th Anniversary Salk Polio Vaccine

KM# 604 • 26.73 g., 0.900 Silver 0.7734 oz. ASW,
38.1 mm. • **Obv.** President Franklin D. Roosevelt
and Dr. Jonas Salk busts right **Rev:** Baby cradled in
hand **Edge:** Reeded

Date	Mintage	MS65	Prf65
2015P	22,606	40.00	—
2015W	124,671	—	55.00

Lions Club - 100th Anniversary

KM# 658 • 26.73 g., 0.900 Silver 0.7734 oz. ASW,
38.61 mm. • **Obv.** Melvin Jones with Lions Club
International Logo **Rev:** Male and female Lions with
cub superimposed over globe

Date	Mintage	MS65	Prf65
2017P	Est. 400000	35.00	—
2017P Proof	Inc. Ab.	—	38.00

MODERN COMMEMORATIVE COINAGE 1982-PRESENT

Boys Town - 100th Anniversary

KM# 660 • 26.73 g., 0.900 Silver 0.7734 oz. ASW, 38.61 mm. • **Obv.** Young girl gazing into the branches of an oak tree **Rev:** Oak tree offering shelter, family, including girl from obverse, holding hands below tree

Date	Mintage	MS65	Prf65
2017P	Est. 350000	33.00	—
2017P Proof	Inc. Ab.	—	35.00

Breast Cancer Awareness

KM# 681 • 26.73 g., 0.900 Silver 0.7734 oz. ASW, 38.61 mm. • **Obv.** Two women battling cancer, with breast cancer awareness ribbon in background and butterfly above **Rev:** Tiger Swallowtail butterfly

Date	Mintage	MS65	Prf65
2018P	Est. 400000	55.00	—
2018P Proof	Inc. Ab.	—	58.00

World War I Centennial

KM# 682 • 26.73 g., 0.900 Silver 0.7734 oz. ASW, 38.61 mm. • **Obv.** Soldier with rifle preparing to charge **Rev:** Poppies entangled with barbed wire

Date	Mintage	MS65	Prf65
2018P	Est. 350000	55.00	—
2018P Proof	Inc. Ab.	—	58.00

$5 (HALF EAGLE)

Statue of Liberty Centennial

KM# 215 • 8.36 g., 0.900 Gold 0.2419 oz. AGW, 21.6 mm. • **Obv.** Statue of Liberty head right **Rev:** Eagle in flight left **Designer:** Elizabeth Jones

Date	Mintage	MS65	Prf65
1986W	95,248	357	—
1986W	404,013	—	357

Constitution Bicentennial

KM# 221 • 8.36 g., 0.900 Gold 0.2419 oz. AGW, 21.6 mm. • **Obv.** Eagle left with quill pen in talon **Rev:** Upright quill pen **Designer:** Marcel Jovine

Date	Mintage	MS65	Prf65
1987W	214,225	357	—
1987W	651,659	—	357

1988 Olympics

KM# 223 • 8.36 g., 0.900 Gold 0.2419 oz. AGW, 21.6 mm. • **Obv.** Nike head wearing olive wreath **Rev:** Stylized Olympic cauldron **Obv. Designer:** Elizabeth Jones **Rev. Designer:** Marcel Jovine

Date	Mintage	MS65	Prf65
1988W	62,913	357	—
1988W	281,456	—	357

Congress Bicentennial

KM# 226 • 8.36 g., 0.900 Gold 0.2419 oz. AGW, 21.6 mm. • **Obv.** Capitol dome **Rev:** Eagle atop of the canopy from the Old Senate Chamber **Designer:** John Mercanti

Date	Mintage	MS65	Prf65
1989W	46,899	357	—
1989W	164,690	—	357

Mount Rushmore 50th Anniversary

KM# 230 • 8.36 g., 0.900 Gold 0.2419 oz. AGW, 21.6 mm. • **Obv.** Eagle in flight towards Mount Rushmore **Rev:** Legend at center **Obv. Designer:** John Mercanti **Rev. Designer:** Robert Lamb and William C. Cousins

Date	Mintage	MS65	Prf65
1991W	31,959	357	—
1991W	111,991	—	357

1992 Olympics

KM# 235 • 8.36 g., 0.900 Gold 0.2419 oz. AGW, 21.6 mm. • **Obv.** Sprinter, U.S. Flag in background **Rev:** Heraldic eagle, Olympic rings above **Obv. Designer:** James C. Sharpe and T. James Ferrell **Rev. Designer:** James M. Peed

Date	Mintage	MS65	Prf65
1992W	27,732	357	—
1992W	77,313	—	357

Columbus Quincentenary

KM# 239 • 8.36 g., 0.900 Gold 0.2419 oz. AGW, 21.6 mm. • **Obv.** Columbus' profile left, at right, map of Western Hemisphere at left **Rev:** Arms of Spain, and parchment map **Obv. Designer:** T. James Ferrell **Rev. Designer:** Thomas D. Rogers, Sr.

Date	Mintage	MS65	Prf65
1992W	24,329	357	—
1992W	79,730	—	357

James Madison - Bill of Rights

KM# 242 • 8.36 g., 0.900 Gold 0.2419 oz. AGW, 21.6 mm. • **Obv.** Madison at left holding document **Rev:** Eagle above legend, torch and laurel at sides **Obv. Designer:** Scott R. Blazek **Rev. Designer:** Joseph D. Peña

Date	Mintage	MS65	Prf65
1993W	22,266	357	—
1993W	78,651	—	357

World War II 50th Anniversary

KM# 245 • 8.36 g., 0.900 Gold 0.2419 oz. AGW, 21.6 mm. • **Obv.** Soldier with expression of victory **Rev:** Morse code dot-dot-dot-dash for V, large in background; V for Victory **Obv. Designer:** Charles J. Madsen and T. James Ferrell **Rev. Designer:** Edward S. Fisher and T. James Ferrell

Date	Mintage	MS65	Prf65
1993W	23,089	357	—
1993W	65,461	—	357

1994 World Cup Soccer

KM# 248 • 8.36 g., 0.900 Gold 0.2419 oz. AGW, 21.6 mm. • **Obv.** World Cup trophy **Rev:** World Cup 94 logo **Obv. Designer:** William J. Krawczewicz **Rev. Designer:** Dean McMullen

Date	Mintage	MS65	Prf65
1994W	22,464	357	—
1994W	89,619	—	357

MODERN COMMEMORATIVE COINAGE 1982-PRESENT

Civil War

KM# 256 • 8.36 g., 0.900 Gold 0.2419 oz. AGW, 21.6 mm. • **Obv.** Bugler on horseback right **Rev:** Eagle on shield **Designer:** Don Troiani and Alfred F. Maletsky

Date	Mintage	MS65	Prf65
1995W	55,246	—	357
1995W	12,735	357	—

1996 Olympics - Flag bearer

KM# 274 • 8.36 g., 0.900 Gold 0.2419 oz. AGW, 21.6 mm. • **Obv.** Flag bearer advancing **Rev:** Atlanta Olympic logo flanked by laurel **Obv. Designer:** Patricia Verani and John Mercanti **Rev. Designer:** William J. Krawczewicz and Thomas D. Rogers, Sr.

Date	Mintage	MS65	Prf65
1996W	9,174	400	—
1996W	32,886	—	357

1996 Olympics - Torch runner

KM# 261 • 8.36 g., 0.900 Gold 0.2419 oz. AGW, 21.6 mm. • **Obv.** Torch runner, Atlanta skyline and logo in background **Rev:** Eagle advancing right **Designer:** Frank Gasparro

Date	Mintage	MS65	Prf65
1995W	14,675	500	—
1995W	57,442	—	357

Smithsonian Institution 150th Anniversary

KM# 277 • 8.36 g., 0.900 Gold 0.2419 oz. AGW, 21.6 mm. • **Obv.** Smithson bust left **Rev:** Sunburst museum logo **Obv. Designer:** Alfred Maletsky **Rev. Designer:** T. James Ferrell

Date	Mintage	MS65	Prf65
1996W	9,068	357	—
1996W	29,474	—	357

1996 Olympics - Stadium

KM# 265 • 8.36 g., 0.900 Gold 0.2419 oz. AGW, 21.6 mm. • **Obv.** Atlanta Stadium and logo **Rev:** Eagle advancing right **Obv. Designer:** Marvel Jovine and William C. Cousins **Rev. Designer:** Frank Gasparro

Date	Mintage	MS65	Prf65
1995W	10,579	625	—
1995W	43,124	—	357

Jackie Robinson

KM# 280 • 8.36 g., 0.900 Gold 0.2419 oz. AGW, 21.6 mm. • **Obv.** Robinson head right **Rev:** Legend on baseball **Obv. Designer:** William C. Cousins **Rev. Designer:** James M. Peed

Date	Mintage	MS65	Prf65
1997W	5,202	1,100	—
1997W	24,072	—	400

1996 Olympics - Cauldron

KM# 270 • 8.36 g., 0.900 Gold 0.2419 oz. AGW, 21.6 mm. • **Obv.** Torch bearer lighting cauldron **Rev:** Atlanta Olympics logo flanked by laurel **Obv. Designer:** Frank Gasparro and T. James Ferrell **Rev. Designer:** William J. Krawczewicz and Thomas D. Rogers, Sr.

Date	Mintage	MS65	Prf65
1996W	9,210	800	—
1996W	38,555	—	357

Franklin Delano Roosevelt

KM# 282 • 8.36 g., 0.900 Gold 0.2419 oz. AGW, 21.6 mm. • **Obv.** Roosevelt bust right **Rev:** Eagle shield **Obv. Designer:** T. James Ferrell **Rev. Designer:** James M. Peed and Thomas D. Rogers, Sr.

Date	Mintage	MS65	Prf65
1997W	11,894	357	—
1997W	29,474	—	357

George Washington Death Bicentennial

KM# 300 • 8.36 g., 0.900 Gold 0.2419 oz. AGW, 21.6 mm. • **Obv.** Washington's head right **Rev:** Eagle with wings outstretched **Designer:** Laura G. Fraser

Date	Mintage	MS65	Prf65
1999W	22,511	357	—
1999W	41,693	—	357

Jamestown - 400th Anniversary

KM# 406 • 8.36 g., 0.900 Gold 0.2419 oz. AGW **Obv.** Settler and Native American **Rev:** Jamestown Memorial Church ruins **Obv. Designer:** John Mercanti **Rev. Designer:** Susan Gamble and Norman Nemeth

Date	Mintage	MS65	Prf65
2007W	18,843	357	—
2007W	47,050	—	357

Capitol Visitor Center

KM# 326 • 8.54 g., 0.900 Gold 0.2471 oz. AGW **Obv.** Column at right **Rev:** First Capital building **Designer:** Elizabeth Jones

Date	Mintage	MS65	Prf65
2001W	6,761	750	—
2001W	27,652	—	357

American Bald Eagle

KM# 440 • 8.36 g., 0.900 Gold 0.2419 oz. AGW, 21.6 mm. • **Obv.** Two eagles on branch **Rev:** Eagle with shield **Obv. Designer:** Susan Gamble and Phebe Hemphill **Rev. Designer:** Don Everhart II

Date	Mintage	MS65	Prf65
2008W	13,467	357	—
2008W	59,269	—	357

2002 Winter Olympics

KM# 337 • 8.36 g., 0.900 Gold 0.2419 oz. AGW, 21.6 mm. • **Obv.** Salt Lake City Olympics logo **Rev:** Stylized cauldron **Designer:** Donna Weaver

Date	Mintage	MS65	Prf65
2002W	10,585	357	—
2002W	32,877	—	357

Medal of Honor

KM# 505 • 8.36 g., 0.900 Gold 0.2419 oz. AGW, 21.1 mm. • **Obv.** 1861 Medal of Honor design for the Navy **Rev:** Minerva standing with shield and Union flag, field artillery cannon flanking **Obv. Designer:** Joseph Menna **Rev. Designer:** Joel Iskowitz and Michael Gaudioso **Edge:** Reeded

Date	Mintage	MS65	Prf65
2011S	18,012	—	357
2011S	8,251	425	—

San Francisco Mint Museum

KM# 395 • 8.36 g., 0.900 Gold 0.2419 oz. AGW **Obv.** Front entrance façade **Rev:** Eagle as on 1860s $5. Gold **Obv. Designer:** Charles Vickers and Joseph Menna **Rev. Designer:** Christian Gobrecht

Date	Mintage	MS65	Prf65
2006S	16,230	357	—
2006S	41,517	—	357

U.S. Army

KM# 508 • 8.36 g., 0.900 Gold 0.2419 oz. AGW, 21.1 mm. • **Obv.** Five Soldiers of different eras **Rev:** Elements from the Army's emblem **Obv. Designer:** Joel Iskowitz and Phebe Hemphill **Rev. Designer:** Joseph Menna **Edge:** Reeded

Date	Mintage	MS65	Prf65
2011P	8,062	357	—
2011W	17,173	—	357

MODERN COMMEMORATIVE COINAGE 1982-PRESENT

Star-Spangled Banner

KM# 531 • 8.36 g., 0.900 Gold 0.2419 oz. AGW, 21.1 mm. • **Obv.** Naval battle scene from the War of 1812. American ship in foreground, damaged British ship in background **Rev:** 15 stars and 15 stripes, opening words to the Star-Spangled Banner: O say can you see. **Obv. Designer:** Donna Weaver **Rev. Designer:** Joseph Menna

Date	Mintage	MS65	Prf65
2012	—	357	—
2012	—	—	357

Five-Star Generals - Douglas MacArthur

KM# 555 • 8.36 g., 0.900 Gold 0.2419 oz. AGW, 21.1 mm. • **Obv.** Head facing at left **Rev:** Lamp

Date	Mintage	MS65	Prf65
2013P	5,658	430	—
2013S	15,843	—	380

Baseball Hall of Fame

KM# 578 • 8.36 g., 0.900 Gold 0.2419 oz. AGW, 21.1 mm. • **Obv.** Baseball glove **Rev:** Baseball

Date	Mintage	MS65	Prf65
2014W	—	550	—
2014W	—	—	525

Mark Twain

KM# 626 • 8.36 g., 0.900 Gold 0.2419 oz. AGW, 21.6 mm. • **Obv.** Twain bust right **Rev:** Steamboat

Date	Mintage	MS65	Prf65
2016W	—	550	—
2016W	—	—	600

National Park Service

KM# 646 • 8.36 g., 0.900 Gold 0.2419 oz. AGW, 21.6 mm. • **Obv.** John Muir and Theodore Roosevelt with Yosemite National Park's Half Dome in background **Rev:** National Park Service Logo

Date	Mintage	MS65	Prf65
2016W	—	400	—
2016W	—	—	400

Boys Town - 100th Anniversary

KM# 661 • 8.36 g., 0.900 Gold 0.2419 oz. AGW, 21.6 mm. • **Obv.** Father Flanagan **Rev:** Outstretched hand holding young oak tree growing from acorn

Date	Mintage	MS65	Prf65
2017W	Est. 50000	—	—
2017W Proof	Inc. Ab.	—	—

Breast Cancer Awareness

KM# 683 • 7.93 g., 0.850 Gold 0.2167 oz. AGW, 21.6 mm. • **Obv.** Two women battling cancer, with breast cancer awareness ribbon in background and butterfly above **Rev:** Tiger Swallowtail butterfly

Date	Mintage	MS65	Prf65
2018W	Est. 50000	390	—
2018W Proof	Inc. Ab.	—	400

MODERN COMMEMORATIVE COINAGE 1982-PRESENT

$10 (EAGLE)

1984 Olympics

KM# 211 • 16.72 g., 0.900 Gold 0.4837 oz. AGW, 27 mm. • **Obv.** Male and female runner with torch **Rev:** Heraldic eagle **Obv. Designer:** James M. Peed and John Mercanti **Rev. Designer:** John Mercanti

Date	Mintage	MS65	Prf65
1984W	75,886	715	—
1984W	381,085	—	715
1984P	33,309	—	715
1984D	34,533	—	715
1984S	48,551	—	715

Library of Congress

KM# 312 • 16.26 g., Bi-Metallic, 48% platinum center in 48% gold ring **Obv.** Torch and partial facade **Rev:** Stylized eagle within laurel wreath **Obv. Designer:** John Mercanti **Rev. Designer:** Thomas D. Rogers, Sr.

Date	Mintage	MS65	Prf65
2000W	6,683	990	—
2000W	27,167	—	800

First Flight Centennial

KM# 350 • 16.72 g., 0.900 Gold 0.4837 oz. AGW **Obv.** Orville and Wilbur Wright busts facing **Rev:** Wright flyer and eagle **Obv. Designer:** Donna Weaver **Rev. Designer:** Norman Nemeth

Date	Mintage	MS65	Prf65
2003P	10,129	715	—
2003W	21,846	—	715

American Liberty Bullion Coinage

KM# 685 • 3.11 g., 0.9999 Gold 0.100 oz. AGW, 16.5 mm. • **Obv.** Lady Liberty with stars, date at right **Rev:** Eagle in flight **Edge:** Reeded

Date	Mintage	MS65	Prf65
2018W Proof	Est. 135000	—	200

$20 (DOUBLE EAGLE)

KM# 464 • 31.11 g., 0.999 Gold 0.999 oz. AGW, 27 mm. • **Obv.** Ultra high relief Liberty holding torch, walking forward **Rev:** Eagle in flight left, sunrise in background **Designer:** Augustus Saint-Gaudens

Date	Mintage	MS65	Prf65
2009	115,178	1,850	—

$100

American Liberty

KM# 617 • 31.10 g., 0.9999 Gold 0.9998 oz. AGW, 30.61 mm. • **Obv.** Modern Liberty **Rev:** Eagle **Edge:** Reeded

Date	Mintage	MS65	Prf65
2015W	1,829,517	1,550	—

225th Anniversary - United States Mint

KM# 668 • 31.10 g., 0.9999 Gold 0.9998 oz. AGW, 30.61 mm. • **Obv.** Lady Liberty with stars divides anniversary dates **Rev:** Eagle in flight **Edge:** Lettered

Date	Mintage	MS65	Prf65
2017W	—	1,550	—

AMERICA THE BEAUTIFUL SILVER BULLION

SILVER QUARTER

KM# 489 HOT SPRINGS NATIONAL PARK • 155.55 g., 0.999 Silver 4.996 oz. ASW **Rev:** Park Headquarters and fountain **Rev. Designer:** Don Everhart II and Joseph Menna

Date	Mintage	MS65	MS69
2010	33,000	248	360
2010P Vapor Blast finish	27,000	230	375

KM# 490 YELLOWSTONE NATIONAL PARK • 155.55 g., 0.999 Silver 4.996 oz. ASW **Rev:** Old Faithful geyser and bison **Rev. Designer:** Don Everhart II

Date	Mintage	MS65	MS69
2010	33,000	320	500
2010P Vapor Blast finish	27,000	240	325

KM# 491 YOSEMITE NATIONAL PARK • 155.55 g., 0.999 Silver 4.996 oz. ASW **Rev:** El Capitan, largest monolith of granite in the world **Rev. Designer:** Joseph Menna and Phebe Hemphill

Date	Mintage	MS65	MS69
2010	33,000	110	220
2010P Vapor blast finish	27,000	230	260

BULLION COINAGE

KM# 492 GRAND CANYON NATIONAL PARK
• 155.55 g., 0.999 Silver 4.996 oz. ASW **Rev:** Grabarues above the Nankoweap Delta in Marble Canyon near the Colorado River **Rev. Designer:** Phebe Hemphill

Date	Mintage	MS65	MS69
2010	33,000	180	220
2010P Vapor blast finish	26,019	230	325

KM# 513 GETTYSBURG NATIONAL MILITARY PARK
• 155.55 g., 0.999 Silver 4.996 oz. ASW **Rev:** 72nd Pennsylvania Infantry Monument on the battle line of the Union Army at Cemetery Ridge **Rev. Designer:** Joel Iskowitz and Phebe Hemphill

Date	Mintage	MS65	MS69
2011	126,700	138	180
2011P Vapor blast finish	24,625	200	240

KM# 493 MOUNT HOOD NATIONAL PARK
• 155.55 g., 0.999 Silver 4.996 oz. ASW **Rev:** Mt. Hood with Lost Lake in the foreground **Rev. Designer:** Phebe Hemphill

Date	Mintage	MS65	MS69
2010	33,000	248	305
2010P Vapor blast finish	25,318	210	260

KM# 514 GLACIER NATIONAL PARK
• 155.55 g., 0.999 Silver 4.996 oz. ASW **Rev:** Northeast slope of Mount Reynolds **Rev. Designer:** Barbara Fox and Charles L. Vickers

Date	Mintage	MS65	MS69
2011	126,700	122	235
2011P Vapor blast finish	20,503	205	240

KM# 515 OLYMPIC NATIONAL PARK • 155.55 g., 0.999 Silver 4.996 oz. ASW **Rev:** Roosevelt elk on a gravel river bar along the Hoh River, Mount Olympus in the background **Rev. Designer:** Susan Gambel and Michael Gaudioso

Date	Mintage	MS65	MS69
2011	85,900	85	150
2011P Vapor blast finish	17,988	200	240

KM# 517 CHICKASAW NATIONAL RECREATION AREA • 155.55 g., 0.999 Silver 4.996 oz. ASW **Rev:** Limestone Lincoln Bridge **Rev. Designer:** Donna Weaver and James Licaretz

Date	Mintage	MS65	MS69
2011	29,700	146	200
2011P Vapor blast finish	16,386	235	240

KM# 516 VICKSBURG NATIONAL MILITARY PARK • 155.55 g., 0.999 Silver 4.996 oz. ASW **Rev:** U.S.S. Cairo on the Yazoo River **Rev. Designer:** Thomas Cleveland and Joseph Menna

Date	Mintage	MS65	MS69
2011	39,500	147	210
2011P Vapor blast finish	18,181	225	240

KM# 536 EL YUNGUE NATIONAL FOREST • 155.55 g., 0.999 Silver 4.996 oz. ASW **Rev:** Coquin tree frog and Puerto Rico parrot

Date	Mintage	MS65	MS69
2012	21,900	224	350
2012P Vapor blast finish	15,271	240	290

BULLION COINAGE

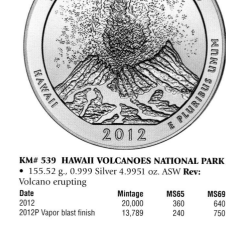

KM# 537 CHACO CULTURE NATIONAL HISTORIC PARK • 155.52 g., 0.999 Silver 4.9951 oz. ASW **Rev:** Two elevated kivas at Chetro Ketl complex

Date	Mintage	MS65	MS69
2012	20,000	185	445
2012P Vapor blast finish	12,679	230	240

KM# 539 HAWAII VOLCANOES NATIONAL PARK • 155.52 g., 0.999 Silver 4.9951 oz. ASW **Rev:** Volcano erupting

Date	Mintage	MS65	MS69
2012	20,000	360	640
2012P Vapor blast finish	13,789	240	750

KM# 538 ACADIA NATIONAL PARK • 155.52 g., 0.999 Silver 4.9951 oz. ASW **Rev:** Bass Harbor Head Lighthouse

Date	Mintage	MS65	MS69
2012	25,400	317	420
2012P Vapor blast finish	13,196	240	575

KM# 540 DENALI NATIONAL PARK • 155.55 g., 0.999 Silver 4.9961 oz. ASW **Rev:** Dall sheep and Mount McKinley

Date	Mintage	MS65	MS69
2012	20,000	255	330
2012P Vapor blast finish	10,180	240	360

BULLION COINAGE

KM# 556 WHITE MOUNTAIN NATIONAL FOREST • 155.55 g., 0.999 Silver 4.996 oz. ASW **Rev:** Mountain vista

Date	Mintage	MS65	MS69
2013	35,000	175	200
2013P Vapor blast finish	20,530	210	240

KM# 558 GREAT BASIN NATIONAL PARK • 155.55 g., 0.999 Silver 4.996 oz. ASW **Rev:** Ancient weatherworn tree

Date	Mintage	MS65	MS69
2013	30,000	138	190
2013P Vapor blast finish	17,792	165	260

KM# 557 PERRY'S VICTORY AND INTERNATIONAL PEACE MEMORIAL • 155.55 g., 0.999 Silver 4.996 oz. ASW **Rev:** Perry standing and Memorial column

Date	Mintage	MS65	MS69
2013	30,000	90	230
2013P Vapor blast finsih	17,707	165	240

KM# 559 FORT MCHENRY NATIONAL MONUMENT AND HISTORIC SITE • 155.55 g., 0.999 Silver 4.996 oz. ASW **Rev:** Fort McHenry and flag

Date	Mintage	MS65	MS69
2013	30,000	130	220
2013 Vapor blast finish	19,802	165	240

BULLION COINAGE

KM# 560 MT. RUSHMORE NATIONAL MEMORIAL • 155.55 g., 0.999 Silver 4.996 oz. ASW **Rev:** Presidential head sculpture on Mt. Rushmore

Date	Mintage	MS65	MS69
2013	35,000	110	230
2013P Vapor blast finish	23,547	165	260

KM# 581 SHENANDOAH NATIONAL PARK • 155.55 g., 0.999 Silver 4.996 oz. ASW **Rev:** Hiker overlooking scenic view

Date	Mintage	MS65	MS69
2014	—	152	165
2014P Vapor blast finish	—	165	240

KM# 580 GREAT SMOKEY MOUNTAINS NATIONAL PARK • 155.55 g., 0.999 Silver 4.996 oz. ASW **Rev:** Historic log cabin

Date	Mintage	MS65	MS69
2014	29,500	190	200
2014P Vapor blast finish	24,705	165	240

KM# 582 ARCHES NATIONAL PARK • 155.55 g., 0.999 Silver 4.996 oz. ASW **Rev:** Famed Delicate Arch

Date	Mintage	MS65	MS69
2014	—	165	175
2014P Vapor blast finish	—	165	240

BULLION COINAGE

KM# 583 GREAT SAND DUNES NATIONAL PARK
• 155.55 g., 0.999 Silver 4.996 oz. ASW **Rev:** Father
and son playing in sand by the creek

Date	Mintage	MS65	MS69
2014	—	130	160
2014P Vapor blast finish	—	165	240

KM# 630 HOMESTEAD NATIONAL MONUMENT OF AMERICA • 155.55 g., 0.999 Silver 4.996 oz. ASW **Rev:** Homestead scene with water pump and corn ears

Date	Mintage	MS65	MS69
2015	35,000	145	180
2015P Vapor blast finish	19,357	190	240

KM# 584 EVERGLADES NATIONAL PARK •
155.55 g., 0.999 Silver 4.996 oz. ASW **Rev:** Bird
with outstretched wings right; bird in water left

Date	Mintage	MS65	MS69
2014	—	137	160
2014P Vapor blast finish	—	165	240

KM# 631 KISATCHIE NATIONAL FOREST •
155.55 g., 0.999 Silver 4.996 oz. ASW **Rev:** Wild
turkey in flight

Date	Mintage	MS65	MS69
2015	42,000	130	275
2015P Vapor blast finish	17,477	190	240

BULLION COINAGE

KM# 632 BLUE RIDGE PARKWAY • 155.50 g., 0.999 Silver 4.9944 oz. ASW **Rev:** Road along side of mountain with flowers

Date	Mintage	MS65	MS69
2015	45,000	133	230
2015P Vapor blast finish	16,000	190	240

KM# 634 SARATOGA NATIONAL HISTORICAL PARK • 155.50 g., 0.999 Silver 4.9944 oz. ASW **Rev:** Military surrender of sword

Date	Mintage	MS65	MS69
2015	45,000	125	190
2015P Vapor blast finish	17,563	190	240

KM# 633 BOMBAY HOOK NATIONAL WILDLIFE REFUGE • 155.50 g., 0.999 Silver 4.9944 oz. ASW **Rev:** Heron in foreground and Egret in background

Date	Mintage	MS65	MS69
2015	45,000	115	260
2015P Vapor blast finish	17,309	190	240

KM# 647 SHAWNEE NATIONAL FOREST • 155.50 g., 0.999 Silver 4.9944 oz. ASW, 76.2 mm. • **Rev:** Camel Rock with vegetation and flying hawk

Date	Mintage	MS65	MS69
2016	—	145	170
2016P Vapor blast finish	—	190	240

BULLION COINAGE

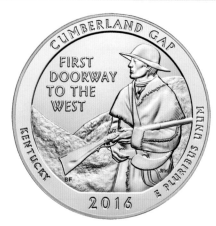

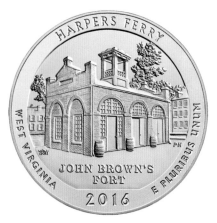

KM# 648 CUMBERLAND GAP NATIONAL HISTORICAL PARK • 155.50 g., 0.999 Silver 4.9944 oz. ASW, 76.2 mm. • **Rev:** Frontiersman looking at mountains

Date	Mintage	MS65	MS69
2016	—	120	160
2016P Vapor blast finish	—	190	240

KM# 650 THEODORE ROOSEVELT NATIONAL PARK • 155.50 g., 0.999 Silver 4.9944 oz. ASW, 76.2 mm. • **Rev:** Theodore Roosevelt on horseback overlooking river

Date	Mintage	MS65	MS69
2016	—	125	170
2016P Vapor blast finish	—	190	240

KM# 649 HARPERS FERRY NATIONAL HISTORICAL PARK • 155.50 g., 0.999 Silver 4.9944 oz. ASW, 76.2 mm. • **Rev:** John Brown's Fort building with barrels along side

Date	Mintage	MS65	MS69
2016	—	125	155
2016P Vapor blast finish	—	190	240

KM# 651 FORT MOULTRIE (FORT SUMTER) NATIONAL MONUMENT • 155.50 g., 0.999 Silver 4.9944 oz. ASW, 76.2 mm. • **Rev:** Soldier carrying flag in foreground with ships in background

Date	Mintage	MS65	MS69
2016	—	118	170
2016P Vapor blast finish	—	190	240

BULLION COINAGE

KM# 662 EFFIGY MOUNDS NATIONAL MONUMENT • 155.50 g., 0.999 Silver 4.9944 oz. ASW, 76.2 mm. • **Rev:** Three animal-shaped effigy mounds.

Date	Mintage	MS65	MS69
2017	—	115	183
2017P Vapor blast finish	—	175	225

KM# 664 OZARK NATIONAL SCENIC RIVERWAYS • 155.50 g., 0.999 Silver 4.9944 oz. ASW, 76.2 mm. • **Rev:** Building with dam next to river.

Date	Mintage	MS65	MS69
2017	—	145	165
2017P Vapor blast finish	—	175	225

KM# 663 FREDERICK DOUGLASS NATIONAL HISTORIC SITE • 155.50 g., 0.999 Silver 4.9944 oz. ASW, 76.2 mm. • **Rev:** Frederick Douglass holding pen poised to write with house in the background.

Date	Mintage	MS65	MS69
2017	—	90	185
2017P Vapor blast finish	—	175	225

KM# 665 ELLIS ISLAND (STATUE OF LIBERTY NATIONAL MONUMENT) • 155.50 g., 0.999 Silver 4.9944 oz. ASW, 76.2 mm. • **Rev:** Immigrants including boy holding flag in foreground; building in background.

Date	Mintage	MS65	MS69
2017	—	112	300
2017P Vapor blast finish	—	175	225

BULLION COINAGE

BULLION COINAGE

KM# 666 GEORGE ROGERS CLARK NATIONAL HISTORICAL PARK • 155.50 g., 0.999 Silver 4.9944 oz. ASW, 76.2 mm. • **Rev:** Three men holding guns.

Date	Mintage	MS65	MS69
2017	—	120	190
2017P Vapor blast finish	—	175	225

KM# 675 APOSTLE ISLANDS NATIONAL LAKESHORE • 155.50 g., 0.999 Silver 4.9944 oz. ASW, 76.2 mm. •

Date	Mintage	MS65	MS69
2018P	—	130	155
2018P Vapor blast finish	—	175	225

KM# 674 PICTURED ROCKS NATIONAL LAKESHORE • 155.50 g., 0.999 Silver 4.9944 oz. ASW, 76.2 mm. •

Date	Mintage	MS65	MS69
2018P	—	135	190
2018P Vapor blast finish	—	175	225

KM# 676 VOYAGEURS NATIONAL PARK • 155.50 g., 0.999 Silver 4.9944 oz. ASW, 76.2 mm. •

Date	Mintage	MS65	MS69
2018P	—	165	173
2018P Vapor blast finish	—	175	225

KM# 677 CUMBERLAND ISLAND NATIONAL SEASHORE • 155.50 g., 0.999 Silver 4.9944 oz. ASW, 76.2 mm. •

Date	Mintage	MS65	MS69
2018P	—	140	190
2018P Vapor blast finish	—	175	225

KM# 678 BLOCK ISLAND NATIONAL WILDLIFE REFUGE • 155.50 g., 0.999 Silver 4.9944 oz. ASW, 76.2 mm. •

Date	Mintage	MS65	MS69
2018P	—	110	173
2018P Vapor blast finish	—	175	225

AMERICAN EAGLE GOLD BULLION COINS

GOLD $5

KM# 216 • 3.39 g., 0.9167 Gold 0.100 oz. AGW, 16.5 mm. • **Obv. Designer:** Augustus Saint-Gaudens **Rev. Designer:** Miley Busiek

Date	Mintage	MS65	PF65
MCMLXXXVI 1986	912,609	153	—
MCMLXXXVII 1987	580,266	153	—
MCMLXXXVIII 1988	159,500	153	—
MCMLXXXVIII (1988)P	143,881	—	145
MCMLXXXIX 1989	264,790	153	—
MCMLXXXIX (1989)P	84,647	—	145
MCMXC 1990	210,210	153	—
MCMXC (1990)P	99,349	—	145
MCMXCI 1991	165,200	153	—
MCMXCI (1991)P	70,334	—	145
1992	209,300	153	—
1992P	64,874	—	145
1993	210,709	158	—
1993P	45,960	—	145
1994W	206,380	153	—
1994	62,849	—	145
1995	223,025	153	—
1995W	62,667	—	145
1996	401,964	158	—
1996W	57,047	—	145
1997	528,515	153	—
1997W	34,977	—	145
1998	1,344,520	153	—
1998W	39,395	—	145
1999W	2,750,338	153	—
1999W	48,428	—	145
1999 Unfinished Proof die	Est. 6000	700	—

Note: The 1999 W issues are standard matte finished gold that were struck with unfinished proof dies.

Date	Mintage	MS65	PF65
2000W	569,153	153	—
2000	49,971	—	145
2001	269,147	153	—
2001W	37,530	—	145
2002	230,027	153	—
2002W	40,864	—	145
2003W	245,029	153	—
2003	40,027	—	145
2004W	250,016	153	—
2004	35,131	—	145
2005W	300,043	153	—
2005	49,265	—	145
2006W	285,006	153	—
2006 Burnished Unc.	20,643	168	—
2006W	47,277	—	145
2007	190,010	153	—
2007W Burnished Unc.	22,501	173	—
2007W	58,553	—	145
2008W	305,000	153	—
2008 Burnished Unc.	12,657	340	—
2008W	Est. 29000	—	145
2009	27,000	153	—
2010	435,000	153	—
2010W	54,285	—	145
2011	350,000	153	—
2011W	42,697	—	145
2012W	315,000	153	—
2012W	20,740	—	145
2013W	535,000	153	—
2013	21,879	—	145
2014	565,000	153	—
2014	22,725	—	145
2015	980,000	153	—
2015	17,444	—	145
2016	—	153	—
2016W	—	—	145
2017	—	153	—
2017	—	—	145
2018	—	153	—
2018	—	—	145

BULLION COINAGE

GOLD $10

KM# 217 • 8.48 g., 0.9167 Gold 0.250 oz. AGW, 22 mm. • **Obv. Designer:** Augustus Saint-Gaudens **Rev. Designer:** Miley Busiek

Date	Mintage	MS65	PF65
MCMLXXXVI 1986	726,031	372	—
MCMLXXXVII 1987	269,255	472	—
MCMLXXXVIII 1988	49,000	—	377
MCMLXXXVIII (1988)P	98,028	657	—
MCMLXXXIX 1989	81,789	657	—
MCMLXXXIX (1989)P	54,170	—	377
MCMXC 1990	41,000	—	377
MCMXC (1990)P	62,674	792	—
MCMXCI 1991	36,100	—	377
MCMXCI (1991)P	50,839	832	—
1992	59,546	—	377
1992P	46,269	592	—
1993	71,864	592	—
1993P	33,775	—	377
1994	72,650	592	—
1994W	47,172	—	377
1995	83,752	592	—
1995W	47,526	—	377
1996	60,318	592	—
1996W	38,219	—	377
1997	108,805	—	377
1997W	29,805	387	—
1998	309,829	—	377
1998W	29,503	387	—
1999	564,232	387	—
1999W	34,417	—	377
1999W Unfinished Proof die	Est. 6000	1,325	—

Note: The 1999 W issues are standard matte finished gold that were struck with unfinished proof dies.

Date	Mintage	MS65	PF65
2000	128,964	387	—
2000W	36,036	—	377
2001	71,280	—	377
2001W	25,613	592	—
2002	62,027	—	377
2002W	29,242	592	—
2003	74,029	387	—
2003W	30,292	—	377
2004	72,014	—	377
2004W	28,839	387	—
2005	72,015	387	—
2005W	37,207	—	377
2006	60,004	387	—
2006W Burnished Unc.	15,188	610	—
2006W	36,127	—	377
2007	34,004	592	—
2007W Burnished Unc.	12,786	660	—
2007W	46,189	—	377
2008	Est. 58000	387	—
2008W Burnished Unc.	8,883	1,450	—
2008W	28,000	421	—
2009	110,000	387	—
2010	86,000	387	—
2010W	44,507	—	377
2011	80,000	—	377
2011W	28,782	387	—
2012	76,000	387	—
2012W	13,375	—	377
2013	122,000	387	—
2013W	12,642	—	377
2014	118,000	387	—
2014W	14,790	—	377

Date	Mintage	MS65	PF65
2015	158,000	387	—
2015W	11,437	—	377
2016	—	387	—
2016W	—	—	377
2017	—	387	—
2017W	—	—	377
2018	—	387	—
2018W	—	—	377

GOLD $25

KM# 218 • 16.97 g., 0.9167 Gold 0.500 oz. AGW, 27 mm. • **Obv. Designer:** Augustus Saint-Gaudens **Rev. Designer:** Miley Busiek

Date	Mintage	MS65	PF65
MCMLXXXVI 1986	599,566	689	—
MCMLXXXVII 1987	131,255	—	684
MCMLXXXVII (1987)P	143,398	899	—
MCMLXXXVIII 1988	45,000	—	684
MCMLXXXVIII (1988)P	76,528	1,399	—
MCMLXXXIX 1989	44,829	1,550	—
MCMLXXXIX (1989)P	44,798	—	684
MCMXC 1990	31,000	1,700	—
MCMXC (1990)P	51,636	—	684
MCMXCI 1991	24,100	—	684
MCMXCI (1991)P	53,125	2,650	—
1992	54,404	—	684
1992P	40,976	724	—
1993	73,324	—	684
1993P	31,130	724	—
1994	62,400	—	684
1994W	44,584	704	—
1995	53,474	—	684
1995W	45,388	1,100	—
1996	39,287	1,000	—
1996W	35,058	—	684
1997	79,605	—	684
1997W	26,344	724	—
1998	169,029	—	684
1998W	25,374	689	—
1999	263,013	689	—
1999W	30,427	—	684
2000	79,287	699	—
2000W	32,028	—	684
2001	48,047	—	684
2001W	23,240	699	—
2002	70,027	699	—
2002W	26,646	—	684
2003	79,029	—	684
2003W	28,270	689	—
2004	98,040	689	—
2004W	27,330	—	684
2005	80,023	—	684
2005W	34,311	689	—
2006	66,004	—	684
2006W Burnished Unc.	15,164	960	—
2006W	34,322	699	—
2007	47,002	699	—
2007W Burnished Unc.	11,458	1,075	—
2007W	44,025	—	684
2008	61,000	689	—
2008W Burnished Unc.	15,683	1,050	—
2008W	27,800	—	684
2009	55,000	689	—
2010	81,000	689	—

Date	Mintage	MS65	PF65
2010W	44,527	—	684
2011	70,000	689	—
2011W	26,781	—	684
2012	71,000	689	—
2012W	12,809	—	684
2013	58,000	689	—
2013W	12,570	—	684
2014	46,000	925	—
2014W	14,693	—	684
2015	75,000	689	—
2015W	9,989	—	684
2016	—	704	—
2016W	—	—	684
2017	—	689	—
2017W	—	—	684
2018	—	689	—
2018W	—	—	684

GOLD $50

Date	Mintage	MS65	PF65
1993W	480,192	1,379	—
1993	34,369	—	1,374
1994W	221,663	1,379	—
1994	46,674	—	1,374
1995W	200,636	1,379	—
1995	46,368	—	1,374
1995W 10th Anniversary	30,125	—	—
1996W	189,148	1,379	—
1996	36,153	—	1,374
1997	664,508	1,379	—
1997W	28,034	—	1,374
1998	1,468,530	1,379	—
1998W	25,886	—	1,374
1999	1,505,026	1,379	—
1999W	31,427	—	1,374
2000	433,319	1,379	—
2000W	33,007	—	1,374
2001	143,605	1,379	—
2001W	24,555	—	1,374
2002	222,029	1,379	—
2002W	27,499	—	1,374
2003	416,032	1,379	—
2003W	28,344	—	1,374
2004	417,149	1,379	—
2004W	28,215	—	1,374
2005W	356,555	1,379	—
2005	35,246	—	1,374
2006	237,510	1,379	—
2006W Burnished Unc.	45,912	1,450	—
2006W	47,000	—	1,374
2006W Reverse Proof	10,000	—	2,600
2007W	140,016	1,379	—
2007W Burnished Unc.	18,609	1,500	—
2007	51,810	—	1,374
2008W	710,000	1,379	—
2008W Burnished Unc.	11,908	2,350	—
2008W Reverse of '07	Est. 47000	—	—
2008W	29,000	—	1,374
2009	122,000	1,379	—
2010W	1,125,000	1,379	—
2010	59,480	—	1,374
2011	857,000	1,379	—
2011 Burnished Unc.	8,729	1,500	—
2011W	48,306	—	1,374
2012W	—	1,379	—
2012 Burnished Unc.	5,829	1,875	—
2013	—	—	1,374
2013W	24,753	1,379	—
2014	—	—	1,374
2014	—	1,379	—
2015	626,500	1,379	—
2015	—	—	1,374
2016	—	1,379	—
2016W	—	—	1,374
2017	—	1,379	—
2017W	—	—	1,374
2018	—	1,379	—
2018W	—	—	1,374

KM# 219 • 33.93 g., 0.9167 Gold 1.000 oz. AGW, 32.7 mm. • **Obv. Designer:** Augustus Saint-Gaudens **Rev. Designer:** Miley Busiek

Date	Mintage	MS65	PF65
MCMLXXXVI (1986)W	446,290	—	1,374
MCMLXXXVI -1986	1,362,650	1,379	—
MCMLXXXVII (1987)W	147,498	—	1,374
MCMLXXXVII -1987	1,045,500	1,379	—
MCMLXXXVIII (1988)W	87,133	—	1,374
MCMLXXXVIII -1988	465,000	1,379	—
MCMLXXXIX (1989)W	54,570	—	1,374
MCMLXXXIX -1989	415,790	1,379	—
MCMXC (1990)W	62,401	—	1,374
MCMXC -1990	373,219	1,379	—
MCMXCI (1991)W	50,411	—	1,374
MCMXCI -1991	243,100	1,399	—
1992W	275,000	1,379	—
1992	44,826	—	1,374

BULLION COINAGE

AMERICAN EAGLE BULLION COINAGE

PALLADIUM $25

KM# 667 • 31.11 g., 0.9995 Palladium 0.9995 oz. APW, 33 mm. • **Obv.** Winged Liberty Mercury Dime style in high relief **Rev:** Standing Eagle from Weinman's 1907 AIA Gold Medal **Designer:** Adolph A. Weinman

Date	Mintage	MS65	PF65
2017	—	289	—

PLATINUM $10

KM# 283 • 3.11 g., 0.9995 Platinum 0.0999 oz. APW, 17 mm. • **Rev:** Eagle flying right over sunrise **Obv. Designer:** John Mercanti **Rev. Designer:** Thomas D. Rogers Sr

Date	Mintage	MS65	PF65
1997	70,250	135	—
1997W	36,996	—	117
1998	39,525	135	—
1999	55,955	135	—
2000	34,027	135	—
2001	52,017	135	—
2002	23,005	135	—
2003	22,007	135	—
2004	15,010	135	—
2005	14,013	135	—
2006	11,001	135	—
2006W Burnished Unc.	3,544	300	—
2007	13,003	135	—
2007W Burnished Unc.	5,566	135	—
2008	17,000	135	—
2008 Burnished Unc.	3,706	180	—

KM# 301 • 3.11 g., 0.9995 Platinum 0.0999 oz. APW, 17 mm. • **Rev:** Eagle in flight over Southeastern Wetlands **Obv. Designer:** John Mercanti

Date	Mintage	MS65	PF65
1999W	19,133	—	117

KM# 314 • 3.11 g., 0.9995 Platinum 0.0999 oz. APW, 17 mm. • **Rev:** Eagle in flight over Heartland **Obv. Designer:** John Mercanti

Date	Mintage	MS65	PF65
2000W	15,651	—	117

KM# 289 • 3.11 g., 0.9995 Platinum 0.0999 oz. APW, 17 mm. • **Rev:** Eagle in flight over New England costal lighthouse **Obv. Designer:** John Mercanti

Date	Mintage	MS65	PF65
1998W	19,847	—	117

KM# 327 • 3.11 g., 0.9995 Platinum 0.0999 oz. APW, 17 mm. • **Rev:** Eagle in flight over Southwestern cactus desert **Obv. Designer:** John Mercanti

Date	Mintage	MS65	PF65
2001W	12,174	—	110

KM# 339 • 3.11 g., 0.9995 Platinum 0.0999 oz. APW, 17 mm. • **Rev:** Eagle fishing in America's Northwest **Obv. Designer:** John Mercanti

Date	Mintage	MS65	PF65
2002W	12,365	—	110

BULLION COINAGE

KM# 351 PATROTIC VIGILANCE • 3.11 g., 0.9995 Platinum 0.0999 oz. APW, 17 mm. • **Rev:** Eagle pearched on a Rocky Mountain Pine branch against a flag backdrop **Obv. Designer:** John Mercanti **Rev. Designer:** Al Maletsky

Date	Mintage	MS65	PF65
2003W	9,534	—	117

KM# 434 JUDICIAL • 3.11 g., 0.9995 Platinum 0.0999 oz. APW, 17 mm. • **Rev:** Justice standing before eagle **Obv. Designer:** John Mercanti

Date	Mintage	MS65	PF65
2008W	8,176	—	495

PLATINUM $25

KM# 364 • 3.11 g., 0.9995 Platinum 0.0999 oz. APW, 17 mm. • **Rev:** Chester French, 1907. The sculpture is outside the N.Y. Customs House, now part of the Smithsonian's Museum of the American Indian **Obv. Designer:** John Mercanti

Date	Mintage	MS65	PF65
2004W	7,161	—	445

KM# 284 • 7.79 g., 0.9995 Platinum 0.2502 oz. APW, 22 mm. • **Rev:** Eagle in flight over sunrise **Obv. Designer:** John Mercanti **Rev. Designer:** Thomas D. Rogers Sr

Date	Mintage	MS65	PF65
1997	27,100	289	—
1997W	18,628	—	294
1998	38,887	289	—
1999	39,734	289	—
2000	20,054	289	—
2001	21,815	289	—
2002	27,405	289	—
2003	25,207	289	—
2004	18,010	289	—
2005	12,013	289	—
2006	12,001	289	—
2006W Burnished Unc.	2,676	475	—
2007	8,402	289	—
2007W Burnished Unc.	3,690	550	—
2008	20,800	289	—
2008 Burnished Unc.	2,481	425	—

KM# 377 • 3.11 g., 0.9995 Platinum 0.0999 oz. APW, 17 mm. • **Rev:** Eagle with cornucopiae **Obv. Designer:** John Mercanti **Rev. Designer:** Donna Weaver

Date	Mintage	MS65	PF65
2005W	8,104	—	265

KM# 389 LEGISLATIVE • 3.11 g., 0.9995 Platinum 0.0999 oz. APW, 17 mm. • **Rev:** Liberty seated writing between two columns **Obv. Designer:** John Mercanti

Date	Mintage	MS65	PF65
2006W	10,205	—	180

KM# 290 • 7.79 g., 0.9995 Platinum 0.2502 oz. APW, 22 mm. • **Rev:** Eagle in flight over New England costal lighthouse **Obv. Designer:** John Mercanti

Date	Mintage	MS65	PF65
1998W	14,873	—	294

KM# 414 EXECUTIVE BRANCH • 3.11 g., 0.9995 Platinum 0.0999 oz. APW, 17 mm. • **Rev:** Eagle with shield **Obv. Designer:** John Mercanti

Date	Mintage	MS65	PF65
2007W	8,176	—	180

KM# 302 • 7.79 g., 0.9995 Platinum 0.2502 oz. APW, 22 mm. • **Rev:** Eagle in flight over Southeastern Wetlands **Obv. Designer:** John Mercanti

Date	Mintage	MS65	PF65
1999W	13,507	—	294

KM# 315 • 7.79 g., 0.9995 Platinum 0.2502 oz. APW, 22 mm. • **Rev:** Eagle in flight over Heartland **Obv. Designer:** John Mercanti

Date	Mintage	MS65	PF65
2000W	11,995	—	294

KM# 328 • 7.79 g., 0.9995 Platinum 0.2502 oz. APW, 22 mm. • **Rev:** Eagle in flight over Southwestern cactus desert **Obv. Designer:** John Mercanti

Date	Mintage	MS65	PF65
2001W	8,847	—	368

KM# 340 • 7.79 g., 0.9995 Platinum 0.2502 oz. APW, 22 mm. • **Rev:** Eagle fishing in America's Northwest **Obv. Designer:** John Mercanti

Date	Mintage	MS65	PF65
2002W	9,282	—	368

KM# 352 PATROTIC VIGILANCE • 7.79 g., 0.9995 Platinum 0.2502 oz. APW, 22 mm. • **Rev:** Eagle perched on a Rocky Mountain Pine branch against a flag backdrop. **Obv. Designer:** John Mercanti **Rev. Designer:** Al Maletsky

Date	Mintage	MS65	PF65
2003W	7,044	—	294

KM# 365 • 7.79 g., 0.9995 Platinum 0.2502 oz. APW, 22 mm. • **Rev:** Chester French, 1907. The sculpture is outside the N.Y. Customs House, now part of the Smithsonian's Museum of the American Indian **Obv. Designer:** John Mercanti

Date	Mintage	MS65	PF65
2004W	5,193	—	1,000

KM# 378 • 7.79 g., 0.9995 Platinum 0.2502 oz. APW, 22 mm. • **Rev:** Eagle with cornucopiae **Obv. Designer:** John Mercanti **Rev. Designer:** Donna Weaver

Date	Mintage	MS65	PF65
2005W	6,592	—	610

KM# 390 LEGISLATIVE • 7.79 g., 0.9995 Platinum 0.2502 oz. APW, 22 mm. • **Rev:** Liberty seated writing between two columns **Obv. Designer:** John Mercanti

Date	Mintage	MS65	PF65
2006W	7,813	—	368

KM# 415 EXECUTIVE • 7.79 g., 0.9995 Platinum 0.2502 oz. APW, 22 mm. • **Rev:** Eagle with shield **Obv. Designer:** John Mercanti

Date	Mintage	MS65	PF65
2007W Polished Freedom	6,017	—	368
2007W Frosted Freedom, Rare	21	—	—

KM# 435 JUDICIAL • 7.79 g., 0.9995 Platinum 0.2502 oz. APW, 22 mm. • **Rev:** Justice holding scales, standing before eagle **Obv. Designer:** John Mercanti

Date	Mintage	MS65	PF65
2008W	6,017	—	715

BULLION COINAGE

PLATINUM $50

KM# 285 • 15.55 g., 0.9995 Platinum 0.4998 oz. APW, 27 mm. • **Rev:** Eagle flying right over sunrise **Obv. Designer:** John Mercanti **Rev. Designer:** Thomas D. Rogers Sr

Date	Mintage	MS65	PF65
1997W	20,500	522	—
1997	15,432	—	562
1998	32,419	522	562
1999	32,309	522	562
2000	18,892	522	562
2001	12,815	522	562
2002	24,005	522	562
2003	17,409	522	562
2004	13,236	522	1,225
2005	9,013	522	—
2006W	9,602	522	—
2006 Burnished Unc.	—	700	—
2007W	7,001	522	—
2007 Burnished Unc.	—	650	—
2008	14,000	522	—
2008W Burnished Unc.	—	850	—

KM# 316 • 15.55 g., 0.9995 Platinum 0.4998 oz. APW, 27 mm. • **Rev:** Eagle in flight over Heartland **Obv. Designer:** John Mercanti

Date	Mintage	MS65	PF65
2000W	11,049	—	562

KM# 329 • 15.55 g., 0.9995 Platinum 0.4998 oz. APW, 27 mm. • **Rev:** Eagle in flight over Southwestern cactus desert **Obv. Designer:** John Mercanti

Date	Mintage	MS65	PF65
2001W	8,254	—	541

KM# 291 • 15.55 g., 0.9995 Platinum 0.4998 oz. APW, 27 mm. • **Rev:** Eagle in flight over New England costal lighthouse **Obv. Designer:** John Mercanti

Date	Mintage	MS65	PF65
1998W	13,836	—	562

KM# 341 • 15.55 g., 0.9995 Platinum 0.4998 oz. APW, 27 mm. • **Rev:** Eagle fishing in America's Northwest **Obv. Designer:** John Mercanti

Date	Mintage	MS65	PF65
2002W	8,772	—	541

KM# 303 • 15.55 g., 0.9995 Platinum 0.4998 oz. APW, 27 mm. • **Rev:** Eagle in flight over Southeastern Wetlands **Obv. Designer:** John Mercanti

Date	Mintage	MS65	PF65
1999W	11,103	—	562

KM# 353 PATRIOTIC VIGILANCE • 15.55 g., 0.9995 Platinum 0.4998 oz. APW, 27 mm. • **Rev:** Eagle perched on a Rocky Mountain Pine branch against a flag backdrop **Obv. Designer:** John Mercanti **Rev. Designer:** Al Maletsky

Date	Mintage	MS65	PF65
2003W	7,131	—	562

BULLION COINAGE

KM# 366 • 15.55 g., 0.9995 Platinum 0.4998 oz. APW, 27 mm. • **Rev:** Chester French, 1907. The sculpture is outside the N.Y. Customs House, now part of the Smithsonian's Museum of the American Indian **Obv. Designer:** John Mercanti

Date	Mintage	MS65	PF65
2004W	5,063	—	1,550

KM# 379 • 15.55 g., 0.9995 Platinum 0.4998 oz. APW, 27 mm. • **Rev:** Eagle with cornucopiae **Obv. Designer:** John Mercanti **Rev. Designer:** Donna Weaver

Date	Mintage	MS65	PF65
2005W	5,942	—	1,088

KM# 391 LEGISLATIVE • 15.55 g., 0.9995 Platinum 0.4998 oz. APW, 27 mm. • **Rev:** Liberty seated writing between two columns **Obv. Designer:** John Mercanti

Date	Mintage	MS65	PF65
2006W	7,649	—	541

KM# 416 EXECUTIVE • 15.55 g., 0.9995 Platinum 0.4998 oz. APW, 27 mm. • **Rev:** Eagle with shield **Obv. Designer:** John Mercanti

Date	Mintage	MS65	PF65
2007W Reverse Proof	22,873	—	790
2007W Frosted Freedom, Rare	21	—	—

KM# 436 JUDICIAL • 15.55 g., 0.9995 Platinum 0.4998 oz. APW, 27 mm. • **Rev:** Justice standing before eagle **Obv. Designer:** John Mercanti

Date	Mintage	MS65	PF65
2008W	22,873	—	638

PLATINUM $100

KM# 286 • 31.11 g., 0.9995 Platinum 0.9995 oz. APW, 33 mm. • **Obv.** Statue of Liberty **Rev:** Eagle in flight over sunrise **Obv. Designer:** John Mercanti **Rev. Designer:** Thomas D. Rogers Sr

Date	Mintage	MS65	PF65
1997W	15,885	—	1,173
1997	56,000	1,083	1,173
1998	133,002	1,083	—
1999	56,707	1,083	—
2000	10,003	1,083	—
2001	14,070	1,083	1,173
2002	11,502	1,083	1,173
2003	8,007	1,083	1,173
2004	7,009	1,083	1,173
2005	6,310	1,083	1,173
2006	6,000	1,083	1,173
2006W Burnished Unc.	—	1,800	—
2007W	7,202	1,083	1,173
2007 Burnished Unc.	—	1,700	—
2008	21,800	1,083	1,675
2008W Burnished Unc.	—	1,700	—
2011	—	—	1,173
2014	—	—	1,173
2017	—	1,083	—
2017W Proof	—	—	1,173
2018	—	1,083	—
2018W Proof	—	—	1,173

BULLION COINAGE

KM# 292 • 31.11 g., 0.9995 Platinum 0.9995 oz. APW, 33 mm. • **Rev:** Eagle in flight over New England costal lighthouse **Obv. Designer:** John Mercanti

Date	Mintage	MS65	PF65
1998W	14,912	—	1,173

KM# 304 • 31.11 g., 0.9995 Platinum 0.9995 oz. APW, 33 mm. • **Rev:** Eagle in flight over Southeastern Wetlands **Obv. Designer:** John Mercanti

Date	Mintage	MS65	PF65
1999W	12,363	—	1,173

KM# 317 • 31.11 g., 0.9995 Platinum 0.9995 oz. APW **Rev:** Eagle in flight over Heartland **Obv. Designer:** John Mercanti

Date	Mintage	MS65	PF65
2000W	12,453	—	1,173

KM# 330 • 31.11 g., 0.9995 Platinum 0.9995 oz. APW, 33 mm. • **Rev:** Eagle in flight over Southwestern cactus desert **Obv. Designer:** John Mercanti

Date	Mintage	MS65	PF65
2001W	8,969	—	1,173

KM# 342 • 31.11 g., 0.9995 Platinum 0.9995 oz. APW, 33 mm. • **Rev:** Eagle fishing in America's Northwest **Obv. Designer:** John Mercanti

Date	Mintage	MS65	PF65
2002W	9,834	—	1,275

KM# 354 PATROTIC VIGILANCE • 31.11 g., 0.9995 Platinum 0.9995 oz. APW, 33 mm. • **Rev:** Eagle pearched on a Rocky Mountain Pine branch against a flag backdrop **Obv. Designer:** John Mercanti **Rev. Designer:** Al Maletsky

Date	Mintage	MS65	PF65
2003W	8,246	—	1,173

KM# 367 • 31.11 g., 0.9995 Platinum 0.9995 oz. APW, 33 mm. • **Rev:** Inspired by the sculpture "America" by Daniel Chester French, 1907. The sculpture is outside the N.Y. Customs House, now part of the Smithsonian's Museum of the American Indian **Obv. Designer:** John Mercanti **Rev. Designer:** Donna Weaver

Date	Mintage	MS65	PF65
2004W	6,007	—	1,950

KM# 380 • 31.11 g., 0.9995 Platinum 0.9995 oz. APW, 33 mm. • **Rev:** Eagle with cornucopiae **Obv. Designer:** John Mercanti **Rev. Designer:** Donna Weaver

Date	Mintage	MS65	PF65
2005W	6,602	—	2,175

BULLION COINAGE

KM# 392 LEGISLATIVE • 31.11 g., 0.9995 Platinum 0.9995 oz. APW, 33 mm. • **Rev:** Liberty seated writing between two columns **Obv. Designer:** John Mercanti

Date	Mintage	MS65	PF65
2006W	9,152	—	1,275

KM# 417 EXECUTIVE BRANCH • 31.11 g., 0.9995 Platinum 0.9995 oz. APW, 33 mm. • **Rev:** Eagle with shield **Obv. Designer:** John Mercanti

Date	Mintage	MS65	PF65
2007W Freedom Frosted	12	—	47,000
2007W Freedom Polished	8,363	—	1,173

KM# 437 JUDICIAL • 31.11 g., 0.9995 Platinum 0.9995 oz. APW, 33 mm. • **Rev:** Justice standing before eagle **Obv. Designer:** John Mercanti

Date	Mintage	MS65	PF65
2008W	8,363	—	1,173

KM# 463 A MORE PERFECT UNION • 31.10 g., 0.9995 Platinum 0.9995 oz. APW, 33 mm. • **Rev:** Four portraits **Obv. Designer:** John Mercanti

Date	Mintage	MS65	PF65
2009W Proof	4,900	—	1,173

KM# 488 TO ESTABLISH JUSTICE • 31.11 g., 0.999 Platinum 0.999 oz. APW, 33 mm. • **Rev:** Statue of Justice holding scales **Obv. Designer:** John Mercanti

Date	Mintage	MS65	PF65
2010W	—	—	1,173

KM# 518 TO INSURE DOMESTIC TRANQUILITY • 31.11 g., 0.9995 Platinum 0.9995 oz. APW, 33 mm. • **Rev:** Female with dove, walking in field

Date	Mintage	MS65	PF65
2011W	10,299	—	1,173

KM# 541 TO PROVIDE FOR THE COMMON DEFENSE • 31.11 g., 0.9995 Platinum 0.9995 oz. APW, 33 mm. • **Rev:** Colonial soldier and flag

Date	Mintage	MS65	PF65
2012	—	—	1,173

KM# 585 TO PROVIDE FOR THE COMMON WELFARE • 31.11 g., 0.9995 Platinum 0.9995 oz. APW, 33 mm. • **Rev:** Female and gears of industry

Date	Mintage	MS65	PF65
2013	—	—	1,173

BULLION COINAGE

KM# 592 TO SECURE THE BLESSINGS OF LIBERTY TO OURSELVES AND OUR PROSPERITY • 31.11 g., 0.9995 Platinum 0.9995 oz. APW, 33 mm. • **Rev:** Girl with torch; landscape scene with sun in background

Date	Mintage	MS65	PF65
2014W	—	—	1,173

KM# 616 LIBERTY NURTURES FREEDOM • 31.12 g., 0.9995 Platinum 1.000 oz. APW, 32.7 mm. • **Rev:** Liberty, American bald eagle **Edge:** Reeded

Date	Mintage	MS65	PF65
2015W	—	—	1,400

KM# 652 LIBERTY AND ENLIGHTENMENT • 31.12 g., 0.9995 Platinum 1.000 oz. APW, 32.7 mm. • **Rev:** Liberty, with torch of enlightenment and olive branch, bald eagle at side **Obv. Designer:** John Mercanti **Rev. Designer:** Paul C. Balan **Edge:** Reeded

Date	Mintage	MS65	PF65
2016W Proof	—	—	1,173

KM# 684 PREAMBLE TO THE DECLARATION OF INDEPENDENCE • 31.12 g., 0.9995 Platinum 1.000 oz. APW, 32.7 mm. • **Obv.** Lady Liberty with child, sowing seeds in field **Rev:** Eagle in flight, olive branch in talons

Date	Mintage	MS65	PF65
2018W Proof	Est. 20000	—	1,220

SILVER DOLLAR

KM# 273 • 31.11 g., 0.9993 Silver 0.9993 oz. ASW, 40.6 mm. • **Obv.** Liberty walking left **Rev:** Eagle with shield **Obv. Designer:** Adolph A. Weinman **Rev. Designer:** John Mercanti **Edge:** Reeded

Date	Mintage	MS65	PF65
1986	5,393,005	26.40	—
1986S	1,446,778	—	45.40
1987	11,442,335	26.40	—
1987S	904,732	—	45.40
1988	5,004,646	26.40	—
1988S	557,370	—	45.40
1989	5,203,327	26.40	—
1989S	617,694	—	45.40
1990	5,840,110	26.40	—
1990S	695,510	—	45.40
1991	7,191,066	26.40	—
1991S	511,924	—	45.40
1992	5,540,068	26.40	—
1992S	498,543	—	45.40
1993	6,763,762	26.40	—
1993P	405,913	—	95.00
1994	4,227,319	56.40	—
1994P	372,168	—	130
1995W	4,672,051	26.40	—
1995	407,822	—	80.00
1995P 10th Anniversary	30,102	3,600	—
1996P	3,603,386	65.00	—
1996	498,293	—	45.40
1997P	4,295,004	26.40	—
1997	440,315	—	45.40
1998P	4,847,547	26.40	—
1998	450,728	—	45.40
1999P	7,408,640	26.40	—
1999	549,330	—	45.40
2000	9,239,132	26.40	—
2000P	600,743	—	45.40
2001	9,001,711	26.40	—
2001W	746,398	—	45.40
2002W	10,539,026	26.40	—
2002	647,342	—	45.40
2003W	8,495,008	26.40	—
2003	747,831	—	45.40
2004	8,882,754	—	45.40
2004W	801,602	26.40	—

Date	Mintage	MS65	PF65
2005	8,891,025	26.40	—
2005W	816,663	—	45.40
2006	10,676,522	26.40	—
2006P Burnished Unc.	468,000	65.00	—
2006W	1,093,600	—	45.40
2006W Reverse Proof	Est. 250000	—	175
2006 20th Aniv. 3 pc. set	—	250	—
2007W	9,028,036	26.40	—
2007W Burnished Unc.	690,891	30.00	—
2007	821,759	—	45.40
2008W	20,583,000	26.40	—
2008 Burnished Unc.	Est. 550000	50.00	—
2008 Reverse of '07, U in United with rounded bottom.	Est. 47000	520	—
2008W	713,353	—	45.40
2009	30,459,000	26.40	—
2010	34,764,500	26.40	—
2010		—	45.40
2011W	39,764,500	26.40	—
2011P Reverse Proof	100,000	—	350
2011 Burnished Unc.	100,000	50.00	—

Date	Mintage	MS65	PF65
2011S Burnished Unc.	—	90.00	—
2011W	850,000	—	45.40
2012		26.40	—
2012S Reverse Proof	—	—	140
2012	60,203	—	45.40
2012W Burnished Unc.	33,742,500	72.00	—
2013W	42,675,000	26.40	—
2013W Burnished Unc.	281,310	50.00	—
2013 Enhanced Unc.	281,310	110	—
2013 Reverse Proof	281,310	—	105
2013W Proof	868,494	—	45.40
2014	44,006,000	26.40	—
2014W	894,614	—	45.40
2015	47,000,000	26.40	—
2015W	699,623	—	45.40
2016		26.40	—
2016W	—	—	45.40
2017		26.40	—
2017W	—	—	45.40
2018		26.40	—
2018W	—	—	45.40

BISON BULLION COINAGE

GOLD $5

KM# 411 • 3.11 g., 0.9999 Gold 0.100 oz. AGW
Obv. Indian Head right **Rev:** Bison

Date	Mintage	MS65	PF65
2008W	17,429	893	—
2008W	18,884	—	109

GOLD $10

KM# 412 • 7.79 g., 0.9999 Gold 0.2503 oz. AGW
Obv. Indian Head right **Rev:** Bison

Date	Mintage	MS65	PF65
2008W	9,949	274	—
2008W	13,125	—	856

GOLD $25

KM# 413 • 15.55 g., 0.999 Gold 0.4995 oz. AGW
Obv. Indian Head right **Rev:** Bison

Date	Mintage	MS65	PF65
2008W	16,908	1,113	—
2008W	12,169	—	547

GOLD $50

KM# 393 • 31.11 g., 0.9999 Gold 0.9999 oz. AGW, 32 mm. • **Obv.** Indian head right **Rev:** Bison standing left on mound **Designer:** James E. Fraser

Date	Mintage	MS65	PF65
2006	337,012	1,095	—
2006W Proof	246,267	—	1,125
2007	136,503	1,095	—
2007W Proof	58,998	—	1,125
2008	189,500	1,095	—
2008W Burnished	18,863	—	2,225
2008W Moy Family Chop, Proof	—	—	1,095
2009	200,000	1,095	—
2009W Proof	49,306	—	1,125
2010	209,000	1,095	—
2010W Proof	49,263	—	1,125
2011W	174,500	1,095	—
2011 Proof	28,693	—	1,125
2012	132,000	1,095	—
2012W Proof	19,765	—	1,225
2013W	—	1,095	—
2013 Reverse Proof	47,836	1,275	—
2014	—	1,095	—
2014W Proof	—	—	1,275
2015	—	1,095	—
2015W Proof	—	—	1,275
2016	—	1,195	—
2016W Proof	—	—	1,275
2017	—	1,250	—
2017W Proof	—	—	1,275
2018	—	1,250	—
2018W Proof	—	—	1,275

BULLION COINAGE

FIRST SPOUSE GOLD COINAGE

GOLD $10

KM# 407 MARTHA WASHINGTON • 15.55 g., 0.9999 Gold 0.500 oz. AGW, 26.5 mm. • **Obv.** Bust 3/4 facing **Rev:** Martha Washington seated sewing **Series:** Presidential Spouse Bullion **Obv. Designer:** Joseph Menna **Rev. Designer:** Susan Gamble and Don Everhart

Date	Mintage	MS65	PF65
2007W	17,661	660	—
2007W	19,169	—	660

KM# 408 ABIGAIL ADAMS • 15.55 g., 0.9999 Gold 0.500 oz. AGW, 26.5 mm. • **Obv.** Bust 3/4 facing **Rev:** Abigail Adams seated at desk writing to John during the Revolutionary War **Series:** Presidential Spouse Bullion **Obv. Designer:** Joseph Menna **Rev. Designer:** Thomas Cleveland and Phebe Hemphill

Date	Mintage	MS65	PF65
2007W	17,142	660	—
2007W	17,149	—	660

KM# 409 JEFFERSON - BUST COINAGE DESIGN • 15.55 g., 0.9999 Gold 0.500 oz. AGW, 26.5 mm. • **Obv.** Bust design from coinage **Rev:** Jefferson's tombstone **Series:** Presidential Spouse Bullion **Obv. Designer:** Robert Scot and Phebe Hemphill **Rev. Designer:** Charles Vickers

Date	Mintage	MS65	PF65
2007W	19,823	670	—
2007W	19,815	—	670

KM# 410 DOLLEY MADISON • 15.55 g., 0.9999 Gold 0.500 oz. AGW, 26.5 mm. • **Obv.** Bust 3/4 facing **Rev:** Dolley standing before painting of Washington, which she saved from the White House

Series: Presidential Spouse Bullion **Obv. Designer:** Don Everhart **Rev. Designer:** Joel Iskowitz and Don Everhart

Date	Mintage	MS65	PF65
2007W	11,813	660	—
2007W	17,661	—	680

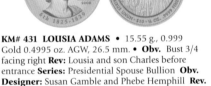

KM# 430 ELIZABETH MONROE • 15.55 g., 0.999 Gold 0.4995 oz. AGW, 26.5 mm. • **Obv.** Bust 3/4 facing right **Rev:** Elizabeth standing before mirror **Series:** Presidential Spouse Bullion **Obv. Designer:** Joel Iskowitz and Don Everhart **Rev. Designer:** Donna Weaver and Charles Vickers

Date	Mintage	MS65	PF65
2008W	4,519	700	—
2008W	7,933	—	680

KM# 431 LOUSIA ADAMS • 15.55 g., 0.999 Gold 0.4995 oz. AGW, 26.5 mm. • **Obv.** Bust 3/4 facing right **Rev:** Lousia and son Charles before entrance **Series:** Presidential Spouse Bullion **Obv. Designer:** Susan Gamble and Phebe Hemphill **Rev. Designer:** Joseph Menna

Date	Mintage	MS65	PF65
2008W	4,223	710	—
2008W	7,454	—	730

KM# 432 JACKSON'S LIBERTY • 15.55 g., 0.999 Gold 0.4995 oz. AGW, 26.5 mm. • **Obv.** Capped and draped bust left **Rev:** Andrew Jackson on horseback right **Series:** Presidential Spouse Bullion **Obv. Designer:** John Reich **Rev. Designer:** Justin Kunz and Don Everhart

Date	Mintage	MS65	PF65
2008W	4,281	760	—
2008W	7,454	—	750

KM# 433 VAN BUREN'S LIBERTY • 15.55 g.,

BULLION COINAGE

BULLION COINAGE

0.999 Gold 0.4995 oz. AGW, 26.5 mm. • **Obv.** Seated Liberty with shield **Rev:** Youthful van Buren seated under tree, family tavern in distance **Series:** Presidential Spouse Bullion **Obv. Designer:** Christian Gobrecht **Rev. Designer:** Thomas Cleveland and James Licaretz

Date	Mintage	MS65	PF65
2008W	3,443	800	—
2008W	6,187	—	770

KM# 456 ANNA HARRISON • 15.55 g., 0.999 Gold 0.4995 oz. AGW, 26.5 mm. • **Obv.** Bust 3/4 left **Rev:** Anna reading to her three children **Series:** Presidential Spouse Bullion **Obv. Designer:** Donna Weaver and Joseph Menna **Rev. Designer:** Thomas Cleveland and Charles Vickers

Date	Mintage	MS65	PF65
2009W	2,993	730	—
2009W	5,801	—	720

KM# 457 LETTIA TYLER • 15.55 g., 0.999 Gold 0.4995 oz. AGW, 26.5 mm. • **Obv.** Bust facing **Rev:** Letitia and two children playing outside of Cedar Grove Plantation **Series:** Presidential Spouse Bullion **Obv. Designer:** Phebe Hemphill **Rev. Designer:** Susan Gamble and Norm Nemeth

Date	Mintage	MS65	PF65
2009W	2,381	750	—
2009W	4,341	—	740

KM# 458 JULIA TYLER • 15.55 g., 0.999 Gold 0.4995 oz. AGW, 26.5 mm. • **Obv.** Bust facing **Rev:** Julia and John Tyler dancing **Series:** Presidential Spouse Bullion **Designer:** Joel Iskowitz and Don Everhart

Date	Mintage	MS65	PF65
2009W	2,188	830	—
2009W	3,878	—	780

KM# 459 SARAH POLK • 15.55 g., 0.999 Gold 0.4995 oz. AGW, 26.5 mm. • **Obv.** Bust 3/4 right **Rev:** Sarah seated at desk as personal secretary to

James Polk **Series:** Presidential Spouse Bullion **Designer:** Phebe Hemphill

Date	Mintage	MS65	PF65
2009W	1,893	710	—
2009W	3,512	—	740

KM# 465 MARGARET TAYLOR • 15.55 g., 0.999 Gold 0.4995 oz. AGW, 26.5 mm. • **Obv.** Bust 3/4 left **Rev:** Margaret Taylor nurses wounded soldier during the Seminole War **Series:** Presidential Spouse Bullion **Obv. Designer:** Phebe Hemphill and Charles Vickers **Rev. Designer:** Mary Beth Zeitz and James Licaretz

Date	Mintage	MS65	PF65
2009W	3,430	700	—
2009W	4,787	—	700

KM# 481 ABIGAIL FILMORE • 15.52 g., 0.999 Gold 0.4985 oz. AGW, 26.5 mm. • **Rev:** Abigail Filmore placing books on library shelf **Series:** Presidential Spouse Bullion **Obv. Designer:** Phebe Hemphill **Rev. Designer:** Susan Gamble and Joseph Menna

Date	Mintage	MS65	PF65
2010W	3,482	700	—
2010W	6,130	—	700

KM# 482 JANE PIERCE • 15.52 g., 0.999 Gold 0.4985 oz. AGW, 26.5 mm. • **Rev:** Jane Pierce seated on porch **Series:** Presidential Spouse Bullion **Obv. Designer:** Donna Weaver and Don Everhart **Rev. Designer:** Donna Weaver and Charles Vickers

Date	Mintage	MS65	PF65
2010W	3,338	710	—
2010W	4,775	—	700

KM# 483 BUCHANAN'S LIBERTY • 15.52 g., 0.999 Gold 0.4985 oz. AGW, 26.5 mm. • **Rev:** Buchanan as clerk **Series:** Presidential Spouse

Bullion **Obv. Designer:** Christian Gobrecht **Rev. Designer:** Joseph Menna

Date	Mintage	MS65	PF65
2010W	5,162	720	—
2010W	7,110	—	720

KM# 484 MARY TODD LINCOLN • 15.52 g., 0.999 Gold 0.4985 oz. AGW, 26.5 mm. • **Rev:** Mary Lincoln visiting soldiers at hospital **Series:** Presidential Spouse Bullion **Obv. Designer:** Phebe Hemphill **Rev. Designer:** Joel Iskowitz and Pheve Hemphill

Date	Mintage	MS65	PF65
2010W	3,965	710	—
2010W	6,861	—	720

KM# 509 ELIZA JOHNSON • 15.55 g., 0.999 Gold 0.4994 oz. AGW, 26.5 mm. • **Obv.** Bust of Eliza Johnson **Series:** Presidential Spouse Bullion

Date	Mintage	MS65	PF65
2011W	2,915	740	—
2011W	3,907	—	710

KM# 510 JULIA GRANT • 15.55 g., 0.999 Gold 0.4995 oz. AGW, 26.5 mm. • **Obv.** Bust of Julia Grant **Series:** Presidential Spouse Bullion

Date	Mintage	MS65	PF65
2011W	2,952	750	—
2011W	3,969	—	710

KM# 511 LUCY HAYES • 15.55 g., 0.999 Gold 0.4995 oz. AGW, 26.5 mm. • **Obv.** Bust of Lucy Hayes **Series:** Presidential Spouse Bullion

Date	Mintage	MS65	PF65
2011W	2,263	840	—
2011W	3,885	—	760

KM# 512 LUCRETIA GARFIELD • 15.55 g., 0.999 Gold 0.4995 oz. AGW, 26.5 mm. • **Obv.** Bust of Lucretia Garfield **Series:** Presidential Spouse Bullion

Date	Mintage	MS65	PF65
2011W	2,498	880	—
2011W	3,652	—	780

KM# 532 ALICE PAUL, SUFFRAGIST • 15.55 g., 0.999 Gold 0.4995 oz. AGW, 26.5 mm. • **Obv.** Bust of Alice Paul **Series:** Presidential Spouse Bullion

Date	Mintage	MS65	PF65
2012W	2,798	730	—
2012W	3,506	—	750

KM# 533 FRANCES CLEVELAND (FIRST TERM) • 15.55 g., 0.999 Gold 0.4995 oz. AGW, 26.5 mm. • **Obv.** Frances Cleveland **Series:** Presidential Spouse Bullion

Date	Mintage	MS65	PF65
2012W	2,454	740	—
2012W	3,158	—	750

KM# 534 CAROLINE HARRISON • 15.55 g., 0.999 Gold 0.4995 oz. AGW, 26.5 mm. • **Obv.** Caroline Harrison **Series:** Presidential Spouse Bullion

Date	Mintage	MS65	PF65
2012W	2,436	740	—
2012W	3,046	—	760

BULLION COINAGE

BULLION COINAGE

KM# 535 FRANCES CLEVELAND (SECOND TERM) • 15.55 g., 0.999 Gold 0.4995 oz. AGW, 26.5 mm. • **Obv.** Frances Cleveland **Series:** Presidential Spouse Bullion

Date	Mintage	MS65	PF65
2012W	2,425	710	—
2012W	3,104	—	720

KM# 561 IDA MCKINLEY • 15.55 g., 0.999 Gold 0.4995 oz. AGW, 26.5 mm. • **Obv.** Bust of Ida McKinley **Series:** Presidential Spouse Bullion

Date	Mintage	MS65	PF65
2013W	—	860	—
2013W	—	—	770

KM# 562 EDITH ROOSEVELT • 15.55 g., 0.999 Gold 0.4995 oz. AGW, 26.5 mm. • **Obv.** Bust of Edith Roosevelt **Series:** Presidential Spouse Bullion

Date	Mintage	MS65	PF65
2013W	—	760	—
2013W	—	—	790

KM# 563 HELEN TAFT • 15.55 g., 0.999 Gold 0.4995 oz. AGW, 26.5 mm. • **Obv.** Bust of Helen Taft **Series:** Presidential Spouse Bullion

Date	Mintage	MS65	PF65
2013W	—	860	—
2013W	—	—	810

KM# 564 ELLEN WILSON • 15.55 g., 0.999 Gold 0.4995 oz. AGW, 26.5 mm. • **Obv.** Bust of Ellen Wilson **Series:** Presidential Spouse Bullion

Date	Mintage	MS65	PF65
2013W	—	840	—
2013W	—	—	780

KM# 565 EDITH WILSON • 15.55 g., 0.999 Gold 0.4995 oz. AGW, 26.5 mm. • **Obv.** Bust of Edith Wilson **Series:** Presidential Spouse Bullion

Date	Mintage	MS65	PF65
2013W	—	860	—
2013W	—	—	780

KM# 593 FLORENCE HARDING • 15.55 g., 0.999 Gold 0.4995 oz. AGW, 26.5 mm. • **Obv.** Bust of Florence Harding **Series:** Presidential Spouse Bullion

Date	Mintage	MS65	PF65
2014W	—	860	—
2014W	—	—	860

KM# 594 GRACE COOLIDGE • 15.55 g., 0.999 Gold 0.4995 oz. AGW, 26.5 mm. • **Obv.** Bust of Grace Coolidge **Series:** Presidential Spouse Bullion

Date	Mintage	MS65	PF65
2014W	—	870	—
2014W	—	—	850

KM# 595 LOU HOOVER • 15.55 g., 0.999 Gold 0.4995 oz. AGW, 26.5 mm. • **Obv.** Bust of Lou Hoover **Series:** Presidential Spouse Bullion

Date	Mintage	MS65	PF65
2014W	—	850	—
2014W	—	—	840

KM# 596 ELEANOR ROOSEVELT • 15.55 g., 0.999 Gold 0.4995 oz. AGW, 26.5 mm. • **Obv.** Bust of Eleanor Roosevelt **Series:** Presidential Spouse Bullion

Date	Mintage	MS65	PF65
2014W	—	1,400	—
2014W	—	—	1,260

KM# 615 CLAUDIA TAYLOR "LADY BIRD" JOHNSON • 15.55 g., 0.999 Gold 0.4995 oz. AGW, 26.5 mm. • **Obv.** Bust of Lady Bird Johnson **Series:** Presidential Spouse Bullion

Date	Mintage	MS65	PF65
2015W	—	820	—
2015W	—	—	830

KM# 612 ELIZABETH TRUMAN • 15.55 g., 0.999 Gold 0.4995 oz. AGW, 26.5 mm. • **Obv.** Bust of Elizabeth Truman **Series:** Presidential Spouse Bullion

Date	Mintage	MS65	PF65
2015W	—	800	—
2015W	—	—	760

KM# 627 PATRICIA RYAN "PAT" NIXON • 15.55 g., 0.999 Gold 0.4995 oz. AGW, 26.5 mm. • **Obv.** Bust of Pat Nixon **Series:** Presidential Spouse Bullion

Date	Mintage	MS65	PF65
2016W	—	890	—
2016W	—	—	840

KM# 613 MAMIE EISENHOWER • 15.55 g., 0.999 Gold 0.4995 oz. AGW, 26.5 mm. • **Obv.** Bust of Mamie Eisenhower **Series:** Presidential Spouse Bullion

Date	Mintage	MS65	PF65
2015W	—	760	—
2015W	—	—	760

KM# 628 ELIZABETH BLOOMER "BETTY" FORD • 15.55 g., 0.999 Gold 0.4995 oz. AGW, 26.5 mm. • **Obv.** Bust of Betty Ford **Series:** Presidential Spouse Bullion

Date	Mintage	MS65	PF65
2016W	—	950	—
2016W	—	—	850

KM# 614 JACQUELINE KENNEDY • 15.55 g., 0.999 Gold 0.4995 oz. AGW, 26.5 mm. • **Obv.** Bust of Jacqueline Kennedy **Series:** Presidential Spouse Bullion

Date	Mintage	MS65	PF65
2015W	—	670	—
2015W	—	—	720

KM# 629 NANCY REAGAN • 15.55 g., 0.999 Gold 0.4995 oz. AGW, 26.5 mm. • **Obv.** Bust of Nancy Reagan **Series:** Presidential Spouse Bullion

Date	Mintage	MS65	PF65
2016W	—	780	—
2016W	—	—	800

BULLION COINAGE

MINT SETS

Mint, or uncirculated, sets contain one uncirculated coin of each denomination from each mint produced for circulation that year. Values listed here are only for those sets sold by the U.S. Mint. Sets were not offered in years not listed. In years when the Mint did not offer the sets, some private companies compiled and marketed uncirculated sets. Mint sets from 1947 through 1958 contained two examples of each coin mounted in cardboard holders, which caused the coins to tarnish. Beginning in 1959, the sets have been packaged in sealed Pliofilm packets and include only one specimen of each coin struck for that year (both P & D mints). Listings for 1965, 1966 and 1967 are for "special mint sets," which were of higher quality than regular mint sets and were prooflike. They were packaged in plastic cases. The 1970 large-date and small-date varieties are distinguished by the size of the date on the coin. The 1976 three-piece set contains the quarter, half dollar and dollar with the Bicentennial design. The 1971 and 1972 sets do not include a dollar coin; the 1979 set does not include an S-mint-marked dollar. Mint sets issued prior to 1959 were double sets (containing two of each coin) packaged in cardboard with a paper overlay. Original sets will always be toned and can bring large premiums if nicely preserved with good color.

Date	Sets Sold	Issue Price	Value	Date	Sets Sold	Issue Price	Value
1947 Est. 5,000	—	4.87	1,300	1981 Type I	2,908,145	11.00	8.00
1948 Est. 6,000	—	4.92	935	1982 Souvenir set	—	—	55.00
1949 Est. 5,200	—	5.45	1,100	1982 & 1983 None issued	—	—	—
1950 None issued	—	—	—	1983 Souvenir set	—	—	60.00
1951	8,654	6.75	875	1984	1,832,857	7.00	3.00
1952	11,499	6.14	780	1985	1,710,571	7.00	3.50
1953	15,538	6.14	660	1986	1,153,536	7.50	6.00
1954	25,599	6.19	360	1987	2,890,758	7.00	3.50
1955 flat pack	49,656	3.57	300	1988	1,646,204	7.00	3.50
1956	45,475	3.34	300	1989	1,987,915	7.00	3.50
1957	32,324	24.50	300	1990	1,809,184	7.00	3.50
1958	50,314	4.43	275	1991	1,352,101	7.00	4.00
1959	187,000	2.40	46.00	1992	1,500,143	7.00	3.50
1960 large date	260,485	2.40	40.00	1993	1,297,094	8.00	3.75
1961	223,704	2.40	38.00	1994	1,234,813	8.00	3.00
1962	385,285	2.40	37.50	1995	1,038,787	8.00	4.00
1963	606,612	2.40	32.00	1996	1,457,949	8.00	14.00
1964	1,008,108	2.40	32.00	1997	950,473	8.00	4.00
1965 Special Mint Set	2,360,000	4.00	8.50	1998	1,187,325	8.00	4.50
1966 Special Mint Set	2,261,583	4.00	8.00	1999 9 piece	1,421,625	14.95	7.00
1967 Special Mint Set	1,863,344	4.00	9.00	2000	1,490,160	14.95	7.00
1968	2,105,128	2.50	6.25	2001	1,066,900	14.95	7.00
1969	1,817,392	2.50	5.50	2002	1,139,388	14.95	7.25
1970 large date	2,038,134	2.50	16.00	2003	1,002,555	14.95	7.75
1970 small date	Inc. above	2.50	44.00	2004	844,484	16.95	7.75
1971	2,193,396	3.50	3.00	2005	—	16.95	7.25
1972	2,750,000	3.50	3.00	2006	—	16.95	7.25
1973	1,767,691	8.00	10.00	2007	—	—	16.00
1974	1,975,981	6.75	5.00	2008	—	—	25.00
1975	1,921,488	6.00	7.50	2009 18 piece clad set	—	—	20.00
1976 3 coins	4,908,319	9.00	15.50	2010 28 piece clad set	—	—	20.00
1976	1,892,513	6.00	7.00	2011 28 piece clad set	532,059	—	21.00
1977	2,006,869	7.00	5.00	2012 28 piece clad set	365,298	—	58.00
1978	2,162,609	7.00	5.50	2013 28 piece clad set	—	31.95	20.00
1979 Susan B Anthony PDS Souvenir Set	—	—	6.50	2014 28 piece clad set	—	27.95	22.00
1979 Type I	2,526,000	8.00	5.00	2015 28 piece clad set	—	28.95	23.00
1980 Susan B. Anthony PDS Souvenir Set	—	—	6.50	2016 27 piece clad set	—	26.95	28.00
1980	2,815,066	9.00	6.00	2017 20 piece clad set	—	20.95	20.00
1981 Susan B. Anthony PDS Souvenir Set	—	—	22.00	2017 Enhanced (S) Unc. clad set	—	29.95	28.00
				2018 20 piece clad set	—	21.95	21.95

SETS & ROLLS

MODERN COMMEMORATIVE COIN SETS

Olympic, 1983-1984

Date	Price
1983 1983S & 1984S 2 coin set: proof dollars.	80.00
1983 1983 collectors 3 coin set: 1983 PDS uncirculated dollars; KM209.	710
1984 1984 collectors 3 coin set: 1984 PDS uncirculated dollars; KM210.	710
1983 1983 & 1984 3 coin set: 1983 and one 1984 uncirculated dollar and 1984W uncirculated gold $10; KM209, 210, 211.	1,460
1983 1983S & 1984S 3 coin set: proof 1983 and 1984 dollar and 1984W gold $10; KM209, 210, 211.	60.00
1983 1983 & 1984 6 coin set in a cherrywood box: 1983S and 1984S uncirculated and proof dollars, 1984W uncirculated and proof gold $10; KM209, 210, 211.	80.00

Statue of Liberty

Date	Price
1986 1986 2 coin set: uncirculated silver dollar and clad half dollar; KM212, 214.	33.00
1986 1986 2 coin set: proof silver dollar and clad half dollar; KM212, 214.	32.00
1986 1986 3 coin set: uncirculated silver dollar, clad half dollar and gold $5; KM212, 214, 215.	378
1986 1986 3 coin set: proof silver dollar, clad half dollar and gold $5; KM212, 214, 215.	378
1986 1986 6 coin set: 1 each of the proof and uncirculated issues; KM212, 214, 215.	750

Constitution

Date	Price
1987 1987 2 coin set: uncirculated silver dollar and gold $5; KM220, 221.	375
1987 1987 2 coin set: proof silver dollar and gold $5; KM220, 221.	375
1987 1987 4 coin set: silver dollar and $5 gold proof and uncirculated issues; KM220, 221.	745

Olympic, 1988

Date	Price
1988 1988 2 coin set: uncirculated silver dollar and gold $5; KM222, 223.	375
1988 1988 2 coin set: proof silver dollar and gold $5; KM222, 223.	375
1988 1988 4 coin set: silver dollar and $5 gold proof and uncirculated issues; KM222, 223.	745

Congress

Date	Price
1989 1989 2 coin set: uncirculated silver dollar and clad half dollar; KM224, 225.	34.00
1989 1989 2 coin set: proof silver dollar and clad half dollar; KM224, 225.	39.00
1989 1989 3 coin set: uncirculated silver dollar, clad half and gold $5; KM224, 225, 226.	380
1989 1989 3 coin set: proof silver dollar, clad half and gold $5; KM224, 225, 226.	385
1989 1989 6 coin set: 1 each of the proof and uncirculated issues; KM224, 225, 226.	765

Mt. Rushmore

Date	Price
1991 1991 2 coin set: uncirculated half dollar and silver dollar; KM228, 229.	454
1991 1991 2 coin set: proof half dollar and silver dollar; KM228, 229.	50.00
1991 1991 3 coin set: uncirculated half dollar, silver dollar and gold $5; KM228, 229, 230.	396
1991 1991 3 coin set: proof half dollar, silver dollar and gold $5; KM228, 229, 230.	393
1991 1991 6 coin set: 1 each of proof and uncirculated issues; KM228, 229, 230.	789

Olympic, 1992

Date	Price
1992 1992 2 coin set: uncirculated half dollar and silver dollar; KM233, 234.	41.00
1992 1992 2 coin set: proof half dollar and silver dollar; KM233, 234.	44.00
1992 1992 3 coin set: uncirculated half dollar, silver dollar and gold $5; KM233, 234, 235.	388
1992 1992 3 coin set: proof half dollar, silver dollar and gold $5; KM233, 234, 235.	391
1992 1992 6 coin set: 1 each of proof and uncirculated issues; KM233, 234, 235.	779

Columbus Quincentenary

Date	Price
1992 1992 2 coin set: uncirculated half dollar and silver dollar; KM237, 238.	48.00
1992 1992 2 coin set: proof half dollar and silver dollar; KM237, 238.	42.00
1992 1992 3 coin set: uncirculated half dollar, silver dollar and gold $5; KM237, 238, 239.	396
1992 1992 3 coin set: proof half dollar, silver dollar and gold $5; KM237, 238, 239.	390
1992 1992 6 coin set: 1 each of proof and uncirculated issues; KM237, 238, 239.	786

Jefferson

Date	Price
1993 1993 Jefferson: dollar, 1994 matte proof nickel and $2 note; KM249, 192.	50.00

Madison / Bill of Rights

Date	Price
1993 1993 2 coin set: uncirculated half dollar and silver dollar; KM240, 241.	58.00
1993 1993 2 coin set: proof half dollar and silver dollar; KM240, 241.	55.00
1993 1993 3 coin set: uncirculated half dollar, silver dollar and gold $5; KM240, 241, 242.	49.00
1993 1993 3 coin set: proof half dollar, silver dollar and gold $5; KM240, 241, 242.	404
1993 Coin and stamp set: KM#240 and 20c stamp	58.00
1993 1993 6 coin set: 1 each of proof and uncirculated issues; KM240, 241, 242.	398

World War II

Date	Price
1993 1993 2 coin set: uncirculated half dollar and silver dollar; KM243, 244.	15.00
1993 1993 2 coin set: proof half dollar and silver dollar; KM243, 244.	57.00
1993 1993 3 coin set: uncirculated half dollar, silver dollar and gold $5; KM243, 244, 245.	58.00
1993 1993 3 coin set: proof half dollar, silver dollar and gold $5; KM243, 244, 245.	407
1993 1993 6 coin set: 1 each of proof and uncirculated issues; KM243, 244, 245.	409

U.S. Veterans

Date	Price
1994 1994 3 coin set: uncirculated POW, Vietnam, Women dollars; KM250, 251, 252.	396
1994 1994 3 coin set: proof POW, Vietnam, Women dollars; KM250, 251, 252.	797

World Cup

Date	Price
1994 1994 2 coin set: uncirculated half dollar and silver dollar; KM246, 247.	156
1994 1994 2 coin set: proof half dollar and silver dollar; KM246, 247.	134
1994 1994 3 coin set: uncirculated half dollar, silver dollar and gold $5; KM246, 247, 248.	52.00
1994 1994 3 coin set: proof half dollar, silver dollar and gold $5; KM246, 247, 248.	44.00
1994 1994 6 coin set: 1 each of proof and uncirculated issues; KM246, 247, 248.	401

SETS & ROLLS

Olympic, 1995-96

Date	Price
1995 1995 4 coin set: uncirculated basketball half, $1 gymnast & blind runner, $5 torch runner; KM257, 259, 260, 261.	1,024
1995 1995 4 coin set: proof basketball half, $1 gymnast & blind runner, $5 torch runner; KM257, 259, 260, 261.	533
1995 1995P 2 coin set: proof $1 gymnast & blind runner; KM259, 260.	82.00
1995 1995P 2 coin set: proof $1 track & field, cycling; KM263, 264.	84.00
1995 1995-96 4 coin set: proof halves, basketball, baseball, swimming, soccer; KM257, 262, 267, 271.	75.00
1995 1995 & 96 8 coins in cherry wood case: proof silver dollars: blind runner, gymnast, cycling, track & field, wheelchair, tennis, rowing, high jump; KM259, 260, 263, 264, 268, 269, 272, 272A.	425
1995 1995 & 96 16 coins in cherry wood case: bu and proof silver dollars: blind runner, gymnast, cycling, track & field, wheelchair, tennis, rowing, high jump; KM259, 260, 263, 264, 268, 269, 272, 272A.	10,400
1995 1995 & 96 16 coins in cherry wood case: proof half dollars: basketball, baseball, swimming, soccer, KM257, 262, 267, 271. Proof silver dollars: blind runner, gymnast, cycling, track & field, wheelchair, tennis, rowing, high jump, KM259, 260, 263, 264, 268, 269, 272, 272A. Proof $5 gold: torch runner, stadium, cauldron, flag bearer, KM 261, 265, 270, 274.	2,370
1995 1995 & 96 32 coins in cherry wood case: bu & proof half dollars: basketball, baseball, swimming, soccer, KM257, 262, 267, 271. BU & proof silver dollars: blind runner, gymnast, cycling, track & field, wheelchair, tennis, rowing, high jump, KM259, 260, 263, 264, 268, 269, 272, 272A. BU & proof $5 gold: torch runner, stadium, cauldron, flag bearer, KM261, 265, 270, 274.	12,800
1996 1996P 2 coin set: proof $1 wheelchair & tennis; KM268, 269.	755
1996 Young collector 4 coin set; Half dollars: KM#257, 262, 267, 271	230
1996 1996P 2 coin set: proof $1 rowing & high jump; KM272, 272A.	514

Civil War

Date	Price
1995 Civil War Young Collectors set KM#245	40.00
1995 1995 2 coin set: uncirculated half and dollar; KM254, 255.	82.00
1995 1995 2 coin set: proof half and dollar; KM254, 255.	76.00
1995 1995 3 coin set: uncirculated half, dollar and gold $5; KM254, 255, 256.	483
1995 1995 3 coin set: proof half, dollar and gold $5; KM254, 255, 256.	426
1995 1995 6 coin set: 1 each of proof and uncirculated issues; KM254, 255, 256.	909

Smithsonian

Date	Price
1996 1996 2 coin set: proof dollar and $5 gold; KM276, 277.	391
1996 1996 4 coin set: proof and B.U. ; KM276, 277.	782

Franklin Delano Roosevelt

Date	Price
1997 1997W 2 coin set: uncirculated and proof; KM282.	500

Jackie Robinson

Date	Price
1997 1997 2 coin set: proof dollar & $5 gold; KM279, 280.	680
1997 1997 4 coin set: proof & BU; KM279, 280.	3,660
1997 1997 legacy set	650

Botanic Garden

Date	Price
1997 1997 2 coin set: dollar, Jefferson nickel and $1 note; KM278, 192.	132

Black Patriots

Date	Price
1998 1998S 2 coin set: uncirculated and proof; KM288.	63.00

Kennedy

Date	Price
1998 1998 2 coin set: proof; KM287.	103
1998 1998 2 coin collectors set: Robert Kennedy dollar and John Kennedy half dollar; KM287, 202b. Matte finished.	218

Dolley Madison

Date	Price
1999 1999 2 coin set: proof and uncirculated silver dollars; KM298.	75.00

Yellowstone National Park

Date	Price
1999 1999 2 coin set: proof and uncirculated silver dollars; KM299.	120

George Washington

Date	Price
1999 1999 2 coin set: proof and uncirculated gold $5; KM300.	675

Millennium Coin & Currency

Date	Price
2000 2000 2 coin set: uncirculated Sacagewea $1, silver Eagle & $1 note.	270

Leif Ericson

Date	Price
2000 2000 2 coin set: proof and uncirculated silver dollars; KM313.	95.00

American Buffalo

Date	Price
2001 2001 2 coin set: 90% silver unc. & proof $1.; KM325.	410
2001 2001 coin & currency set 90% unc. dollar & replicas of 1899 $5 silver cert.; KM325.	387

Capitol Visitor Center

Date	Price
2001 3 coin set: proof half, silver dollar, gold $5; KM323, 324, 326.	162

Winter Olympics - Salt Lake City

Date	Price
2002 2002 2 coin set: proof 90% silver dollar KM336 & $5.00 Gold KM337.	774
2002 2002 4 coin set: 90% silver unc. & proof $1, KM336 & unc. & proof gold $5, KM337.	38.00

Thomas Alva Edison

Date	Price
2004 2004 Uncirculated silver dollar and light bulb.	55.00

Lewis and Clark Bicentennial

Date	Price
2004 2004 Coin and pouch set.	50.00
2004 2004 coin and currency set: Uncirculated silver dollar, two 2005 nickels, replica 1901 $10 Bison note, silver plated peace medal, three stamps & two booklets.	60.00
2004 2004 Westward Journey Nickel series coin and medal set: Proof Sacagawea dollar, two 2005 proof nickels and silver plated peace medal.	58.00

Chief Justice John Marshall

Date	Price
2005 2005 Coin and Chronicles set: Uncirculated silver dollar, booklet and BEP intaglio portrait.	57.00

U.S. Marine Corps

Date	Price
2005 2005 Uncirculated silver dollar and stamp set.	63.00

Benjamin Franklin Tercentennary

Date	Price
2006 2006 Coin and Chronicles set: Uncirculated "Scientist" silver dollar, four stamps, Poor Richards Almanac and intaglio print.	60.00

Central High School Desegregation

Date	Price
2007 2007 Little Rock Dollar and medal set, KM#418	55.00

American Bald Eagle

Date	Price
2008 2008 Proof half dollar, dollar and $5 gold, KM438, KM439, KM440	400
2008 2008 Bald Eagle young collector's set; Half Dollar, KM#438	20.00

Louis Braille

Date	Price
2009 Braille Education set, KM#455	38.00

Star Spangled Banner

Date	Price
2012 Star Spangled Banner 2-coin set: Proof silver dollar and gold $5 coin, KM #530, 51	375

Infantry Soldier

Date	Price
2012 Infantry Soldier Defenders of Freedom set, proof silver dollar KM #529, dogtag in folder	60.00

5-Star Generals

Date	Price
2013 5-Star Generals 3-coin set: clad half dollar, silver dollar, gold $5 coin, KM #553, 554. 555	425

March of Dimes

Date	Price
2015 March of Dimes 3-coin set: Proof silver dollar, proof and reverse proof silver dimes, KM #604, 195b	75.00

U.S. Marshals Service

Date	Price
2015 U.S. Marshals Service 3-coin proof set, KM #608, 609, 610	370

National Park Service

Date	Price
2016 National Park Service 3-coin proof set, KM #644, 645, 646	425

Boys Town

Date	Price
2017 Boys Town 3-coin proof set, KM #659, 660, 661	450

PROOF SETS

Proof coins are produced through a special process involving specially selected, highly polished planchets and dies. They usually receive two strikings from the coin press at increased pressure. The result is a coin with mirror-like surfaces and, in recent years, a cameo effect on its raised design surfaces. Proof sets have been sold off and on by the U.S. Mint since 1858. Listings here are for sets from what is commonly called the modern era, since 1936. Values for earlier proofs are included in regular date listings. Sets were not offered in years not listed. Since 1968, proof coins have been produced at the San Francisco Mint; before that they were produced at the Philadelphia Mint. In 1942 the five-cent coin was struck in two compositions. Some proof sets for that year contain only one type (five-cent set); others contain both types. Two types of packaging were used in 1955 -- a box and a flat, plastic holder. The 1960 large-date and small-date sets are distinguished by the size of the date on the cent. Some 1968 sets are missing the mint mark on the dime, the result of an error in the preparation of an obverse die. The 1970 large-date and small-date sets are distinguished by the size of the date on the cent. Some 1970 sets are missing the mint mark on the dime, the result of an error in the preparation of an obverse die. Some 1971 sets are missing the mint mark on the five-cent piece, the result of an error in the preparation of an obverse die. The 1976 three-piece set contains the quarter, half dollar and dollar with the Bicentennial designs. The 1979 and 1981 Type II sets have clearer mint marks than the Type I sets for those years. Some 1983 sets are missing the mint mark on the dime, the result of an error in the preparation of an obverse die. Prestige sets contain the five regular-issue coins plus a commemorative silver dollar from that year. Sets issued prior to 1956 came in transparent envelopes stapled together in a small square box. In mid 1955 sets were changed to a flat clear cellophane envelope. In 1968 sets were changed to a clear hard plastic case as they still are currently issued.

Date	Sets Sold	Issue Price	Value	Date	Sets Sold	Issue Price	Value
1936	3,837	1.89	6,000	1970S large date	2,632,810	5.00	9.00
1937	5,542	1.89	2,600	1970S small date	Inc. above	5.00	77.00
1938	8,045	1.89	1,100	1970S no mint mark dime	Inc. above	5.00	750
1939	8,795	—	1,000	1971S	3,224,138	5.00	3.25
1940	11,246	—	925	1971S no mint mark nickel	1,655	5.00	1,100
1941	15,287	—	800	Est. 1,655			
1942 6 coins	21,120	1.89	840	1972S	3,267,667	5.00	3.75
1942 5 coins	Inc. above	1.89	800	1973S	2,769,624	7.00	7.50
1950	51,386	2.10	500	1974S	2,617,350	7.00	8.00
1951	57,500	2.10	460	1975S no mint mark dime	Inc. above	7.00	220,000
1952	81,980	2.10	230	1975S	2,909,369	7.00	7.50
1953	128,800	2.10	175	1976S 3 coins	3,998,621	13.00	21.00
1954	233,300	2.10	90.00	1976S	4,149,730	7.00	8.00
1955 box	378,200	2.10	115	1977S	3,251,152	9.00	6.00
1955 flat pack	Inc. above	2.10	95.00	1978S	3,127,788	9.00	5.25
1956	669,384	2.10	58.00	1979S Type I	3,677,175	9.00	6.50
1957	1,247,952	2.10	23.00	1979S Type II	Inc. above	9.00	45.00
1958	875,652	2.10	25.00	1980S	3,547,030	9.00	4.50
1959	1,149,291	2.10	25.00	1981S Type I	4,063,083	7.00	4.50
1960 large date	1,691,602	2.10	25.00	1981S Type II	Inc. above	11.00	250
1960 small date	Inc. above	2.10	28.00	1982S	3,857,479	11.00	4.50
1961	3,028,244	2.10	20.00	1983S	3,138,765	11.00	3.00
1962	3,218,019	2.10	19.00	1983S Prestige Set	140,361	59.00	38.50
1964	3,950,762	2.10	19.00	1983S no mint mark dime	Inc. above	11.00	650
1968S	3,041,509	5.00	5.50	1984S	2,748,430	11.00	5.00
1968S no mint mark dime	Inc. above	5.00	13,000	1984S Prestige Set	316,680	59.00	22.00
1969S	2,934,631	5.00	5.50	1985S	3,362,821	11.00	3.00

SETS & ROLLS

Date	Sets Sold	Issue Price	Value	Date	Sets Sold	Issue Price	Value
1986S	2,411,180	11.00	5.00	2007S 5 quarter set	—	13.95	6.25
1986S Prestige Set	599,317	48.50	26.00	2007S Silver 5 quarter set	—	22.95	21.00
1987S	3,972,233	11.00	3.50	2007S 14 piece clad	—	—	18.00
1987S Prestige Set	435,495	45.00	23.00	2007S Silver 14 piece	—	—	38.00
1988S	3,031,287	11.00	4.00	2007S Presidental $ set	—	—	5.00
1988S Prestige Set	231,661	45.00	27.00	2007S American Legacy	—	—	66.00
1989S	3,009,107	11.00	3.75	2008S 5 quarter clad set	—	22.95	22.00
1989S Prestige Set	211,087	45.00	26.50	2008S 5 quarter silver set	—	—	23.00
1990S	2,793,433	11.00	4.00	2008S 14 piece clad set	—	—	35.00
1990S no S 1¢	3,555	11.00	4,100	2008S 14 piece silver set	734,045	—	45.00
1990S Prestige Set	506,126	45.00	24.00	2008S Presidental $ set	—	—	10.00
1990S Prestige Set, no S 1¢	Inc. above	45.00	4,300	2008S American Legacy	—	—	75.00
1991S	2,610,833	11.00	3.50	2009S 18 piece clad set	1,477,967	—	19.00
1991S Prestige Set	256,954	59.00	42.00	2009S 18 piece silver set	694,406	—	39.00
1992S	2,675,618	12.00	3.50	2009S Presidential $ set	627,925	—	7.25
1992S Prestige Set	183,285	59.00	46.00	2009S Lincoln Chronicle	—	—	75.00
1992S Silver	1,009,585	21.00	16.00	2009S Lincoln 4 piece	—	—	9.00
1992S Silver premier	308,055	37.00	21.00	2009S 6 quarter clad set	—	—	5.75
1993S	2,337,819	12.50	4.00	2009S 6 quarter silver set	—	—	27.00
1993S Prestige Set	224,045	57.00	31.00	2010S 14 piece clad set	1,103,950	—	28.00
1993S Silver	570,213	21.00	21.00	2010S 14 piece silver set	583,912	—	42.00
1993S Silver premier	191,140	37.00	30.00	2010S Presidential $ set	535,463	—	20.50
1994S	2,308,701	13.00	4.50	2010S 6 quarter set	276,335	—	12.00
1994S Prestige Set	175,893	57.00	31.00	2010S 5 quarter silver set	274,003	—	21.00
1994S Silver	636,009	21.00	20.00	2011S 5 quarter silver set	147,005	—	23.00
1994S Silver premier	149,320	37.50	30.00	2011S 14 piece silver set	572,247	—	55.00
1995S	2,010,384	12.50	7.50	2011S 5 quarter clad set	151,434	—	14.50
1995S Prestige Set	107,112	57.00	72.00	2011S Presidential $ set	299,161	—	26.00
1995S Silver	549,878	21.00	42.00	2011S 6 quarter set	—	—	12.00
1995S Silver premier	130,107	37.50	48.00	2011S 14 piece clad set	1,095,318	—	28.00
1996S	2,085,191	16.00	6.00	2012S 5 quarter silver set	—	—	27.00
1996S Prestige Set	55,000	57.00	285	2012S 14 piece silver set	—	—	210
1996S Silver	623,655	21.00	22.00	2012S 5 quarter clad set	—	—	13.75
1996S Silver premier	151,366	37.50	27.50	2012S 14 piece clad set	—	—	110
1997S	1,975,000	12.50	6.00	2012S Presidential $ set	—	—	60.00
1997S Prestige Set	80,000	57.00	53.00	2012S 8 piece Limited	—	—	220
1997S Silver	605,473	21.00	26.00	Edition			
1997S Silver premier	136,205	37.50	34.00	2013S 5 quarter silver set	—	36.95	32.00
1998S	2,078,494	12.50	8.00	2013S 14 piece silver set	—	60.95	63.00
1998S Silver	638,134	21.00	18.00	2013S 5 quarter clad set	—	14.95	13.00
1998S Silver premier	240,658	26.50	26.00	2013S 14 piece clad set	—	31.95	28.00
1999S 9 piece	2,557,899	19.95	11.25	2013S Presidential $ set	—	18.95	15.00
1999S 5 quarter set	1,169,958	13.95	5.75	2013S 8 piece Limited	—	139	165
1999S Silver	804,565	31.95	92.00	Edition			
2000S 10 piece	3,097,442	19.95	9.00	2014S 5 quarter silver set	—	36.95	32.00
2000S 5 quarter set	995,803	13.95	4.75	2014S 14 piece silver set	—	60.95	51.00
2000S Silver	965,421	31.95	32.00	2014S 5 quarter clad set	—	14.95	14.00
2001S 10 piece	2,249,498	19.95	13.00	2014S 14 piece clad set	—	31.95	28.00
2001S 5 quarter set	774,800	13.95	5.25	2014S Presidential $ set	—	18.95	16.00
2001S Silver	849,600	31.95	45.00	2014S 8 piece Limited	—	139	165
2002S 10 piece	2,319,766	19.95	11.00	Edition			
2002S 5 quarter set	764,419	13.95	6.50	2015S 5 quarter silver set	—	31.95	25.00
2002S Silver	892,229	31.95	34.00	2015S 14 piece silver set	—	53.95	46.00
2003S 10 piece	2,175,684	16.75	9.75	2015S 5 quarter clad set	—	14.95	14.00
2003S 5 quarter set	1,225,507	13.95	5.00	2015S 14 piece clad set	—	32.95	30.00
2003S Silver	1,142,858	31.95	32.00	2015S Presidential $ set	—	18.95	16.00
2004S 11 piece	1,804,396	22.95	15.00	2016S 5 quarter silver set	—	31.95	25.00
2004S 5 quarter set	987,960	23.95	6.00	2016S 13 piece silver set	—	52.95	55.00
2004S Silver 11 piece	1,187,673	37.95	34.00	2016S 5 quarter clad set	—	14.95	14.00
2004S Silver 5 quarter set	594,137	—	22.00	2016S 13 piece clad set	—	31.95	40.00
2005S American Legacy	—	—	66.00	2016S Presidential $ set	—	17.95	14.00
2005S 11 piece	—	22.95	9.50	2016S 8 piece Limited	—	139	165
2005S 5 quarter set	—	15.95	4.25	Edition			
2005S Silver 11 piece	—	37.95	34.00	2017S 5 quarter silver set	—	31.95	25.00
2005S Silver 5 quarter set	—	23.95	21.00	2017S 10 piece silver set	—	47.95	40.00
2005S American Legacy	—	—	84.50	2017S 5 quarter clad set	—	14.95	14.00
2006S 10 piece clad	—	22.95	11.75	2017S 10 piece clad set	—	26.95	25.00
2006S 5 quarter set	—	15.95	3.00	2017S 8 piece Limited	—	139	165
2006S Silver 10 piece	—	37.95	34.00	Edition			
2006S American Legacy	—	—	68.00	2018S 10 piece silver set	—	49.95	60.00
2006S Silver 5 quarter set	—	23.95	21.00	2018S 10 piece clad set	—	27.95	35.00

UNCIRCULATED ROLLS

Listings are for rolls containing uncirculated coins. Large date and small date varieties for 1960 and 1970 apply to the one cent coins.

Date	Cents	Nickels	Dimes	Quarters	Halves
1934	585	3,500	2,350	1,650	2,350
1934D	2,650	4,350	2,950	9,000	—
1934S	—	—	—	—	—
1935	885	1,700	1,450	1,725	1,250
1935D	750	3,150	2,950	8,850	4,000
1935S	2,500	1,725	1,950	4,650	6,500
1936	285	1,450	885	1,300	1,750
1936D	400	1,450	1,700	—	2,750
1936S	885	1,800	1,675	6,250	3,500
1937	250	1,100	710	1,250	1,150
1937D	250	1,200	1,550	3,450	5,000
1937S	335	1,285	1,650	4,850	3,450
1938	665	535	1,100	3,100	1,850
1938D Buffalo	—	1,065	—	—	—
1938D	710	485	1,000	—	—
1938S	440	355	1,350	3,250	—
1939	180	160	630	1,040	1,250
1939D	535	3,850	610	1,875	1,975
1939S	265	2,750	1,900	3,200	2,350
1940	225	145	535	1,850	975
1940D	265	120	780	5,350	—
1940S	300	265	675	1,275	1,200
1941	170	215	430	475	750
1941D	335	330	710	2,750	1,200
1941S	360	295	535	2,450	3,000
1942	140	315	465	450	690
1942P	—	600	—	—	—
1942D	140	2,550	740	1,060	1,350
1942S	585	525	1,050	5,350	1,475
1943	60.00	275	470	365	725
1943D	170	210	610	2,000	1,775
1943S	310	325	650	2,100	1,365
1944	30.00	720	460	280	715
1944D	38.00	680	635	725	1,250
1944S	120	565	660	950	1,300
1945	125	375	410	325	730
1945D	110	315	500	1,000	1,000
1945S	80.00	270	525	575	950
1946	39.00	80.00	140	365	1,025
1946D	36.50	75.00	140	380	900
1946S	185	50.00	140	275	900
1947	220	58.00	215	735	1,000
1947D	46.50	72.00	275	385	1,000
1947S	39.00	72.00	210	415	—
1948	72.50	55.00	188	270	450
1948D	175	155	325	645	425
1948S	165	80.00	255	475	—
1949	180	330	1,200	2,350	1,300
1949D	125	215	550	1,285	1,475
1949S	140	138	2,350	—	2,250
1950	115	120	525	395	750
1950D	42.00	385	200	440	875
1950S	78.00	—	1,550	850	—
1951	165	230	140	435	390
1951D	26.50	285	140	325	800
1951S	60.00	265	690	1,350	750
1952	165	145	140	535	385
1952D	26.50	260	140	300	230
1952S	300	42.00	290	1,000	1,585
1953	42.00	24.50	140	635	490
1953D	22.50	17.00	140	280	280
1953S	35.00	39.00	140	280	850
1954	39.00	57.50	140	280	280
1954D	22.50	24.00	140	280	280
1954S	22.50	39.50	140	280	400
1955	24.50	19.00	140	280	300
1955D	19.00	7.00	170	280	—
1955S	27.50	—	140	—	—
1956	10.50	7.50	140	280	280
1956D	12.50	9.25	140	280	—
1957	10.00	12.50	140	280	280
1957D	9.50	4.75	140	280	280

SETS & ROLLS

Date	Cents	Nickels	Dimes	Quarters	Halves
1958	10.50	6.50	140	280	280
1958D	9.75	5.50	140	280	280
1959	2.50	5.00	140	280	280
1959D	2.10	5.25	140	280	280
1960 large date	1.60	4.40	140	280	280
1960 small date	220	—	—	—	—
1960D large date	1.60	5.00	140	280	280
1960D small date	2.85	—	—	—	—
1961	1.60	4.25	140	280	280
1961D	1.90	4.50	140	280	280
1962	1.65	5.25	140	280	280
1962D	1.65	5.50	140	280	280
1963	1.50	4.25	140	280	280
1963D	1.65	4.75	140	280	280
1964	1.50	3.50	140	280	280
1964D	1.60	3.50	140	280	280
1965	2.25	8.75	8.00	25.00	120
1966	3.75	6.00	10.00	53.00	120
1967	4.50	9.75	8.50	25.00	120
1968	1.75	—	8.50	25.00	—
1968D	1.70	6.00	9.50	33.00	120
1968S	1.90	6.25	—	—	—
1969	7.75	—	44.00	100	—
1969D	2.00	6.25	21.50	82.00	120
1969S	3.75	6.75	—	—	—
1970	2.10	—	8.00	26.00	—
1970D	2.10	4.00	7.75	16.00	235
1970S	3.00	4.50	—	—	—
1970S small date	2,650	—	—	—	—
1971	17.00	26.50	16.00	50.00	26.00
1971D	3.00	7.50	9.50	19.50	15.50
1971S	4.00	—	—	—	—
1972	2.00	6.50	11.00	23.00	32.00
1972D	6.00	5.75	10.00	21.50	23.00
1972S	4.75	—	—	—	—
1973	1.75	6.25	10.50	22.00	25.50
1973D	1.75	6.25	9.00	23.00	18.00
1973S	3.00	—	—	—	—
1974	1.75	4.50	7.50	18.50	15.00
1974D	1.75	5.75	7.75	17.50	21.00
1974S	3.50	—	—	—	—
1975	3.75	12.50	8.75	—	—
1975D	1.75	5.25	15.50	—	—
1976	1.75	13.50	21.00	17.50	18.00
1976D	2.50	11.00	18.00	17.50	15.50
1977	1.75	6.25	9.75	16.50	21.50
1977D	2.85	5.75	8.50	17.50	24.00
1978	3.00	4.50	7.25	16.00	32.00
1978D	10.00	5.00	8.00	16.50	46.50
1979	1.75	4.75	8.75	17.00	22.50
1979D	3.00	5.75	8.00	22.50	22.50
1980	1.75	4.25	8.00	16.50	20.50
1980D	2.50	4.50	7.50	16.50	20.50
1981	1.75	4.25	7.50	16.50	16.50
1981D	1.85	4.25	8.00	16.50	19.00
1982 Large date	2.50	—	—	—	—
1982 Small date	25.00	325	270	250	98.00
1982D Large date	4.00	54.00	66.00	165	80.00
1982 Copper plated Zinc	8.00	—	—	—	—
1982 Small date, copper plated zinc	3.00	—	—	—	—
1982D Large date, copper plated zinc	35.00	—	—	—	—
1982D Small date, copper plated zinc	2.50	—	—	—	—
1983	7.50	90.00	235	945	80.00
1983D	17.50	39.00	39.00	410	120
1984	5.50	22.00	8.50	17.00	26.00
1984D	14.50	6.50	21.00	29.00	37.00
1985	4.25	10.00	9.75	31.00	76.00
1985D	9.75	8.00	9.25	22.00	44.00
1986	20.00	8.75	25.00	85.00	75.00
1986D	31.50	24.50	22.50	210	90.00
1987	6.50	6.00	7.75	15.50	52.00
1987D	13.50	4.50	8.75	15.50	52.00
1988	6.25	5.50	9.75	39.00	75.00
1988D	12.50	9.00	9.25	22.50	45.00
1989	3.25	5.50	12.00	19.50	42.00
1989D	3.50	8.75	12.50	17.00	25.00
1990	4.00	11.50	14.50	20.00	39.00

Date	Cents	Nickels	Dimes	Quarters	Halves
1990D	5.85	13.75	10.00	25.00	52.00
1991	2.60	12.00	10.00	29.00	37.50
1991D	11.50	12.00	11.00	31.00	33.00
1992	3.00	46.00	8.00	42.00	21.00
1992D	5.00	9.00	8.00	27.50	50.00
1993	3.25	13.50	9.50	39.00	64.00
1993D	7.50	17.50	13.00	36.00	17.00
1994	2.00	7.75	12.00	42.00	15.00
1994D	2.00	8.00	12.00	47.50	20.00
1995	1.85	10.50	16.50	45.00	17.00
1995D	2.00	20.00	19.50	53.00	40.00
1996	2.25	8.75	11.00	19.00	17.00
1996D	2.85	8.25	11.50	27.50	19.00
1997	2.75	14.50	29.00	22.50	20.00
1997D	3.35	60.00	11.00	39.00	16.50
1998	2.00	13.75	9.75	17.00	20.00
1998D	1.85	14.00	12.00	18.00	16.50
1999P	2.35	5.50	8.50	—	20.00
1999D	2.25	6.25	8.50	—	19.00
2000P	2.50	6.25	7.75	—	15.00
2000D	1.75	4.75	7.00	—	17.00
2001P	3.75	4.75	7.75	—	16.50
2001D	2.00	6.50	7.25	—	16.00
2002P	2.00	4.00	7.25	—	20.00
2002D	3.25	4.10	7.25	—	20.00
2003P	3.35	7.50	7.00	—	22.50
2003D	2.00	3.50	7.00	—	19.50
2004P Peace Medal Nickel	1.75	6.75	7.00	—	30.00
2004D Peace Medal Nickel	2.50	7.00	7.00	—	30.00
2004P Keelboat Nickel	—	4.00	—	—	—
2004D Keelboat Nickel	—	3.50	—	—	—
2005P Bison Nickel	1.75	3.25	7.00	—	21.00
2005D Bison Nickel	2.75	3.25	7.00	—	21.00
2005P Ocean in view Nickel	—	3.25	—	—	—
2005D Ocean in view Nickel	—	3.25	—	—	—
2006P	2.75	3.25	8.50	—	29.00
2006D	1.75	3.25	8.50	—	29.00
2007P	1.75	3.50	8.00	—	21.00
2007D	1.75	3.50	7.75	—	21.00
2008P	1.75	3.75	8.00	—	24.50
2008D	1.75	3.75	7.50	—	25.50
2009P Log Cabin	2.00	23.00	13.50	—	18.50
2009D Log Cabin	2.15	13.50	13.50	—	18.50
2009P Log Splitter	1.75	—	—	—	—
2009D Log Splitter	1.75	—	—	—	—
2009P Professional	1.75	—	—	—	—
2009D Professional	1.75	—	—	—	—
2009P President	2.00	—	—	—	—
2009D President	2.00	—	—	—	—

UNCIRCULATED ROLLS - 50 STATE QUARTERS

Date	Philadelphia	Denver	Date	Philadelphia	Denver
1999 Delaware	16.50	14.50	2004 Michigan	11.00	11.25
1999 Pennsylvania	21.00	21.00	2004 Florida	12.00	11.50
1999 New Jersey	13.00	17.00	2004 Texas	12.25	12.25
1999 Georgia	14.00	14.00	2004 Iowa	12.25	11.00
1999 Connecticut	12.00	12.00	2004 Wisconsin	14.00	15.00
2000 Massachusetts	11.50	12.00	2005 California	13.50	13.00
2000 Maryland	12.00	12.00	2005 Minnesota	13.50	11.00
2000 South Carolina	12.00	11.50	2005 Oregon	11.50	12.00
2000 New Hampshire	12.00	11.50	2005 Kansas	11.00	11.00
2000 Virginia	12.00	12.00	2005 West Virginia	11.50	11.00
2001 New York	13.00	12.00	2006 Nevada	12.00	12.00
2001 North Carolina	12.00	11.00	2006 Nebraska	11.50	11.50
2001 Rhode Island	12.50	12.50	2006 Colorado	12.00	11.50
2001 Vermont	12.50	12.50	2006 North Dakota	12.50	12.00
2001 Kentucky	12.50	14.00	2006 South Dakota	11.75	11.75
2002 Tennessee	18.50	22.00	2007 Montana	12.00	12.00
2002 Ohio	113	12.00	2007 Washington	13.00	16.00
2002 Louisiana	11.50	12.00	2007 Idaho	13.00	15.50
2002 Indiana	11.50	12.50	2007 Wyoming	12.00	12.00
2002 Mississippi	14.50	14.50	2007 Utah	12.00	13.00
2003 Illinois	32.00	33.00	2008 Oklahoma	11.50	11.50
2003 Alabama	15.00	16.00	2008 New Mexico	15.00	15.00
2003 Maine	16.50	22.00	2008 Arizona	13.00	13.00
2003 Missouri	12.00	20.00	2008 Alaska	12.00	12.50
2003 Arkansas	13.00	14.00	2008 Hawaii	13.00	13.00

SETS & ROLLS

COLONIAL AMERICA

North America was initially explored by the Vikings, but it was not until the age of Discovery, that active and expansive colonization began. The French, Spanish, Dutch, English and Portuguese were all involved in colonizing North, Central and South America.

The Spanish were strongest in Central and South America, taking that whole continent except for Brazil, which went to Portugal. Their expansion also spread into what became modern day Florida, Texas, and California.

The French settled in the Mississippi River Delta, from New Orleans northward to St. Louis, then east to the Ohio River basin, and west to the Rockies; they also progressed to the north, in the St. Lawrence River area in Canada; Quebec and Montreal being their principal cities.

The Dutch had a presence from the 1620s through 1664, mainly in the New York region, but lost that territory to the English, and never again gained a stronghold on the mainland during this period.

The English settled on the East Coast of the United States, from Georgia north to what later became Maine, and east of the Allegheny and Appalachian Mountains. To the north in Canada, they worked their way into Nova Scotia, Newfoundland, and north of the French in Quebec, Ontario, and with the explorers of the Hudson Bay Company, westward on the plains to the Pacific North West.

On the basis of the voyage of John Cabot to the North American mainland in 1497, England initially claimed the entire continent. The first permanent English settlement was established at Jamestown, Va., in 1607. France and Spain had also claimed extensive territory in North America, but at the end of the French and Indian Wars in 1763, England acquired all of the territory east of the Mississippi River, including east and west Florida. From 1776 to 1781, the States were governed by the Continental Congress. From 1781 to 1789, they were organized under the Articles of Confederation, during which period the individual States, formed from the former 13 British-American colonies; New York, New Jersey, New Hampshire, Massachusetts, Rhode Island, Connecticut, Pennsylvania, Delaware, Maryland, Virginia, North Carolina, South Carolina and Georgia, had the right to issue money.

While British and Spanish silver coins circulated freely in the American Colonies, several of the Colonies and later States did issue copper or silver coins. In addition, both merchant and political tokens, mainly in copper, were issued in several locations. The most popularly circulated, and now collected, of these Colonial and State issues are listed here.

The population of the colonies during this political phase of America's history (1781-1789) was about 3 million, most of whom lived on self-sufficient family farms. Fishing, lumbering and the production of grains for export were major economic endeavors. Rapid strides were also being made in industry and manufacturing by 1775, when the North American colonies were accounting for one-seventh of the world's production of raw iron.

Independence from Great Britain was attained with the American Revolution in 1776. The Constitution organized and governs the present United States. It was ratified on Nov. 21, 1788.

MONETARY SYSTEM

12 Pence = 1 Shilling   5 Shillings = 1 Crown   21 Shillings = 1 Guinea

COLONIAL COINAGE

MARYLAND

LORD BALTIMORE

PENNY (DENARIUM)

KM# 1 • Copper **Obv. Legend:** CAECILIVS Dns TERRAE MARIÆ

Date	F12	VF20	XF40	MS60
(ca.1659) 9 known	65,000	120,000	185,000	—

Note: Stack's Auction 5-04, Proof realized $241,500

4 PENCE (GROAT)

KM# 2 • Silver **Obv.** Large bust **Rev:** Large shield
Obv. Legend: CAECILIVS Dns TERRAE MARIÆ

Date	AG3	G4	VG8	F12	VF20	XF40	MS60
(ca.1659)	1,350	2,750	5,500	10,000	22,500	35,000	—

KM# 3 • Silver **Obv.** Small bust **Rev:** Small shield
Obv. Legend: CAECILIVS Dns TERRAE MARIÆ

Date	VG8	F12	VF20	XF40	MS60
(ca.1659) unique	—	—	—	—	—

Note: Norweb $26,400

6 PENCE

KM# 4 • Silver **Obv.** Small bust **Obv. Legend:** CAECILIVS Dns TERRAE MARIÆ **Note:** Known in two other rare small-bust varieties and two rare large-bust varieties.

Date	AG3	G4	VG8	F12	VF20	XF40	MS60
(ca.1659)	850	1,400	2,400	5,000	9,500	15,000	—

SHILLING

KM# 6 • Silver **Obv. Legend:** CAECILIVS Dns TERRAE MARIÆ **Note:** Varieties exist; one is very rare.

Date	AG3	G4	VG8	F12	VF20	XF40	MS60
(ca.1659)	1,200	2,000	3,750	7,000	13,500	20,000	—

MASSACHUSETTS
NEW ENGLAND

3 PENCE

KM# 1 • Silver **Obv.** NE **Rev:** III

Date	AG3	G4	VG8	F12	VF20	XF40	MS60
(ca. 1652) Unique	—	—	—	—	—	—	—

Note: Massachusetts Historical Society specimen

6 PENCE

KM# 2 • Silver **Obv.** NE **Rev:** VI

Date	G4	VG8	F12	VF20
(ca. 1652) 8 known	45,000	85,000	170,000	295,000

Note: Garrett $75,000

SHILLING

KM# 3 • Silver **Obv.** NE **Rev:** XII

Date	G4	VG8	F12	VF20	XF40	MS60
(ca. 1652)	40,000	75,000	120,000	195,000	295,000	—

WILLOW TREE

3 PENCE

KM# 4 • Silver **Obv.** Willow tree

Date	AG3	G4	VG8	F12	VF20	XF40	MS60
1652 3 known	—	—	—	—	—	—	—

6 PENCE

KM# 5 • Silver **Obv.** Willow tree

Date	AG3	G4	VG8	F12	VF20	XF40
1652 14 known	9,500	18,500	32,000	60,000	150,000	270,000

SHILLING

KM# 6 • Silver **Obv.** Willow tree

Date	AG3	G4	VG8	F12	VF20	XF40
1652	9,000	17,500	30,000	55,000	125,000	245,000

COLONIAL COINAGE

OAK TREE

2 PENCE

KM# 7 • Silver **Obv.** Oak tree **Note:** Small 2 and large 2 varieties exist

Date	AG3	G4	VG8	F12	VF20	XF40	MS60
1662	—	500	900	2,000	3,850	6,500	15,000

3 PENCE

KM# 8 • Silver **Obv.** Oak tree **Note:** Two types of legends.

Date	AG3	G4	VG8	F12	VF20	XF40	MS60
1652	350	650	1,250	3,000	6,500	12,500	40,000

6 PENCE

KM# 9 • Silver **Obv.** Oak tree **Note:** Three types of legends.

Date	AG3	G4	VG8	F12	VF20	XF40	MS60
1652	400	850	1,350	3,250	7,500	15,000	35,000

SHILLING

KM# 10 • Silver **Obv.** Oak tree **Note:** Two types of legends.

Date	AG3	G4	VG8	F12	VF20	XF40	MS60
1652	375	750	1,250	3,000	6,200	11,500	32,000

PINE TREE

3 PENCE

KM# 11 • Silver **Obv.** Pine tree without berries

Date	AG3	G4	VG8	F12	VF20	XF40	MS60
1652	250	500	775	1,650	3,250	6,500	18,500

KM# 12 • Silver **Obv.** Pine tree with berries

Date	AG3	G4	VG8	F12	VF20	XF40	MS60
1652	250	500	775	1,650	3,500	6,750	19,500

6 PENCE

KM# 13 • Silver **Obv.** Pine tree without berries; spiney tree

Date	AG3	G4	VG8	F12	VF20	XF40	MS60
1652	350	675	1,200	2,000	4,000	7,000	22,000

KM# 14 • Silver **Obv.** Pine tree with berries

Date	AG3	G4	VG8	F12	VF20	XF40	MS60
1652	300	600	1,000	1,850	3,750	6,000	20,000

SHILLING

KM# 15 • Silver **Obv.** Pine tree **Note:** Large planchet. Many varieties exist; some are very rare.

Date	AG3	G4	VG8	F12	VF20	XF40	MS60
1652	375	700	1,100	2,250	4,750	8,250	27,000

KM# 16 • Silver **Obv.** Pine tree **Note:** Small planchet; large dies. All examples are thought to be contemporary fabrications.

Date	AG3	G4	VG8	F12	VF20	XF40	MS60
1652	—	—	—	—	—	—	—

KM# 17 • Silver **Obv.** Pine tree **Note:** Small planchet; small dies. Many varieties exist; some are very rare.

Date	AG3	G4	VG8	F12	VF20	XF40	MS60
1652	285	550	900	1,850	4,000	7,000	24,000

COLONIAL COINAGE

NEW JERSEY

ST. PATRICK OR MARK NEWBY

FARTHING

KM# 1 • Copper **Obv. Legend:** FLOREAT REX **Rev. Legend:** QUIESCAT PLEBS

Date	AG3	G4	VG8	F12	VF20	XF40	MS60
(ca. 1682)	65.00	115	300	825	2,750	7,500	18,500

Note: One very rare variety is known with reverse legend: QUIESAT PLEBS

KM# 1a • Silver **Obv. Legend:** FLOREAT REX **Rev. Legend:** QUIESCAT PLEBS

Date	AG3	G4	VG8	F12	VF20	XF40	MS60
(ca. 1682)	800	1,750	3,250	9,000	18,500	27,500	—

HALFPENNY

KM# 2 • Copper **Obv. Legend:** FLOREAT REX **Rev. Legend:** ECCE GREX

Date	AG3	G4	VG8	F12	VF20	XF40	MS60
(ca. 1682)	185	365	850	1,450	3,250	11,500	—

EARLY COLONIAL AMERICAN TOKENS

AMERICAN PLANTATIONS

1/24 REAL

KM# Tn5.1 • Tin **Obv. Legend:** ET HIB REX

Date	AG3	G4	VG8	F12	VF20	XF40	MS60
(ca. 1688)	125	220	325	550	1,150	2,150	—

KM# Tn5.2 • Tin **Obv.** Rider's head left of "B" in legend **Note:** Restrikes made in 1828 from broken obverse die.

Date	AG3	G4	VG8	F12	VF20	XF40	MS60
(ca. 1688)	60.00	100	150	225	400	550	1,250

KM# Tn5.3 • Tin **Rev:** Horizontal 4

Date	AG3	G4	VG8	F12	VF20	XF40	MS60
(ca. 1688)	285	425	950	1,850	4,250	6,750	—

KM# Tn5.4 • Tin **Obv. Legend:** ET. HB. REX.

Date	AG3	G4	VG8	F12	VF20	XF40	MS60
(ca. 1688)	—	250	450	875	1,950	3,250	11,500

KM# Tn6 • Tin **Rev:** Arms of Scotland left, Ireland right

Date	AG3	G4	VG8	F12	VF20	XF40	MS60
(ca. 1688)	450	750	1,350	2,750	6,750	11,000	—

CHALMERS

3 PENCE

KM# Tn45 • Silver

Date	AG3	G4	VG8	F12	VF20	XF40	MS60
1783	650	1,150	2,200	4,250	9,500	20,000	—

COLONIAL COINAGE

6 PENCE

KM# Tn46.1 • Silver **Rev:** Small date

Date	AG3	G4	VG8	F12	VF20	XF40	MS60
1783	900	1,650	2,750	7,000	16,500	29,500	—

KM# Tn46.2 • Silver **Rev:** Large date

Date	AG3	G4	VG8	F12	VF20	XF40	MS60
1783	775	1,450	2,250	6,000	14,500	27,500	—

SHILLING

KM# Tn47.1 • Silver **Rev:** Birds with long worm

Date	AG3	G4	VG8	F12	VF20	XF40	MS60
1783	450	775	1,350	2,750	7,500	13,500	—

KM# Tn47.2 • Silver **Rev:** Birds with short worm

Date	AG3	G4	VG8	F12	VF20	XF40	MS60
1783	450	750	1,250	2,350	6,500	12,000	—

KM# Tn48 • Silver **Rev:** Rings and stars

Date	AG3	G4	VG8	F12	VF20	XF40	MS60
1783 5 known	—	—	—	—250,000	—	—	

Note: Garrett $75,000

ELEPHANT

KM# Tn1.1 • 15.55 g., Copper **Note:** Thick planchet.

Date	AG3	G4	VG8	F12	VF20	XF40	MS60
(ca. 1664)	125	200	300	550	1,000	1,750	4,500

KM# Tn1.2 • Copper **Note:** Thin planchet.

Date	AG3	G4	VG8	F12	VF20	XF40	MS60
(ca. 1664)	175	300	500	950	3,200	5,500	12,500

KM# Tn2 • Copper **Rev:** Diagonals tie shield

Date	AG3	G4	VG8	F12	VF20	XF40	MS60
(ca. 1664)	250	450	650	2,000	5,000	7,750	37,500

KM# Tn3 • Copper **Rev:** Sword right side of shield

Date	G4	VG8	F12	VF20	XF40	MS60
(ca. 1664) 3 known	—	—	—25,000	—	—	—

Note: Norweb $1,320

KM# Tn4 • Copper **Rev. Legend:** LON DON

Date	AG3	G4	VG8	F12	VF20	XF40	MS60
(ca. 1684)	340	650	1,100	2,350	4,750	8,500	25,000

KM# Tn7 • Copper **Rev. Legend:** GOD / PRESERVE / NEW / ENGLAND

COLONIAL COINAGE

Date	VG8	F12	VF20	XF40	MS60
1694 2 known	95,000	125,000	175,000	225,000	—

Note: Norweb $25,300

KM# Tn8.1 • Copper Obv. Elephant **Rev. Legend:** GOD / PRESERVE / CAROLINA / AND THE LORDS / PROPRIETORS

Date	VG8	F12	VF20	XF40	MS60
1694 5 known	12,000	27,000	37,000	55,000	135,000

Note: Norweb $35,200

KM# Tn8.2 • Copper Obv. Elephant **Rev. Legend:** GOD / PRESERVE / CAROLINA / AND THE LORDS / PROPRIETORS **Note:** O over E in Proprietors

Date	AG3	G4	VG8	F12	VF20	XF40	MS60
1694	1,350	2,650	5,500	8,500	14,500	37,500	115,000

Note: Norweb $17,600

GLOUCESTER

KM# Tn15 • Copper Obv. Legend: GLOVCESTER • COVRTHOVSE • VIRGINIA / XII **Rev. Legend:** RIGHAVLT • DAWSON • ANNO • DOM • 1714 •

Date	AG3	G4	VG8	F12	VF20	XF40	MS60
(ca. 1714) 2 known	—	—	—	—	—	—	—

Note: Garrett $36,000

HIBERNIA-VOCE POPULI

FARTHING

KM# Tn21.1 • Copper Note: Large letters

Date	AG3	G4	VG8	F12	VF20	XF40	MS60
1760	145	250	375	750	1,850	3,500	11,500

KM# Tn21.2 • Copper Note: Small letters

Date	AG3	G4	VG8	F12	VF20	XF40	MS60
1760	—	—	3,250	6,500	25,000	60,000	—

Note: Norweb $5,940.

HALFPENNY

KM# Tn22 • Copper

Date	AG3	G4	VG8	F12	VF20	XF40	MS60
1700 Extremely rare	—	—	—	—	—	—	—

Note: Date is in error; ex-Roper $575. Norweb $577. Stack's Americana, VF, $2,900

Date	AG3	G4	VG8	F12	VF20	XF40	MS60
1760		40.00	75.00	145	185	365	675	2,500
1760 P below bust		65.00	120	200	375	750	1,750	8,250
1760 P in front of bust	55.00	110	180	325	650	1,450	6,500
1760		50.00	80.00	135	195	425	775	3,750

Note: legend VOOE POPULI

HIGLEY OR GRANBY

KM# Tn16 • Copper Obv. Legend: CONNECTICVT **Rev. Legend:** THE VALVE OF THREE PENCE

Date	AG3	G4	VG8	F12	VF20	XF40	MS60
1737	—	10,000	18,500	40,000	85,000	—	—

Note: Garrett $16,000

KM# Tn17 • Copper Obv. Legend: THE VALVE OF THREE PENCE **Rev. Legend:** I AM GOOD COPPER

Date	G4	VG8	F12	VF20	XF40	MS60
1737 3 known	12,000	25,000	50,000	100,000	—	—

Note: ex-Norweb $6,875

KM# Tn18.1 • Copper Obv. Legend: VALUE ME AS YOU PLEASE **Rev. Legend:** I AM GOOD COPPER

Date	AG3	G4	VG8	F12	VF20	XF40	MS60
1737	6,500	10,000	18,500	42,000	87,500	—	—

COLONIAL COINAGE

KM# Tn18.2 • Copper **Obv. Legend:** VALVE.ME.AS. YOU.PLEASE. **Rev. Legend:** I AM GOOD COPPER.

Date	AG3	G4	VG8	F12	VF20	XF40	MS60
1737 3 known	—	—	—	—	—	275,000	—

KM# Tn19 • Copper **Rev:** Broad axe

Date	AG3	G4	VG8	F12	VF20	XF40	MS60
(ca. 1737)	—	10,000	20,000	45,000	125,000	—	—

Note: Garrett $45,000

| 1739 5 known | — | — | — | — | — | — | — |

Note: Eliasberg $12,650. Oechsner $9,900. Steinberg (holed) $4,400.

KM# Tn20 • Copper **Obv.** Wheel **Rev:** Broad axe **Obv. Legend:** THE WHEELE GOES ROUND **Rev. Legend:** J CUT MY WAY THROUGH

Date	AG3	G4	VG8	F12	VF20	XF40	MS60
(ca. 1737) unique	—	—	—	150,000	—	—	—

Note: Roper $60,500

NEW YORKE

KM# Tn9 • Brass **Obv.** Eagle **Obv. Legend:** NEW • YORKE • IN • AMERICA

Date	AG3	G4	VG8	F12	VF20	XF40	MS60
1700	1,800	3,750	7,500	16,500	28,500	57,500	—

KM# Tn9a • White Metal **Obv.** Eagle **Obv. Legend:** NEW • YORKE • IN • AMERICA

Date	AG3	G4	VG8	F12	VF20	XF40	MS60
1700 4 known	—	—	10,000	22,500	35,000	75,000	—

PITT

FARTHING

KM# Tn23 • Copper

Date	AG3	G4	VG8	F12	VF20	XF40	MS60
1766	—	3,750	7,000	11,500	28,500	42,500	—

HALFPENNY

KM# Tn24 • Copper

Date	AG3	G4	VG8	F12	VF20	XF40	MS60
1766	145	275	450	750	1,650	3,000	9,500

KM# Tn24a • Silver Plated Copper

Date	AG3	G4	VG8	F12	VF20	XF40	MS60
1766	—	—	—	—	2,250	5,000	12,500

RHODE ISLAND SHIP

KM# Tn27a • Brass **Obv.** Without wreath below ship.

Date	AG3	G4	VG8	F12	VF20	XF40	MS60
1779	—	—	325	550	1,000	2,000	7,500

KM# Tn27b • Pewter **Obv.** Without wreath below ship.

Date	AG3	G4	VG8	F12	VF20	XF40	MS60
1779	—	—	—	—	4,750	8,500	18,500

KM# Tn28a • Brass **Obv.** Wreath below ship.

Date	AG3	G4	VG8	F12	VF20	XF40	MS60
1779	—	—	—	675	1,100	2,100	7,750

KM# Tn28b • Pewter **Obv.** Wreath below ship.

Date	AG3	G4	VG8	F12	VF20	XF40	MS60
1779	—	—	—	5,500	9,000	20,000	

KM# Tn29 • Brass **Obv.** VLUGTENDE below ship

Date	AG3	G4	VG8	F12	VF20	XF40	MS60
1779 unique	—	—	—	—	—	35,000	—

Note: Garrett $16,000

ROYAL PATENT COINAGE
HIBERNIA
FARTHING

KM# 20 • Copper **Note:** Pattern.

Date	AG3	G4	VG8	F12	VF20	XF40	MS60
1722	135	250	425	700	1,750	3,500	13,500

KM# 24 • Copper **Obv.** 1722 obverse **Obv. Legend:** ...D:G:REX.

Date	AG3	G4	VG8	F12	VF20	XF40	MS60
1723	20.00	75.00	120	200	325	600	1,250

KM# 25 • Copper **Obv. Legend:** DEI • GRATIA • REX •

Date	AG3	G4	VG8	F12	VF20	XF40	MS60
1723	25.00	45.00	60.00	180	300	550	1,000
1724	—	90.00	125	225	700	1,750	4,250

KM# 25a • Silver

Date	AG3	G4	VG8	F12	VF20	XF40	MS60
1723	—	—	1,600	2,250	4,200	6,500	15,000

HALFPENNY

KM# 21 • Copper **Obv.** Bust right **Rev:** Harp left, head left **Obv. Legend:** GEORGIUS • DEI • GRATIA • REX • **Rev. Legend:** • HIBERNIA • 1722 •

Date	AG3	G4	VG8	F12	VF20	XF40	MS60
1722	50.00	90.00	110	160	325	700	1,750

KM# 22 • Copper **Obv.** Bust right **Rev:** Harp left, head right **Obv. Legend:** GEORGIVS D: G: REX **Rev. Legend:** • HIBERNIÆ • **Note:** Rocks Reverse pattern.

Date	AG3	G4	VG8	F12	VF20	XF40	MS60
1722	—	—	—	5,000	7,750	12,500	42,000

KM# 23.1 • Copper **Rev:** Harp right

Date	AG3	G4	VG8	F12	VF20	XF40	MS60
1722	35.00	60.00	80.00	120	285	600	1,950
1723	20.00	35.00	45.00	75.00	190	285	850
1723/22	35.00	60.00	80.00	150	400	850	2,500
1724	25.00	50.00	90.00	160	400	850	2,500

KM# 23.2 • Copper **Obv.** DEII error in legend

Date	AG3	G4	VG8	F12	VF20	XF40	MS60
1722	75.00	125	160	325	750	1,500	3,250

KM# 26 • Copper **Rev:** Large head **Note:** Rare. Generally mint state only. Probably a pattern.

Date	AG3	G4	VG8	F12	VF20	XF40	MS60
1723	—	—	—	—	—	—	—

KM# 27 • Copper **Rev:** Continuous legend over head

Date	AG3	G4	VG8	F12	VF20	XF40	MS60
1724	45.00	80.00	150	300	900	1,850	4,500

COLONIAL COINAGE

ROSA AMERICANA

KM# 1 • Copper **Obv. Legend:** • D : G : REX •

Date	AG3	G4	VG8	F12	VF20	XF40	MS60
1722	20.00	50.00	140	250	525	1,050	4,000

KM# 2 • Copper **Obv.** Uncrowned rose **Obv. Legend:** ... • DEI • GRATIA • REX • **Note:** Several varieties exist.

Date	AG3	G4	VG8	F12	VF20	XF40	MS60
1722	50.00	90.00	135	250	450	975	3,500
1723	385	700	850	1,750	3,600	5,500	—

KM# 5 • Copper **Note:** Several varieties exist. Also known in two rare pattern types with long hair ribbons, one with V's for U's on the obverse.

Date	AG3	G4	VG8	F12	VF20	XF40	MS60
1722	18.00	35.00	150	275	750	1,450	6,000

KM# 3 • Copper **Rev. Legend:** VTILE DVLCI

Date	AG3	G4	VG8	F12	VF20	XF40	MS60
1722	250	450	950	2,250	4,000	7,500	—

KM# 10 • Copper **Note:** Several varieties exist.

Date	AG3	G4	VG8	F12	VF20	XF40	MS60
1723	40.00	75.00	110	175	425	875	3,600

KM# 9 • Copper **Rev:** Crowned rose

Date	AG3	G4	VG8	F12	VF20	XF40	MS60
1723	45.00	85.00	110	165	425	900	4,500

KM# 12 • Copper **Note:** Pattern.

Date	AG3	G4	VG8	F12	VF20	XF40	MS60
1724 2 known	—	—	—	—	—	—	—

PENNY

KM# 13 • Copper **Rev. Legend:** ROSA: SINE: SPINA •

Date	AG3	G4	VG8	F12	VF20	XF40	MS60
(ca. 1724) 5 known	—	—	—	—	—	—	—

Note: Stack's Bowers 5-05, VF realized $21,850; Norweb $2,035

KM# 14 • Copper **Obv.** George II **Note:** Pattern.

Date	AG3	G4	VG8	F12	VF20	XF40	MS60
1727 2 known	—	—	—	—	—	—	—

KM# 4 • Copper **Rev. Legend:** UTILE DULCI **Note:** Several varieties exist.

Date	AG3	G4	VG8	F12	VF20	XF40	MS60
1722	60.00	100	135	240	450	950	3,750

COLONIAL COINAGE

2 PENCE

KM# 6 • Copper **Rev:** Motto in scroll

Date	AG3	G4	VG8	F12	VF20	XF40	MS60
(ca.1722)	80.00	150	200	425	750	1,650	7,000

KM# 7 • Copper **Rev:** Motto without scroll

Date	AG3	G4	VG8	F12	VF20	XF40	MS60
(ca.1722) 3 known	—	—	—	—	—	—	—

KM# 8.1 • Copper **Rev:** Dated **Obv. Legend:** ...REX •

Date	AG3	G4	VG8	F12	VF20	XF40	MS60
1722	70.00	125	175	275	750	1,500	5,500

KM# 8.2 • Copper **Obv. Legend:** ...REX

Date	AG3	G4	VG8	F12	VF20	XF40	MS60
1722	70.00	125	175	275	775	1,600	6,000

KM# 11 • Copper **Obv.** No stop after REX **Rev:** Stop after 1723 **Note:** Several varieties exist.

Date	AG3	G4	VG8	F12	VF20	XF40	MS60
1723	65.00	125	175	300	550	1,200	3,500

KM# 15 • Copper **Note:** Pattern. Two varieties exist; both extremely rare.

Date	AG3	G4	VG8	F12	VF20	XF40	MS60
1724	—	—	—	—	—	—	—
Note: Stack's Bowers 5-05 choice AU realized $25,300. Ex-Garrett $5,775. Stack's Americana, XF, $10,925

KM# 16 • Copper **Obv.** Bust left **Rev:** Crowned rose **Note:** Pattern.

Date	AG3	G4	VG8	F12	VF20	XF40	MS60
1733 4 known	—	—	—	—	—	—	—
Note: Stacks-Bowers 5-05, Gem Proof realized $63,250; Norweb $19,800

VIRGINIA HALFPENNY

KM# Tn25.1 • Copper **Rev:** Small 7s in date. **Note:** Struck on Irish halfpenny planchets.

Date	AG3	G4	VG8	F12	VF20	XF40	MS60
1773							

KM# Tn25.2 • Copper **Rev:** Varieties with 7 or 8 strings in harp **Obv. Legend:** GEORGIVS •...

Date	AG3	G4	VG8	F12	VF20	XF40	MS60
1773	30.00	50.00	70.00	110	225	425	1,000

KM# Tn25.3 • Copper **Rev:** Varieties with 6, 7 or 8 strings in harp **Obv. Legend:** GEORGIVS...

Date	AG3	G4	VG8	F12	VF20	XF40	MS60
1773	35.00	60.00	75.00	135	275	525	1,350

KM# Tn25.4 • Copper **Rev:** 8 harp strings, dot on cross **Obv. Legend:** GEORGIVS...

Date	AG3	G4	VG8	F12	VF20	XF40	MS60
1773	—	—	—	—	—	—	—
Note: ex-Steinberg $2,600

KM# Tn26 • Silver **Note:** So-called "shilling" silver proofs.

Date	AG3	G4	VG8	F12	VF20	XF40	MS60
1774 6 known	—	—	—	—	—	—	—
Note: Garrett $23,000

CONTINENTAL CURRENCY

CONTINENTAL "DOLLAR"

KM# EA1 • Pewter **Obv. Legend:** CURRENCY.

Date	AG3	G4	VG8	F12	VF20	XF40	MS60
1776	—	7,500	9,350	12,000	22,000	33,500	70,000

KM# EA2 • Pewter **Obv. Legend:** CURRENCY, EG FECIT.

Date	AG3	G4	VG8	F12	VF20	XF40	MS60
1776	—	8,000	10,500	14,500	27,500	40,000	80,000

KM# EA2a • Silver **Obv. Legend:** CURRENCY, EG FECIT.

Date	VG8	F12	VF20	XF40	MS60
1776 2 known	—	—	450,000	650,000	—

KM# EA3 • Pewter **Obv. Legend:** CURRENCEY

Date	G4	VG8	F12	VF20	XF40	MS60
1776 Rare	—	—	—	—	150,000	—

KM# EA4 • Pewter **Rev:** Floral cross. **Obv. Legend:** CURRENCY.

Date	G4	VG8	F12	VF20	XF40	MS60
1776 3 known	—	—	—	—	400,000	—

Note: Norweb $50,000. Johnson $25,300.

KM# EA5 • Pewter **Obv. Legend:** CURENCY.

Date	AG3	G4	VG8	F12	VF20	XF40	MS60
1776	—	7,500	9,500	12,000	22,500	35,000	75,000

KM# EA5a • Brass **Obv. Legend:** CURENCY. **Note:** Two varieties exist.

Date	AG3	G4	VG8	F12	VF20	XF40
1776	—	22,500	28,500	40,000	75,000	145,000

KM# EA5b • Silver **Obv. Legend:** CURENCY.

Date	AG3	G4	VG8	F12	VF20	XF40
1776 2 known	—	—	—	285,000	425,000	—

Note: Stacks-Bowers 5-2005, VF $345000; Romano $99,000.

COLONIAL COINAGE

POST REVOLUTIONARY AMERICA

CONNECTICUT

STATE COINAGE

KM# 1 • Copper **Obv.** Bust facing right.

Date	AG3	G4	VG8	F12	VF20	XF40	MS60
1785	35.00	55.00	90.00	200	650	1,750	—

KM# 2 • Copper **Obv.** African head.

Date	AG3	G4	VG8	F12	VF20	XF40	MS60
1785	55.00	85.00	150	600	1,500	3,800	—

KM# 3.1 • Copper **Obv.** Mailed bust facing left.

Date	AG3	G4	VG8	F12	VF20	XF40	MS60
1785	125	220	375	750	1,800	3,850	—
1786	30.00	50.00	90.00	175	500	1,400	—
1787	30.00	50.00	85.00	160	450	1,350	—
1788	30.00	50.00	80.00	160	435	1,150	—

KM# 3.3 • Copper **Obv.** Perfect date. **Rev. Legend:** IN DE ET.

Date	AG3	G4	VG8	F12	VF20	XF40	MS60
1787	50.00	80.00	125	350	750	1,850	—

KM# 3.4 • Copper **Obv. Legend:** CONNLC.

Date	AG3	G4	VG8	F12	VF20	XF40	MS60
1788	44.00	65.00	130	265	700	2,150	—

KM# 4 • Copper **Obv.** Small mailed bust facing left. **Rev. Legend:** ETLIB INDE.

Date	AG3	G4	VG8	F12	VF20	XF40	MS60
1786	45.00	90.00	175	400	1,100	2,750	—

KM# 5 • Copper **Obv.** Small mailed bust facing right. **Rev. Legend:** INDE ET LIB.

Date	AG3	G4	VG8	F12	VF20	XF40	MS60
1786	60.00	100	175	450	2,000	4,250	—

KM# 6 • Copper **Obv.** Large mailed bust facing right.

Date	AG3	G4	VG8	F12	VF20	XF40	MS60
1786	55.00	90.00	160	400	1,750	3,750	—

KM# 7 • Copper **Obv.** Hercules head.

Date	AG3	G4	VG8	F12	VF20	XF40	MS60
1786	60.00	110	220	600	2,500	5,800	—

KM# 8.1 • Copper **Obv.** Draped bust.

Date	AG3	G4	VG8	F12	VF20	XF40	MS60
1786	50.00	100	200	500	1,250	2,850	—

COLONIAL COINAGE

KM# 8.2 • Copper **Obv.** Draped bust. **Note:** Many varieties.

Date	AG3	G4	VG8	F12	VF20	XF40	MS60
1787	28.00	42.00	70.00	115	325	775	—

KM# 8.3 • Copper **Obv. Legend:** AUCIORI.

Date	AG3	G4	VG8	F12	VF20	XF40	MS60
1787	30.00	55.00	90.00	175	450	1,100	—

KM# 8.4 • Copper **Obv. Legend:** AUCTOPI.

Date	AG3	G4	VG8	F12	VF20	XF40	MS60
1787	35.00	65.00	110	200	650	1,650	—

KM# 8.5 • Copper **Obv. Legend:** AUCTOBI.

Date	AG3	G4	VG8	F12	VF20	XF40	MS60
1787	35.00	65.00	110	200	625	1,550	—

KM# 8.6 • Copper **Obv. Legend:** CONNFC.

Date	AG3	G4	VG8	F12	VF20	XF40	MS60
1787	32.00	60.00	95.00	185	525	1,100	—

KM# 8.7 • Copper **Obv. Legend:** CONNLC.

Date	AG3	G4	VG8	F12	VF20	XF40	MS60
1787	60.00	90.00	180	375	950	3,000	—

KM# 8.8 • Copper **Rev. Legend:** FNDE.

Date	AG3	G4	VG8	F12	VF20	XF40	MS60
1787	35.00	55.00	85.00	175	525	1,650	—

KM# 8.9 • Copper **Rev. Legend:** ETLIR.

Date	AG3	G4	VG8	F12	VF20	XF40	MS60
1787	32.00	50.00	75.00	160	475	1,275	—

KM# 8.10 • Copper **Rev. Legend:** ETIIB.

Date	AG3	G4	VG8	F12	VF20	XF40	MS60
1787	35.00	50.00	75.00	160	485	1,300	—

KM# 9 • Copper **Obv.** Small head. **Rev. Legend:** ETLIB INDE.

Date	AG3	G4	VG8	F12	VF20	XF40	MS60
1787	65.00	110	180	425	1,750	4,300	—

KM# 10 • Copper **Obv.** Small head. **Rev. Legend:** INDE ET LIB.

Date	AG3	G4	VG8	F12	VF20	XF40	MS60
1787	75.00	135	200	525	2,300	4,600	—

KM# 11 • Copper **Obv.** Medium bust. **Note:** Two reverse legend types exist.

Date	AG3	G4	VG8	F12	VF20	XF40	MS60
1787	60.00	90.00	150	400	1,750	3,450	—

KM# 12 • Copper **Obv.** Muttonhead variety. **Note:** Extremely rare with legend INDE ET LIB.

Date	AG3	G4	VG8	F12	VF20	XF40	MS60
1787	60.00	90.00	175	575	2,550	5,200	—

KM# 13 • Copper **Obv.** Laughing head

Date	AG3	G4	VG8	F12	VF20	XF40	MS60
1787	35.00	60.00	120	240	650	1,800	—

KM# 14 • Copper **Obv.** Horned head

Date	AG3	G4	VG8	F12	VF20	XF40	MS60
1787	30.00	50.00	80.00	165	450	1,200	—

KM# 15 • Copper **Rev. Legend:** IND ET LIB

Date	AG3	G4	VG8	F12	VF20	XF40	MS60
1787/8		100	150	250	750	2,000	5,000	—
1787/1887	85.00	150	225	600	1,750	4,750	—

KM# 16 • Copper **Obv. Legend:** CONNECT. **Rev. Legend:** INDE ET LIB. **Note:** Two additional scarce reverse legend types exist.

Date	AG3	G4	VG8	F12	VF20	XF40	MS60
1787	35.00	50.00	120	240	675	1,750	—

KM# 20 • Copper **Obv.** Mailed bust facing right.

Date	AG3	G4	VG8	F12	VF20	XF40	MS60
1788	28.00	45.00	90.00	200	650	1,650	—

KM# 21 • Copper **Obv.** Small mailed bust facing right.

Date	AG3	G4	VG8	F12	VF20	XF40	MS60
1788	850	1,650	3,750	5,500	12,500	22,500	—

KM# 22.1 • Copper **Obv.** Draped bust facing left. **Rev. Legend:** INDE ET LIB.

Date	AG3	G4	VG8	F12	VF20	XF40	MS60
1788	49.50	75.00	140	325	750	1,800	—

COLONIAL COINAGE

KM# 22.2 • Copper **Rev. Legend:** INDLET LIB.

Date	AG3	G4	VG8	F12	VF20	XF40	MS60
1788	60.00	90.00	195	425	875	1,950	—

KM# 22.3 • Copper **Obv. Legend:** CONNEC. **Rev. Legend:** INDE ET LIB.

Date	AG3	G4	VG8	F12	VF20	XF40	MS60
1788	58.00	85.00	190	400	875	1,850	—

KM# 22.4 • Copper **Obv. Legend:** CONNEC. **Rev. Legend:** INDL ET LIB.

Date	AG3	G4	VG8	F12	VF20	XF40	MS60
1788	58.00	85.00	190	400	925	2,250	—

MASSACHUSETTS
STATE COINAGE

HALFPENNY

KM# 17 • Copper

Date	AG3	G4	VG8	F12	VF20	XF40	MS60
1776 unique	—	—	—	200,000	—	—	—

Note: Garrett $40,000

PENNY

KM# 18 • Copper

Date	AG3	G4	VG8	F12	VF20	XF40	MS60
1776 unique	—	—	—	—	—	—	—

HALF CENT

KM# 19 • Copper **Note:** Varieties exist; some are rare.

Date	AG3	G4	VG8	F12	VF20	XF40	MS60
1787	60.00	90.00	140	225	575	1,000	3,250
1788	70.00	115	175	275	600	1,100	3,500

CENT

KM# 20.1 • Copper **Rev:** Arrows in right talon

Date		G4	VG8	F12	VF20	XF40	MS60
1787 7 known		9,500	17,500	30,000	55,000	75,000	175,000

Note: Ex-Bushnell-Brand $8,800. Garrett $5,500

KM# 20.2 • Copper **Rev:** Arrows in left talon

Date	AG3	G4	VG8	F12	VF20	XF40	MS60
1787	60.00	90.00	165	240	650	1,350	6,250

KM# 20.3 • Copper **Rev:** Horned eagle die break

Date	AG3	G4	VG8	F12	VF20	XF40	MS60
1787	70.00	110	190	275	775	1,550	6,000

COLONIAL COINAGE

KM# 20.4 • Copper **Rev:** Without period after Massachusetts

Date	AG3	G4	VG8	F12	VF20	XF40	MS60
1788	70.00	105	190	260	675	1,600	6,250

KM# 20.5 • Copper **Rev:** Period after Massachusetts, normal Ss

Date	AG3	G4	VG8	F12	VF20	XF40	MS60
1788	60.00	90.00	170	235	600	1,350	5,750

KM# 20.6 • Copper **Rev:** Period after Massachusetts, Ss like 8s

Date	AG3	G4	VG8	F12	VF20	XF40	MS60
1788	50.00	75.00	135	200	575	1,250	5,250

NEW HAMPSHIRE
STATE COINAGE

KM# 1 • Copper

Date	AG3	G4	VG8	F12	VF20	XF40
1776 extremely rare	—	—	110,000	—	—	—

Note: Garrett $13,000

NEW JERSEY
STATE COINAGE

KM# 8 • Copper **Obv.** Date below draw bar.

Date	G4	VG8	F12	VF20	XF40
1786 extremely rare	—	—	80,000	135,000	225,000

Note: Garrett $52,000

KM# 9 • Copper **Obv.** Large horse head, date below plow, no coulter on plow.

Date	AG3	G4	VG8	F12	VF20	XF40	MS60
1786	450	850	1,500	2,750	6,500	22,500	—

KM# 10 • Copper **Rev:** Narrow shield, straight beam.

Date	AG3	G4	VG8	F12	VF20	XF40	MS60
1786	38.00	60.00	140	210	550	1,350	—

KM# 11.1 • Copper **Rev:** Wide shield, curved beam.
Note: Varieties exist.

Date	AG3	G4	VG8	F12	VF20	XF40	MS60
1786	45.00	75.00	150	225	600	2,000	—

KM# 11.2 • Copper **Obv.** Bridle variety (die break).
Note: Reverse varieties exist.

Date	AG3	G4	VG8	F12	VF20	XF40	MS60
1786	45.00	70.00	145	235	650	2,400	—

KM# 12.1 • Copper **Rev:** Plain shield. **Note:** Small planchet. Varieties exist.

Date	AG3	G4	VG8	F12	VF20	XF40	MS60
1787	35.00	55.00	110	200	500	950	—

KM# 12.2 • Copper **Rev:** Shield heavily outlined.
Note: Small planchet.

Date	AG3	G4	VG8	F12	VF20	XF40	MS60
1787	38.00	60.00	120	215	550	1,150	—

KM# 13 • Copper **Obv.** Serpent head.

Date	AG3	G4	VG8	F12	VF20	XF40	MS60
1787	55.00	85.00	200	375	1,650	4,200	—

KM# 14 • Copper **Rev:** Plain shield. **Note:** Large planchet. Varieties exist.

Date	AG3	G4	VG8	F12	VF20	XF40	MS60
1787	45.00	60.00	135	240	750	1,650	—

KM# 15 • Copper **Rev. Legend:** PLURIBS.

Date	AG3	G4	VG8	F12	VF20	XF40	MS60
1787	85.00	150	275	500	1,500	3,250	—

KM# 16 • Copper **Obv.** Horse head facing right.
Note: Varieties exist.

Date	AG3	G4	VG8	F12	VF20	XF40	MS60
1788	42.00	60.00	115	190	700	1,275	—

KM# 17 • Copper **Rev:** Fox before legend. **Note:**
Varieties exist.

Date	AG3	G4	VG8	F12	VF20	XF40	MS60
1788	75.00	145	295	575	2,150	4,750	—

KM# 18 • Copper **Obv.** Horse head facing left.
Note: Varieties exist.

Date	AG3	G4	VG8	F12	VF20	XF40	MS60
1788	235	425	900	1,650	4,800	13,000	—

NEW YORK
STATE COINAGE

KM# 1 • Copper **Obv.** Bust right **Obv. Legend:**
NON VI VIRTUTE VICI. **Rev. Legend:** NEO-
EBORACENSIS

Date	AG3	G4	VG8	F12	VF20	XF40	MS60
1786	3,250	5,000	8,000	16,000	35,000	65,000	—

COLONIAL COINAGE

KM# 2 • Copper **Obv.** Eagle on globe facing right. **Obv. Legend:** EXCELSIOR **Rev. Legend:** E. PLURIBUS UNUM

Date	AG3	G4	VG8	F12	VF20	XF40	MS60
1787	1,400	2,250	3,850	7,500	20,000	37,500	—

KM# 6 • Copper **Obv.** Indian. **Rev:** New York arms. **Obv. Legend:** LIBERNATUS LIBERTATEM DEFENDO **Rev. Legend:** EXCELSIOR

Date	AG3	G4	VG8	F12	VF20	XF40	MS60
1787	4,500	7,500	12,500	35,000	80,000	170,000	—

KM# 3 • Copper **Obv.** Eagle on globe facing left. **Obv. Legend:** EXCELSIOR **Rev. Legend:** E. PLURIBUS UNUM

Date	AG3	G4	VG8	F12	VF20	XF40	MS60
1787	1,250	2,000	3,500	7,000	15,000	30,000	—

KM# 7 • Copper **Obv.** Indian. **Rev:** Eagle on globe. **Obv. Legend:** LIBERNATUS LIBERTATEM DEFENDO **Rev. Legend:** NEO EBORACUS EXCELSIOR

Date	AG3	G4	VG8	F12	VF20	XF40	MS60
1787	6,500	11,500	17,500	37,500	75,000	160,000	—

KM# 8 • Copper **Obv.** Indian. **Rev:** George III.

Date	AG3	G4	VG8	F12	VF20	XF40	MS60
1787 3 Known	—	—	—	—	—	—	—

MACHIN'S MILL

KM# 13 • Copper **Note:** Crude, lightweight imitations of the British Halfpenny were struck at Machin's Mill in large quantities bearing the obverse legends: GEORGIVS II REX, GEORGIVS III REX, and GEORGIUS III REX, with the BRITANNIA reverse. There are many different mulings. Plain crosses in the shield of Britannia are noticeable on high grade pieces, unlike common British made imitations, which usually have outlined crosses in the shield. Some Machin's Mill varieties are very rare.

Date	AG3	G4	VG8	F12	VF20	XF40	MS60
(1747-1788)	40.00	75.00	145	325	800	2,250	—

Note: Prices are for most common within date ranges. Examples are dated: 1747, 1771, 1772, 1774, 1775, 1776, 1777, 1778, 1784, 1785, 1786, 1787 and 1788. Other dates may exist

KM# 4 • Copper **Rev:** Large eagle, arrows in right talon. **Obv. Legend:** EXCELSIOR **Rev. Legend:** E. PLURIBUS UNUM

Date	AG3	G4	VG8	F12	VF20	XF40	MS60
1787	—	4,500	9,000	16,500	35,000	55,000	—

Note: Norweb $18,700

KM# 5 • Copper **Obv.** George Clinton. **Rev. Legend:** EXCELSIOR

Date	AG3	G4	VG8	F12	VF20	XF40	MS60
1787	5,000	9,500	17,500	45,000	95,000	250,000	450,000

COLONIAL COINAGE

NOVA EBORACS

KM# 9 • Copper **Obv.** Bust right **Rev:** Figure seated right. **Obv. Legend:** NOVA EBORAC. **Rev. Legend:** VIRT.ET.LIB.

Date	AG3	G4	VG8	F12	VF20	XF40	MS60
1787	75.00	115	220	360	1,150	2,700	—

KM# 10 • Copper **Obv.** Bust right **Rev:** Figure seated left. **Obv. Legend:** NOVA EBORAC **Rev. Legend:** VIRT.ET.LIB.

Date	AG3	G4	VG8	F12	VF20	XF40	MS60
1787	60.00	100	200	325	825	1,750	—

KM# 11 • Copper **Obv.** Small head, star above. **Rev:** Figure seated left **Obv. Legend:** NOVA EBORAC. **Rev. Legend:** VIRT.ET.LIB.

Date	AG3	G4	VG8	F12	VF20	XF40	MS60
1787	2,450	3,750	5,500	9,500	22,500	—	—

KM# 12 • Copper **Obv.** Large head, two quatrefoils left. **Rev:** Figure seated left **Obv. Legend:** NOVA EBORAC. **Rev. Legend:** VIRT.ET.LIB.

Date	AG3	G4	VG8	F12	VF20	XF40	MS60
1787	350	600	1,250	2,500	7,750	15,000	—

VERMONT

STATE COINAGE

KM# 1 • Copper **Rev. Legend:** IMMUNE COLUMBIA

Date	AG3	G4	VG8	F12	VF20	XF40	MS60
1785	4,000	6,000	9,500	13,750	35,000	—	—

KM# 2 • Copper **Obv.** Sun rising over field with plow **Rev:** Eye, with rays and stars **Obv. Legend:** VERMONTIS. RES. PUBLICA. **Rev. Legend:** QUARTA. DECIMA. STELLA.

Date	AG3	G4	VG8	F12	VF20	XF40	MS60
1785	140	300	750	1,650	5,250	12,500	—

KM# 3 • Copper **Obv.** Sun rising over field with plow **Rev:** Eye, with rays and stars **Obv. Legend:** VERMONTS. RES. PUBLICA. **Rev. Legend:** QUARTA. DECIMA. STELLA.

Date	AG3	G4	VG8	F12	VF20	XF40	MS60
1785	150	285	550	1,150	2,250	7,500	—

KM# 4 • Copper **Obv.** Sun rising over field with plow **Rev:** Eye, with pointed rays and stars **Obv. Legend:** VERMONTENSIUM.RES.PUBLICA **Rev. Legend:** QUARTA. DECIMA. STELLA.

Date	AG3	G4	VG8	F12	VF20	XF40	MS60
1786	140	235	425	775	2,000	4,500	13,500

COLONIAL COINAGE

KM# 5 • Copper **Obv.** Baby head. **Rev:** Seated figure left **Obv. Legend:** AUCTORI: VERMON: **Rev. Legend:** ET:LIB: INDE

Date	AG3	G4	VG8	F12	VF20	XF40	MS60
1786	200	350	650	1,250	3,500	9,500	—

KM# 9.1 • Copper **Obv.** Bust right **Rev:** Seated figure left **Obv. Legend:** VERMON. AUCTORI. **Rev. Legend:** INDE . ET LIB. **Note:** Varieties exist.

Date	AG3	G4	VG8	F12	VF20	XF40	MS60
1788	65.00	125	200	450	950	2,250	—

KM# 6 • Copper **Obv.** Bust facing left. **Rev:** Seated figure left **Obv. Legend:** VERMON: AUCTORI: **Rev. Legend:** INDE ETLIB

Date	AG3	G4	VG8	F12	VF20	XF40
1786	115	175	325	750	2,250	3,850
1787 extremely rare	—	4,500	10,000	22,500	42,500	—

KM# 9.2 • Copper **Obv.** Bust right. "C" backward in AUCTORI. **Rev:** Seated figure left

Date	AG3	G4	VG8	F12	VF20	XF40
1788 extremely rare	—	4,200	7,000	17,500	38,000	—

Note: Stack's Americana, Fine, $9,775

KM# 10 • Copper **Obv.** Bust right **Rev:** Seated figure left **Rev. Legend:** .ET LIB. .INDE.

Date	AG3	G4	VG8	F12	VF20	XF40	MS60
1788	200	325	675	1,750	3,500	11,500	—

KM# 7 • Copper **Obv.** Bust facing right. **Rev:** Seated figure left **Obv. Legend:** VERMON. AUCTORI. **Rev. Legend:** INDE ETLIB **Note:** Varieties exist.

Date	AG3	G4	VG8	F12	VF20	XF40	MS60
1787	70.00	150	260	575	1,450	3,000	—

KM# 11 • Copper **Obv.** Bust right **Rev:** Seated figure left **Note:** George III Rex mule.

Date	AG3	G4	VG8	F12	VF20	XF40	MS60
1788	300	500	850	2,000	4,750	12,500	—

KM# 8 • Copper **Obv.** Bust right **Rev:** Seated figure left **Obv. Legend:** VERMON AUCTORI **Note:** Britannia mule.

Date	AG3	G4	VG8	F12	VF20	XF40	MS60
1787	65.00	120	170	300	700	1,650	—

COLONIAL COINAGE

POST REVOLUTION AMERICAN TOKENS

ALBANY CHURCH "PENNY"

CASTORLAND "HALF DOLLAR"

KM# Tn54.1 • Copper **Obv.** Without "D" above church. **Note:** Uniface.

Date	AG3	G4	VG8	F12	VF20	XF40
(ca. 1790) 5 known	—	—	10,000	25,000	45,000	75,000

KM# Tn54.2 • Copper **Obv.** With "D" above church. **Note:** Uniface.

Date	AG3	G4	VG8	F12	VF20	XF40
(ca. 1790) rare	—	—	9,000	22,500	42,500	67,500

AUCTORI PLEBIS

KM# Tn50 • Copper **Obv.** Bust left **Rev:** Seated figure left **Obv. Legend:** AUCTORI: PLEBIS: **Rev. Legend:** INDEP: ET. LIBER

Date	AG3	G4	VG8	F12	VF20	XF40	MS60
1787	—	100	165	340	700	1,650	15,000

BAR "CENT"

KM# Tn49 • Copper **Obv.** USA monogram **Rev:** Horizontal bars

Date	AG3	G4	VG8	F12	VF20	XF40	MS60
(ca.1785)	—	1,400	1,750	3,100	6,250	9,500	27,500

KM# Tn87.1 • Silver **Obv. Legend:** FRANCO • AMERICANA / COLONIA **Edge:** Reeded.

Date	AG3	G4	VG8	F12	VF20	XF40	MS60
1796	—	—	—	—	—	4,500	12,500

KM# Tn87.1a • Copper **Obv. Legend:** FRANCO • AMERICANA / COLONIA **Edge:** Reeded.

Date	AG3	G4	VG8	F12	VF20	XF40	MS60
1796 3 known	—	—	—	—	—	3,500	—

KM# Tn87.1b • Brass **Obv. Legend:** FRANCO • AMERICANA / COLONIA **Edge:** Reeded

Date	AG3	G4	VG8	F12	VF20	XF40	MS60
1796	—	—	—	—	—	275	700

KM# Tn87.2 • Copper **Obv. Legend:** FRANCO • AMERICANA / COLONIA **Edge:** Plain. **Note:** Thin planchet.

Date	AG3	G4	VG8	F12	VF20	XF40	MS60
1796 unique	—	—	—	—	—	—	—

KM# Tn87.3 • Silver **Obv. Legend:** FRANCO • AMERICANA / COLONIA **Edge:** Reeded. **Note:** Thin planchet. Restrike.

Date	G4	VG8	F12	VF20	XF40	MS60	PF60
1796	—	—	—	—	—	1,450	—

KM# Tn87.3a • Copper **Obv. Legend:** FRANCO • AMERICANA / COLONIA **Edge:** Reeded. **Note:** Thin planchet. Restrike.

Date	G4	VG8	F12	VF20	XF40	MS60	PF60
1796	—	—	—	—	—	350	—

KM# Tn87.4 • Silver **Obv. Legend:** FRANCO • AMERICANA / COLONIA **Edge:** Lettered. **Edge Lettering:** ARGENT. **Note:** Thin planchet. Restrike.

Date	G4	VG8	F12	VF20	XF40	MS60	PF60
1796	—	—	—	—	—	75.00	—

KM# Tn87.5 • Copper **Obv. Legend:** FRANCO • AMERICANA / COLONIA **Edge:** Lettered. **Edge Lettering:** CUIVRE. **Note:** Thin planchet. Restrike.

Date	G4	VG8	F12	VF20	XF40	MS60	PF60
1796	—	—	—	—	—	45.00	—

COLONIAL COINAGE

COPPER COMPANY OF UPPER CANADA

HALFPENNY

KM# Tn86 • Copper **Obv. Legend:** BRITISH SETTLEMENT KENTUCKY

Date	G4	VG8	F12	VF20	XF40	MS60	PF60
1796	—	—	—	—	—	—	9,500

FRANKLIN PRESS

KM# Tn73 • Copper **Obv.** Printing press **Obv. Legend:** SIC ORITUR DOCTRINA SURGETQUE LIBERTAS **Rev. Inscription:** PAYABLE AT THE FRANKLIN PRESS LONDON **Edge:** Plain.

Date	AG3	G4	VG8	F12	VF20	XF40	MS60
1794	30.00	75.00	110	150	285	450	1,350

KENTUCKY TOKEN

KM# Tn70.1 • Copper **Obv. Legend:** UNANIMITY IS THE STRENGTH OF SOCIETY **Rev. Legend:** E. PLURIBUS UNUM **Edge:** Plain. **Note:** 1793 date is circa.

Date	AG3	G4	VG8	F12	VF20	XF40	MS60
(ca. 1793)	12.00	25.00	40.00	150	200	375	1,150

KM# Tn70.2 • Copper **Obv. Legend:** UNANIMITY IS THE STRENGTH OF SOCIETY **Rev. Legend:** E. PLURIBUS UNUM **Edge:** Engrailed.

Date	AG3	G4	VG8	F12	VF20	XF40	MS60
(ca. 1793)	35.00	75.00	125	200	500	950	3,250

KM# Tn70.3 • Copper **Obv. Legend:** UNANIMITY IS THE STRENGTH OF SOCIETY **Rev. Legend:** E. PLURIBUS UNUM **Edge:** Lettered. **Edge Lettering:** PAYABLE AT BEDWORTH.

Date	AG3	G4	VG8	F12	VF20	XF40
(ca. 1793) unique	—	—	—	—	—	2,500

KM# Tn70.4 • Copper **Obv. Legend:** UNANIMITY IS THE STRENGTH OF SOCIETY **Rev. Legend:** E. PLURIBUS UNUM **Edge:** Lettered. **Edge Lettering:** PAYABLE AT LANCASTER.

Date	AG3	G4	VG8	F12	VF20	XF40	MS60
(ca. 1793)	14.00	28.00	45.00	65.00	225	400	1,250

KM# Tn70.5 • Copper **Obv. Legend:** UNANIMITY IS THE STRENGTH OF SOCIETY **Rev. Legend:** E. PLURIBUS UNUM **Edge:** Lettered. **Edge Lettering:** PAYABLE AT I.FIELDING.

Date	AG3	G4	VG8	F12	VF20	XF40
(ca. 1793) unique	—	—	—	—	—	—

KM# Tn70.6 • Copper **Obv. Legend:** UNANIMITY IS THE STRENGTH OF SOCIETY **Rev. Legend:** E. PLURIBUS UNUM **Edge:** Lettered. **Edge Lettering:** PAYABLE AT W. PARKERS.

Date	AG3	G4	VG8	F12	VF20	XF40
(ca. 1793) unique	—	—	—	—	20,000	—

KM# Tn70.7 • Copper **Obv. Legend:** UNANIMITY IS THE STRENGTH OF SOCIETY **Rev. Legend:** E. PLURIBUS UNUM **Edge:** Ornamented branch with two leaves.

Date	AG3	G4	VG8	F12	VF20	XF40	MS60
(ca. 1793) unique	—	—	—	—	—	—	—

MOTT TOKEN

KM# Tn52.1 • Copper **Obv.** Clock **Rev:** Eagle with shield **Note:** Thin planchet.

Date	AG3	G4	VG8	F12	VF20	XF40	MS60
1789	50.00	80.00	150	300	550	1,200	1,750

KM# Tn52.2 • Copper **Obv.** Clock **Rev:** Eagle with shield **Note:** Thick planchet. Weight generally about 170 grams.

Date	AG3	G4	VG8	F12	VF20	XF40	MS60
1789	60.00	95.00	175	325	525	1,000	—

KM# Tn52.3 • Copper **Obv.** Clock **Rev:** Eagle with shield **Edge:** Fully engrailed. **Note:** Specimens struck with perfect dies are scarcer and generally command higher prices.

Date	AG3	G4	VG8	F12	VF20	XF40	MS60
1789	90.00	160	325	450	700	1,750	4,800

COLONIAL COINAGE

MYDDELTON TOKEN

KM# Tn85 • Copper **Obv. Legend:** BRITISH
SETTLEMENT KENTUCKY **Rev. Legend:** PAYABLE
BY P • P • P • MYDDELTON •

Date	G4	VG8	F12	VF20	XF40	MS60	PF60
1796	—	—	—	—	—	—	18,500

KM# Tn85a • Silver

Date	G4	VG8	F12	VF20	XF40	MS60	PF60
1796	—	—	—	—	—	—	24,500

NEW YORK THEATRE

KM# Tn90 • Copper **Obv.** Theater building **Rev:**
Ships at sea, viewed from dock **Obv. Legend:** THE
• THEATRE • AT • NEW • YORK • / AMERICA **Rev.
Legend:** MAY • COMMERCE • FLOURISH

Date	G4	VG8	F12	VF20	XF40	MS60	PF60
(ca. 1796)	—	—	—	—	—	—	35,000

NORTH AMERICAN
HALFPENNY

KM# Tn30 • Copper **Obv.** Seated figure left, with
harp **Rev:** Ship **Obv. Legend:** NORTH AMERICAN
TOKEN **Rev. Legend:** COMMERCE

Date	AG3	G4	VG8	F12	VF20	XF40	MS60
1781	32.00	50.00	70.00	140	300	750	3,250

STANDISH BARRY
3 PENCE

KM# Tn55 • Silver **Obv.** Bust left **Rev:**
Denomination **Obv. Legend:** BALTIMORE • TOWN
• JULY • 4 • 90 • **Rev. Legend:** STANDISH BARRY •

Date	AG3	G4	VG8	F12	VF20	XF40	MS60
1790	—	—	15,000	25,000	55,000	75,000	125,000

TALBOT, ALLUM & LEE
CENT

KM# Tn71.1 • Copper **Rev:** NEW YORK above ship
Edge: Lettered. **Edge Lettering:** PAYABLE AT THE
STORE OF

Date	AG3	G4	VG8	F12	VF20	XF40	MS60
1794	32.00	50.00	85.00	165	275	550	1,850

KM# Tn71.2 • Copper **Rev:** NEW YORK above ship
Edge: Plain. **Note:** Size of ampersand varies on
obverse and reverse dies.

Date	AG3	G4	VG8	F12	VF20	XF40	MS60
1794 4 known	—	—	—	—	15,000	27,000	—

KM# Tn72.1 • Copper **Rev:** Without NEW YORK
above ship **Edge:** Lettered. **Edge Lettering:**
PAYABLE AT THE STORE OF

Date	AG3	G4	VG8	F12	VF20	XF40	MS60
1794	200	375	600	1,250	3,750	7,500	22,000

KM# Tn72.2 • Copper **Edge:** Lettered. **Edge
Lettering:** WE PROMISE TO PAY THE BEARER ONE
CENT.

Date	AG3	G4	VG8	F12	VF20	XF40	MS60
1795	30.00	50.00	75.00	135	250	400	1,200

COLONIAL COINAGE

KM# Tn72.3 • Copper **Edge:** Lettered. **Edge Lettering:** CURRENT EVERYWHERE.

Date	AG3	G4	VG8	F12	VF20	XF40	MS60
1795 unique	—	—	—	—	—	—	—

KM# Tn72.4 • Copper **Edge:** Olive leaf.

Date	AG3	G4	VG8	F12	VF20	XF40	MS60
1795 unique	—	—	—	—	—	18,000	—

Note: Norweb $4,400

KM# Tn72.5 • Copper **Edge:** Plain.

Date	AG3	G4	VG8	F12	VF20	XF40	MS60
1795 Lettered edge; unique	—	—	—	—	—	18,000	—

Note: Edge: Cambridge Bedford Huntington.X.X.; Norweb, $3,960

1795 plain edge; 2 known	—	—	—	—	—	—	—

WASHINGTON PIECES

KM# Tn35 • Copper **Obv. Legend:** GEORGIVS TRIUMPHO.

Date	AG3	G4	VG8	F12	VF20	XF40	MS60
1783	—	95.00	135	285	550	850	—

KM# Tn36 • Copper **Obv.** Large military bust.
Note: Varieties exist.

Date	AG3	G4	VG8	F12	VF20	XF40	MS60
1783	—	—	50.00	90.00	185	450	2,600

KM# Tn37.1 • Copper **Obv.** Small military bust.
Edge: Plain.

Date	AG3	G4	VG8	F12	VF20	XF40	MS60
1783	—	—	70.00	95.00	220	525	3,800

Note: One proof example is known. Value: $25,000

KM# Tn37.2 • Copper **Obv.** Small military bust.
Edge: Engrailed.

Date	AG3	G4	VG8	F12	VF20	XF40	MS60
1783	—	75.00	110	150	300	750	4,750

KM# Tn38.1 • Copper **Obv.** Draped bust, no button on drapery.

Date	AG3	G4	VG8	F12	VF20	XF40	MS60
1783	—	40.00	60.00	95.00	175	350	2,250

KM# Tn38.2 • Copper **Obv.** Draped bust, button on drapery.

Date	AG3	G4	VG8	F12	VF20	XF40	MS60
1783	—	75.00	110	150	300	600	4,500

KM# Tn38.4 • Copper **Edge:** Engrailed. **Note:** Restrike.

Date	G4	VG8	F12	VF20	XF40	MS60	PF60
1783	—	—	—	—	—	—	800

KM# Tn38.4a • Copper **Note:** Bronzed. Restrike.

Date	G4	VG8	F12	VF20	XF40	MS60	PF60
1783	—	—	—	—	—	—	—

KM# Tn83.3 • Copper **Obv.** Large modern lettering. **Edge:** Plain. **Note:** Restrike.

Date	G4	VG8	F12	VF20	XF40	MS60	PF60
1783	—	—	—	—	—	—	950

KM# Tn83.4b • Silver **Note:** Restrike.

Date	G4	VG8	F12	VF20	XF40	MS60	PF60
1783	—	—	—	—	—	—	1,750

COLONIAL COINAGE

KM# Tn83.4c • Gold AGW **Note:** Restrike.

Date	AG3	G4	VG8	F12	VF20	XF40	MS60
1783 2 known	—	—	—	—	—	—	—

SECURITY. Edge: Lettered. **Note:** "Penny."

Date	AG3	G4	VG8	F12	VF20	XF40	MS60
(ca. 1795)	70.00	110	165	300	500	850	3,500

KM# Tn60.1 • Copper **Obv. Legend:** WASHINGTON PRESIDENT. **Edge:** Plain.

Date	AG3	G4	VG8	F12	VF20	XF40	MS60
1792	1,150	2,850	6,500	12,500	27,500	47,500	—

Note: Steinberg $12,650. Garrett $15,500

KM# Tn60.2 • Copper **Obv. Legend:** WASHINGTON PRESIDENT. **Edge:** Lettered. **Edge Lettering:** UNITED STATES OF AMERICA.

Date	AG3	G4	VG8	F12	VF20	XF40	MS60
1792	—	—	—	—	—	—	—

KM# Tn77.2 • Copper **Edge:** Plain. **Note:** "Penny."

Date	AG3	G4	VG8	F12	VF20	XF40	MS60
(ca. 1795)	—	—	—	—	—	—	—
extremely rare							

KM# Tn77.3 • Copper **Note:** "Penny." Engine-turned borders.

Date		G4	VG8	F12	VF20	XF40	MS60
(ca. 1795) 12 known		275	450	650	1,250	2,400	7,500

KM# Tn78 • Copper **Note:** Similar to "Halfpenny" with date on reverse.

Date	AG3	G4	VG8	F12	VF20	XF40	MS60
1795 very rare	—	—	—	—	—	—	—
Note: Roper $6,600							

HALFPENNY

KM# Tn56 • Copper **Obv. Legend:** LIVERPOOL HALFPENNY

Date	AG3	G4	VG8	F12	VF20	XF40	MS60
1791	40.00	70.00	1,000	125	300	550	3,250

KM# Tn61.1 • Copper **Obv. Legend:** BORN VIRGINIA. **Note:** Varieties exist.

Date	AG3	G4	VG8	F12	VF20	XF40	MS60
(ca.1792)	500	1,000	2,000	4,000	7,500	12,000	—

KM# Tn61.1a • Silver **Edge:** Plain.

Date	AG3	G4	VG8	F12	VF20	XF40
(ca.1792) 4 known	—	—	—	—	—250,000	
Note: Roper $16,500						

KM# Tn61.2 • Silver **Edge Lettering:** UNITED STATES OF AMERICA •

Date	AG3	G4	VG8	F12	VF20	XF40
(ca.1792) 2 known	—	—	—	—	—	—

KM# Tn62 • Silver **Rev:** Heraldic eagle. 1792 half dollar. **Note:** Mule.

Date	AG3	G4	VG8	F12	VF20	XF40
(ca.1792) 3 known	—	—	—	—60,000	85,000	

KM# Tn66.1 • Copper **Rev:** Ship **Edge:** Lettered.

Date	AG3	G4	VG8	F12	VF20	XF40	MS60
1793	25.00	45.00	85.00	225	450	825	3,500

KM# Tn66.2 • Copper **Rev:** Ship **Edge:** Plain.

Date	AG3	G4	VG8	F12	VF20	XF40	MS60
1793 5 known	—	—	—	—15,000	—	—	—

KM# Tn77.1 • Copper **Obv. Legend:** LIBERTY AND

KM# Tn75.1 • Copper **Obv.** Large coat buttons **Rev:** Grate **Edge:** Reeded.

Date	AG3	G4	VG8	F12	VF20	XF40	MS60
1795	—	—	70.00	110	200	400	900

COLONIAL COINAGE

KM# Tn75.2 • Copper **Rev:** Grate **Edge:** Lettered.

Date	AG3	G4	VG8	F12	VF20	XF40	MS60
1795	90.00	140	210	275	400	800	2,800

KM# Tn75.3 • Copper **Obv.** Small coat buttons
Rev: Grate **Edge:** Reeded.

Date	AG3	G4	VG8	F12	VF20	XF40	MS60
1795	50.00	75.00	120	190	275	575	2,550

KM# Tn76.1 • Copper **Obv. Legend:** LIBERTY AND SECURITY. **Edge:** Plain.

Date	AG3	G4	VG8	F12	VF20	XF40	MS60
1795	18.00	35.00	60.00	160	350	650	3,250

KM# Tn76.2 • Copper **Edge:** Lettered. **Edge Lettering:** PAYABLE AT LONDON ...

Date	AG3	G4	VG8	F12	VF20	XF40	MS60
1795	40.00	65.00	90.00	140	300	600	3,000

KM# Tn76.3 • Copper **Edge:** Lettered. **Edge Lettering:** BIRMINGHAM ...

Date	AG3	G4	VG8	F12	VF20	XF40	MS60
1795	55.00	85.00	125	175	350	750	3,500

KM# Tn76.4 • Copper **Edge:** Lettered. **Edge Lettering:** AN ASYLUM ...

Date	AG3	G4	VG8	F12	VF20	XF40	MS60
1795	18.00	35.00	60.00	275	600	1,500	6,250

KM# Tn76.5 • Copper **Edge:** Lettered. **Edge Lettering:** PAYABLE AT LIVERPOOL ...

Date	AG3	G4	VG8	F12	VF20	XF40	MS60
1795 unique	—	—	—	—	—	—	—

KM# Tn76.6 • Copper **Edge:** Lettered. **Edge Lettering:** PAYABLE AT LONDON-LIVERPOOL.

Date	AG3	G4	VG8	F12	VF20	XF40	MS60
1795 unique	—	—	—	—	—	—	—

KM# Tn81.1 • Copper **Rev. Legend:** NORTH WALES **Edge:** Plain.

Date	AG3	G4	VG8	F12	VF20	XF40	MS60
(ca.1795)	60.00	110	175	265	625	1,750	—

KM# Tn81.2 • Copper **Rev. Legend:** NORTH WALES **Edge:** Lettered.

Date	AG3	G4	VG8	F12	VF20	XF40	MS60
(ca.1795)	350	550	1,150	1,750	5,500	9,500	—

KM# Tn82 • Copper **Rev:** Four stars at bottom **Rev. Legend:** NORTH WALES

Date	AG3	G4	VG8	F12	VF20	XF40	MS60
(ca.1795)	1,250	2,250	4,750	7,750	21,500	—	—

CENT

KM# Tn39 • Copper **Obv.** Draped Bust left **Rev:** Denomination in wreath **Obv. Legend:** WASHINGTON & INDEPENDENCE **Rev. Legend:** UNITY STATES OF AMERICA

Date	AG3	G4	VG8	F12	VF20	XF40	MS60
1783	30.00	50.00	70.00	100	265	550	2,150

KM# Tn40 • Copper **Note:** Double head.

Date	AG3	G4	VG8	F12	VF20	XF40	MS60
(ca. 1783)	25.00	45.00	60.00	95.00	250	500	2,650

KM# Tn41 • Copper **Obv.** Ugly head. **Note:** 3 known in copper, 1 in white metal.

Date	AG3	G4	VG8	F12	VF20	XF40	MS60
1784	80,000	120,000	—	—	—	—	—

Note: Roper $14,850. Heritage PCGS Poor $9,775 (2010)

COLONIAL COINAGE

KM# Tn57 • Copper Obv. Military bust left **Rev:** Small eagle **Obv. Legend:** WASHINGTON PRESIDENT.

Date	AG3	G4	VG8	F12	VF20	XF40	MS60
1791	—	—	350	500	725	1,000	4,250

KM# Tn58 • Copper Obv. Military bust left **Rev:** Large eagle **Obv. Legend:** WASHINGTON PRESIDENT

Date	AG3	G4	VG8	F12	VF20	XF40	MS60
1791	—	200	325	485	650	900	3,200

KM# Tn65 • Copper Obv. Roman head **Obv. Legend:** WASHINGTON PRESIDENT.

Date	G4	VG8	F12	VF20	XF40	MS60	PF60
1792	—	—	—	—	—	—	75,000

HALF DOLLAR

KM# Tn59.1 • Copper Edge Lettering: UNITED STATES OF AMERICA

Date	AG3	G4	VG8	F12	VF20	XF40	MS60
1792 2 known	—	—	—	—	—	—150,000	—

Note: Roper $2,860. Benson, EF, $48,300.

KM# Tn59.1a • Silver Edge Lettering: UNITED STATES OF AMERICA

Date	AG3	G4	VG8	F12	VF20	XF40
1792 rare	—	—	—	—	70,000	120,000

Note: Roper $35,200

KM# Tn59.1b • Gold AGW **Edge Lettering:** UNITED STATES OF AMERICA

Date	AG3	G4	VG8	F12	VF20	XF40	MS60
1792 unique	—	—	—	—	—	—	—

KM# Tn59.2 • Copper Edge: Plain.

Date	AG3	G4	VG8	F12	VF20	XF40
1792 3 known	—	—	—	—	145,000	225,000

KM# Tn59.2a • Silver Edge: Plain.

Date	AG3	G4	VG8	F12	VF20	XF40	MS60
1792 rare	—	—	—	—	—	—	—

KM# Tn63.1 • Silver Rev: Small eagle **Edge:** Plain.

Date	AG3	G4	VG8	F12	VF20	XF40	MS60
1792	—	—	—	—250,000	350,000	—	

KM# Tn63.1a • Copper Edge: Plain.

Date	AG3	G4	VG8	F12	VF20	XF40	MS60
1792	—	4,000	6,500	12,500	32,000	48,000	95,000

Note: Garrett $32,000

KM# Tn63.2 • Silver Edge: Ornamented, circles and squares.

Date	G4	VG8	F12	VF20	XF40	MS60
1792 5 known	—	—	—100,000	175,000	400,000	

KM# Tn63.3 • Silver Edge: Two olive leaves.

Date	AG3	G4	VG8	F12	VF20	XF40	MS60
1792 unique	—	—	—	—	—	—	—

KM# Tn64 • Silver Rev: Large heraldic eagle

Date	G4	VG8	F12	VF20	XF40	MS60
1792 unique	—	—	—	120,000	—	—

Note: Garrett $16,500

COLONIAL COINAGE

FEDERAL AMERICA

EARLY FEDERAL PATTERNS

NOVA CONSTELLATIO

KM# EA6.1 • Copper **Obv.** Pointed rays **Rev:** Small "U•S **Obv. Legend:** NOVA • CONSTELLATIO •

Date	AG3	G4	VG8	F12	VF20	XF40	MS60
1783	50.00	70.00	100	225	440	950	3,250

KM# EA6.2 • Copper **Obv.** Pointed rays **Rev:** Large "US **Obv. Legend:** NOVA • CONSTELLATIO •

Date	AG3	G4	VG8	F12	VF20	XF40	MS60
1783	55.00	75.00	110	250	600	1,400	7,000

KM# EA7 • Copper **Obv.** Blunt rays **Obv. Legend:** NOVA • CONSTELATIO •

Date	AG3	G4	VG8	F12	VF20	XF40	MS60
1783	50.00	75.00	110	250	575	1,350	5,000

KM# EA8 • Copper **Obv.** Blunt rays **Obv. Legend:** NOVA • CONSTELATIO •

Date	AG3	G4	VG8	F12	VF20	XF40	MS60
1785	50.00	75.00	110	260	650	1,550	6,500

KM# EA9 • Copper **Obv.** Pointed rays **Obv. Legend:** NOVA • CONSTELLATIO •

Date	AG3	G4	VG8	F12	VF20	XF40	MS60
1785	—	—	100	225	450	1,000	3,600

KM# EA10 • Copper **Note:** Contemporary circulating counterfeit. Similar to previously listed coin.

Date	AG3	G4	VG8	F12	VF20	XF40	MS60
1786 extremely rare	—	—	—	—	—	—	—

5 UNITS

KM# EA12 • Copper **Obv.** Eye, with pointed rays & stars **Obv. Legend:** NOVA CONSTELLATIO **Rev. Legend:** • LIBERTAS • JUSTITIA •

Date	AG3	G4	VG8	F12	VF20	XF40	MS60
1783 unique	—	—	—	—	—	—	—

100 (BIT)

KM# EA13.1 • Silver **Obv.** Eye, with pointed rays & stars **Obv. Legend:** NOVA CONSTELLATIO **Rev. Legend:** • LIBERTAS • JUSTITIA • **Edge:** Leaf.

Date	AG3	G4	VG8	F12	VF20	XF40	MS60
1783 2 known	—	—	—	—	—	—	—

Note: Garrett $97,500. Stack's auction, May 1991, $72,500

KM# EA13.2 • Silver **Obv.** Eye, with pointed rays & stars **Obv. Legend:** NOVA CONSTELLATIO **Rev. Legend:** • LIBERTAS • JUSTITIA • **Edge:** Plain

Date	AG3	G4	VG8	F12	VF20	XF40	MS60
1783 unique	—	—	—	—	—	—	—

Note: Newman, AU55, $705,000

COLONIAL COINAGE

500 (QUINT)

KM# EA14 • Silver **Obv.** Eye with pointed rays & stars **Obv. Legend:** • LIBERTAS • JUSTITIA • **Rev. Legend:** NOVA CONSTELLATIO **Rev.**

Date	AG3	G4	VG8	F12	VF20	XF40	MS60
1783 unique	—	—	—	—	—	—	—

Note: Garrett $165,000

KM# EA15 • Silver **Obv.** Eye, with rays & stars, no legend **Rev. Legend:** • LIBERTAS • JUSTITIA •

Date	AG3	G4	VG8	F12	VF20	XF40	MS60
1783 unique	—	—	—	—	—	—	—

Note: Perschke, AU53, $1,175,000. Garrett $55,000

1000 (MARK)

KM# EA16 • Silver **Obv.** Eye, with pointed rays & stars **Obv. Legend:** • LIBERTAS • JUSTITIA • **Rev. Legend:** NOVA CONSTELLATIO **Rev.**

Date	AG3	G4	VG8	F12	VF20	XF40	MS60
1783 unique	—	—	—	—	—	—	—

Note: Garrett $190,000

IMMUNE COLUMBIA

KM# EA17 • Copper **Rev:** Eye, with pointed rays

& stars **Obv. Legend:** IMMUNE COLUMBIA. **Rev. Legend:** NOVA • CONSTELLATIO

Date	AG3	G4	VG8	F12	VF20	XF40	MS60
1785	—	—	—	—	25,000	45,000	115,000

KM# EA17a • Silver **Rev:** Eye, with pointed rays & stars **Obv. Legend:** IMMUNE COLUMBIA • **Rev. Legend:** NOVA CONSTELLATIO

Date	AG3	G4	VG8	F12	VF20	XF40	MS60
1785	—	—	—	—	45,000	75,000	150,000

KM# EA18 • Copper **Rev:** Eye, with pointed rays & stars. Extra star in reverse legend **Obv. Legend:** IMMUNE COLUMBIA • **Rev. Legend:** NOVA • CONSTELLATIO *

Date	AG3	G4	VG8	F12	VF20	XF40	MS60
1785	—	—	—	—	25,000	45,000	115,000

Note: Caldwell $4,675

KM# EA19 • Copper **Rev:** Blunt rays **Obv. Legend:** IMMUNE COLUMBIA • **Rev. Legend:** NOVA CONSTELATIO

Date	AG3	G4	VG8	F12	VF20	XF40	MS60
1785 2 known	—	—	—	—	—	—	—

Note: Partrick, XF40, $54,050. Norweb $22,000

KM# EA19a • Gold AGW **Rev:** Blunt rays **Obv. Legend:** IMMUNE COLUMBIA • **Rev. Legend:** NOVA CONSTELATIO •

Date	AG3	G4	VG8	F12	VF20	XF40	MS60
1785 Unique	—	—	—	—	—	—	—

Note: In the Smithsonian Collection

KM# EA20 • Copper **Obv.** George III **Obv. Legend:** GEORGIVS III • REX • **Rev. Legend:** IMMUNE COLUMBIA •

Date	AG3	G4	VG8	F12	VF20	XF40	MS60
1785	3,500	5,250	7,750	12,500	22,500	37,500	—

KM# EA21 • Copper **Obv.** Head right **Obv. Legend:** VERMON AUCTORI **Rev. Legend:** IMMUNE COLUMBIA •

Date	AG3	G4	VG8	F12	VF20	XF40	MS60
1785	—	6,000	9,500	14,500	37,500	—	—

COLONIAL COINAGE

KM# EA24 • Copper **Obv.** Washington **Rev:** Stars
in rayed circle **Rev. Legend:** • CONFEDERATIO •

Date	AG3	G4	VG8	F12	VF20	XF40	MS60
1786 3 known	—	—	—	—60,000	—	—	

Note: Garrett $50,000. Steinberg $12,650

KM# EA25 • Copper **Obv.** Eagle, raw shield **Rev:**
Shield **Obv. Legend:** * E • PLURIBUS UNUM • **Rev.
Legend:** * E * PLURIBUS * UNUM *

Date	AG3	G4	VG8	F12	VF20	XF40	MS60
1786 unique	—	—	—	—	—	—	—

Note: Garrett $37,500

KM# EA26 • Copper **Obv.** Washington **Rev:** Eagle
Obv. Legend: GEN • WASHINGTON •

Date	AG3	G4	VG8	F12	VF20	XF40	MS60
1786 2 known	—	—	—	—	—	—	—

KM# EA27 • Copper **Rev:** Shield **Obv. Legend:**
IMMUNIS COLUMBIA • **Rev. Legend:** * E *
PLURIBUS * UNUM *

Date	AG3	G4	VG8	F12	VF20	XF40	MS60
1786	—	—	—	—	—	65,000	137,500

Note: Rescigno, AU, $33,000. Steinberg, VF $11,000

KM# EA28 • Copper **Rev:** Eagle **Obv. Legend:**
IMMUNIS COLUMBIA **Rev. Legend:** * E *
PLURIBUS * UNUM *

Date	AG3	G4	VG8	F12	VF20	XF40	MS60
1786	—	—	—	—	—	80,000	165,000

CONFEDERATIO

KM# EA22 • Copper **Obv.** Standing figure with
bow & arrow **Rev:** Small circle of stars **Obv. Legend:**
INIMICA TYRANNIS • AMERICANA • **Rev. Legend:**
• CONFEDERATIO •

Date	AG3	G4	VG8	F12	VF20	XF40	MS60
1785	—	—	—	—	70,000	116,500	

KM# EA23 • Copper **Obv.** Standing figure with
bow & arrow **Rev:** Large circle of stars **Obv. Legend:**
INIMICA TYRANNIS • AMERICANA • **Rev. Legend:**
• CONFEDERATIO • **Note:** The Confederatio
dies were struck in combination with 13 other
dies of the period. All surviving examples of these
combinations are extremely rare.

Date	AG3	G4	VG8	F12	VF20	XF40	MS60
1785	—	—	—	—	80,000	137,500	—

Note: Newman, MS63, $352,500

KM# EA23a • Silver **Obv.** Standing figure with bow
& arrow **Rev:** Large circle of stars **Obv. Legend:**
INIMICA TYRANNIS • AMERICANA • **Rev. Legend:**
• CONFEDERATIO • **Note:** Only known example
is holed

Date	AG3	G4	VG8	F12	VF20	XF40	MS60
1785 Unique	—	—	—	—	—	—	—

Note: Partrick, VF, $44,650

FUGIO "CENT"

KM# EA30.1 • Copper **Obv.** Club rays, round ends.

Date	AG3	G4	VG8	F12	VF20	XF40	MS60
1787	225	325	450	950	2,000	3,850	—

KM# EA30.2 • Copper **Obv.** Club rays, concave
ends.

Date	AG3	G4	VG8	F12	VF20	XF40	MS60
1787	1,500	2,500	4,500	9,000	27,500	—	

COLONIAL COINAGE

KM# EA30.3 • Copper **Obv. Legend:** FUCIO.

Date	AG3	G4	VG8	F12	VF20	XF40	MS60
1787	—	2,000	3,000	7,000	25,000	35,000	—

KM# EA31.1 • Copper **Obv.** Pointed rays. **Rev:** UNITED above, STATES below.

Date	AG3	G4	VG8	F12	VF20	XF40	MS60
1787	600	950	1,500	3,250	8,000	11,500	—

KM# EA31.2 • Copper **Rev:** UNITED STATES at sides of ring.

Date	AG3	G4	VG8	F12	VF20	XF40	MS60
1787	110	175	275	550	900	1,800	3,500

KM# EA31.3 • Copper **Rev:** STATES UNITED at sides of ring.

Date	AG3	G4	VG8	F12	VF20	XF40	MS60
1787	110	190	275	550	850	1,650	2,500

KM# EA31.4 • Copper **Rev:** Eight-pointed stars on ring.

Date	AG3	G4	VG8	F12	VF20	XF40	MS60
1787	150	285	475	700	1,250	2,750	9,000

KM# EA31.5 • Copper **Rev:** Raised rims on ring, large lettering in center.

Date	AG3	G4	VG8	F12	VF20	XF40	MS60
1787	185	325	550	950	2,750	6,000	18,500

KM# EA32.1 • Copper **Obv.** No cinquefoils, cross after date. **Obv. Legend:** UNITED STATES.

Date	AG3	G4	VG8	F12	VF20	XF40	MS60
1787	300	—	750	1,450	3,750	5,750	—

KM# EA32.2 • Copper **Obv.** No cinquefoils, cross after date. **Obv. Legend:** STATES UNITED.

Date	AG3	G4	VG8	F12	VF20	XF40	MS60
1787	175	350	750	1,500	4,000	7,200	—

KM# EA32.3 • Copper **Obv.** No cinquefoils, cross after date. **Rev:** Raised rims on ring.

Date	AG3	G4	VG8	F12	VF20	XF40	MS60
1787	—	—	—	—	27,500	—	—

KM# EA33 • Copper **Obv.** No cinquefoils, cross after date. **Rev:** With rays. **Rev. Legend:** AMERICAN CONGRESS.

Date	VG8	F12	VF20	XF40	MS60
1787 extremely rare	—	—	225,000	300,000	—

Note: Norweb $63,800

KM# EA34 • Brass **Note:** New Haven restrike.

Date	AG3	G4	VG8	F12	VF20	XF40	MS60
1787 (ca.1858)	—	—	—	—	—	450	950

KM# EA34a • Copper **Note:** New Haven restrike.

Date	AG3	G4	VG8	F12	VF20	XF40	MS60
1787 (ca.1858)	—	—	—	—	—	450	750	1,250

KM# EA34b • Silver **Note:** New Haven restrike.

Date	AG3	G4	VG8	F12	VF20	XF40	MS60
1787 (ca. 1858)	—	—	—	—	—	2,750	6,750

KM# EA34c • Gold AGW **Note:** New Haven restrike.

Date	AG3	G4	VG8	F12	VF20	XF40	MS60
1787 (ca. 1858)	—	—	—	—	—	—	—

2 known

Note: Norweb (holed) $1,430

BRASHER

KM# Tn51.1 • Gold AGW **Obv.** Sunrise over mountains. **Rev:** Displayed eagle with shield on breast, EB counterstamp on wing.

Date	AG3	G4	VG8	F12	VF20	XF40	MS60
1787 6 known	—	—	—	—	—	—	—

Note: Heritage FUN Sale, January 2005, AU-55, $2,415,000.

COLONIAL COINAGE

KM# Tn51.2 • Gold AGW **Obv.** Sunrise over mountains **Rev:** Displayed eagle with shield on breast. EB counterstamp on breast.

Date	AG3	G4	VG8	F12	VF20	XF40	MS60
1787 unique	—	—	—	—	—	—	—

Note: Heritage FUN sale, January 2005, XF-45, $2,9900. Foreign gold coins with EB counterstamp exist. These are valued at over $5,000, with many much higher.

ISSUES OF 1792

CENT

KM# PnE1 • Bi-Metallic, Silver center in Copper ring

Date	VG8	F12	VF20	XF40	MS60
1792 14 known	—	185,000	325,000	475,000	950,000

Note: Norweb, MS-60, $143,000; Heritage 4-12; MS61 $1.15 million

KM# PnF1 • Copper **Note:** No silver center.

Date	VG8	F12	VF20	XF40	MS60
1792 9 known	—	250,000	550,000	800,000	—

Note: Norweb, EF-40, $35,200; Benson, VG-10, $57,500

KM# PnG1 • Copper **Edge:** Plain **Note:** Commonly called "Birch cent."

Date	AG3	G4	VG8	F12	VF20	XF40	MS60
1792 unique	—	—	—	—	—	850,000	—

KM# PnH1 • Copper **Obv.** One star in edge legend **Note:** Commonly called "Birch cent."

Date	G4	VG8	F12	VF20	XF40	MS60
1792 2 known	—	—	—	—	650,000	750,000

Note: Norweb, EF-40, $59,400

KM# PnI1 • Copper **Obv.** Two stars in edge legend **Note:** Commonly called "Birch cent."

Date	G4	VG8	F12	VF20	XF40	MS60
1792 8 known	—	100,000	200,000	400,000	550,000	—

Note: Partrick, MS65, $2,585,000. Hawn, strong VF, $57,750.

KM# PnJ1 • White Metal **Rev:** G.W.Pt. below wreath tie **Note:** Commonly called "Birch cent."

Date	AG3	G4	VG8	F12	VF20	XF40	MS60
1792 unique	—	—	—	—	—	—	—

Note: Garrett, $90,000

COLONIAL COINAGE

HALF DISME

KM# 5 • Silver

Date	AG3	G4	VG8	F12	VF20	XF40	MS60
1792	20,000	25,000	45,000	65,000	90,000	125,000	325,000

KM# PnA1 • Copper

Date	AG3	G4	VG8	F12	VF20	XF40	MS60
1792 unique	—	—	—	—	—	—	—
Note: Heritage 4-06, Sp-67, $1,322,500							

DISME

KM# PnB1 • Silver

Date	VG8	F12	VF20	XF40	MS60
1792 3 known		—	700,000	1,000,000	—
Note: Norweb, EF-40, $28,600					

KM# PnC1 • Copper **Edge:** Reeded

Date	VG8	F12	VF20	XF40	MS60
1792 14 known		—	150,000	250,000	500,000
Note: Hawn, VF, $30,800; Benson, EF-45, $109,250					

KM# PnD1 • Copper **Edge:** Plain

Date	G4	VG8	F12	VF20	XF40	MS60
1792 2 known	—	—	—450,000	750,000	—
Note: Garrett, $45,000						

QUARTER

KM# PnK1 • Copper **Edge:** Reeded **Note:** Commonly called "Wright quarter."

Date	AG3	G4	VG8	F12	VF20	XF40	MS60
1792 2 known	—	—	—	—	—	—	—
Note: Patrick, MS63, $2,232,500							

KM# PnL1 • White Metal **Edge:** Plain **Note:** Commonly called "Wright quarter."

Date	AG3	G4	VG8	F12	VF20	XF40	MS60
1792 4 known	—	—	—	—	—	400,000	—
Note: Patrick, XF45, $376,000. Norweb, VF-30 to EF-40, $28,600							

KM# PnM1 • White Metal **Note:** Commonly called "Wright quarter."

Date	AG3	G4	VG8	F12	VF20	XF40	MS60
1792 die trial	—	—	—	—	—	—	—
Note: Garrett, $12,000							

COLONIAL COINAGE

PRIVATE GOLD

Private gold pieces (also referred to as "Territorial" and "Pioneer" gold) are those struck outside the U.S. Mint and not recognized as official issues by the federal government. The pieces so identified are of various shapes, denominations, and degrees of intrinsic value, and were locally required because of the remoteness of the early gold fields from a federal mint and/or an insufficient quantity of official coinage in frontier areas.

The legality of these privately issued pieces derives from the fact that federal law prior to 1864 prohibited a state from coining money, but did not specifically deny that right to an individual, providing that the privately issued coins did not closely resemble those of the United States.

In addition to coin-like gold pieces, the private minters of the gold rush days also issued gold in ingot and bar form. Ingots were intended for circulation and were cast in regular values and generally in large denominations. Bars represent a miner's deposit after it had been assayed, refined, cast into convenient form (generally rectangular), and stamped with the appropriate weight, fineness, and value. Although occasionally cast in even values for the convenience of banks, bars were more often of odd denomination, and when circulated were rounded off to the nearest figure. Ingots and bars are omitted from this listing.

CALIFORNIA
Fractional and Small Size Gold Coinage

During the California gold rush a wide variety of U.S. and foreign coins were used for small change, but only limited quantities of these coins were available. Gold dust was in common use, although this offered the miner a relatively low value for his gold.

By 1852 California jewelers had begun to manufacture 25¢, 50¢ and $1 gold pieces in round and octagonal shapes. Makers included M. Deriberpe, Antoine Louis Nouizillet, Isadore Routhier, Robert B. Gray, Pierre Frontier, Eugene Deviercy, Herman J. Brand, and Herman and Jacob Levison. Reuben N. Hershfield and Noah Mitchell made their coins in Leavenworth, Kansas and most of their production was seized in August 1871. Herman Kroll made California gold coins in New York City in the 1890s. Only two or three of these companies were in production at any one time. Many varieties bear the makers initials. Frontier and his partners made most of the large Liberty Head, Eagle reverse, and Washington Head design types. Most of the small Liberty Head types were made first by Nouizillet and later by Gray and then the Levison brothers and lastly by the California Jewelry Co. Coins initialed "G.G." are apparently patterns made by Frontier and Deviercy for the New York based firm of Gaime, Guillemot & Co.

Most of the earlier coins were struck from gold alloys and had an intrinsic value of about 50-60 percent of face value. They were generally struck from partially hubbed dies and with reeded collars. A few issues were struck with a plain collar or a collar with reeding on only 7 of the 8 sides. Many issues are too poorly struck or too thin to have a clear and complete image of the collar. The later coins and some of the earlier coins were struck from laminated or plated gold planchets, or from gold plated silver planchets. Most of the last dates of issue are extremely thin and contain only token amounts of gold.

Circumstantial evidence exists that the coins issued through 1856 circulated as small change. The San Francisco mint was established in 1854, and by 1856 it had ramped up its production enough to satisfy the local need for small change. However, some evidence exists that these small gold coins may have continued to circulate on occasion through to 1871. After 1871, the gold content of the coins dramatically decreases and it is very unlikely that any of these last issues circulated.

Although the Private Coinages Act of 1864 outlawed all private coinage, this law was not enforced in California and production of small denominated gold continued through 1882. In the spring of 1883, Col. Henry Finnegass of the U.S. Secret Service halted production of the denominated private gold pieces. Non-denominated tokens (lacking DOLLARS, CENTS or the equivalent) were also made during this latter period, sometimes by the same manufacturing jeweler using the same obverse die and the same planchets as the small denomination gold coins. Production of these tokens continues to this day, with most issues made after the 1906 earthquake and fire being backdated to 1847-1865 and struck from brass or gold plated brass planchets.

Approximately 25,000 pieces of California small denomination gold coins are estimated to exist, in a total of over 500 varieties. A few varieties are undated, mostly gold rush era pieces; and a few of the issues are backdated, mostly those from the 1880s. This listing groups varieties together in easily identified categories. The prices quoted are for the most common variety in each group.

US PRIVATE GOLD

UNC prices reflect the median auction prices realized of MS60 to MS62 graded coins. BU prices reflect the median auction prices realized of MS63 to MS64 graded coins. Pre-1871 true MS-65 coins are rare and sell for substantial premiums over the prices on this list. Post-1871 coins are rarely found with wear and often have a cameo proof appearance. Auction prices realized are highly volatile and it is not uncommon to find recent records of sales at twice or half of the values shown here. Many of the rarity estimates published in the 1980s and earlier have proven to be too high, so caution is advised when paying a premium for a rare variety. In addition, many varieties that have a refined appearance command higher prices than equivalent grade but scarcer varieties that have a more crude appearance.

Several counterfeits of California Fractional Gold coins exist. Beware of 1854 and 1858 dated round 1/2 dollars, and 1871 dated round dollars that have designs that do not match any of the published varieties. Beware of reeded edge Kroll coins being sold as originals.

For further information consult *California Pioneer Fractional Gold, 2nd Edition* by W. Breen and R.J. Gillio and "The Brasher Bulletin" the official newsletter of The Society of Private and Pioneer Numismatists. The bulletin has not been published recently due to a lack of new material.

CALIFORNIA

1/4 DOLLAR (OCTAGONAL)

KM# 1.1 • Gold **Obv.** Large Liberty head, left **Rev:** Value and date within beaded circle

Date	XF40	AU50	MS60	MS63	MS65
1853	—	175	300	400	1,000
Note: BG-102					
1854	—	175	250	300	800
Note: BG-103, BG-104, BG-105					
1855	—	175	250	350	800
Note: BG-106					
1856 FD	—	175	310	425	1,200
Note: BG-107, BG-704A					

KM# 1.2 • Gold **Obv.** Liberty head, left **Rev:** Value and date within wreath

Date	XF40	AU50	MS60	MS63	MS65
1859	—	140	200	300	500
Note: BG-701, BG-702, BG-703, BG-704, BG-705					
1864	—	150	300	1,000	—
Note: BG-706, BG-707					
1866	—	150	250	400	—
Note: BG-708					
1867	—	140	250	325	800
Note: BG-709					
1868	—	145	200	300	550
Note: BG-710, BG-711					
1869	—	145	200	350	600
Note: BG-712					
1870	—	145	200	350	—
Note: BG-713					
1871	—	140	200	300	500
Note: BG-714, BG-715, BG-716 BG-716A, BG-717, BG-718, BG-719, BG-719A, BG-720					

KM# 1.3 • Gold **Obv.** Large Liberty head, left, above date **Rev:** 1/4 DOLLAR and CAL within wreath

Date	XF40	AU50	MS60	MS63	MS65
1872	—	125	250	400	—
Note: BG-725, BG-726					
1873	—	110	175	300	700
Note: BG-727, BG-728					

KM# 1.4 • Gold **Obv.** Small Liberty head, left **Rev:** Value and date within beaded circle

Date	XF40	AU50	MS60	MS63	MS65
1853	200	300	1,000	3,000	—
Note: BG-101					

KM# 1.5 • Gold **Obv.** Small Liberty head, left, above date **Rev:** Value within wreath

Date	XF40	AU50	MS60	MS63	MS65
1854	—	200	300	400	—
Note: BG-108, BG-109					

KM# 1.6 • Gold **Obv.** Small Liberty head, left **Rev:** Value and date within wreath

Date	XF40	AU50	MS60	MS63	MS65
1855	—	200	300	400	—
Note: BG-110					
1856	—	175	250	300	550
Note: BG-111					
1857 Plain edge	—	—	150	200	—
Note: BG-1301, Plain edge. Kroll type date.					
1857 Reeded edge	—	—	75.00	110	—
Note: BG-1301A Reeded edge. Kroll type date.					
1860 Rare	—	—	—	—	—
Note: BG-729, Rare					
1860 G	—	200	300	750	—
Note: BG-730, BG-731, BG-732					
1870 G	—	160	250	400	—
Note: BG-753, BG-754, BG-755					

KM# 1.7 • Gold **Obv.** Liberty head, left **Rev:** 1/4 in shield, DOLLAR and date below, all within wreath

Date	XF40	AU50	MS60	MS63	MS65
1863 G	—	200	500	—	—
Note: BG-733, BG-734					
1864 G	—	140	240	350	—
Note: BG-735					

Date	XF40	AU50	MS60	MS63	MS65
1865 G	—	160	250	550	—

Note: BG-736

Date	XF40	AU50	MS60	MS63	MS65
1866 G	—	160	300	750	—

Note: BG-737, BG-738, BG-739, BG-740

| 1867 G | — | 150 | 250 | 600 | — |

Note: BG-741, BG-742, BG-743

| 1868 G | — | 150 | 250 | 400 | — |

Note: BG-744, BG-745, BG-746, BG-747

| 1869 G | — | 150 | 250 | 450 | — |

Note: BG-748, BG-749, BG-750, BG-751

| 1870 G | — | 150 | 250 | 450 | — |

Note: BG-752

KM# 1.8 • Gold **Obv.** Small Liberty head, left, above date **Rev:** 1/4 DOLLAR and CAL, all within wreath

Date	XF40	AU50	MS60	MS63	MS65
1870 G	—	140	250	350	—

Note: BG-756, BG-757, BG-758, BG-759, BG-760, BG-761, BG-762, BG-763

| 1871 G | — | 175 | 250 | 350 | — |

Note: BG-764, BG-765, BG-766, BG-767, BG-768, BG-769

| 1871 L | — | 140 | 250 | 350 | — |

Note: BG-770, BG-771

| 1873 | — | 225 | 400 | 1,000 | — |

Note: BG-772

| 1874 | — | 140 | 300 | 700 | — |

Note: BG-773, BG-774, BG-775, BG-776

| 1875/3 | — | 400 | 1,000 | — | — |

Note: BG-777

| 1876 | — | 140 | 300 | 400 | 1,000 |

Note: BG-778, BG-779, BG-780

KM# 1.9 • Gold **Obv.** "Goofy" Liberty head, left **Rev:** Value and date within wreath

Date	XF40	AU50	MS60	MS63	MS65
1870	—	150	200	350	1,000

Note: BG-789

KM# 1.10 • Gold **Obv.** Oriental Liberty head, left, above date **Rev:** 1/4 CALDOLL within wreath

Date	XF40	AU50	MS60	MS63	MS65
1881	—	—	1,000	3,000	—

Note: BG-799Z

KM# 1.11 • Gold **Obv.** Large Liberty head, left, above 1872 **Rev:** Value and 1871 within wreath

Date	XF40	AU50	MS60	MS63	MS65
1872-71	—	—	1,000	3,000	—

Note: BG-721, BG-721a

KM# 2.1 • Gold **Obv.** Large Indian head, left, above date **Rev:** Value within wreath

Date	XF40	AU50	MS60	MS63	MS65
1852	—	200	340	500	1,500

Note: BG-799U, BG-799V, BG-799DD. Back dated issue.

Date	XF40	AU50	MS60	MS63	MS65
1868	—	200	340	500	1,500

Note: BG-799R, BG-799S, BG-799T. Back dated issue.

| 1874 | — | 185 | 320 | 450 | 1,500 |

Note: BG-799P, BG-799P2, BG-799Q. Back dated issue.

| 1876 | — | 150 | 320 | 375 | 800 |

Note: BG-799A, BG-799B, BG-799C, BG-799D, BG-799F, BG-799BA (a.k.a. BG-799GG)

| 1878/6 | — | 300 | 400 | 500 | 1,000 |

Note: BG-799E, BG-799G

| 1880 | — | 125 | 200 | 300 | 750 |

Note: BG-799H, BG-799I, BG-799J, BG-799K, BG-799L

| 1881 | — | 125 | 200 | 300 | 750 |

Note: BG-799M, BG-799N, BG-799O

KM# 2.2 • Gold **Obv.** Large Indian head, left, above date **Rev:** Value and CAL within wreath

Date	XF40	AU50	MS60	MS63	MS65
1872	100	125	260	350	800

Note: BG-790, BG-791

| 1873/2 | 200 | 250 | 600 | 2,000 | — |

Note: BG-792

| 1873 | 120 | 150 | 300 | 400 | 800 |

Note: BG-793, BG-794

| 1874 | 100 | 125 | 260 | 350 | 600 |

Note: BG-795

| 1875 | 120 | 150 | 300 | 400 | 800 |

Note: BG-796, BG-797, BG-798

| 1876 | 120 | 150 | 300 | 400 | 800 |

Note: BG-799

KM# 2.3 • Gold **Obv.** Small Indian head, left, above date **Rev:** 1/4 DOLLAR and CAL, all within wreath

Date	XF40	AU50	MS60	MS63	MS65
1875	—	175	300	500	2,000

Note: BG-781, BG-782, BG-783, BG-784

| 1876 | — | 200 | 300 | 500 | — |

Note: BG-785, BG-786, BG-787

| 1881 | — | — | 500 | 1,100 | — |

Note: BG-788

KM# 2.4 • Gold **Obv.** Aztec Indian head, left, above date **Rev:** Value and CAL within wreath

Date	XF40	AU50	MS60	MS63	MS65
1880	—	150	210	250	600

Note: BG-799W, BG-799X, BG-799Y

KM# 2.6 • Gold **Obv.** Dumb Indian head, left, date below **Rev:** Value and CAL within wreath

Date	XF40	AU50	MS60	MS63	MS65
1881	—	—	1,800	—	—

Note: BG-799AA

KM# 2.7 • Gold **Obv.** Young Indian head, left, above date **Rev:** Value within wreath

Date	XF40	AU50	MS60	MS63	MS65
1881	—	—	500	1,800	—

Note: BG-799BB

US PRIVATE GOLD

KM# 2.8 • Gold **Obv.** Indian head, left, above date **Rev:** 1/4 DOLLAR and CAL, all within wreath

Date	XF40	AU50	MS60	MS63	MS65
1882	—	—	500	1,000	—
Note: BG-799CC					

KM# 5.3 • Gold **Obv.** Small Liberty head, left **Rev:** 25 CENTS within wreath

Date	XF40	AU50	MS60	MS63	MS65
ND	1,000	1,650	2,450	3,500	—
Note: BG-201, BG-202					

KM# 3 • Gold **Obv.** Washington head, left, above date **Rev:** Value and CAL within wreath

Date	XF40	AU50	MS60	MS63	MS65
1872	—	750	1,000	1,100	3,000
Note: BG-722, BG-723, BG-724					

KM# 5.4 • Gold **Obv.** Small Liberty head, left **Rev:** 1/4 DOLL. or "DOLLAR" and date in wreath

Date	XF40	AU50	MS60	MS63	MS65
1853	500	800	1,200	2,500	—
Note: BG-208, BG-209					
ND	115	175	225	375	—
Note: BG-203, BG-204, BG-204A, BG-204B, BG-204C BG-205, BG-206, BG-207, BG-209A, BG-209B, BG-209C, BG-221, BG-222, BG-223, BG-224. Rare counterfeit exists.					
1855 10 stars	145	225	300	400	—
Note: BG-225, BG-226, BG-226A, BG-227, 10 stars					
1855 11 stars	—	—	50.00	100	—
Note: BG-1302, 11 stars. Kroll type.					
1856	125	200	275	375	—
Note: BG-228, BG-229, BG-230, BG-818A					
1860	90.00	135	200	300	—
Note: BG-819, BG-866					
1864	100	150	225	325	—
Note: BG-821, BG-821A					
1865	115	160	250	375	—
Note: BG-822					
1866 G	150	235	625	375	—
Note: BG-823, BG-824					
1867 G	90.00	135	200	375	—
Note: BG-825					
1869 G	90.00	125	200	325	—
Note: BG-826, BG-827, BG-828, BG-829, BG-830, BG-831					
1870 G	150	235	275	475	—
Note: BG-832, BG-833					

1/4 DOLLAR (ROUND)

KM# 4 • Gold **Obv.** Defiant eagle above date **Rev:** 25 CENTS within wreath

Date	XF40	AU50	MS60	MS63	MS65
1854	11,000	22,000	33,000	44,000	—
Note: BG-220					

KM# 5.1 • Gold **Obv.** Large Liberty head, left **Rev:** Value and date within wreath

Date	XF40	AU50	MS60	MS63	MS65
1853	400	700	1,000	1,500	—
Note: BG-213, BG-214, BG-215					
1853 F.D.	600	950	1,500	2,250	—
Note: BG-210, BG-211, BG-212					
1853 G.G.	600	950	1,500	2,250	—
Note: BG-217, BG-217A, BG-218, BG-219					
1854	175	275	425	625	—
Note: BG-216					
1858 Rare	—	—	—	—	—
Note: BG-800, Rare					
1859	95.00	145	250	300	—
Note: BG-801					
1865	115	185	275	375	—
Note: BG-802, BG-803					
1866	—	—	250	350	—
Note: BG-804					
1867	—	—	250	350	—
Note: BG-805					
1868	—	—	250	350	—
Note: BG-806					
1870	—	—	250	350	—
Note: BG-807, BG-808, BG-808A					
1871	—	—	250	350	—
Note: BG-809, BG-810, BG-811, BG-812					

KM# 5.2 • Gold **Obv.** Large Liberty head, left, above date **Rev:** Value and CAL within wreath

Date	XF40	AU50	MS60	MS63	MS65
1871	—	—	250	325	—
Note: BG-813					
1872	—	—	300	375	—
Note: BG-814, BG-815, BG-816					
1873	—	—	230	300	—
Note: BG-817					

KM# 5.5 • Gold **Obv.** Small Liberty head, left **Rev:** Value in shield and date within wreath

Date	XF40	AU50	MS60	MS63	MS65
1863/1860 Rare	—	—	—	—	—
Note: BG-820A, Rare. Struck over 1/4 Dollar KM#5.4.					
1863	80.00	160	200	—	—
Note: BG-820					
1870 G Rare	—	—	—	—	—
Note: BG-831A, Rare. 1/4 Dollar KM#1.7 on a round planchet.					

KM# 5.6 • Gold **Obv.** Small Liberty head, left, above date **Rev:** 1/4 DOLLAR CAL within wreath

Date	XF40	AU50	MS60	MS63	MS65
ND G	120	175	500	—	—
Note: BG-834					
1870 G	100	160	200	250	—
Note: BG-835, BG-835A, BG-836					
1871 G	100	160	200	250	—
Note: BG-837, BG-838, BG-839, BG-840					
1871 L	—	—	210	350	—
Note: BG-841					
1873	—	—	300	500	—
Note: BG-842					
1874	—	—	300	500	—

US PRIVATE GOLD

Date	XF40	AU50	MS60	MS63	MS65
Note: BG-843, BG-844, BG-845					
1875	—	—	250	475	—
Note: BG-846					
1876	—	—	225	400	—
Note: BG-854, BG-855, BG-856					

KM# 5.7 • Gold **Obv.** Goofy Liberty head, left **Rev:** Value and date within wreath

Date	XF40	AU50	MS60	MS63	MS65
1870	110	160	220	275	—
Note: BG-867					

KM# 5.8 • Gold **Obv.** Liberty head left, H and date below **Rev:** 1/4 DOLLAR CAL within wreath

Date	XF40	AU50	MS60	MS63	MS65
1871 H	180	125	225	375	—
Note: BG-857A, BG-857, BG-859, BG-860, BG-861, BG-862, BG-864, BG-864A, BG-865					

KM# 6.1 • Gold **Obv.** Large Indian head left, date below **Rev:** Value within wreath

Date	XF40	AU50	MS60	MS63	MS65
1852	—	—	350	450	—
Note: BG-891. Back dated issue.					
1868	—	—	400	525	—
Note: BG-889, BG-890. Back dated issue.					
1874	—	—	350	425	—
Note: BG-888. Back dated issue.					
1876	—	—	350	475	—
Note: BG-880, BG-881, BG-882					
1878/6	—	—	350	450	—
Note: BG-883, BG-884					
1880	—	—	250	375	—
Note: BG-885					
1881	—	—	250	375	—
Note: BG-886, BG-887					

KM# 6.2 • Gold **Obv.** Large Indian head left, date below **Rev:** 1/4 DOLLAR CAL within wreath

Date	XF40	AU50	MS60	MS63	MS65
1872/1	—	—	250	350	—
Note: BG-868, BG-869, BG-870					
1873	—	—	325	425	—
Note: BG-871, BG-872, BG-873, BG-874					
1874	—	—	230	325	—
Note: BG-875, BG-876					
1875	—	—	250	350	—
Note: BG-877, BG-878					
1876	—	—	250	350	—
Note: BG-879					

KM# 6.3 • Gold **Obv.** Small Indian head left, date below **Rev:** Value within wreath

Date	XF40	AU50	MS60	MS63	MS65
1875	125	175	300	450	—
Note: BG-847, BG-847A, BG-848					

Date	XF40	AU50	MS60	MS63	MS65
1876	115	160	250	400	—
Note: BG-849, BG-850, BG-851, BG-852, BG-853					
1881 Rare	—	—	—	—	—
Note: BG-853A, Rare					

KM# 6.4 • Gold **Obv.** Young Indian head left, date below **Rev:** 1/4 DOLLAR CAL within wreath

Date	XF40	AU50	MS60	MS63	MS65
1882	400	725	1,225	1,750	—
Note: BG-892					

KM# 7 • Gold **Obv.** Washington head left, date below **Rev:** 1/4 DOLLAR CAL within wreath

Date	XF40	AU50	MS60	MS63	MS65
1872	—	550	1,100	1,450	—
Note: BG-818					

1/2 DOLLAR (OCTAGONAL)

KM# 8.1 • Gold **Obv.** Liberty head left, date below **Rev:** 1/2 DOLLAR in beaded circle, CALIFORNIA GOLD around

Date	XF40	AU50	MS60	MS63	MS65
1853 FD	165	280	350	450	—
Note: BG-304					
1854	110	225	285	350	—
Note: BG-304A, BG-304B, BG-305. Rare counterfiet exists.					
1854 FD	165	280	350	450	—
Note: BG-306					
1856	165	285	365	450	—
Note: BG-307					

KM# 8.2 • Gold **Obv.** Liberty head, left **Rev:** Small eagle with rays ("peacock")

Date	XF40	AU50	MS60	MS63	MS65
1853 FD	800	600	2,000	3,000	—
Note: BG-302, BG-303					

KM# 8.3 • Gold **Obv.** Large Liberty head, left **Rev:** Large eagle with date

Date	XF40	AU50	MS60	MS63	MS65
1853 FD	5,000	7,500	10,000	—	—
Note: BG-301					

KM# 8.4 • Gold **Obv.** Liberty head, left **Rev:** Value and date within wreath

Date	XF40	AU50	MS60	MS63	MS65
1859	—	155	225	300	—
Note: BG-901, BG-902					
1866	—	225	325	425	—

US PRIVATE GOLD

Date	XF40	AU50	MS60	MS63	MS65
Note: BG-903, BG-904					
1867	—	155	250	325	—
Note: BG-905					
1868	—	155	250	325	—
Note: BG-906					
1869	—	155	275	375	—
Note: BG-907					
1870	—	155	275	375	—
Note: BG-908, BG-909					
1871	—	155	250	325	—
Note: BG-910, BG-911, BG-912					

KM# 8.5 • Gold **Obv.** Large Liberty head left, date below **Rev:** HALF / DOLLAR / CAL within wreath

Date	XF40	AU50	MS60	MS63	MS65
1872	—	155	275	375	—
Note: BG-913, BG-914					
1873	—	155	250	325	—
Note: BG-915					

KM# 8.6 • Gold **Obv.** Liberty head, left **Rev:** HALF DOL. CALIFORNIA GOLD around wreath, date within

Date	XF40	AU50	MS60	MS63	MS65
1854 N	100	250	350	500	—
Note: BG-308					
1855 N	90.00	200	300	400	—
Note: BG-309					
1856 N	90.00	200	265	325	—
Note: BG-310, BG-311, BG-915A					
1856 G N	165	350	1,100	—	—
Note: BG-916. Back date issue struck in 1864.					
1868	70.00	110	185	275	—
Note: BG1303. Kroll type.					

KM# 8.7 • Gold **Obv.** Small Liberty head left **Rev:** HALF / DOLLAR /date all within wreath

Date	XF40	AU50	MS60	MS63	MS65
1864 G	—	175	275	350	—
Note: BG-917, BG-917a, BG-918. A rare silver strike of 1864G is known.					
1870 G	—	175	275	—	—
Note: BG-921					

KM# 8.8 • Gold **Obv.** Liberty head left **Rev:** CAL. GOLD / HALF DOL and date within wreath

Date	XF40	AU50	MS60	MS63	MS65
1869 G	—	175	200	350	—
Note: BG-919					
1870 G	—	175	200	350	—
Note: BG-920					

KM# 8.9 • Gold **Obv.** Small Liberty head left, date below **Rev:** HALF DOLLAR CAL within wreath

Date	XF40	AU50	MS60	MS63	MS65
1870 G	75.00	110	200	300	—
Note: BG-922					
1871 G	75.00	110	200	250	—
Note: BG-923, BG-924, BG-925					
1871 L	75.00	100	165	250	—
Note: BG-926, BG-927					
1873	95.00	200	300	600	—
Note: BG-928					
1874	95.00	200	300	600	—
Note: BG-929, BG-930					
1875	250	475	1,000	—	—
Note: BG-930A, BG-931					
1876	75.00	110	200	250	—
Note: BG-932, BG-932A					

KM# 8.10 • Gold **Obv.** Goofy Liberty head, left **Rev:** Value and date within wreath

Date	XF40	AU50	MS60	MS63	MS65
1870	75.00	110	200	300	—
Note: BG-936					

KM# 8.11 • Gold **Obv.** Oriental Liberty head left, date below **Rev:** 1/2 CALDOLL within wreath

Date	XF40	AU50	MS60	MS63	MS65
1881	250	450	750	1,150	—
Note: BG-964					

KM# 9.1 • Gold **Obv.** Large Indian head left, date below **Rev:** Value within wreath

Date	XF40	AU50	MS60	MS63	MS65
1852	—	—	700	1,100	—
Note: BG-962. Back dated issue.					
1868	—	—	850	1,200	—
Note: BG-961. Back dated issue.					
1874	—	175	700	1,100	—
Note: BG-959. Back dated issue.					
1876	—	—	350	450	—
Note: BG-953					
1880	—	—	350	450	—
Note: BG-954					
1881	—	—	350	450	—
Note: BG-956					

KM# 9.2 • Gold **Obv.** Large Indian head left, date below **Rev:** 1/2 DOLLAR CAL within wreath

Date	XF40	AU50	MS60	MS63	MS65
1852	—	—	500	750	—
Note: BG-963. Back dated issue.					
1868	—	—	300	600	—
Note: BG-960. Back dated issue.					
1872	—	—	250	350	—
Note: BG-937, BG-938, BG-939, BG-940					
1873/2	—	—	250	450	—
Note: BG-941					
1873	—	—	250	350	—
Note: BG-942					
1874/3	—	—	300	400	—
Note: BG-943					
1874	—	—	250	475	—

US PRIVATE GOLD

Date	XF40	AU50	MS60	MS63	MS65
Note: BG-944, BG-944A, BG-945, BG-958					
1875	—	—	300	350	—
Note: BG-946, BG947, BG-948					
1876	—	—	300	450	—
Note: BG-949, BG-950, BG-951					
1878/6	—	—	300	450	—
Note: BG-952					
1880	—	—	550	1,050	—
Note: BG-955					
1881	—	—	300	450	—
Note: BG-952A, BG-952B, BG-957					

KM# 9.3 • Gold **Obv.** Small Indian head left, date below **Rev:** Value and CAL within wreath

Date	XF40	AU50	MS60	MS63	MS65
1875	—	265	350	525	—
Note: BG-933, BG-934					
1876	—	265	350	525	—
Note: BG-935					

KM# 9.4 • Gold **Obv.** Young Indian head left, date below **Rev:** 1/2 DOLLAR CAL within wreath

Date	XF40	AU50	MS60	MS63	MS65
1881	—	—	550	850	—
Note: BG-965, BG-965A					
1882 Rare	—	—	—	—	—
Note: BG-966, Rare					

1/2 DOLLAR (ROUND)

KM# 10 • Gold **Obv.** Arms of California and date **Rev:** Eagle and legends

Date	XF40	AU50	MS60	MS63	MS65
1853	—	3,500	—	—	—
Note: BG-435					

KM# 11.1 • Gold **Obv.** Liberty head, left **Rev:** Large eagle and legends

Date	XF40	AU50	MS60	MS63	MS65
1854	1,000	2,700	6,000	—	—
Note: BG-436. Similar obverse paired with reverse of KM#12.2, or an eagle with no denomination are modern counterfeits.					

KM# 11.2 • Gold **Obv.** Liberty head left, date below **Rev:** HALF DOL. CALIFORNIA GOLD around wreath

Date	XF40	AU50	MS60	MS63	MS65
1854	200	300	450	600	—
Note: BG-431					

KM# 11.3 • Gold **Obv.** Liberty head left **Rev:** Date in wreath, value and CALIFORNIA GOLD around wreath

Date	XF40	AU50	MS60	MS63	MS65
1852	195	280	375	500	—
Note: BG-401, BG-426, BG-427					
1852 DN	195	280	375	500	—
Note: BG-407					
1853 DN	195	280	375	500	—
Note: BG-408, BG-409					
1853 D	215	300	400	525	—
Note: BG-420, BG-421, BG-422					
1853	215	300	400	525	—
Note: BG-415, BG-415A, BG-416, BG-416A, BG-417, BG-418, BG-419, BG-428, BG-429, BG-430					
1854 D	300	500	750	1,000	—
Note: BG-422A, BG-423, BG-424					
1854 Large head, small stars	750	950	1,500	3,000	—
Note: BG-425, Large head, small stars					
1854 Small head, small stars	—	—	200	300	—
Note: BG-1304, Small head, small stars. Kroll type.					
1854 Large stars	—	—	—	—	—
Note: BG-1304A, Large stars. Common counterfeit.					
1855	225	310	425	650	—
Note: BG-432, BG-433					
1856 N	150	235	325	425	—
Note: BG-434					
1860/56	175	285	350	500	—
Note: BG-1014					

KM# 11.4 • Gold **Obv.** Liberty head, left **Rev:** Small eagle and legends

Date	XF40	AU50	MS60	MS63	MS65
1853 Rare	—	—	—	—	—
Note: BG-402, Rare					
1853 GG	5,000	8,000	10,000	15,000	—
Note: BG-410, BG-411, BG-412, BG-413					

KM# 11.5 • Gold **Obv.** Liberty head left **Rev:** Value in wreath; CALIFORNIA GOLD and date around wreath

Date	XF40	AU50	MS60	MS63	MS65
1853 GG	150	250	750	1,500	—
Note: BG-414					

KM# 11.6 • Gold **Obv.** Liberty head left **Rev:** Value and date within wreath

Date	XF40	AU50	MS60	MS63	MS65
1854 12 stars	—	—	—	—	—
Note: BG-1321, 12 stars. Rare counterfeit without "FD" beneath truncation.					
1854 FD 13 stars	850	2,000	3,000	—	—
Note: BG-403, BG-404, 13 stars					
ND Rare	—	—	—	—	—
Note: BG-1078, BG-1079, Rare					
1855 FD	180	325	450	600	—
Note: BG-405, BG-406					

Date	XF40	AU50	MS60	MS63	MS65
1859 FD	275	375	750	1,000	—
Note: BG-1001					
1859	—	175	275	425	—
Note: BG-1002, BG-1003, BG-1004					
1865	—	175	250	375	—
Note: BG-1005					
1866	—	190	275	425	—
Note: BG-1006					
1867	—	175	250	375	—
Note: BG-1007					
1868	—	190	275	425	—
Note: BG-1008					
1869	—	190	275	425	—
Note: BG-1009					
1870	—	155	250	375	—
Note: BG-1010					
1871	—	150	225	325	—
Note: BG-1011					
1873	—	195	275	475	—
Note: BG-1012. A rare counterfeit exists for this date.					

KM# 11.7 • Gold **Obv.** Liberty head left, date below **Rev:** Value and CAL within wreath

Date	XF40	AU50	MS60	MS63	MS65
1870 G	—	175	300	450	—
Note: BG-1023, BG-1024					
1871 G	—	175	300	450	—
Note: BG-1025, BG-1026, BG-1027, BG-1028. Common, yet deceptive, counterfeits exist.					
1871 L	—	250	450	—	—
Note: BG-1029, BG-1030					
1872	—	—	300	450	—
Note: BG-1013					
1873	—	250	450	1,000	—
Note: BG-1031, BG-1032					
1874	—	175	300	750	—
Note: BG-1033, BG-1034					
1875	—	175	350	800	—
Note: BG-1035					
1876	—	150	300	—	—
Note: BG-1039, BG-1039A, BG-1040					

KM# 11.8 • Gold **Obv.** Liberty head left **Rev:** Value and date within wreath, CALIFORNIA GOLD around

Date	XF40	AU50	MS60	MS63	MS65
1863	275	425	675	950	—
Note: BG-1305. This issue is a rare Kroll type. All 1858 dates of this type are counterfeits.					

KM# 11.9 • Gold **Obv.** Liberty head left **Rev:** HALF DOLLAR and date within wreath

Date	XF40	AU50	MS60	MS63	MS65
1864	150	215	300	400	—
Note: BG-1015, BG-1015A, BG1015a, BG-1016, BG1016A, BG-1016a. A rare silver strike is known.					
1866 G	330	500	800	1,000	—
Note: BG-1017					
1867 G	150	215	300	375	—
Note: BG-1018					
1868 G	150	215	300	375	—
Note: BG-1019					
1869 G	175	250	350	—	—
Note: BG-1020, BG-1021					

Date	XF40	AU50	MS60	MS63	MS65
1870 G	—	250	400	—	—
Note: BG-1022					

KM# 11.11 • Gold **Obv.** Goofy Liberty head, left **Rev:** Value and date within wreath

Date	XF40	AU50	MS60	MS63	MS65
1870	150	225	400	700	—
Note: BG-1047					

KM# 11.12 • Gold **Obv.** Liberty head left, H and date below **Rev:** Value and CAL within wreath

Date	XF40	AU50	MS60	MS63	MS65
1871 H	210	275	500	575	—
Note: BG-1041, BG-1042, BG-1043, BG-1044, BG-1045, BG-1046					

KM# 12.1 • Gold **Obv.** Large Indian head left, date below **Rev:** Value within wreath **Note:** 1852, 1868 and 1874 are backdated issues

Date	XF40	AU50	MS60	MS63	MS65
1852	—	—	375	675	—
Note: BG-1075, BG-1076					
1868	—	—	325	600	—
Note: BG-1073, BG-1074					
1874	—	—	325	600	—
Note: BG-1071, BG-1072. Similar obverse paired with reverse of KM#11.2 or an eagle with no denomination are modern counterfeits.					
1876	—	—	225	275	—
Note: BG-1064, BG-1065					
1878/6	—	—	325	475	—
Note: BG-1066					
1880	—	—	275	425	—
Note: BG-1067, BG-1068					
1881	—	—	275	425	—
Note: BG-1069, BG-1070					

KM# 12.2 • Gold **Obv.** Large Indian head left, date below **Rev:** Value and CAL within wreath

Date	XF40	AU50	MS60	MS63	MS65
1872	—	—	250	350	—
Note: BG-1048, BG-1049					
1873/2	—	—	400	700	—
Note: BG-1050					
1873	—	—	250	350	—
Note: BG-1051					
1874/3	—	—	350	500	—
Note: BG-1052					
1874	—	—	250	350	—
Note: BG-1053, BG-1054, BG-1055					
1875/3	—	—	250	350	—
Note: BG-1058					
1875	—	—	350	550	—
Note: BG-1056, BG-1057					
1876/5	—	—	250	350	—
Note: BG-1059					
1876	—	—	400	650	—
Note: BG-1060, BG-1061, BG-1062, BG-1063					

US PRIVATE GOLD

KM# 12.3 • Gold **Obv.** Small Indian head left, date below **Rev:** Value and CAL within wreath

Date	XF40	AU50	MS60	MS63	MS65
1875	100	165	300	500	—
Note: BG-1036, BG-1037					
1876	75.00	100	250	350	—
Note: BG-1038					

KM# 12.4 • Gold **Obv.** Young Indian head left, date above **Rev:** Value and CAL within wreath

Date	XF40	AU50	MS60	MS63	MS65
1882	—	375	850	—	—
Note: BG-1077					

DOLLAR (OCTAGONAL)

KM# 13.1 • Gold **Obv.** Liberty head left **Rev:** Large eagle and legends

Date	XF40	AU50	MS60	MS63	MS65
ND	1,000	1,500	2,200	4,000	—
Note: BG-501					
1853	3,500	5,000	7,500	—	—
Note: BG-502, BG-503					
1854	1,500	2,000	3,200	5,000	—
Note: BG-504, BG-534					

KM# 13.2 • Gold **Obv.** Liberty head left **Rev:** Value and date in beaded circle; CALIFORNIA GOLD and initials around

Date	XF40	AU50	MS60	MS63	MS65
1853 DERI	275	500	750	1,100	—
Note: BG-514, BG-515, BG-516, BG-517, BG-518, BG-519, BG-520, BG-521, BG-522, BG-523, BG-524					
1853 DERIB	450	800	1,100	—	—
Note: BG-525, BG-526					
1853 FD	300	450	900	—	—
Note: BG-505					
1853 N	325	550	900	1,450	—
Note: BG-530, BG-531					
1854 DERI	550	950	1,300	—	—
Note: BG-527, BG-528, BG-529					
1854 FD	350	600	1,100	1,900	—
Note: BG-506, BG-507, BG-508, BG-509, BG-510					
1855 FD	425	725	1,100	—	—
Note: BG-511					
1856	2,100	3,300	5,000	—	—
Note: BG-512					
1863 Reeded edge, restrike	—	125	175	275	—
Note: BG-1307A, Reeded edge. Kroll type restrike.					
1863 Plain edge	—	—	150	250	—
Note: BG1307, Plain edge. Kroll type.					

KM# 13.3 • Gold **Obv.** Liberty head left **Rev:** Value and date inside wreath; legends outside

Date	XF40	AU50	MS60	MS63	MS65
1854 GL Rare	—	—	—	—	—
Note: BG-513, Rare. Bowers and Marena sale 5-99, XF $9,775.					
1854	325	600	900	1,300	—
Note: BG-532					
1855 NR	325	600	900	1,300	—
Note: BG-533					
1858 K	180	300	425	725	—
Note: BG-1306. 1858 dates are Kroll types.					
1859 FD	1,900	—	—	—	—
Note: BG-1101					
1860	—	550	900	1,200	—
Note: BG-1102, BG-1103					
1868 G	—	550	900	1,300	—
Note: BG-1105					
1869 G	—	425	800	1,100	—
Note: BG-1106					
1870 G	—	425	725	1,100	—
Note: BG-1107, BG-1108					
1871	—	350	475	1,000	—
Note: BG-1104					

KM# 13.4 • Gold **Obv.** Goofy Liberty head, left **Rev:** Value and date within wreath

Date	XF40	AU50	MS60	MS63	MS65
1870	—	300	1,200	1,800	—
Note: BG-1118. Deceptive counterfeits exist.					

KM# 13.5 • Gold **Obv.** Liberty head left, date below **Rev:** Value and date within wreath; CALIFORNIA GOLD around

Date	XF40	AU50	MS60	MS63	MS65
1871 G	—	425	725	1,100	—
Note: BG-1109					
1874	—	3,000	—	—	—
Note: BG-1110					
1875	—	3,000	—	—	—
Note: BG-1111					
1876	—	2,000	—	—	—
Note: BG-1117, BG-1117A					

KM# 14.1 • Gold **Obv.** Large Indian head left, date below **Rev:** 1 DOLLAR within wreath; CALIFORNIA GOLD around

Date	XF40	AU50	MS60	MS63	MS65
1872	—	525	900	1,350	—
Note: BG-1119, BG-1129					
1873/2	—	600	1,050	1,650	—
Note: BG-1121, BG-1122					
1873	—	900	1,150	—	—
Note: BG-1123					
1874	—	800	1,300	1,950	—
Note: BG-1124					
1875	—	725	900	1,500	—
Note: BG-1125, BG-1126, BG-1127					
1876/5	—	1,050	1,500	1,950	—
Note: BG-1128, BG-1129					

US PRIVATE GOLD

KM# 14.2 • Gold **Obv.** Small Indian head left, date below **Rev:** 1 DOLLAR CAL within wreath

Date	XF40	AU50	MS60	MS63	MS65
1875	1,050	1,350	1,800	—	—
Note: BG-1112					
1876	—	1,500	2,100	—	—
Note: BG-1113					

KM# 15.3 • Gold **Obv.** Liberty head left, date below **Rev:** Value within wreath; CALIFORNIA GOLD around

Date	XF40	AU50	MS60	MS63	MS65
1870 G	750	1,500	2,100	3,000	—
Note: BG-1203					
1871 G	750	1,500	2,100	3,000	—
Note: BG-1204					

KM# 14.3 • Gold **Obv.** Indian head left, date below **Rev:** 1 DOLLAR within wreath; CALIFORNIA GOLD around

Date	XF40	AU50	MS60	MS63	MS65
1876	—	750	1,150	—	—
Note: BG-1114, BG-1115, BG-1116, BG-1116A					

DOLLAR (ROUND)

KM# 15.1 • Gold **Obv.** Liberty head left **Rev:** Large eagle and legends

Date	XF40	AU50	MS60	MS63	MS65
1853 GG Rare	—	—	—	—	—
Note: BG-604, Rare. Superior sale Sept. 1987 MS-63 $35,200.					

KM# 15.2 • Gold **Obv.** Liberty head left **Rev:** Value and date within wreath; CALIFORNIA GOLD around

Date	XF40	AU50	MS60	MS63	MS65
1854 GL	3,000	5,500	—	—	—
Note: BG-605, BG-606					
1854 FD	5,000	7,500	—	—	—
Note: BG-602, BG-603					
1854 Rare	—	—	—	—	—
Note: BG-601, BG-603A, Rare. Superior sale Sept. 1988 Fine $13,200					
1857 4 known	—	—	—	—	—
Note: BG-607, 4 known					
1870 G	750	1,900	3,000	—	—
Note: BG-1202					
1871	1,300	2,200	3,750	—	—
Note: Counterfeit exists. BG-1201					

KM# 15.4 • Gold **Obv.** Goofy Liberty head left **Rev:** Value and date within wreath; CALIFORNIA GOLD around

Date	XF40	AU50	MS60	MS63	MS65
1870	600	1,500	2,250	—	—
Note: BG-1205					

KM# 16 • Gold **Obv.** Large Indian head left, date below **Rev:** Value within wreath; CALIFORNIA GOLD outside

Date	XF40	AU50	MS60	MS63	MS65
1872	975	1,650	2,700	3,600	—
Note: BG-1206, BG-1207, BG-1208					

PRIVATE ASSAY OFFICE ISSUES

CALIFORNIA

Norris, Grieg & Norris produced the first territorial gold coin struck in California, a $5 piece struck in 1849 at Benicia City, though it bears the imprint of San Francisco. The coining facility was owned by Thomas H. Norris, Charles Greig, and Hiram A. Norris, members of a New York engineering firm. A unique 1850 variety of this coin has the name STOCKTON beneath the date, instead of SAN FRANCISCO.

Early in 1849, John Little Moffat, a New York assayer, established an assay office at San Francisco in association with Joseph R. Curtis, Philo H. Perry, and Samuel Ward. The first issues of the **Moffat & Co.** assay office consisted of rectangular $16 ingots and assay bars of various and irregular denominations. In early August, the firm began striking $5 and $10 gold coins which resemble those of the U.S. Mint in design, but carry the legend S.M.V. (Standard Mint Value) CALIFORNIA GOLD on the reverse. Five-dollar pieces of the same design were also issued in 1850.

On Sept. 30, 1850, Congress directed the Secretary of the Treasury to establish an official Assay Office in California. Moffat & Co. obtained a contract to perform the duties of the U.S. Assay Office. **Augustus Humbert**, a New York watchcase maker, was appointed U.S. Assayer of Gold in California. Humbert stamped the first octagonal coin-ingots of the Provisional Government Mint on Jan. 31, 1851. The $50 pieces were accepted at par with standard U.S. gold coins, but were not officially recognized as coins. Officially, they were designated as "ingots." Colloquially, they were known as slugs, quintuple eagles, or 5-eagle pieces.

The $50 ingots failed to alleviate the need of California for gold coins. The banks regarded them as disadvantageous to their interests and utilized them only when compelled to do so by public need or convenience. Being of sound value, the ingots drove the overvalued $5, $10, and $20 territorial gold coins from circulation, bringing about a return to the use of gold dust for everyday transactions. Eventually, the slugs became so great a nuisance that they were discounted 3 percent when accepted. This unexpected turn of events forced Moffat & Co. to resume the issuing of $10 and $20 gold coins in 1852. The $10 piece was first issued with the Moffat & Co. imprint on Liberty's coronet, and later with the official imprint of Augustus Humbert on reverse. The $20 piece was issued with the Humbert imprint.

On Feb. 14, 1852, John L. Moffat withdrew from Moffat & Co. to enter the diving bell business, and Moffat & Co. was reorganized as the **United States Assay Office of Gold**, composed of Joseph R. Curtis, Philo H. Perry, and Samuel Ward. The U.S. Assay Office of Gold issued gold coins in denominations of $50 and $10 in 1852, and $20 and $10 in 1853. With the exception of the $50 slugs, they carry the imprint of the Assay Office on reverse. The .900 fine issues of this facility reflect an attempt to bring the issues of the U.S. Assay Office into conformity with the U.S. Mint standard.

The last territorial gold coins to bear the imprint of Moffat & Co. are $20 pieces issued in 1853, after the retirement of John L. Moffat. These coins do not carry a mark of fineness, and generally assay below the U.S. Mint standard.

Templeton Reid, previously mentioned in connection with the private gold issues of Georgia, moved his coining equipment to California when gold was discovered there, and in 1849 issued $10 and $25 gold pieces. No specimens are available to present-day collectors. The only known $10 piece is in the Smithsonian Collection. The only known specimen of the $25 piece was stolen from the U.S. Mint Cabinet Collection in 1858 and was never recovered.

Little is known of the origin and location of the **Cincinnati Mining & Trading Co.** It is believed that the firm was organized in the East and was forced to abandon most of its equipment while enroute to California. A few $5 and $10 gold coins were struck in 1849. Base metal counterfeits exist.

The **Massachusetts & California Co.** was organized in Northampton, Mass., in May 1849 by Josiah Hayden, S. S. Wells, Miles G. Moies, and others. Coining equipment was taken to San Francisco where $5 gold pieces were struck in 1849. The few pieces extant are heavily alloyed with copper.

Wright & Co., a brokerage firm located in Portsmouth Square, San Francisco, issued an undated $10 gold piece in the autumn of 1849 under the name of **Miners' Bank**. Unlike most territorial gold pieces, the Miners' Bank eagle was alloyed with copper. The coinage proved to be unpopular because of its copper-induced color and low intrinsic value. The firm was dissolved on Jan. 14, 1850.

US PRIVATE GOLD

In 1849, Dr. **J. S. Ormsby** and Major William M. Ormsby struck gold coins of $5 and $10 denominations at Sacramento under the name of Ormsby & Co. The coinage, which is identified by the initials J. S. O., is undated. Ormsby & Co. coinage was greatly over-valued, the eagle assaying at as little as $9.37.

The **Pacific Co.** of San Francisco issued $5 and $10 gold coins in 1849. The clouded story of this coinage is based on conjecture. It is believed that the well-struck pattern coins of this type were struck in the East by the Pacific Co. that organized in Boston and set sail for California on Feb. 20, 1849, and that the crudely hand-struck pieces were made by the jewelry firm of Broderick and Kohler after the dies passed into their possession. In any event, the intrinsic value of the initial coinage exceeded face value, but by the end of 1849, when they passed out of favor, the coins had been debased so flagrantly that the eagles assayed for as little as $7.86.

Dubosq & Co., a Philadelphia jewelry firm owned by Theodore Dubosq Sr. and Jr. and Henry Dubosq, took melting and coining equipment to San Francisco in 1849, and in 1850 issued $5 and $10 gold coins struck with dies allegedly made by U.S. Mint Engraver James B. Longacre. Dubosq & Co. coinage was immensely popular with the forty-niners because its intrinsic worth was in excess of face value.

The minting equipment of David C. Broderick and Frederick D. Kohler (see Pacific Co.) was acquired in May 1850 by San Francisco jewelers George C. Baldwin and Thomas S. Holman, who organized a private minting venture under the name of **Baldwin & Co.** The firm produced a $5 piece of Liberty Head design and a $10 piece with Horseman device in 1850. Liberty Head $10 and $20 pieces were coined in 1851. Baldwin & Co. produced the first $20 piece issued in California.

Schultz & Co. of San Francisco, a brass foundry located in the rear of the Baldwin & Co. establishment, and operated by Judge G. W. Schultz and William T. Garratt, issued $5 gold coins from early 1851 until April of that year. The inscription "SHULTS & CO." is a misspelling of SCHULTZ & CO.

Dunbar & Co. of San Francisco issued a $5 gold piece in 1851, after Edward E. Dunbar, owner of the California Bank in San Francisco, purchased the coining equipment of the defunct Baldwin & Co.

The San Francisco-based firm of **Wass, Molitor & Co.** was owned by 2 Hungarian exiles, Count S. C. Wass and A. P. Molitor, who initially founded the firm as a gold smelting and assaying plant. In response to a plea from the commercial community for small gold coins, Wass, Molitor & Co. issued $5 and $10 gold coins in 1852. The $5 piece was coined with small head and large head varieties, and the $10 piece with small head, large head, and small close-date varieties. The firm produced a second issue of gold coins in 1855, in denominations of $10, $20, and $50.

The U.S. Assay Office in California closed its doors on Dec. 14, 1853, to make way for the newly established San Francisco Branch Mint. The Mint, however, was unable to start immediate quantity production due to the lack of refining acids. During the interim, John G. Kellogg, a former employee of Moffat & Co., and John Glover Richter, a former assayer in the U.S. Assay Office, formed **Kellogg & Co.** for the purpose of supplying businessmen with urgently needed coinage. The firm produced $20 coins dated 1854 and 1855, after which Augustus Humbert replaced Richter and the enterprise reorganized as Kellogg & Humbert Melters, Assayers & Coiners. Kellogg & Humbert endured until 1860, but issued coins, $20 pieces, only in 1855.

BALDWIN & COMPANY
5 DOLLARS

KM# 17 • Gold Obv. Liberty head left, date below
Rev: Eagle

Date	F12	VF20	XF40	AU50	MS60	MS63
1850	7,500	12,000	22,500	30,000	47,500	—

10 DOLLARS

KM# 18 • Gold Obv. Figure on horseback right, swinging rope, date and value below Rev: Eagle
Obv. Legend: CALIFORNIA GOLD. / 1850 / CALIFORNIA. Rev. Legend: BALDWIN & Co. / SAN FRANCISCO.

Date	F12	VF20	XF40	AU50	MS60
1850 Horsemab	32,500	65,000	97,500	125,000	200,000

Note: Bass Sale May 2000, MS-64 $149,500

KM# 19 • Gold **Obv.** Coronet head left within circle of stars, date below **Rev:** Eagle **Rev. Legend:** S.M.V. CALIFORNIA GOLD

Date	F12	VF20	XF40	AU50	MS60	MS63
1851	10,000	22,000	37,500	55,000	125,000	—

20 DOLLARS

KM# 20 • Gold **Obv.** Coronet head, left, within circle of stars, date below **Rev:** Eagle **Rev. Legend:** S.M.V. CALIFORNIA GOLD

Date	F12	VF20	XF40	AU50	MS60	MS63
1851 Rare	—	—	—	—	—	—

Note: Stack's Superior Sale Dec. 1988, XF-40 $52,800; Beware of copies cast in base metals

BLAKE & COMPANY

KM# 21 • Gold **Obv.** Value within small center circle, legend around **Rev:** Coining screw press at centre, date and value below **Obv. Legend:** BLAKE & CO. ASSAYERS **Rev. Legend:** ...CALIFORNIA GOLD

Date	F12	VF20	XF40	AU50	MS60	MS63
1855	—	—	—	—	—	—

Note: No original specimens are known. Most experts believe this to be a counterfeit circa 1950. Many modern copies exist

J. H. BOWIE
5 DOLLARS

KM# 22 • Gold **Obv.** Value at center, Company name above **Rev:** Pine tree **Rev. Legend:** CAL. GOLD 1849

Date	F12	VF20	XF40	AU50	MS60	MS63
1849 Rare	—	—	—	—	—	—

Note: Americana Sale Jan. 2001, AU-58 $253,000

CINCINNATI MINING AND TRADING COMPANY

KM# 23 • Gold **Obv.** Draped bust with headress left **Rev:** Eagle with shield left, date below **Obv. Legend:** CINCINNATI MINING & TRADING COMPANY.

Date	F12	VF20	XF40	AU50	MS60	MS63
1849 Unique	—	—	—	—	—	—

10 DOLLARS

KM# 24 • Gold **Obv.** Draped bust with headdress left **Rev:** Eagle with shield left, date below **Obv. Legend:** CINCINNATI MINING & TRADING COMPANY.

Date	F12	VF20	XF40	AU50	MS60	MS63
1849 Rare	—	—	—	—	—	—

Note: Stack's-Bowers sale 2004, XF realized $431,250; Brand Sale 1984, XF $104,500

DUBOSQ & COMPANY
5 DOLLARS

KM# 26 • Gold **Obv.** Coronet head left, within circle of stars, date below **Rev:** Eagle **Rev. Legend:**

US PRIVATE GOLD

S.M.V. CALIFORNIA GOLD

Date	F12	VF20	XF40	AU50	MS60	MS63
1850	120,000	225,000	—	—	—	—

10 DOLLARS

KM# 27 • Gold **Obv.** Coronet head left, within circle of stars, date below **Rev:** Eagle **Rev. Legend:** S.M.V. CALIFORNIA GOLD

Date	F12	VF20	XF40	AU50	MS60	MS63
1850	120,000	200,000	300,000	—	—	—

DUNBAR & COMPANY

5 DOLLARS

KM# 28 • Gold **Obv.** Coronet head left, within circle of stars, date below **Rev:** Eagle **Rev. Legend:** S.M.V. CALIFORNIA GOLD.

Date	F12	VF20	XF40	AU50	MS60	MS63
1851	125,000	200,000	350,000	—	—	—

Note: Spink & Son Sale 1988, AU $62,000

AUGUSTUS HUMBERT / UNITED STATES ASSAYER

10 DOLLARS

KM# 29.1 • Gold **Obv.** Eagle with ribbon, value below **Rev:** Inscription and date **Obv. Legend:** UNITED STATES OF AMERICA. **Note:** "AUGUSTUS HUMBERT" imprint.

Date	F12	VF20	XF40	AU50	MS60	MS63
1852/1	3,000	5,300	8,500	15,000	30,000	—
1852	2,750	4,000	7,250	10,000	23,500	—

KM# 29.2 • Gold **Obv.** Eagle with ribbon, value below **Rev:** Inscription and date **Note:** Error: IINITED in obverse legend

Date	F12	VF20	XF40	AU50	MS60	MS63
1852/1 Rare	—	—	—	—	—	—
1852 Rare	—	—	—	—	—	—

20 DOLLARS

KM# 30 • Gold **Obv.** Eagle with ribbon and shield **Rev:** Inscription and date **Obv. Legend:** UNITED STATES OF AMERICA, 884 THOUS on ribbon

Date	F12	VF20	XF40	AU50	MS60	MS63
1852/1	6,500	10,000	22,500	40,000	—	—

Note: Mory Sale June 2000, AU-53 $13,800; Garrett Sale March 1980, Humbert's Proof $325,000; Private Sale May 1989, Humbert's Proof (PCGS Pr-65) $1,350,000; California Sale Oct. 2000, Humbert's Proof (PCGS Pr-65) $552,000

50 DOLLARS

KM# 31.1 • Gold **Obv.** Eagle with ribbon and shield **Rev:** Target, 50 stamped incuse in center **Obv. Legend:** UNITED STATES OF AMERICA, 880 THOUS on ribbon **Edge:** Lettered

Date	F12	VF20	XF40	AU50	MS60	MS63
1851	22,500	40,000	65,000	90,000	—	—

KM# 31.1a • Gold **Obv.** 887 THOUS **Rev:** 50 in center **Obv. Legend:** UNITED STATES OF AMERICA

Date	F12	VF20	XF40	AU50	MS60	MS63
1851	20,000	32,500	55,000	85,000	150,000	—

US PRIVATE GOLD

KM# 32.2 • Gold **Obv.** Eagle with ribbon and shield **Rev:** Target, small design **Obv. Legend:** UNITED STASTES OF AMERICA

Date	F12	VF20	XF40	AU50	MS60	MS63
1851		10,000	17,500	35,000	50,000	—	—
1852		9,500	16,500	32,000	42,000	80,000	—

Note: Bloomfield Sale December 1996, BU $159,500

KM# 31.2 • Gold **Obv.** Eagle with ribbon and shield **Rev:** Target design, without value **Obv. Legend:** UNITED STATES OF AMERICA, 880 THOUS on ribbon

Date	F12	VF20	XF40	AU50	MS60	MS63
1851	17,500	28,500	50,000	75,000	130,000	—

KM# 31.2a • Gold **Obv.** Eagle with ribbon and shield **Rev:** Target design without value **Obv. Legend:** UNITED STATES OF AMERICA, 887 THOUS on ribbon

Date	F12	VF20	XF40	AU50	MS60	MS63
1851	—	45,000	70,000	125,000	—	—

KM# 31.3 • Gold **Obv.** Eagle with ribbon and shield **Rev:** Target design, without value **Obv. Legend:** UNITED STATES OF AMERICA **Note:** ASSAYER inverted on edge.

Date	F12	VF20	XF40	AU50	MS60	MS63
1851 Unique	—	—	—	—	—	—

KM# 31.4 • Gold **Obv.** Eagle with ribbon and shield **Rev:** Target design, rays from center, without value **Obv. Legend:** UNITED STATES OF AMERICA, 880 THOUS on ribbon

Date	F12	VF20	XF40	AU50	MS60	MS63
1851 Unique	—	—	—	—	—	—

KELLOGG & COMPANY
20 DOLLARS

KM# 33.1 • Gold **Obv.** Coronet head left, thick date **Rev:** Eagle with shield, short arrows **Rev. Legend:** SAN FRANCISCO CALIFORNIA

Date	F12	VF20	XF40	AU50	MS60	MS63
1854	2,500	3,500	5,500	7,750	19,500	—

KM# 33.2 • Gold **Obv.** Coronet head left, medium date **Rev:** Eagle with shield

Date	F12	VF20	XF40	AU50	MS60	MS63
1854	2,500	3,500	5,500	7,750	19,500	—

KM# 33.3 • Gold **Obv.** Coronet head left, thin date **Rev:** Eagle with shield, short arrows **Rev. Legend:** SAN FRANCISCO CALIFORNIA

Date	F12	VF20	XF40	AU50	MS60	MS63
1854	2,500	3,500	5,500	7,750	19,500	—

KM# 32.1 • Gold **Obv.** Eagle with ribbon and shield **Rev:** Target with circular center **Obv. Legend:** UNITED STATES OF AMERICA, 880 THOUS on ribbon

Date	F12	VF20	XF40	AU50	MS60	MS63
1851	12,000	20,000	30,000	45,000	75,000	—

Note: Garrett Sale March 1980, Humberts Proof $500,000

US PRIVATE GOLD

KM# 33.4 • Gold **Obv.** Coronet head left, thick date
Rev: Eagle with shield, large and long arrows **Rev.**
Legend: SAN FRANCISCO CALIFORNIA

Date	F12	VF20	XF40	AU50	MS60	MS63
1854	2,500	3,500	5,750	8,250	20,000	—
1855	2,650	3,750	6,500	9,250	22,000	—

Note: Garrett Sale March 1980 Proof $230,000

KM# 33.5 • Gold **Obv.** Coronet head left, thick date
Rev: Eagle with shield, medium arrows **Rev. Legend:**
SAN FRANCISCO CALIFORNIA

Date	F12	VF20	XF40	AU50	MS60	MS63
1855	2,650	3,750	6,500	9,250	22,000	—

KM# 33.6 • Gold **Obv.** Coronet head left **Rev:** Eagle
with shield, short arrows

Date	F12	VF20	XF40	AU50	MS60	MS63
1855	2,650	3,750	6,000	8,500	20,000	—

50 DOLLARS

KM# 34 • Gold **Obv.** Coronet head left, within circle
of stars **Rev:** Banner above eagle, FIFTY DOLLS. in
legend **Rev. Legend:** SAN FRANCISCO CALIFORNIA.

Date	F12	VF20	XF40	AU50	MS60	MS63
1855	—	—	—	—	—	—

Note: Heritage FUN Sale January 2007, Pr64 $747,500.
Heritage ANA Sale August 1977, Proof $156,500

MASSACHUSETTS AND CALIFORNIA COMPANY
5 DOLLARS

KM# 35 • Gold **Obv.** Rearing equestrian figure
within shield with bear and dear supporters **Rev:**
Value within wreath, date below **Rev. Legend:**
MASSACHUSETTS & CALIFORNIA CO.

Date	F12	VF20	XF40	AU50	MS60	MS63
1849	120,000	170,000	260,000	—	—	—

MINERS BANK
10 DOLLARS

KM# 36 • Red Gold **Obv.** Value at center **Rev:** Eagle
with shield **Rev. Legend:** CALIFORNIA.

Date	F12	VF20	XF40	AU50	MS60	MS63
ND-1849	—	18,500	35,000	50,000	90,000	—

Note: Garrett Sale March 1980, MS-65 $135,000

KM# 36a • Yellow Gold **Obv.** Value within legend
Rev: Eagle with shield

Date	F12	VF20	XF40	AU50	MS60	MS63
ND-1849	—	—	—	—	—	—

Note: Rare, as most specimens have heavy copper alloy

MOFFAT & COMPANY
5 DOLLARS

KM# 37.1 • Gold **Obv.** Coronet head left, within
circle of stars, date below **Rev:** Eagle with shiled **Rev.**
Legend: S.M.V. CALIFORNIA GOLD.

Date	F12	VF20	XF40	AU50	MS60	MS63
1849	1,350	2,400	3,750	5,500	12,500	—

KM# 37.2 • Gold **Obv.** Coronet head left, within
circle of stars, date below **Rev:** Eagle with shield, die
break at DOL

Date	F12	VF20	XF40	AU50	MS60	MS63
1849	1,350	2,400	3,750	5,500	12,500	—

US PRIVATE GOLD

KM# 37.3 • Gold **Obv.** Coronet head left, within circle of stars, date below **Rev:** Eagle with shield, die break on shield

Date	F12	VF20	XF40	AU50	MS60	MS63
1849	1,350	2,400	3,750	5,500	12,500	—

KM# 37.4 • Gold **Obv.** Coronet head left, within circle of stars, date below **Rev:** Eagle with shield, small letters **Rev. Legend:** S.M.V. CALIFORNIA GOLD

Date	F12	VF20	XF40	AU50	MS60	MS63
1850	1,450	2,750	4,500	5,800	14,000	—

KM# 37.5 • Gold **Obv.** Coronet head left, within circle of stars, date below **Rev:** Eagle with shield, large letters

Date	F12	VF20	XF40	AU50	MS60	MS63
1850	1,450	2,750	4,500	5,800	14,000	—

Note: Garrett Sale March 1980, MS-60 $21,000

10 DOLLARS

KM# 38.1 • Gold **Obv.** Coronet head left, within circle of stars, date below **Rev:** Eagle with shield, TEN DOL., middle arrow points below period at end of GOLD **Rev. Legend:** S.M.V. CALIFORNIA GOLD.

Date	F12	VF20	XF40	AU50	MS60	MS63
1849	3,250	6,000	12,000	20,000	35,000	—

KM# 38.2 • Gold **Obv.** Coronet head left, within circle of stars, date below **Rev:** Eagle with shield, middle arrow points above period at end of GOLD.

Date	F12	VF20	XF40	AU50	MS60	MS63
1849	3,250	6,000	12,000	20,000	35,000	—

KM# 38.3 • Gold **Obv.** Coronet head, left, within circle of stars, date below **Rev:** Value: "TEN D.", large letters

Date	F12	VF20	XF40	AU50	MS60	MS63
1849	3,500	6,500	13,500	22,500	40,000	—

KM# 38.4 • Gold **Obv.** Coronet head left, within circle of stars, date below **Rev:** Eagle with shield, small letters

Date	F12	VF20	XF40	AU50	MS60	MS63
1849	3,500	6,500	13,500	22,500	40,000	—

KM# 39.1 • Gold **Obv.** Coronet head left, within circle of stars, wide date below **Rev:** Eagle with ribbon and shield **Rev. Legend:** 264 GRS. CALIFORNIA GOLD **Note:** "MOFFAT & CO." imprint

Date	F12	VF20	XF40	AU50	MS60	MS63
1852	3,750	37,500	12,500	30,000	70,000	—

KM# 39.2 • Gold **Obv.** Coronet head left, within circle of stars, date below, close date **Rev:** Eagle with ribbon and shield, 880 THOUS. above **Rev. Legend:** 264 GRS. CALIFORNIA GOLD **Note:** Struck by Augustus Humbert.

Date	F12	VF20	XF40	AU50	MS60	MS63
1852	3,500	6,000	11,500	30,000	70,000	—

20 DOLLARS

KM# 40 • Gold **Obv.** Coronet head left, within circle of stars, date below **Rev:** Eagle and shield, circle of stars and rays above **Rev. Legend:** SAN FRANCISCO CALIFORNIA **Note:** Struck by Curtis, Perry, & Ward.

Date	F12	VF20	XF40	AU50	MS60	MS63
1853	4,250	6,750	10,000	15,000	32,500	—

NORRIS, GREIG, & NORRIS
HALF EAGLE

KM# 41.1 • Gold **Obv.** Date in center of circle of stars and legend **Rev:** Eagle with laurel and arrows,

US PRIVATE GOLD

period after ALLOY **Rev. Legend:** CALIFORNIA GOLD • WITHOUT ALLOY. • **Edge:** Plain

Date	F12	VF20	XF40	AU50	MS60	MS63
1849	4,250	6,750	13,500	17,500	32,500	—

KM# 41.2 • Gold **Obv.** Date in center of circle of stars and legend **Rev:** Eagle with laurel and arrows, period after ALLOY **Rev. Legend:** CALIFORNIA GOLD • WITHOUT ALLOY. •

Date	F12	VF20	XF40	AU50	MS60	MS63
1849	4,250	6,750	13,500	17,500	32,500	—

KM# 41.3 • Gold **Obv.** Date in center of stars and legend **Rev:** Eagle with laurel and arrows, period after ALLOY **Edge:** Reeded

Date	F12	VF20	XF40	AU50	MS60	MS63
1849	3,750	6,000	12,500	16,500	32,000	—

KM# 41.4 • Gold **Obv.** Date in center of circle of stars and legend **Rev:** Eagle with laurel and arrows, without period after ALLOY

Date	F12	VF20	XF40	AU50	MS60	MS63
1849	3,750	6,000	12,500	16,500	32,000	—

KM# 42 • Gold **Obv.** STOCKTON beneath date **Rev:** Eagle with laurel and arrows

Date	F12	VF20	XF40	AU50	MS60	MS63
1850 Unique	—	—	—	—	—	—

J. S. ORMSBY
5 DOLLARS

KM# 43.1 • Gold **Obv.** J.S.O. in center **Rev:** Value within circle of stars **Obv. Legend:** UNITED STATES OF AMERICA **Edge:** Plain

Date	F12	VF20	XF40	AU50	MS60	MS63
ND-1849 Unique	—	—	—	—	—	—

KM# 43.2 • Gold **Obv.** J.S.O. in center **Rev:** Value within circle of stars **Edge:** Reeded

Date	F12	VF20	XF40	AU50	MS60	MS63
ND-1849 Unique	—	—	—	—	—	—

Note: Superior Auction 1989, VF $137,500

10 DOLLARS

KM# 44 • Gold **Obv.** J.S.O. in center **Rev:** Value in center circle of stars **Obv. Legend:** UNITED STATES OF AMERICA

Date	F12	VF20	XF40	AU50	MS60	MS63
ND-1849 Rare	—	—	—	—	—	—

Note: Garrett Sale March 1980, F-12 $100,000; Ariagno Sale June 1999, AU-50 $145,000

PACIFIC COMPANY
1 DOLLAR

KM# A45 • Gold **Obv.** Liberty cap on pole, stars and rays around, value below **Rev:** Eagle

Date	F12	VF20	XF40	AU50	MS60	MS63
ND-1849 Rare	—	—	—	—	—	—

Note: Stack's Old West Sale August 2006, AU $126,500. Mory Sale June 2000, EF-40 $57,500

5 DOLLARS

KM# 45 • Gold **Obv.** Liberty cap on pole, stars and rays around, value below **Rev:** Eagle **Rev. Legend:** PACIFIC COMPANY CALIFORNIA

Date	F12	VF20	XF40	AU50	MS60	MS63
1849 Rare	—	—	—	—	—	—

Note: Garrett Sale March 1980, VF-30 $180,000

10 DOLLARS

KM# 46.1 • Gold **Obv.** Liberty cap on pole, stars and rays around, value below **Rev:** Eagle, date below **Rev. Legend:** PACIFIC COMPANY CALIFORNIA **Edge:** Plain

Date	F12	VF20	XF40	AU50	MS60	MS63
1849 Rare	—	—	—	—	—	—

Note: Waldorf Sale 1964, $24,000

KM# 46.2 • Gold **Obv.** Liberty cap on pole, stars and rays around **Rev:** Eagle **Edge:** Reeded

Date	F12	VF20	XF40	AU50	MS60	MS63
1849 Rare	—	—	—	—	—	—

TEMPLETON REID

10 DOLLARS

KM# 47 • Gold **Obv.** Date in center **Rev:** Value in center **Obv. Legend:** TEMPLETON... **Rev. Legend:** CALIFORNIA * GOLD *

Date	F12	VF20	XF40	AU50	MS60	MS63
1849 Unique	—	—	—	—	—	—

20 DOLLARS

KM# 48 • Gold

Date	F12	VF20	XF40	AU50	MS60	MS63
1849 Unknown	—	—	—	—	—	—

Note: The only known specimen was stolen from the U.S. Mint in 1858 and has never been recovered. For additional listings of Templeton Reid, see listings under Georgia

SCHULTZ & COMPANY

5 DOLLARS

KM# 49 • Gold **Obv.** Coronet head left, within circle of stars, date below **Rev:** Eagle, shield on breast, value below **Rev. Legend:** PURE CALIFORNIA GOLD.

Date	F12	VF20	XF40	AU50	MS60	MS63
1851	25,000	55,000	85,000	145,000	—	—

UNITED STATES ASSAY OFFICE OF GOLD

10 DOLLARS

KM# 51.1 • Gold **Obv.** Eagle with ribbon and shield **Rev:** O of OFFICE below I of UNITED **Obv. Legend:** UNITED STATES OF AMERICA TEN DOLS 884 THOUS

Date	F12	VF20	XF40	AU50	MS60	MS63
1852	—	—	—	—	—	—

Note: Garrett Sale March 1980, MS-60 $18,000

KM# 51.2 • Gold **Obv.** Eagle with ribbon and shield **Rev:** O below N, strong beads **Obv. Legend:** UNITED STATES OF AMERICA TEN DOLS 884 THOUS

Date	F12	VF20	XF40	AU50	MS60	MS63
1852	1,750	3,000	5,000	7,250	17,500	—

KM# 51.3 • Gold **Obv.** Eagle with ribbon and shield **Rev:** Weak beads **Obv. Legend:** UNITED STATES OF AMERICA TEN DOLS 884 THOUS

Date	F12	VF20	XF40	AU50	MS60	MS63
1852	1,750	3,000	5,000	7,250	17,500	—

KM# 52 • Gold **Obv.** Eagle with ribbon and shield **Rev:** Inscription, date **Obv. Legend:** UNITED STATES OF AMERICA TEN D, 884 THOUS

Date	F12	VF20	XF40	AU50	MS60	MS63
1853	7,500	13,500	25,000	37,500	—	—

KM# 52a • Gold **Obv.** Eagle with ribbon and shield **Rev:** Inscription, date **Obv. Legend:** UNITED STATES OF AMERICA TEN D. 900 THOUS

Date	F12	VF20	XF40	AU50	MS60	MS63
1853	42,000	6,500	10,000	16,000	27,500	—

Note: Garrett Sale March 1980, MS-60 $35,000

20 DOLLARS

KM# 53 • Gold **Obv.** Eagle with ribbon and shield **Rev:** Inscription, date **Obv. Legend:** UNITED STATES OF AMERICA TWENTY D. 884/880 THOUS

Date	F12	VF20	XF40	AU50	MS60	MS63
1853	8,500	12,500	18,500	28,000	47,500	—

US PRIVATE GOLD

KM# 53a • Gold **Obv.** Eagle with ribbon and shield **Rev:** Inscription, date **Obv. Legend:** UNITED STATES OF AMERICA TWENTY D. 900/880 THOUS

Date	F12	VF20	XF40	AU50	MS60	MS63
1853	2,250	3,250	5,000	6,750	12,500	—

Note: 1853 Liberty Head listed under Moffat & Company

50 DOLLARS

KM# 54 • Gold **Obv.** Eagle with ribbon and shield **Rev:** Target **Obv. Legend:** UNITED STATES OF AMERICA FIFTY FOLLS. 887 THOUS **Shape:** 8-sided

Date	F12	VF20	XF40	AU50	MS60	MS63
1852	12,500	20,000	32,000	45,000	77,500	—

KM# 54a • Gold **Obv.** Eagle and ribbon with shield **Rev:** Target **Obv. Legend:** UNITED STATES OF AMERICA FIFTY DOLLS. 900 THOUS **Shape:** 8-sided

Date	F12	VF20	XF40	AU50	MS60	MS63
1852	12,500	20,000	33,500	47,500	82,500	—

WASS, MOLITOR & COMPANY
5 DOLLARS

KM# 55.1 • Gold **Obv.** Small Liberty head, rounded bust **Rev:** Eagle, shield on breast **Rev. Legend:** • IN CALIFORNIA GOLD • FIVE DOLLARS

Date	F12	VF20	XF40	AU50	MS60	MS63
1852	4,500	10,000	20,000	35,000	67,500	—

KM# 55.2 • Gold **Obv.** Coronet head, left, within circle of stars **Rev:** Eagle, shield on breast **Rev. Legend:** • IN CALIFORNIA GOLD • FIVE DOLLARS
Note: Thick planchet.

Date	F12	VF20	XF40	AU50	MS60	MS63
1852 Unique	—	—	—	—	—	—

KM# 56 • Gold **Obv.** Large Liberty head, pointed bust **Rev:** Eagle, shield on breast **Rev. Legend:** • IN CALIFORNIA GOLD • FIVE DOLLARS

Date	F12	VF20	XF40	AU50	MS60	MS63
1852	4,000	9,000	17,500	32,000	60,000	—

10 DOLLARS

KM# 57 • Gold **Obv.** Liberty head with long neck, large date **Rev:** Eagle, shield on breast **Rev. Legend:** • S.M.V. CALIFORNIA GOLD • TEN D.

Date	F12	VF20	XF40	AU50	MS60	MS63
1852	5,500	9,500	18,500	32,000	—	—

KM# 58 • Gold **Obv.** Liberty head, short neck, wide date **Rev:** Eagle, shield on breast **Rev. Legend:** • S.M.V. CALIFORNIA GOLD • TEN D.

Date	F12	VF20	XF40	AU50	MS60	MS63
1852	2,800	4,650	7,500	12,500	27,500	—

US PRIVATE GOLD

KM# 59.1 • Gold **Obv.** Liberty head, short neck, small date **Rev:** Eagle, shield on breast **Rev. Legend:** • S.M.V. CALIFORNIA GOLD • TEN D.

Date	F12	VF20	XF40	AU50	MS60	MS63
1852	13,500	28,000	50,000	—	—	—

Note: Eliasberg Sale May 1996, EF-45 $36,300; S.S. Central America Sale December 2000, VF-30 realized $12,650

KM# 59.2 • Gold **Obv.** Plugged date **Rev:** Eagle, shield on breast **Rev. Legend:** S.M.V.CALIFORNIA GOLD.

Date	F12	VF20	XF40	AU50	MS60	MS63
1855	9,000	14,500	22,000	30,000	55,000	—

20 DOLLARS

KM# 60 • Gold **Obv.** Large Liberty head **Rev:** Eagle, shield on breast, value in banner above **Rev. Legend:** SAN FRANCISCO CALIFORNIA TWENTY DOL. 900 THOUS

Date	F12	VF20	XF40	AU50	MS60	MS63
1855 Rare	—	—	—	—	—	—

KM# 61 • Gold **Obv.** Small head **Rev:** Eagle, shield on breast, value in banner above **Rev. Legend:** SAN FRANCISCO CALIFORNIA TWENTY DOL.

Date	F12	VF20	XF40	AU50	MS60	MS63
1855	12,500	25,000	45,000	55,000	—	—

Note: Heritage CSNS Sale May 2007, AU55 $43,125

50 DOLLARS

KM# 62 • Gold **Obv.** Coronet head, left, within circle of stars, date below **Rev:** Value within wreath **Rev. Legend:** SAN FRANCISCO CALIFORNIA WASS MOLITOR & Co 50 DOLLARS

Date	F12	VF20	XF40	AU50	MS60	MS63
1855	22,500	32,500	55,000	75,000	165,000	—

Note: Heritage Baltimore Sale July-August 2008, MS-61 $207,000, AU-50 $63,250. Heritage FUN Sale January 2008, MS-60 $161,000. Bloomfield Sale December 1996, BU $170,500

COLORADO

The discovery of gold in Colorado Territory was accompanied by the inevitable need for coined money. Austin M. Clark, Milton E. Clark, and Emanuel H. Gruber, bankers of Leavenworth, Kansas, moved to Denver where they established a bank and issued $2.50, $5, $10, and $20 gold coins in 1860 and 1861. To protect the holder from loss by abrasion, Clark, Gruber & Co. made their coins slightly heavier than full value required. The 1860 issues carry the inscription PIKE'S PEAK GOLD on reverse. CLARK, GRUBER & CO. appears on the reverse of the 1861 issues, and PIKE'S PEAK on the coronet of Liberty. The government purchased the plant of Clark, Gruber & Co. in 1863 and operated it as a federal Assay Office until 1906.

In the summer of 1861, John Parsons, an assayer whose place of business was located in South Park at the Tarryall Mines, Colorado, issued undated gold coins in the denominations of $2.50 and $5. They, too, carry the inscription PIKE'S PEAK GOLD on reverse.

J. J. Conway & Co., bankers of Georgia Gulch, Colorado operated the Conway Mint for a short period in 1861. Undated gold coins

US PRIVATE GOLD

in the denominations of $2.50, $5, and $10 were issued. A variety of the $5 coin does not carry the numeral 5 on reverse. The issues of the Conway Mint were highly regarded for their scrupulously maintained value.

CLARK, GRUBER & COMPANY

2-1/2 DOLLARS

KM# 63 • Gold **Obv.** Coronet head, left, within circle of stars, date below **Rev:** Eagle, shield on breast **Rev. Legend:** • PIKES PEAK GOLD DENVER • 2 1/2 D.

Date	F12	VF20	XF40	AU50	MS60	MS63
1860	1,500	2,500	3,750	6,000	12,500	40,000

Note: Garrett Sale March 1980, MS-65 $12,000

KM# 64.1 • Gold **Obv.** Coronet head, left, within circle of stars, date below **Rev:** Eagle, shield on breast **Rev. Legend:** • CLARK GRUBER & CO DENVER • 2 1/2 D

Date	F12	VF20	XF40	AU50	MS60	MS63
1861	1,650	2,750	4,000	6,000	13,500	—

KM# 64.2 • Gold **Obv.** Coronet head, left, within circle of stars, date below **Rev:** Eagle, shield on breast **Rev. Legend:** • CLARK, GRUBER & CO. DENVER • 2 1/2 D **Note:** Extra high edge.

Date	F12	VF20	XF40	AU50	MS60	MS63
1861	1,750	3,000	4,500	7,000	14,500	—

5 DOLLARS

KM# 65 • Gold **Obv.** Coronet head, left, within circle of stars, date below **Rev:** Eagle, shield on breast **Rev. Legend:** • PIKES PEAK GOLD DENVER • 2 1/2 D

Date	F12	VF20	XF40	AU50	MS60	MS63
1860	2,000	3,200	4,500	6,500	12,500	—

Note: Garrett Sale March 1980, MS-63 $9,000

KM# 66 • Gold **Obv.** Coronet head, left, within circle of stars, date below **Rev:** Eagle, shield on breast **Rev. Legend:** • CLARK GRUBER & CO DENVER • 2 1/2 D

Date	F12	VF20	XF40	AU50	MS60	MS63
1861	2,500	3,650	6,000	10,000	35,000	—

10 DOLLARS

KM# 67 • Gold **Obv.** Mountain above value **Rev:** Eagle, shield on breast **Obv. Legend:** PIKES PEAK GOLD / DENVER / TEN D. **Rev. Legend:** CLARK GRUBER & CO.

Date	F12	VF20	XF40	AU50	MS60	MS63
1860	7,250	11,000	17,500	26,500	47,500	—

KM# 68 • Gold **Obv.** Coronet head, left, within circle of stars, date below **Rev:** Eagle, shield on breast **Rev. Legend:** * CLARK GRUBER & CO DENVER * TEN D.

Date	F12	VF20	XF40	AU50	MS60	MS63
1861	2,500	3,850	6,750	11,500	27,500	—

20 DOLLARS

KM# 69 • Gold **Obv.** Mountain above value **Rev:** Eagle, shield on breast **Obv. Legend:** PIKES PEAK GOLD / DENVER / TWENTY D. **Rev. Legend:** CLARK GRUBER & CO.

Date	F12	VF20	XF40	AU50	MS60	MS63
1860	50,000	100,000	175,000	320,000	525,000	—

Note: Heritage FUN Sale January 2006, MS-64 $690,000. Eliasberg Sale May 1996, AU $90,200. Schoonmaker Sale June 1997, VCF $62,700

US PRIVATE GOLD

KM# 70 • Gold **Obv.** Coronet head, left, within circle of stars, date below **Rev:** Circle of stars and rays above eagle **Rev. Legend:** CLARK GRUBER & CO DENVER .TWENTY D.

Date	F12	VF20	XF40	AU50	MS60	MS63
1861		14,500	32,500	57,500	85,000	—	—

J. J. CONWAY
2-1/2 DOLLARS

KM# 71 • Gold **Obv.** legend **Rev:** Value in center **Obv. Legend:** * J.J. CONWAY * / & CO. / BANKERS **Rev. Legend:** * PIKES PEAK * 2 1/2 DOLS

Date	F12	VF20	XF40	AU50	MS60	MS63
ND-1861		—	140,000	180,000	—	—	—

5 DOLLARS

KM# 72.1 • Gold **Obv.** Legend, ring of stars within **Rev:** Large 5 in center **Obv. Legend:** * J.J. CONWAY * / & CO. / BANKERS **Rev. Legend:** PIKES PEAK / FIVE DOLLARS

Date	F12	VF20	XF40	AU50	MS60	MS63
ND-1861 Rare	—	—	—	—	—	—

Note: Brand Sale June 1984, XF-40 $44,000

KM# 72.2 • Gold **Obv.** Legend **Rev:** Legend without large 5 in center **Obv. Legend:** * J.J. CONWAY * / & CO. / BANKERS

Date	F12	VF20	XF40	AU50	MS60	MS63
ND-1861 Unique	—	—	—	—	—	—

10 DOLLARS

KM# 73 • Gold **Obv.** & CO. within circle **Rev:** Numeral value within circle of stars **Obv. Legend:**

* J.J. CONWAY * / & CO. / BANKERS **Obv.**
Inscription: * J.J. CONWAY * BANKERS **Rev.**
Legend: * PIKES PEAK * TEN DOLLARS

Date	F12	VF20	XF40	AU50	MS60	MS63
ND-1861 Rare	—	—	—	—	—	—

JOHN PARSONS
2-1/2 DOLLARS

KM# 74 • Gold **Obv.** Assay office window and minting machine **Rev:** Eagle, shield on breast, value below **Obv. Legend:** J PARSON & Co / ORO **Rev. Legend:** PIKES PEAK GOLD / 2 1/2 D

Date	F12	VF20	XF40	AU50	MS60	MS63
ND-1861 Rare	—	—	—	—	—	—

Note: Garrett Sale March 1980, VF-20 $85,000

5 DOLLARS

KM# 75 • Gold **Obv.** Assay office window and minting machine **Rev:** Eagle, shield on breast, value below **Obv. Legend:** J N. PARSON & Co. / ORO **Rev. Legend:** PIKES PEAK GOLD / TEN D.

Date	F12	VF20	XF40	AU50	MS60	MS63
ND-1861 Rare	—	—	—	—	—	—

Note: Garrett Sale March 1980, VF-20 $100,000

GEORGIA

The first territorial gold pieces were struck in 1830 by **Templeton Reid**, a goldsmith and assayer who established a private mint at Gainesville, Georgia, at the time gold was being mined on a relatively large scale in Georgia and North Carolina. Reid's pieces were issued in denominations of $2.50, $5, and $10. Except for an undated variety of the $10 piece, all are dated 1830.

CHRISTOPHER BECHTLER
2-1/2 DOLLARS

KM# 76.1 • Gold **Obv.** 2.50 in center **Rev:** 64. G. / 22. in center **Obv. Legend:** BECHTLER . RUTHERF :

Rev. Legend: :GEORGIA GOLD: CARATS

Date	F12	VF20	XF40	AU50	MS60	MS63
ND-1831	4,200	6,750	12,500	15,000	28,500	—

KM# 76.2 • Gold **Obv.** 2.50 in center **Rev:** 64. G. / 22. in center, even 22 **Obv. Legend:** BECHLER . RUTHERF : **Rev. Legend:** GEORGIA GOLD : CATATS :

Date	F12	VF20	XF40	AU50	MS60	MS63
ND-1831	4,500	7,500	13,750	17,500	37,500	—

5 DOLLARS

KM# 77 • Gold **Obv.** Value in center **Rev:** 128 G / * in center **Obv. Legend:** C. BECHTLER. AT RUTHERF * 5 DOLLARS **Rev. Legend:** GEORGIA GOLD. 22 CARATS.

Date	F12	VF20	XF40	AU50	MS60	MS63
ND-1831	4,000	7,000	11,000	14,500	28,500	—

KM# 78.1 • Gold **Obv.** Value in center **Rev:** 128. G. / * in center **Obv. Legend:** C. BECHTLER. AT RUTHERFORD * 5 DOLLARS **Rev. Legend:** GEORGIA GOLD. / 22 CARATS.

Date	F12	VF20	XF40	AU50	MS60	MS63
ND-1831	4,000	7,500	12,000	15,500	32,000	—

KM# 78.2 • Gold **Obv.** Value in center **Rev:** 128 G: in center **Obv. Legend:** C. BECHTLER. AT RUTHERFORD / 5 DOLLARS. **Rev. Legend:** GEORGIA GOLD. 22 CARATS.

Date	F12	VF20	XF40	AU50	MS60	MS63
ND-1831 Rare	—	—	—	—	—	—

Note: Stack's Americana Sale January 2008 AU-58 $115,000. Akers Pittman Sale October 1997, VF-XF $26,400.

TEMPLETON REID
2-1/2 DOLLARS

Rev. Legend: :GEORGIA GOLD: CARATS

KM# 79 • Gold **Obv.** Date in center **Rev:** Value in center **Obv. Legend:** GEORGIA /GOLD. / 1830 **Rev. Legend:** T. REID / ASSAYER.

Date	F12	VF20	XF40	AU50	MS60	MS63
1830	55,000	85,000	165,000	275,000	—	—

Note: Stack's Berngard/S.S. New York Sale July 2008 VF35 $103,500. Stack's Norweb Sale November 2006 AU55 $299,000

5 DOLLARS

KM# 80 • Gold **Obv.** Value in center **Rev:** Value in center **Obv. Legend:** GEORGIA GOLD. / 1830 / $5 **Rev. Legend:** TEMPLETON REID / ASSAYER. / $5

Date	VF20	XF40	AU50	MS60	MS63
1830 Rare, 7 known	—	—	—	—	—

Note: Garrett Sale November 1979, XF-40 $200,000

10 DOLLARS

KM# 81 • Gold **Obv.** Date at center **Rev:** Written value at center **Obv. Legend:** GEORGIA / GOLD / 1830 **Rev. Legend:** TEMPLETON REID / ASSAYER / TEN / DOLLARS

Date	VF20	XF40	AU50	MS60	MS63
1830 Rare, 6 known	—	—	—	—	—

KM# 82 • Gold **Obv.** Without date at center **Rev:** Written value at center **Obv. Legend:** GEORGIA / GOLD **Rev. Legend:** TEMPLETON REID / ASSAYER / TEN / DOLLARS

Date	F12	VF20	XF40	AU50	MS60	MS63
ND-1830 Rare, 3 known	—	—	—	—	—	—

Note: Also see listings under California

NORTH CAROLINA

The southern Appalachians were also the scene of a private gold minting operation conducted by Christopher Bechtler Sr., his son August, and nephew Christopher Jr. The Bechtlers, a family of German metallurgists, established a mint at Rutherfordton, North Carolina, which produced territorial gold coins for a longer period than any other private mint in American history. Christopher Bechtler Sr. ran the Bechtler mint from July 1831 until his death in 1842, after which the

US PRIVATE GOLD

mint was taken over by his son August who ran it until 1852.

The Bechtler coinage includes but 3 denominations -- $1, $2.50, and $5 - but they were issued in a wide variety of weights and sizes. The coinage is undated, except for 3 varieties of the $5 piece which carry the inscription "Aug. 1, 1834" to indicate that they conform to the new weight standard adopted by the U.S. Treasury for official gold coins. Christopher Bechtler Sr. produced $2.50 and $5 gold coins for Georgia, and $1, $2.50, and $5 coins for North Carolina. The dollar coins have the distinction of being the first gold coins of that denomination to be produced in the United States. While under the supervision of August Bechtler, the Bechtler mint issued $1 and $5 coins for North Carolina.

AUGUST BECHTLER
DOLLAR

KM# 83.1 • Gold **Obv.** Large 1 in center **Rev:** 27. G. in center **Obv. Legend:** A. BECHTLER. / 1 / DOL: * **Rev. Legend:** CAROLINA GOLD. / 21C. **Edge:** Plain

Date	F12	VF20	XF40	AU50	MS60	MS63
ND(1842-52)	900	1,450	2,250	3,200	5,000	7,500

KM# 83.2 • Gold **Obv.** Value in center **Rev:** 27 G. in center **Obv. Legend:** A. BECHTLER . / 1 /DOL: **Rev. Legend:** CAROLINA GOLD . / 21 C. **Edge:** Reeded

Date	F12	VF20	XF40	AU50	MS60	MS63
ND(1842-52)	900	1,450	2,250	3,200	5,000	7,500

5 DOLLARS

KM# 84 • Gold **Obv.** Value in two lines in center **Rev:** 134 G. at center **Obv. Legend:** A. BECHTLER. RUTHERFORD * / 5 / DOLLARS **Rev. Legend:** CAROLINA GOLD. / 21/ CARATS.

Date	F12	VF20	XF40	AU50	MS60	MS63
ND(1842-52)	2,650	5,300	9,000	12,000	32,500	—

KM# 85 • Gold **Obv.** Value in two lines in center **Rev:** 128 G. in center **Obv. Legend:** A. BECHTLER.

RUTHERFORD / 5 / DOLLARS **Rev. Legend:** CAROLINA GOLD. / 22 / CARATS

Date	F12	VF20	XF40	AU50	MS60	MS63
ND(1842-52)	7,000	12,500	18,000	28,500	42,500	—

KM# 86 • Gold **Obv.** Value in two lines in center **Rev:** 141. G: in center **Obv. Legend:** A. BECHTLER. RUTHERFORD / 5 / DOLLARS. **Rev. Legend:** CAROLINA GOLD. / 20 / CARATS

Date	F12	VF20	XF40	AU50	MS60	MS63
ND(1842-52)	6,500	11,500	17,000	24,000	38,500	—
ND(1842-52)	PF60 37,500					

Proof restrike

Note: Struck from original dies by Henry Chapman in 1908. Stack's Nerngard/S.S. New York Sale July 2008 Pr63 sold for $34,500. Akers Pittman Sale October 1997 chPr $14,300

CHRISTOPHER BECHTLER
DOLLAR

KM# 87 • Gold **Obv.** 28 G. in center **Rev:** ONE in center, N reversed **Obv. Legend:** * BECHTLER RUTHERF: / 28. G. **Rev. Legend:** * CAROLINA DOLLAR / ONE

Date	F12	VF20	XF40	AU50	MS60	MS63
ND(1831-42)	1,250	2,200	3,000	4,250	7,500	—

KM# 88.1 • Gold **Obv.** 28. G. centered in center **Rev:** ONE at center **Obv. Legend:** C: BECHTLER. RUTHERF: **Rev. Legend:** N: CAROLINA GOLD. DOLLAR. / ONE

Date	F12	VF20	XF40	AU50	MS60	MS63
ND(1831-42)	2,400	4,000	6,000	11,000	24,000	—

KM# 88.2 • Gold **Obv.** 28 G high in center **Rev:** ONE in center **Obv. Legend:** C: BECHTLER RUTHERF: / 28 G. **Rev. Legend:** N. CAROLINA GOLD DOLLAR / ONE

Date	F12	VF20	XF40	AU50	MS60	MS63
ND(1831-42)	5,000	8,500	12,500	22,000	32,500	—

KM# 89 • Gold **Obv.** 30 G. /* in center **Rev:** ONE at center **Obv. Legend:** C. BECHTLER. RUTHERF: / 30 G. / * **Rev. Legend:** N: CAROLINA GOLD. DOLLAR. / ONE

Date	F12	VF20	XF40	AU50	MS60	MS63
ND(1831-42)	1,650	2,750	4,250	7,750	15,000	—

US PRIVATE GOLD

2-1/2 DOLLARS

KM# 90 • Gold Obv. 250 in center **Rev:** 67 G. 21 CARATS at center **Obv. Legend:** BECHTLER RUTHERF: **Rev. Legend:** CAROLINA GOLD.

Date	F12	VF20	XF40	AU50	MS60	MS63
ND(1831-42)	2,500	5,500	11,500	14,500	27,000	—

Note: Stack's Old Coloney Sale December 2005 MS62 $23,000

KM# 91 • Gold Obv. 250 in center **Rev:** 70 G. 20 CARATS at center **Obv. Legend:** BECHTLER. RUTHERF. **Rev. Legend:** CAROLINA GOLD

Date	F12	VF20	XF40	AU50	MS60	MS63
ND(1831-42)	2,750	5,750	12,000	16,000	29,500	—

Note: Stack's Norweb Sale November 2006 MS60 $26,450. Stack's Allison Park Sale August 2004 MS62 $28,750. Bowers and Merena Long Sale May 1995, MS-63 $31,900

KM# 92.1 • Gold Obv. RUTHERFORD in a circle, border of large beads **Rev:** 250 / 20 C. / 75 G. in center **Obv. Legend:** C. BECHTLER, ASSAYER. **Rev. Legend:** NORTH CAROLINA GOLD

Date	F12	VF20	XF40	AU50	MS60	MS63
ND(1831-42)	12,500	22,500	34,500	45,000	75,000	—

KM# 92.2 • Gold Obv. RUTHERFORD in circle **Rev:** 250. / wide 20 C. in center **Obv. Legend:** C. BECHTLER, ASSAYER. **Rev. Legend:** NORTH CAROLINA GOLD

Date	F12	VF20	XF40	AU50	MS60	MS63
ND(1831-42)	15,000	25,000	35,000	50,000	85,000	—

Note: Stack's Norweb Sale November 2006 MS62 $83,375

KM# 92.3 • Gold Obv. 250 / narrow 20 C in center **Series:** RUTHERFORD in circle in center **Obv. Legend:** C. BECHTLER, ASSAYER **Rev. Legend:** NORTH CAROLINA GOLD

Date	F12	VF20	XF40	AU50	MS60	MS63
ND(1831-42)	15,000	25,000	35,000	50,000	85,000	—

KM# 93.1 • Gold Obv. RUTHERFORD in a circle **Rev:** 250 / 20 G in center **Obv. Legend:** C. BECHTLER, ASSAYER. **Rev. Legend:** NORTH CAROLINA GOLD.

Date	VF20	XF40	AU50	MS60	MS63
ND(1831-42) Unique	—	—	—	—	—

KM# 93.2 • Gold Obv. * / 75 G in center, border finely serrated **Rev:** 250. / 20 G. in center **Obv. Legend:** C. BECHLER ASSAYER / 75 G **Rev. Legend:** NORTH CAROLINA GOLD

Date	F12	VF20	XF40	AU50	MS60	MS63
ND(1831-42) Rare	—	—	—	—	—	—

5 DOLLARS

KM# 94 • Gold Obv. two-line value in center **Rev:** 134 G. / * in center **Obv. Legend:** C. BECHTLER. AT RUTHFER. * / 5 / DOLLARS * **Rev. Legend:** CAROLINA GOLD: / 21 CARATS

Date	F12	VF20	XF40	AU50	MS60	MS63
ND(1831-42)	2,750	5,500	8,500	13,000	22,500	—

KM# 95 • Gold Obv. Two-line value in center **Rev:** 134. G at center, 21 above CARATS, no star **Obv. Legend:** C. BECHTLER. AT RUTHERF / 5 / DOLLARS **Rev. Legend:** CAROLINA GOLD / 21 / CARATS

Date	F12	VF20	XF40	AU50	MS60	MS63
ND(1831-42) Unique	—	—	—	—	—	—

KM# 96.1 • Gold Obv. Value in center **Rev:** 140 G. in center **Obv. Legend:** C. BECHTLER. AT RUTHERFORD. **Rev. Legend:** CAROLINA GOLD. / 20 / CARATS **Edge:** Plain

Date	F12	VF20	XF40	AU50	MS60	MS63
1834	2,500	5,000	8,000	14,000	25,000	—

KM# 96.2 • Gold Obv. Value in center **Rev:** 140. G. in center **Obv. Legend:** C. BECHTLER. AT RUTHERFORD / 5 / DOLLARS **Rev. Legend:** CAROLINA GOLD / 20 / CARATS **Edge:** Reeded

Date	F12	VF20	XF40	AU50	MS60	MS63
1834	7,500	14,500	27,500	40,000	65,000	—

US PRIVATE GOLD

US PRIVATE GOLD

KM# 97.1 • Gold **Obv.** Value at center **Rev:** 140 / G / in center, 20 close to CARATS **Obv. Legend:** C. BECHTLER. AT RUTHERF: **Rev. Legend:** CAROLINA GOLD. / 20 / CARATS **Edge:** Plain

Date	F12	VF20	XF40	AU50	MS60	MS63
1834	4,000	8,500	16,500	28,500	47,500	—

KM# 97.2 • Gold **Obv.** Value in center **Rev:** 140 / G in center, 20 far away from CARATS **Obv. Legend:** C. BECHTLER. AT RUTHERF: / 5 / DOLLARS **Rev. Legend:** CALIFORNIA GOLD. / 20 / CARATS **Edge:** Plain

Date	F12	VF20	XF40	AU50	MS60	MS63
1834		2,500	6,500	11,500	14,500	32,500	—

Note: Stack's Berngard/S.S. New York Sale July 2008 AU58 $29,900

KM# 98 • Gold **Obv.** Value in center **Rev:** 141. G: in center **Obv. Legend:** C. BECHTLER. AT RUTHERF: / 5 / DOLLARS. **Rev. Legend:** CAROLINA GOLD. / 20 CARATS

Date	F12	VF20	XF40	AU50	MS60	MS63
ND(1831-42)	PF60 40,000					

Proof restrike

Note: Struck from original dies by Henry Chapman in 1908. Heritage ANA Sale Auguust 2007 Pr65 $37,375

KM# 99.1 • Gold **Obv.** Legend in double circle **Rev:** 5 / DOLLARS / 20 CARATS / 150 G in center **Obv. Legend:** C. BECHTLER, ASSAYER. / RUTHERFORD COUNTY. **Rev. Legend:** NORTH CAROLINA GOLD.

Date	F12	VF20	XF40	AU50	MS60	MS63
ND(1831-42)	12,000	20,000	35,000	45,000	85,000	—

Note: Stack's Berngard/S.S. New York Sale July 2008 AU50 $69,000. Stack's Americana Sale January 2008 AU55 $74,750. Heritage ANA Sale August 2007 MS62 $97,750

KM# 99.2 • Gold **Obv.** Legend in two circles **Rev:** 5 / DOLLARS / 20 CARATS. in center **Obv. Legend:** C. BRECHTLER, ASSAYER. / RUTHERFORD COUNTY. **Rev. Legend:** NORTH CAROLINA GOLD.

Date	VF20	XF40	AU50	MS60	MS63
ND(1831-42) Rare	—	—	—	—	—

OREGON

The Oregon Exchange Co., a private mint located at Oregon City, Oregon Territory, issued $5 and $10 pieces of local gold in 1849. The initials K., M., T., A., W. R. C. (G on the $5 piece), and S. on the obverse represent the eight founders of the **Oregon Exchange Co.:** William Kilborne, Theophilus Magruder, James Taylor, George Abernathy, William Willson, William Rector, John Campbell, and Noyes Smith. Campbell is erroneously represented by a G on the $5 coin. For unknown reasons, the initials A and W are omitted from the $10 piece. O.T. (Oregon Territory) is erroneously presented as T.O. on the $5 coin.

OREGON EXCHANGE COMPANY

5 DOLLARS

KM# 100 • Gold **Obv.** Beaver above date and sprigs **Rev:** Weight and value in center **Obv. Legend:** R. M. T. A. W. R. C. S. / T. O. / 1849 **Rev. Legend:** OREGON EXCHANGE COMPANY / 130 G. / NATIVE / GOLD. / 5 D.

Date	F12	VF20	XF40	AU50	MS60	MS63
1849	22,500	37,500	70,000	120,000	—	—

Note: Heritage Internet Sale February 2009 AU53 $69,000. Heritage FUN Sale January 2009 VF25 $37,375

10 DOLLARS

KM# 101 • Gold **Obv.** Beaver above date and sprigs **Rev:** Weight and value within wreath **Obv. Legend:** R. M. T. R. C. S. / O. T. / 1849 **Rev. Legend:** OREGON EXCHANGE COMPANY. / 10 D. 20 G. / NATIVE / GOLD / TEN D.

Date	F12	VF20	XF40	AU50	MS60	MS63
1849	65,000	125,000	225,000	—	—	—

Note: Heritage Long Beach Sale September 2002 XF40 $126,500

UTAH

In 1849, the **Mormons** settled in the Great Salt Lake Valley of Utah and established the Deseret Mint in a small adobe building in Salt Lake City. Operating under the direct supervision of Brigham Young, the Deseret Mint issued $2.50, $5, $10, and $20 gold coins in 1849. Additional $5 pieces were struck in 1850 and 1860, the latter in a temporary mint set up in Barlow's jewelry shop. The Mormon $20 piece was the first of that denomination to be struck in the United States. The initials G.S.L.C.P.G. on Mormon coins denotes "Great Salt Lake City Pure Gold." It was later determined that the coinage was grossly deficient in value, mainly because no attempt was made to assay or refine the gold.

MORMON ISSUES
2-1/2 DOLLARS

KM# 102 • Gold **Obv.** Hat design above eye **Rev:** Clasped hands above date **Obv. Legend:** HOLINESS • TO • THE • LORD • **Rev. Legend:** G. S. L. C. P. C. / TWO . AND . HALF . DO.

Date	F12	VF20	XF40	AU50	MS60	MS63
1849	11,500	17,500	28,500	47,500	75,000	—

5 DOLLARS

KM# 103 • Gold **Obv.** Hat design above eye **Rev:** Clasped hands above date **Obv. Legend:** HOLINESS • TO • THE • LORD • **Rev. Legend:** G. S. L. C. P. C. / FIVE.DOLLARS

Date	F12	VF20	XF40	AU50	MS60	MS63
1849	7,750	18,500	24,500	32,000	70,000	—

KM# 104 • Gold **Obv.** Hat design above eye and stars **Rev:** Clasped hands above date **Obv. Legend:** HOLINESS •TO • THE • LORD • **Rev. Legend:** G. S. L. C. P. C. / FIVE DOLLARS

Date	F12	VF20	XF40	AU50	MS60	MS63
1850	9,500	18,500	32,000	45,000	80,000	—

Note: Heritage Long Beach Sale February 2009 MS61 $54,625

KM# 105 • Gold **Obv.** Seated lion facing left above date **Rev:** Beehive design on eagle breast

Date	F12	VF20	XF40	AU50	MS60	MS63
1860	13,500	27,500	45,000	65,000	85,000	—

Note: Heritage Los Angeles Sale August 2009 AU55 $63,250.
Stack's Bergstrom/Husky Sale June 2008 MS61 $74,750

10 DOLLARS

KM# 106 • Gold **Obv.** Hat design above eye **Rev:** Clasped hands above date **Obv. Legend:** HOLINESS • TO • THE • LORD **Rev. Legend:** PURE GOLD. / TEN DOLLARS

Date	F12	VF20	XF40	AU50	MS60	MS63
1849	175,000	275,000	385,000	575,000	—	—

Note: Heritage ANA Sale July 1988, AU $93,000

20 DOLLARS

KM# 107 • Gold **Obv.** Hat design above eye **Rev:** Clasped hands above date **Obv. Legend:** HOLINESS • TO • THE • LORD **Rev. Legend:** G. S. L. C. P. C. / TWENTY. DOLLARS

Date	F12	VF20	XF40	AU50	MS60	MS63
1849	75,000	145,000	225,000	—	—	—

Note: Stack's Old West Sale August 2006 XF45 $207,000

US PRIVATE GOLD

HAWAII

Hawaii, the 50th state, consists of eight main islands and numerous smaller islets of coral and volcanic origin. Situated in the central Pacific Ocean, 2,400 miles from San Francisco, the Hawaiian archipelago has an area of 6,450 square miles. Capital: Honolulu. The principal sources of income are in order: tourism, defense, and agriculture.

The Hawaiian Islands, originally populated by Polynesians from the Society Islands, were rediscovered by British navigator Capt. James Cook in 1778. He named them the Sandwich Islands. King Kamehameha I (the Great) united the islands under one kingdom, which endured until 1893, when Queen Lilioukalani was deposed and a provisional government established. This was followed in 1894 by a republic, which governed Hawaii until 1898, when the islands were ceded to the United States. Hawaii was organized as a territory in 1900 and attained statehood on Aug. 21, 1959.

Official coinage issued under the Kingdom of Hawaii was limited. The 1847 cent or Hapa Haneri coins were ordered by the Minister of Finance through an agent by the name of James Jackson Jarves. Jarves contracted the striking of 100,000 large copper coins from an unknown firm located somewhere in New England. The lack of acceptance by merchants limited the success of the 1847 coppers, which lead to a long gap before the next Hawaiian coinage issue in 1883.

The 1883 Kingdom coinage was contracted through Claus Spreckels, with circulation coins being struck at the San Francisco Mint. Very limited numbers of proof strikes were completed at the Philadelphia Mint, where Charles E. Barber designed these coins. Weights and measures on the 1883 Hawaiian coinage are the same as standard U.S. coins of the time period.

RULERS
Kamehameha I, 1795-1819
Kamehameha II, 1819-1824
Kamehameha III, 1825-1854
Kamehameha IV, 1854-1863
Kamehameha V, 1863-1872
Lunalilo, 1873-1874
Kalakaua, 1874-1891
Liliuokalani, 1891-1893
Provisional Government, 1893-1894
Republic, 1894-1898
Annexed to U.S., 1898-1900
Territory, 1900-1959

MONETARY SYSTEM
100 Hapa Haneri - Akahi Dala
100 Cents - 1 Dollar (Dala)

CENT

KM# 1a • Copper Obv. Uniformed bust, facing **Rev:** Value within wreath **Obv. Legend:** KAMEHAMEHA III. KA. MOI. **Rev. Legend:** AUPUNI HAWAII

Date	Mintage	F12	VF20	XF40	MS60	MS63
1847 Plain 4, 13 berries (6 left, 7 right)	100,000	375	475	775	1,150	2,200

KM# 1b • Copper Obv. Uniformed bust, facing **Rev:** Value within wreath **Obv. Legend:** KAMEHAMEHA III. KA. MOI. **Rev. Legend:** AUPUNI HAWAII

Date	Mintage	F12	VF20	XF40	MS60	MS63
1847	Inc. above	375	475	775	1,100	2,200
Note: Plain 4, 15 berries (8 left, 7 right)						

KM# 1c • Copper Obv. Uniformed bust, facing **Rev:** Value within wreath **Obv. Legend:** KAMEHAMEHA III. KA. MOI. **Rev. Legend:** AUPUNI HAWAII

Date	Mintage	F12	VF20	XF40	MS60	MS63
1847	Inc. above	400	500	800	1,300	2,500
Note: Plain 4, 17 berries (8 left, 9 right)						

HAWAII, PHILIPPINES, PUERTO RICO

KM# 1d • Copper **Obv.** Uniformed bust, facing **Rev:** Value within wreath **Obv. Legend:** KAMEHAMEHA III. KA. MOI. **Rev. Legend:** AUPUNI HAWAII

Date	Mintage	F12	VF20	XF40	MS60	MS63
1847	Inc. above	375	475	750	1,100	2,200

Note: Crosslet 4, 15 berries (7 left, 8 right)

KM# 1e • Copper **Obv.** Uniformed bust, facing **Rev:** Value within wreath **Obv. Legend:** KAMEHAMEHA III. KA. MOI. **Rev. Legend:** AUPUNI HAWAII

Date	Mintage	F12	VF20	XF40	MS60	MS63
1847	Inc. above	450	600	900	3,500	4,200

Note: Crosslet 4, 18 berries (9 left, 9 right)

KM# 1f • Copper **Obv.** Uniformed bust, facing **Rev:** Value within wreath **Obv. Legend:** KAMEHAMEHA III.KA.MOI. **Rev. Legend:** AUPUNI HAWAII

Date	Mintage	F12	VF20	XF40	MS60	MS63
1847	Inc. above	800	1,500	2,000	2,800	3,250

Note: Plain 4, 15 berries (7 left, 8 right)

5 CENTS (PATTERN)

KM# 2 • Nickel **Obv.** Head left, date below **Rev:** Value within crowned belt **Obv. Legend:** KALAKAUA KING OF SANDWICH ISLANDS

Date	Mintage	F12	VF20	XF40	MS60	MS63
1881	200	6,500	9,500	14,000	22,000	27,000

Note: Original examples of this pattern were struck on thin nickel planchets, presumably in Paris and some have "MAILLECHORT" stamped on the edge. In the early 1900's, deceptive replicas of the issue were produced in Canada, on thick and thin nickel and aluminum planchets, and thin copper planchets (thick about 2.7 to 3.1mm; thin about 1.4 to 1.7mm). The original patterns have a small cross atop the crown, the replicas do not have the cross.

10 CENTS (UMI KENETA)

KM# 3 • 2.50 g., 0.900 Silver 0.0723 oz. **Obv.** Head right, date below **Rev:** Crown and value within wreath **Obv. Legend:** KALAKAUA I KING OF HAWAII

Date	Mintage	F12	VF20	XF40	MS60	MS63
1883	26	PF63 14,000	PF65 20,000			
1883	250,000	65.00	95.00	250	950	2,700

1/8 DOLLAR (HAPAWALU)

KM# 4 • 0.900 Silver **Obv.** Head right **Obv. Legend:** KALAKAUA I KING OF HAWAII **Note:** Pattern issue.

Date	Mintage	F12	VF20	XF40	MS60	MS63
1883	20	PF63 45,000	PF65 50,000			

KM# 4a • Copper **Obv.** Head right **Obv. Legend:** KALAKAUA I KING OF HAWAII **Note:** Pattern issue.

Date	Mintage	F12	VF20	XF40	MS60	MS63
1883	18	PF63 20,000	PF65 30,000			

1/4 DOLLAR (HAPAHA)

KM# 5 • 6.22 g., 0.900 Silver 0.180 oz. **Obv.** Head right, date below **Rev:** Crowned arms divides value **Obv. Legend:** KALAKAUA I KING OF HAWAII **Rev. Legend:** UA MAU KE...

Date	Mintage	F12	VF20	XF40	MS60	MS63
1883	500,000	55.00	75.00	125	250	400
1883/3	Inc. above	65.00	95.00	150	300	500
1883	—	PF63 16,000	PF65 25,000			

KM# 5a • Copper **Obv.** Head right, date below **Rev:** Crowned arms divides value **Obv. Legend:** KALAKAUA I KING OF HAWAII **Rev. Legend:** UA MAU KE... **Note:** Pattern issue.

Date	Mintage	F12	VF20	XF40	MS60	MS63
1883	18	PF63 17,000	PF65 27,000			

HAWAII, PHILIPPINES, PUERTO RICO

1/2 DOLLAR (HAPALUA)

KM# 6 • 12.50 g., 0.900 Silver 0.3617 oz. **Obv.**
Head right, date below **Rev:** Crowned arms divides
value **Obv. Legend:** KALAKAUA I KING OF HAWAII
Rev. Legend: UA MAU KE...

Date	Mintage	F12	VF20	XF40	MS60	MS63
1883	700,000	150	200	300	1,000	3,000
1883	—	PF60 14,000	PF63 20,000		PF65 30,000	

KM# 6a • Copper **Obv.** Head right, date below
Rev: Crowned arms divides value **Obv. Legend:**
KALAKAUA I KING OF HAWAII **Rev. Legend:** UA
MAU KE... **Note:** Pattern issue.

Date	Mintage	F12	VF20	XF40	MS60	MS63
1883	18	PF63 13,000		PF65 16,000		

DOLLAR (AKAHI DALA)

KM# 7 • 26.73 g., 0.900 Silver 0.7734 oz. **Obv.**
Head right, date below **Rev:** Crowned arms with
supporters within crowned mantle **Obv. Legend:**
KALAKAUA I KING OF HAWAII **Rev. Legend:** UA
MAU KE...

Date	Mintage	F12	VF20	XF40	MS60	MS63
1883	500,000	375	500	800	4,000	10,000
1883	—	PF60 20,000	PF63 35,000		PF65 60,000	

KM# 7a • Copper **Obv.** Head right, date below **Rev:**
Crowned arms with supporters within crowned
mantle **Obv. Legend:** KALAKAUA I KING OF
HAWAII **Rev. Legend:** UA MAU KE... **Note:** Pattern
issue.

Date	Mintage	F12	VF20	XF40	MS60	MS63
1883	18	PF63 25,000		PF65 50,000		

Note: Official records indicate the following quantities of
the above issues were redeemed and melted: KM#1 -
88,405; KM#3 - 79; KM#5 - 257,400; KM#6 - 612,245;
KM#7 - 453,652. That leaves approximate net mintages
of: KM#1 - 11,600; KM#3 - 250,000; KM#5 (regular
date) - 242,600, (unknown) 40,000; KM#6 - 87,700;
KM#7 - 46,300.

PHILIPPINES
United States Administration
1899-1946

The Philippines, an archipelago in the western Pacific 500 miles (805 km.) from the southeast coast of Asia, has an area of 115,830 square miles (300,000 sq. km.) and a current population of 64.9 million. Its capital city is Manila. From its acquisition in 1898 until 1992, the U.S. has had a military presence in the Philippines.

Migration to the Philippines began about 30,000 years ago when land bridges connected the islands with Borneo and Sumatra. Ferdinand Magellan claimed the islands for Spain in 1521. Miguel de Legazpi established the first permanent settlement at Cebu in April 1565. Manila was established in 1572. A British expedition captured Manila and occupied the Spanish colony in October 1762, but returned it to Spain by the treaty of Paris, 1763. Spain held the Philippines despite growing Filipino nationalism until 1898 when they were ceded to the United States at the end of the Spanish-American War.

A military government was established on the Islands until a civil administration was put in place in 1901. The Philippines became a self-governing commonwealth under the United States in 1935. In 1942, during the Second World War, the Philippines were occupied by the Japanese. U.S forces and Filipinos both fought during 1944-45 to regain control of the Islands. On July 4, 1946, the Philippines became an independent Republic.

The coins listed here were issued under United States Administration of the Philippines. Coins dated 1903 to 1919 were struck at both the Philadelphia and San Francisco Mints, while coins dated 1920 and after were produced at the Manila Mint in the Philippines. With Japanese forces advancing in 1942, much of the Philippine Treasury's silver coinage was returned to the United States for safekeeping. Coinage that remained at the Mint in Manila was crated and dumped in the bay before the Japanese arrived. During the struggle to regain control of the Philippines near the end of WWII, coins dated 1944 to 1945 were struck by the U.S. Mint at Denver, San Francisco and Philadelphia.

Symbolically the first series of U.S. Philippines coins with its American eagle perched on a stars and stripes shield places emphasis on U.S. dominance of the islands. The second series, struck under Commonwealth authority began the move towards independence by placing a new Commonwealth of the Philippines shield on the reverses of all denominations.

MINT MARKS
D - Denver, 1944-1945
S - San Francisco, 1903-1947
M – Manila, 1920-1941

MONETARY SYSTEM
4 Quartos = 1 Real
8 Reales = 1 Peso
1 Peso = 100 Centavos

1/2 CENTAVO

KM# 162 • Bronze **Obv.** Man seated beside hammer and anvil **Rev:** Eagle above stars and striped shield

Date	Mintage	F12	VF20	XF40	MS60	MS63
1903	12,084,000	0.50	1.25	2.50	10.00	25.00
1903	2,558	PF60 50.00	PF63 110	PF65 150		
1904	5,654,000	1.00	1.75	3.50	20.00	50.00
1904	1,355	PF60 75.00	PF63 175	PF65 300		
1905	471	PF60 175	PF63 300	PF65 500		
1906	500	PF60 150	PF63 275	PF65 500		
1908	500	PF60 150	PF63 250	PF65 500		

CENTAVO

KM# 163 • 4.70 g., Bronze **Obv.** Man seated beside hammer and anvil **Rev:** Eagle above stars and striped shield

Date	Mintage	F12	VF20	XF40	MS60	MS63
1903	10,790,000	0.50	1.25	2.50	15.00	35.00
1903	2,558	PF60 70.00	PF63 100	PF65 190		
1904	17,040,000	0.50	1.25	2.75	20.00	45.00
1904	1,355	PF60 75.00	PF63 125	PF65 350		
1905	10,000,000	0.75	1.25	3.50	20.00	45.00
1905	471	PF60 175	PF63 300	PF65 750		
1906	500	PF60 150	PF63 275	PF65 750		
1908	500	PF60 150	PF63 275	PF65 700		
1908 S	2,187,000	2.50	4.00	8.00	40.00	100
1908 S/S	—	20.00	30.00	50.00	150	330
1909 S	1,738,000	7.00	10.00	20.00	100	225

HAWAII, PHILIPPINES, PUERTO RICO

Date	Mintage	F12	VF20	XF40	MS60	MS63
1910 S	2,700,000	2.00	4.00	9.00	35.00	60.00
1911 S	4,803,000	1.00	2.50	5.00	30.00	60.00
1912 S	3,000,000	3.50	7.50	15.00	75.00	125
1913 S	5,000,000	2.00	4.00	7.00	25.00	75.00
1914 S	5,000,000	1.75	3.50	5.00	45.00	75.00
1915 S	2,500,000	30.00	40.00	90.00	550	1,250
1916 S	4,330,000	6.00	7.50	12.50	90.00	150
1917/6 S	7,070,000	40.00	55.00	160	500	750
1917 S	Inc. above	2.00	4.00	10.00	75.00	150
1918 S	11,660,000	2.00	5.00	12.50	100	200
1918 S Large S	Inc. above	125	150	250	1,000	1,900
1919 S	4,540,000	2.50	5.00	15.00	75.00	125
1920 S	2,500,000	4.50	3.50	20.00	50.00	175
1920	3,552,000	2.00	5.00	10.00	125	225
1921	7,283,000	1.00	2.50	5.00	35.00	85.00
1922	3,519,000	0.50	3.00	6.00	25.00	70.00
1925 M	9,332,000	0.50	2.50	7.50	35.00	85.00
1926 M	9,000,000	0.50	2.50	5.00	30.00	55.00
1927 M	9,270,000	0.50	2.50	5.00	25.00	45.00
1928 M	9,150,000	0.50	2.00	5.00	30.00	75.00
1929 M	5,657,000	1.00	3.00	6.00	40.00	85.00
1930 M	5,577,000	0.50	2.00	4.50	30.00	50.00
1931 M	5,659,000	0.50	2.25	5.00	35.00	60.00
1932 M	4,000,000	1.00	3.00	7.50	50.00	75.00
1933 M	8,393,000	0.25	2.00	3.00	20.00	50.00
1934 M	3,179,000	0.75	2.50	4.50	50.00	70.00
1936 M	17,455,000	0.50	2.50	4.00	35.00	65.00

5 CENTAVOS

KM# 164 • 5.25 g., Copper-Nickel, 21.3 mm. • **Obv.** Man seated beside hammer and anvil **Rev:** Eagle above stars and striped shield

Date	Mintage	F12	VF20	XF40	MS60	MS63
1903	8,910,000	0.50	1.25	2.50	18.00	30.00
1903	2,558	**PF60** 75.00	**PF63** 135	**PF65** 250		
1904	1,075,000	0.75	2.50	5.00	20.00	45.00
1904	1,355	**PF60** 75.00	**PF63** 130	**PF65** 250		
1905	471	**PF60** 85.00	**PF63** 160	**PF65** 250		
1906	500	**PF60** 175	**PF63** 250	**PF65** 550		
1908	500	**PF60** 200	**PF63** 300	**PF65** 575		
1916 S	300,000	50.00	85.00	150	800	1,500
1917 S	2,300,000	2.25	5.00	12.50	130	300
1918 S/S	—	—	150	200	450	—
1918 S	2,780,000	3.00	8.00	15.00	140	300
1919 S	1,220,000	4.00	15.00	30.00	175	450
1920	1,421,000	3.00	8.50	30.00	175	375
1921	2,132,000	3.00	8.00	20.00	115	225
1925 M	1,000,000	8.00	20.00	30.00	175	300
1926 M	1,200,000	4.00	6.00	17.50	120	200
1927 M	1,000,000	2.50	5.00	10.00	70.00	110
1928 M	1,000,000	3.00	6.00	12.50	75.00	150

KM# 173 • Copper-Nickel **Obv.** Man seated beside hammer and anvil **Rev:** Eagle above stars and striped shield **Note:** Mule.

Date	Mintage	F12	VF20	XF40	MS60	MS63
1918 S	—	175	475	1,200	4,500	9,500

KM# 175 • 4.75 g., Copper-Nickel, 19 mm. • **Obv.** Man seated beside hammer and anvil **Rev:** Eagle above stars and striped shield

Date	Mintage	F12	VF20	XF40	MS60	MS63
1930 M	2,905,000	1.00	2.50	6.00	45.00	85.00
1931 M	3,477,000	1.00	2.50	7.50	70.00	150
1932 M	3,956,000	1.00	2.00	4.00	50.00	130
1934 M	2,154,000	1.00	3.50	9.00	75.00	200
1934 M recut 1	—	5.00	10.00	35.00	125	250
1935 M	2,754,000	1.00	2.50	8.00	85.00	220

10 CENTAVOS

KM# 165 • 2.69 g., 0.900 Silver 0.0779 oz. **Obv.** Female standing beside hammer and anvil **Rev:** Eagle above stars and striped shield

Date	Mintage	F12	VF20	XF40	MS60	MS63
1903	5,103,000	2.50	4.00	5.00	35.00	75.00
1903	2,558	**PF60** 100	**PF63** 150	**PF65** 250		
1903 S	1,200,000	20.00	30.00	50.00	350	950
1904	11,000	20.00	30.00	55.00	90.00	150
1904	1,355	**PF60** 125	**PF63** 175	**PF65** 285		
1904 S	5,040,000	2.50	4.00	9.00	60.00	120
1905	471	**PF60** 150	**PF63** 325	**PF65** 650		
1906	500	**PF60** 135	**PF63** 225	**PF65** 625		

KM# 169 • 2.00 g., 0.750 Silver 0.0482 oz. **Obv.** Female standing beside hammer and anvil **Rev:** Eagle above stars and striped shield **Edge:** Reeded

Date	Mintage	F12	VF20	XF40	MS60	MS63
1907	1,501,000	1.75	4.00	7.50	60.00	175
1907 S	4,930,000	1.75	2.00	5.00	40.00	90.00
1908	500	**PF60** 150	**PF63** 200	**PF65** 600		
1908 S	3,364,000	BV	2.00	5.00	40.00	70.00
1909 S	312,000	25.00	30.00	65.00	450	1,200
1910 S	—	—	—	—	—	—
Note: Unknown in any collection. Counterfeits of the 1910S commonly encountered						
1911 S	1,101,000	2.50	10.00	15.00	150	500
1912 S	1,010,000	2.50	6.00	12.00	125	275
1912 S S/S	—	—	50.00	75.00	200	500
1913 S	1,361,000	2.00	9.00	12.00	85.00	150
1914 S Short bar on "4"	1,180,000	2.00	6.00	15.00	175	350
1914 S Long bar on "4"	—	2.00	7.50	15.00	125	300
1915 S	450,000	12.50	25.00	45.00	250	750
1917 S	5,991,000	BV	2.50	5.00	50.00	100
1918 S	8,420,000	—	2.00	3.00	20.00	50.00
1919 S	1,630,000	BV	2.50	5.00	35.00	110
1920	520,000	3.00	6.00	15.00	100	200
1921	3,863,000	BV	2.00	5.00	25.00	50.00

Date	Mintage	F12	VF20	XF40	MS60	MS63
1929 M	1,000,000	BV	2.00	5.00	25.00	45.00
1935 M	1,280,000	BV	2.00	4.00	20.00	50.00

20 CENTAVOS

Eagle above stars and striped shield **Note:** Mule.

Date	Mintage	F12	VF20	XF40	MS60	MS63
1928 M	100,000	10.00	20.00	60.00	900	1,800

50 CENTAVOS

KM# 166 • 5.38 g., 0.900 Silver 0.1558 oz. **Obv.** Female standing beside hammer and anvil **Rev:** Eagle above stars and striped shield **Edge:** Reeded

Date	Mintage	F12	VF20	XF40	MS60	MS63
1903	5,353,000	BV	5.00	8.00	45.00	100
1903	2,558	PF60 100	PF63 150		PF65 250	
1903 S	150,000	15.00	25.00	50.00	600	1,900
1904	11,000	25.00	30.00	45.00	125	200
1904	1,355	PF60 110	PF63 175		PF65 275	
1904 S	2,060,000	5.00	7.00	11.00	100	200
1905	471	PF60 225	PF63 375		PF65 625	
1905 S	420,000	7.50	20.00	35.00	400	1,250
1906	500	PF60 175	PF63 325		PF65 600	

KM# 167 • 13.48 g., 0.900 Silver 0.390 oz. **Obv.** Female standing beside hammer and anvil **Rev:** Eagle above stars and striped shield

Date	Mintage	F12	VF20	XF40	MS60	MS63
1903	3,102,000	—	10.00	15.00	70.00	125
1903	2,558	PF60 100	PF63 175		PF65 300	
1903 S 2 Known	—	—	—	22,000	—	—
1904	11,000	25.00	50.00	90.00	150	250
1904	1,355	PF60 150	PF63 400		PF65 550	
1904 S	2,160,000	—	12.00	25.00	125	225
1905	471	PF60 275	PF63 475		PF65 675	
1905 S	852,000	BV	20.00	50.00	700	2,100
1906	500	PF60 225	PF63 425		PF65 575	

KM# 170 • 4.00 g., 0.750 Silver 0.0965 oz. **Obv.** Female standing beside hammer and anvil **Rev:** Eagle above stars and striped shield **Edge:** Reeded

Date	Mintage	F12	VF20	XF40	MS60	MS63
1907	1,251,000	3.50	6.00	13.00	200	450
1907 S	3,165,000	BV	4.00	5.00	75.00	175
1908	500	PF60 175	PF63 325		PF65 600	
1908 S	1,535,000	3.00	4.00	10.00	100	325
1909 S	450,000	12.50	25.00	50.00	400	1,500
1910 S	500,000	15.00	30.00	60.00	400	1,000
1911 S	505,000	10.00	25.00	45.00	325	900
1912 S	750,000	5.00	12.00	30.00	200	400
1913 S/S	949,000	7.50	12.50	35.00	200	350
1913 S	Inc. above	4.00	10.00	15.00	150	200
1914 S	795,000	4.50	10.00	30.00	150	450
1915 S	655,000	15.00	20.00	55.00	475	1,600
1916 S	1,435,000	6.00	10.00	25.00	150	500
1917 S	3,151,000	3.00	5.50	8.00	75.00	200
1918 S	5,560,000	3.00	4.50	6.00	50.00	125
1919 S	850,000	3.50	7.25	12.50	125	225
1920	1,046,000	4.00	8.00	20.00	125	225
1921	1,843,000	—	3.00	5.50	50.00	100
1929 M	1,970,000	—	3.00	5.00	40.00	100
1929 M/M	—	—	—	100	250	400

Note: Portions of the date have been repunched,

KM# 171 • 10.00 g., 0.750 Silver 0.2411 oz. **Obv.** Female standing beside hammer and anvil **Rev:** Eagle above stars and striped shield **Edge:** Reeded

Date	Mintage	F12	VF20	XF40	MS60	MS63
1907	1,201,000	BV	15.00	40.00	150	325
1907 S	2,112,000	BV	11.00	30.00	150	325
1908	500	PF60 200	PF63 400		PF65 550	
1908 S	1,601,000	BV	15.00	40.00	325	1,500
1909 S	528,000	10.00	20.00	60.00	350	850
1917 S	674,000	BV	12.50	35.00	200	550
1918 S	2,202,000	BV	7.50	15.00	125	190
1919 S	1,200,000	BV	7.50	20.00	125	225
1920	420,000	BV	7.50	11.00	70.00	100
1921	2,317,000	BV	7.50	11.00	50.00	85.00

KM# 174 • 4.00 g., 0.750 Silver 0.0965 oz. **Obv.** Female standing beside hammer and anvil **Rev:**

HAWAII, PHILIPPINES, PUERTO RICO

PESO

KM# 168 • 26.96 g., 0.900 Silver 0.780 oz. **Obv.**
Female standing beside hammer and anvil **Rev:**
Eagle above stars and striped shield

Date	Mintage	F12	VF20	XF40	MS60	MS63
1903	2,791,000	25.00	35.00	45.00	190	550
1903	2,558	**PF60** 200	**PF63** 400		**PF65** 800	
1903 S	11,361,000	25.00	30.00	40.00	150	325
1904	11,000	65.00	80.00	115	300	625
1904	1,355	**PF60** 250	**PF63** 500		**PF65** 900	
1904 S	6,600,000	25.00	35.00	40.00	175	375
1905 S curved serif on 1	6,056,000	25.00	40.00	60.00	350	750
1905 S straight serif on 1	—	40.00	50.00	90.00	900	3,500
1905	471	**PF60** 700 2,000	**PF63** 1,500		**PF65**	
1906	500	**PF60** 700 1,500	**PF63** 1,200		**PF65**	
1906 S	201,000	1,000	1,500	3,000	17,500	32,500

Note: Counterfeits of the 1906S exist

KM# 172 • 20.00 g., 0.800 Silver 0.5144 oz. **Obv.**
Female standing beside hammer and anvil **Rev:**
Eagle above stars and striped shield **Edge:** Reeded

Date	Mintage	F12	VF20	XF40	MS60	MS63
1907 Proof, 2 known	—	**PF63** 165,000				

Note: Gem $165,000, 6/10/12 Pineda Sale.

Date	Mintage	F12	VF20	XF40	MS60	MS63
1907 S	10,276,000	14.00	17.50	22.00	90.00	250
1908	500	**PF60** 650	**PF63** 1,000		**PF65** 1,500	
1908 S	20,955,000	14.00	17.50	22.00	90.00	250
1909 S	7,578,000	18.00	24.00	30.00	115	300
1909 S S/S	—	—	—	100	225	450
1910 S	3,154,000	20.00	25.00	35.00	225	450
1911 S	463,000	30.00	40.00	75.00	750	4,250
1912 S	680,000	40.00	50.00	85.00	2,000	5,000

UNITED STATES ADMINISTRATION
Commonwealth

CENTAVO

KM# 179 • 5.30 g., Bronze, 25 mm. • **Obv.** Male
seated beside hammer and anvil **Rev:** Eagle above
shield

Date	Mintage	VF20	XF40	MS60	MS63	MS65
1937 M	15,790,000	2.00	3.00	20.00	45.00	100
1938 M	10,000,000	1.50	2.50	15.00	35.00	65.00
1939 M	6,500,000	2.50	3.50	17.50	40.00	75.00
1940 M	4,000,000	1.25	3.00	15.00	25.00	75.00
1941 M	5,000,000	3.50	7.50	18.00	50.00	90.00
1944 S	58,000,000	0.25	0.50	2.00	4.00	35.00

5 CENTAVOS

KM# 180 • 4.80 g., Copper-Nickel **Obv.** Male
seated beside hammer and anvil **Rev:** Eagle with
wings open above shield

Date	Mintage	VF20	XF40	MS60	MS63	MS65
1937 M	2,494,000	5.00	7.50	50.00	75.00	125
1938 M	4,000,000	1.00	2.75	20.00	45.00	125
1941 M	2,750,000	4.00	8.00	70.00	150	375

KM# 180a • 4.92 g., Copper-Nickel-Zinc, 19 mm.
• **Obv.** Male seated beside hammer and anvil **Rev:**
Eagle with wings open above shield

Date	Mintage	VF20	XF40	MS60	MS63	MS65
1944	21,198,000	0.50	1.00	2.00	3.00	15.00
1944 S	14,040,000	0.25	0.50	1.00	2.00	12.00
1945 S	72,796,000	0.25	0.50	1.00	2.00	11.00

10 CENTAVOS

KM# 181 • 2.00 g., 0.750 Silver 0.0482 oz. ASW,
16.7 mm. • **Obv.** Female standing beside hammer
and anvil **Rev:** Eagle with wings open above shield
Edge: Reeded

Date	Mintage	VF20	XF40	MS60	MS63	MS65
1937 M	3,500,000	2.25	3.50	15.00	30.00	90.00
1938 M	3,750,000	1.85	2.25	12.50	25.00	70.00
1941 M	2,500,000	1.85	2.25	7.50	15.00	50.00
1944 D	31,592,000	—	1.50	3.00	4.00	10.00
1945 D	137,208,000	—	1.50	3.00	4.00	10.00

Note: 1937, 1938, and 1941 dated strikes have inverted W's
for M's

1945 D/D	—	8.50	15.00	30.00	50.00	100

20 CENTAVOS

KM# 182 • 4.00 g., 0.750 Silver 0.0965 oz. ASW, 21
mm. • **Obv.** Female standing beside hammer and
anvil **Rev:** Eagle with wings open above shield **Edge:**
Reeded

Date	Mintage	VF20	XF40	MS60	MS63	MS65
1937 M	2,665,000	3.00	5.00	35.00	50.00	80.00
1938 M	3,000,000	3.00	3.75	15.00	30.00	50.00
1941 M	1,500,000	3.00	3.75	12.50	20.00	45.00
1944 D	28,596,000	—	2.00	3.00	5.00	7.00
1944 D/S	—	5.00	8.00	25.00	50.00	110
1945 D	82,804,000	—	2.00	3.00	5.00	7.00

50 CENTAVOS

Establishment of the Commonwealth

KM# 176 • 10.00 g., 0.750 Silver 0.2411 oz. ASW,
27.5 mm. • **Obv.** Murphy-Quezon busts facing
each other **Rev:** Eagle above shield **Designer:**
Ambrosia Morales

Date	Mintage	VF20	XF40	MS60	MS63	MS65
1936	20,000	25.00	50.00	100	200	375

KM# 183 • 10.00 g., 0.750 Silver 0.2411 oz. ASW,
27.5 mm. • **Obv.** Female standing beside hammer
and anvil **Rev:** Eagle with wings open above shield
Edge: Reeded

Date	Mintage	VF20	XF40	MS60	MS63	MS65
1944 S	19,187,000	5.00	6.00	8.50	12.50	50.00
1945 S	18,120,000	5.00	6.00	8.50	12.50	50.00
1945 S/S	—	12.00	30.00	80.00	180	240

PESO

Establishment of the Commonwealth

KM# 177 • 20.00 g., 0.900 Silver 0.5787 oz. ASW,
35 mm. • **Obv.** Roosevelt-Quezon conjoined
busts left **Rev:** Eagle with wings open above shield
Designer: Ambrosia Morales

Date	Mintage	VF20	XF40	MS60	MS63	MS65
1936	10,000	70.00	85.00	200	300	450

KM# 178 • 20.00 g., 0.900 Silver 0.5787 oz. ASW,
35 mm. • **Obv.** Murphy-Quezon conjoined
busts left **Rev:** Eagle with wings open above shield
Designer: Ambrosia Morales

Date	Mintage	VF20	XF40	MS60	MS63	MS65
1936	10,000	70.00	85.00	200	350	550

PUERTO RICO

The Commonwealth of Puerto Rico, the eastern-most island of the Greater Antilles in the West Indies, has an area of approximately 3,435 square miles (9,104 sq. km.), with sandy beaches on the costal areas and much mountainous territory inland. Puerto Rico's capital, San Juan, affords the island one of the best natural harbors in the Caribbean and has become an important stop on the Mona Passage shipping route to the Panama Canal.

Columbus discovered Puerto Rico (Rich Port) and took possession for Spain on Nov. 19, 1493 - the only time Columbus set foot on the soil of what is now a possession of the United States. The first settlement, Caparra, was established by Ponce de Leon in 1508. The early years of the colony were not promising. Considerable gold was found, but the supply was soon exhausted. Efforts to enslave the Indians caused violent reprisals. Hurricanes destroyed crops and homes. French, Dutch, and English freebooters burned the towns. Puerto Rico remained a Spanish possession until 1898, when it was ceded to the United States following the Spanish-American War.

When the Spanish first colonized Puerto Rico, native populations were operating on a barter system of exchange. Spanish coinage was introduced and eventually accepted for exchange. As mints developed in the Americas, their coins, first cobs and later milled coins, were also circulated in Puerto Rico. This mix of Spanish and Spanish Colonial coins served Puerto Rico for several centuries, though copper and bronze coins were easier to keep in circulation, while silver and gold tended to be taken away by traders. Paper money was also used in Puerto Rico from the mid 18th century on, though counterfeiting lead to the devaluation of many of these banknotes. Economic conditions were in great disarray by the early part of the 19th century. All sorts of currency and coinage were in circulation with counterfeits diluting the money supply. Cob coins, Spanish coins, cut and countermarked coins of the various West Indies, along with several issues of bank notes were all in circulation, leading to confusion and lack of fluid acceptance.

In 1895 the first coinage specifically struck for the Island of Puerto Rico was produced by Spain. Additional denominations were struck in 1896 completing Puerto Rico's only official coinage series. These coins brought some semblance of order to the daily economic transactions on the island and remained in use until Puerto Rico was taken over by the United States in 1898. Redemption of all peso denominated coins took place from July 1900 until March 1901 at the rate of 60 U.S. cents to the peso.

RULER	ASSAYERS' INITIALS	MONETARY SYSTEM
Spanish, until 1898	G - Antonio Garcia Gonzalez P - Felix Miguel Peiro Rodrigo	100 Centavos = 1 Peso

5 CENTAVOS

KM# 20 • 1.25 g., 0.900 Silver 0.0362 oz. **Obv.** Value, date **Rev:** Crowned arms, pillars

Date	Mintage	F12	VF20	XF40	MS60	MS63
1896 PGV	600,000	30.00	50.00	90.00	200	325

10 CENTAVOS

KM# 21 • 2.50 g., 0.900 Silver 0.0723 oz. **Obv.** Young head left **Rev:** Crowned arms, pillars

Date	Mintage	F12	VF20	XF40	MS60	MS63
1896 PGV	700,000	25.00	55.00	165	375	675

20 CENTAVOS

KM# 22 • 5.00 g., 0.900 Silver 0.1447 oz. **Obv.** Young head left **Rev:** Crowned arms, pillars

Date	Mintage	F12	VF20	XF40	MS60	MS63
1895 PGV	3,350,000	35.00	90.00	185	425	750

40 CENTAVOS

KM# 23 • 10.00 g., 0.900 Silver 0.2894 oz. **Obv.** Young head left **Rev:** Crowned arms, pillars

Date	Mintage	F12	VF20	XF40	MS60	MS63
1896 PGV	725,000	250	375	875	2,850	—

PESO

KM# 24 • 25.00 g., 0.900 Silver 0.7234 oz. **Obv.** Young head left **Rev:** Crowned arms, pillars

Date	Mintage	F12	VF20	XF40	MS60	MS63
1895 PGV	8,500,000	275	475	875	2,250	4,500

Glossary

Adjustment marks: Marks made by use of a file to correct the weight of overweight coinage planchets prior to striking. Adjusting the weight of planchets was a common practice at the first U.S. Mint in Philadelphia and was often carried out by women hired to weigh planchets and do any necessary filing of the metal.

Altered coin: A coin that has been changed after it left the mint. Such changes are often to the date or mintmark of a common coin in an attempt to increase its value by passing to an unsuspecting buyer as a rare date or mint.

Alloy: A metal or mixture of metals added to the primary metal in the coinage composition, often as a means of facilitating hardness during striking. For example, most U.S. silver coins contain an alloy of 10 percent copper.

Anneal: To heat in order to soften. In the minting process planchets are annealed prior to striking.

Authentication: The act of determining whether a coin, medal, token or other related item is a genuine product of the issuing authority.

Bag marks: Scrapes and impairments to a coin's surface obtained after minting by contact with other coins. The term originates from the storage of coins in bags, but such marks can occur as coins leave the presses and enter hoppers. A larger coin is more susceptible to marks, which affect its grade and, therefore, its value.

Base metal: A metal with low intrinsic value.

Beading: A form of design around the edge of a coin. Beading once served a functional purpose of deterring clipping or shaving parts of the metal by those looking to make a profit and then return the debased coin to circulation.

Blank: Often used in reference to the coinage planchet or disc of metal from which the actual coin is struck. Planchets or blanks are punched out of a sheet of metal by what is known as a blanking press.

Business strike: A coin produced for circulation.

Cast copy: A copy of a coin or medal made by a casting process in which molds are used to produce the finished product. Casting imparts a different surface texture to the finished product than striking and often leaves traces of a seam where the molds came together.

Center dot: A raised dot at the center of a coin caused by use of a compass to aid the engraver in the circular positioning of die devices, such as stars, letters, and dates. Center dots are prevalent on early U.S. coinage.

Chop mark: A mark used by Oriental merchants as a means of guaranteeing the silver content of coins paid out. The merchants' chop marks, or stamped insignia, often obliterated the original design of the host coin. U.S. Trade dollars, struck from 1873 through 1878 and intended for use in trade with China, are sometimes found bearing multiple marks.

Clash marks: Marks impressed in the coinage dies when they come together without a planchet between them. Such marks will affect coins struck subsequently by causing portions of the obverse design to appear in raised form on the reverse, and vice versa.

Clipping: The practice of shaving or cutting small pieces of metal from a coin in circulation. Clipping was prevalent in Colonial times as a means of surreptitiously extracting precious metal from a coin before placing it back into circulation. The introduction of beading and a raised border helped to alleviate the problem.

Coin alignment: U.S. coins are normally struck with an alignment by which, when a coin is held by the top and bottom edge and rotated from side-to-side, the reverse will appear upside down.

Collar: A ring-shaped die between which the obverse and reverse coinage dies are held during striking. The collar contains the outward flow during striking and can be used to produce edge reeding.

Commemorative: A coin issued to honor a special event or person. United States commemorative coins have historically been produced for sale to collectors and not placed in circulation, though the 50-states quarters are circulating commemoratives.

Copy: A replica of an original issue. Copies often vary in quality and metallic composition from the original. Since passage of the Hobby Protection Act (Public Law 93-167) of Nov. 29, 1973, it has been illegal to produce or import copies of coins or other numismatic items that are not clearly and permanently marked with the word "Copy."

Counterfeit: A coin or medal or other numismatic item made fraudulently, either for entry into circulation or sale to collectors.

Denticles: The toothlike pattern found around a coin's obverse or reverse border.

Die: A cylindrical piece of metal containing an incuse image that imparts a raised image when stamped into a planchet.

Die crack: A crack that develops in a coinage die after extensive usage, or if the die is defective or is used to strike harder metals. Die cracks, which often run through border lettering, appear as raised lines on the finished coin.

Device: The principal design element.

Double eagle: Name adopted by the Act of March 3, 1849, for the gold coin valued at 20 units or $20.

Eagle: Name adopted by the Coinage Act of 1792 for a gold coin valued at 10 units or $10. Also a name used to refer to gold, silver, and platinum coins of the American Eagle bullion coinage program begun in 1986.

Edge: The cylindrical surface of a coin between the two sides. The edge can be plain, reeded, ornamented, or lettered.

Electrotype: A copy of a coin, medal, or token made by electroplating.

Exergue: The lower segment of a coin, below the main design, generally separated by a line and often containing the date, designer initials, and mintmark.

Face value: The nominal legal-tender value assigned to a given coin by the governing authority.

Fasces: A Roman symbol of authority consisting of a bound bundle of rods and an axe.

Field: The flat area of a coin's obverse or reverse, devoid of devices or inscriptions.

Galvano: A reproduction of a proposed design from an artist's original model produced in plaster or other substance and then electroplated with metal. The galvano is then used in a reducing lathe to make a die or hub.

Glory: A heraldic term for stars, rays or other devices placed as if in the sky or luminous.

Grading: The largely subjective practice of providing a numerical or adjectival ranking of the condition of a coin, token, or medal. The grade is often a major determinant of value.

Gresham's law: The name for the observation made by Sir Thomas Gresham, 16th century English financier, that when two coins with the same face value but different intrinsic values are in circulation at the same time, the one with the lesser intrinsic value will remain in circulation while the other is hoarded.

Half eagle: Name adopted by the Coinage Act of 1792 for a gold coin valued at five units or $5.

Hub: A piece of die steel showing the coinage devices in relief. The hub is used to produce a die that, in contrast, has the relief details incuse. The die is then used to produce the final coin, which looks much the same as the hub. Hubs may be reused to make new dies.

Legend: A coin's principal lettering, generally shown along its outer perimeter.

Lettered edge: Incuse or raised lettering on a coin's edge.

Matte proof: A proof coin on which the surface is granular or dull. On U.S. coins this type of surface was used on proofs of the early 20th century. The process has since been abandoned.

Magician's coin: A term sometimes used to describe a coin with two heads or two tails. Such a coin is considered impossible in normal production due to physical differences in obverse and reverse die mountings, though as of 2001 two have been certified as genuine by professional coin authenticators. The vast majority are products made outside the Mint as novelty pieces.

Medal: Made to commemorate an event or person. Medals differ from coins in that a medal is not legal tender and, in general, is not produced with the intent of circulating as money.

Medal alignment: Medals are generally struck with the coinage dies facing the same direction during striking. When held by the top and bottom edge and rotated from side-to-side, a piece struck in this manner will show both the obverse and reverse right side up.

Mintage: The total number of coins struck during a given time frame, generally one year.

Mintmark: A letter or other marking on a coin's surface to identify the mint at which the coin was struck.

Mule: The combination of two coinage dies not intended for use together.

Numismatics: The science, study or collecting of coins, tokens, medals, paper money, and related items.

Obverse: The front or "head" side of a coin, medal, or token.

Overdate: Variety produced when one or more digits of the date are re-engraved over an old date on a die at the Mint, generally to save on dies or correct an error. Portions of the old date can still be seen under the new one.

Overmintmark: Variety created at the Mint when a different mintmark is punched over an already existing mintmark, generally done to make a coinage die already punched for one mint usable at another. Portions of the old mintmark can still be seen under the new one.

Overstrike: A coin, token or medal struck over another coin, token, or medal.

Pattern: A trial strike of a proposed coin design, issued by the Mint or authorized agent of a governing authority. Patterns can be in a variety of metals, thicknesses, and sizes.

Phrygian cap: A close-fitting, egg-shell-shaped hat placed on the head of a freed slave when Rome was in its ascendancy. Hung from a pole, it was a popular symbol of freedom during the French Revolution and in 18th century United States.

Planchet: A disc of metal or other material on which the image of the dies are impressed, resulting in a finished coin. Also sometimes called a blank.

Proof: A coin struck twice or more from specially polished dies and polished planchets. Modern proofs are prepared with a mirror finish. Early 20th century proofs were prepared with a matte surface.

Prooflike: A prooflike coin exhibits some of the characteristics of a proof despite having been struck by regular production processes. Many Morgan dollars are found with prooflike surfaces. The field will have a mirror background similar to that of a proof, and design details are frosted like some proofs.

Quarter eagle: Name adopted by the Coinage Act of 1792 for a gold coin valued at 2.5 units or $2.50.

Reeding: Serrated (toothlike) ornamentation applied to the coin's edge during striking.

Relief: The portion of a design raised above the surface of a coin, medal, or token.

Restrike: A coin, medal or token produced from original dies at a later date, often with the purpose of sale to collectors.

Reverse: The backside or "tail" side of a coin, medal or token, opposite from the principal figure of the design or obverse.

Rim: The raised area bordering the edge and surrounding the field.

Series: The complete group of coins of the same denomination and design and representing all issuing mints.

Token: A privately issued piece, generally in metal, with a represented value in trade or offer of service. Tokens are also produced for advertising purposes.

Type coin: A coin from a given series representing the basic design. A type coin is collected as an example of a particular design rather than for its date and mintmark.

Variety: Any coin noticeably different in dies from another of the same design, date and mint. Overdate and overmintmarks are examples of varieties.

Wire edge: Created when coinage metal flows between the coinage die and collar, producing a thin flange of coin metal at the outside edge or edges of a coin.

Index

INDEX